P9-DZX-994

ROBES AND HONOR

THE NEW MIDDLE AGES

BONNIE WHEELER

Series Editor

The New Middle Ages presents transdisciplinary studies of medieval cultures. It includes both scholarly monographs and essay collections.

PUBLISHED BY PALGRAVE:

Women in the Medieval Islamic World: Power, Patronage, and Piety
edited by Gavin R. G. Hambly

The Ethics of Nature in the Middle Ages: On Boccaccio's Poetaphysics
by Gregory B. Stone

Presence and Presentation: Women in the Chinese Literati Tradition
by Sherry J. Mou

The Lost Love Letters of Heloise and Abelard: Perceptions of Dialogue in Twelfth-Century France
by Constant J. Mews

Understanding Scholastic Thought with Foucault
by Philipp W. Rosemann

For Her Good Estate: The Life of Elizabeth de Burgh
by Frances Underhill

Constructions of Widowhood and Virginity in the Middle Ages
edited by Cindy L. Carlson and Angela Jane Weisl

Motherhood and Mothering in Anglo-Saxon England
by Mary Dockray-Miller

Listening to Heloise: The Voice of a Twelfth-Century Woman
edited by Bonnie Wheeler

The Postcolonial Middle Ages
edited by Jeffrey Jerome Cohen

Chaucer's Pardoner and Gender Theory: Bodies of Discourse
by Robert S. Sturges

Crossing the Bridge: Comparative Essays on Medieval European and Heian Japanese Women Writers
edited by Barbara Stevenson and Cynthia Ho

Engaging Words: The Culture of Reading in the Later Middle Ages
by Laurel Amtower

Robes and Honor: The Medieval World of Investiture
edited by Stewart Gordon

ROBES AND HONOR

THE MEDIEVAL WORLD OF INVESTITURE

edited by
Stewart Gordon

palgrave

ROBES AND HONOR: THE MEDIEVAL WORLD OF INVESTITURE
Copyright © Stewart Gordon, 2001. All rights reserved.
Printed in the United States of America. No part of this book may be used or reproduced in any manner whatsoever without written permission except in the case of brief quotations embodied in critical articles or reviews. For information, address Palgrve, 175 Fifth Avenue, New York, N.Y. 10010.

First published 2001 by
PALGRAVE™
175 Fifth Avenue, New York, N.Y. 10010 and
Houndmills, Basingstoke, Hampshire, England RG21 6XS
Companies and representatives throughout the world.

PALGRAVE™ is the new global publishing imprint of St. Martin's Press LLC Scholarly and Reference Division and Palgrave Publishers Ltd (formerly Macmillan Press Ltd).

ISBN 0-312-21230-5

Library of Congress Cataloging-in-Publication Data

Robes and honor: the medieval world of investiture / edited by Stewart Gordon.
p. cm. (New Middle Ages)
Includes bibliographical references and index.
ISBN 0-312-21230-5
1. Costume—History—Medieval, 500–1500—Social aspects.
2. Rites and ceremonies—History—To 1500. 3. Investiture—History.
I. Gordon, Stewart, 1945-.
GT575.R63 1999
394'.4—dc21 99–27770

A catalogue record for this book is available from the British Library.

Design by Letra Libre, Inc.

First edition: January 2001
10 9 8 7 6 5 4 3 2 1

CONTENTS

SERIES EDITOR'S FOREWORD

The *New Middle Ages* contributes to lively transdisciplinary conversations in medieval cultural studies through its scholarly monographs and essay collections. This series provides new work in a contemporary idiom about precise (if often diverse) practices, expressions, and ideologies in the Middle Ages.

With *Robes and Honor,* Stewart Gordon and his collaborators break new ground in the study of ceremony, symbolism, and material culture, presenting diverse readings of the ambiguous semiotics of robing. This volume takes the reader across languages and cultures to explore possible relationships between the (seemingly) disparate medieval traditions of investiture. The essays explore "robes of honor" as material markers of diplomacy and government—and religious and artistic emblems—in several cultures. These essays invite us to think about robing as a "ceremonial metalanguage," but they also remind us that robes themselves as well as robing ceremonials have particular, local resonance.

Bonnie Wheeler
Southern Methodist University

BRIDWELL LIBRARY
SOUTHERN METHODIST UNIVERSITY
DALLAS, TEXAS 75275

ACKNOWLEDGMENTS

I presented the basic ideas for this book at an Association for Asian Studies annual meeting and a seminar at the University of Minnesota. It was Richard Eaton who moved the study beyond India by identifying a similar robing custom in Persia. To the dozens of friends, colleagues, and bare acquaintances who responded to my questions about investiture in areas far beyond my expertise, I appreciate your tolerance and patience. David Sa'adah translated the article by Dominique Sourdel with care and thoroughness. Bob Frost translated the chapter by Bernard Berthod as only a fellow historian of France could. My thanks go to Paul Legutko for work on the Byzantine Greek and Eric Hanna for checking many of the Arabic transliterations.

ILLUSTRATIONS

CHAPTER 1

A WORLD OF INVESTITURE

Stewart Gordon

At its most general, investiture involves re-clothing a person in special garments for an occasion before an audience that acknowledges and celebrates the new and "suitable" persona. Today, if we think of investiture at all, what comes to mind are coronations of European royalty and the ceremonial surrounding the installation of a new pope. A bit more consideration, however, brings investiture much closer to home. Judges and academics are robed, as are barristers in England. Recall that brides are dressed in a once-only gown and "shown" in it before an approving audience. Catholic clergy receive robes for their ranks and change them for various occasions. The Masonic orders use elaborate robes to designate ranks and functions. Some Jewish rabbis don robes for services. A bit further afield, robes would probably be given to the architect on completion of a building in Saudi Arabia. All of these investitures have roots that go well back into the Middle Ages where, as we shall see, robes were far more than "apparel." The ceremony surrounding robes brought together the high art of luxury fabrics and the high-stakes politics of kingship.

For the editor of this volume, awareness of the power of investiture began with a personal incident more than a quarter of a century ago. In the late fall and winter of 1973, my wife Sara and I traveled overland from Istanbul to Delhi. At Meshed, just into Afghanistan, Sara met a group of tribal women. They liked her and allowed her to purchase an old, black, full-length, elaborately embroidered cloak. With no common language, Sara could not ask the women anything about the cloak. Nevertheless, the women showed her how to wear it, and the cloak was her outer garment all across Afghanistan. Unlike other Western women in our group, Sara was treated with the highest courtesy and respect in bazaars, shops, and all other public spaces. Weeks later in Kabul, someone explained that the cloak's embroidery signaled that the wearer was under the protection of one of the most powerful border tribes of western Afghanistan; anything less than courtesy might provoke armed retaliation.

As a historian of precolonial India, I began my study of investiture just a few years later. I came across the term *sirpau* (head-foot) as an obscure but consistent item of government expenditure in Marathi revenue documents of seventeenth-century Western India. A few years later, a Persian historian easily identified the term as a local variant of *sarupa* (from head to foot), an old and common honorific robing custom in Persia. Further research revealed that this custom was central to the politics of the Mughal Empire in India (ca. 1500–1800 CE); honorific robing was one of the most common incidents in all official court biographies, and figured prominently in accounts by travelers and ambassadors. Luxurious robes were part of large transfers of gems, gold, and precious objects to princes of the blood. They were used to personalize and solidify relations between the emperor and his nobility. For example, the *Humayun-nama* (an imperial biography of the mid-sixteenth century) describes a feast by one of the emperor's principal wives at which 7,000 luxury robes were bestowed. The same source mentions important diplomatic uses; 12,000 robes of honor were carried to Mecca by the leader of a special caravan sponsored by the Mughal Emperor.[1] The official chronicle of Humanyan's famous son, the Emperor Akbar, records that court officials kept 1,000 full sets of luxury robes—made in the emperor's workshops—ready at all times for bestowal.[2] Throughout the Mughal years, honorific robes went "from the hand of the Emperor" to nobles on regular occasions in a yearly cycle, as well as at births and marriages of royal children, and various anniversaries. Investiture with luxury robes figured prominently in the shifting alliances around every succession.[3]

An incident of the mid-seventeenth century well illustrates the shared "metalanguage" of robes of honor and the conjoining of luxury textiles and serious politics at the Mughal court in India. In 1666, Shivaji (a highly successful local rebel military leader in western India near present-day Bombay) when surrounded by Mughal forces reluctantly agreed as part of the settlement to come to Delhi under the protection of a high Mughal noble. He was to accept the "largesse" of the emperor, receive honorific robes, and become a ranked military leader in Mughal service. The emperor sent Shivaji what his accompanying letter described as a "resplendent robe" on his departure for the Mughal capital.[4]

After a leisurely progress of two months, Shivaji, elegantly attired and served by a retinue of several thousand men, arrived with much pomp at Agra, the Mughal capital. A few days later, a high noble conducted Shivaji into the Mughal court, then in full session in the hall of public audience; nobles—more than a hundred—stood in rows, lower ranks further away, higher ranks within a silver railing, all dressed in luxurious silk robes. On a jeweled throne at the front sat the emperor receiving petitions and reports from officials. Nobles were required to stand quietly facing the emperor during the entire session. (Many Mughal paintings portray just such scenes.) Shivaji was announced by the court chamberlain and ushered forward; he offered his presents (1,000 gold coins and 2,000 silver coins) to the emperor, who neither acknowledged them nor spoke. Then, robes were given to princes and high nobles but not to Shivaji, who was conducted far back in the audience hall. Shivaji became so angry that he turned his back on the emperor and began to walk away. Nobles asked what was the matter and Shivaji shouted insults, the essence of which were that he refused to stand behind men whose backs he had already seen when they were fleeing from his army. Nearby nobles attempted to mollify him with a robe of honor, but he threw it on the floor of the audience hall. This is about as serious a breach of court etiquette as one can imagine. Both Shivaji and the Emperor Aurangzeb knew precisely what the robe of honor and its rejection meant. The chronicles report that Shivaji said, "Kill me, imprison me if you like, but I will not wear the khilat [robe of honor]." It is no wonder that chronicles of the day expected Shivaji and his entire entourage to be killed immediately. They were all imprisoned and survived only through the intercession of the high Mughal noble, who brought Shivaji to Delhi. Months went by while the court speculated on Shivaji's fate. He pled for the life of his retainers, who were released. Possibly with the connivance of his patron, Shivaji finally escaped Delhi—without elephants, jewels, or robes—and fled south to his home area.[5]

I next found that this custom of honorific robing was equally common throughout the Muslim world and had been for centuries before the Mughal Empire in India. To get a sense of this "world," I examined the career of perhaps the most widely traveled man in the whole of the Middle Ages. In 1325 CE, Ibn Battuta set out from his native Morocco on the first of several expeditions that would take much of his life and encompass much of the Middle East, some of Central Asia, parts of India and China, and sub-Saharan Africa. One of the noteworthy features of his extraordinary narrative is how often Ibn Battuta was honored with investiture of costly robes, sometimes because of his Islamic learning, sometimes because of his pilgrimages to Mecca, sometimes just because he told good stories of his adventures. We can track his acquisition of high-value garments through all the small courts of central and western Turkey, across Persia, and on to the lavish court of the sultan of Delhi. Further afield, Ibn Battuta was presented robes by the rulers of Ethiopia and Sumatra.

At Mali, in West Africa, Ibn Battuta knew he was beyond the edge of the world of robes of honor.

> Ibn al-Faqih came hurrying out of his house saying "Stand up; here comes the sultan's stuff and gift to you." So I stood up thinking [since he had called it "stuff"] that it consisted of robes of honour and money, and lo! it was three cakes of bread, and a calabash of sour curds. When I saw this I burst out laughing, and thought it a most amazing thing that they could be so foolish and make so much of such a paltry matter.[6]

The evidence from Ibn Battuta's memoirs is very clear, however, that the use of honorific robing was wider even than the vast Islamic world. Ibn Battuta received robes from the Christian emperor of Constantinople, from a Hellenic queen of Muhammad Uzbeg Khan (ruled 1312–1341) of the Crimea, and from the local magnate in Hangchow, China. While our traveler was in Delhi, he witnessed the sultan receiving jeweled robes as part of a diplomatic mission from China and sending fine robes in return. This evidence suggests an investiture custom far older than Islam that perhaps began somewhere in the vast plains of Central Asia or even in China.

I set out to explore these ideas though aware of a daunting geographic spread, variety of languages and cultures, and complexity of textual and visual evidence. It was apparent from the start that any conclusions based on local primary materials would require a collaborative effort of several different specialists. I corresponded with individual contributors who had expertise in one of the relevant historical periods and regions and some research interest in robing and ceremony. During two years of research and writing, the contributors stayed in touch through a bimonthly newsletter that I had the pleasure of editing and distributing. New ideas and drafts were "floated," discussion promoted, and common threads discovered.

We sought something considerably more specific than the well-known one-way movement of silk out of China and down what is now termed the Silk Road to the Middle East and Europe. Such trade is found in the Greek and Roman eras, but no dominant use of the silk can be found in this period. It was used for shrouds in Egypt, condemned as "too feminine" for men's garments in Rome, and widely used for elite clothes in Persia. Likewise, we found ourselves well beyond simple assertions that ceremonial robing—like pasta, gunpowder, paper, various art motifs, and the button—somehow made its way out from China to the rest of the world.

In this volume, we examine a certain "something," a ceremony with common attributes whose beginning and development can be historically located. Our primary interest, however, is not that an identifiable ceremonial tradition moved from one local setting to another over time (a simple diffusionist viewpoint). Rather, we are interested in what happened in each local setting and the choices and opportunities that accompanied investiture's adoption. One way to view this process is in semiotic terms. A robe of luxury fabric from the hand of a king would be seen as an extraordinarily rich, complex, ambiguous, and multivalent sign. Such a semiotic viewpoint would focus attention on meanings that varied with audience, location, and political situation. Meanings could be actively contested by those involved in the ceremony.

Our story begins in the first few centuries BCE among the nomads west and north of the Great Wall of China. As Xinru Liu lays out in her chapter, trade, marriage alliance, and war between the sedentary culture inside the Wall and the nomads moved large quantities of silk and grain west in return for large numbers of horses and cattle that moved within the Wall. Horses were in constant demand by the elite, and cattle were essential for sedentary agriculture. For the steppe nomad confederations, silk and grain were equally essential for holding together fragile alliances. Grain was food that allowed the band to stay together through the winter. Silk not only gave the tribe something to trade for necessities like iron but also provided the leader with a means to reward and retain the loyalty of his followers. It appears that investiture with luxurious robes began among these nomads, first perhaps as a semi-diplomatic relation with the sedentary culture but soon as a prerogative of the nomadic leader.[7]

Use among these early Central Asian nomads set some of the most enduring features of the investiture ceremony.

> First, presentation was highly personalized. In its earliest use, silk and robes came from the sedentary silk-producing states solely to the nomadic band leader. In these nomadic bands, the leader by custom provided food, clothing, and shelter; his followers literally ate his "salt" at his table. Luxurious robing reinforced existing relations between a leader and his men.
>
> Second, the robe was granted "from the hand of the leader" before the whole band. This public presentation and donning before the whole court represented a form of solidarity within the band, cross-cutting familial ties.
>
> Third, the robe was given in conjunction with the items of war as fought in Central Asia. As the ceremony developed over the next thousand years and across thousands of miles, we see kings giving luxurious robes along with swords, daggers, quivers, and bows.
>
> Fourth, there was a central and enduring connection between robing and horses. Along with the robe, a king commonly bestowed a horse and decorated trappings.

Fifth, the robe in Central Asian use was always a sewn garment, rather than a wrapped or draped one, and always compatible with riding a horse. In its many later local manifestations, honorific robes often had side or back slits for ease of riding. It was the outermost and most visible garment of courtly dress.

Sixth, while the robe was itself a form easily transportable wealth, it was almost always accompanied by something gold.

Over the ensuing centuries, ceremonial robing, of course, continued to develop in the core area of Central Asia and moved eastward into China, Korea, and Japan. Robes became central to the practice of Buddhism and to the theocracy of Tibet. They were regularly used in diplomatic exchanges between China and Southeast Asia.

Our study, however, traces the movement of this tradition into the Middle East and on to Europe. What of the ancient investiture traditions indigenous to the Middle East? A long section in Leviticus 8.1–36, for example, presents detailed instructions for the investiture of the high priest of the house of Aaron. Over the course of seven days, the candidate was first washed, then robed in a full ritual outfit—tunic, sash, purple robe, ephod (vest), breastplate, turban, and gold turban ornament. The ceremony continued with the anointing with fragrant oils; the sacrifice of a bull and a ram; the application of the blood to the ear, hand, and toe; sprinkling the blood on the vestments; special breads; and a meal by the priests of the sacrificed animals.

My only reason for recounting the details of this investiture is to suggest that its dynamic and purpose were utterly different from the tradition that developed millennia later in Central Asia and entered the Middle East. This early Old Testament investiture was centrally focused on the holiness and practices of the Jews; it was a ceremony that separated Jews from non-Jews, just as it separated priests from followers. There was no sharing or presentation of garments. It was unconnected to horses or the objects of war. The priestly ceremony had no "secular" analogue for use in kingly legitimacy and loyalty.

Moving forward from the ancient period to the Greek period, it is suggestive that the Central Asian investiture tradition is not found in Herodotus (dated 450 BCE), though his history is rich with incidents of diplomacy negotiated, submission offered, loyalty tested, legitimacy asserted, and good work recognized. Herodotus also noted that the Scythians—nomads from the steppe—dressed exclusively in leather; there was no mention of luxurious robes or robing.[8] Therefore, I place Herodotus well before Central Asian investiture reached the Middle East.

The histories of Alexander the Great (ruled 335–345 BCE) are tantalizing but inconclusive. No contemporary account survives, nor is robing found in any of the fragments specifically quoted by later writers. For example, Alexander honored both the commander and the pilot of his naval expedition upon their return from a voyage of many months to India; he gave them golden crowns, made sacrifices to the gods, held a banquet, and sponsored games—but bestowed no robes.[9]

The first intact history of Alexander is by Diodorus of Sicily and was written nearly 300 years later (ca. 45 BCE). There is no mention of robes or investiture until Alexander successfully invaded Persia. Diodorus writes of the many luxurious robes found when Alexander overran the camp of the defeated Persian king at Issus and an even larger number seized in the sack of Persepolis, the Persian capital.[10] Two days after the sack, Alexander "put on the Persian diadem and dressed himself in the white robe and Persian sash and everything else except the trousers and the long-sleeved upper garment. He distributed to his companions cloaks with purple borders and dressed the horses in Persian harness. . . . Many, it is true, did reproach him for these things, but he silenced them with gifts."[11] Whether this is a sober description of events or a wholly fanciful narrative depends on one's assessment of Diodorus's sources.[12] Even if it was suggestive of existing Persian practice, Alexander's investiture of his companions was a one-time event not repeated in any of his subsequent history.

One likely transmitter of the Central Asian robing custom to Persia and the Middle East was the Yuezhi, a nomadic people whom the Chinese official histories first mention in the second century BCE as "moving with their flocks" in an area southeast of the Gobi desert only a couple of hundred miles west of the Wall. Forced west by politics and extended war with the Hsiung-nu, the Yuezhi crossed more than 5,000 miles of dessert and steppe, sometimes defeating and sometimes being defeated by other nomadic groups they encountered. The Chinese histories give 145 BCE as the date of the arrival of one large branch of the Yuezhi in Bactria (in northern Afghanistan).[13] There, the five clan groups competed for power with at least four indigenous groups and adopted the Greek alphabet found on all of the early coins. In the last decades BCE, the five clans were unified under a ruler named Ch'iu-chiu-chuch in the Chinese sources and Kujula Kadphises in the Greek sources, who extended his kingdom south into northern Afghanistan; from his reign onward, the Yuezhi became known as the Kushans. Within a century, King Kanishka I extended conquest from his core provinces in northern and eastern Afghanistan and Pakistan into eastern Persia, parts of Uzbekistan, Kashmir, and the plains of India at least as far as the upper Gangetic valley. Several features suggest transmission of the robing ceremony. First, the Yuezhi were nomads in the right place and time to have had the silk-horses relationship with China. Second, we know that they maintained a trade relationship in silk because

BRIDWELL LIBRARY
SOUTHERN METHODIST UNIVERSITY

it went through their kingdom from China to Rome.[14] Third, the Kushan kingdom was famous for the peace and prosperity it brought to the entire region and for its role as a transmitter of cultural artifacts and ideas.[15] For example, under Kushan sovereignty and patronage, Buddhism moved from India to Turkestan and China. Lastly, the visual evidence from the Kushans suggests an active royal use of robes. On their coinage, most of the post-Alexander kingdoms of the region continued to portray sovereigns (whether Selucid, Sogdian, Parthian, or Scythian) in a "Greek" idiom—that is, a bust in profile with a diadem. The reverse was a Greek god or goddess in predictably draped garments. There had indeed been exceptions—Parthian kings on horses with Hindu gods on the reverse—but nothing on the scale of change the Kushans were to introduce. Even the earliest coinage from the reign of Kujula Kaphises shows the king in full figure, frontal, in trousers. His successor, Vima, portrayed himself in what would become typical royal dress of the Kushan coinage, an elaborate, shin-length sewn outer robe, a lighter and slightly shorter tunic, leggings, high felt boots, and a complex hat.[16] Pearls and buttons abound; some of the fabrics are patterned. On the coinage, the style of robes shows exuberant change from reign to reign and sometimes within a reign, with at least ten variants in the two centuries of the Kushan kingdom (200–400 CE). A few of the robes look somewhat like Parthian royal attire, but most look like no previous coinage or representations in the region.[17]

In the absence of any documented Kushan textiles, let alone robes or any texts describing courtly ritual, any conclusions must be speculative. Nevertheless, we do know that the Yuezhi were receivers of silk robes, like other nomads living outside the Wall. Like other nomads, they perhaps used investiture as a ceremony of fealty. When the Yuezhi became the Kushans in their new kingdom more than five thousand miles west, we know that they had access to silk and the prosperity to buy it, plus a continued need to integrate families and ethnic groups as the kingdom expanded. The coins strongly suggest at least ongoing royal use of elaborate sewn robes. All of this makes it likely that the Kushans continued and developed a familiar investiture ceremony that they brought from Central Asia.

One of the earliest clear references to Central Asian investiture practice in the Middle East is in the Book of Esther, a late book of the Old Testament. In spite of many attempts by biblical scholars, there is no convincing evidence of the historicity of the basic story. For the last fifty years, biblical researchers have agreed that the Book of Esther is literature, a kind of historical novel, perhaps a merging of two or even three stories. It circulated in as many as four versions. In spite of these problems, it is clear that the Book of Esther is set in Persia, and many researchers suggest on the basis of internal evidence that it was written down in a final form by

BRIDWELL LIBRARY
SOUTHERN METHODIST UNIVERSITY

the middle of the second century BCE (though certain "Greek" interpolations, not central to the section on robing, were added later). Datable commentary on the book of Esther, however, begins only after about 150 CE. Thus, it seems that the robing incident in the Book of Esther cannot be later than the second century CE and could be a century or more earlier, putting it in a time and place influenced by the Kushans.[18]

The king rhetorically asks Haman the suitable forms of honor.

> What should be done for the man whom the king especially wants to honor? . . . Haman said to the king, "All right. Have them bring a royal robe which the king has worn and horse that the king has ridden, one with a royal crown on its head. Then have them hand the robe and the horse over to one of the kings most noble princes and have him robe the man whom the king especially wants to honor and have the prince lead him on horseback through the city square, proclaiming before him, 'This is what is done for the man the king especially wants to honor.'"[19]

Many of the features of this ceremony seem familiar from Central Asian practice—the luxury garment, the bestowal from the hand of the king, the association with horses, the donning of the robe in court, and the public parade of the honored one. Immediately following in the story, Mordecai the Jew was so honored and robed, much to the consternation of Haman, who thought he was to be the recipient of these honors.[20]

In the Sasanian Empire (fourth-seventh centuries), which conquered and displaced the Kushans, Jenny Rose's chapter shows that investiture was not central to the accession of kings but was important in two other settings. The first was as a regular feature of the yearly cycle of kingly ceremony. In what seems to be a merging of Central Asian nomadic practice and local custom, each fall and each spring the king gave his followers his used clothes, along with weapons, jewels, gold, silver, and horses. Bestowing the king's old clothes is an early manifestation of a theme widely found in later robing ceremonial, that some of a king's "essence" remained with the clothing. Thus, as in the Book of Esther, robes a king had actually worn were the most prized of all honorific clothing.

This ceremonial investiture tradition moved west in the centuries after the founding of Constantinople. These were centuries of warfare and ambassadorial contact between the Sasanian Empire and Constantinople, with considerable cultural borrowing by Constantinople of art motifs, kingly symbolism such as the diadem, and court dress.

In the Byzantine Empire, we seem to have the interplay of many factors influencing investiture. One was the flow of high-value textiles. Initially, silks came mainly from China and Central Asia, but production developed in Persia and later within the Byzantine Empire. Availability of these fabrics was essential to a developing investiture tradition both for imperial bestowal and church relations. This history still has many unanswered questions, such as the relation of private silk guilds to the imperial workshops, the extent of imperial dominance of high-value textiles, how aggressively Byzantine dominance of silk was used as a political lever abroad, and the impact of silk on the imperial economy.[21]

Investiture in the Byzantine Empire was also affected by the continued influence of Roman dress. The relatively spare military uniforms of Roman soldiers remained a strong image. For example, elaborate robing played no part in the appointment by Emperor Constantius of Julian as caesar of the West in 355 CE. Julian simply had his hair trimmed short and his beard shaved and put on military garments. Representations of both emperors and empresses in sculpture, consular diptychs, ivories, and mosaics show them in classical, draped Roman robes. None of this precluded honorific robing; it just influenced content and form of the robes. Two centuries later (mid-sixth century), however, the Ravenna mosaics depict very different robes for the Emperor Justinian, his wife Theodora, and their attendants. While still nominally clasped garments, these robes have a fullness, a layering, and general richness of fabric that seem as much Persian as Roman.

In the fourth and the fifth centuries, ecclesiastical garments emerged. The early Church had had no special dress for clerics or for services. In form, these new clerical garments were Roman dress retained for ritual use when styles changed—the chlamys derived from the military cloak, the dalmitic from an upper garment of senators and distinguished persons, the chausable from a late Roman cloak, and archaic peasant dress for monks and nuns. Both Augustine and Theodoret of Cyrrhus (ca. 330 CE) railed against a clergy that they observed using luxury fabrics for special garments and embellishing them with embroidery. Augustine also argued against the prevailing trend of differentiating levels of clergy, especially by form of dress.[22] Nevertheless, the endless, bitter sectarian strife throughout the period provided the unstoppable dynamic for investiture and defining priestly robes. Given the wide powers of bishops in their respective cities, robing was one means of promoting loyalty to Constantinople, as well as promoting loyalty within each bishop's jurisdiction. By the mid-sixth century, in both the eastern and western churches, there were written regulations for priestly wear. The garments of even monks and nuns must have been distinctive; in 546 CE, a law of the Empire threatened actors who impersonated monks and nuns with beating and exile.[23]

Another factor favoring investiture was a steady replacement of Roman patrician and citizen traditions by proliferating bureaucracy. More and more, hierarchy—civil, military, and ecclesiastical—came to be expressed in a hierarchy of dress employing luxury fabrics. Later codes were explicit on the centrality of robing for accession to office.[24] For example, a candidate for the guild of notaries appeared before the prefect of the city and the full guild in a special robe, was examined, took a complicated oath of office, and was confirmed in office by the prefect.

> Upon leaving the tribunal he goes to the church closest to his home, and there, in the presence of all other notaries wearing their cloaks, he takes off his own, puts on a surplice, and is consecrated by the priest's prayers. All of the notaries, wearing their cloaks, fall into a line behind him, the primikerios himself holding the censor and directing the smoke toward the newly elected one, who has the Bible in his hands and carries it in front of him. The straight and narrow paths upon which he is expected to walk are symbolized by the incense smoke directed in front of the Lord. The elected one takes possession of the post that has been conferred upon him amidst this pompous display of ceremonial garments; he remains in his robes when he returns home, to celebrate and rejoice with everyone in attendance.[25]

Constantinople in these centuries was the location of a vast development in the production and display of Christian relics. The relics were sometimes themselves cloth, such as Jesus' seamless garment or the robe of Mary (see the chapter by Annemarie Weyl-Carr); reliquaries were generally draped in luxury fabric. This use reinforced the passing of an "essence" to the fabric.

Thus, well before 500 CE, honorific investiture became fully integrated into the courtly life of the Byzantine Empire. It was used for church accessions, ambassadorial exchanges, bureaucratic promotion, and personal recognition by the emperor. An interesting far flung diplomatic use was the robes sent by Byzantium to Clovis in 481 CE (see Michael Moore's chapter). In this early Frankish kingdom, the embassy with its presentation of silk robes was exotic and unique. The ceremony was neither adopted nor emulated by later Frankish war bands. Forty years later, we have the interchange (described by Malalas) between Emperor Justinian and the "emperor of Laz" who came to court seeking an alliance and conversion to Christianity. He received not only a Roman wife but an imperial crown and a white tunic and cloak of pure silk, both with a gold border and a portrait medallion of the emperor.[26] The same year, Justinian won over the queen of the Sabir Huns with imperial robes, "a variety of silver vessels, and not a little money."[27]

Given that silk and luxury fabrics were entering the region and the pervasive influence of the Sasanian Empire, it seems likely that investiture spread rapidly into smaller courts and kingdoms. For example, as early as the fourth century, we find vestments with gold threads brought by "barbarian" ambassadors (likely from Southern Arabia) and offered to Emperor Constantine.[28]

It is certainly suggestive that explicit ceremonial robing is mentioned several times in the Koran (compiled 630–640 CE). There are three similar descriptions of the rewards awaiting the faithful on judgment day.

> Allah will deliver them from the evil of that day and make their faces shine with joy. He will reward them for their steadfastness with robes of silk and the delights of Paradise. . . . They shall be arrayed in garments of fine green silk and rich brocade and adorned with bracelets of silver.[29]

In the "Home of Imran" section, another passage makes explicit the importance of robing symbolism in the relation of man to God. "And hold you fast to the robe of God, do not forget and do not scatter."[30] It seems quite likely that even for smaller players residing far away from major imperial capitals, investiture was an established and understood ceremony, though the evidence is stronger for the ninth and tenth centuries than earlier (see the chapter by Jones and Eastmond).

Constantinople has been the focal point of this introductory chapter because it was the critical precursor to the essays that follow. The Byzantine Empire in 600 CE stretched past Egypt and along the North African coast, included almost the entire Black Sea region, present-day Greece, Bulgaria, Rumania, and Hungary.[31] The region of honorific robing was, however, far larger. The ceremony was already in use in Central Asia and the Sasanian Empire, whose influence extended east into Afghanistan. Descriptions of diplomatic encounters imply that robing was familiar to all who had dealings with the Byzantine and Sasanian Empires.

Let me suggest that Byzantium and the Sasanian Empire are the reasons that an honorific robing tradition became so central to state practice in Islam. In the early years, the fierce monotheism of Islam, espousal of the Prophet, and ideological egalitarianism were enough to tie together men of different language, ethnic background, and family. Once Islam developed into larger state structures, especially the Caliphate, additional mechanisms were needed to tie groups in loyalty across distances and across ethnic and familial lines.

Investiture was one obvious choice to fill this need of the Caliphate. If we trace the extent of the rapid Muslim conquests of the seventh and eight centuries, all of them were in preexisting "regions of robing" defined by the Byzantine and Sasanian Empires. Thus, honorific investiture had for two centuries been an established, complex ceremony, full of meanings that could legitimate the giver, subordinate the receiver, define groups, and reward individual actions. It does not seem surprising, therefore, that the ceremony became central to all states that developed out of Islamic conquests.

Medieval Europe, as our essays show, had a more problematic relation to this robing tradition.[32] In Eastern Europe, the robing ceremony closely followed the influence of Constantinople. The South Slavs, Bulgars, Serbs, and Ukranians, for example, accepted much from Constantinople—religion, trade, recruitment—and the concomitant robing tradition.[33] Hungary, in contrast, rejected both the Constantinople association and robing. I find it suggestive that the robes sent by Constantinople to the Frankish war bands in the fourth through the seventh centuries did not "plant" the custom; rather, these ambassadorial robings remained exotic, one-time events. In Western Europe, only Venice, which had a long and intense relationship with Constantinople, developed its own full tradition of luxury honorific robing for secular office.[34] West of the Greek-Latin divide, robes were indeed used in coronation (though anointing was more important), and some of the fabrics of coronation were of "Eastern" origin.[35] Medieval kings of Western Europe, however, did not follow the particulars of the Central Asian robing tradition—regularly bestowing on family and nobility luxurious robes accompanied by horses, jeweled daggers, and gold. Fealty had other ceremonies. Nor was robing a common part of ambassadorial exchanges within this region. The one serious attempt by the later Carolingians to introduce an imperial robing tradition failed.

Nevertheless, investiture flourished in the developing hierarchy of the Roman church. Our essays show that the "meaning" of robes and fine attire was debated and contested over the entire Middle Ages. Roman clerics often looked to Old Testament use for meaning, rather than ritual in rival Constantinople. Letters of appointment and public vows routinely supplemented and clarified the meaning of investiture ceremonies. Throughout our period, the uses of colors and fabrics signaled not only hierarchy but tensions and politics within the Church.[36] Our essays suggest that it overstates the case to argue that robing played no role in the power and politics of kings in Western Europe. It was precisely at the intersections of the church and kings that luxurious robing and its complex semiotics were most important. Robes were central to developing notions of sacral kingship. Copes and chausables of kings carried the complex signs of their authority; their luxury and cost signified power and wealth.[37]

By the middle centuries of the medieval period, our honorific robing custom was perceived in Western Europe as "Islamic," belonging to a different and somewhat alien culture. Thus, as Martial Rose's chapter shows, luxurious "Eastern" robes were the standard dress of the powerful villains of the English mystery plays—Pilate, Pharaoh, and Herod. Nevertheless, a few fascinating incidents suggest that kings and popes well understood the essential features of the Central Asian robing ceremony. In the thirteenth century, for example, two envoys from the Tartar confederacy arrived in Rome on a secret ambassadorial mission concerning Frederick's Greek son-in-law. The pope gave the envoys "some costly clothes, which we commonly call robes, of choice scarlet, together with cloaks, and furs made of the pelts of squirrels. He conversed freely, favourably and frequently with them through interpreters, and he secretly gave them precious gifts of gold and silver."[38]

Why did this robing tradition fail to develop among kings in Western Europe? It would be easy enough to argue that none of the war bands had the wealth to use luxury robes in ceremonies of loyalty with their own nobility. I believe that the issue goes much deeper and would like to offer a speculation. Though this robing ceremony started among nomads of Central Asia, it connected these peoples with the sedentary empire of China. Over the centuries of its spread, I believe that this robing ceremony developed as a profoundly imperial and cosmopolitan custom. It flourished in empires—Sasanian, Byzantine, Mughal, Mongolian, and Chinese. A large part of the semiotic meaning of this robing ceremony was the embedded association with a metropolitan power and perceived advantages of such an association. We can trace a "frontier" on the fringes of Europe beyond which the association with Constantinople did not provide enough perceived benefit to take up its robing customs.

In Western Europe, no strong center developed from which a new imperial tradition and patronage might spread. Instead, the crucial fifth through eighth centuries saw considerable decline in population, cities, cash economy, and central government. Unlike the Byzantine Empire, military leaders, their castles, and their estates became the largest political unit. These nobles held heritable rights and perquisites never surrendered by the Byzantine Empire to its nobility.[39] I find it suggestive that the artwork of the fourth through seventh centuries in Western Europe retains draped garments throughout and a predominantly "Roman" look for kings without a new metropolitan center to set a new style.

Western Europe is hardly unique in having a "frontier" with luxury honorific robing in active use on one side and nonadoption of the custom on the other. We can trace a similar "frontier" appearing when Buddhist pilgrimage brought large quantities of Chinese silk and the robing custom from Tang China to India in the seventh and eighth centuries. The custom and the materials were there, but the ceremony remained "exotic" and was not adopted.[40] It was not until India became part of the larger Islamic world with the development of Islamic empires half a millennium later that robing became common currency in India. A similar frontier is found in Southeast Asia, where Chinese embassies and robing remained an exotic custom. Even when Islamic robing arrived in Southeast Asia, the custom was strongly and successfully resisted by the nobility of the court of Siam.

I believe that the existence of these "frontiers" only underscores the variety of functions of honorific robing in the Middle Ages. The practice connected individuals to a particular patron as well as to a broader political area. Investiture bridged ethnic and familial divisions. In the world of investiture, robes were sought as frequently as they were bestowed. Acceptance could mean military defeat or splendid opportunity. Either way, the hand of the giver left its "essence" on the robe. As an imperial and cosmopolitan tradition, investiture by luxurious robes signaled suitability for courtly presence and the solidarity of elite culture. Besides a transfer of real wealth, luxurious robes were used to designate rank and attendant responsibilities. The ceremony might have severe sanctions for nonperformance of duties or such minimal sanctions that it connected distant allies or subordinates in bonds more emotional and imagined than operational. The ceremony eventually found a home among Christians, Jews, Muslims, Hindus, Confucians, and Buddhists. Perhaps its crucial features were semiotic complexity and ambiguity, lack of any particular "religious" connection, and ease of merger with older traditions. Throughout, these splendid, luxurious garments represented a medieval meeting of high politics and high art.

An incident late in our medieval period well illustrates robing at its most artistic and most political. Shortly before the defeat of the Spanish Armada, Elizabeth I established diplomatic ties with Ottoman Turkey. Both kingdoms had good reason to view Spain as a common enemy. On the advice of a young and ambitious ambassador, in 1594 Elizabeth promoted the connection by sending presents (including pieces of gold cloth and a jeweled portrait miniature) and a letter to the Walide Safiye, mother of the sultan and at the time one of the most powerful individuals in the empire.[41] Along with a reply to Elizabeth's letter, Safiye sent "an upper gowne of cloth of gold very rich, and under gowne of cloth of silver, and a girdle of Turkie worke, rich and faire," plus a crown studded with pearls and rubies. In hopes of strengthening the connection, Elizabeth eventually sent a second letter, accompanied by handsome coach. Safiye in response sent robes, jewels, and assurances that she was promoting Elizabeth's interests with her son, the sultan.

Elizabeth apparently enjoyed wearing the Turkish luxury robes. It could only have discomfited the Spanish spies at her court to see her flaunting a possible Turkish connection. The robes, as they had in so many situations, had just the right degree of semiotic ambiguity. Perhaps they were a mere fashion, the splendor of luxury silks, but they might mean a new alliance and shifting power relationships. Master politician that she was, Elizabeth likely kept her court and the Spanish spies guessing.

Notes

1. Gul-Badan Begam, *The History of Humayan,* trans. A. S. Beveridge (Delhi: Low Price Publications, 1989), pp. 107–109.
2. Abu l-Fazl, *Ain-I Akbari,* trans. H. Blochman (Delhi: Low Price Publications, 1997), p. 96.
3. *Tuzuk-I-Jahangiri,* ed. and trans. Alexander Rogers and Henry Beveridge (Delhi: Mushiram Manoharlal, 1968), pp. 69, 114, 126.
4. One full set of newswriter's letters is translated in Jadunath Sarkar, *House of Shivaji* (Calcutta: M. C. Sarkar, 1955).
5. An even fuller account of the incident is found in Jadunath Sarkar, *Shivaji and His Times* (Calcutta: M. C. Sarkar, 1961), pp. 103–17.
6. Ibn Batuta, *Travels in Asia and Africa, 1325–1354,* trans. H. A. R. Gibb (London: Hakluyt Society,1929), p. 325.
7. See also Thomas Barfield, *The Perilous Frontier: Nomadic Empires and China* (Cambridge, MA: B. Blackwell, 1989), chapters 1 and 2.
8. See also Dennis Sinor, ed., *Cambridge History of Inner Asia* (Cambridge: Cambridge University Press, 1990), pp. 97–117.
9. See the narrative translated in Charles A. Robinson, *History of Alexander the Great* (Providence: Brown University Press, 1953), pp. 120, 126, 150.
10. Robes, for example, played no part in negotiations with the Greek states upon his succession. See Diodorus of Sicily, *Library of History,* Book 7, trans. C. Bradford Wells (Cambridge: Harvard University Press, The Loeb Classical Library, 1963), 7: 119–156, 217.
11. Diodorus, *Library,* 7:341–43.
12. Considerable scholarly writing, both in English and German, has addressed the chronology and reliability of the contemporary writers on Alexander. A substantial critical literature likewise addresses the question of what sections of the extant histories (including Diodorus) derive from which source. For example, Hammond finds the quote in question derived from Cleitarchus, a source prone to inflate and embellish everything from battles scenes to Alexander's nobility of action. See N. G. L. Hammond, *Three Histories of Alexander the Great* (Cambridge: Cambridge University Press, 1983), p. 59. For a sampling of these debates, see A. B. Bosworth, *From Arrian to Alexander* (Oxford: Oxford University Press,1988) and Lionel Pearson, *The Lost Histories of Alexander the Great* (Chico, California: Scholars Press, reprinted edition, 1983).
13. For a discussion of the Chinese sources on the Yuezhi, see John M. Rosenfield, *The Dynastic Arts of the Kushans* (Berkeley: University of California Press, 1967), p. 281.
14. Many examples of high-value luxury silks bound for the Mediterranean were found by Aurel Stein during his excavation of Loulan, a Chinese fort

on the Silk Road occupied from the second century BCE to the second or third century CE. The find of plain, batik, and patterned silks was divided between the British Museum and the National Museum (Delhi). See *Fabrics from the Silk road: The Stein Collection, National Museum, Delhi* (Kyoto: Shikosha, 1979), pp. i–iv. Rosenfield believes that this trade was the source for the gold of the Kushan coinage, the first in the region in several centuries. See Rosenfield, pp. 19–22.

15. Evidence from images on tiles suggests that the stupa form patronized by King Kanishka had an elaborate, multistoried roof and may have been the prototype of the Far Eastern pagoda. See Rosenfield, p. 36.
16. Rosenfield, p. 25.
17. More than 250 examples of Kushan coins are illustrated in Rosenfield, following p. 377. Some are also illustrated and discussed in *The Crossroads of Asia: Transformation of Image and Symbol* (Cambridge, England: The Ancient India and Iran Trust, 1992), pp. 63–88.
18. These issues are argued in the articles reprinted in Carey A. Moore, ed., *Studies in the Book of Esther* (New York: KTAV Publishing House, Inc., 1982).
19. *Esther,* trans. Carey A. Moore (Garden City, New York: Doubleday & Company, 1971), pp. 62–63.
20. See Nielson C. Debevoise, *A Political History of Parthia,* reprinted edition (Chicago: University of Chicago Press, 1969) and Richard N. Frye, *The Heritage of Central Asia* (Princeton: Marcus Weiner Publishers, 1996). See also F. Grenet and N. Sims-Williams, "The historical context of the Sogdian ancient letters," *Studia Iranica* 5 (1987), pp.101–22.
21. See the excellent review article by Anna Muthesius, "Crossing traditional boundaries: Grub to glamour in Byzantine silk weaving," *Byzantine and Modern Greek Studies* 15 (1991): 326–65.
22. V. Pavani, "Vestments," *Encyclopedia of the Early Church* (New York: Oxford University Press, 1992).
23. John Moorhead, *Justinian* (New York: Longman, 1994), p.117.
24. The emperor, at the top of this hierarchy, was robed in a complex and luxurious yearly rhythm. The descriptions in the Book of Ceremonies, however, present many problems. There are no remaining Byzantine court fabrics, and the visual record is relatively skimpy. See Elizabeth Piltz, "Middle Buzantine Court Costume," in Henry Maguire, ed., *Byzantine Court Culture from 829 to 1204* (Washington, DC: Dumbarton Oaks Research Library and Collection, 1979), pp. 39–53.
25. From the Book of the Prefect, translated in Andre Guillou, "Functionaries," in Guglielmo Cavallo, ed., *The Byzantines* (Chicago: University of Chicago Press, 1997), p. 201.
26. *The Chronicle of John Malalas,* trans. Elizabeth Jeffreys and Roger Scott (Melbourne: Australian Association of Byzantine Studies, 1986), pp. 233–34.
27. *Malalas,* p. 249.

28. Irfan Shahid, *Byzantium and the Arabs in the Fourth Century* (Washington, D.C: Dumbarton Oaks Research Library, 1984), p. 55. The source is the Vita Constantini.
29. *Al-Qur an: A Contemporary Translation,* trans. Ahmed Ali (Princeton: Princeton University Press, 1988), p. 18.
30. Verse 3/103.
31. Mark Whittow, *The Making of Orthodox Byzantium, 600–1025* (London: Macmillan Press, Inc., 1996), p. 39.
32. For a fascinating analysis of the divergence between Byzantium and the West of anointing in kingly accession ritual of this period, see Janet L. Nelson, "Symbols in Context: Rulers' Inauguration Rituals in Byzantium and the West in the Early Middle Ages," in Derek Baker, ed., *The Orthodox Churches and the West* (Oxford: Ecclesiastical History Society, 1976), pp. 97–120.
33. Speros Vyronis, "Byzantine civilization, a world civilization," in Angelilki E. Laiou and Henry Maguire, *Byzantium: A World Civilization* (Washington, DC: Dumbarton Oaks Research Library and Collection, 1992), pp. 19–37.
34. See Donald M. Nicol, *Byzantium and Venice: A Study in Diplomatic and Cultural Relations* (Cambridge: Cambridge University Press, 1988).
35. I found useful the introductory review article by Richard A. Jackson in Heinz Duchhardt, Richard A. Jackson, and David Sturdy, eds., *European Monarchy: Its Evolution and Practice from Roman Antiquity to Modern Times* (Stuttgart: Franz Steiner, 1992). Also see Janos M. Bak, "Coronation studies—past, present, and future" in Janos M. Bak, ed., *Coronations: Medieval and Early Modern Monarchic Ritual* (Berkeley: University of California Press, 1990) pp. 1–13.
36. For example, the dress of pious women and nuns was the site of considerable tension and politics within the medieval church. There was an appropriation of mourning and other "plain" garments by married women seeking direct spiritual association with Christ. St. Augustine and St. Jerome, of course, disapproved. See Dyann Elliott, "Dress as mediator between inner and outer self: The pious matron of the high and later Middle Ages," *Medieval Studies* 53 (1991): 279
37. See, for example, the famous cope of Henry VII woven in Florence around 1500 CE (currently in the collection of Stonyhurst College). It was emblazoned with the king's devices—the portcullis of the city of London and the Tudor rose. Illustrated in Jennifer Harris, ed., *Textiles, 5,000 Years: An International History and Illustrated Survey* (New York: Harry N. Abrams, 1993), p. 170.
38. *The Illustrated Chronicles of Matthew Paris: Observations of Thirteenth-Century Life,* trans. Richard Vaughan (Cambridge, England: Alan Sutton, 1984), p. 77.
39. For the nonspecialist, a helpful discussion can be found in Angeliki E. Lailou, "Byzantium and the West" in Lailou and Macguire, pp. 61–80.

40. Xinru Liu, *Silk and Religion: An Exploration of Material Life and the Thought of People, AD 600–1200* (Delhi: Oxford University Press, 1996), chapters 1 and 2.
41. The letters are translated and the incident thoroughly discussed in S. A. Skilliter, "Three letters from the Ottoman 'Sultana' Safiye to Queen Elizabeth" in Samuel M. Stern, ed., *Documents from Islamic Chanceries* (Oxford: Bruno Cassier, Ltd., 1965), pp. 119–59. The garments appear in an inventory of Elizabeth's clothes. See Janet Arnold, *Queen Elizabeth's Wardrobe Unlock'd: The Inventories of the Wardrobe of Robes Prepared in July, 1600* (Leeds: Money, 1988).

PART ONE

THE BEGINNINGS: 100 CE–500 CE

CHAPTER 2

SILK, ROBES, AND RELATIONS BETWEEN EARLY CHINESE DYNASTIES AND NOMADS BEYOND THE GREAT WALL

Xinru Liu

Soon after agriculture appeared on the North China plain, the relationship between sedentary agricultural societies and nomads on the steppe became a serious issue in Chinese history. Warfare with various nomadic groups was recorded from the times of the Shang (ca. sixteenth to eleventh centuries BCE) and the Zhou (ca. eleventh century to 771 BCE) dynasties. A more diplomatic means in dealing with the nomads, using silk products as an expression of good will, began with the Former Han dynasty. Han rulers sent silk as gifts and dowry for princesses who were married to the nomads, functionally a bribe to prevent invasion of the frontier. At the same time, they also used silks to form alliances with the sedentary societies on the oases of Central Asia against the nomads.

Special silk robes for diplomatic relationships, however, have not been recorded until the Sui (581–618 CE) and the Tang (618–907 CE) dynasties, when silk regalia were established for expression of political and social hierarchy in China. We should note, however, that the nomads to the north were not only passive recipients of silk products. They frequently intruded inside the Great Wall; they also migrated in and out, and some were eventually transformed into sedentary people. Silk transactions and the formation of a code of silk regalia played a role both in the transformation of these groups from a nomadic to a sedentary life and also in the relationship between nomads outside the Great Wall and Chinese government of the early dynasties.

Formation of the Code of Silk Regalia

The Former Han dynasty established itself on the ruins of the Qin dynasty. Because the devastating dynastic transition impoverished the whole country, the founding ruler of the dynasty, Gaozu, and his retinue had limited resources to clothe themselves as a ruling elite. In addition, the emperor himself and most of his followers came from lower social strata and knew little of the royal life of the former rulers. The court therefore lacked rituals and etiquette. After unifying the country with military force, the emperor realized that he needed institutions to establish his authority. He employed a Confucian scholar, Shusun Tong, to enact various rituals and rules in the court, which finally took shape after several rehearsals. The emperor rejoiced and said: "Now I know the taste of being an emperor!"[1] A set of regalia for the emperor and his followers was necessary to show the order of the court. Nevertheless, it took several centuries for clothing to be fully codified at the Han court. Mingdi (ruled 58–75 CE) of the Later Han was the first Han emperor who had a code of ritual clothes declared.[2] Han rules of clothing and carriage are detailed in the chapter on carriages and clothing in the *Houhan Shu* (*History of the Later Han*).

The *Houhan Shu* was, in fact, written after the fall of the Later Han dynasty. Thus, the chapter on carriages and clothing is a summary of the court regulations established in the four centuries of the two Han dynasties. The chapter begins with regulations for carriages, horses, chariots, and their decorations for various members of the royal family and different levels of court officials. Turning to clothing, the most prominent concern was with headgear. There were regulations about what kind of crown or hat the emperor should wear at worship and sacrifices, and what he should wear at daily audience with his ministers at the court. Rules about other parts of the regalia specified colors, types of textiles, and embroidered or woven symbols. Clothes were divided into upper and lower parts. On ceremonies of sacrifice to the heaven and the earth, the emperor wore a black upper part and a purple lower part, embroidered with twelve symbols, including the sun, the moon, stars, etc. His ministers were ranked by the numbers of the symbols—nine, seven, five, and three (*HHS* 30/3663). The upper parts of the outfit looked like a robe, but with long splits on both sides.[3]

While the ruler and officials wore these glittering silk clothes, women of the court—empresses, princesses, and wives of officials—also wore colorful clothes.[4] It was understood that commoners were forbidden to wear these courtly fabrics and dress. The only possible offenders were traders, who had wealth and access to these luxury fabrics. Sumptuary laws permitted traders to wear only plain silk with yellowish or bluish colors.[5]

It is noteworthy, however, that among the variety of clothes for the wardrobe of the emperors and officers, "robe" was not in a conspicuous item. In the entire two chapters on "Carriages and Clothing," robes were referred to only twice. The text said that in the ancient times the robe was used to match a kind of headgear, but currently even the officials at the lowest level could wear it.[6] It seems that robe was not a prestigious style in the Han dynasties. Artworks from that period also show that most people wore two-piece outfits. Women of the court—princesses and concubines of the emperors and princes—wore robes for weddings.[7] Obviously, robes had not yet become an important style denoting ritual and status.

Silk in Diplomacy

As the Han dynasty consolidated its rule of China, simple silk textiles became one of the major forms of wealth. Silk tabby was a large component of the taxes that farming households paid to the government; it was also a commonly traded commodity in the marketplace. Exquisite silk textiles such as embroidery and brocade were reserved exclusively for ritual apparel at court. The sedentary agricultural empire thus was well known for its silk textiles among its nomadic neighbors.

Silk trading along the frontiers with the nomads has a very long history, even predating the Han dynasty. According to Sima Qian, the earliest Chinese historian, a pastoral people who lived in Wuzhi county (in modern Ningxia Autonomous Region) in northwest China (probably related to the Yuezhi people who appeared in history slightly later) traded their cattle for silk textiles during the Qin dynasty. They then sold the silk to nomad chiefs, who paid them ten times the value in horses and cattle. Their mediation between the nomadic and sedentary society was so important that the first emperor of the Qin dynasty granted the chief of that tribe, Luo, the title of noble, which enabled him to stand in the audience of the emperor along with other ministers in the court.[8] It is clear that the dissemination of Chinese silk textiles through frontier chieftains had by the time of the Han already spread the fame of these fabrics and bred a greed for them among the nomads.

The most serious threat to the Han frontier was the Xiongnu, a nomadic people who rose as a powerful confederacy to the north of the Han territory. During the transitional chaos between the Qin and the Han dynasties, the Xiongnu often broke into the Great Wall to loot properties and carry away the local population. The founding emperor—Gaozu—of the Han felt his regime was too weak to cope with the invasions by military means. Even after the humiliation of being surrounded in Pingcheng (a city in modern Datong, Shanxi province) by the Xiongnu for seven days,

Gaozu dared not attack. Instead, the Han ruler chose to pacify the nomads by marrying one of his princesses to Maodun, the Shanyu (chief) of the Xiongnu. Thereafter, the emperor sent annual gifts of silk textiles, floss, wine, and the other products of an agricultural society to the Xiongnu; the humiliation of making tributes to a "barbarian" chief was avoided by terming them "obligations by marriage."[9]

The turbulent relationship between the Xiongnu and the Han has been well researched by Yu Yingshih and Thomas Barfield.[10] Both emphasize the Xiongnu's dependence on Han agricultural products as the prime reason for the incessant raids and Han efforts to pacify them. Barfield further explains the Xiongnu's need for silk and other luxurious products by an intrinsically unstable political structure. The chief needed silks, grains, and wine to maintain a courtly style and to buy the loyalty of his otherwise quite autonomous chiefs.[11] Unfortunately, there is no remaining eyewitness account from the time of the Xiongnu of the grandeur of a tent-court decorated with silk drapery and filled with nobles dressed in silks. The closest that we have is the description of the court of the Yabgu Khan of the Western Turks by the seventh-century Chinese pilgrim, Xuanzang. It details the true magnificence of a tent-court of a nomadic chief furnished with silk decorations.[12]

Silk and Horses

Soon after the Han rulers felt more secure in their power, making peace with aggressive nomads was no longer the only incentive to marry their princesses and send gifts to the nomads. The rulers of this sedentary agricultural society depended on the nomads of the steppe for horses and cattle as much as the nomads depended on the sedentary state for wine and silks. The First Emperor of the Qin dynasty (which precedes the Han), for example, made the chief of the Wuzhi a noble because he supplied many horses and cattle to the empire. Even so, the number of horses available to the Qin empire was limited. The evidence consists of the terracotta troops in the tomb of the First Emperor, which were mainly infantry. In the early Han, the country was so poor that even the Emperor Gaozu could not afford the four horses of the same color for his carriages while the ministers of the court had often put up with bull carts.[13] In the course of the Han dynasty, horses evidently became much more common among the elite. Many of the terracotta soldiers in the Han tombs were cavalry rather than infantry. In addition, the code of carriages and clothes provided such details for horse decorations that horses must have been abundant in courtly life. Actually, horses were as important symbols as silk clothes for establishing the status of the royal family and the court elite.

The increase of horses in Han life demonstrates that even though the Han empire never really tamed the Xiongnu or even confined them to the area beyond the Great Wall, they benefited from their interactions with the nomads. For example, during the time of the Emperor Xiaohui (194–188 BCE), the empress dowager sent two chariots and two horses to the Shanyu of the Xiongnu as a token of goodwill. The Shanyu sent back many horses, perhaps a thousand, according to a later source.[14]

Besides the three strategies discussed—marrying princesses with a large dowry to Xiongnu, making alliances with other nomadic groups on the steppe, and sending envoys to the Central Asian states against the Xiongnu—all of which essentially exchanged silks and other products for horses and cattle, one other strategy brought these much needed and desired animals within the Great Wall. Horses and cattle (and prisoners) were the principal war booty in campaigns against the Xiongnu and other nomads. When the Xiongnu expelled the Yuezhi tribe from Central Asia and established the confederacy of twenty-six nomadic tribes on the steppe in 176 BCE, the Shanyu informed the Han court of his victory and sent a camel, two riding horses, and two drawing horses to express his favorable attitude toward a marriage alliance.[15] During a campaign with the Xiongnu in the year 72 BCE, the Han court sent five expeditions, all together more than 100,000 cavalry, beyond the Wall. The five generals of the expeditions reported to the court their captures: about 90,000 horses, cattle, and sheep in addition to the thousands of killed and captured enemies. In the same campaign, the Wusun tribe, then an ally of the Han mobilized by the military governor of the Han in Central Asia, attacked the Xiongnu from the west and captured more than 700,000 animals in addition to 39,000 Xiongnu people killed and captured, including the Shanyu himself.[16] These various strategies—in war and peace—demonstrate the growing importance of horses and cattle to the sedentary agricultural economy, the military, and the expression of courtly culture during the Han period.

At the same time, the Xiongnu built up a taste for Chinese material culture represented by silk products. In the last decades BCE, the Xiongnu confederacy disintegrated, at least in part because of its interactions with the Han empire. After the surrender of Huhanxie the Shanyu (52 BCE) to the Han court, the Xiongnu's acceptance of the value of the Han culture accelerated. When Huhanxie sent a delegation to the court of the Han emperor to accept the suzerainty of the latter in the year 51 BCE, he received a whole set of regalia that symbolized his status as equivalent to a Han prince, including chariots, horses, saddles, clothes, and weapons. Huhanxie also received major wealth—20 catties of gold, 200,000 coins, 77 sets of clothes, 8,000 bolts of silks varying from brocade to embroidery and tabby, and 6,000 catties of silk floss.[17]

The quantity of gifts only seems to have increased with Huhanxie's and his successors' visits to the Han court. By the year 1 BCE, the number of silk garments increased to 370 sets, along with 30,000 bolts of all variety of silk textiles and 30,000 catties of silk floss, as well as other forms of wealth.[18]

We do not know whether the Shanyu distributed the wealth to his followers or sold them to the West. The purpose of the Han court was to help him please or pacify his followers by pursuing friendly relationships with the Han. The records show that the Han government continuously sent food grains to the Xiongnu when requested by the Shanyu.[19] Among the gifts to the Shanyu, silk floss was used primarily for padded clothes to resist the cold temperature on the steppe and was probably much less valuable for spinning into fabrics. Thus, silk floss was probably intended for use by the nomadic people themselves rather than trading it for profit. The food grains were certainly not aimed at pleasing the ruling elite but as an effort to help the whole tribe overcome difficult times.

The peaceful side of the nomadic-sedentary state relationship in this period is illustrated by the story of Wang Zhojun. In the year 33 BCE, Huhanxie asked for the hand of a Han princess to secure his relationship with the Han court. A beauty from the emperor Yuandi's harem volunteered.[20] This girl's name, Wang Zhaojun, became legendary in Chinese history and folklore and is much better known than many genuine princesses who married nomadic chiefs before and after her. Perhaps she was more accomplished and more beautiful than other princesses, but she also lived in a time when the Xiongnu and the Han had a long-lasting, harmonious relationship; thus, her peace mission was particularly successful.

Overall, the mutual dependence of the Chinese sedentary society and the nomads outside the Wall was the dynamic of warfare and peacemaking. Silk clothes and fabrics, wine, and grains were essential for the nomadic empire to keep the loyalty of nobles and, thus, the entire state structure. Horses and cattle were equally necessary for the Han empire and later Chinese empires to maintain their state machinery, specifically court rituals and the military forces. Therefore, the transactions of silks and horses—through conquest, loot, or trade—remained a major theme of the frontier history in China until the modern period.

It is important to note, however, that over the centuries, the nomadic-sedentary relationship along the Wall involved the peoples who were not totally separated by the Wall. More precisely, groups of people did not permanently remain on one side or the other. The Great Wall functioned rather like a lever to keep a periodic balance of power on both sides than as a wall literally stopping warfare, trade, or even migration. Thus, the persistent theme of sedentary-nomadic relationships or silk and horse transactions involved different peoples in different historical periods. As early as the Later Han, the Xiongnu confederacy began to break up. In 48 CE, the northern tribes migrated to the northwest (further on to the steppe), while the southern groups migrated within the Wall. About the same period, more names of nomadic peoples appear in the records. In the centuries following the collapse of the Han empire, many of these tribes migrated within the Wall. Most of the immigrants gradually settled there to participate in creating dynasties. Others migrated out again to join the new arrivals of nomads to the north of the Wall. It was this process that reshaped the culture of north China; silk textiles became more and more important in diplomacy and eventually developed into the institution of silk-robe granting.

Sedentarization of Nomads and Silk Robes

By the time of the Later Han (first century CE), the government seems to have built up a set of strategies to deal with the nomadic barbarians and a ritual to receive their chiefs as vassals at the court. In the history of the Later Han, the chapter on official positions explains that foreign kings and vassals who accepted Han suzerainty should be administered by an assistant chief, the same as in a jun (prefecture), and Xian (county) of the Han administration unit.[21] The clothing of those chiefs and their assistants were probably the same as that of the Chinese officials of their levels.

In the same period or later, it seems that the peoples who lived outside the Wall also accepted Chinese silk clothes as regalia, at least on occasions of dealing with Chinese regime. For example, the Fuyu, a semipastoral and semiagricultural people who lived north of the Great Wall, wore white linen at home but put on all their embroidery, brocade, silks, and fine woollen textiles when going abroad. As this was recorded by Chinese, this probably refers to the occasions of their meeting with Chinese. Chiefs among them would wear furs of fox, black sable, and gold-and-silver-decorated hats in addition to their silk clothes in order to show their status.[22]

With the collapse of the Later Han regime and the disintegration of the Xiongnu confederacy, the Great Wall served neither as a buffer between peoples who lived inside and those who lived outside nor as a lever to keep the balance of power. In the following centuries, many historical records refer to nomads settling in sedentary areas inside the Wall and to military officials of the Han who went outside the Wall with their followers to conquer and rule new territories. Political alliances across the Wall were not infrequent. Many chiefs outside the Wall became involved in the politics of the post-Han period. Around the end of the Later Han, the prefect of

Zhongshan under the Han defected to a nomadic tribe—Wuwan—outside the Wall, then became the confederate leader of the three tribes of the Wuwan. His encroachments along the frontier regions with his new followers chagrined the Later Han frontier officials so much that in spite of the fragility of the Later Han polity at that time, the prefect of Youzhou, a frontier station, hired a "barbarian" to assassinate him.[23] The Wuwan tribe, however, remained involved with politics within the Wall. One of its chiefs, Tadun, formed an alliance with the warlord, Yuan Shao, of north China and helped him to defeat his enemy.[24]

The most influential nomadic group that appeared when the Xiongnu confederacy was breaking up was the Xianbi. Like the term Xiongnu, the term Xianbi referred to several tribes; they lived east of the Xiongnu's territory outside the Wall and owed them fealty. The Xianbi formed their own confederacy with an unstable structure similar to the Xiongnu during the latter's decline. Some of the tribes entered the Wall and established political regimes there. The most powerful one was the Northern Wei dynasty (386–534 CE).

Let us now consider some events and stories about the process by which the Xianbi peoples and other nomads from beyond the Wall were transformed from outsiders to Chinese culture to insiders. We will note the key role of silk textiles and apparel. Our analysis of this process may also reveal how the silk robe was established as an institution in the sedentary-nomadic relationship along the Wall.

While the hegemony of the Xiongnu outside the Wall was declining, the presence of Xianbi on the Han border became more and more obvious. The story begins when some Xianbis invaded the Wall in 106 CE and killed the prefect of Yuyang (a prefecture near the border).[25] Thereafter, the Xianbis occasionally made peace with the Later Han in order to trade in the border markets and obtain silk grants from Han court. At other times they betrayed the Han court and attacked the border. Peace or war often depended on the Han relationship with other nomads—the Xiongnu, the Wuwan, etc. In the final year of the Later Han, Yuan Shao, the warlord, controlled north China. Political disturbances and warfare disrupted life in that region and many of Chinese people migrated outside the Wall. They carried with them the technology and culture of a sedentary society. Some of the Xianbi tribes learned from them how to read and write and how to make certain kinds of weapons. The military maneuvers of the Xianbi tribes became more organized by adopting standards and drums in the style of Han.[26]

The interactions between the Xianbi and north Chinese regimes continued in the same pattern after the Han. The Wei State of the Three Kingdoms period (220–265 CE), for example, adopted the same policy as the Han in dealing with the Xianbi. Nevertheless, the political coherence of north China continued to degenerate. After the court of the Jin dynasty took refuge in the south in 317 CE under the pressure of numerous invasions of "barbarians," north China experienced a period called Sixteen Kingdoms of Five Barbarians in Chinese historiography. Short-lived kingdoms built by the five former nomadic peoples—the Xiongnu, the Xianbi, the Qing, the Di, and the Jie—appeared and disappeared for more than one hundred years.

The Tuoba lineage of the Xianbi gradually gained hegemony and eventually put north China under the rule of the Northern Wei dynasty in the early fifth century. Once becoming rulers inside the Wall, the Tuoba family and the entire Northern Wei court changed quickly. One of the factors that facilitated these changes was that the Xianbi regime faced the same problems as that of the Han rulers in dealing with the nomads outside the Wall. In the reign of Taiwu (424–452), a chief of the nomadic Tuyuhun sent an envoy to the Northern Wei court in hopes of developing a closer relationship. In his petition for gifts, the chief stated that his tribe adopted the Chinese use of chariots and displaying standards. The wealth under his control, however, was not enough to distribute to his followers in order to maintain this style.

As the Northern Wei court counted on him to defend the border, he argued, he hoped the emperor would grant him some wealth, presumably silks. The emperor presented this request to his consultants to discuss. After the learned ones among them quoted precedents from the Han period, ministers and consultants deliberated how much should be given to the Tuyuhun. The final decision of the emperor was to increase the gifts only modestly according to the status and contribution of the Tuyuhun.27 This procedure shows how thoroughly the Northern Wei ruler assumed the role of a regime inside the Wall.

These Tuyuhuns were nomads whose territory encompasses the modern Qinghai province and who were famous for high-quality horses. A legendary species of "dragon horses" was cross-bred between the local horses and some Persian horses.[28] In the fifth century, men of the tribe, especially the distinguished men, wore clothes in Chinese style and silk hats.[29] Thus it is understandable that they had a constant demand for Chinese silks. In the year 477, Tuyuhun fought with another nomadic group, the Dangchang. The Northern Wei court sent 120 bolts of brocade and colored silk textiles to the Tuyuhun to persuade them to make peace with Dangchang.[30] The possession of silks and other products of an agricultural society thus enabled the Northern Wei to impose their influence on the nomads.

Silk Robes Become Regalia

The Northern Wei dealt with other nomads in ways similar to their relationship to the Tuyuhun. For example, the Gaoche (a branch of the Xiongnu) in the later fifth and early sixth centuries was an ally of the Northern Wei against another nomadic group known as the Ruru. The Gaoch sent horses, camels, furs and other products of the steppe to the Northern Wei court, and in return the Northern Wei ruler sent them silk clothes and textiles, music instruments and musicians to make them more civilized.[31]

For our purposes, the crucial event in these centuries of warfare negotiation and acculturation of nomadic tribes comes in the year 520. One of the Ruhu chiefs named Anahuan defected to the camp of the Northern Wei after a dispute in the ruling family. The Northern Wei ruler, Mingdi, granted much wealth to him. The next year when Anahuan was leaving the Northern Wei court to return to the steppe, he received "an embroidered silk robe and hat made in the workshop of the inner-court."[32]

This probably is the earliest recorded instance in which a royal robe was granted to a nomadic chief. We may recall that all the ritual clothes at the end of the Han period were divided into upper and lower parts, and the robe was not a garment used in courtly ritual. It seems that robes evolved into ritual clothes in the court of the Northern Wei, a dynasty built by a former nomads. It is quite possible that ritual robes represented a style arising from mutual influences between the sedentary Chinese and nomadic cultures. However, this remains speculation because the regalia of the Northern Wei has not been so clearly recorded as that of the Han or later dynasties. Probably due to the nomadic origin of the Northern Wei, their garments inevitably showed transitional features from the steppe life to Chinese culture and thus caused difficulties for later historians who attempted to record their ritual clothes in details. One may only assume that, as the robe arose from the Northern Wei period as a ritual style, the style might have its origin from the nomadic life of the Xianbi people.

What is clear is that by the sixth century, silk robes were established as the most formal ritual garments and regalia. For example, consider interactions between the Turks and the rulers of the Sui dynasty (581–618). In the middle of the sixth century, Turks had started coming to the gates of the Great Wall to buy silks and floss and tried to contact the various Chinese rulers of that time. In 551, a princess of the Western Wei was married to a chief of the Turks—Tumen—presumably with a dowry including many silks.[33] The Turks also sent 200 horses to the Western Wei court when the emperor died.[34]

Turks continued these interactions with Chinese rulers when the Sui dynasty took over. In 611, for example, a Turkish chief defected to the Sui court. A princess of the Sui emperor was married to him in the year of 614 with a dowry of much brocade, 1,000 sets of "robe clothes," and 10,000 bolts of colored silks.[35]

The story of nomads obtaining silks and migrating within the Great Wall continued in Chinese history. Nevertheless, my story of the silk robe as regalia and ritual apparel should stop here, as the role of silks and silk robes in the dynamics of the sedentary-nomadic relationship has been demonstrated. Silks and silk robes were not just favors that the ruling Chinese dynasties bestowed on nomads outside the Great Wall. Silk was used to secure a relatively safe environment for agricultural production along the borders between sedentary and nomadic peoples, where silk transactions represented good will and a friendly relationship. Silk robes developed into a style of prestige and sacredness by absorbing style from both the sedentary culture and that of nomadic horse-riding peoples.

Notes

1. Ban Gu, *Hanshu* [History of the Former Han Dynasty], chapter 22 (Beijing: Zhonghua Shuju, 1962), p. 1030.
2. Yuqing Wang, *Mianfu Fuzhang zhi Yanjiu* [A Study of Regalia] (Taibei: National Museum of History, 1966), p. 101.
3. For illustrations of the ritual apparel in the Han period, see Wang, *Mianfu Fuzhang zhi Yanjiu;* Yushito Harada, *Chinese Dress and Personal Ornaments in the Han and Six Dynasties* (Tokyo: The Toyo Bunko, 1937).
4. Sima Biao, *Yufu Zhi* [Carriages and Clothes], included in Fan Ye, *Hou-Han Shu* [History of the Later Han], Monograph 30 (Beijing: Zhonghua Shuju, 1973), pp. 3676–77.
5. Sima Biao, *Yufu Zhi,* p. 3677.
6. Sima Biao, *Yufu Zhi,* p. 3666.
7. Sima Biao, *Yufu Zhi,* p. 3677.
8. Sima Qian, *Shi Ji* [The History], chapter 129 (Beijing: Zhonghua Shuju, 1959), p. 3260.
9. Ban Gu, *Hanshu,* chapter 94, p. 3754.
10. Yu Yingshih, *Trade and Expansion in Han China* (Berkeley and Los Angeles: University of California Press, 1967) and Thomas Barfield, "The Hsiung-nu Imperial Confederacy: Organization and Foreign Policy," *The Journal of Asian studies* 41.1 (1981): 45–62.
11. Barfield, "The Hsiung-nu Imperial Confederacy," p. 53.
12. Xinru Liu, *Silk and Religion, an Exploration of Material Life and Thought of People, A.D. 600–1200* (Delhi: Oxford University Press, 1996), p. 56.
13. Ban Gu, *Hanshu,* chapter 24a, p. 1126.
14. Ban Gu, *Hanshu,* chapter 94a, p .3755; Li Yanshou, *Beishi* [History of the Northern Dynasties], chapter 96 (Beijing: Zhonghua Shuju, 1974), p. 3181.
15. Ban Gu, *Hanshu,* chapter 94a, p. 3756.

16. Ban Gu, *Hanshu,* chapter 94a, pp. 3785–86.
17. Ban Gu, *Hanshu,* chapter 94b, p. 3798.
18. Ban Gu, *Hanshu,* chapter 94b, p. 3817.
19. Ban Gu, *Hanshu,* chapter 94b, p. 3798.
20. Ban Gu, *Hanshu,* chapter 94b, p. 3803.
21. Sima Biao, *Bai Guan* [Positions and Offices], included in Fan Ye, *Hou-Han Shu* [History of the Later Han], Monograph 28 (Beijing: Zhonghua Shuju, 1973), p. 3632.
22. Chen Shou, *Sanguo Zhi* [History of the Three Kingdoms], chapter 30 (Beijing: Zhonghua Shuju, 1959), p. 841.
23. Hu, probably a member of a nomadic people. Chen Shou, *Sanguo Zhi,* chapter 30, p. 834.
24. Chen Shou, *Sanguo Zhi,* chapter 30, p. 834.
25. Chen Shou, *Sanguo Zhi,* chapter 30, p. 837.
26. Chen Shou, *Sanguo Zhi,* chapter 30, p. 838.
27. Li Yanshou, *Beishi* [History of the Northern Dynasties], chapter 96 (Beijing: Zhonghua Shuju, 1974), p. 3180–182.
28. Li Yanshou, *Beishi,* chapter 96, p. 3186.
29. Li Yanshou, *Beishi,* chapter 96, p. 3186.
30. Li Yanshou, *Beishi,* chapter 96, p. 3184.
31. Li Yanshou, *Beishi,* chapter 98, pp. 3274–75.
32. Li Yanshou, *Beishi,* chapter 98, p. 3260.
33. Li Yanshou, *Beishi,* chapter 99, p. 3287.
34. Li Yanshou, *Beishi,* chapter 99 p. 3287
35. Li Yanshou, *Beishi,* chapter 99, p. 3302.

CHAPTER 3

SASANIAN SPLENDOR:
THE APPURTENANCES OF ROYALTY

Jenny Rose

Kingship was a central institution for the Sasanian dynasty (ca. 224–651 CE). The King of Kings (*Shāhānshāh*) was regarded as "a cosmic figure, the first among men,"[1] and a representative of Ahura Mazda (the "Lord of Wisdom," which becomes *Ohrmazd* in Middle Persian). In his person, he embodied the order of society and the interdependence of the Zoroastrian religion and state. One ninth-century Zoroastrian text, the *Dēnkard,* states that "The king's way is religion,"[2] and asserts that it was the king's duty to defend the Zoroastrian faith and to mediate its wisdom in order to ensure a stable, lasting government.[3] The Sasanians believed that the royalty of Iran was divinely chosen and that the *khwarrah,* divine fortune or glory, was conferred upon the king by Ohrmazd, consecrating his rule.[4]

The bestowal of royal fortune is symbolized in various investiture scenes on Sasanian rock reliefs, where Ohrmazd is portrayed handing the diadem of kingship to the monarch.[5] Those kings who commissioned only a single rock relief, such as Bahrām I (273–276 CE) at Bīshāpūr, and Narseh (293–302 CE) at Naqsh-i Rustam, chose the theme of divine investiture above all others.[6] Even Shāpūr I (241–272 CE), whose political leadership and military prowess was established by his victories over the Romans, and who celebrated this achievement several times on rock reliefs, also felt the need to record his investiture twice, once at Naqsh-i Rajab and once at Bīshāpūr.[7] Such spiritual legitimation of rule is also depicted on the coins of successive Sasanian rulers, in which each king is identified by the distinctive crown he wears, encircled by a diadem with ribbon ties.[8]

I intend here to consider some of the examples of Sasanian royal robing that are still available to us, primarily in the dynastic rock reliefs, but also in silver vessels, coins depicting the insignia of specific kings, contemporary Middle Persian (Pahlavi) and foreign (Latin, Armenian, and Greek) texts, and later accounts by Muslim authors, such as Tabari and Hamza al-Isfahānī, who relied on Middle Persian sources. Since the majority of Sasanian monarchs during the dynasty's 400 years' duration were men, and the extant artistic and textual evidence refers mostly to them, the discussion will focus on the ceremonial clothing and accoutrements worn by kings rather than queens.[9]

Robes of Power and Emblems of Royalty

The monumental rock reliefs, mostly located in Pārs, the dynastic homeland of the Sasanians, were intended to glorify and immortalize the Sasanian kings.[10] Of the twenty-nine known sculptures, most were carved between the beginning of the dynasty and the early fourth century and depict a single scene. They provide almost the only contemporary internal information we have on the structure of Sasanian society, illustrating mainly royal investitures, battles, and hunts. As the central positional figure in the rock reliefs, the monarch is not usually identified by particular facial features but is distinguished from his subordinates by specific insignia of power, such as the distinctive crown, the style of the hair and beard, his jewelry and ornaments, and his apparel.

The Sasanian kings are also portrayed on silver dishes, several fine examples of which are extant. By the beginning of the fourth century CE, the production of silver had become a royal prerogative in Iran, and the depiction of human figures on silverware was limited to the image of the king.[11] We know that some of the silver vessels bearing the king's portrait were intended for use by the monarch himself and that some were given as gifts at royal banquets or to foreign rulers, whose recipients in some way participated in the king's *khwarrah*.[12] The concept of divinely blessed kingship inspired the Sasanian decorative arts as a whole, which may be said to begin "with the creation of the iconography of the official portrait and the triumphal composition."[13]

Each Sasanian monarch had one or more characteristic crowns, so that most can easily be identified on coinage and rock reliefs. Many monarchs favored a winged crown, perhaps because in the Avesta and in a later Pahlavi text, the *khwarrah,* the divine fortune or glory, manifests itself as a falcon.[14] It was the crown, more than any other of the royal appurtenances which distinguished the monarch from predecessors and that set him apart from the other nobles. For it was the crown that symbolized the divine fortune that blessed his rule.

Such devices as the crown, hat, and belt *(tāj, kolāh, kamar)* are frequently referred to in the *Shāhnāma* (the Iranian *Book of Kings*) as the particular appurtenances of royalty. For instance, Jamshid, one of the first (mythical) kings of the world, is described as wearing a golden crown around his hat and a diadem tied around his waist.[15] Jamshid represents the Iranian ideal of kingship,[16] and he is purported to have established the tradition of holding the coronation ceremony on the first No Ruz (New Year) following the accession of a new monarch.[17] He is also said to have spent fifty years considering matters relating to dress, such as what clothing was appropriate for feasting or battle: he "contrived materials of linen, silk, wool and floss as well as rich brocades and satins. He taught men how to spin and weave and how to interlace the warp with the weft; then, when the weaving was completed, they learnt from him how to wash the materials, how to sew."[18] Although Firdausi (ca. 932–1021 CE) compiled and wrote the *Shāhnāma* over three hundred years after the fall of the Sasanian empire, this passage seems to reflect the tradition of superior Iranian craftsmanship in the production and design of textiles.

Apart from the king, members of the nobility were also identified by specific devices indicating rank.[19] According to the *Letter of Tansar* (Tosar), a sixth-century CE work that appears to contain some genuine third-century material,[20] the king "established a visible and general distinction between men of noble birth and common people with regard to horse and clothes, houses and gardens, women and servants."[21] The distinction of the nobles from artisans and tradespeople by their dress involved wearing specific trousers, headgear, and silken garments, as well as "clothes for travel and for home."[22]

Another way of distinguishing the ranks and professions from each other was through the wearing of particular colors. The priests normally wore white and the warriors wore reds and purples.[23] According to Islamic sources, red seems to have been the most dominant color of the boots, tunics, and trousers worn by Sasanian monarchs.[24] Hamza al-Isfahānī (ca. 893–961 CE), apparently using an official Sasanian work as his source, provides information in his "Chronology of Ancient Nations" about the robe and trousers of each Sasanian king, identifiable by his particular colors.[25] In his fifth-century history of Armenia, Faustus of Byzantium records that Shāpūr II (309–379 CE) presented the Armenian queen Zarmandukht with a red tent with blue drapes.[26] The color is also evident in textiles from outside Iran, which reflect Sasanian motifs and style, such as the sixth- or seventh-century red woollen coat from Antinoe, in Egypt, or the red background to a Sasanian-style tapestry, also said to have been found in Egypt.[27]

From one of the third-century Sasanian rock reliefs at Bīshāpūr, it is clear that traditional "Iranian dress" was in vogue over a wide area of the empire, from Syria to Central Asia and northern India. Iranian peoples, probably from Central Asia, are shown bringing gifts of homage to Shāpūr I, wearing "typical Iranian clothing: a knee-length, belted tunic over loose leggings or trousers tucked into calf-high boots."[28] This outfit—a tunic and trousers—remained acceptable male dress throughout the Sasanian period.[29]

The earliest Sasanian depictions of monarchs in the various investiture scenes show them wearing variations on this type of dress, more elaborately cut and ornamented. At Naqsh-i Rustam, Ardashīr I and Ohrmazd are depicted on horseback, trampling the heads of their respective enemies, while the latter hands the diadem of kingship to the former. Both wear cloaks draped over the shoulders of tight-fitting, knee-length tunics over wide trousers that hang loosely to cover the feet.[30] In contrast to Ohrmazd, who wears a mural crown, Ardashīr wears his hair in a *korymbos,* a huge ball of hair on top of the head, covered with a silk cloth and drawn through the diadem.[31] Ardashīr was the first to adopt the *korymbos,* as is evident also from a gold dinar, although on the Firūzābād relief his head is (unusually) bare, with just the diadem around the forehead. The *korymbos* style of crown was later worn by Shāpūr I. Another fashion employed by Ardashīr I on the Naqsh-i Rustam investiture relief is the beard bound by a ring, leaving a tuft of hair below. The king also wears this style of beard on the investiture relief at Firūzābād but not on his coins.[32] The beard ring became a symbol of royalty, and is found on later portraits of Shāpūr I, and Bahrām II.[33]

In the above depiction of Ohrmazd (figure 3.1), and in other early Sasanian representations of royal and divine figures (such as Narseh at Naqsh-i Rustam, and Shāpūr at Dārāb), the top cloak is fastened with two circular clasps tied with short ribbons.[34] In these instances, the cloak, worn with a broad collar of flat discs or jewels (perhaps a chain of office, as Hermann has suggested)[35] was evidently a symbol of power and authority.[36] The collar was replaced in later reliefs with a necklace of pearls, which became a royal motif until the end of the dynasty, as attested also by portraits on coins and silver vessels, and designs on textiles.[37]

The cloak was frequently ornamented with round medallions on the shoulders. These radial epaulettes, decorated with "dotted circles, rays, scallops, dots and star rosettes"[38] can be found until the end of the fourth century on royal tunics represented on silver bowls and plates, such as the "Shāpūr plate," now located in the British Museum.[39] That entire royal garments were often patterned with "triple dots, circles or

Figure 3.1. Investiture of Ardashir I at Naqsh-i Rustam. Photo by Georgina Herrmann. Used by permission.

beaded bands" is evident from silver vessels dated from the late third to the seventh centuries.[40]

The quintessential Sasanian royal garb was identified for the first time on the mid-third-century reliefs at Dārāb in southern Iran: "It was worn in depictions of both kings and gods and, once developed and codified under Shāpūr I, became standard royal attire in representations on rock reliefs and 'hunting' plates until late in the fourth century."[41] In contrast to Ardashīr's investiture reliefs, Shāpūr I's carving at Naqsh-i Rustam, depicting his triumphs over the Romans, places more emphasis "on fluttering and billowing clothes," with the king's dress "carved in a complicated mass of curves, pleats and folds."[42] This suggests a development toward more elaborate robes of power (see figure 3.2).

Shāpūr's relief at Dārāb dates from the time of the battle of Edessa against Valerian (260 CE). Although there is some damage to the face, Shāpūr can be seen wearing his beard through a gold hoop (as he does on the Bīshāpūr relief and as crown prince at Salmas) and a necklace of pearls around his neck. As another sign of ruling power, fluttering ribbons appear in three places: from the diadem around the *korymbos,* from the neck, and from the elegantly pleated trousers fastened in front to the shoe strap.[43] This style of trousers was apparently pulled over narrower, shorter leggings, "and secured at the upper thigh with a button and strap leading under the tunic to an innerbelt."[44] Shāpūr's fluttering cloak is fastened at the chest with a clasp consisting of two large circles, which Hinz supposes to be made of gold, as well as the belt around his waist.[45] The rest of the king's attire consists of a short tunic gathered at the waist by a ribbon belt with round clasps, worn above trousers of a soft material with pleated ribbons.

The bright colors and the silky textures of Shāpūr's Persian warriors' clothing made a vivid impression on Ammianus Marcellinus, writing in the latter half of the fourth century, but he makes no mention of patterns: "Most of them are so covered with clothes gleaming with many shimmering colors, that although they leave their robes open in front and on the sides, and let them flutter in the wind, yet from their head to their shoes no part of the body is seen uncovered. To the use of golden amulets and neck chains, gems, and especially pearls, of which they possess a great number, they first became accustomed after their victory over Lydia and Croesus [546 BCE]."[46]

Another investiture scene found at Naqsh-i Rustam is that of Narseh, which depicts the king wearing a similar costume to that of his father, Shāpūr I. In this relief, there are five figures: the king, in the center, receives the diadem from Anāhīd in his right hand; underneath the diadem is a boy; and there are two attendants behind the king, one incomplete.[47] The king is depicted frontally, with his head in right profile. He wears a

Figure 3.2. Bishapur II, a victory of Shāpūr I over the Romans. Photo by Georgina Herrmann. Used by permission.

fluted crown with *korymbos,* circled by a diadem with long fluted ribbons, and his beard is carefully bound. Here also, his clothing consists of a long-sleeved tunic of what appears to be a soft material, tied at the waist with ribbon above the remains of his sword belt. He wears the cloak draped back over the shoulders and fastened with two circular clasps on the chest. His trousers are fastened in a bow at the ankle with long ties hanging symmetrically on either side of the feet. He wears shoes with a T-strap along the bridge of the foot and another strap under the instep, with a disc near the ankle. As jewelry, he wears earrings and a necklace of large, spherical beads, presumably pearls.[48]

The attendant closest to the king is dressed in similar trousers and shoes. His long-sleeved tunic is also tied with a ribbon bow at the waist, the two ends hanging down. Instead of a crown, he wears a courtier's high hat (*kolāh*) with a diadem fastened by short ties in a bow at the back. The attendant raises his right hand with a crooked forefinger in a gesture of respect.[49]

The high relief and rich decoration of the victory carvings of Shāpūr were imitated by Bahrām II (276–293 CE) and resumed later in the reliefs of Ardashīr II (379–383 CE) at Tāq-i Bustān, near Kirmanshah. In the rock relief at Sar Mashhad depicting Bahrām II killing a lion, the king wears wide, ankle-length trousers under a knee-length, close-fitting tunic with long, narrow sleeves and a cloak fastened at the chest by a buttonlike clasp and hanging over the shoulders to the knees.[50] His shoes are no longer discernible. He wears his personal crown and a necklace made of large pearls. The material of the tunic appears to be a soft, flowing, relatively thin stuff, possibly silk, which clings to the body.[51] From the way the cloak hangs, it appears to be made of a heavier material. Both the cloak and belt fastenings are decorated with short ribbons, and another pair of ribbons hangs from the hem of the tunic.[52]

In an investiture scene at Tāq-i Bustān, which resembles that of Narseh, Ardashīr II, in between Ohrmazd and Mithra, wears a somewhat modified form of royal apparel (see figure 3.3): "the hem of the tunic seems to have been gathered at the sides by rings and ribbons, producing a rounded panel like an apron in front."[53] This fashion seems to have continued into the late sixth century, being found on silver plates dated to the time of Shāpūr II and Yazdagird I (399–420 CE),[54] and on a Sasanian seal now in the British Museum, which shows Bahrām IV (388–399 CE) standing on the corpse of his enemy and wearing the same distinctive apron skirt.[55] It is also found on coin reverses of Kavad I (488–497; 499–531 CE), Khosrow I (531–579 CE) and Khosrow II (591–628 CE).[56]

Another new element that had developed by the mid- to late fourth century, and that Ardashīr II wears on the relief at Tāq-i Bustān, is a halter strapped around the upper torso, replacing the cloak with fibula.[57] Herrmann contends that by the fourth century "a single necklace was no longer sufficient to express the king's magnificence, and so a chest harness . . . was

Figure 3.3. Investiture of Adashīr II at Tāq-I Bustān. Photo by Georgina Herrmann. Used by permission.

worn as well."[58] This chest harness seems to be the most important insignia of royalty on the silver plates depicting royal hunters, and it is found also on seals, coins, and stucco reliefs.[59] It consists of diagonal, jeweled, or beaded shoulder straps across the chest, attached by a central boss or rosette to a horizontal strap encircling the upper chest and tied at the back with two long ribbons ending in jewels or bells. Two centuries later, on an investiture relief at Tāq-i Bustān, it appears on the image of the king in its most elaborate form, decorated "with bands of beads and square gems."[60]

The later Tāq-i Bustān carvings, as well as illustrating court ritual, are a significant source of information concerning late Sasanian textiles and costume detail, particularly the woven patterning and decoration. It seems that an even more elaborate form of costume had developed toward the end of the Sasanian period, probably influenced by eastern fashion. Textual sources record the legendary splendor of the Sasanian court under the later kings, especially Khosrow I and II, paying particular attention to "the great quantities of rich textiles which were in use."[61] One Byzantine eyewitness at the coronation of Hormizd IV (579–590 CE, successor to Khosrow I) describes his awe at the ornately bejewelled, glittering attire of the new king as he is seated on the throne: Theophylactus writes of the splendid golden, jewel-encrusted tiara worn by the monarch, his handwoven, gold-decorated trousers, and the general ostentation of his dress.[62] Tabari (839–923 CE) remarks that Khosrow II was more greedy than anyone else for jewels and costly vessels, and that he had collected more gold than any previous king.[63] In the eighteenth year of his reign, Khosrow assessed his wealth, which included, according to Tabari's account, "such a quantity of jewels and clothes that only God could tally its worth."[64]

This preoccupation with extravagance is echoed on the later reliefs in the grotto, or *ayvān,* at Tāq-i Bustān, which demonstrate "a concern with decorative motifs and minutiae of detail not known before in Sasanian sculpture."[65] In the investiture scene, the king (accepted by most scholars, following Herzfeld and Ghirshman, as Khosrow II)[66] is shown wearing a fantastic amount of jewelry, and the motifs decorating his apparel are clearly visible. The king's tunic, which has the shape and cut of a caftan, seems to be made of quite a stiff material, and is "trimmed with beads and square gems, and strewn with ovoid gems dangling from smaller beads and discs."[67] The leggings are also jewel-encrusted. The caftan, like those of the nobles, is embroidered or appliqued with patterns of flowers, birds, and animals.[68] As well as his sumptuous costume, the king wears a massive winged crown (so heavy it would have needed to be suspended),[69] long earrings, a large, decorated necklace, jeweled chest harness, belt, sword belt, and scabbard.[70]

In the boar hunt scene at Tāq-i Bustān, the king's clothes are equally elaborate. His coat is decorated with the *sēnmurv* motif[71] and floral designs, and he is wearing a necklace with many pendants, a jewelled belt also holding many pendants, and bracelets on each arm.[72] In the relief, the king and his fellow hunters are clothed in close-fitting, intricately patterned caftans with high, embroidered collars and long, narrow sleeves, belted at the waist with wide jewelled belts from which hang ornamented thongs.[73] The king's caftan differs from those of the courtiers in that it appears to be fastened down the front, like a coat. Both the caftan and trousers of the chief riders are woven or embroidered with designs, mostly of animals, birds, and plants.[74] Some of the garments incorporate large medallions with pearled borders. The coats of most of the riders reach to above the knee, and then fall like a skirt on each side in two narrow scallops.[75] A late fashion peculiar to the hunting reliefs is "the low, square cap worn by the king and his entourage."[76] The king is not wearing a ceremonial crown but a plain flat cap tied at the back with short, fluttering ribbons.

There are parallels between the robes in these carvings and the so-called Cup of Khosrow, in the Bibliothèque Nationale, which depicts an enthroned monarch carved on a central medallion of rock crystal, set into a gold plate with colored glass inlays. The king wears a long-sleeved, tight-fitting robe, with pointed hems at the sides richly decorated with embroidery patterns and appliqués.[77]

That the *avyān* (grotto) at Taq-i Bustān presents such a detailed representation of the king, his courtly rituals and activities, leads Shepherd to speak of the whole design as symbolic of the *khwarrah*—the "Divine Destiny"—of Khosrow II: "The great diadem which frames the arch" and is reproduced throughout the iconography of the relief "consecrates the entire grotto and informs us that this is a sacred place."[78]

Some of the garments on these later reliefs at Tāq-i Bustān, such as the high-collared robes and the headdresses worn by both men and women, are unique to the site and suggest the influence of eastern design on existing Sasanian traditions.[79] One element that particularly suggests eastern influence is the high, pointed top boot with decorated surfaces, worn by the elephant drivers in the boar hunt relief over their leggings. Such boots seem to have been introduced into Iran from Central Asia in the sixth century and are seen again on courtiers and the king on silverware of the same period.[80] In the hunting reliefs, however, the king and his courtiers wear "shin guards which resemble the boots in having a peak at the front, but which do not cover the feet."[81] The fashion continued in post-Sasanian Iran until the ninth century.

Robes of Honor

Although there is no record of the king being specifically invested with a coronation robe on his accession to the throne, there are several references to robes of honor being bestowed on worthy members of the Sasanian court, and on visiting dignitaries. Yazdagird I (399–421 CE) once conferred a robe and presents upon one of his palace guards when he learned that the guard had physically prevented thirteen-year old prince Bahrām from gaining admittance to a part of the palace to which he was forbidden.[82] Shāpūr II gave silks as gifts to Armenian dignitaries[83] and presented his Armenian general, Manuel, with a royal robe, an ermine fur, and other decorations of royalty, such as a chest harness and chest and helmet ornaments.[84]

Ibn Khaldun relates that such robes of honor generally had a portrait of the king or illustrations of the symbols of royal dignity woven into them.[85] The custom of bestowing a robe of honor is of ancient origin and continued well after the end of the Sasanian dynasty throughout the eastern Islamic countries.

According to one later Islamic source, certain monarchs, such as Ardashīr I, Bahrām I, and Khosrow I gave away their old robes to deserving courtiers: at No Ruz, in the spring, they donated winter clothes that were no longer of use to them, and at the autumn festival of Mehregan they gave away their summer clothes.[86] Evidently, the king and his courtiers had clothing made of different materials for the different seasons.[87] The king would also mark his coronation by opening the treasury and giving gifts of "gold, silver, jewels, robes and fabrics, mounts and armor to the nobles and to his army."[88] Such gifts were also customarily given on national festivals, and important events, such as the birth of an heir to the throne or a military victory.[89]

J̌uanšer, a prince from Albania who fought for Yazdagird III (632–651 CE) against the Arabs and was wounded, was rewarded splendidly by the king after his recovery. He received a palace and the insignia and honors due to a general, and the king invested him "with a belt of gold studded with pearls, a sword of wrought gold, bracelets for his arms, and set a coveted crown upon his head. He gave him also leggings sewn with pearls and as many pearls again [on a collar] round his neck. They clothed him in a dark tunic with four hems, and taffeta and silken Persian coats with fringes of spun gold. . . ."[90] According to Procopius, "in that country [Persia] no one is allowed to wear a ring or a belt, a clasp or any other object of gold without royal bestowal."[91]

The practice of presenting a *kolāh* (tiara, or hat denoting noble rank) to a visiting noble was also well established by Sasanian times. The Arsacid kings are recorded as handing over the royal hat to local kings, and Ammianus Marcellinus writes that the merchant Antoninus, a deserter from the Roman camp, was brought to the winter quarters of Shāpūr II and was "received with open arms, being graced with the distinction of the turban,[92] an honor shared by those who sit at the royal table, and allowing men of merit among the Persians to speak words of advice and to vote in the assemblies."[93] According to Procopius, a golden diadem embellished with pearls was one of the greatest signs of honor.[94]

An Enduring Influence

Sasanian royal iconography continued for many decades after the end of the dynasty, influencing courtly fashion in Islamic Iran as well as in Byzantium and Central Asia, where some of the nobility took refuge. The son of Yazdagird III, Piruz, fled to the western region of the T'ang dynasty in China, in an attempt to set up a government in exile. Sasanian merchants, already familiar with the trade routes along the Silk Road, also established themselves and their craftsmen in areas under T'ang control, so that we find T'ang silks with typical Sasanian designs on them. For instance, the imperial treasure of the Shoso-in at Nara contains ornaments that were influenced by Sasanian decorative art, including a textile with stenciled rams on it probably deriving from the seventh century.[95] The rams, representing the *khwarrah,* the emblem of royal power as found on the apparel of the helmsmen at Tāq-i Bustān,[96] are also found on clothing in frescoes at Pyanjikent, Kucha, and Turfan[97] and on a fragment of silk from the cemetery at Antinoe in Egypt.[98]

Although no garments have survived from within Sasanian Iran, many of the bird and animal motifs connected with royal authority, such as the boar's head or birds holding pearl necklaces, reappear on textiles and in wall paintings at Central Asian sites, such as Afrasiab (ancient Samarqand), Varaksha near Bokhara, and Bāmīān.[99] The boar's head motif is usually said to represent the Zoroastrian deity Verethragna.[100] It appears on the clothing of one of the helmsmen at Tāq-i Bustān and on one of the few specimens of Sasanian jewelry that have survived—a pendant in the form of a wild boar.[101] The motif is found again on a fragment of woven silk discovered in the tombs at Astana in the Turfan oasis (Chinese Turkestan),[102] on the clothing of one of the ambassadors in the sixth- or seventh-century wall paintings at Afrasiab,[103] and on sixth-century representations at Bāmīān, Damghan, and Balalik-Tepe.[104] Other textiles from Astana show Iranian-style animal motifs set in a beaded medallion.[105] From China, such designs, particularly hunting scenes, became popular in Japan.[106] Silk fragments containing other Sasanian motifs have also been discovered in Antinoe and among church treasures in Europe, whence they accompanied holy relics from the east or were used as door hangings or altar screens.[107]

The iconography of the royal hunt, one of the main symbolic themes of official Sasanian art as found at Tāq-i Bustān and on court silverware,[108] reappears also in Byzantine imagery,[109] as do the fluttering ribbons that adorn the Sasanian kings.[110] Those fluttering ribbons are also to be found, alongside Persian-like crowns and long, narrow-sleeved garments, on the wall paintings of Cave 257 at Tun-Huang, where the Buddhist Deer Jataka is portrayed,[111] adorning Buddha images at Bāmīān,[112] and on a frieze of beribboned ducks holding pearl necklaces in their beaks at a cave in Qizil, Chinese Turkestan.[113]

Concluding Remarks

Although the royal apparel was obviously a significant element of the king's public persona, it seems in itself to have conveyed no power of authority. Rather, it was the stylized patterns symbolizing the royal fortune, or the embroidered image of the king on the robe of honor, that incorporated the notion that divine grace had been bestowed upon the wearer. The Sasanian kings were regarded as conduits of power, dignity, and faith, and rulers and affluent members of society sought to emulate them in later years. Of the many emblems of Sasanian royalty that were consciously assimilated into the art of the surrounding cultures, the robe itself is less significant than the accoutrements associated with the *khwarrah,* the divine fortune: the crown, with its elaborate ornamentation; the necklace or diadem of pearls; the fluttering ribbons; and the various symbols associated with the deities.

Such features of Sasanian decorative art were incorporated into the art of the surrounding peoples but reinterpreted according to each culture's perception of the relationship between the monarchy and religion. For example, in the paintings at Sogdiana, where wealthy merchants lived in great prosperity and power, royal symbolism was not used to express official grandeur; rather, "a king's portrait was used to create the model for a deity on a throne, and a king's hunt was transformed into an informal hunting scene or into a mythological scene depicting the struggle of a god with a monster."[114] Elsewhere, such as on the royal Hephthalite portrait near Bāmīān,[115] or the Byzantine mosaics at Ravenna, a deliberate attempt seems to have been made to revive the model of Sasanian imperial iconography.

It has been suggested that the Byzantine emperors so admired the pomp and wealth of the Sasanian court, particularly the jewelled, colorful attire of the monarch and courtiers, that they consciously imitated this style.[116] There are several instances of the adoption of Sasanian elements of apparel by the emperor and his wife,[117] in an attempt to reflect or surpass the standard of splendor set by the renowned Sasanian monarchy. Indeed, Ghirshman maintains that the image of the King of Kings surrounded by his court dignitaries was so powerful that it served as a model for the Byzantine depictions of Christ Pantocrator surrounded by the heavenly host.[118]

Notes

1. J. R. Russell "Sages and Scribes at the Courts of Ancient Iran," *The Sage in Israel and the Ancient Near East,* ed. J. G. Gammie and L. G. Perdue (Winona Lake, Indiana: Eisenbrauns, 1990), 141–46:142.
2. Dēnkard 6. 173; S. Shaked, trans., *The Wisdom of the Sasanian Sages (Dēnkard VI)* (Boulder, CO: Westview Press, 1979), 69.
3. Dēnkard 4.13.
4. This concept dates back to the Avesta in which *khwarenah* (Pahlavi: *Khwarr, khwarrah,* Persian: *farr*), is the hypostasis of the divine grace or fortune that cleaves to those kings and worthy Iranians who are deserving and makes them strong, brave, healthy, wise, fulfilled, and powerful rulers; see Yasht 19.64, 72. If the king errs in some way, such as by telling lies, then *khwarenah* may depart from him, and he is disgraced; see Yasht 19.34f. The Sasanian inscription at Paikuli tells of the punishment of one person, driven by Ahriman (the "destructive spirit" of Zoroastrian mythology) and the devils to place the diadem representing the *khwarrah* on the head of a false ruler; see P. O. Skjaervo, trans., *The Sasanian Inscription of Paikuli* 3.1 (Wiesbaden: Dr. Ludwig Reichelt Verlag, 1983) 21f, 29.
5. In the investiture of Narseh at Naqsh-i Rustam, however, it is the goddess Anāhīd who bestows the diadem, and at Tāq-i Bustān, the king (whom most scholars accept as Khosrow II; see n. 66 below) is handed two diadems, one from Ohrmazd, on the right, and the other from Anāhīd, on the left.
6. G. Herrmann, "Shāpūr I in the East," *The Art and Archaeology of Ancient Persia,* ed. V. S. Curtis, R. Hillenbrand, and J. M. Rogers (London and New York: I. B. Tauris, 1998): 38–51: 46 n.6.
7. Herrmann, "Shāpūr," 39.
8. The Sasanians adopted and Iranized the Greek symbol of Victory, the diadem (*stemma*) with its long ribbon ties, as their symbol of kingship. The diadem is first found on coinage of the Parthian Mithradates I. Sasanian coins, mostly silver drachms, express the Sasanian view of world order, with the king and his crown surrounded by the diadem, often in the form of a ring of pearls, representing the *khwarrah*. According to the ninth-century history of Armenia attributed to Mousēs Xorenac'i,"the right to wear a headband of pearls" was a royal privilege; see V. Langlois, *Collection*

des histoires anciens et modernes de l'Arménie II (Paris: Firmin-Didot frères, 1869), 66.

9. For information and references concerning women's attire, see E. H. Peck, "Clothing in the Sasanian Period, IV," *Encyclopaedia Iranica* V (1992): 739–752, particularly 739–743. See also J. Rose, "Three Queens, Two Wives, and a Goddess: Roles and Images of Women in Sasanian Iran," *Women in the Medieval Islamic World: Power Patronage and Piety,* ed. G. Hambly (New York: St. Martin's Press, 1998): 29–54.
10. See D. Shepherd, "Sasanian Art," *Cambridge History of Iran* 3.1, ed. E. Yarshater (Cambridge: Cambridge University Press, 1983): 1055–1112; 1077.
11. P. O. Harper, *The Royal Hunter: Art of the Sasanian Empire* (New York: The Asia Society, 1998), 32.
12. B. I. Marshak, "The decoration of some late Sasanian Silver Vessels and its Subject-Matter," *The Art and Archaeology of Ancient Persia,* ed. V. S. Curtis, R. Hillenbrand, and J. M. Rogers (London and New York: I. B. Tauris, 1998): 84–92, 84.
13. V. Loukonine and A. Ivanov, *Lost Treasures of Persia* (Washington, DC: Mage, 1996), 25.
14. See Yasht 19.35. In the fifth-century *Kārnāmag ī Ardashīr,* the *khwarrah* appears again as a falcon and dashes a cup of poison from the king's hand; see Boyce, *History of Zoroastrianism II,* 104.
15. This occurs at the beginning of the Jamshid story, as pointed out by Vesta Curtis in a lecture, "Symbols of Kingship in Ancient Iran," presented to the British Institute of Persian Studies at the British Academy, London, June 1, 1998. [To be published in the forthcoming William Sumner festschrift]
16. In the *Shāhnāma,* the early, mythical kings are modeled on Sasanian monarchs: "The standard image of a king in the national history presents him as superior among men in physical strength, good looks, wisdom and eloquence. . . . Kings are also law-givers and great organizers. This is particularly true of the 'great kings' such as the founders of dynasties;" E. Yarshater "Iranian National History," *Cambridge History of Iran* 3.1: 359–477; 405.
17. See A. S. Shahbazi, "Coronation," *Encyclopaedia Iranica* VI (1993): 277–279; 278.
18. R. Levi, *The Epic of the Kings* (1967; repr. London: Routledge & Kegan Paul, 1985), 9.
19. There were four different levels of nobility: *āzādān*—the nobility, "consisting mostly of landed gentry;" *vuzurgān*—"the heads of noble clans, semi-independent rulers of small provinces and high ranking state officials"; *vāspuhragān*—"persons close to the royal house, normally related to the king"; and *shahrdārān*—"the rulers of major provinces and local dynasts;" E. Yarshater, "Introduction," *Cambridge History of Iran* 3.1: xvii-lxxv; xli.
20. See M. Boyce, trans., *The Letter of Tansar,* (Rome: Istituto Italiano per il Medio ad Estremo Oriente, 1968), 15, 20.
21. Boyce, *Letter of Tansar,* 44.
22. Boyce, *Letter of Tansar,* 48, 67.

23. M. Boyce, *History of Zoroastrianism* II (Leiden and Cologne: E. J. Brill, 1982), 21.
24. See C. Manson-Bier, "Textiles," Harper, *The Royal Hunter:* 119–125; 123.
25. See J. Wiesehöfer, *Ancient Persia From 550 BC to 650 AD,* trans. A. Azodi (London and New York: I. B. Tauris, 1996), 289 n.1.
26. B. Overlaet, D. De Jonghe, and S. Daemen, "Pfister's Sasanian Cocks Tapestry Reconsidered: A Rediscovery at the Biblioteca Apostolica Vaticana," *Iranica Antiqua* XXXI (1996): 179–211; 204.
27. B. Overlaet, "Pfister's Tapestry," 204. See also Manson-Bier, "Textiles," 123.
28. Herrmann, "Shāpūr," 45. See the articles on "Clothing," *Encyclopaedia Iranica* V, for the origins and development of this style of dress. The gifts brought include bolts of material, vessels, and jewelry.
29. Peck, "Clothing," 747. Peck elsewhere considers the antecedents and later examples of leggings; see E. H. Peck "The Representation of Costumes in the Reliefs of Tāq-i Bustān," *Artibus Asia* XXXI, 2/3 (1969): 101–24: 112f.
30. F. Sarre and E. Herzfeld, *Iranische Felsreliefs* (Berlin: E. Wasmuth, 1910), 68.
31. Göbl suggests that the ball of hair might have been a wig and that the silk was brightly colored; R. Göbl, "Sasanian Coins," *Cambridge History of Iran* 3.1: 322–339, 325. Possibly, the silk was lowered to hide the face as a veil. Milani conjectures that the titles *Pardeh dar* and *Hajeb* (curtain holder, veil), "which came to mean the intermediary between the king and his people, could have its etymological basis in this tradition;" F. Milani, *Veils and Words: The Emerging Voices of Iranian Women Writers* (New York: Syracuse University Press, 1992), 2.
32. Sarre, *Iranische Felsreliefs,* 68. Hinz maintains that the beard ring was made of gold wire; W. Hinz, *Altiranische Funde und Forschungen* (Berlin: De Gruyter, 1969), 127, 130, fig. 63.
33. Hinz claims that this style of wearing the beard was a privilege of the ruler alone and that princes wore a shorter frizzy beard, and other dignitaries half-length or shorter beards; Hinz, *Altiranische Funde,* 146.
34. See Peck, "Clothing" 745.
35. G. Herrmann, "The Dārābgird Relief—Ardashīr or Shāpūr?," *Iran* 7 (1969), 85.
36. That the high priest Kerdīr is portrayed at Naqsh-i Rustam wearing a cloak secured with a double clasp and ribbons indicates his elevated standing. In two reliefs at Naqsh-i Rustam and one at Naqsh-i Bahrām, Kerdīr wears on his *kolāh* (headgear) a coat of arms in the form of a huge pair of scissors. Hinz regards this symbol as signifying that he is the highest judge of the kingdom, having the power to cut through the most difficult problems; Hinz, *Altiranische Funde,* 191.
37. At Ctesiphon, seed pearls were found, sewn onto clothing, belts and headdresses, or as earrings; St. John Simpson, "Sasanian Arts and Crafts," lecture delivered at the Lukonin seminar, British Museum, London, July 14, 1997.
38. Peck, "Clothing," 748.

39. Harper, *Silver Vessels of the Sasanian Period: I Royal Imagery* (New York: The Metropolitan Museum of Art, 1981), pl. 13. See also 36, and pls. 3, 4 6, 10, 11a, 23, 24.
40. Peck, "Clothing," 748.
41. Peck, "Clothing," 746f.
42. G. Herrmann "The Art of the Sasanians," *The Arts of Persia,* ed. R. W. Ferrier (New York and London: Yale University Press, 1989): 61–79; 67.
43. The long ribbons, although worn by both nobles and rulers, are considered to be more characteristic of royalty; Peck, "Clothing," 747.
44. Peck, "Clothing," 747.
45. Hinz, *Altiranische Funde,* 146.
46. Ammianus Marcellinus XXIII, 6, 84; J.C. Rolfe, trans., *Ammianus Marcellinus* II, Books XX-XXVI (1940; rev. and repr., London: William Heinemann, 1972), 397.
47. See G. Herrmann "Naqsh-i Rustam 5 & 8: Sasanian Reliefs attributed to Hormuzd II and Narseh," *Iranische Denkmäler* 8 (1977), 10.
48. Sarre, *Iranische Felsreliefs,* 85.
49. "A sketch of the bas-relief of Mithridates II of Parthia at Behistun . . . shows that a Parthian gesture of salutation consisted of raising the right hand with the fist partially closed i.e., with the forefinger and middle finger extended, slightly bent, towards the saluted individual. The Sasanians continued to use this gesture . . . but in most instances they simplified it by showing the raised right hand with the forefinger pointing. The gesture was used both towards divinities and kings, and it survived the fall of the Sasanian Empire"; A. S. Shahbazi, "Iranian Notes 7–13," *Archaeologische Mitteilungen aus Iran* (1986), 163- 170; 166f. Ardashīr I makes this gesture of respect to Ohrmazd on the Firūzābād investiture relief; Hinz, *Altiranische Funde,* 119.
50. L. Trümpelmann, "Das Sasanidische Felsrelief von Sar Mashhad," *Iranische Denkmäler* 5 (1975), 8.
51. For references to Persians wearing silk, see Trümpelmann, "Das Sasanidische Felsrelief," 8. Sasanian Iran controlled the western extremity of the Silk Road and thus trade between Byzantium and other parts of the near east and the Far East.

    Shāpūr II is recorded by the tenth-century Muslim historian Mas'udi as settling Syrian silk weavers from Mesopotamia in Susa and other cities in Khuzistan, where they created new types of silks and brocades that were able to be exported outside Iran; see A. Christensen, *L'Iran sous les Sassanides* (Copenhagen: Munksgaard, 1936), 127. According to Jeroussalimskaja, this account is somewhat exaggerated, in that silk production had already begun in the third century, and the Iranian towns cited by Mas'udi did not, in fact, become famous for their silks until his own time; A. Jeroussalimskaja, "Soieries sassanides," *Splendeur des Sassanides* (Brussels: Musées royaux d'Art et d'Histoire, 1993), 113. We do know, however, that sixth- and seventh-century Greek writers were impressed by the quantity and quality of Iranian silk; ibid.

52. Trümpelmann, "Das Sasanidische Felsrelief," 9.
53. Peck, "Clothing," 749. See also Peck, "Tāq-i Bustān," 111.
54. Harper, *Silver Vessels,* 83 and pls. 16, 24, 29.
55. G. Herrmann, *The Iranian Revival* (Oxford: Elsevier Phaidon, 1977), 112.
56. Harper, *Silver Vessels,* 113. Peck discusses the possible origins and prevalence of this fashion in "Tāq-i Bustān," 110ff.
57. Herrmann, *The Iranian Revival,* 136.
58. P. O. Harper, "Art in Iran V. Sasanian," *Encyclopaedia Iranica* II (1987): 585–594: 588.
59. Peck, "Clothing," 749. See also Harper, *The Royal Hunter,* 33, 41.
60. Peck, "Clothing," 749. See Harper, *Silver Vessels,* pls. 10, 14, 15, 16, 17.
61. Shepherd, "Sasanian Art," 1108.
62. See Christensen, *L'Iran,* 393.
63. Tabari, *Geshichte der Perser und Araber zur Zeit der Sasaniden, aus der Arabischen Chronik des Tabari,* trans. Th. Nöldeke, (Leyden: E. J. Brill, 1879), 352f.
64. Tabari, *Geschichte der Perser,* 354. When toward the end of the dynasty Khosrow II's army was defeated by Heraclius in 628 CE, booty taken from the palace of Dastagird included embroidered carpets and silken garments; Christensen, *L'Iran,* 469. See also Shepherd, "Sasanian Art," 1108.
65. Shepherd, "Sasanian Art," 1088.
66. Erdmann maintains that this is the investiture of Peroz (457–483 CE), not Khosrow II. For a summary of the arguments concerning the dating of these reliefs, see Peck, "Tāq-i Bustān," 102ff.
67. Peck, "Clothing," 751. In contrast, Ohrmazd is depicted in the traditional soft tunic with a ribbon belt at the waist, and a cloak fastened by two round clasps.
68. Peck, "Clothing," 751. Tabari describes Khosrow II as sitting on his throne behind a screen or curtain, on a cushion of gold brocade, dressed in a tunic of rich material, embroidered in gold thread; Herrmann, *The Iranian Revival,* 128: see also Tabari, *Geschichte der Perser,* 367.
69. By the later Sasanian period, the ceremonial crown had developed into such an elaborate and cumbersome headgear that it was too heavy for the king to wear and was instead suspended from the ceiling of the throne hall at Ctesiphon. A mid-eighth-century account by Ibn Ishaq states that Khosrow I (Anoshirvan) "used to sit in his audience hall where was his crown like a mighty bowl . . . set with rubies, emeralds and pearls, with gold and silver, suspended by a chain of gold from the top of an arch in this his audience hall, and his neck could not support the crown, but he was veiled by draperies till he had taken his seat in this his audience hall, and had introduced his head within his crown, and had settled himself in his place, whereupon the draperies were withdrawn"; cited in R. Ettinghausen, *From Byzantium to Sasanian Iran and the Islamic World* (Leiden: E. J. Brill, 1972), 28. This custom seems to have been adopted by subsequent Sasanian kings. Both Tabari and Tha'ālībi (961–1038 CE) report the practice as being associated with Khosrow II (Parviz). In the *Shāhnāma,* Firdausi mentions that

several mythical kings and actual Sasanian rulers followed this practice of suspending the crown wherever a royal audience was held; Ettinghausen, *From Byzantium,* 29.

70. See Herrmann, *The Iranian Revival,* 136.
71. The *sēnmurv* was a royal symbol, also said to represent the royal fortune. It is embroidered in two different variations on the king's robe at Tāq-i Bustān; see Jeroussalimaja, "Soieries Sassanides," 117. The motif derives from the Saena bird (Avestan: *Saēna meregha;* Pahlavi: *sēnmurv;* Persian: *sīmurgh*) of Zoroastrian mythology. It appears in at least one version of the *Shāhnāma,* in stories about Zal and his son Rustam, and is depicted in later texts, silverware, and illustrations as a composite creature with the head of a dog, the wings of a bird, the tail of a peacock, and the scales of a fish. The *sēnmurv* appears again on a silk from Antinoe, and on an ambassador's garment at Afrasiab; Jeroussalimskaja, "Soieries sassanides," 117.
72. Herrmann, *The Iranian Revival,* 136.
73. Peck, "Tāq-i Bustān," 115, 117f. This style of caftan, without the high collar, is also found on silver plates and on seventh-century wall paintings at Pyanjikent and at Afrasiab; see Peck, 112, 115.
74. Jeroussalimskaja, "Soieries sassanides," fig. 99. Peck, "Tāq-i Bustān," pls. VI, XII; see also Harper, "Art in Iran," 591.
75. Peck, "Clothing," 749f.
76. Peck, "Clothing," 750.
77. Peck, "Tāq-i Bustān," 111. See Harper, *Silver Vessels,* pl. 33.
78. Shepherd, "Sasanian Art," 1086.
79. Peck, "Tāq-i Bustān," 121. Both the caftan and the thonged belts seem to be of eastern origin, coming to Iran via Central Asia; Peck, ibid., 118.
80. Peck, "Clothing," 750, Harper, *Silver Vessels,* 111.
81. Harper, *Silver Vessels,* 111.
82. Christensen, *L'Iran,* 400f.
83. Overlaet, "Pfister's Tapestry," 204.
84. See Christensen, *L'Iran,* 404, referring to an account by Faustus of Byzantium.
85. See Christensen, *L'Iran,* 403f.
86. See Christensen, *L'Iran,* 403, referring to Jahiz (b. 776 CE).
87. Christensen, *L'Iran,* 467, referring to Tha'ālibī's account of Khosrow's discussion with his page, which is missing from the extant Pahlavi text.
88. Yarshater, "Iranian National History," 407.
89. Yarshater, "Iranian National History," 408.
90. C. J. F. Dowsett, trans., *The History of the Caucasian Albanians by Mousēs Dasxuranç̣i* (London: Oxford University Press, 1961), 111.
91. Christensen, *L'Iran,* 404.
92. Latin *apex,* referring to the hat or tiara of eastern kings and satraps.
93. Ammianua Marcellinus XVII, 5, 3; J.C. Rolfe, trans. *Ammianus Marcellinus* I, Books XIV-XIX (1935; rev. and rep. London: William Heinemann, 1971), 333.

94. Christensen, *L'Iran,* 404.
95. Rowland, *Central Asia,* 201.
96. In the legendary history of Ardashīr I, the *khwarrah* is said to have departed from the last Parthian king, Ardabān, in the form of a winged ram, and to have chased after Ardashīr and leapt onto his horse, signifying that the kingly glory was now his; Boyce, *History of Zoroastrianism I* (Leiden/ Cologne: E. J. Brill, 1975), 68. See also Levy, *Epic of the Kings,* 260f. Ammianus records that Shāpūr I "rode before the whole army, wearing in place of a diadem a golden image of a ram's head set within precious stones"; *Ammianus Marcellinus* I, 471.
97. Jeroussalimskaja, "Soieries sassanides," 117.
98. Ghirshman, *Persian Art,* 229.
99. Rowland, *Central Asia,* 71, 73f., 95.
100. Verethragna (Pahlavi: *Vahrām;* Persian: *Bahrām*) is the *yazata* ("being worthy of worship") of victory. In his *Yasht* ("hymn") he is embodied in ten incarnations, one of which is a fierce boar; see Boyce, *History of Zoroastrianism* I, 63. There is another fragment from Antinoe showing the winged horse, another incarnation of Verethragna; ibid. The winged horse motif is found also on textiles from Astana; B. Rowland, *The Art of Central Asia* (New York: Crown Publishers, 1970), 191.
101. Ghirshman, *Persian Art,* 223.
102. See Rowland, *Central Asia,* 97, 191. Other typical Sasanian motifs found on the Afrasiab frescoes include the *sēnmurv,* "birds bearing beribboned necklaces, rams and elephants;" ibid.
103. Rowland, *Central Asia,* 71.
104. Jeroussalimskaja, "Soieries sassanides," 117.
105. W. Watson, "Iran and China," *Cambridge History of Iran* 3.1, 537–558: 555.
106. Jeroussalimskaja, "Soieries Sassanides," 118; Rowland, *Central Asia,* 95f.
107. R. Ghirshman, *Persian Art: The Parthian and Sassanian Dynasties 249 BC–AD 651,* trans., S. Gilbert and J. Emmons (New York: Golden Press, 1962) 227, 232–235. For example, the *sēnmurv* motif appears on a Sasanian silk that was once used to cover the bones of St. Lupus; ibid, 228. Jeroussalimskaja discusses those textiles that she considers to be genuinely Sasanian and the various motifs which decorate them; Jeroussalimskaja, "Soieries Sassanides," 115ff.
108. See Harper, *The Royal Hunter,* 40ff.
109. A. Grabar, *L'empéreur dans l'art byzantin* (1936; repr. London: Variorum Reprints, 1971), 134. The Byzantine imagery appears to be modeled largely on Sasanian illustrations of Bahrām V (Gur: 420–438 CE) killing a lion; ibid., 60.
110. D. Talbot Rice, *Art of the Byzantine Era* (London: Thames & Hudson, 1963), 34, 71.
111. Watson, "Iran and China," 555.
112. Rowland, *Central Asia,* 113.
113. Rowland, *Central Asia,* 160.

114. A. M. Belenitskii and B. Marshak, "The Paintings of Sogdiana," *Sogdian Painting: The Pictorial Epic in Oriental Art,* ed. G. Azarpay (Berkeley and Los Angeles: University of California Press, 1981): 11–73; 27.
115. G. Azarpay, "Sogdian Painting," *Sogdian Painting:* 79–184, 93.
116. Talbot Rice, *Byzantine Era,* 44.
117. For instance, the high soft boots of Justinian in the Ravenna mosaics, Theodora's crown on coins, and the shoulder clasps worn by the emperor on the Barberini ivory; see Talbot Rice, *Byzantine Era,* 49f.
118. Ghirshman, *Persian Art,* 305.

PART TWO

EARLY MEDIEVAL DEVELOPMENT AND SPREAD: CA. 500 CE–CA. 1000 CE

CHAPTER 4

THREADS OF AUTHORITY: THE VIRGIN MARY'S VEIL IN THE MIDDLE AGES

Annemarie Weyl Carr

In 1031/32 the monastery of New Minster in Winchester, England, commemorated benefactions from the reigning king, Cnut, and his spouse, Queen Emma, by creating a *Liber Vitae* for the altar of its church.[1] The book's text—a list of benefactors and the order for prayers on behalf of their salvation[2]—is prefaced by three full-page illuminations. The first shows Cnut and Emma making their gift by placing a large cross on New Minster's altar (see figure 4.1); the following pair shows the afterlife, where the Devil garners the damned from his book of sins while the blessed—introduced to Peter by the *Liber Vitae* itself[3]—enjoy the rewards of their benefactions in Heaven. The theme of generosity rewarded is anticipated already in the opening scene, where—before the approving eyes of New Minster's monks at the lower margin—the royal donation is acknowledged with divine recompense. Christ himself in a mandorla hovers over the cross, flanked on his right by his Mother and on his left by Peter, the two patron saints of New Minster. Below St. Peter, an angel lowers a crested crown onto Cnut's head, and below Mary, a similar angel lowers a veil onto Emma's.

The miniature presents the first surviving image of an English queen, a distinction reinforced by the placement of Emma below Mary on Jesus's right hand, a place of honor in which one might have expected to find Cnut. Emma's eminence reflects, in fact, her prominence in the political conditions of Cnut's reign; Pauline Stafford, her modern apologist, calls Emma the "apotheosis of English queenship."[4] No less striking in the miniature is Emma's receipt of the veil. The visual alignment of their placement and clothing links Emma and Mary together with the veil: as Cnut

Figure 4.1 *Liber Vitae* commemorating King Cnut and Queen Emma, 1031/32 AD. After frontispiece, Walter Gray, ed., *Liber Vitae: Register and Martyrology of New Minster and Hyde Abbey, Winchester* (London: Simpkin and Co., Ltd., 1892).

receives the crown of kingship from Christ through St. Peter, Emma receives a veil associated with the Virgin.

A ruler's receipt of a crown from Christ or Mary is an image well entrenched in Christian art and one that Cnut assuredly found useful in England.[5] The conferral of a veil, on the other hand, is singular. The veil seems inevitably to be a confirming sign of Mary's power and approval: a confirmation of Emma's queenship through her vestment in the veil of Mary. And so the New Minster *Liber Vitae* leads us to the issue at hand: the Virgin's veil and its role as an instrument of investiture.

The Virgin's veil is a largely modern figure of speech used to cover (among others) a range of legitimately medieval images and objects. The questions it poses are legion; important for us will be: What deserves to be called a veil of the Virgin? When, where, and how did such objects appear? How were they utilized or displayed? What does this say about the distinctive kind of power attributed to the Virgin Mary? How was this power imagined to be linked to that of earthly rulers? And to what extent was it used to distinguish women's from men's power?

The idea of the veil may initially have emerged from a relic cult. As Mary's tomb in Gethsemane had been left without bodily remains, she was served—when her relics began to appear—by secondary relics, especially clothing. These collected above all in Constantinople, where their advent is linked by legend with the great partisan of the Mother of God, the empress Pulcheria (450–53). Among these relics, one came to be known as the "maphorion" of Mary, that is, the cloth enveloping her head and shoulders. This seems to have been the initial veil.

This relic was housed in a circular church sheathed in silver known as the Soros, or Reliquary, adjoining the basilica of the Virgin at Blachernai.[6] Blachernai occupied an exposed position at the northern end of the Constantinopolitan land walls. Its vulnerability is reflected in the annual feast of the deposition of its relic on July 2. This commemorated not the garment's arrival in Constantinople, but its restitution to Blachernai in 620 after removal for safekeeping during Avar raids during the preceding year. Blachernai's great moment came soon thereafter, in 626, when the Patriarch Sergios repulsed an Avar assault by taking holy objects (variously identified in historical reports) onto the walls there;[7] a similar defense ended the terrible Arab siege of Constantinople in 718. Mary's protection manifested in these events was—and continues to be—celebrated in the annual singing of Romanos the Melode's great Akathistos Hymn, modified by the addition of a prooimion lauding Mary as the "invincible general."[8] Then again in 860 Mary was summoned to Constantinople's defense: the Patriarch Photios, bearing Blachernai's relic in his hands, routed marauding Russian invaders.[9]

Blachernai was a site of imperial as well as episcopal display and included, along with the basilica and the reliquary church, a *metatorikion* or imperial vesting apartment for the emperors when they visited the complex for official ceremonies.[10] They did this on a number of feast days and anniversaries,[11] as well as on Fridays to bathe in Blachernai's sacred spring. On these latter occasions the ritual included a visit to the Soros, as we learn from Constantine VII's *Book of Ceremonies.*[12] Constantine gives no indication whether these visits were in any way coordinated with another famous Friday event at Blachernai: an all-night vigil in honor of Mary held each week and attended by the populace at large.[13] Known as the "Presbeia," or Intercession, the vigil was accompanied by a procession across Constantinople to the church of the Virgin Chalkoprateia near Hagia Sophia, also equipped with a Soros housing Marian garments.[14] The vigil must have acquired a spectacular aspect, for it figures in a range of visions in ninth- and tenth-century saints' lives that refer to the Virgin Mary in a radiance of light.[15] Its showmanship seems to have culminated in the famous "usual miracle" described in 1075 by Michael Psellos and known to pilgrim literature throughout Europe in the later eleventh and twelfth centuries.[16] In the "usual miracle" a veiled icon of Mary was mysteriously exposed and became luminous when the veil rose at dusk on Fridays; it fell again on Saturday evening. The "usual miracle" is cited for the last time in about 1200 by the Russian pilgrim Anthony of Novgorod, and it seems, like the Soros, to have fallen victim to the Latin Interregnum (1204–61).[17] The basilica itself, still majestic in 1400, was destroyed in 1434 in a fire lit by youngsters chasing pigeons.

The *Book of Ceremonies* makes it clear that the Soros figured in imperial ceremonial, and the recurrent reference to the vigil shows that Blachernai was a major center of Marian veneration, known both within Byzantium and to pilgrims from abroad. The nature of the relic housed there is far less clear.[18] Three legends are recorded in Byzantium about its origin. One, best told in a sermon by a certain Theodore Synkellos, relates how two Constantinopolitan patricians named Galbios and Kandidos stole from a pious Jewish widow a casket containing one of the two garments that Mary had willed on her deathbed to needy friends.[19] Calling it simply ἐσΘής—that is, "garment"—, Theodore asserts that Mary not only wore it, but "received and nursed the Christ Child in it."[20] A sermon delivered at Blachernai and attributed to the eighth-century Andrew of Crete cites droplets of milk on the cloth, but calls it the ζώνη, or belt, of Mary.[21] A second narrative is preserved in the anonymous *Euthymiac History;* this tells how Juvenal, Patriarch of Jerusalem, responding to empress Pulcheria's demand for a relic of the Virgin Mary, sent a sealed casket containing the Virgin's two dresses (ἱμάτια) and burial shroud (ἐντάφια), which Pulcheria installed with due reverence at Blachernai.[22] A third narrative, finally, given in the late tenth-century Menologion of Basil II (Vatican, gr. 1613) and cited already in a sermon for 2 July by the Patriarch Euthymius (907–912), says the emperor Arcadius (395–424) received the belt that Mary had worn at the first Christmas; deposited in Blachernai, the garment was taken briefly from its reliquary in 906 in order to liberate from demons the empress Zoe, wife of the emperor Leo VI (886–912).[23]

These narratives yield at least three definitions of the garment—as belt, shroud, and dress—; they link it with three different moments in Mary's life—her new motherhood, her death, and her assumption—; and they describe three different moments of deposition. They have been variously interpreted by modern scholars. Martin Jugie, who attributed both the *Euthymiac History* and the sermon associated with Theodore Synkellos to the second half of the ninth century, asserted firmly that no relic of Mary could be associated with Blachernai before the ninth century when the Patriarch Photios enshrined it in Byzantine history and sensibility by involving it in the Russian defeat of 860.[24] A decade after Jugie, however, Antoine Wenger identified Theodore Synkellos as an eye-witness of the Avar siege of 626, thus creating a far earlier context for the association of a relic with Blachernai.[25] Lodged in Constantinople already before the tumultuous years of the Avar raids, he sees it thrust into mythic eminence by the events surrounding these raids. Van Esbroeck, finally, based on his study of an Arabic text related to the *Euthymiac History,* sees the Marian relics forged in the yet earlier crucible of the Chalcedonian controversies that wracked the later fifth and sixth centuries.[26] He reconstructs a veritable laundry-chute of Marian garments imported to bolster Chalcedonian Christology by recreating in Constantinople the sacred topography of Sion and Gethsemane, sites of Mary's dormition and assumption.

Wenger's and Van Esbroeck's textual attributions seem, indeed, to have located a Marian relic at Blachernai long before the Patriarch Photios mobilized it to defeat Russian marauders in 860. Yet Jugie retains his grandeur. For the relic seems to have became a *veil* only at a time near if not during the miracle of 860. It is only after Photios' use of it that the relic acquires its identity as the Virgin's veil or *maphorion* (also omophorion), a word that seems to have been applied to the relic for the first time by Photios himself.[27]

The volatile identity of the Blachernai relic throws into relief the complex persona of Mary herself in Constantinople. Each of the three eras singled out above was crucial to her configuration. Ephesus, Chalcedon, and their great sponsor, Pulcheria, elevated Mary to the majestic status of godbearer that permitted her to intervene in the fate of empires.[28] The metaphor of textile-weaving is so powerful in the Marian rhetoric of this era that the textile relics—whatever their identity—find a compelling context here.[29] Thus Nicholas Constas has brought out the rich nuances given to textile metaphors in the Marian sermons of Pulcheria's confessor, Patriarch Proclus, and the intimate bond he knit by their means between the virgin empress and the Mother of God. Speaking of Christ's flesh as a luxurious toga woven on the textile-loom of Mary's womb, Proclus promised also that Pulcheria could, by her pious chastity, make her own flesh a loom of Christ.[30] The empress inscribed her vow of chastity on an altar in the cathedral church of Hagia Sophia, presenting her own robe as its altar cloth; "like her exemplar the Virgin Mary who wove a robe of flesh that was draped around the divinity," Constas writes, "the virgin empress wove a robe of cloth that served as both a covering for the body of the altar and a shroud for the symbolic body of Christ."[31] An echo of this strong, somatic imagery may reverberate still in Cosmas Vestitor's fourth sermon on the Dormition, known only in its Latin translation from Reichenau, which glosses the *Euthymiac History* by saying that Pulcheria placed the casket with Mary's garments on Blachernai's altar "veluti si dixerim, in sinibus Dei Genitricis Christum portatum"—as if, so to say, Christ upon [Mary's dress spread upon] the altar were borne on the lap of the Mother of God.[32]

If Mary attained imperial agency with Pulcheria, however, it was only later, in the fierce crucible of the later sixth and early seventh centuries, that the distinctive character of her agency begins to emerge.[33] Her motherhood, reflected in the droplets of milk; her ascetic and virginal purity, reflected in her meagre bequest of two dresses; her mysterious ascent to the realm of the ruler of the angels, reflected in her empty shroud were all threads in the fabric of her being. But as Averil Cameron has argued, these themes—which were to be so important to the formation of the western medieval Mary—did not have the power to focus firmly the identity of the chameleonlike "ἐσΘής" interred in the Soros at Blachernai.[34] Instead, Mary assumed an eminence analogous to that being forged in the same centuries by the earthly Augustae: she became the guarantor of eternal victory. As Diliana Angelova has shown, the empresses acquired an imagery of authority rooted in their intercessory participation as partners in victory, an imagery that merged with—rather than diverged from—the imagery of the emperors, welding them together, male and female, as shared faces of one ideal.[35] So, too, with Mary. She became the embodiment of the imperial virtue of eternal victory, the sure intercessor whose protection safeguarded the integrity of the realm. The concreteness of Mary's bond with victory comes out powerfully in the panegyric composed by George of Pisidia to celebrate the triumph of 626, which opens with a metaphor likening Mary to a victory standard:

If a painter wished to show the tropaion of this battle,
he would raise high the one who conceived without seed,
and paint her image.
She alone can triumph forever over nature,
first in her conception and second in battle.[36]

Finally, in the ninth century, the city found a fitting fabric in which to clothe this concept of Mary. This occurred with the identification of the relic as the cloth veiling Mary's head and shoulders. It refers to the heavy mantle that cloaks the head and shoulders of the Byzantine figure of Mary, falling in deep swags over her chest and cascading over her arms to deeply fringed hems at knee-level, known as the maphorion. Photius himself calls it her περιβολή or stole, but it is clear from his language that it is a protective mantle, and accounts of the miracle of 860 from the tenth century on call it her maphorion. In Photios' words, it is mobilized by compassion, deployed in intercession, and enfolds the city like a sheltering cloak pulled around the shoulders:

> When, moreover, as the whole city was carrying with me her raiment for the repulse of the besiegers and the protection of the besieged, we offered freely our prayers and performed the litany, thereupon with ineffable compassion she spoke out in motherly intercession: God was moved, His anger was averted, and the Lord took pity of His inheritance. Truly is this most-holy garment the raiment of God's Mother! It embraced the walls, and the foes inexplicably showed their backs; the city put it around itself, and the camp of the enemy was broken up as at a signal; the city bedecked itself with it, and the enemy were deprived of the hopes which bore them on. For immediately as the Virgin's garment went around the walls, the barbarians gave up the siege and broke camp.[37]

Photios ends his sermon with a prayer to Mary: "We put thee forward as our arms, our rampart, our shield, our general: do thou fight for thy people."[38] It is her sure intercession that the maphorion signals. Notably, the visual aspect so central to our conception of the veil—as something that hides—is absent from Photius's language. No less absent is the strong, somatic association with Mary's delivery and death seen in the Pulcherian rhetoric.

The maphorion linked effectively the relic of Mary's garment and the potent myth of her protection in times of war. To the modern imagination these elements coalesce readily in an image of Mary's veil. In Byzantium, by contrast, the iconography of the relic remains elusive. To our knowledge—though the point is much debated—there was no Byzantine icon conceived specifically to represent the protective power of the relic at

Blachernai.[39] The icon of the orante Virgin spreading her maphorion in the gesture of prayer is often associated with Blachernai, but we have little understanding as yet of when and how dogmatically this association was made in Byzantium: many icons of the orante Virgin must have lived out their serviceable lives without ever evoking the relic of the veil, while the name "Blachernitissa" appears on images of Mary that are not in the orante pose, as well.[40] By the same token, though Mary is depicted conferring garments like the episcopal pallium upon St. Nicholas, she was never shown conferring her maphorion. Mary does confer regalia on rulers. We see this in images from precisely the centuries in which the maphorion served as a major repository of the distinctive persona of Mary as the protector of Constantinople and its rulers in times of war. In these images Mary places a crown upon the head of the ruler and so confirms the divine origin of the ruler's authority. The emperors, as Henry Maguire has shown, wore the garb of angels, expressing their place in the hierarchy of the cosmic court of God.[41] Mary at her assumption had risen to the side of the ruler of the angels,[42] and it is this role that she assumes here. She is the peerless intercessor between Christ and the angelic host of his court. This was the role in which Photios, too, had cast the Mary of the maphorion. In the images of crowning, this Mary exercises the right of investiture. In contrast to the investiture depicted in the *Liber Vitae* of New Minster with which this article opened, the investiture she enacts is represented by a crown, and it is gender-indifferent: be it the emperor Leo VI on his ivory knop,[43] be it the warrior-emperor John I Tzimiskes (969–976) crowned by Mary on his gold coins,[44] be it the eleventh-century empress Theodora (1055–1056), crowned in exactly the same way on her coins,[45] the investiture received is one only, conferred on the unpartible head of empire. Conferred upon emperor alone, empress alone, emperor and empress together, or emperor and son(s), the investiture is one, and expressed in the same garment: not a veil, but a crown.

The Virgin of the maphorion co-existed at Blachernai with many other faces of Mary. These lived largely in icons, and Blachernai became a very busy locus of Marian invocation.[46] The maphorion's role in the ongoing rituals of imperial and civic devotion in Constantinople is not easy to discern, for its active interventions in the City's life are few. They are concentrated in the tenth and early twelfth centuries—assuredly not accidentally in the reigns of warrior rulers. The best-known use of the maphorion was by Romanos I (920–944), who wrapped it around his body as an impregnable armor when he departed Constantinople on November 9, 926, to engage his arch-enemy, the Bulgarian Tsar Symeon, in peace negotiations.[47] It can not have been long thereafter that the *Life* of St. Andrew the Fool in Christ was composed in Constantinople; a story of apocalyptic foreboding, the *Life* is directed to heavenly, not earthly, threats, but it buffers these with a brilliant vision of holy protection set in the Soros at Blachernai, when Andrew beholds the Virgin herself, moving on the path the emperors used, to the sanctuary where she kneels in prayer, lifting her veil till it floats like a luminous cloud over the assembled crowd.[48] The *Life* tells us that the maphorion had a deep root in the imagination of contemporaries, and this impression is reinforced by the fact that it was among the palatine relics of which small fragments were sent to war with the emperors in spectacular reliquaries—including the Limburg Reliquary of 963.[49]

The maphorion next emerges in 1093, when the splenetic metropolitan, John Oxites—upbraiding the emperor Alexios I Komnenos (1081–1118) for lack of piety—invoked the miracle of the maphorion as exemplary of the invincibility that that proper piety conferred.[50] The use of this example may well have been a special dig at Alexios, for we know that Alexios did employ the maphorion; he is the last emperor whom we know to have done so. Alexios' relation to the Marian cult at Blachernai has been a matter of some conjecture: he made his home in the Blachernai palace, and the *Alexiad* reports his hurried return to Constantinople from the outset of his campaign against the Normans in March, 1107,[51] after Blachernai's "usual miracle" had failed to occur on the Friday of his departure. This passage is often understood to indicate his customary engagement in the ritual. In fact, however, we have no evidence that Alexios (or any other emperor) ever participated in the "usual miracle." A different story in the *Alexiad* may throw clearer light on his relation to the shrine.[52] This reports that when Alexios went onto the battlefield against the Cumans in 1089 he carried a sword in one hand and in the other the maphorion of the Mother of God as a battle standard. The emperor must have gone to Blachernai to get the veil/standard, and with it the Virgin's blessing, before going to war. Under these circumstances the failure of the "usual miracle" on the eve of battle might well have aroused a popular anxiety deep enough to compel his return.

Alexios' use of the maphorion as a battle standard is otherwise unknown in Byzantium, though it recalls George of Pisidia's metaphor of Mary as tropaion centuries earlier.[53] It was not a success: Alexios was so badly beaten by the Cumans that he was forced to stuff the veil into the crux of a tree and flee the field.[54] The maphorion was surely not lost to history at this point. But it does not figure again in military history. As a myth it was still strong. This is proved by the decision of the Andrej Bogoljubskij (+1174), prince of Suzdal, to adopt as a major cult in his realm the cult of the Pokrov, the protection and intercession of Mary.[55] The liturgy of the Pokrov-feast was based upon that of the 2 July feast at Blachernai;[56] Bogoljubskij also dedicated the famous church on the Nerl River commemorating his victory over the Bulgarians in 1164 to the Pokrov. Thus he bound victory, protection and intercession together in the language of the Blachernai shrine, surely adopting for his own regime the protection under Mary's maphorion that Byzantium claimed.[57] Notably, however, we have no evidence that Bogoljubskij acquired from Constantinople an actual fragment of the maphorion, or of any other Blachernai relic. Rather, it is with icons that his veneration of Mary is associated, and eventually the feast of Pokrov acquired its own icon, depicting the vision at the Soros of Andrej's saintly namesake, Andrew the Fool in Christ.[58]

The linkage of Bogoljubskij's cult with an icon is suggestive. For in Constantinople, too, the maphorion was being preempted by an icon: the icon of the Mother of God Hodegetria was taking over the veil's traditional role as the sign of the City's Marian protection.[59] A relic continued to grace Blachernai: Russian pilgrims venerated Mary's robe, belt, and cap (literally, scullcap) there;[60] the fourteenth-century historian Nikephoros Kallistos inventoried quite a complex cluster of textile relics associated with Mary's motherhood and death there;[61] and the Roman church of Santa Maria Maggiore eventually, in 1453, received a belt of Mary reputed to have come from Blachernai.[62] But these were no longer the maphorion—in all his careful inventory Nikephoros Kallistos never so much as uses the word.[63] Alexios I's own daughter, Anna Komnene, writing in the second quarter of the twelfth century, is among the last to use it.[64] The relics Nikephoros cites spoke of a different identity of Mary, and served a different purpose. Singled out in the ninth century from the dress, the shroud, and the milk-stained belt, the maphorion had played its role, and—after passing its identity on to the icon of the Hodegetria—had succumbed once again to the relics bound to the more corporeal life of Mary.[65]

A further indication of a shift in the imagery of the Virgin's veil in the decades of Alexios I's crucial reign occurs in painting. It is seen in the iconographic elaboration—not so much of the maphorion—but of the clustered folds depicted around Mary's head in certain icons. Perhaps the earliest instance of this occurs in the famous icon of the Virgin with Prophets preserved at Mount Sinai: here Christ draws the eye specifically to the headdress of his mother by clutching it.[66] The gesture has been variously interpreted: as a reference to the imperial celebration of the feast of the Presentation at Blachernai;[67] as a reference to the veil of flesh that Mary gave to her son's divinity;[68] as the veil of his divinity that he is said to cast over her in the fourth oikos of the Akathistos hymn.[69] This variability shows that the iconography is arcane: bound to some specific, presumably literate key. But it does not seem to open upon the militant messages of Blachernai's maphorion. In time this image of Jesus clutching Mary's veil became widespread, and a striking number of the icons that display it became charismatically charged and served as the focus of devotional cults.[70] Only fitfully, for short periods, did any of them assume a role in military events, though, and none shared the charge of the maphorion. The same can surely be said of a variant of the so-called Pelagonitissa, again a widely-disseminated thaumaturgic type, that also showed a twisting child clutching his mother's veil.[71]

The maphorion's role as the protective mantle of eternal victory might seem to be linked more justly with another instance of a conspicuously painted veil that appeared in the century after Alexios. This is the heavy red and gold veil worn over Mary's maphorion in a pair of icons from the Crusader period, one of about 1200 in Paphos on Cyprus, and another of about 1280 at St. Catherine's monastery, Mount Sinai.[72] These icons show the Mother of God cradling a recumbent Child, and both are paired with an icon of a military saint. The pairing is striking: for all her martial presence in Byzantium, Mary is rarely linked with military saints in Byzantine art. The same iconography of Mary cradling a recumbent Christ recurs in a fourteenth-century icon in Athens that is inscribed with the name ἡ ἀκαταμάχητος—the invincible—, echoing the militant Prooimion to the Akathistos Hymn.[73] If protective, however, the icon in Athens lacks the heavy red veil and so challenges this garment's association with the maphorion and its myth. The veil itself, moreover, appears in a range of other contexts that speak not to war, but to more specifically womanly conditions, veiling the virginal Mary of the Annunciation, the child Mary at her Presentation in the Temple, and the aged Anna with the infant Mary in her arms.[74] The garment is significant in illustrating attention to the veil of Mary from the twelfth century on. But it is a new attention, that finds its roots in contexts different from those of the maphorion.

This heavily embroidered, red veil was, moreover, joined by other veil images: the veil embroidered in its hem with the words of Psalm 45,[75] or the veil grasped in one hand by a snuggling Christ depicted as the Lamb of the Passion.[76] These images appear in Palaiologan art and reflect the richly nuanced, highly semiotic visual language that Chrysanthe Baltoyanni has identified in Palaiologan icons.[77] Rooted in homilies and Scripture, this is an idiom deeply steeped in the intensity of the anticipated Passion. It is physically associative and corporeal, pointing in the direction of birth, death, obedience, and virginity intimated by Mary's dress, shroud, and belt. It is plausibly regal, as illustrated by the images of sainted princesses like Helena, Catherine, and Barbara, who wear similar veils, or by the beautiful Poganovo icon in which the donor, Helena Palaiologina, mourns the death of her father and son through the image of a mourning

Mary who clutches her heavily fringed veil about her.[78] But it is an imagery adapted to rulers as women: as mothers and queens. It does not merge with, but differentiates itself from, the imagery of male rulers. It is in this sense an imagery unlike that of the warrior goddess of the maphorion.

The protective role of Mary's maphorion did not vanish: the folklore of Athos, Cyprus, and the city of Siena all draw upon legends of the Virgin's protecting an endangered site by veiling it in fog;[79] in the nineteenth century the feast of the Pokrov was introduced as the feast of the Skepe or veil into the Greek Orthodox Church;[80] and still in the Second World War, war posters showed the Mother of God with her mantle thrown over Greek soldiers.[81] But these stories—linked more with the mantle than the veil as such—led an existence alongside another and more intimate imagery that spoke to the veil of the flesh.[82]

Linking the two changes operating here—from relic to icon and maphorion to veil—may be a yet deeper shift signalled by the spectacular events of the "usual miracle." In the "usual miracle" we encounter for the first time a veil that is not a protective cover but a concealment: a cloth that functions to hide from view. The drama of concealment and revelation became a familiar aspect of icon culture in late eleventh and twelfth-century Byzantium. Like modern ones, the great charismatic icons of Byzantium were "brought out" only on certain occasions, for ceremonial appearances in vigils and processions. Some of these great images were veiled by embroidered covers: Alexios I himself, for instance, recovered from serious illness after being covered with the veil from the icon of Christ in the Chalke Gate.[83] Valerie Nunn has collected eleven epigrams from the late eleventh and twelfth centuries that were composed for embroidered covers given in thanks or supplication to icons.[84] Many of the donors belonged to the imperial family, and half of the covers are destined for "the Hodegetria"—either the great palladion itself, or precious private replicas venerated under her name. Such covers were a form of display, for they were rich and precious. But they were also a form of concealment, mystifying and making desirable the icon beneath. They played, thus, upon a fundamental dialectic of vision, both creating a display and withdrawing its object into the realm of desire. Like the very objects they covered, they belonged to a realm of spectacle. As the great sacred objects of Byzantium became drawn ever more into the play of spectacle, these instruments of vision—the icon and the veil—come into their own.

It has been noted that Andrej Bogoljubskij's devotion to the Pokrov became associated above all with icons, and not with a relic. This was not the case with rulers linked at earlier moments with Byzantium's rituals of imperial presence. Focal in this context is Charlemagne, a figure scarcely less mythic than the maphorion itself, and fundamental to the legends of Mary's relics in western Europe.[85] If the Virgin's garments had originated within what was, in around 400, still Byzantine territory, and so belonged to Byzantium's own heritage, such items were available to western Europe only from outside: from the "east." Charlemagne acquired sacred objects from Jerusalem and cultivated an enthusiasm for Holy Land relics in his courtier-abbots. But Charlemagne also had the example of the imperial capital of the east, Constantinople. Constantinopolitan habits of relic acquisition and display assuredly affected his own. He takes us into another—if interestingly interlocked—story of Mary's veil.

"Veil" is the identification given repeatedly to the relic of the Virgin's vesture housed in the great Marian shrine in Aachen and traced back by both legend and learned association—medieval as well as modern—to Charles the Great and his Palace Chapel.[86] This definition met a formidable challenge when the shrine was opened and yielded not a veil, at all, but a fully intact dress.[87] The dress is of western medieval origin, and reflects the fashions of the early thirteenth century. It must have been made for the ceremonies surrounding the dedication of Aachen's Court Style Gothic apse, consecrated to Mary in 1238 and furnished with trappings of a sanctity capable of withstanding the glare of Louis IX's Passion relics at the Sainte-Chapelle.[88]

But the story is not quite so simple as this. The Aachen couture tells us that the appropriate form for a Marian garment in 1238 was as a dress. It does not tell us that the tradition requiring a Marian garment at Aachen had originated in the thirteenth century, or that that tradition had been served throughout its life by the same conception of the garment. The tradition assuredly antedated 1238, and there is every reason to expect that it was as volatile as the one that spawned it in Constantinople. As Heinrich Schiffers notes, it is probable that a relic or relics of Marian garments were among the sacred items assembled at Aachen in Carolingian times: Angilbert of Centula, who claimed to have a sample of every relic in Aachen, had among others a relic of a Marian "vestimentum,"[89] and according to a monastic inventory of 1003 Charlemagne's grandson, Lothair I, had given another to the monastery of Prüm.[90] The earliest inventory of the Aachen relics is no earlier than the late twelfth century and so not long before the apse of 1238.[91] It, however, speaks of a "velum" of Mary. With this, an interesting pattern emerges, as a "vestimentum" gives way to a "velum" that reverts in the thirteenth century to a dress, a dress now stained with droplets of milk from the Nativity.[92] The articles of clothing, and perhaps more notably their sequence, recall the shifting habit of Blachernai.

A curiously convergent picture is offered by the most famous off-spring of Charlemagne's legendary Marian relic.[93] This, of course, is the "chemise" of Christmas night preserved at Chartres, supposed to have come to Chartres as a gift of Charles the Bald. The relic is first attested by Dudo of St.-Quentin between 994 and 1015 in his account of Chartres's miraculous triumph over Rollo the Norman, an account repeated in several eleventh-century Norman texts and eventually implanted in early twelfth-century compilations of Marian miracles at Chartres itself, and in England.[94] As Dudo tells it, the story has clear reverberations of the accounts of the defenses of Constantinople at Blachernai: threatened by Norse invasion, Chartres's bishop, Walter, summons the Duke of Burgundy and the Count of Poitou to defend his city and, as combat is engaged, marches himself toward the enemy holding up the cross and the tunic of Mary; Rollo flees—in other accounts he is blinded—and the city is saved. The story of Blachernai had reached the West already by 800 with the translation of the Akathistos Hymn by a Venetian bishop named Christophoros, who was in France in 807–13;[95] Paul the Deacon recounted it,[96] so one gathers that it was known in the West, and the legend of Chartres seems to have appropriated it. Progressively, as Chartres' story was told, the role of the relic became more central until, as Gabriela Signori notes,[97] William of Malmesbury omits the warlords entirely and focuses on the relic, reporting that:

> . . . the townspeople, relying neither on arms nor fortifications, piously implored the assistance of the blessed Virgin Mary. The shift, too, of the Virgin, which Charles the Bald (literally, "unus ex Karolis") had brought with other relics from Constantinople, they displayed to the winds on the ramparts, thronged by the garrison, after the fashion of a banner ("in modum vexilli").[98]

The account of the miracle preserved at Chartres itself, composed perhaps a century after William of Malmesbury's and transmitted by Vincent Sablon in 1671, uses much the same image, saying that the bishop "raised [the tunic] like a banner."[99] That the relic had, indeed, been singled out for exceptional veneration at Chartres is attested by its installation in a rich reliquary by the goldsmith Tendon in the very years around 1000 when Dudo was writing.[100] It remained there until 1717.

William of Malmesbury's account of the siege of Chartres is interesting in many ways: it links the relic with the Carolingians and before them with Constantinople, offering in the guise of history a clear picture of its legend's geneaology, running back from the emperor of the West to the imperial city of Constantinople; it focuses the city's salvation upon the relic alone; it identifies the relic clearly as Mary's tunic. But it also adds an interesting detail. Rather than stating that Bishop Walter was carrying the tunic in his hands ("in manibus ferens") as Dudo had, he says that it was set up as a battle standard. All western authors are agreed that the garment invoked during the siege of Chartres was a tunic. But the reference to its being carried as a battle standard has a parallel only in Anna Komnene's description of Alexios I carrying the maphorion. The convergence of William of Malmesbury's and Anna Komnene's conceptions—both set down in the first half of the twelfth century—is striking. It suggests that the relic at Chartres not only drew upon a deep and ancient linkage with Constantinople, but that it continued to be conceived in parallel with what—in Constantinople—had become the maphorion. This suggestion receives support from an unexpected piece of evidence. When Tendon's reliquary was opened at Chartres in 1717, what lay within was a white silk veil, wrapped in a long, tirazlike swath of Byzantine silk of tenth- or early eleventh-century manufacture.[101] The latter textile is now displayed behind the altar at Chartres; it tells us that the relic deposed in Tendon's shrine was conceived in around 1000 as being linked to Constantinople. The fabric that it enfolded tells us something else: the "tunic" of the Virgin was a veil. As Aachen's "vestimentum" had emerged in 1238 from what had earlier been a "velum," so the "tunicam" of Chartres emerged from its eleventh-century reliquary as a veil.

The relics at Aachen and Chartres represent no more than a tiny fraction of the Marian garments that were gathering in châsses throughout Europe in the course of the early medieval centuries;[102] the value of these two, very eminent examples lies in the glimpse they afford into the volatile history of the relics' role as they lived in the imaginations of successive centuries of Christians. Both examples were bound in this rich imaginative life with the city of Constantinople, and one feels in their shifting shape and stories how strongly the history of the Marian relics in Constantinople paralleled that in western Europe. During the centuries of the maphorion's ascendancy in Byzantium, the Chartres and Aachen relics, too, assumed aspects of veils.

We argued earlier that the maphorion had been a way of linking the relics resident at Blachernai in Constantinople with a conception of Mary as the "invincible general," the peerless intercessor whose protection guaranteed eternal victory and safeguarded the integrity of the City. More than in any imagery of her own imperial status, this role as the embodiment of eternal victory bound Mary to the emperors as the guarantor of their rule. It was a guarantee that embraced not just the emperor but the head of empire, be that head male or female, single or—through marriage or co-rulership—conjoint.

In western Europe, too, the centuries of the maphorion saw a heightening of Mary's royalty, though by interestingly different means. She was associated with royal persons; but she was also—as she was not in Byzantium—imaged as royal. It was, thus, in exactly the years that Dudo wrote about the siege of Chartres that Bishop Aethelwold's magnificent Benedictional was illuminated at Winchester with an image of Mary receiving a crown and scepter at her Dormition, a motif repeated with focal clarity in the slightly later Sacramentary of Robert of Jumièges;[103] in the early years of the new millennium, Mary was depicted with crown and scepter in the Bury Psalter and the Arenburg and Pembroke Gospels; and in the famous "Winchester Quinity," possibly drawn by the artist of the New Minster *Liber Vitae,* she is conspicuously crowned.[104] In bearing the scepter, she bears regalia belonging to the king, but not—as Pauline Stafford has shown—accorded to queens.[105] She is in this sense beyond gendered definitions of regal authority, a status perhaps confirmed by the fact that in several of these images she also carries a book and so "has voice." Ottonian Germany, too, in the same years at the turn of the millennium, saw a cluster of imperial representations of Mary, dressed in jeweled garments recalling those of Byzantium.[106]

The figure of Mary is also associated in varied ways with images of rulers. This is most visible Germany under Otto III (991–1002) and his Salian successors, Henry II (1002–1024) and Conrad II (1024–1039). A range of iconographic conventions rooted in Byzantium link these emperors with Mary in a pattern that was itself very probably rooted in Byzantine political rhetoric. Thus, the miniature of Mary crowning Otto III in the Sacramentary of Warmund of Ivrea is readily paralleled with the just slightly earlier formula found on Byzantine coins of John I Tzimiskes (969–976), with Mary crowning him.[107] The use of August 15, the day of Mary's Dormition, as a time for imperial ceremonies,[108] may also be rooted in Byzantium.[109] It was at her Dormition, as Aethelwold's Benedictional had shown, that Mary ascended to queenship of Heaven, and so the emperors celebrated their own power on that day, paralleling it with Mary's assumption to be, in the words of Brunon de Querfurt (ca. 1002), "bona angelorum imperatrix augusta."[110] A magnificent Byzantine ivory of the Dormition was inset in the cover of the Gospel Book of Otto III (Munich, Bayerische Staatsbibl., clm. 4453); Otto's successor, Henry II, celebrated August 15 with pomp; and Conrad II scheduled both of his coronations—in Germany in 1024 and in Rome in 1033—on Marian feasts, and had himself depicted with his family before an image of Mary in the apse of Aquileia cathedral in a composition reminiscent of the image of Leo I at Blachernai.[111]

Paralleling these public and Byzantine-inflected images associating the emperors with Mary, however, a second iconographic current of Marian regal imagery appeared. This one is more strictly western, though it assumes especially clear visual form in a depiction of Otto III's Byzantine mother, Theophano. This current is focused on women. It is seen clearly in the well-known ivory in the Castel Sforzesco, Milan, showing Otto II and Theophano kneeling beneath an enthroned Christ, who is flanked by intercessors.[112] Otto's protector, the soldier-saint Maurice, stands over Otto to Christ's right. At Christ's left, Mary looms above the kneeling Theophano, who holds her infant son Otto III before body as if he were virtually being born. As St. Maurice guards the emperor in war, Mary guards Theophano, bending her grace to the empress specifically in the female terms of her fertility.

Characteristically, we assign the elaboration of a Marian rhetoric of queenship to the later eleventh and twelfth centuries, based in Gergory VII's famous letters to Mathilda of Tuscany and Adelaide of Hungary. But Dominique Iogna-Prat has traced it back already to the Carolingian coronation *ordines.*[113] She identifies as an echo of the *ordo* for Louis the Pious's wife Irmingart the words attributed by Ermold le Noir to Pope Stephen IV during Louis's anointing, with their resonance of the Annunciation: "Hail, woman loved of God. May life and health be accorded to you for long years."[114] Mary's bond to the theme of fertility is stronger in the surviving *ordines* of Charles the Bald's wives, Ermentrude and Richildis—crowned only after they were pregnant—who are admonished to imitate Mary's chastity by consecrating their ready fertility to the realm.[115] Where Mary figures in male *ordines* as a protection and rampart, she figures for queens in terms of grace and fecundity.[116] Iogna-Prat thus singles out a phenomenon seen more fully in the Ottonian use of Mary: two iconographies of Mary evolve around the royal couple, one for males and one for females. The ivory of Otto II and Theophano illustrates this clearly, and this differentiation continues even in the Ottonian era that produced many images of the ruling couple equally disposed on either side of Christ: the Codex Aureus of Speyer shows Mary receiving the manuscript from the emperor Henry III (1028–56) while laying her hand on the head of his wife, Agnes.[117]

The ivory in Milan is the image most consistently associated by scholars with the frontispiece in the *Liber Vitae* with which we began. In both, Christ in a mandorla sits flanked by a royal couple for whom saintly protectors intercede, a male saint for the male ruler and the Virgin Mary for his consort. In the *Liber Vitae,* however, as noted, Mary and the queen are at Christ's right, and the queen receives a veil. The veil is paralleled with the crown conferred on the king by Christ, and it echoes the crown's dual theme of confirmation and investiture. At the same time, it is closely associated with Mary and her grace. Like her placement at Christ's right, the veil gives signal distinction to the queen, Emma. But what is signalled by the veil? To Renate Kroos, it signals the *stola secunda* worn by the blessed at the Last Judgment.[118] The Last Judgment follows this frontispiece in the manuscript; nonetheless, the visual parallel of crown and veil is too overt to believe that they do not have a shared dimension of worldly meaning. To Dominique Iogna-Prat, this shared dimension lies in their reference to coronation, the veil signalling the chaste marital fertility invoked by Carolingian *ordines* and imaged in Mary's protection of Theophano with her tiny son in the Milan ivory.[119] But Pauline Stafford points out that the coronation *ordines* of English queens are striking precisely for their omission of fertility as a theme.[120] The rite used in Emma's coronation in 1017 in particular emphasizes other duties, calling upon her to "be a peace-weaver, to bring tranquillity in her days, to be an English queen, and to be a consort in royal power."[121] It is likely that the veil, too, spoke the language of English *ordines.*

Emma was crowned at much the time that Dudo wrote about the defense of Chartres by the Virgin's relic; the *Liber Vitae* was written before Dudo's death but not before his account of Chartres' protection had reached England. At Wincester, where the *Liber Vitae* was made, it reached a community distinguished for its veneration of Mary, where Marian relics rested, and where the imagery of Mary's royalty flourished. Winchester's Marian relics are recorded in the *Liber Vitae* itself: several relics of Mary's garments (*vestimenta*) and one of her sepulcher.[122] A century after the *Liber Vitae,* the "Byzantine diptych" in the Winchester Psalter would display the sepulchre relic as the sarcophagus in a potent image of Mary's assumption to be the "reine de ciel."[123] But the Winchester manuscripts of the *Liber Vitae*'s own era show that the royalty that Mary reached through her sarcophagus was already particularly Winchester's own.

The royal Mary of Winchester oversees Emma as her fellow patron of New Minster, St. Peter, oversees Cnut. We have seen above that in the art of the medieval West the Virgin's relation to queens was not the same as that to kings; a particular relationship is formulated in the veil that links Emma and Mary. We have seen, too, that the terminology of coronation in England does not readily furnish the relationship of chaste fertility that had linked Mary and the queen in the Carolingian coronation *ordines.* Emma had been crowned with an admonition to be a consort not in the royal bed but "in royal power."[124] Mary, too, had assumed a heroic dimension in Emma's day: this was the era of the victor-Virgin of Blachernai and Chartres, who had given Blachernai's relic its distinctive definition as a maphorion. The imaginative form of the "garment" housed in western relic collections, too, was volatile. Interred in Tendon's reliquary at Chartres in the form of a veil, Mary's signature garment may well have assumed that form in Winchester, too, when called upon to image the special grace of a queen who was as "gerant" as she was "germinant."

The image in the *Liber Vitae* is unique in the history of medieval art. It is central to our quest because it is the unique instance in which a garment of Mary constitutes an instrument of investiture. It arises from a very particular conjunction of circumstances: a particular phase in the persona of Mary, a particular phase in the imaginative history of her relics, a particular place in the geography of Europe with its distinctive patterns of Christian rulership and worship, and a particular woman's queenship. The moment that produced the *Liber Vitae* was fleeting. Especially for the Virgin's relics, the European West was even less hospitable to the concept of a garment abstracted from the somatic story of birth and Passion than Byzantium was, and the great majority of the textile relics in the West got swept into the embrace of the Nativity or the Passion. Fashion, too, was important, for Romanesque images of the Virgin rarely wear a maphorion; they wear a mantle and a headcloth. Where Mary's protection survives as a theme, it is bound largely to Mary's mantle. The veil slowly assumed a different life, as it did also in Byzantium.

This story can be observed most compactly in the city of Siena, where the Virgin's veil became the locus for at least four different significations during the two-generation span between about 1260 and 1320. A first occurs with Coppo di Marcovaldo's majestic Madonna del bordone, painted in 1261 in the wake of Ghibelline Siena's dramatic victory over the Florentines at the battle of Montaperti the year before.[125] In a composition notable for its Byzantine character, echoing the pose of the Hodegetria, Coppo nonetheless retains the Romanesque clothing of the Virgin, her dress cloaked not by a maphorion but by a heavy stole and white veil. In this huge and somber panel whose iconography deliberately conjures the Hodegetria's role as guardian of cities and emperors, the conspicuous white wimple offers itself as the logical nesting point for metaphors of Mary's clothing. Sienese legend assigns the victory at Montaperti to the protection of the Virgin, who veiled the battlefield in white mist and so bewildered the enemy.[126] This metaphor of protection—a topos in Byzantine legends, too[127]—seems to find its visualization in the white wimple that the Madonna del bordone bequeathed in turn upon the whole generation of Virgins dominated by the models of Coppo and Guido da Siena.

That the metaphor of Mary's protection was, in fact, linked with her clothing in Siena as in Constantinople is demonstrated by a second significant image. This is Duccio's well-known Madonna of the Franciscans of around 1280–85.[128] Surely produced for private devotion, this tiny panel uses a composition known hitherto only in the Crusader Levant,[129] with Mary throwing open the long fringe of her maphorion to cloak kneeling devotees, in this case three Franciscan friars huddled in the Byzantine devotional posture of proskynesis. Reflecting a fusion of Byzantium's legend of the maphorion and the western understanding of Mary's robe as a cloak, this short-lived but eloquent iconographic formula exposes with momentary, dramatic clarity the rich processes of mutual accommodation as the visual imaginations of two cultures converged on common myths.

If the protective mantle/maphorion was a factor in the Sienese iconography of Mary's veil, as the Madonna del bordone and Madonna of the Franciscans attest, this metaphor was being joined by a different image of Mary's clothing, now rooted not in the robe but in the white, wimplelike veil itself. This third face of Siena's veil-imagery was developed once again by Duccio, who pioneered it in his early Stoclet Madonna, developed it in his Perugia Madonna, and brought it to its exquisite fulfilment in the triptych in the National Gallery in London.[130] In this case, Mary is shown wearing something very like the maphorion. But it is not this garment that is mobilized iconographically. It is, rather, her fine, white veil, worn under the maphorion, that is brought into play, as her infant child pulls at it. In his seemingly innocent play, he draws it across his own, scantly clad body. With this, Duccio activates a new and extraordinarily provocative realm of imagery, as the delicate clothing of Mary's head and heart both cloak her child's divinity and shroud his mortality. Powerless to protect, this fabric can only veil the inexpressible mysteries of maternity and mortality.

As the veil had triumphed over the maphorion in Byzantine iconography, so in Siena it was the veil, not the mantle, that was bequeathed by Duccio's generation on the art of its successors. This is illustrated by a fourth Sienese image, whose pan-European dissemination must stand in the limited scope of this article for the broader processes of European image-making. A product of the circle of the Lorenzetti, this image is preserved for us in the great miracle-worker, the Madonna of Cambrai.[131] Copied countless times in the northern Europe, the panel itself seems to have originated in Siena in the 1330s, and shows the Virgin cuddling a twisting child who clutches with one hand at the rich hem of her maphorion as it laps onto her breast. Less explicit than Duccio's veil, the veil of the Virgin of Cambrai stands as a quiet, portentious sign of the vast body of associative significations embraced by the bond of matter—of material stuff—that binds mother and child. Hans Belting has traced the image itself to Byzantium. But in this Sienese form it exercised vast, evocative power over western European art.

Richard Trexler sums up his study on clothing and unclothing holy images with the conclusion that to clothe an image is to feminize it.[132] Veiling, with its visual dialectic of transformation and mystification, occlusion and desire, evokes the same patterns of response that Trexler singled out in his investigation of clothing. Our overview of the story of Mary's veil has shown that this highly visual, speculative and specular response to the veil is not the only one possible. Most notably, this is not the way the mythology of the maphorion functioned. Yet it is a response that appeals to the modern imagination. The deeply somatic mystery of Mary—mother of god, daughter of her child, spouse of her son—demands a veil before its suggestive immensity. What is beneath the clothing of Mary? The early medieval answer—that it is we ourselves—cannot satisfy the yearning curiosity to lift the veil that covers Mary's head and heart and see into that deep vessel where the physical facts of god's life were weighed. So it is that the relics of Mary's garments—varied as they may have been in both name and mythic interpretations during the Middle Ages—have become in our modern vocabulary her "veil." In the vast economy of textile exchange, it should perhaps surprise us that Mary's robes, so potent as the armor of just rulers, were but rarely drafted into the role of investiture. It cannot surprise us, however, so long as we veil our own imagination with the potent and feminizing "veil of the Virgin."

Notes

1. Elizabeth Temple, *Anglo-Saxon Manuscripts 900–1066,* Manuscript Books from the British Isles 2 (London: Harvey Miller, 1976), no. 78. The manuscript is London, British Library, Stowe 944, folio 6r.
2. Jan Gerchow, "Prayers for King Cnut: The Liturgical Commemoration of a Conqueror," in *England in the Eleventh Century,* Harlaxton Medieval Studies 2 (Stamford: Paul Watkins, 1992), 230–37.
3. On the books' identification see Gershow, "Prayers," 231.
4. Pauline Stafford, *Queen Emma and Queen Edith* (Cambridge, Mass.: Blackwell Publishers, 1997), 175–79, esp. 178.
5. For late ninth- and tenth-century examples preceding Cnut's portrait see the Byzantine emperors Leo VI (886–912) crowned by the Virgin (Kathleen Corrigan, "The Ivory Scepter of Leo VI: A Statement of Post-Iconoclastic Imperial Ideology," *Art Bulletin* 60 [1978]: 407–16, and Helen C. Evans and William D. Wixom, eds., *The Glory of Byzantium. Art and Culture of the Middle Byzantine Era, A.D. 843–1261,* exhibition catalogue, Metropolitan Museum of Art, New York, 11 March 1997–6 July 1997 [New York, 1997], 201–2, no. 138), Constantine VII (913–959) crowned by Christ (Evans and Wixom, eds., *The Glory,* 203–4, no. 140), and Romanos and Eudokia crowned by Christ (Ibid., 500; see most recently Anthony Cutler, "A Byzantine Triptych in Medieval Germany and Its Modern Recovery," *Gesta* 37 [1998]: 9–10 for the date of this plaque and thus of its imperial pair). In the West see Otto II (967–983) and Theophano (972–991) crowned by Christ in their ivory plaque in the Musée de Cluny in Paris (Evans and Wixom, eds., *The Glory,* 499–501, no. 337), Otto III (991–1002) crowned by Mary in Ivrea, Biblioteca capitolare, MS LXXXVI, fol. 16v (Robert Deshman, "Otto III and the Warmund Sacramentary. A Study in Political Theology,"

Zeitschrift für Kunstgeschichte 34 [1971]: fig. 1), and Henry II (1002–1024) crowned by Christ in Munich, Staatsbibliothek, cod. lat. 4456, folio 11r (Percy Ernst Schramm, *Die deutschen Kaiser und Könige in Bilder ihrer Zeit 751–1190,* 2nd ed., ed. Florentine Mütherich [Munich: Prestel Verlag, 1983], no. 124).

6. On the Blachernai complex see Raymond Janin, *La Géographie ecclésiastique de l'empire byzantin, I: Le Siège de Constantinople et le patriachat oecuménique, 3: Les Églises et les monastères* (Paris: Centre national des recherches scientifique, 1969), 161–70.
7. On the siege of 626 see most recently J. Howard-Johnston, "The Siege of Constantinople in 626," in *Constantinople and Its Hinterland,* ed. Cyril Mango and Gilbert Dagron (Aldershot: Variorum, 1995), 131–42, and Cyril Mango's commentary in *The Chronicle of Theophanes the Confessor,* trans. and with commentary by Cyril Mango and Roger Scott (Oxford: Clarendon, 1997), 477.
8. On the Akathistos and its relation to the events of 626, see Egon Wellesz, "The 'Akathistos': A Study in Byzantine Hymnography," *Dumbarton Oaks Papers* 9–10 (1956): 143–76; Paul Speck, *Zufälliges zum Bellum avaricum des Georgios Pisides,* Miscellanea Byzantina Monacensia 24 (Munich: Institut für Byzantinistik, neugriechische Philologie und byzantinische Kunstgeschichte der Universität, 1980), 58–59; and Nancy Patterson Ševčenko, "Icons in the Liturgy," *Dumbarton Oaks Papers* 45 (1991): 49 n30.
9. A good summary of this event's complex historiography is given in Cyril Mango, *The Homilies of Photios, Patriarch of Constantinople. English Translation, Introduction and Commentary,* Dumbarton Oaks Studies 3 (Cambridge: Haarvard University Press, 1958), 74–82.
10. See Alexander P. Kazhdan, ed., *The Oxford Dictionary of Byzantium,* 3 vols. (New York: Oxford University Press, 1991), 2: 1353, s.v. "Metatorion."
11. They visited Blachernai on Good Friday; on the Virgin's feasts of the Presentation of Christ in the Temple (Feb. 2), the Dormition (Aug. 15), and her Synax (Dec. 26); on July 2 and on the anniversary of the dedication of the church on August 31; on the eve of the Feast of Orthodoxy (first Sunday in Lent); on the anniversaries of the victory over the Arabs in 718 (June 20), the victory over the Avars in 626 (Aug. 7), and the earthquake of 740 (Oct 26).
12. Constantini Porphyrogeniti, "De Cerimoniis Aulae Byzantinae,"in *Patrologiae Cursus Completus, Series Graeca* [henceforth *PG*], ed. J.-P. Migne, 161 vols. in 166 (Paris: Garnier Fratres, 1857–1887), 112: col. 1021 A: Εἶθ'οὕτως δεέρχονται διὰ τοῦ πρὸς ἀνατολὴν δεξιοῦ μέρους τοῦ βήματος καὶ τοῦ σκευοφυλακίου, καὶ εἰσέρχονται εἰς τὸν νάρθηκα τῆς ἁγίας σοροῦ . . . [Then the emperors leave the bema to the east through the right side of the bema and the skevophylakion, and they enter the narthex of the Soros . . .]. It is not easy to see the point at which the emperors actually acknowledge the Virgin's garment. With Venance Grumel, "Sur l'*Episkepsis* des Blachernes," *Echos d'Orient* 33 (1930): 334, I

suspect that this occurred at the "Episkepsis" cited at col. 1021 B: Εἶτα ἐκβάλλουσι τὰ τούτων σαγία, καὶ λαμβάνει ὁ πρῶτος βασιλεὺς παρὰ τοῦ πραιποσίτου τὸ ἀπὸ ταωνοπτέρων ῥιπίδιον, καὶ φιλοκαλεῖ πέριξ τῆς ἁγίας τραπέζης, καὶ ἐξέρχονται τοῦ βέματος, καὶ ἀπέρχονται ἀπὸ δεξιᾶς εἰς τὴν ἐπίσκεψιν, καὶ ἅπτουσιν κἀκεῖσε κηροὺς καὶ προσκυνοῦσιν [Then, the emperors get out of their sagia, and the senior emperor takes the riphidion made of peacock feathers from the praepositos, and he goes around the altar, and they go out of the bema, and go out on the right into the Episkepsis, and light candles there and venerate]. This seems to refer not to an icon, as usually maintained, but rather—as Reiskius proposed in his translation given in Ibid., col. 1022 B—to the site of the relic: . . . et abeunt a dextra parte ad episkepsin [seu visitationem atque adorationem sacrarum B.Virginis reliquiarum], et ibi quoque accendunt cereos et [reliquias] adorant. See, however, Lennart Rydén, "The Vision of the Virgin at Blachernae and the Feast of the Pokrov," *Analecta Bollandiana* 94 (1976): 70, who cites a similar use of the word in reference to an icon at the Myrelaion church.

13. On the vigil and procession see most recently Ševčenko, "Icons in the Liturgy," 50–54. Constantine's predecessor by a century, the Iconoclast emperor Theophilos (829–842), is reported by both Michael Glykas and Kedrenos to have gone each week to venerate at Blachernai, but while his visit is likely to have been made on Fridays, we don't know if it bore any relation to the vigil. See Michael Glykas, "Annales, IV," in *PG,* 158: col. 537 B: οὗτος καθ'ἑκάστην ἑβδομάδα διὰ τῆς ἀγορᾶς ἔφιππος εἰς τὸν ἐν Βλαχέρναις ναὸν ἀπήρχετο· εἰ γὰρ καὶ τιμὴν ταῖς ἁγίαις εἰκόσιν οὐκ ἔνεμεν, τῷ Σωτῆρι καὶ αὐτῇ τῇ Θεομητόρι πίστιν ἐτήρει, ὡς ἔλεγεν [He went each week on horseback through the agora to the church of Blachernai; if he did not have honor for the holy icons, he nonetheless did have faith in the Savior and the Mother of God].
14. For the Chalkoprateia church, see Janin, *La Géographie,* 241–53.
15. See in particular the vision of St. Andrew the Fool in Christ, quoted in translation by Rydén, "The Vision," 66, and the visionary dream of St. Irene of Chysobalanton, in Jan Olaf Rosenqvist, *The Life of St. Irene Abbess of Chrysobalanton* (Uppsala: Almqvist and Wiksell, 1986), 58–59.
16. Psellos's text, composed in 1075, is given in translation and the western European descriptions of the miracle are cited in Venance Grumel, "Le 'Miracle habituel' de Notre-Dame des Blachernes," *Echos d'Orient* 24 (1931): 129–46.
17. Ibid., 141.
18. Note Nikephoros Kallistos Xanthopoulos's extremely complicated narrative of Constantinople's Marian relics, analyzed by Michel Van Esbroeck, "Le Culte de la Vierge de Jérusalem à Constantinople aux 6e–7e siècles," *Revue des études byzantines* 46 (1988): 185–86, quoting from Nicephori Callisti Xanthopouli, "Historia Ecclesiastica," in *PG,* 146: col. 1061 A-B and 147: cols. 41 D, 44 B-45 B. Nikephoros has Pulcheria place at Blachernai with

her own hands two caskets received from Jerusalem, one with the *shroud* (τὰ ἐντάφια σπάργανα) and one with what must be the two *robes (. . .* μετὰ τῶν ἱερῶν ἐκείνων ἀμφίων . . .), and then adds that "the venerable *garment* was placed there not long afterward under Leo ('Η γὰρ τιμία ἐσΘὴς ἐπί λέοντος οὐ πολλῷ ὕστερον ἐκοιμίζετο.)"The genuine confusion over the matter is amusingly reflected in the illuminations for 15 August in three Metaphrastian Menologia of the eleventh century (Moscow, Historical Museum, gr. 382, Athos, Dionysiou 50, and Paris, Bibliothèque nationale, gr. 1528), which conflate elements of Blachernai and Chalkoprateia, and of the ceremonies of July 2 and August 15: Sirarpie Der Nersessian, "The Illustrations of the Metaphrastian Menologium," in *Late Classical and Mediaeval Studies in Honor of Albert Mathias Friend, Jr.,* ed. George Forsyth and Kurt Weitzmann (Princeton: Princeton University Press, 1955), 230–31. Pilgrim accounts are no more consistent. The early twelfth-century English Pilgrim, for instance, reports that "Ad sanctam Mariam Blachernes . . . est posita argentea archa, et iacet intus cinctura sanctae Dei genitricis," while William of Tyre says nothing about the Soros. See Krijne N. Ciggaar, "Une description de Constantinople traduite par un pèlerin anglais," *Revue des études byzantines* 34 (1976): 260; E.M. Langille, "La Constantinople de Guillaume de Tyre," *Byzantion* 63 (1993): 195.

19. "Narratio in Depositionem Vestis S. Mariae = Εἰς κατάΘεσιν τῆς τιμίας ἐσΘῆτος τῆς ἱεομήτορος ἐν Βλαχέρναις," in François Combefis, *Historia haeresis monotheletarum sanctaeque in eam sextae synodi actorum vindiciae . . .* (Paris: Antonii Bertier, 1648), 751–88.
20. Ibid., 782 A: ἣν οὐ μόνον αὐτὴν πεπιστεύκαμεν ἠμφιέσΘαι τὴν τοῦ Θεοῦ λόγου μητέρα · ἀλλ' ἐν ᾗ καὶ αὐτὸν πάντως ἔτι νήπιου ὄντα τὸν Θεὸν λόγον, ἐδέξατό τε, καὶ ἐγαλούχησεν.
21. Andrew of Crete, "Εγκόμιον εἰς τὴν κατάΘεσιν τῆς τιμίας ζώνης τῆς ὑπεραγίας δεσποίνης ἡμῶν Θεοτόκου," in Combefis, *Historia,* 789–804. Accordingly, the sermon by Patriarch Germanos (730–33) honoring a church of the Virgin and its milk-stained relic of the ζώνη is often assigned to Blachernai: S. Germani Patriarchae Constantinopolitanae, "Oratio I in Encaenia venerandae aedis sanctissimae Dominae nostrae Dei Genitricis, inque sanctas fascias Domini nostri Jesu Christi," in *PG,* 98 (1865): 371–84. This or another ζώνη was venerated along with the saddling clothes of Christ from the early tenth century onward at the Chalkopraeia church; another ζώνη was brought to Chalkoprateia in 942. See Nancy Patterson Ševčenko, "The Limburg Staurothek and Its Relics," in *ίΥΜΙΑΜΑ στην μνήμη της Θασκαρίνας Μπούρα* (Athens: Benaki Museum, 1994), 291.
22. The Euthymiac History is preserved as an interpolation into John of Damascus's second sermon on the Dormition and in the eighth-century Sinai MS gr. 491: see Antoine Wenger, A.A., *L'Assomption de la T.S. Vierge dans la tradition byzantine du VIe au Xe siècle. Études et documents,* Archives de l'orient chrétien 5 (Paris: Institut français d'études byzantines, 1955), 136–40.

As seen in S. Joannis Damasceni, "Homilia II in Dormitionem B.V. Mariae," in *PG,* 96: cols. 721–54, this speaks indeed of the Virgin's burial shroud (col. 749 B: Καὶ τὸ μὲν σῶμα αὐτῆς τὸ πανύμνητον οὐδαμῶς εὑρεῖν ἠδυνήσαν, μόνα δὲ αὐτῆς τὰ ἐντάφια κείμενα εὑρόντες [And her all-glorious body could not be found at all; only the empty winding cloths could be found]), but it is the dresses that are cited in the reliquary sent by Patriarch Juvenal (col. 752 A: Καὶ ταῦτα οἱ βασιλεῖς ἀκούσαντες, ἤτησαν αὐτὸν τὸν ἀρχιεπίσκοπον Ἰουενάλιον τὴν ἁγίαν ἐκείνην σορὸν μετὰ τῶν ἐν αὐτῇ τῆς ἀνδόξου καὶ παναγίας ἱεοτόκου Μαρίας ἱματίων βεβουλλωμένην ἀσφαλῶς αὐτοῖς ἀποσταλῆναι . . . [And hearing these things the emperors asked the Patriarch Juvenal to send them that holy casket carefully sealed up with the dresses of the glorious and all-holy Theotokos Mary inside . . .).

23. Martin Jugie, *La Mort et l'assomption de la sainte Vierge. Étude historico-doctrinale,* Studi e testi 114 (Città del Vaticano: Biblioteca Apostolica Vaticana, 1944), 695–96, where the text is quoted. The sermon of Euthymios is given in the *Patrologia orientalia* 17: 484–85, 511.
24. Ibid., 688–707.
25. Wenger, *L'Assomption,* 111–39.
26. Van Esbroeck, "Le Culte," 181–90. The Arabic text, cited on page 187, is not fully identified.
27. In his Fourth Homily on the Russian siege in Mango, *Homilies* (as in note 9 above), 95–110, Photios does not use "maphorion" but his term περιβολή means something "thrown around," like a stole: see note 37 below. The word maphorion appears in the tenth-century chronicle known under the name of its scribe, Leo Grammatikos (Immanuelis Bekkari, ed., *Leonis Grammatici Chronographia,* Corpus Scriptorum Historiae Byzantinae 26 [Bonn: Weber, 1842], 241, ll. 4–12) and its various plagiarisms describing the event of 860; in the chronicle of Theophanes Continuatus describing Romanos I's departure to parley with Tsar Symeon of Bulgaria in 926 (Immanuelis Bekkeri, ed., *Theophanes Continuatus, Ioannes Cameniata, Symeon Magister, Georgius Monachus,* Corpus Scriptorum Historiae Byzantinae 43 [Bonn: Weber, 1838], 406, l. 19–407, l. 7); in a reference to the event of 860 in one of the diatribes of John Oxites against Alexios I Komnenos composed around 1093 (Paul Gautier, "Diatribes de Jean l'Oxite contre Alexis Ier Comnène," *Revue des études byzantines* 28 [1970]: 38–39, ll. 17–27); and in a description of Alexios I Komnenos's battle against the Cumans in 1089 in the *Alexiad* of Anna Komnene (Bernard Leib, ed., *Anne Comnène Alexiade,* 3 vols. [Paris: Société d'édition 'Les belles lettres', 1933], 2: 98).
28. On Pulcheria see recently Vasiliki Limberis, *Divine Heiress. The Virgin Mary and the Creation of the Christian Constantinople* (London and New York: Routledge, 1994), and Nicholas P. Constas, "Weaving the Body of God: Proclus of Constantinople, the Theotokos, and the Loom of the Flesh," *Journal of Early Christian Studies* 3,2 (1995): 169–94.

29. See in particular Constas, "Weaving," 176–94.
30. Ibid., 183, 173.
31. Ibid., 189.
32. Antoine Wenger, A.A., "Les Homélies inédites de Cosmas Vestitor sur la Dormition," *Revue des études byzantines* 11 (1953): 295.
33. See in particular Averil Cameron, "The Theotokos in Sixth-Century Constantinople," *Journal of Theological Studies* NS 29 (1978): 79–108; Idem, "Images of Authority: Elites and Icons in Late Sixth-Century Byzantium," *Past and Present* 84 (1979): 3–35; and Idem, "The Virgin's Robe: An Episode in the History of Early Seventh-Century Constantinople," *Byzantion* 49 (1979): 42–56. These are reprinted in Averil Cameron, *Continuity and Change in Sixth-Century Byzantium* (Aldershot: Variorum, 1981), articles XIII, XVI, and XVII.
34. Cameron, "The Theotokos," 103–4 and passim.
35. Diliana Nikolova Angelova, "The Ivories of Ariadne and the Construction of the Image of the Empress and the Virgin Mary in Late Antiquity," M.A. thesis, Southern Methodist University, 1998.
36. Agostino Pertusi, *Giorgio di Pisidia. Poemi, I: Panegyrici epici,* Studia patristica et byzantina 7 (Ettal: Buch-Kunstverlag, 1959), 176:

> Τῶν ζωγράφων τις εἰ Θέλει τὰ τῆς μάχης
> τρόπαια δεῖξαι, τὴν Τεκοῦσαν ἀσπόρως
> μόνην προτάξοι καὶ γράφοι τὴν εἰκόνα˙
> ἀεί γὰρ οἶδε τὴν φύσιν νικᾶν μόνη,
> τόκῳ τὸ πρῶτον καὶ μάχῃ τὸ δεύτερον:

37. Cyril Mango, *The Homilies* (as in note 9 above), 102–3; S. Aristarches, *Τοῦ ἐν ἁγίοις πατρὸς ἡμῶν Φωτίου . . . λόγοι καὶ ὁμιλίαι ὀγδοήκοντα τρεῖς,* vols. (Constantinople, 1990), 2: 41–42: 'Ης καὶ τὴν περιβολὴ εἰς ἀναστολὴ μέν τῶν πολιορκούντων, φυλακὴν δέ τῶν πολιορκουμένων σὺν ἐμοί πᾶσα ἡ πόλις ἐπιφερόμενοι τὰς ἑκουσίας ἑκουσιαζόμεΘα, τὴν λιτανείαν ἐποιούμεΘα, ἐφ' οἷς ἀράτῳ φιλανΘρωπίᾳ, μητρικῆς παρρησιασαμένης ἐντεύξεως, καὶ τὸ Θεῖον ἐπεκλίΘη, καὶ ὁ Θυμὸς ἀπεστράφη, καὶ, 'Ηλέησε κύριος τὴν κληρονομίαν αὑτοῦ. "οντως μητρὸς Θεοῦ περιβολὴ ἡ πάνσεπτος αὕτη στολή! αὕτη περιεκύκου τὰ τεΘχη, καὶ τὰ τῶν πολεμίων ἀρρήτῳ λόγῳ ἐδείκνυτο νῶτα ˙ ἡ πόλις ταύτην περιεβάλλετο, καὶ τὸ χαράκωμα τῶν πολεμίων ὡς ἐκ συνΘήματος διελύετο ˙ αὕτη ταύτην ἐστολίζετο, καὶ τῆς ἐλπίδος αὑτῶν, ἐφ' ἧς ἐπωχοῦντο, ἐγυμνοῦτο τὸ πολέμιον. ''Αμα γὰρ τὸ τεῖχος ἡ παρΘενικὴ στολὴ περιελήλυΘε, καὶ τῆς πολιορκίας οἱ βάρβαροι ἀπειπόντες ἀνεσκευάσαντο, καὶ τῆς προσδοκωμένης ἁλώσεως ἐλυτρώΘημεν, καὶ τῆς ἀδοκήτου σωτηρίας ἠξιώμεΘα.
38. Cyril Mango, *The Homilies,* 110; Aristarches, *Τοῦ ἐν ἁγίοις,* 2: 56: 'Ημεῖς τὴν πρὸς σὲ πίστιν καὶ τὸν πόΘον ἀδιστάκτως φυλάξομεν, αὐτὴ τὴν

σὴν πόλιν, ὡς οἶδας, ὡς βούλει, περίσωσον · ὅπλα σὲ καὶ τεῖχος καὶ Θυρεοὺς καὶ στρατηγὸν αὐτὸν προβαλλόμεΘα, αὐτὴ τοῦ λαοῦ σου ὑπερμάχησον.

39. The *locus classicus* for the imagery of the Virgin of Blachernai is the fundamental study of Christa Belting-Ihm, *"Sub Matris Tutula." Untersuchungen zur Vorgeschichte der Schutzmantel Madonna* (Heidelberg: Karl Winter–Universitätsverlag, 1976). With extensive bibliography see also John Cotsonis, "The Virgin with the 'Tongues of Fire' on Byzantine Lead Seals," *Dumbarton Oaks Papers* 48 (1994): 221–27 discussing an image perhaps associated with the icon of the "usual miracle," and Annemarie Weyl Carr, "Court Culture and Cult Icons in Middle Byzantine Constantinople," in *Byzantine Court Culture from 829 to 1204,* ed. Henry Maguire (Washington, D.C.: Dumbarton Oaks, 1997), 92.
40. Ibid., 92, note 78; see also the twelfth-century icon on Mount Sinai depicting miracle-working icons in Constantinople, that shows the Blachernitissa (at far left) as holding a standing child who seems to run along the lower frame of the image: Anthony Cutler and Jean-Michel Spieser, *Byzance médiévale, 700–1204* (Paris: Gallimard, 1997), pl. 310.
41. Henry Maguire, "The Heavenly Court," in *Byzantine Court Culture from 829 to 1204,* ed. Henry Maguire (Washington, D.C.: Dumbarton Oaks, 1997), 95–99 and passim.
42. Mary's status above the angels is expressed with particular intensity by the late tenth-century John Geometres in a passage translated by Antoine Wenger, A.A., "Foi et piété mariales à Byzance," in *Maria. Études sur la sainte Vierge,* ed. Hubert du Manoir, S.J. (Paris: Beauchesne, 1958), 5: 942: " . . . elle est plus élevée que les thrônes, plus redoutable que les chérubins; remplie d'une sagesse plus grande que les séraphins; ou mieux, elle est révérée des thrônes, elle est redoutable aux chérubins, incomprehensible aux séraphins; elle est la commune reine de l'universe, détenant un règne indestructible, au deuxième rang après la royale Trinité, et remplie à satieté du toute la Trinité . . .
43. Corrigan, "The Ivory Scepter" (as in note 5 above). On the object's function see Anthony Cutler, *The Hand of the Master. Craftsmanship, Ivory and Society in Byzantium (9th–11th Centuries)* (Princeton: Princeton University Press, 1994), 200–1.
44. Philip Grierson, *Catalogue of the Byzantine Coins in the Dumbarton Oaks Collection and in the Whittemore Collection, 3: Leo III to Nicephorus III, 717–1081, 2: Basil I to Nicephorus III (867–1081)* (Washington, D.C.: Dumbarton Oaks, 1973), 589, pl. XLII, 19.1–19.4.
45. Ibid., 749, pl. LXII, 1a.1–1.d.
46. See Ševčenko, "Icons in the Liturgy" (as in note 8 above), 51 n. 41; the Life of St. Thomais of Lesbos in Alice-Mary Talbot, ed., *Holy Women of Byzantium. Ten Saints' Lives in English Translation* (Washington, D.C.: Dumbarton Oaks, 1996), 297–322, esp. 309; and Rosenqvist, *The Life of St. Irene* (as in note 15 above), 58–59.

47. Described in Theophanes Continuatus, as cited in note 27 above (. . . τὸ ἅγιον οὖν κιβώτιον διανοίξαντες ἐν ᾧ τὸ σεπτὸν τῆς ἁγίας Θεοτόκου τεθησαύριστο ὠμοφόριον . . .), and repeated in John Skylitzes: Ioannes Thurn, ed., *Ioannis Scylitzae Synopsis Historiarum,* Corpus Fontium Historiae Byzantinae 5 (Berlin: Walter de Gruyter, 1973), 219, ll. 31–35; translated in Hans Thurn, trans., *Byzanz wieder ein Weltreich,* Byzantinische Geschichtschreiber 15 (Graz: Verlag Styria, 1983), 257: ὁ δὲ βασιλεὺς ἐν τῷ ναῷ γενόμενος τῶν Βλαχερνῶν ἅμα τῷ πατριάρχῃ, καὶ ἐν τῇ ἁγίᾳ σορῷ εἰσελιὼν καὶ ἱκετηρίας ᾠδὰς ἀποδοὺς τῷ ἱεῷ, τὸ ὠμοφόριον τῆς Θεοτόκου λαβὼν ἐξῄει τοῦ ναοῦ, ὅπλοις ἀσφαλέσι φραξάμενος (Der Kaiser begab sich mit Patriarchen Nikolaos in die Blachernenkirche, trat in die Kapelle des heiligen Reliquienschreins ein und sang Bittgesänge an Gott. Mit dem Omophorion der Gottesmutter verliess er sicher gewaffnet die Kirche).
48. The vision at Blachernai is given in English translation in Rydén, "The Vision" (as in note 12 above), 66, and extensively analyzed on 66–73.
49. Ševčenko, "The Limburg Staurothek" (as in note 21 above), 291.
50. Gautier, "Diatribes" (as in note 27 above), 38–39, ll. 17–27: . . . τὸ Θεῖον τῆς Θεομήτορος ῥάκος (μαφόριον σύνηθες τοῦτο καλεῖν) . . . (the sacred scrap of God's Mother, commonly called the maphorion).
51. Leib, ed., *Anne Comnène* (as in note 27 above), 3: 87, ll. 15–23; in E. R. A. Sewter, trans., *The Alexiad of Anna Comnena* (Harmondsworth: Penguin Books, 1969), 395.
52. Leib, ed., *Anne Comnène,* 2: 98, ll. 23–29; translated in Sewter, *The Alexiad,* 225: ὁ μέντοι βασιλεὺς προβέβλητο τῆς οἰκείας δυνάμεως καὶ ξιφηφόρος εἱστήκει, τῇ ἑτέρᾳ δὲ τῶν χειρῶν τῆς τοῦ Λόγου μητρὸς τὸ ὠμόφορον σημαίαν κατέχων ἵστατο (The emperor, however, still stood with sword in hand beyond his own front line. In the other hand he grasped like a standard the Cape of the Mother of the Word).
53. In 971 John I Tzimiskes went with the standard of the Cross to Blachernai before departing for war, but we do not know what he did there and have no intimation that he adopted the relic as a battle standard. See Michael McCormick, *Eternal Victor. Triumphal Rulership in Late Antiquity, Byzantium, and the Early Medieval West* (Cambridge: Cambridge University Press, 1986), 249, citing Leo Diakonos. It is hard to guess how characteristic of Byzantine habit Alexios's use of the maphorion was. We know about the use of icons in the army and about battle standards, often painted with holy images, but not about textile relics in this role. On the use of banners and icons in the Byzantine army, see George T. Dennis, "Religious Services in the Byzantine Army," in *ΕΥΛΟΓΗΜΑ. Studies in Honor of Robert Taft, S.J., Studia Anselmiana 110,* ed. E. Carr, S. Parenti, A.A. Thiermeyer, E. Volkovska (Rome, 1993), 109–13; John F. Haldon, *Constantine Porphyrogenitus. Three Military Treatises on Imperial Military Expeditions* (Vienna, 1990), 270–71.
54. Leib, *Anne Comnène,* 2: 110; Sewter, *The Alexiad,* 227.

55. Alice Christ, "Calendar and Liturgy in the Icon of the Pokrov," *Byzantinorussica* 1 (1995): 126–37; Rydén, "The Vision" (as in note 12 above), 74–82; Belting-Ihm, *"Sub Matris Tutula"* (as in note 39 above), 58–61.
56. Belting-Ihm, *"Sub Matris Tutula,"* 59.
57. Certainly it is a veil-like garment that figures centrally in the icon eventually formulated for the Pokrov feast, illustrating the vision of Andrew the Fool in Christ, with Mary's veil spread like an arc over crowds in her Soros. See Rydén, 74–82. See the fifteenth-century icon of the "Suzdal" version of the Pokrov with Mary holding the veil in Engelina Smirnova, *Moscow Icons 14th–17th Century* (Oxford: Phaidon, 1989), pl. 416; Kurt Weitzmann, Gaiané Alibegašvili, Aneli Volskaja, Manolis Chatzidakis, Gordana Babić, Mihail Alpatov, Teodora Voinescu, *The Icon* (New York: Knopf, 1982), 297–98 gives an example of the "Novgorod" version of the Pokrov in which angels hold the veil.
58. Ibid., 275 for the famous fifteenth-century icon of the battle of the Novgorodians with the Suzdalians (Novgorod, Museum of Architecture and Ancient Monuments) that shows the image being carried in war. The icon itself is now damaged on the front: see Engelina Smirnova, "Some Contributions to the Iconography of the Blachernitissa (The Study of Two Russian Icons of the 12th–13th Centuries)," *Βυζαντινή Μακεδονία,* forthcoming. It is closely copied in the thirteenth-century icon of Our Lady of the Sign in the Korin Collection: Konrad Onasch and Annemarie Schnieper, *Icons. The Fascination and the Reality,* trans. Daniel G. Conklin (New York: Riverside Book Company, Inc., 1995), pl. p. 158. I am very much indebted to Dr. Smirnova for her generosity in showing me a typescript of her article—and in so many other contexts.
59. Carr, "Court Culture" (as in note 39 above), 94–99. The Hodegetria's symbolic role as the guardian of the city is summed up well in the exasperated comment of Eustathios, Bishop of Thessaloniki, that the Constantinopolitans shrug off their military weakness by saying that "the Hodegetria, the protectress of our city, will be enough, without anyone else, to secure our welfare": J.R. Melville Jones, trans., *Eustathios of Thessalonike: The Capture of Thessalonike,* Byzantina Australiensia 8 (Canberra: Australian Association for Byzantine Studies, 1988), 42–43, ll. 11–12.
60. George P. Majeska, *Russian Travelers to Constantinople in the Fourteenth and Fifteenth Centuries,* Dumbarton Oaks Studies 19 (Washington, D.C.: Dumbarton Oaks, 1984), 44, where Stephen of Novgorod speaks of the robe *(riza),* belt *(poias)* and cap *(skufiia)* of Mary at Blachernai (Lacherniu).
61. See note 18 above.
62. Janin, *La Géographie* (as in note 6 above), 170.
63. This is true not only of the *Historia Ecclesiastica* cited above, but of the sermon for the Feast of the Akathistos formerly attributed to George of Pisidia and now attributed to Nikephoros: Georgii Pisidii, "In Hymnum Acathistum," *PG* 92: cols. 1348–52, esp. 1350 D where the acheiropoietas

icon of Christ and the ἐσίῆς are cited, and 1352 D where the True Cross and the icon of the Hodegetria are named.

64. See note 27 above.
65. Belting-Ihm, *"Sub Matris Tutula"* (as in note 39 above), 45, notes that a relic of the veil is recorded in San Marco in Venice after 1204; if this was, indeed, from Blachernai, it is notable both that Venice succeeded in acquiring it—as she had not managed to do with the Hodegetria—and that it drifted into indifference thereafter.
66. Evans and Wixom, eds., *The Glory* (as in note 5 above), 372–73, no. 244, and with earlier bibliography, Annemarie Weyl Carr, "The Presentation of an Icon on Sinai," *Δελτίον τῆς χριστιανικῆς ἀρχαιολογικῆς ἑταιρείας* ser. 4, 17 (1993–94): 239–48.
67. Ibid., 242.
68. Hans Belting, *Likeness and Presence. A History of the Image Before the Era of Art,* trans. Edmund Jephcott (Chicago: University of Chicago Press, 1994), 291.
69. Efthalia C. Constantinides, *The Wall Paintings of the Panagia Olympiotissa at Elasson in Northern Thessaly,* 2 vols. (Athens: Canadian Archaeological Institute at Athens, 1992), 1: 142–44, and 169 where she links this imagery with the church at Blachernai.
70. On its future as the Mother of God of Kykkos Monastery in Cyprus, see Olga Gratziou, "Μεταμορφώσεις μίας Θαυματουργής εικόνας. Σημειώσεις στις όψιμες παραλλαγές της Παναγίας του Κύκκου," *Δελτίον τῆς χριστιανικῆς ἀρχαιολογικῆς ἑταιρείας,* ser. 4, 17 (1933–94): 317–29 with English summary on 330; George A. Soteriou, "Η Κυκκιώτισσα," *Νέα Εστία* (Christmas issue 1939): 3–6. On its future in Italy see Paola Santa Maria Mannino, "Vergine 'Kykkotissa' in due icone Laziali del Duecento," in *Roma Anno 1300,* Atti del Congresso internazionale di storia dell'arte medievale, Roma, 19–24 Maggio, 1980 (Rome: L'Erma di Bretschneider, 1983), 487–92.
71. This type is postulated by Belting, *Likeness and Presence,* 438, on the basis of its appropriation in Italy for the type later famous as the Madonna of Cambrai. It is significant because it draws even more closely together the Pelagonitissa type with the type seen in the Sinai icon of the Virgin and Prophets, eventually famous as the Kykkotissa.
72. Evans and Wixom, eds., *The Glory* (as in note 5 above), 127–28, no. 75 and A. Papageorghiou, *Icons of Cyprus* (Nicosia: Holy Archbishopric of Cyprus, 1992), pls. 15 a and b; Doula Mouriki, "Icons from the Twelfth to the Fifteenth Century," in *Sinai. Treasures of the Monastery of Saint Catherine,* ed. Konstantinos A. Manafēs (Athens: Ekdotike Athenon, 1990), 118–19, pl. 65.
73. *Κατάλογος: 'ΕκΘεση για τα εκατό χρόνια της Χριστιανικής 'Αρχαιολογικής Εταιρείας,* exhibition catalogue, Byzantine and Christian Museum, Athens, 6 October 1984–30 June 1985 (Athens, 1985), 22–23, no. 9 (entry by Manolis Chatzidakis).
74. Annemarie Weyl Carr, "Byzantines and Italians on Cyprus: Images from Art," *Dumbarton Oaks Papers* 49 (1995): 335–36.

75. Gordana Babić, "Le Maphorion de la Vierge et la Psaume 44 (45) sur les images du XIVe siècle," in Εὐφρόσυνον ἀφιέρωμα στον Μανόλη Χατζηδάκη, ed. Myrtile Acheimastou-Potamianou, 2 vols. (Athens, 1991), 1: 57–64.
76. Weitzmann et al., *The Icon* (as in note 57 above), 180 (Virgin and Child, Monastery of Dečani, altar screen of the Katholikon, ca. 1350).
77. Chrysanthe Baltogianne, *Εικόνες. Μήτηρ Θεού βρεφοκρατούσα στην ενσάρκωση και το πάθος* (Athens: ADAM, 1994), 107 and passim.
78. Gordana Babić, "Sur l'Icone de Poganovo et la Vasilissa Hélène," in *Thessalonique et les pays balkaniques et les courants spirituels au XIVe siècle. Receuil des rapports du IVe colloque serbo-grec (Belgrade 1985),* Académie Serbe des sciences et des arts, Institute des études balkaniques, Editions speciales 31 (Belgrade: GRO Kultura, 1987), 57–65.
79. For Paphos and Siena, see Carr, "Byzantines and Italians," 356; for Athos, see R.M. Dawkins, *The Monks of Mount Athos* (London: George Allen and Unwin, Ltd., 1936), 281–83.
80. John Wortley, "Hagia Skêpe and Pokrov Bogoroditsi," *Analecta Bollandiana* 89 (1971): 149.
81. Richard A. Clogg, *A Concise History of Greece* (Cambridge: Cambridge University Press, 1992), 122, fig. 39, showing George Gounaropoulos's "Νική, λευτερία, Η Παναγία μαζί του."
82. The theme deserves exploration on the level of folk devotion: see the fascinating nineteenth-century Finnish icon with Mary's upper body rising from a "skirt" of walls and bearing a Child who grasps her white veil: Mikhail Kraslin, "Ikonograficheskii arkhetip i narodnoe pochitanie chudotbori'ch obrazov = The Iconographic Archetype and Folk Worship of Miracle-Working Icons," in *Chudotvoriia Ikona v Vizantii i drevnei Rusi,* ed. A.M. Lidov (Moscow: Martis, 1996), fig. 1.
83. B. G. Niebuhr, ed., *Ioannes Zonaras,* 3 vols., Corpus Scriptorum Historiae Byzantinae 46 (Bonn: Weber, 1897), 3: 751, translated in Joannes Zonaras, *Militärs und Höflinge Ringen um das Kaisertum. Byzantinische Geschichte von 969 bis 1118,* trans. E. Trapp (Graz: Verlag Styria, 1986), 173.
84. Valerie Nunn, "The Encheirion as Adjunct to the Icon in the Middle Byzantine Period," *Byzantine and Modern Greek Studies* 5 (1986): 73–102.
85. On the relics collected at Aachen see Heinrich Schiffers, *Karls des Grossen Reliquienschatz und die Anfänge der Aachenfahrt* (Aachen: J. Volk, 1951).
83. "Schleier" is the favored noun of Stephan Beissel, S. J., *Geschichte der Verehrung Marias in Deutschland während des Mittelalters* (Freiburg im Breisgau: Herdersche Verlagshandlung, 1909), of Walter Pötzl, "Marianischen Brauchtum an Wallfahrtsorten," in *Handbuch der Marienkunde,* ed. Wolfgang Beinert and Heinrich Petri (Regensburg: F. Pustet, 1982), 883–926, and of Schiffers himself.
87. Schiffers, *Karls des Grossen,*" pl. III.
88. As argued with piercing scorn by Professor Dr. H, Disselnkötter, *Aachens grosse Heilingtümer und geschichtliche Beglaubung* (Bonn: Universitäts-buchdruckerei und Verlag, 1909), 57 and passim.

89. Schiffers, *Karls Des Grossen,* 57. Belting-Ihm, *"Sub Matris Tutula"* (as in note 39 above), 45, endorses Schiffers' conclusions.
90. Schiffers, *Karls des Grossen,* 13.
91. Ibid., 32.
92. Ibid., 55, quotes the inventory of 1238, which lists "Das Hemd der seligen Jungfrau, mit dem sie bekleidet gewesen, als sie Christus gebar."
93. Documents on the history of the relic at Chartres are compiled and translated in Robert Branner, *Chartres Cathedral,* Norton Critical Studies in Art History (London: Thames and Hudson, 1969), 107–14.
94. This genealogy is spelled out with particular clarity by J.C. Jennings, "The Origins of the 'Elements Series' of the Miracles of the Virgin," *Mediaeval and Renaissance Studies* 6 (1968): 87–90. I am indebted to Rachel Fulton for showing me this helpful article.
95. Belting-Ihm, *"Sub Matris Tutula,"* 41.
96. Jennings, "The Origins," 90.
97. Gabriela Signori, *Maria zwischen Kathedrale, Kloster und Welt* (Sigmaringen: Jan Thorbecke Verlag, 1995), 179.
98. J.A. Giles, D. C. L., *William of Malmesbury's Chronicle of the Kings of England* (London: Henry G. Bohn, 1847), 125. The Latin, cited by Signori, *Maria,* 180 n35, reads: Namque cives, nec armis nec muris confisi, Beate Marie auxillium implorant camisiamque gloriosissime Virginis quam, a Constantinopoli sibi allatum, unus ex Karolis ibi posuerat, super propugnacula in modum vexilli ventis exponunt.
99. Branner, *Chartres Cathedral,* 112. The account forms part of a history of the relic that draws in its earlier portions on the story of the patricians Kandidos and Galbios, recounted by Theodore Synkellos.
100. André Chédeville, *Histoire de Chartres et du pays chartrain* (Toulouse: Editions Privat, 1983), 61.
101. Ibid., 61. Chédeville calls the fabric eighth- or ninth-century; this is too early for its tiraz-like design, and it seems more nearly contemporary with the relic's installation in Tendon's reliquary.
102. For inventories of these relics, see Beissel, *Geschichte* (as in note 86 above), 293–94, and Charles Rohault de Fleury, *La sainte Vierge; études archéologiques et iconographiques,* 2 vols. (Paris: Poussielgne, 1878), 1: 290–93. Beissel, 293–94, points out that many textile relics of Mary were portions of fabrics used to dress either altars or images of Mary. The close bond of such textiles to Mary herself is seen already clearly in the robe placed by Pulcheria upon the altar in Hagia Sophia, which was interpreted by Cosmas Vestitor's translator as the dress on Mary's lap upon which Christ sat when he was present upon the altar (see note 32 above).
103. Robert Deshman, *The Benedictional of St. Aethelwold,* Studies in Manuscript Illumination 9 (Princeton: Princeton University Press, 1995); Mary Clayton, *The Cult of the Virgin Mary in Anglo-Saxon England* (Cambridge: Cambridge University Press, 1990), 162–65, pls. VI and VII. The manuscripts in question are London, British Library, Additional 49598, folio 102v, and Rouen, Bibliothèque municipale, 369, folio 54v.

104. Clayton, *The Cult,* 166–71; Stafford, *Queen Emma* (as in note 4 above), 172–74. The manuscripts are: Vatican, Biblioteca Apostolica Vaticana, Reg. Lat. 12, folio 62r; New York, Pierpont Morgan Library, MS M 869, folio 11r (Clayton, pl. X); Cambridge, Pembroke College, MS 301, folio 2v (Ibid., pl. XII); and London, British Library, Cotton, Titus D. xxvii, folio 75v (Ibid., pl. VIII).
105. Stafford, *Queen Emma,* 179.
106. See recently Patrick Corbet, "Les Impératrices ottoniennes et le modèle mariale. Autour de l'ivoire du Château Sforza de Milan," in *Marie. Le Culte de la Vierge dans la société médiévale,* ed. Dominique Iogna-Prat, Eric Palazzo, Daniel Russo (Paris: Beauchesne, 1996), 127, 129, citing in particular an image of Mary in clothing reminiscent of Byzantium in the Petershausen Sacramentary (see Anton Van Euw, *Vor dem Jahre 1000. Abendländische Buchkunst zur Zeit der Kaiserin Theophanu, Ausstellungskatalog, Köln, 1991,* 122, no. 32), the Ivrea Sacramentary studied by Deshman, "Otto III" (as in note 5 above), the Seeon Lectionary in which Henry II is shown presenting the manuscript to an imperially clad Virgin, and the Rich Gospels of St. Bernward of Hildesheim (Rainer Kahsnitz, *Das kostbare Evangeliar des heiligen Bernwards* [Munich: Prestel Verlag, 1993], 27–30).
107. Deshman, "Otto III," fig. 1; Grierson, *Catalogue* (as in note 44 above).
108. Henry Mayr-Harting, *Ottonian Book Illumination,* 2 vols. (London: Harvey Miller Publishers, 1991), 1: 140–54. The miniatures he cites are all reproduced in Rainer Kashnitz, "Koimesis-dormitio-assumptio. Byzantinisches und Antikes in den Miniaturen der Liuthargruppe," in *Florilegium Carl Nordenfalk,* ed. P. Bjurström, N.-G. Hökby, F. Mütherich (Stockholm: National Museum, 1987), 91–122.
109. Van Esbroeck, "Le Culte" (as in note 18 above), 184, on the celebration of imperial acclamations at Blachernai on 15 August.
110. Quoted by Corbet, "Les Impératrices," 131. Compare this with the language of the late tenth-century Byzantine John Geometres (note 42 above).
111. Mary-Harting, *Ottonian Book Illumination,* 1: 140–41; Corbet, "Les Impératrices," 128–31.
112. Corbet, "Les Impératrices," 118 and passim.
113. Dominique Iogna-Prat, "La Vierge et les *ordines* de couronnement des reines au IXe siècle," in *Marie. Le Culte de la Vierge dans la société médiévale,* ed. Dominique Iogna-Prat, Eric Palazzo, Daniel Russo (Paris: Beauchesne, 1996), 100–7; Idem, "Le Culte de la Vierge sous le regne de Charles le Chauve," *Les Cahiers de Saint-Michel de Cuxa* 23 (1992): 97–116.
114. Iogna-Prat, "Le Culte," 115: Ave femina amata Deo! Sit tibi vita, salus longos distenta per annos; conjugis observes semper amata thorum.
115. Iogna-Prat, "La Vierge," 106–7.
116. Iogna-Prat, "Le Culte," 115.
117. Escorial, Cod. Vitrinas 17, fol. 3r: Schramm, *Die deutschen Kaiser* (a in note 5 above), pl. 157. Compare this with the ivory of Otto II and Theophano, cited in note 5 above, or with the frontispiece on folio 2r of the Speyer

manuscript itself showing the Conrad II and Gisela symmetrically at the feet of Christ: Schramm, *Die deutschen Kaiser,* pl. 143.

118. Renate Kroos, *Der Schrein des hl. Servatius in Maastricht und die vier zugehörigen Reliquiare in Brüssel* (Munich: Deutscher Kunstverlag, 1985), 176.
119. Iogna-Prat, "La Vierge," 103–7.
120. Stafford, *Queen Emma* (as in note 4 above), 167–68.
121. Ibid., 177–78.
122. Clayton, *The Cult* (as in note 103 above), 138; Walter de Gray Birch, F.S.A., ed., *Liber Vitae: Register and Martyrology of New Minster and Hyde Abbey, Winchester* (London: Simpkin and Company, Ltd., 1892), 147 ("De uestimento SANCTE MARIE"), 148 ("De Sepulcro SANCTE MARIE"); 150 ("De uestimento Sancte MARIE matris domini"), 151 ("De uestimento Sancte MARIE"). A half century later, Exeter recorded relics (in Oxford, Bodleian Library, Auct.D.2.16) of Mary's headdress and hair. This suggests a veil, but the word itself is different: not "cuffia" but "heafoðclade."
123. Holger A. Klein, "The so-called Byzantine Diptych in the Winchester Psalter, British Library, MS Cotton Nero C. IV," *Gesta* 37 (1998): 26–43, and Kristine Edmondson Haney, *The Winchester Psalter: An Iconographic Study* (Leicester: University of Leicester Press, 1986), 44–46, 125, and passim, discuss the sarcophagus without specific reference to the relic at Winchester, as I did, too, in Evans and Wixom, eds. *The Glory* (as in note 5 above), 474–85, no. 312. Relics of Mary's sepulchre were, admittedly, legion in western Europe.
124. Stafford, *Queen Emma,* 178.
125. Rebecca Corrie, "The Political Meaning of Coppo di Marcovaldo's Madonna and Child in Siena," *Gesta* 29 (1990): 61–75, and Idem, "Coppo di Marcovaldo's *Madonna del bordone* and the Meaning of the Bare-Legged Christ Child in Siena and the East," *Gesta* 35 (1996): 43–65.
126. Corrie, "The Political Meaning," 65.
127. See note 79 above.
128. John White, *Duccio. Tuscan Art and the Medieval Workshop* (London: Thames and Hudson, 1979), 46–48, fig. 18.
129. See Sirarpie Der Nersessian, "Deux examples arméniennes de la Vierge de Miséricorde," *Revue des études arméniennes* NS 7 (1970): 187–202; Belting-Ihm, *"Sub Matris Tutula"* (as in note 39 above), 68–69. Three examples survive from the Crusader Levant, all from the later thirteenth century: the huge panel of the Virgin protecting Carmelite monks in the Byzantine Museum of the Holy Archiepiscopate of Cyprus in Nicosia (Papageorghiou, *Icons* [as in note 72 above], 46–49, pl. 31); the mural painting with a Frankish family in the southern conch of the narthex at Asinou (Ewald Hein, Andrija Jakovljević, Brigitte Kleidt, *Zypern–byzantinische Kirchen und Klöstern. Mosaiken und Fresken* [Ratingen: Melina-Verlag, 1996], fig. 26); and in a Cilician Armenian miniature, now in theMertopolitan Museum of Art in New York, showing Marshal Oshin and his sons protected by Mary (Sirarpie Der Nersessian, *Miniature Painting from the*

Armenian Kingdom of Cilicia from the Twelfth to the Fourteenth Century, Dumbarton Oaks Studies 31, 2 vols. (Washington, D.C.: Dumbarton Oaks, 1993), 1: 158–59; 2: fig. 646; a similar composition used with a standing Virgin appears in the Cilician Prince Vasak Gospels in Jerusalem (Ibid., 1: 158–59, 2: fig. 647).

130. White, *Duccio,* 63, fig. 30 (Brussels, Feron-Stoclet Collection); 63, fig. 31 (Perugia, Galleria nazionale dell'Umbria); 52, fig. 22 (London, National Gallery). On the latter see also David Bomford, Jill Dunkerton, Gillian Gordon, Ashok Roy, *Art in the Making. Italian Painting Before 1400,* exhibition catalogue, National Gallery, London, 29 November 1989–28 February 1990 (London, 1989), 90–97, no. 4.

131. Belting, *Likeness and Presence* (as in note 68 above), 438–40, color plate X.

132. Richard C. Trexler, "Habiller et déshabiller les images: Esquisse d'une analyse," in *L'image et la production du sacré: Actes du colloque de Strasbourg (20–21 janvier 1988) organisé par le Centre d'histoire des religions de l'Université de Strasbourg II, group "Theorie et pratique de l'image culturelle,"* ed. F.Dunand, J.-M. Spieser, and J. Wirth (Paris: Klincksieck, 1991), 195–231.

CHAPTER 5

THE KING'S NEW CLOTHES: ROYAL AND EPISCOPAL REGALIA IN THE FRANKISH EMPIRE

Michael Moore

On the eve of Easter in 841, Charles the Bald was having a bath. The king and his army had been in the field for months, in a struggle with Charles's older brother Lothar for control of the Carolingian empire. Warfare among the sons of Louis the Pious had broken out even before the death of the old emperor the previous year. Lothar had then inherited the imperial crown, and was trying to assert his dominance over the entire Empire. Charles, for his part, wanted to get hold of those portions of the kingdom that his father had promised him. As portrayed by the historian and warrior Nithard, his king was in a weak and vulnerable position. Lost somewhere in the forests along the Seine, in pursuit of Lothar and his army and pursued by them, it was by no means clear that Charles would manage to save himself or gain his kingdom.

In his history of these events, written just months afterward, Nithard recounted something remarkable that occurred as Charles arose from his bath.[1] The king intended to put on the same dusty clothes he had shed before entering the water, when messengers suddenly arrived from Aquitaine, bearing royal and religious garments (*ornatus*).[2] To Nithard, the arrival of these robes was a miracle; they had come safely across a war-torn countryside, arriving at the right place and at "the right day and hour, when even Charles did not know where he and his followers were."[3] The story is striking for its layered symbolism. At a moment when his fortunes seemed bleakest, the viability of Charles's kingship was made clear by a miraculous robing scene with baptismal overtones. The garments had arrived, moreover, at Easter, the traditional time of year for baptism. Charles was thus able to appear before his army on Easter Sunday in royal robes, surrounded by clerics wearing ecclesiastical vestments that had arrived at the same time. Charles the Bald suddenly looked like a king. It is possible that Charles knew the robes were coming—it has even been suggested that he staged the entire scene in order to boost the morale of his army with a show of divine favor.[4] From Nithard's perspective, however, the robing of Charles was a genuine religious event that marked a crucial turning point in the civil war. Two months later, Charles went on to defeat his brother Lothar in the horrible slaughter at Fontenoy, after which his possession of a kingdom was no longer in doubt. By wrapping himself in this symbol of kingship, Charles set in motion a series of events that ensured that he would no longer be lost and vulnerable, a king without a kingdom.

Nevertheless, the royal garments that Charles received remain a mystery to us. It is impossible to say what they looked like, what their origins were, or if Charles had ever seen or worn them before. It is difficult, more generally speaking, to establish from literary accounts what the garments associated with kingship might have looked like, because the language of the sources is so opaque.[5] Very little physical evidence has survived that might be compared to such descriptions.[6] Even lifelike paintings in manuscripts cannot be accepted as straightforward renditions of a king and his regalia.[7] Detailed catalogues have been assembled, for example, that show how the shape of Frankish crowns changed over time, according to royal portraits. But to what extent is one looking at changes in actual garments and emblems, or at changes in an iconographic tradition?[8]

The two questions are doubtless related. It seems likely that the shape of crowns actually worn by kings was in a dynamic relation with the crowns depicted in paintings or on coins. These considerations point out the failings of an antiquarian approach, like that of Schramm's, to the problem of regalia. Frankish kings came to surround themselves with an imposing array of regal symbols. In what follows, my object is not to provide a history of the specific forms of these robes, crowns, thrones, and scepters but to examine the meanings attached to them by Frankish kings, their bishops, and those who lived under them. More specifically, what did the robes that Charles assumed on Easter 841 mean to him and his followers?

The study of royal symbology has long been pursued as a means of tracing the rise of the later medieval state.[9] Percy Schramm argued that one could locate its origins in the accoutrements of early medieval kings: the state first emerged as an abstract concept of kingship, expressed in symbolic objects such as crowns and robes. A guiding interest in developments of the later Middle Ages and the early modern period has often formed an anachronistic backdrop for the study of early medieval regalia.[10] Whether or not coronation rites were a festal display of royal equipment or an official ceremony for making a king is also to one side of this study. My focus instead is on the social and religious concepts concentrated in regal and episcopal garments, from the Carolingian usurpation in 751 to the imperial coronation of Charles the Bald in 875. The regalia of Carolingian kings expressed the hope that kingship could be something sacred and good. Where did these symbolic objects come from, and, more importantly, how could such a hope be attached to them?

The problem to be addressed here is not the origins of the state but how a group of symbolic objects, all extremely old, were taken up as expressions of a new kind of kingship.[11] This social change was accompanied by a continuous reinterpretation of the past, in which old symbols were filled with new meaning. The historical and theological views of bishops played an important role in the development of royal symbology. Believing that Christian society inherited the priestly and royal nature of Christ, bishops interpreted their garments and symbols from this perspective and went on to think of royal robes and crowns along the same lines. As a result, the regalia of Frankish kings and bishops were thought to reflect one another as two visible aspects of a single, indivisible Christian reality.

To a significant extent the immediate origins of Frankish royal and episcopal garments lay in the symbols of Roman and Byzantine sovereignty.[12] Despite these origins, however, the paraphernalia associated with Frankish kings and bishops came to be viewed through the lens of new religious and social ideals. The first dynasty of Frankish kings (the Merovingian family, which ruled from ca. 450 to ca. 751), made only a tentative use of such symbols, preferring to mark their status by the traditional signs of a Germanic war-chief. With the rise of the Carolingian dynasty in 751, however, the nature of kingship and the use of royal signs changed considerably.

The garments and emblems associated with kingship became more elaborate during the reign of Charlemagne (768–814), and reached a high point with his grandson Charles the Bald (843–877). In order to highlight the changes in royal symbology over this period of some seventy years, it is necessary not only to glance back at the earlier Merovingian kings but also to examine the garments of bishops and the complex meanings attached to them. Frankish kings surrounded themselves with robes, crowns, scepters, and thrones as a Christian understanding of society transformed the meaning of kingship.

Regalia in Death

Our starting point is the remarkable grave of Childeric I (d. 481), the first Frankish king about whom there is any historical certainty.[13] His tomb was discovered near Tournai in 1653, and its contents were published with important engravings by Jean-Jacques Chifflet.[14] Much of the astonishing treasure found with the body of Childeric was subsequently stolen from the Cabinet des Medailles in Paris in 1831. Among the objects found in the grave, Childeric's seal-ring has perhaps attracted the most attention. Here we have an engraved frontal portrait of a king wearing his hair long, parted in the middle and bound in pony-tails or braids on each side of his head. The carefully modeled figure wears an armored breastplate, and holds a spear in his right hand (fig.5.1). Taking these items together, the seal-ring confirms what is known from so many other sources for the Merovingian period—that the Merovingian kings were primarily distinguished by their long hair.[15]

It is also clear that the king, as portrayed by an impression of this ring, was above all a military figure, a warrior whose chief attribute was the spear.[16] Through much of Merovingian history, the spear was both a basic instrument of royal power and its preeminent symbol. The spear embodied the king's ability to lead and to compel. When King Gunthram (d. 593) gave his kingdom to Childebert II (d. 596), he expressed this by handing him a spear.[17] But for the fact that the image on Childeric's ring was without a helmet, it is like the later figure of Clothar II (d. 629), as described in the *Liber historiae francorum:* "But the king was standing there, dressed in his leather breastplate, helmet on his head, and his long hair, bespeckled with grey, bound up."[18] In death, the body of King Childeric was displayed as a prominent, successful warrior. The other contents of his grave consisted of warlike finery: strap-ends, a battle-axe, a sword that had rusted away in its fine garnet-inlayed sheath, and of course a spear. Alongside these items were hundreds of little bees of gold, which may have adorned a purple mantle.[19] With the grave of Childeric we are able to peer into the very origins of Frankish kingship, and what we find is a warlord's display of wealth and prestige with little that seems distinctively kingly. The lavish purple robe in which he was buried shows only that Childeric was a victorious warrior and a prosperous Roman ally.[20] Likewise, when Chilperic I was assassinated by his wife Fredegund in 584, his body was "dressed in royal robes" and taken to Saint-Vincent's in Paris for interment.[21] And yet members of the royal family other than the king were buried in similar garments.[22] If the king were by nature a singular figure in his kingdom, then one would expect a special royal garment to be restricted to his unique person.[23]

Unlike the pagan Childeric, whose body was lain in a burial mound, later monarchs were interred in monasteries or churches, such as Saint-Denis or Saint-Germain-des-Prés.[24] One aspect of the rise of Christian kingship among the Franks was the promotion of monasticism within

Figure 5.1. The warlike finery of a Merovingian king: spear, breastplate and royal long hair. A plaster-cast made from the seal-ring of Childeric, courtesy of the Ashmolean Museum, Oxford

their kingdoms. Accordingly this new royal ideal was expressed in the burial of the king in a monastery and the performance there of a perpetual liturgy on behalf of his soul. As Frankish kingship became associated with Christianity, this was expressed in new insignia, prominently displayed in royal burials.

In addition to robes, the evidence of early Frankish royal tombs shows that crowns were also associated with Frankish kings. The tomb of King Childeric II (d. 675), in the monastery of Saint-Germain-des-Prés, was opened by royal command in 1656.[25] Like the tomb of Childeric I, two hundred years earlier, the grave-goods represented the wealth and power of a successful war-lord. But there was also a significant difference. A braid of gold had been placed like a crown on the head of the corpse.[26] The appearance of a crown on the brow of a dead king, long before the Frankish kings had adopted the diadem as part of the regalia they displayed in life,[27] suggests an eschatological dimension for this symbol.

The Franks were well aware that the Roman emperors, whose empire once incorporated the lands they now occupied, had worn a diadem on their heads. The ancient Persian diadem had first become a feature of Roman imperial insignia under Constantine I (ca. 274–337), sometime after his conversion to Christianity.[28] It is certainly possible that the imperial diadem was from the first a religious sign. The religious and royal significance of the diadem had already gained a firm hold on the imagination of Christians, as expressed in the *De Corona* of Tertullian (ca. 150–230).[29] On Constantine's coinage, a diadem was shown being placed on his head by the hand of God in place of the laurel wreath that had adorned the imperial heads of earlier coinage.[30] Constantine's diadem, which later emperors also adopted, was related to the religious associations of the crown in Scripture, where it was often used as a metaphor for victorious religious qualities such as the "crown of dignity" or the "crown of life."[31] Christ was sometimes pictured receiving a crown, signifying his victory over the world.[32] In the same way, crowns became associated with the victory of the Apostles and martyrs over the world and death.[33] Childeric's death-crown represented such a "crown of glory," placing his personal, earthly royalty in a direct antinomy with the royalty of the saints. It signified that like the martyrs, he had died in the faith.[34] The death-crown of Childeric II may therefore be related not so much to the Roman and imperial connotations of the diadem as to the sentiment embodied in the votive crowns that Visigothic and Frankish monarchs donated to their churches. These votive crowns represented the royalty of the martyrs, but the presentation of such gifts was also an expression of royal power.[35]

The later Carolingian kings, for their part, went to their graves clothed in an array of regal signs. Charlemagne's grave was said to have been opened by Otto III in the year 1000, but the contemporary account of what was found within it is unreliable and fantastic.[36] In 1239, however, a large number of graves were unearthed at the basilica of St. Arnulf in Metz. The evidence is difficult to assess, but Metz had long been at the heart of the Carolingian domains, and many of the family had been buried there, including Louis the Pious.[37] The contemporary account of the discovery of these graves, by Abbot Thibault, lacks precision (the inscriptions could not be read even in the thirteenth century), but the bodies were said to wear crowns and silk robes, and some to hold scepters.[38] Such death-regalia had an eschatological dimension. The scepter, for example, recalled the accoutrements of Davidic kingship and thence also the risen Christ of the Book of Revelation.[39] With the Carolingian dynasty, however, symbols that formerly had signified kingship in death were now also worn in life.

Crowns, Robes, Thrones

Distinctive dress has always been used for the marking of social categories and stature.[40] However, the clothing worn by kings and bishops in the new kingdoms of Europe was significant not only because it served to mark and distinguish individuals but because to contemporaries, these garments seemed to express the nature and meaning of society. In addition to the diadem, other imperial signs, such as the scepter and the throne, also made an impression on the Franks, as upon all the peoples who established kingdoms within the former territories of the Roman Empire. These signs were already old when the Romans adopted them.[41] The purple mantle, or *chlamys,* was a soldier's cloak that came to form part of the increasingly military "look" of the late Roman emperors, signifying victory and prosperity.[42] Like the diadem, the chlamys and scepter had also been given Christian associations.[43] These and other symbols worn by the emperors of Rome and Byzantium were well known in the kingdoms that succeeded the western Empire. Bishops and kings in these new kingdoms were fascinated by the impressive model of ancient Rome and tentatively adopted the symbols of that empire even as they created new societies based upon non-Roman ideals. This was especially true of the Visigothic kingdom, which had more dealings, both peaceful and violent, with Byzantium than the other Germanic kingdoms, and which struggled to work out its own identity in the shadow of the Empire.[44]

The Visigothic kingdom played a leading role in developing institutions adapted to a sub-Roman, Christian world. The Visigothic model of a sacralized kingship, with close cooperation between kings and bishops, later had a significant impact on the Franks.[45] Some of these institutions were a continuation of Roman customs, while others, such as anointing, were innovations.[46] The adoption of imperial regalia also took place in Spain earlier than among the Franks.[47] Leovigild (569–586) was the first king of Visigothic Spain to adopt the Byzantine regalia of diadem, scepter, and throne.[48] At the same time, the coins minted by Visigothic kings began to depict these regalia in imitation of Byzantine coins.[49] Drawing on Byzantine iconography, the coins of Leovigild showed the king wearing a cloak over his shoulders and a diadem, sometimes surmounted by a cross.[50] The Franks also minted coins patterned on those of Rome and Byzantium, but unlike the Visigoths, their kings seem not to have taken the step of actually wearing all the royal symbols depicted on them.[51] Such coins represented royal power, but the images stamped on them did not portray the king who had them made. They served to publicize royal prestige and even to embody this power like a magical amulet.[52]

Gregory of Tours (ca. 539–594), in his *Ten Books of Histories*[53] related one striking instance of a Frankish king dressing in imperial regalia, bestowed on him by emissaries from Byzantium. This was King Clovis (481–511), the first Christian king of the Franks. In 508, Clovis returned to Tours with his army, having forced the Visigoths out of Gaul in a tremendous battle.[54] Byzantine ambassadors met Clovis with letters from Emperor Anastasius, conferring on him the consulate. This led to a remarkable ceremony in the church of Saint-Martin, at which Clovis put on Roman-style regalia: a purple tunic and cloak (the chlamys) and a diadem.[55] Dressed in this manner, he rode out from the church, throwing coins to the assembled people. Like other late-antique barbarian chieftans, Clovis thus appeared as a double figure: a Roman governor as well as a king.[56] Gregory did not portray any other kings in possession of such regalia, and the event therefore seems to have been a unique, honorific occasion, driven by the demands of Byzantine diplomacy—perhaps misunderstood by Gregory (and no doubt by Clovis himself).[57] The "consulate" of Clovis may be seen as the vaunting of Roman garments in a purely Frankish context, as a display of prestige by a successful warlord, "in the lap of his own people."[58]

But for the ambiguous case of Clovis, there was a break with Roman insignia in the representation of Frankish royal power. Their kings continued to distinguish themselves with a spare, warlike set of symbols. Their unusual status was shown primarily by their long hair and an official seat of power. Essentially their regalia was the battle-equipment of a Frankish warrior: a brandished spear, a shield, and the royal helmet.[59] Added to these were the king's seal-ring and its impression in wax, which could carry his presence throughout the realm, staring out at the viewer with his long hair and spear, like a threatening magical sign.[60]

Among bishops in the Frankish kingdom, however, might it not have been the case that Roman insignia would retain their antique value and meaning, given that so many of them, Gregory included, were from families that thought of themselves as Roman?[61] Bishops had long worn a special garment, the *pallium,* which was in origin a sign of consular status.[62] This long scarf of white wool was marked with black crosses at each end and draped over the shoulders so that both ends came straight down in front.[63] In Gaul and Spain it became a general mark of episcopal authority in the sixth century—that is to say, during this very period.[64] It was felt "that no bishop should presume to conduct a mass without the pallium."[65] We should bear in mind, however, that the bishops of Gaul did not think of the pallium as a Roman garment, despite its origins.

Bishops believed that the pallium was much older than Rome: its origins lay far back in ancient Judaism. As the *Exposition of the Ancient Galli-*

can Liturgy explained: "The pallium, which goes around the neck down to the breast, is called a rationale in the Old Testament, a sign of sanctity. . . ." The *Exposition* went on to say that "Ancient custom adorns the neck because kings and priests were enveloped with a pallium over their shining vestments which was a sign of grace."[66] Origins are meanings, and where an historian sees a different origin for a garment than did the person who wore it, he may be missing much of its significance. Despite their Roman background, bishops prized the pallium not because of its consular origin but because they believed it to be a garment that had been worn by the kings and priests of the Old Testament.

Other ecclesiastical garments were also drawn from the official garments of the Roman Empire. Bishops wore a light-colored tunic covered by a brown or violet *planeta,* or cloak.[67] The dalmatic, a sleeved gown sometimes richly decorated, went over the tunic, which could be seen under it. It often had vertical stripes.[68] The chasuble (*casula*), a richer development of the *planeta,* was a costly, luxurious garment that few could afford and that came to be restricted to priests and bishops.[69] In Spain and in Gaul, the crozier and ring were later added to the assemblage of episcopal signs.[70]

The vestments of bishops, with their ancient Roman origins, were the specialized garments of a group who claimed rulership, and their style and form were retained even while the clothing of those around them was transformed with the rise of the Frankish kingdom. In the cities of Gaul, this meant that the identity of bishops as scions of the old Gallo-Roman nobility could be seen in their dress. And yet the bishops of Gaul thought about their own past along the lines laid down in the *Exposition,* not seeing their garments as a Roman holdover. It is therefore not enough to remark on the traditionalism that makes for the conservation of religious garments over time.[71] As will be seen, for clerics these garments were the mark not of their Roman background but of a prerogative to rule, based upon their inheritance of the Old Testament offices of priest and king.[72]

Gregory of Tours was intrigued by Roman imperial accession ceremonies and was well aware of the regalia involved. In his account of the accession of Tiberius II in 578, for example, he was careful to mention his assumption of a purple robe, his crowning with a diadem, and his ascent of the imperial throne.[73] For Gregory the diadem was strongly associated with Roman (Byzantine) imperial accessions and not with Frankish kings, except for the odd case of Clovis.[74]

Tiberius ascended a throne (*thronus*), but Gregory did not use this word to refer to the thrones of Frankish kings. After the ceremony in which Clovis put on the *chlamys* and diadem, according to Gregory, the king went on to establish the seat of his government in Paris.[75] The word used to describe this seat, *cathedra,* was freighted with significance, especially for a bishop such as Gregory, for this was also the characteristic word for a bishop's chair of office.[76] In late antiquity bishops had adopted a throne, perhaps in imitation of the Roman emperor, although they came to think of this *cathedra* in relation to the thrones of King Solomon and King David.[77] In this and in a number of other passages, Gregory seems to have pointed to a parallel that he saw between two powers in the Frankish kingdom, that of bishop and king, expressed in two parallel seats: the *cathedra episcopalis* and the *cathedra regis.*[78] He thus also expressed the fact that episcopal territories were the building blocks of kingdoms.[79]

The significance of this pairing of royal and episcopal attributes is far-reaching, since bishops believed that they stood side by side with kings at the head of the Christian people. Indeed, there was a kind of partnership between Frankish bishops and the kings who relied on their role as powerful regional lords.[80] Bishops believed in their capacity to govern despite the fact that Merovingian kings persistently intervened in episcopal elections. The imposition of royal power did not alter the self-perception of bishops that they "ruled."[81] After death, a bishop was often remembered as having "sat" for so many years, in a reference to his chair of authority.[82] From late antiquity onward, such a seat occupied a central position in a bishop's church.[83] In attributing a similar chair to the Frankish kings, Gregory indicated the overlapping government of king and bishop. In later royal ordinations, the two chairs of royal and episcopal power would be placed in a direct and dramatic pairing before the assembled people.[84]

King and Priest

The similitude of kings and bishops was expressed, in a limited way, in symbols associated with Merovingian kingship. With the rise of the Carolingian dynasty in 751, however, the paraphernalia of the old warrior-kings was exchanged for a more deliberately symbolic regalia. Changes in royal dress and insignia made the equivalence between king and priest more obvious. As was mentioned, the garments adopted by bishops were Roman in origin but were seen by them as reflections of the garments of the ancient priests and kings of Israel. The regalia of Carolingian kings came to express a similar historical perspective.[85] The changes in royal symbology may be better understood by an examination of theological concepts about the nature of Christian society. Frankish bishops drew upon these notions as they thought about their own role and that of kings. Much of this reflection centered upon study of the Bible, especially the Old Testament, which was viewed as a prefiguration of Christian reality.

With their depiction of peoples divided by tribal distinctions, dominated by priests and kings, and involved in constant warfare, the historical narratives of the Old Testament seemed directly relevant to those who read them in the Frankish kingdoms of the sixth and seventh centuries.[86] Because Christians believed that their societies were a culmination or an actualization of things only foreshadowed in ancient Israel, they scoured the texts of the Old Testament for an understanding of their own times and institutions.[87] The clothing that adorned the kings and priests of Israel seemed meaningful and significant to bishops, in part because of the similarities between them. What sort of kings and priests did they find there?

Over time the garments of the kings and priests of ancient Israel had come to resemble each other, as the priesthood adopted royal symbols.[88] Both kings and priests were endowed with religious power; and yet the origins of Jewish kingship, as portrayed in 1 Samuel, were ambiguous. In the view of the Deuteronomist, by insisting on having a king like her neighbors had, Israel had abandoned the direct government of its God in favor of a human ruler—merely human and hence capable of error and abuse.[89] Nevertheless these kings were also exalted figures, chosen by God to govern his people.[90] The king was sacrosanct because he was anointed with sacred oil and inaugurated in a ceremony in which he ascended a throne and was clothed with a diadem, scepter, vestments, and bracelets. In taking up these signs the kings of Israel availed themselves of the ancient royal symbology of Near Eastern empires.[91]

The similarities between king and priest were considerable: the priests of Israel were also anointed, sacrosanct, and chosen by God. The tiara worn by the ancient Jewish priests was adorned with a diadem on which was fixed the ancient symbol of a golden flower.[92] Their headgear thus combined a priestly garment (the tiara, or turban) with a royal symbol, the diadem. In addition, the levitical priests wore a tunic, cloak, the *ephod,* and yet another royal symbol—the breastplate or *pectoral*. The parallels between the signs of kingship and priesthood, as thus portrayed in the Bible, fascinated later Christian thinkers. Christians believed that the priests and kings of ancient Israel presaged the coming of Christ. This was why, as bishops came into prominence in the early Church, they likened their clothing and rituals to the code of the levitical priesthood.[93]

The theologian Jerome (348–420), famous for his translation of the Bible into Latin (the Vulgate), undertook to explain the relation between the vestments of the Christian priesthood and those of the Jewish priesthood in a letter to Fabiola.[94] The ancient priest who "wore a turban (*cidarim*) and bore the name of God on his brow, adorned with a royal diadem," was surpassed by the appearance of Christ.[95] It was the duty of the Christian priesthood to live up to the example of Christ, the "great Priest," who brought into the light of day all the hidden meaning of those ancient priests.[96] An understanding of the ancient priesthood was therefore of direct importance to Christians, the "royal and priestly people."[97]

Jerome went on to describe in detail the emblems associated with the Jewish priesthood. The tiara, he pointed out, was shaped "as if a sphere were cut in half, and one half placed on the head. . . ."[98] Jerome believed that universal themes were wrapped up in these garments. The four colors of the priestly robes: "linen," hyacinth, purple and scarlet, represented the four elements.[99] However, the universality hidden in the vestments and actions of the ancient priest did not come to fruition until the appearance of Christ. Moses may have washed Aaron—but only Christian baptism offered to cleanse the whole world.[100] For that reason, Christians were given a white gown when they arose naked from the baptismal bath. They merited the shining robes of Christ—they had become like David.[101] The white robe of Christ represented synthesis and completion. But one should bear in mind another mantle of Christ—the robe stained red with blood at the Judgment.[102]

Christ encompassed and surpassed Judaism in his own person and hence could be thought of as a king and priest.[103] Members of the Christian Church were thought to participate in the nature of Christ, because they were the Body of Christ.[104] By means of baptism, the new Christian took on the royal and priestly qualities of Christ, and for this reason the rite came to include anointing with sacred oil. The connection between baptismal anointing and the anointed kings and priests of ancient Israel was explained by John the Deacon, in a well-known letter to Senarius:

> Having put on the white vestments, his head is anointed with the unction of the sacred chrism, so that the baptized might know that he has assumed a kingdom and a priestly mystery. In fact priests and princes are anointed with the oil of the chrism. . . .[105]

Through baptism, every Christian became part of the Body of Christ, and as such a member of the "royal and priestly people"(1 Peter 2.9). This was why the new Christian was given a white robe, like the seamless tunic of Christ.

In the new kingdoms of Europe, all such imagery took on a social dimension that it had not possessed for Jerome. The ancient priests and the kings whose vagaries and violence were nevertheless joined to their sacred standing seemed true and alive in societies that were searching to establish a meaningful identity in the ruins of the Roman Empire. It was in the Visigothic kingdom that the political and social implications of baptism were first realized.

For Visigothic and Frankish bishops, the most authoritative book on the nature of their office was Isidore's *On Ecclesiastical Offices,* written sometime between 598 and 615.[106] Isidore believed that the royal and priestly nature of Christ, exceeding and encompassing ancient Judaism, could also be seen in the Christian Church and those who governed it. This was symbolized in the characteristic hairstyle of clerics, the circular, crown-shaped tonsure:[107]

> the head being shaved on top, a lower circular crown is left, and I judge that it symbolizes their priesthood and government of the church. Indeed, among the ancients, a tiara was placed on the head of priests (this was made of cotton, and circular as if it were a half-sphere), and this is symbolized in the shaved part of the head. A crown, on the other hand, is the golden circular band which adorns the heads of kings . . . that sign is expressed on the head of clerics. . . ."[108]

As was mentioned earlier, the Visigothic kings had long expressed their royalty by wearing a diadem in imitation of the Byzantine emperors. According to Isidore, bishops also wore such a crown in their symbolic hairstyle. He therefore intimated that the governing figures of Visigothic society—king and bishop—were mirror-images of each other, as had been the ancient kings and priests of Israel. Like John the Deacon, he also saw this parallel in the baptismal anointing with oil, drawing upon ancient traditions about the nature of the Church as forming a "mystical body."[109]

The imagery of baptism, with its allusions to ancient kings and priests, must have seemed appropriate to the bishops who participated in the baptismal anointing of newly converted kings, such as Clovis in 508,[110] or at the conversion of the Visigothic King Reccared in 589.[111] For their part, bishops drew upon this imagery in understanding their own role as governors of the Church. Like the ancient kings and priests, Frankish bishops were anointed with sacred oil at their ordinations from the early eighth century onward.[112]

In the Christian kingdoms of Europe, theological ideas associated with baptism gave birth to social concepts, as these societies endeavored to erect a new identity around their governing persons. The ultimate expression of this was in rites of crowning and anointing kings.[113] The first known instance of this ritual was thirty years after Isidore's death, when King Wamba was anointed by Julian of Toledo in 672, in a ceremony full of priestly allusions.[114] The idea of royal anointing was later adopted by the Franks in 751, when Pippin, the first king of the Carolingian dynasty, was anointed in Soissons.[115] Pippin also tonsured the last Merovingian king, Childeric

III, imprisoning him in a monastery. As we shall see, royal anointing became a regular feature of Frankish kingship, and the Franks looked for the origins of this ritual in the distant past. The baptismal anointing of Clovis in 508 came to be seen as an earlier example of what was in fact an innovation. As so often, the emergence of a new institution was accompanied by a reinterpretation of the past.

The conceptualization of Christian society as the Body of Christ became one of the main principles of Carolingian kingship.[116] The liturgical *ordines* for blessing and anointing a king, which flourished under the Carolingian kings, associated the themes of crowning and anointing with the figures of Samuel and David and with the kingship of Christ over his people.[117] Ideals of kingship in Visigothic Spain and Frankish Gaul thus came to absorb the imagery of kingship to be found in the Old Testament.[118] This is why the Carolingian kings were so often compared to King David and why they and their bishops clothed themselves in the sacred raiment and symbols of ancient Jewish kings and priests.[119] However, in the ensuing discussion it should be kept in mind that anointing and crowning did not have an "official" character, and did not amount to an act of king-making. The number and kind of objects involved were flexible and subject to improvisation.[120]

Robing and Disrobing

Charlemagne, as Einhard famously pointed out, preferred to dress as an ordinary Frank, distinguishing himself only by the blue cloak and jeweled sword he wore on especially important occasions. As mentioned at the outset of this essay, literary descriptions of clothing are often hard to assess because of their ambiguity. In his description of Charlemagne's "Frankish" clothing, for example, Einhard quoted passages from Suetonius' biography of Augustus.[121] But on feast days, according to Einhard, Charlemagne would wear robes of gold, begemmed sandals, and a "diadem glittering with gold and gems."[122]

Charlemagne seemed at times to serve as a kind of mannequin whom others dressed up to express their own social ideals. Despite Charlemagne's preference for Frankish clothing, Pope Hadrian once asked him to dress as a Roman; the same thing happened again at his coronation as Emperor of the Romans on Christmas Day 800 at the behest of Pope Leo III. On these occasions, according to Einhard, Charlemagne was dressed in a long, sleeved tunic, over which was thrown a short military cloak (*chlamys*).[123] Charlemagne's desire to stand as an equal of the Byzantine emperors led to the creation of a new crowning ritual but one based on Byzantine accession ceremonies and thought of as old.[124] Political desires of the papacy, first made clear in the *Donation of Constantine,* played a central role in this innovation.[125] In this forged document, some radical proponent of priestly government imagined that Constantine had ceded to the bishops of Rome an imperial regalia, complete with crown, scepter, and robes of purple.[126] By means of this ceremony on Christmas Day, the pope could stand forth as a priest-king, anointing a preeminent king-priest, just as Samuel had anointed David.[127] In a famous mosaic in the Lateran, made to celebrate the coronation of Charlemagne, the emperor and pope were paired as agents of the governing majesty of St. Peter, who handed a royal banner to Charlemagne and a pallium to Pope Leo. The author of the *Royal Frankish Annals* believed that the coronation was the revival of this ancient ceremony.[128] In Charlemagne's imperial coronation, clothing was used to express an imperial ideal blending Roman and Christian themes.

Charlemagne's continuously successful expansion of the Frankish kingdom was viewed by contemporaries as a favorable judgment of God on the religious ideals of his empire. The king was the pinnacle and center of these sacred ideals, and his royal accoutrements were reinterpreted in this light. The ancient duty of allegiance to the king itself took on a religious significance.[129] His son, Louis the Pious (814–840), presented his own government as an intensification of those same concepts,[130] although he was not always able to live up to them.[131] Louis was in his turn crowned as emperor by Pope Stephen IV. Although the ritual took place in Reims rather than Rome, the ideal of a Christian Roman Empire was still the dominant theme.[132] Contemporaries believed that the crown placed on Louis's head was the actual diadem of Constantine the Great.[133]

Thinking ahead toward his death, Louis arranged a division of the empire among his sons in the *Ordinatio imperii* of 817.[134] When he later had another son, the future Charles the Bald, he sought to overturn this arrangement. Louis's renunciation of the *Ordinatio* seemed like an injustice to his older sons, and the resulting civil wars were cruel and long-lasting. As internecine strife consumed the Frankish empire, harsh acts of war were interpreted as sins that violated the religious principles of Carolingian kingship.

At Attigny, in 822, Louis made a public confession for the wrongful imprisonment of his brothers, and for the death of Bernard of Italy, who died after his eyes were gouged out. Louis also endured a public penance.[135] In 833, another rebellion left Louis abandoned by his nobles and bishops at the Field of Lies and then imprisoned. Soon afterward he was compelled to make a second public penance by an assembly at Compiègne. In the church of Saint Médard, Louis held a list of his crimes in his hand and lay outstretched on the floor before the altar, tearfully asking forgiveness. The expected result of this public penance was that the emperor, deprived of his royal military gear (*cingulum militiae*), would wear the white robes of a penitent for the rest of his life, precluded from engaging in public life and incapable of being a king, since a king was still expected to be a warrior.[136] This aspect of the penance endured by Louis shows that the regalia had taken on a new significance. No longer merely a festal display of kingly power, royal dress and paraphernalia now signified a king's competence to govern, functioning like the long hair of the Merovingian kings.[137] When Louis was restored to power in a dramatic reversal of fortune, the occasion was marked by the joyful return of his royal robes and military gear in the basilica of Saint-Denis.[138] Years later, as Louis lay on his deathbed, he sent the scepter and crown to his eldest son Lothar, thereby respecting, in part, the old arrangement of the *Ordinatio*.[139]

The religious ideals of Carolingian kingship were displayed in every medium available—not only on the person of the king, but also in laws, letters and diplomacy, building programs, and ostentatious protocols of Church reform.[140] Perhaps the most preeminent of these expressions, however, was the display of royal tackle in liturgical settings. Robes of purple or gold were prominent in such displays.[141] The sons of Louis, especially Lothar and Charles the Bald, frequently resorted to the symbols of empire. By giving prominence to their crowns and robes, they could emphasize the continuity that each of them claimed with their father and grandfather and at the same time drive home their claims against each other. The purposive, sophisticated use of regalia in the 840s may also be attributed to the fact that the brothers had more than once seen their father stripped of his royal attire.

The Naked King

Let us return, then, to the role of royal garments in the reign of Charles the Bald. As his career progressed, from his isolated position before gaining a kingdom to his accession as emperor of the Romans, each advance was marked by a crowning ceremony, three in all. In 848, Charles was anointed and crowned as king of the western Frankish kingdom at Orléans, in a newly created ritual.[142] Charles was consecrated by the assembled bishops as a kind of priest-king, in a ceremony resembling the ordination of a priest.[143] The king and his bishops stood together at the head of a kingdom conceived of as the Body of Christ, as Charles was endowed with diadem, scepter, and throne.[144]

The regalia of the Carolingian kings increasingly became the primary symbolic assertion of royal legitimacy and efficacy. Thus Pippin II of Aquitaine, who rebelled against Charles in 853, was forced to don a monk's habit to mark his surrender and submission.[145] Three years later, when the

Aquitanians again sought Pippin's leadership, they brought him out of the monastery and "made him look like a king."[146] At the end of his life, the ailing Lothar voluntarily put on a monk's habit, signaling by this change of habiliment that he had abandoned both the world and his royal position.[147] When he died in 855, the kingdom of Lorraine passed on to his son, Lothar II.

From the beginning, the exploitation of rituals and signs of kingship figured prominently in Charles's royal program. This became even more pronounced after the death of Lothar II in 869. Soon afterward Charles was anointed and crowned as king of Lorraine in an elaborate ceremony, composed and presided over by Hincmar, Archbishop of Reims.[148] Once again a Frankish king served as a sort of mannequin. The coronation took place in St. Arnulf's basilica in Metz, resting place of so many of Charles's ancestors. Hincmar believed that in anointing Charles he was repeating and reproducing the anointing of Clovis. Not only was Charles a descendent of Clovis, Hincmar declared, but the church of Reims was still in possession of the same oil that St. Remigius, founder of the See of Reims, had used in that long-ago baptism.[149] Hincmar poured this ancient sacred oil over Charles's head, from back to front, and from side to side in the shape of a cross, as seven bishops pronounced in unison the words "*Coronet te Dominus.*"[150] The king received at that moment a "crown of glory" that preceded the imposition of a physical crown. Charles was also given palm branches and a scepter.[151]

The religious ideals expressed at this coronation and the historical perspective that connected it to the Merovingian past had long been preoccupations of Hincmar.[152] Sometime after 835, in his *Deeds of King Dagobert,* he sought to associate the powerful King Dagobert (629–638) with his own abbey of Saint-Denis.[153] At the same time, he gave the Carolingian kings a distant and exalted origin in the Merovingian past. He imagined Dagobert as an impressive figure, crowned and seated on a golden throne "as was the custom of Frankish kings."[154] This had not been their custom, as we have seen—but Dagobert had become the simulacrum of a social ideal, as did Charles himself when Hincmar poured the sacred oil over his head.

After this ceremony, redolent of the past, Charles the Bald went on to present himself in ever more imposing grandeur. It was perhaps about this time that a great ivory-paneled throne was made for him, covered with allegorical pictures.[155] On one of the panels is carved the figure of a king, probably meant to be Charles, wearing a mantle and crown, holding an orb in his left hand and a scepter in his right. On either side of the king, an angel leans forward proferring a crown to him. Here the earthly and religious connotations of crowns were mingled.

When Charles traveled to Rome late in 875, he was anointed and crowned for a third time, now as Emperor of the Romans, as Charlemagne had been seventy-five years earlier, on Christmas Day.[156] Charles may then have taken the ivory throne to Rome as a present for John VIII. The gift of a throne invoked the ancient parallel between king and priest, once again culminating in emperor and pope.[157] Charles had now reached the height of his ambitions and vaunted his new persona in the Frankish kingdom with a flourishing of garments.

Despite the important role that bishops had come to play in the assertion of royal status, Charles went on to impose his authority harshly over them. In 876, at a council of bishops called to Ponthion, Charles (with the aid of a papal letter, and accompanied by legates from the Apostolic See) attempted to install the canonist Ansegesis as a primate with special powers over the Frankish church.[158] According to Hincmar, who rebelled against this infringement of his authority, Charles ascended the imperial throne wearing a golden robe over his Frankish clothing. The bishops and other assembled clerics, for their part, were also wearing their liturgical vestments. The resemblance of royal and episcopal power was brought to the fore even as they came into conflict.[159] As Charles pressed forward his ambition to reorganize the Frankish church, the war of garments came to a head in a further meeting of the synod. While the bishops appeared again in liturgical dress, Charles was now resplendent in Byzantine imperial regalia, flanked by the papal legates in their Roman vestments.[160] With this theatrical assertion of power, Ansegesis was imposed on the Frankish bishops in spite of their protest.

Charles often wore his regalia on important occasions. He was also frequently portrayed wearing his crown and robes in manuscript paintings.[161] The pictures functioned as a further means by which the king could display his royal presence, not unlike the ancient seal-ring of Childeric. We should keep in mind that the representation of kingship in such paintings was not simply mimetic but was intended to convey a complex story about royal power. In effect these were parables in paint. The depiction of a king and his regalia was an act of the imagination, dominated by the desire to set down social ideals in a permanent form. Moreover, in a set of paintings, every possible resonance of royal symbols could be laid out in visual contrast and comparison.[162] In the course of the invention and reinvention of Frankish kingship, garments and other royal signs served as a fluid language that responded readily to political desire and historical understanding.[163] These paintings were another aspect of the manipulation and continuous rethinking of royal symbols.

Like his forebears, Charles expressed the ideals of his kingship through an extensive patronage of the arts, from book-production to architecture.

But he did so on an unprecedented scale. In a prayerbook made for him sometime between 845 and 866, the artist brought forward a group of images comparing Charles to the figures of King David and Christ.[164] In the principal illustration of the prayerbook, Charles was shown in full regalia, kneeling and reaching forward to embrace the foot of the Cross—in a pious, imperial gesture known as *proskynesis.* The prayerbook represented Charles as one whose humble religious devotion was the source of his exaltation as a ruler.[165]

Perhaps the best-known of the books associated with Charles is the *First Bible of Charles the Bald,* probably completed in 845. Two paintings in this Bible may serve to summarize the themes that have been pursued here. In the famous "presentation miniature," King Charles was shown seated on a raised throne, receiving the Bible from the abbot and monks of the monastery of Saint-Martin in Tours, where the Bible was made. The figure of Charles is draped in a luxurious long cloak, fastened at the right shoulder, a crown on his head, and a long wand in his left hand.[166] Here in a grand ceremonial occasion, the king was imagined to be larger than life (larger than the other figures), in full regalia, flanked by nobles and soldiers (fig. 5.2).

A second painting, of King David, was intended as a companion picture to the throne-scene of Charles the Bald. The dedication poem of the *First Bible* played upon the parallels that might be seen between King Charles and the ancient King David: "O glory, O venerable salvation, O brilliant David . . . King Charles, flourish with the power of the Almighty. . . ."[167] King David, traditionally believed to be the author of the Psalms, was appropriately shown playing a harp. On his head is a crown with the same complicated form as that in the portrait of King Charles.[168] David is clad only in a purple cloak, as indicated by his bare legs. The king is notionally naked (fig. 5.3). The idea of a naked King David comes from 2 Samuel, which tells how David led the ark into Jerusalem, dancing like an ecstatic prophet, wearing only a linen *ephod* (2 Sam. 6.12–23). This "lowering" of David before his Lord was a turning point before he was anointed as king to replace Saul. The striking image of a naked King David was a comparison to Charles, illustrating his struggle against Lothar.[169] The same image, of David "exalted in humility," was alluded to at the coronation of Charles in 848.

Nakedness and humility, succeeded by anointing and a new garment, also suggest the rite of baptism. As has been seen, Jerome and John the Deacon connected the baptism of a new Christian to the ancient custom of clothing him or her in a white robe. In the liturgy of Gaul, likewise, baptism and anointing were associated with being given such a vestment.[170] In its directions for applying the chrism, the *Missale Gothicum* said that this garment was first worn by Christ.[171] The immersion in water was a moment of deliverance and rebirth, as the initiate was liberated from the

Figure 5.2. Charles the Bald, shown seated on a throne, wearing a fine robe and elaborate crown, and holding a wand. He is being presented with the Bible in which the illustration appears. The First Bible of Charles the Bald. BN lat. 1, fol. 423r. Cliché Bibliotheque nationale de France.

weak and vulnerable nakedness of sin by the waters of salvation, like Jonah delivered from the whale, or Noah from the Ark. With the white garment, he or she was now "clothed in Christ," overcoming the primordial nudity of Adam and Eve.[172] Amnesty was declared on the exile of mankind, as it is on the straining newborn child, wrapped and given to her mother's arms. Royal vestments captured some of these associations: as mentioned earlier, the political rebirth of Louis the Pious after his abandonment and defeat had been marked by the restoration of his robes in a jubilant ceremony in the basilica of Saint-Denis.[173]

At the outset of this essay, I argued that to look for the origins of the state in a taxonomy of early medieval royal symbols is anachronistic. Such studies often lapse into antiquarianism and sometimes indulge an interest in the trappings of power tied to nostalgic sentiments about the origins of modern national identity. Historians such as Schramm thereby sought to place Carolingian kingship within a larger narrative regarding the rise of the modern state. In abandoning this larger narrative for the purposes of this study, I have attempted to recover the contemporary historical perspective in which the Franks adopted their royal symbols. By looking at the origins of royal and priestly symbols in this way, a different and older layer of meaning emerges, centered in hieratic prototypes rather than our own view of historical origins. If the origin of the state is to be found here, it should be located in the continuous reinterpretation of the past that gave birth to royal symbols rather than in the symbols themselves. The atmosphere of that long-vanished world was so bounded and inward-looking as to produce a sense of claustrophobia in the historian. Nevertheless, the Franks were aware that within the strident array of royal signs lay a nagging question. Where had social power come from—and how did kings get hold of it? The very origins of kingship were troubling. Was not King David himself a "man of blood" (2 Sam. 16.7)? For this reason, it may possible, at this point, to say something relevant to the rise of the modern state.

Robe, crown, scepter, and throne became major expressions of the ideals of Carolingian kingship, a language of "clean power" that sought to wash the hands of kingship, sullied by its intimate connection to violence.[174] It seemed apparent that the Frankish king combined in himself both royal and priestly qualities—he could even be thought of as a "Christ."[175] Bishops meanwhile continued to speculate on the ancient, exalted origins of their chasuble, dalmatic and sandals.[176] Royal and episcopal regalia shared the crown, throne, and robe. They resembled one another because both displayed the religious hopes attached to Christian society.

When Charles the Bald arose from his bath on Easter Eve of 841, he was at a low point in his struggle against Lothar. The weakness and isolation he

Figure 5.3. King David, playing a harp and wearing a crown. His bare legs indicate his nakedness. The First Bible of Charles the Bald. BN lat. 1, fol 215v. Cliché Bibliotheque nationale de France.

suffered would later be compared to the apparent hopelessness of King David as he danced naked before the Lord.[177] In telling this story, Nithard implied that Charles was also like a new Christian at baptism. When he drew on the mantle that arrived from Aquitaine, he thereby clothed his nakedness with a potent image, a robe like the shining white gown of Christ.

Charles the Bald, like all kings, sought to dominate people and land. But his royal program was also directed toward a symbolic realm. By dressing in his robe, Charles showed his weary men that he had been chosen by God to take his place at the head of "a royal and priestly people." The symbolic objects that have been discussed here—thrones, robes, crowns, and scepters—may all be traced back to early antiquity. Despite their ancient association with royalty, however, they did not move through time with a fixed meaning. They were continuously reinterpreted and put to new uses. As we have seen, bishops traced these objects back to the kings and priests of ancient Israel. Historical reinterpretation thus played a role in the transformation of Frankish kingship.

As a visual language, royal symbols circumvented all the compromise and discord of reality, offering only pure, ideal statements. Nevertheless, violence always lurked in the vicinity of royal power. Naked power was decently covered by the crown and robe of a king, but only on ceremonial occasions or in the frozen gesture of a painted king. Nithard was among the warriors who went on to fight for Charles at the Battle of Fontenoy. The hopes inspired by the marvelous robing scene were suddenly overshadowed by the darker side of royal power, still symbolized by helmet and spear. Two months later, the historian recorded his horror at the great slaughter of that day; and as he was writing his account of the battle, the sun was blotted out in an eclipse.[178]

Notes

I indebted to Sir Hugh Lloyd-Jones and to Nancy Aykanian for their help with this essay and to Jon Knudsen (d. 1999), to whom it is dedicated.

CSEL = *Corpus Scriptorum Ecclesiasticorum Latinorum*
CCCM = *Corpus Christianorum, Continuatio Medievalis*
CCSL = *Corpus Christianorum, Series Latina*
MGH = *Monumenta Germaniae Historica*
Capit. = *Capitularia*
SS= *Scriptores*
SRM = *Scriptores Rerum Merovingicarum*
SRG = *Scriptores Rerum Germanicarum*
SRG in us. schol. = *Scriptores Rerum Germanicarum in usum scholarum*

1. Nithard's history was written to support the cause of Charles the Bald: Janet L. Nelson, "Public *Histories* and Private History in the Work of Nithard," in her *Politics and Ritual in Early Medieval Europe* (London: The Hambledon Press, 1986), pp. 195–237.
2. " . . . repente ab Aquitania missi pro foribus adstiterant, qui coronam et omnem ornatem tam regium quam et quicquid ad cultum divinum pertinebat ferebant." (2.8, year 841) Nithard, *Histoire des fils de Louis le Pieux,* ed. Philibert Lauer (Paris: Société d'édition "Les belles lettres," 1964), p. 60.
3. "Et, quod maxime mirandum fateor fore, qualiter ad definitum locum vel certe ad statutam diem et horam venire poterant, cum nec idem Karolus ubi se suosque oporteret sciebat." 2.8 (year 841) Nithard, *Histoire,* p. 60.
4. Janet L. Nelson, "Public *Histories* and Private History," p. 205f.; likewise her *Charles the Bald* (London: Longman, 1992), p. 114.
5. In regard to the later Middle Ages, see Odile Blanc, "Histoire du costume: l'objet introuvable," *Médiévales* 29 (1995), 65–82.
6. Hervé Pinoteau, "Les insignes du roi vers l'an Mil," in Michel Parisse and Xavier Barral I Altet, eds., *Le roi de France et son royaume autour de l'an mil. Actes du colloque Hugues Capet 987–1987,* Paris–Senlis, 22–25 juin 1987 (Paris: Picard, 1992), pp. 73–88. See p. 74f.
7. A portrait of Charles the Bald in the *First Bible of Charles the Bald,* from sometime after 845, shows the king being presented with the Bible in which the painting was made. In other words, it is a painting of an imagined scene, hence making the robes and crown of the king difficult to assess. See the discussion of Herbert L. Kessler, "A Lay Abbot as Patron: Count Vivian and the First Bible of Charles the Bald," *Settimane di Studi del Centro Italiano di Studi sull' Alto Medioevo* 39 (1992), 649–79. See p. 651f.
8. See the table of crowns in Percy Ernst Schramm, *Die deutschen Kaiser und Könige in Bildern ihrer Zeit, 751–1190,* ed. Florentine Mütherich (Munich: Prestel Verlag, 1983), pp. 142–143; as of this writing, I have been unable to see Joachim Ott, *Krone und Krönung. Die Verheissung und Verleihung von Kronen in der Kunst von der Spätantike bis um 1200 und die geistige Auslesung der Krone* (Mainz am Rhein: P. von Zabern, 1997)
9. J. M. Bak, "Medieval Symbology of the State: Percy E. Schramm's Contribution" *Viator* 4 (1973), 33–63. See also Carlrichard Brühl, "Kronen- und Krönungsbrauch im frühen und hohen Mittelalter," *Historische Zeitschrift* 234 (1982), 1–31. See p.1f.; Peter Classen, "Corona imperii," in *Festschrift Percy Ernst Schramm,* ed. Peter Classen and Peter Scheibert, 2 vols. (Wiesbaden: F. Steiner, 1964), 1:90–101. See p. 90.
10. See the treatment of the early Middle Ages in Josef Deér, "Die abendländische Kaiserkrone des Hochmittelalters," *Schweizer Beitrage zur allgemeinen Geschichte* 7 (1949): 53–86.
11. On the newness of medieval kingship, see Jacques Le Goff, "Le roi dans l'occident médiévale: caracteres originaux," in *Kings and Kingship in Medieval Europe,* ed. Anne J. Duggan, King's College London Medieval Stud-

ies 10 (London: Kings College London Centre for Late Antique and Medieval Studies, 1993), pp. 1–39.

12. On the Roman origins of episcopal garments, see Theodor Klauser, *Der Ursprung der bischöflichen Insignien und Ehrenrechte* (Krefeld, 1949). Repr. in Gesammelte Arbeiten zur Liturgiegeschichte, Kirchengeschichte und christlichen Archäologie, ed. Ernst Dassmann, Jahrbuch für Antike und Christentum, Ergänzungsband 3 (Munster: Aschendorff, 1974), pp. 195–211.
13. For the historian Gregory of Tours, intent on discovering the origins of Frankish kingship, Childeric was definitely a king: "De Childerico rege et Egidio" (chapter headings for Book 2). *Gregorii episcopi Turonensis Libri historiarum X,* ed. Bruno Krusch and Wilhelm Levison, MGH, SRM 1.1, p. 35.
14. Jean-Jacques Chifflet, *Anastasis Childerici I. Francorum regis, sive Thesaurus sepulchralis Tornaci Neruiorum effossus, et commentario illustratus* (Antwerp: Ex officina Plantiniana, B. Moreti, 1655). Chifflet must be used with caution because of his political views: Fritz Wagner, "Die politische Bedeutung des Childerich-Grabfundes von 1653," *Bayerische Akademie der Wissenschaften,* philosophisch-historische Klasse, Sitzungsberichte 2 (Munich, 1973). On Childeric and his grave, see also Ian Wood, *The Merovingian Kingdoms 450–751* (London: Longman, 1994), pp. 38–41; Joachim Werner, "Das Grab des Frankenkönigs Childerich in Tournai," *Bayerische Akademie der Wissenschaften,* philosophisch-historische Klasse, Sitzungsberichte (Munich, 1971); and Percy Ernst Schramm, *Herrschaftszeichen und Staatssymbolik. Beiträge zu ihrer Geschichte vom dritten bis zum sechzehnten Jahrhundert,* Schriften der Monumenta Germaniae historica (Deutsches Institut für Erforschung des Mittelalters) 13; 3 vols. (Stuttgart: Hiersemann, 1954–1956), 1:213–15.
15. Averil Cameron, "How did the Merovingian Kings Wear their Hair?" *Revue Belge de philologie et histoire* 43 (1965), 1203–1216. See also Schramm, *Herrschaftszeichen,* 1:229.
16. A symbol also used by the Romans: Andreas Alföldi, "Zum Speersymbol der Souveränität im Altertum," in *Festschrift Percy Ernst Schramm,* op. cit., 1:3–6.
17. "Post haec rex Gunthchramnus, data in manu regis Childeberthi hasta, ait: 'Hoc est indicium, quod tibi omne regnum meum tradedi'" (7.33), Gregory of Tours, *Libri historiarum,* op. cit., p. 353. For a diffuse discussion, see Olivier Bouzy, "Les armes symboles d'un pouvoir politique: L'épée du sacre, la sainte lance, l'oriflamme, aux VIIIe–XIIe siècles," *Francia* 22 (1995), 45–57.
18. Trans. Richard A. Gerberding, *The Rise of the Carolingians and the Liber Historiae Francorum* (Oxford: Clarendon Press, 1987), p. 64.
19. These "bees" are sometimes interpreted as "cicadas." Alaine Erlande-Brandenburg, *Le roi est mort. Étude sur les funérailles les sépultures et les tombeaux des rois de France jusqu'à la fin du XIIIe siècle,* Bibliothèque de la société

française d'archéologie 7 (Paris: Arts et métiers graphiques, 1975), p. 33. But it seems that bees would make more sense as a royal symbol: W. Deonna, "L'abeille et le roi," *Révue Belge d'archéologie et d'histoire de l'art* 25 (1956), 105–131. See pp. 107–11; on bees at the anointing of Wamba, see Roger Collins, "Julian of Toledo and the Royal Succession in Late Seventh-Century Spain," in P. H. Sawyer and I. N. Wood, eds., *Early Medieval Kingship* (Leeds: University of Leeds, 1979), pp. 30–49. See p. 46f.

20. J. M. Wallace-Hadrill, *The Long-Haired Kings and Other Studies in Frankish History* (New York: Barnes and Noble, 1962), p. 162f.
21. " . . . indutumque eum vestibus regalibus . . ." (c. 35) *Liber historiae francorum,* ed. B. Krusch ed., MGH SRM 2 (Hanover, 1888), p. 304.
22. As for example Queen Arnegund (d. ca. 565–570): Erlande-Brandenburg, *Le roi est mort,* p. 33.
23. "Der Herrscher ist nicht unus ex multis." Eduard Eichmann, "Von der Kaisergewandung im Mittelalter," *Historische Jahrbuch* 58 (1938), 268–304. See p. 268.
24. Margarete Weidemann, *Kulturgeschichte der Merowingerzeit nach den Werken Gregors von Tours,* Römisch-germanisches Zentralmuseum, Monographien 3; 2 vols. (Mainz: Verlag des Römisch-germanisches Zentralmuseums, 1982), 2:17f.
25. Erlande-Brandenburg, *Le roi est mort,* p. 34; on Childeric's reign, see Wood, *Merovingian Kingdoms,* pp. 225–28.
26. Kurt-Ulrich Jäschke, "Frühmittelalterliche Festkrönungen? Überlegungen zu Terminologie und Methode," *Historische Zeitschrift* 211 (1970), 556–88. See p. 582.
27. Janet L. Nelson, "Inauguration Rituals," in *Early Medieval Kingship,* op. cit., pp. 50–71. See p. 62.
28. On the Persian backdrop of the diadem, see Hans Werner Ritter, *Diadem und Königsherrschaft. Untersuchungen zu Zeremonien und Rechtsgrundlagen des Herrschaftsantritts bei den Persern, bei Alexander dem Grossen und im Hellenismus, Vestigia* 7 (Munich: Beck, 1965); for its adoption in Rome: Nikolaus Gussone and Heiko Steuer, art. "Diadem," Reallexikon der germanischen Altertumskunde 5 (Berlin: De Gruyter, 1983), pp. 351–75. See pp. 358–61. See also Jäschke, "Frühmittelalterliche Festkrönungen?" p. 575; Brühl, "Kronen- und Krönungsbrauch," p. 19; and Gussone, "Diadem," pp. 361–63. The related ceremony of crowning with a torque was adopted as a makeshift by Julian the Apostate (361–363), and imitated for a time by other emperors: Wilhelm Ensslin, "Zur Torqueskrönung und Schilderhebung bei der Kaiserwahl," *Klio* 35 (1942), 268–98.
29. "Nam reges nos Deo et patri suo fecit Christus Iesus." (15.2) *Q. Septimi Florentis Tertulliani De corona / Tertullien, Sur la couronne,* Jacques Fontaine, ed., *Érasme* 18 (Paris: Presses universitaires de France, 1966), p. 179. This royal imagery was also drawn upon by the author of the Apocalypse (19.12–15; 20.11), in which Christ was associated with a throne, diadems,

and a scepter: Leonard L. Thompson, *The Book of Revelation: Apocalypse and Empire* (New York: Oxford University Press, 1990), pp. 43–45 and 57–63.

30. Sabine G. MacCormack, *Art and Ceremony in Late Antiquity* (Berkeley: University of California Press, 1981), p. 189; Andreas Alföldi, "Insignien und Tracht der römischen Kaiser," *Mitteilungen des Deutschen Archäologischen Instituts,* Römischen Abteilung 50 (1935), 3–158. See pp. 145–50; Jäschke, "Frühmittelalterliche Festkrönungen?" p. 572.
31. Classen, "Corona imperii," p. 91.
32. In a painting in the Catacombs: Fabrizio Bisconti, "La 'coronatio' de Pretestato. Storia delle manomissioni del passato e riflessioni sui recenti restauri," *Rivista di archeologia christiana* 73 (1997) 7–49.
33. In origin, the crown of martyrs was a wreath of victory: Ernst H. Kantorowicz, "*Pro patria mori* in Medieval Political Thought," in his *Selected Studies* (Locust Valley: J. J. Augustin Publisher, 1965), pp. 308–24. See p. 309. On the ancient backdrop of this wreath, see Michael Blech, *Studien zum Kranz bei den Greichen,* Religionsgeschichtliche Versuche und Vorarbeiten 38 (Berlin: De Gruyter, 1982); and Karl Baus, *Der Kranz in Antike und Christentum. Eine religionsgeschichtliche Untersuchung mit besonderer Berucksichtigung Tertullians,* Theophaneia, Beitrage zur Religions- und Kirchengeschichte des Altertums 2 (Bonn: P. Hanstein, 1940). See also Michael Roberts, *Poetry and the Cult of the Martyrs: The* Liber Peristephanon *of Prudentius* (Ann Arbor: University of Michigan Press, 1993), pp. 33–34.
34. By placing his tomb to the right of the "tomb of the holy martyrs," Dagobert (d. 639) may have emphasized a similar association. Erlande-Brandenburg, *Le roi est mort,* p. 69.
35. Herwig Wolfram, *The Roman Empire and its Germanic Peoples,* trans. Thomas Dunlap (Berkeley: University of California Press, 1997), p. 270. Jäschke, "Frühmittelalterliche Festkrönungen?" p. 585; Schramm, *Herrschaftszeichen,* 3:910–12; On the votive crown that Clovis donated to the shrine of St. Peter, see Ian N. Wood, "Gregory of Tours and Clovis," *Revue belge de philologie et d'histoire* 63 (1985), 249–72. See p. 254.
36. Helmut Beumann, "Grab und Thron Karls des Grossen zu Aachen," in *Karl der Grosse. Lebenswerk und Nachleben,* 4 vols., 2d ed. (Dusseldorf L. Swann, 1967) 4:9–38; Erlande-Brandenburg, *Le roi est mort,* p.63; and Henri Focillon, *The Year 1000,* n.t., (New York: Harper Torchbooks, 1969), p. 173f.
37. Brühl, "Kronen- und Krönungsbrauch," p. 16f.; on the burial of Louis: "corpusque eius Mettis civitatem perlatum in basilica sancti Arnulfi confessoris honorifice sepultum est" (Year 840). *Annales Fuldenses,* ed. G. H. Pertz, Friedrich Kurze, MGH SRG in us. schol. (Hanover, 1891), p. 31; St. Arnulf, whose bones protected the church, was himself an ancestor of the Carolingians: Friedrich Prinz, *Frühes Mönchtum im Frankenreich. Kultur und Gesellschaft in Gallien, den Rheinlanden und Bayern am Beispiel der monastischen Entwicklung (4. bis 8. Jahrhundert),* (Munich: R. Oldenbourg Verlag, 1965), pp. 138–40.

38. I have been unable to examine the account in Martin Meurisse, *Histoire des évesques de l'église de Metz* (Metz: Jean Antoine, 1634), pp. 29–30, cited in Erlande-Brandenburg, *Le roi est mort,* p. 38.
39. Pinoteau, "Les insignes du roi," p. 80; on Christ, see Rev. 19.15.
40. Odile Blanc, "Historiographie du vêtement: un bilan," ed. *Le Vêtement. Histoire, archéologie et symbolique vestimentaires au Moyen Age,* ed. M. Pastoureau, *Cahiers du leopard d'or 1* (Paris: Leopard d'or, 1989), pp. 7–33.
41. All these signs had associations with royal and imperial power among the Greeks and in the ancient Near East. On the sceptre, see the *Iliad,* 2.100f; Sophocles, *Oedipus at Colonus,* 2.425; alongside Ferdinand Joseph M. de Waele, *The Magic Staff or Rod in Graeco-Italian Antiquity* (Ghent: Drukkerij Erasmus, 1927); on the antiquity of the throne, H. U. Instinsky, *Bischofsstuhl und Kaiserthron* (Munich: Kosel, 1955), pp. 11–25; much earlier, Zeus was imagined to have a throne: Aeschylus, *Prometheus Bound,* 910; Sophocles, *Oedipus Tyrannus,* 237; *Antigone,* 1041; Theocritus, *Idylls,* 7.93; human kings were also thought to have or to merit thrones: King Midas donated his throne to the shrine at Delphi, Herodotus, 1.14; see also Aeschylus, *Libation-Bearers,* 973; according to Theocritus, Ptolemy had a golden throne in the household of Zeus: Idyll 17. On the diadem, see Gussone, "Diadem," pp. 352–56; and Alföldi, "Insignien und Tracht," pp. 150–52; On the "purple" see Heinke Stulz, *Die Farbe purpur im frühen Griechentum. Beobachtet in der Literatur und in der bildenden Kunst,* Beiträge zur Altertumskunde 6 (Stuttgart: Teuber, 1990)
42. MacCormack, *Art and Ceremony,* p. 251.
43. In addition to the crown, Christ could also be portrayed wearing the purple *chlamys:* Bisconti, "La 'coronatio' de Pretestato," p. 40. In the earliest Christian writings, Christ was thought of as bearing a sceptre: Philippe Henne, "Le sceptre de la majesté en Clem. 16,2," *Studia Patristica* 21 (Louvain, 1989) 101–105.
44. Abilio Barbero de Aguilera, "El pensiamiento político visigodo y las primeras unciones regias en la Europa medieval," in his *La sociedad visigoda y su entorno histórico* (Madrid: Siglo Veintiuno, 1992), pp. 1–77; p.4f.; see also Luis A. García Moreno, "The Creation of Byzantium's Spanish Province. Causes and Propaganda," *Byzantion* 66 (1996) 101–19.
45. Hans Hubert Anton, "Der König und die Reichskonzilien im westgotischen Spanien," *Historisches Jahrbuch* 92 (1972) 257–81.
46. Roger Collins, "Julian of Toledo and the Royal Succession," p. 43.
47. On the "precocity" of the Visigoths in developing a new kind of kingship, see Jean Comte de Pange, *Le roi très chrétien. Essai sur la nature du pouvoir royal en France* (Paris: A. Fayard, 1949), pp. 120–28.
48. Roger Collins, *Early Medieval Spain. Unity in Diversity, 400–1000* (New York: St. Martin's Press, 1983), p. 49f. Herwig, *The Roman Empire,* pp. 260–78.
49. Felipe Mateu Llopis, "El arte monetario visigodo. Las monedas como monumentos. (Un ensayo de interpretacion)," *Archivo español de arqueologia* 58 (1945), 34–58.

50. G. C. Miles, *The Coinage of the Visigoths of Spain. Leovigild to Achila II,* Hispanic Numismatic Series 2 (New York: American Numismatic Society, 1952), pp. 21–23 and 57f.
51. Despite R. C.Van Caenegem, *De Instellingen van de Middeleeuwen. Geschiednis van de westerse Staatsinstellingen van de Ve tot de XVe Eeuw,* 2 vols. (Ghent: Wetenschappelijke Uitgeverij en Boekhandel, 1967), 1:36. On Merovingian coinage, see Philip Grierson and Mark Blackburn, *Medieval European Coinage, with a Catalogue of the Coins in the Fitzwilliam Museum, Cambridge,* vol.1: *The Early Middle Ages (5th–10th Centuries),* (Cambridge: Cambridge University Press, 1986), pp. 111–46, and plates at 460–511.
52. Henry Maguire, "Magic and Money in the Early Middle Ages," *Speculum* 72 (1997), pp. 1037–54.
53. See above, n.13. On Gregory, see Walter Goffart, *The Narrators of Barbarian History (A.D. 550–800) : Jordanes, Gregory of Tours, Bede, and Paul the Deacon* (Princeton: Princeton University Press, 1988), pp.112–234; Marc Reydellet, *La Royauté dans la littérature latine de Sidoine Apollinaire à Isidore de Séville;* Bibliothèque des Écoles Françaises d'Athènes et de Rome 243 (Rome: École Française de Rome, 1981) pp. 345–437; Giselle de Nie, *Views from a Many-Windowed Tower. Studies of Imagination in the Work of Gregory of Tours,* Studies in Classical Antiquity 7 (Amsterdam: Rodopi, 1987)
54. L. Levillain, "La crise des années 507–508 et les rivalités d'influence en Gaule de 508 à 514" in *Mélanges offerts à M. Nicolas Iorga par ses amis de France et des pays de langue française* (Paris: J. Gamber, 1933), 537–67.
55. "Igitur ab Anastasio imperatore codecillos de consolato accepit, et in basilica beati Martini tunica blattea indutus et clamide, inponens vertice diademam" (2.38). Gregory of Tours, *Libri historiarum,* p. 88f.; Jäschke, "Frühmittelalterliche Festkrönungen?" p. 580f.; Brühl, "Kronen- und Krönungsbrauch," p. 18; Marc Bloch, *The Royal Touch: Sacred Monarchy and Scrofula in England and France,* trans. J. E. Anderson (London: Routledge and Kegan Paul, 1973), p. 34.
56. Ian Wood, "Kings, Kingdoms and Consent," in *Early Medieval Kingship,* op. cit., pp. 6–29. See p. 25. It has been argued that this event was a genuine survival of Roman traditions among the Franks: Michael McCormick, "Clovis at Tours, Byzantine Public Ritual and the Origins of Medieval Ruler Symbolism," in Evangelos K. Chrysos and Andreas Schwarcz, eds., *Das Reich und die Barbaren* (Vienna: Bohlau, 1989), pp. 155–80; or an imitation of Roman imperial accessions: so Van Caenegem, *De Instellingen,* 1:35f.
57. Ian Wood, *Merovingian Kingdoms,* p. 48. Wallace-Hadrill pointed out that in fact the items mentioned by Gregory were imperial, not consular, in association: *Long-Haired Kings,* p.175.
58. The phrase is from Pierre Clastres, "La question du pouvoir dans les sociétés primitives," in his *Recherches d'anthropologie politique* (Paris: Seuil, 1980), pp.103–109. See p. 106.
59. Weidemann, *Kulturgeschichte der Merowingerzeit,* 1:20–23. On the helmet as a royal sign, see Schramm, *Herrschaftszeichen,* 2:389–95.

60. Wallace-Hadrill, *Long-Haired Kings,* p.209.
61. Martin Heinzelmann, *Bischofsherrschaft in Gallien. Zur Kontinuität römischer Führungsschichten vom 4. bis zum 7. Jahrhundert. Soziale, prosopographische und bildunsgeschichtliche Aspekte,* Beihefte der Francia 5 (Zurich: Artemis, 1976). Such was the perception of Gregory of Tours: see for example "Eustochius ordinatur episcopus, vir sanctus et timens Deum, ex generesenatorio . . ." (10.5) Gregory of Tours, Libri historiarum, p. 529.
62. On the origins of the *pallium,* see Louis Duchesne, *Christian Worship, its Origin and Evolution. A Study of the Latin Liturgy up to the Time of Charlemagne,* trans. M. L. McClure, 5th ed. (London: Society for the Promotion of Christian Knowledge, 1931), p. 385; and J. Braun, *Die liturgische Gewandung im Occident und Orient. Nach Ursprung und Entwicklung, Verwendung und Symbolik* (Freiburg im Breisgau: Herder, 1907), pp. 652–64; and Schramm, *Herrschaftszeichen,* 1:28–30.
63. Duchesne, *Christian Worship,* p. 387.
64. Duchesne, *Christian Worship,* pp. 384–90. Braun, *Die liturgische Gewandung,* p. 675f.
65. "Ut episcopus sine palleo missas dicere non praesumat" (canon 6). 1 Macon, A. 581–83, *Concilia Galliae,* Charles de Clerq, ed. CCSL 148A (Turnhout: Brepols, 1963).
66. The *Exposition* was written in Gaul at the end of the seventh century: "Pallium uero quod circa collum usque ad pectus uenit rationale 'testamento:uocabatur in ueteri scilicet signum sanctitatis. . . . 'super:antiquae consuetudinis est quia reges et sacerdotes circumdati erant pallio 'm_m:ueste[m] fulgente quod gratia praesignabat." (2.16) *Expositio antiquae liturgiae gallicanae,* ed., E. C. Ratcliff, Henry Bradshaw Society 98 (London: Henry Bradshaw Society, 1971), p. 23.
67. Duchesne, Christian Worship, p. 380. W. B. Marriott, Vestiarum Christianum: The Origin and Gradual Development of the Dress of Holy Ministry in the Church (London: Rivingtons, 1868), p. xlviiff.
68. Louis Trichet, Le costume du clergé: ses origines et son évolution en France, d'après les règlements de l'Église (Paris: Éditions du Cerf, 1986), p. 22ff.
69. Duchesne, Christian Worship, p. 381; Braun, Die liturgische Gewandung, p. 156f.
70. Duchesne, *Christian Worship,* p. 397f.
71. M. E. Roach, and J. B. Eicher, "The Language of Personal Adornment," in J. M. Cordwell and R. A. Schwartz, eds., *The Fabrics of Culture. The Anthropology of Clothing and Adornment* (The Hague: Mouton, 1979), pp. 7–21. See p. 17.
72. Braun, *Die liturgische Gewandung,* p. 702
73. "Dehinc indutus purpora, diademate coronatus, throno imperiale inpositus . . ." (5.30) Gregory of Tours, *Libri historiarum,* p. 235. Note that Gregory did use this word to describe a bishop's throne, when Bishop Namatius discovered a demonic woman "in throni illius cathedra resedentem" (2.21). Gregory of Tours, *Libri historiarum,* p. 67.

74. Gregory of Tours, *Libri historiarum* (5.30), p. 235; (6.30), p. 98; Nevertheless, Brühl argued that the consular accession of Clovis was part of a "western crowning tradition," although it was not followed up for more than two hundred years. Brühl, "Kronen- und Krönungsbrauch," pp.18–20. The only evidence that he adduces between Clovis and the crowning of Pippin in 751 is the grave of Childeric II, mentioned above at note 26.
75. "Egressus autem a Turonus Parisius venit ibique cathedram regni constituit." (2.38) Gregory of Tours, *Libri historiarum,* p. 89.
76. Bernhard Jussen, "Über 'Bischofsherrschaften' und die Prozeduren politisch-sozialer Umordnung in Gallien zwischen 'Antike' und 'Mittelalter,'" *Historische Zeitschrift* 260 (1995), 673–718. See pp. 699–702; and Schramm, *Herrschaftszeichen,* 1:321–23; Nikolaus Gussone, *Thron und Inthronisation des Papstes von den Anfängen bis zum 12. Jahrhundert,* Bonner historische Forschungen 41 (Bonn: Rohrscheid, 1978), pp. 29–59.
77. Instinsky, *Bischofsstuhl,* p. 27.
78. For episcopal *cathedrae,* see Gregory of Tours, *Libri historiarum* (2.1), p. 38; (2.13), p. 63; (3.2), p. 98; (4.5), p. 138; (9.18), p. 432, and elsewhere. For royal *cathedrae,* see *Libri historiarum:* (2.7), p. 50; (2.38), p. 89; (4.22), p. 155; (5.17), p. 216; (10.28), p. 521. Similarly, Gregory sometimes described kings as having a *sedes*—a "seat," or "see," again using a term often used of bishop's seat of power. For royal *sedes,* see (4.22), p. 154; (4.22), p. 155; (7.27), p. 346. For episcopal *sedes,* see (2.1), p. 38; (4.26), p. 158.
79. Fabienne Cardot, *L'espace et le pouvoir. Étude sur l'Austrasie mérovingienne,* Histoire ancienne et médiévale 17 (Paris: Publications de la Sorbonne, 1987), pp.139–63.
80. Reinhold Kaiser, "Royauté et pouvoir épiscopal au nord de la Gaule (VIIe–IXe siècles)," in *La Neustrie. Les pays au nord de la Loire de 650 à 850.* Beihefte der *Francia* 16, vol. 1 (Sigmaringen: J. Thorbecke, 1989), pp. 143–60. See pp. 144–52.
81. A. Hauck, *Die Bischofswahlen unter den Merovingern* (Erlangen: Andreas Reichert, 1883), pp. 1–19. The length of a bishop's term was called the time when he ruled (*rexit*): Louis Duchesne, *Fastes épiscopaux de l'ancienne Gaule,* 3 vols. (Paris: A. Fontemoing, 1907–1915), 1:189. See also "[Agilmarius] qui rexit ecclesiam suam . . ." Duchesne, *Fastes épiscopaux,* 1:201. See also, in the case of a 'joint appointment,' "rexeruntque ecclesiam Turonicam simul annis duobus et sepultli sunt in basilica sancti Martini." (10.31) Gregory of Tours, *Libri historiarum,* p. 532.
82. This is used throughout the "Nomina pontificum Mettensis sedis et actus hoc obitus seriem codice scripta lege": Duchesne, *Fastes épiscopaux,* 3:48f.; see also "Sedit autem annos XII, menses II, dies XXV et sepultus est in basilica sancti Martini." (10.31) Gregory of Tours, *Libri historiarum,* p. 532.
83. Theodor Klauser, *A Short History of the Western Liturgy. An Account and Some Reflections,* trans. J. Halliburton, 2d ed., repr. (Oxford: Oxford University Press, 1979), p. 144. See also Marriott, *Vestiarum Christianum,* pp. xli-xliii; and J. A. Jungmann, *The Early Liturgy to the Time of Gregory the Great,* trans.

F. A. Brunner, University of Notre Dame Liturgical Studies 6, repr. (Notre Dame: University of Notre Dame Press, 1980), p. 118f.

84. Reinhard Elze, "Le consacrazione regie," Segni e riti nella chiesa alto medievale occidentale, *Settimane di Studio del Centro Italiano de Studi sull' Alto Medioevo* 33; 2 vols. (Spoleto, 1987), 1:43–55. See p. 48.
85. What Carolingian kings wore was different from the Roman models emulated on their royal seals. For Pippin, Carlomann, Charlemagne, Louis the Pious, and Lothar, see Otto Posse, *Die Siegel der deutschen Kaiser und Könige von 751–1806,* 4 vols. (Dresden:Verlag von Wilhelm Baensch, 1909–1913), table 1.
86. 1 and 2 Samuel and Chronicles were influential in regard to both kingship and the role of the priesthood. Leviticus, detailing the regulations of the priesthood, was especially important to bishops. See Raymund Kottje, *Studien zum Einfluss des Alten Testamentes auf Recht und Liturgie des frühen Mittelalters (6.–8. Jahrhundert),* Bonner historische Forschungen 23 (Bonn: L. Rohrscheid, 1970), pp. 101, 104.
87. For Isidore of Seville, exegesis was the basis of Christian culture, itself a summation of all prior knowledge: Jacques Fontaine, "Isidore de Séville pédagogue et théoricien de l'exégèse," in *Stimuli. Exegese und ihre Hermeneutik in Antike und Christentum. Festschrift für Ernst Dassman,* Jahrbuch für Antike und Christentum, Ergänzungsband 23 (Munster: Aschendorff, 1996), pp. 423–34. See p. 428.
88. Roland De Vaux, *Ancient Israel, Its Life and Institutions,* trans. John McHugh (Grand Rapids: Eerdmans, 1997), p. 400.
89. On the ambiguity of this account, see Robert Polzin, *Samuel and the Deuteronomist: A Literary Study of the Deuteronomic history,* Part Two: *1 Samuel* (Bloomington: Indiana University Press, 1989), pp. 80–88; also De Vaux, *Ancient Israel,* p. 99.
90. De Vaux, *Ancient Israel,* p. 96f.
91. Geo Widengren, *Sakrales Königtum im Alten Testament und im Judentum,* Franz Delitzsch-Vorlesungen 1952 (Stuttgart: W. Kohlhammer, 1955), pp. 44–53; De Vaux, *Ancient Israel,* pp. 102–07; Gussone, "Diadem," pp. 352–56; Instinsky, *Bischofsstuhl,* pp. 11–25; Ritter, *Diadem und Königsherrschaft,* p. 167f.
92. With the flower, priests adopted an old symbol for the life-giving force of nature: A. de Buck, "La fleur au front du grand-prêtre," *Oudtestamentische Studien* 9 (1951), 18–29.
93. Alexandre Faivre, Ordonner la fraternité. Pouvoir d'innover et retour à l'ordre dans l'Église ancienne (Paris: Cerf, 1992), pp. 78–84; J. Coppens, *Le sacerdoce chretien. Ses origines et son développement, Analecta lovaniensia biblica et orientalia,* Ser. 5, Fasc. 4–5. (Leiden: Séminaire biblique, 1970), p. 38. As early as Paul's Epistle to the Hebrews, Christian writers had viewed the levitical priesthood as a foreshadowing of Christian priesthood. See M. E. Isaacs, Sacred Space. An Approach to the Theology of the Epistle to the Hebrews,

Journal for the Study of the New Testament, Supplement Series 73 (Sheffield: JSOT Press, 1992), p. 55.

94. Jerome, *Letter to Fabiola,* 64, in *Sancti Eusebii Hieronymi epistulae,* part 1, ed. Isidor Hilberg, CSEL 54 (Vienna: F. Tempsky, 1910), pp. 586–615. I thank Nancy Aykanian for directing my attention to this text.
95. "Caput, inquit suum non discoperiet. habet cidarim et nomen dei portat in fronte, diademate ornatus est regio, ad perfectam Christi uenit aetatem, semper eius gloria protegendus est et uestimenta sua non scindet, quia candida sunt, quia inpolluta . . ." (3) Jerome, *Letter to Fabiola,* p. 591.
96. " . . . audi, Iesu, sacerdos magne . . ." (6) Jerome, *Letter to Fabiola,* p. 594.
97. "genus regale et sacerdotale sumus." (4) Jerome, *Letter to Fabiola,* p. 592.
98. " . . . quasi sphaera media sit diuisa et pars una ponatur in capite . . ." (13) Jerome, *Letter to Fabiola,* p. 599.
99. " . . . byssus terrae deputatur, quia ex terra gignitur, purpura mari, quia ex eius cocleolis tinguitur, hyacinthus aeri propter coloris similitudinem, coccus igni et aetheri . . ." (17) Jerome, *Letter to Fabiola,* p. 605.
100. "legimus in Leuitico iuxta praeceptum dei Moysen lauisse Aaron et filios eius: iam tunc purgationem mundi et rerum omnium sactitatem baptismi sacramenta signabant." (19) Jerome, *Letter to Fabiola,* p. 609.
101. "praeceptis dei lauandi sumus et, cum parati ad indumentum Christi tunicas pellicias deposuerimus, tunc induemur ueste linea nihil in se mortis habente, sed tota candida, ut de baptismo consurgentes cingamus lumbos in ueritate et tota pristinorum peccatorum turpitido celetur. unde et Dauid . . ." (19) Jerome, *Letter to Fabiola,* p. 610.
102. Rev. 19.13. See G. B. Caird, *A Commentary on the Revelation of St. John the Divine* (New York: Harper and Row, 1966), p. 242f.
103. Peter Beskow, *Rex Gloriae. The Kingship of Christ in the Early Church,* trans. E. Sharpe (Uppsala: Almqvist & Wiksell, 1962); Lucien Cerfaux, "Le titre Kyrios et la dignité royale de Jesus," *Recueil Lucien Cerfaux,* 2 vols. (Gembloux: J. Duculot, 1954), 1:1–63; on the importance of these concepts for the ideals of Frankish kingship, see Jean Sainsaulieu, "De Jérusalem à Reims. Origines et évolution des sacres royaux," in *Le Sacre des rois, Actes du Colloque international d'histoire sur les sacres et couronnements royaux,* Reims 1975, (Paris: Les Belles Lettres, 1975), pp. 17–26.
104. Henri de Lubac, *Corpus mysticum. L'Eucharistie et l'église au môyen age. Étude historique,* 2d ed. rev. (Paris: Aubier, 1949).
105. "Sumptis dehinc albis vestibus, caput eius sacri chrismatis unctione perungitur, ut intellegat baptizatus regnum in se ac sacerdotale convenisse mysterium. Chrismatis enim oleo sacerdotes et principes unguebantur. . . . Ad imaginem quippe sacerdotii plenius exprimendam renascentis caput lintei decore conponitur. Nam sacerdotes illius temporis quodam mystico velamine caput semper ornabant." John the Deacon, *Epistola ad Senarium,* VI, ed. A. Wilmart, "Un florilège carolingien sur le symbolisme des cérémonies du baptême, avec un Appendice sur la lettre

de Jean Diacre," *Analecta Reginensia,* Studi e Testi 59 (Rome, 1933), p. 174. See also M. P. Vanhengel, "Le Rite et la Formule de la chrismation postbaptismale en Gaule et en Haute-Italie du IVe au VIIIe siècle d'apres les sacramentaires gallicans. Aux origines du rituel primitif," *Sacris Erudiri* 21 (1972/73), 209–12. See p. 214.

106. Isidore of Seville (ca. 560–636), *Sancti Isidori episcopi Hispalensis, De ecclesiasticis officiis,* ed. Christopher M. Lawson, CCSL, 108 (Turnhout: Brepols, 1989), p. 14. On Isidore, see Jacques Fontaine, *Isidore de Séville et la culture classique dans l'Espagne wisigothique,* 2 vols. (Paris: Études augustiniennes, 1959); *Isidoriana, Estudios sobre San Isidoro de Sevilla en el XIV centenario de su nacimiento* (Centro de estudios "San Isidoro," 1961); H. J. Diesner, *Isidor von Sevilla und seine Zeit* (Berlin: Akademie-Verlag, 1973); P. D. King, *Law and Society in the Visigothic Kingdom,* Cambridge Studies in Medieval Life and Thought, 3d ser., 5 (Cambridge: Cambridge University Press, 1972); J. N. Hillgarth, "The Position of Isidorian Studies: A Critical Review of the Literature 1936–1975," *Studi medievali* 3d ser., 24 (1983), 817–905.

107. Louis Trichet, La Tonsure. Vie et mort d'une pratique ecclésiastique (Paris: Éditions du Cerf, 1990).

108. "Quod uero, detonso superius capite, inferius circuli corona relinquitur, sacerdotium regnumque ecclesiae in eis existimo figurari. Thiara enim apud ueteres constituebatur in capite sacerdotum (haec ex bysso confecta rotunda erat quasi sfera media), et hoc significatur in parte capitis tonsa; corona autem latitudo aurea est circuli quae regum capita cingit. Utrumque itaque signum exprimitur in capite clericorum ut impleatur etiam corporali quadam similtudine quod scriptum est Petro apostolo perdocente: *Vos estis genus electum regale sacerdotium* (I Pet. 2,9)." Isidore, *De ecc.,* 2.4, p. 55f.

109. J. G. Sagüés, "La doctrina del Cuerpo mistico en San Isidoro," *Estudios eclesiasticos* 17 (1943), 227–57, 329–60, 517–46. See pp. 354–60.

110. On the baptism of Clovis, see Wood, "Gregory of Tours and Clovis," pp. 267–72. It has even been argued that the baptismal anointing of Clovis amounted to the first royal anointing: Jean de Pange, "Doutes sur la certitude de cette opinion que le sacre de Pépin est la première époque du sacre des rois de France," in *Mélanges d'histoire du Moyen Âge dédiés a la mémoire de Louis Halphen,* ed. Charles-Edmond Perrin, (Paris: Presses universitaires de France, 1951), pp. 557–564; similarly, L. L. Mitchell, *Baptismal Anointing* Alcuin Club Collections 48 (London: S.P.C.K., 1966), p.121.

111. " . . . de eius conversione quam de gentis Gothorum innovatione in Domino exultarent et divinae dignationi pro tanto munere gratias agerent." Third Council of Toledo (589), in José Vives, *Concilios visigóticos e hispano-romanos,* España Cristiana. Textos 1 (Madrid: Consejo Superior de Investigaciones Cientificas, Instituto Enrique Florez, 1963), pp. 107–45. See p.107. J. Orlandis and D. Ramos-Lisson, *Die Synoden auf der Iberischen Halbinsel bis zum Einbruch des Islam (711),* Konziliengeschichte, Reihe A: Darstellung (Paderborn: F. Schöningh, 1981), pp. 95–117.

112. Gerald Ellard, *Ordination Anointings in the Western Church before 1000 A.D.,* Mediaeval Academy of America Publications 16 (Cambridge: Medieval Academy of America, 1933), p. 19f.
113. Reinhard Elze, "Le consacrazione regie," pp. 49–51.
114. It has been argued that the rite was earlier adopted in Dal Riada: Michael J. Enright, *Iona, Tara and Soissons. The Origin of the Royal Anointing Ritual,* Arbeiten zur Frühmittelalterforschung, Schriftenreihe des Instituts für Frühmittelalterforschung der Universität Münster 17 (Berlin: Walter De Gruyter, 1985). See, within a vast literature, Eduard Eichmann, *Königs- und Bischofsweihe,* Sitzungsberichte der Bayerischen Akademie der Wissenschaften. Philosophisch-philologische und historische Klasse 6 (1928), pp.1–71. See p. 24; Roger Collins, "Julian of Toledo," op. cit.; C. A. Bouman, *Sacring and Crowning. The Development of the Latin Ritual for the Anointing of Kings and the Ordination of an Emperor before the Eleventh Century,* Bijdragen van het Instituut voor Middeleeuwse geschiedenis der Rijks-Universiteit te Utrecht 30 (Gröningen: J. B. Wolters, 1957), p.xi; Jean Devisse, "Le sacre et le pouvoir avant les carolingiens, l'héritage wisigothique," in *Le Sacre des rois,* op. cit., pp. 27–38.
115. Werner Affeldt, "Untersuchungen zur Königsherbung Pippins," *Frühmittelalterlichen Studien* 14 (1980) 95–187; and Walter Schlesinger, "Karlingische Königswahlen," in his *Beiträge zur deutschen Verfassungsgeschichte des Mittelalters,* vol. 1, *Germanen, Franken, Deutsche* (Göttingen: Vandenhoek und Ruprecht, 1963), pp. 88–138.
116. Johannes Fried, "Der karolingische Herrschaftsverband im 9. Jh. zwischen 'Kirche' und 'Königshaus'," *Historische Zeitschrift* 235 (1982), 1–43. See pp. 21–26.
117. See for example the blessings in the *Sacramentary of Gellone* (ca. 790–800): Richard A. Jackson, *Ordines Coronationis Franciae: Texts and Ordines for the Coronation of Frankish and French Kings and Queens in the Middle Ages,* Vol. 1 (Philadelphia: University of Pennsylvania Press, 1995), pp. 51–54; Bouman, *Sacring and Crowning,* pp. 92–93.
118. Gerd Tellenbach, *Römischer und christlicher Reichsgedanke in der Liturgie des frühen Mittelalters,* Sitzungsberichte der Heidelberger Akademie der Wissenschaften, Philosophisch-historische Klasse (Heidelberg: C. Winter, 1934), p. 21f.
119. Bouman, *Sacring and Crowning,* p. 108f. On Charlemagne as David, see Percy Ernst Schramm, *Kaiser, Könige und Päpste. Gesammelte Aufsätze zur Geschichte des Mittelalters,* 4 vols. in 5 (Stuttgart: Hiersemann, 1968–1971), 1:214; Wallace-Hadrill, "The *Via Regia* of the Carolingian Age" in his *Early Medieval History* (Oxford: Blackwell, 1975), pp. 181–200; and many examples cited in Hans Hubert Anton, *Fürstenspiegel und Herrscherethos in der Karolingerzeit,* Bonner Historische Forschungen 32 (Bonn: L. Rohrscheid, 1968)
120. Jürgen Petersohn, "Über monarchische Insignien und ihre Funktion im mittelalterlichen Reich," *Historische Zeitschrift* 266 (1998), 47–96. See pp. 47–52.

121. "Vestitu patrio, id est Francico, utebatur. Ad corpus camisam lineam; et feminalibus lineis induebatur; deinde tunicam, quae limbo serico ambiebatur, et tibialia . . ." (c. 23). Einhard, *Vita Karoli Magni,* O. Holder-Egger, ed., MGH SRG in us. schol (Hanover, 1911), p. 27. Compare Suetonius' description of the winter garments favored by the Emperor Augustus: "Hieme quaternis cum pingui toga tunicis et subucula et thorace laneo et feminalibus et tibialibus muniebatur . . ." (2:82). Suetonius, *Lives of the Caesars,* ed. J. C. Rolfe, Loeb Classical Library (Cambridge, Mass.: Harvard University Press, 1913), p. 248.
122. "In festivitatibus veste auro texta et calciamentis gemmatis et fibula aurea sagum adstringente, diademate quoque ex auro et gemmis ornatus incedebat" (c. 23). Einhard, *Vita Karoli Magni,* p. 28. See Jäschke, "Frühmittelalterliche Festkrönungen?" p. 563.
123. "Peregrina vero indumenta, quamvis pulcherrima, respuebat nec umquam eis indui patiebatur, excepto quod Romae semel Hadriano pontifice petente et iterum Leone successore eius supplicante longa tunica et clamide amictus, calceis quoque Romano more formatis induebatur" (c.23). Einhard, *Vita Karoli Magni,* p. 28; P. Classen, "*Romanum gubernans imperium.* Zur Vorgeschichte der Kaisertitulatur Karl des Grossen," *Deutsches Archiv* 9 (1951), 103–21. Folz and others tend to follow the account of the *Annales Laureshamenses,* ed. G. Pertz, MGH SS 1 (Hanover, 1826), pp. 22–30.
124. On the importance of the Byzantine model, see Werner Ohnsorge, "Orthodoxus Imperator. Vom religiösen Motiv für das Kaisertum Karls des Grossen," in his *Abendland und Byzanz. Gesammelte Aufsätze zur Geschichte der byzantinisch- abendländischen Beziehungen und des Kaisertums* (Darmstadt: H. Gentner, 1958), pp. 64–78; See also Van Caenegem, *De Instellingen,* 1:86–87; Tellenbach, *Römischer und christlicher,* pp. 29–33; Robert Folz, *Le couronnement impérial de Charlemagne, 25 Décembre 800,* Trente journees qui ont fait la France 3 (Paris: Gallimard, 1964), p. 171.
125. *Das Constitutum Constantini (Konstantinische Schenkung),* ed. Horst Fuhrmann, Fontes iuris germanici antiqui 10 (Hanover, 1968). See Folz, *Le couronnement,* pp. 128–133; and Peter Llewellyn, "Le contexte romain du couronnement de Charlemagne. Le temps de l'Avent de l'année 800," *Moyen Âge* 96, 5th ser. 4 (1990) 209–25; Raymond- J. Loenertz, "En marge de Constitutum Constantini. Contribution à l'histoire du texte," *Revue des sciences philosophiques et théologiques* 59 (1975) 289–294
126. Raymond- J. Loenertz, "*Constitutum Constantini.* Destination, destinataires, auteur, date," *Aevum* 48 (1974) 199–245. See p. 227. Nicolas Huyghebaert, "Une légende de fondation: Le Constitutum Constantini," *Moyen Âge* 85, 4th ser. 34 (1979) 177–209.
127. Peter Classen, *Karl der Grosse, das Papsttum und Byzanz. Die Begründung des karolingischen Kaisertums,* Beiträge zur Geschichte und Quellenkunde des Mittelalters 9 (Sigmaringen: J. Thorbecke, 1985), pp. 54–57; Folz, *Le couronnement,* pp. 118–120.

128. " . . . more antiquorum principum . . ." (Year 801) *Annales regni Francorum,* MGH SRG in us. schol., ed. G.H. Pertz and Friedrich Kurze, (Hanover, 1895), p. 112.
129. Herbert Helbig, "Fideles Dei et regis. Zur Bedeutungsentwicklung von Glaube und Treue im hohen Mittelalter," *Archiv für Kulturgeschichte* 33 (1951), 275–306.
130. On the religious exaltation of Louis' kingship, see Michel Perrin, "La représentation figurée de César-Louis le Pieux chez Raban Maur en 835: Religion et idéologie," *Francia* 24 (1997), 39–64.
131. The stasis of the empire under Louis, in itself an accomplishment, was a source of restlessness: see Timothy Reuter, "The End of Carolingian Military Expansion," in P. Godman and R. Collins, eds., *Charlemagne's Heir. New Perspectives on the Reign of Louis the Pious (814–840)* (Oxford: Clarendon Press, 1990), pp. 391–405; on the other hand, Louis was in many ways a vigorous and successful ruler right until his death. See Janet L. Nelson, "The Last Years of Louis the Pious," also in *Charlemagne's Heir,* pp.147–159; see especially Peter McKeon, "The Empire of Louis the Pious. Faith, Politics and Personality," *Revue Bénédictine* 90 (1980), 50–62.
132. Carlrichard Brühl, Reims als Krönungsstadt des franzosischen Königs bis zum Ausgang des 14. Jahrhunderts (Frankfurt am Main: R. Heil, 1950), p. 7.
133. Walter Mohr, "Reichspolitik und Kaiserkrönung in den Jahren 813 und 816," *Die Welt als Geschichte* 20 (1960) 168–86. See pp. 174f. Likewise Schramm, *Herrschaftszeichen,* 1:304.
134. *Ordinatio imperii* (817), MGH Capit. 1.2, pp. 270–73. On the crisis that provoked this document, see Peter R. McKeon, "817: Une année désastreuse et presque fatale pour les Carolingiens," *Moyen Âge* 84, 4th ser. 33 (1978) 5–12; see also Mayke de Jong, "Power and Humility in Carolingian Society: The Public Penance of Louis the Pious," *Early Medieval Europe* 1 (1992) 29–52. See p. 40f.; D. Hägermann, "Reichseinheit und Reichsteilung Bemerkungen zur *Divisio regnorum* von 806 und zur *Ordinatio Imperii* von 817," *Historische Jahrbuch* 95 (1975), 278–307.
135. On the Council of Attigny (822), see de Clercq, "La législation religieuse franque" *Revue de Droit Canonique* 5 (1955), pp. 5–7. On the concept of public penance, see R. Meens, "Paenitentia publica en paenitentia privata. Aantekeningen bij de oorsprong van de zogeheten Karolingische dichotomie," in P. Bange and P. M. J. C. de Kort, eds., *Die Fonteyn der Ewiger Wijsheit. Opstellen aangeboden aan prof. dr A. G. Weiler,* Middeleeuwse Studies 5 (Nijmegen: Centrum voor Middeleeuwse Studies, Katholieke Universiteit Nijmegen, 1989), pp. 65–73. See pp. 65f. and 68f. Agobard was present at this public penance and discussed it in his *De dispensatione ecclesiasticarum rerum,* in Agobard of Lyon, *Opera Omnia,* ed. L. Van Acker, CCCM 52 (Turnhout: Brepols, 1981), pp. 119–42.
136. De Jong, "Power and Humility," pp. 29f. and 36–43; Caenegem, *De Instellingen,* 1:86. Public penance could also result in imprisonment in a monastery: Robert Folz, "La pénitence publique au IXe siècle d'après les

canons de l'évêque Isaac de Langres," in *L'encadrement religieux des fidèles au moyen âge et jusqu'au concile de Trente. Actes du 109e congrès national des Sociétés Savants,* Dijon 1984, Histoire médiévale et philologie 1 (Paris, 1985), pp. 331–343. See p. 337.

137. Merovingian royalty could lose their status by having their hair cut: Wallace-Hadrill, *Long-Haired Kings,* p. 245f. It was once argued that forced tonsures amounted to scalping: J. Hoyoux, "Reges criniti. Chevelures, tonsures et scalps chez les mérovingiens," *Révue belge de philologie et d'histoire* 26 (1948), 479–508; but see Charles Lelong, "Note sur le prétendu scalp mérovingien," *Moyen Âge* 70, 4th ser. 19 (1964) 349–354. On the crown serving a parallel function: Van Caenegem, *De Instellingen,* 1:62.
138. " . . . et in ecclesia Sacti Dionisii domnum imperatorem reconciliauerunt et regalibus uestibus armisque induerunt" (year 834). *Annales de Saint-Bertin,* ed. Felix Grat, Jeanne Vielliard and Suzanne Clémencet, Société de l'histoire de France 470 (Paris: C. Klincksieck, 1964), p. 12. See also the commentary and translation in *The Annals of St. Bertin,* trans. Janet L. Nelson, Ninth-Century Histories 1 (Manchester: Manchester University Press, 1991)
139. "Hunc enim ferunt imperatorem morientem designasse, ut post se regni gubernacula susciperet, missis ei insigniis regalibus, hoc est sceptro imperii et corona" (Year 840) *Annales Fuldenses,* p. 31.
140. M. Jean-Pierre Brunterc'h, "Moines bénédictins et chanoines réformés au secours de Louis le Pieux (830–834)," *Bulletin de la société nationale des antiquaires de France* (1986), 70–85.
141. Pinoteau, "Les insignes du roi," p. 78.
142. Nelson, "Inauguration Rituals," p. 62f.; L. Levillain, "Le sacre de Charles le Chauve à Orléans," *Bibliothèque de l'École des Chartes* 64 (1903), 31–53. See p. 33. Guy Lanoë, "L'*ordo* de couronnement de Charles le Chauve à Sainte-Croix d'Orléans (6 Juin 848)," in *Kings and Kingship,* op. cit., pp. 41–68.
143. " . . . msacroque crismate delibutum et benedictione episcopali solemniter consecrant" (year 848). *Annales de Saint-Bertin,* p. 55; see Levillain, "Le sacre de Charles," p. 49.
144. Robert Folz, "Les trois couronnements de Charles le Chauve," *Byzantion* 61 (1991), 93–111. See p. 95.
145. "Pippinus Karolo regi sacramentum fidelitatis iurat et insuper habitum monachi suscipit . . ." (year 853). *Annales de Saint-Bertin,* p. 66f.; On the authorship and perspective of these annals, see Janet L. Nelson, "The Annals of St. Bertin," in her *Politics and Ritual,* op. cit., pp. 173–194.
146. "regem simulant . . ." (year 856). *Annales de Saint-Bertin,* p. 72. See also the later, poignant tale of Charles the Fat. When the devil told him he would become sole ruler of the kingdom, in terror he tried to tear off the sword-belt and clothing that marked his princely status: " . . . se uellet balteo discingere et uestimento exuere . . ." (year 873). *Annales de Saint-Bertin,* p. 191.
147. " . . . seculoque et regno penitus abrenuntians, tonsus est, uitam habitumque monachi humiliter sumens" (year 855). *Annales de Saint-Bertin,* p.71.

148. Hincmar, who by this point had replaced Prudentius as the author of the Annals of St. Bertin, recorded the ceremony in detail: (year 869) *Annales de Saint-Bertin,* pp. 157–164; see also the "Ordo of Charles the Bald," in Jackson, *Ordines Coronationis,* pp. 87–109; and Bouman, *Sacring and Crowning,* p. 132; also the *Adnuntiatio Adventii episcop I . . . Benedictiones super regem Karolum ante missam et altare sancti Stephani,* MGH Capit. 2:337–341 and 456–58; see also Folz, "Les trois couronnements," pp. 95–103. The accession of Charles to the kingdom of Lorraine required considerable stage-management: Walter Schlesinger, "Zur Erhebung Karls des Kahlen zum König von Lothringen 869 in Metz," in *Ausgewählte Aufsätze von Walter Schlesinger 1965–1979,* ed. Hans Patze and Fred Schwind, Vorträge und Forschungen 34 (Sigmaringen: J. Thorbecke, 1987), pp. 173–98. See pp. 181–83.
149. On the importance of Remigius for Charles the Bald, see Philippe Depreux, "Saint Remi et la royauté carolingienne," *Revue Historique* 578 (1991) 235–60; De Pange, "Doutes," p. 557.
150. Folz, "Les trois couronnements," p. 102.
151. "Ad ista verba, "Coronet te Dominus," inunxit eum Hincmarus archiepiscopus de chrismate ad dextram auriculam, et in fronte usque ad sinistram auriculam, et in capite." Jackson, *Ordines Coronationis,* p. 104. See Janet L. Nelson, "Inauguration Rituals," p. 62; On the crown, palm-branches and scepter, see Brühl, *Reims als Krönungsstadt,* p. 16.
152. Brühl, *Reims als Krönungsstadt,* p. 15. On Hincmar's interest, see Janet L. Nelson, "Hincmar of Reims on King-making: The Evidence of the *Annals of St. Bertin,* 861–882," in János M. Bak, ed., *Coronations. Medieval and Early Modern Monarchic Ritual* (Berkeley: University of California Press, 1990), pp. 16–34.
153. On the motivations of Hincmar in writing the *Gesta Dagoberti Regis* and the *Vita Remigii,* see Wallace-Hadrill, *Long-Haired Kings,* pp. 97–105. Nevertheless, John J. Contreni assigns both works to Hilduin: "The Carolingian Renaissance: Education and Literary Culture," in the *New Cambridge Medieval History,* ed. Rosamond McKitterick, vol. 2: *c. 700–c. 900* (Cambridge: Cambridge University Press, 1995), pp. 709–57. See p. 751.
154. "Cumque, ut Francorum regibus moris erat, super solium aureum coronatus resideret . . ." attributed to Hincmar, *Gesta Dagoberti Regis,* ed. Bruno Krusch, MGH SRM 2 (Hanover, 1888), pp. 396–425.
155. Known as the "Cathedra Petri" because it was donated to the popes, it still resides in the Vatican, in St. Peter's Basilica. Lawrence Nees, "Charles the Bald and the *Cathedra Petri,*" in Margaret T. Gibson and Janet T. Nelson, eds., *Charles the Bald, Court and Kingdom,* 2d ed. rev. (Aldershot: Variorum, 1990), pp. 340–47; also Schramm, *Herrschaftszeichen,* 3:694–707.
156. "in imperatorem unctus et coronatus atque imperator Romanorum est appellatus" (year 876). *Annales de Saint-Bertin,* p. 200; see Folz, "Les trois couronnements," pp. 104–108.
157. The popes, like other bishops, had long possessed a throne: Instinsky, *Bischofsstuhl,* pp. 83–102; Gussone, *Thron und Inthronisation,* pp. 59–78.

158. Folz, "Les trois couronnements," p.109f.
159. On the garments of the bishops: " . . . episcopis ceterisque clericis uestibus ecclesiasticis indutis . . ." On the garments of Charles: " . . . uenit domnus imperator Karolus in uestitu deaurato, habitu francico . . ." (year 876). *Annales de Saint-Bertin,* p. 201.
160. " . . . mane circa horam nonam uenit imperator grecisco more paratus et coronatus, deducentibus eum apostolici legatis more romano uestitis ac episcopis aecclesiasticis uestimentis indutis . . ." (year 876). *Annales de Saint-Bertin,* p. 205. These events have drawn considerable attention: see Brühl, "Kronen- und Krönungsbrauch," p. 21f.; Jäschke, "Frühmittelalterliche Festkrönungen?" p. 563; Eichmann, "Von der Kaisergewandung," p. 278; Robert Deshman, "The Exalted Servant: The Ruler Theology of the Prayerbook of Charles the Bald," *Viator* 11 (1980), pp. 385–433. See p. 395.
161. Paul Edward Dutton and Herbert L. Kessler, *The Poetry and Paintings of the First Bible of Charles the Bald* (Ann Arbor: University of Michigan Press, 1997), pp. 71–87; on the function of such ruler portraits, see Kessler, "A Lay Abbot as Patron," pp. 653–657. In a Bible produced much later (perhaps shortly after 866), Charles was portrayed in a very similar set of regalia but holding a disk with his monogram rather than a wand: Ernst H. Kantorowicz, "The Carolingian King in the Bible of San Paolo Fuori le Mura," in his *Selected Studies,* op. cit., pp. 82–94. Charles was sometimes portrayed in a tunic spangled with stars: Pinoteau, "Les insignes du roi," p.79.
162. Nikolaus Staubach, *Rex christianus. Hofkultur und Herrschaftspropaganda im Reich Karls des Kahlen,* part two: *Die Grundlegung der 'religion royale,'* Pictura et Poesis 2.2 (Cologne: Böhlau, 1993), pp. 221–81.
163. Roland Barthes, "Histoire et sociologie du vêtement. Quelques observations méthodologiques," *Annales E.S.C.* 12 (1957), 430–41.
164. Deshman, "The Exalted Servant," pp. 410, 414.
165. Deshman, "The Exalted Servant," pp. 397–400.
166. Reproduced in Dutton and Kessler, *Poetry and Paintings,* pl. IV, following p. 50.
167. (10.1–2) Edition and translation in Dutton and Kessler, *Poetry and Paintings,* p. 116f.
168. Reproduced in Dutton and Kessler, *Poetry and Paintings,* pl. II, following p. 50. Likewise, the ivory covers of the Prayerbook of Charles the Bald brought forward a concatenation of themes linking Charles to King David. Deshman, "The Exalted Servant," pp. 406–11.
169. Here I have followed Kessler, "A Lay Abbot as Patron," pp. 662–64.
170. "Accipe vestem candidam quam inmacolatam perferas ante tribunal christi." *The Bobbio Missal, a Gallican Mass-book (MS. Paris. Lat. 13246),* ed. E. A. Lowe, Henry Bradshaw Society 58 (London: Henry Bradshaw Society, 1920), p. 75.
171. "Perungo te crisma santitatis Tonicam inmortalitatis qua[m] dominus noster iesus christus traditam a patre primus accepit ut eam integram et inlibatam perferas ante tribunal christi et uiuas in saecula saeculorum."

"Missale Gothicum." A Gallican Sacramentary. MS. Vatican. Regin. Lat. 317, ed. H. M. Bannister, Henry Bradshaw Society 52, 54; 2 vols. (London: Henry Bradshaw Society, 1916–1917), 1:77.

172. Jungmann, *Early Liturgy,* p. 85f.; and Jonathan Z. Smith, "The Garments of Shame," in his *Map Is Not Territory* (Chicago: University of Chicago Press, 1978), pp. 1–23. See p. 5. In addition to the citations provided by Smith, see also the bibliography in Cyril Vogel, *Medieval Liturgy: An Introduction to the Sources,* trans. William G. Storey and Niels Krogh Rasmussen (Washington: The Pastoral Press, 1986), p. 213f.
173. The restoration of Louis was also recalled in Hincmar's coronation ceremony for Charles the Bald, but the focus was on his crown: " . . . per domini sacerdotes acclamatione fidelis populi, sicut vidimus qui adfuimus, corona regni est imperio restitutus . . ." Jackson, *Ordines Coronationis,* p. 104f.
174. The phrase "clean power" is Peter Brown's: *The Cult of the Saints* (Chicago: University of Chicago Press, 1981), p. 102f.
175. On Charlemagne as Christ, see Schramm, *Kaiser, Könige,* 1:308–11; on Louis the Pious as Christ, Ph. Le Maître, "Image du Christ, image de l'empereur. L'exemple du culte du Saint Sauveur sous Louis le pieux," *Revue d'histoire de l'église de France* 68 (1982), 201–212; see also Tellenbach, *Römischer und christlicher,* p. 41. On Charles the Bald as Christ, see Deshman, "The Exalted Servant," p. 402.
176. As in the ninth-century handbook *Liber Quare,* ed. G. P. Glötz, CCCM 60 (Turnhout: Brepols, 1983), pp.97–104.
177. "dauid humilitate exaltatus," Lanoë, "L'*ordo* de couronnement," p.61.
178. "Dum haec . . . scriberem, ecclipsis solis hora prima, feria tertia, XV kal. novembris, in Scorpione contigit." (2.10, year 841) Nithard, *Histoire,* p.76.

CHAPTER 6

ROBES OF HONOR IN 'ABBASID BAGHDAD DURING THE EIGHTH TO ELEVENTH CENTURIES

Dominique Sourdel

Translated by David M. Sa'adah

Granting a costume that we usually call a "robe of honor" (in Arabic *khil'a*)[1] to certain persons whom one wishes to distinguish has been practiced in the Orient since ancient times. In the countries of Islam, it appeared only in the eighth/second century and seems to have become widespread during the ninth through eleventh / third through fifth centuries.

Indeed, at least in the sources that have come to us, there is no concern over "robes of honor" during the time of the Umayyad caliphs who ruled over the world of Islam from 650/29 to 749/132. On the other hand, we note that the very first 'Abbasid caliph, al-Saffāḥ (749/132–754/136), sent a robe of honor (if this is the correct interpretation of the verb *khala'*) to Abu Salama; he was the emissary of al-Saffāḥ who directed the movement culminating in the triumph of the 'Abbasid revolution and whom, before having him executed for treason, al-Saffāḥ wished to honor, undoubtedly to counter suspicion of things to come.[2] The next caliph, al-Man#sūr, who would reign from 754/136 to 775/158, did not as a practice grant robes of honor to dignitaries. We note that when he appointed a chamberlain, al-Rabī'a, he had him sent the costume that he was supposed to wear to present himself at the palace; however, the term that would be used to denote robes of honor is not employed on this occasion.[3]

Only in the ninth/third century, during the time when the caliphs had moved from Baghdad to the new residence of Samarra,[4] can we find episodes described by the chroniclers, in which the sovereigns granted to persons they wished to distinguish robes of honor, crowns, bracelets, and swords. This recognition varied according to the office of the beneficiary and the type of services given. Thus in 838/223 the general al-Afshīn, after his victory over the rebel Bābak, received a crown and bracelets,[5] and in 843/228, it was the Turkish commander Ashnās, left in Baghdad as the representative of the sovereign, who was entitled to the same treatment.[6] The first vizier to receive a robe of honor was 'Ubayd Allah ibn Yaḥyā, the vizier of the Caliph al-Mutawakkil who, in 851/237, was charged with the control of the central administration and given officially the title of vizier (*wazīr*).[7]

Consequently, the use of these recognitions seems to have spread. Thus in 866/252 the recently proclaimed Caliph al-Mu'tazz granted to his vizier Aḥmad ibn Isrā'īl a robe of honor and a crown, while the Baghdad chief of police had the right to a set of five robes and a sword.[8] Sometime afterwards, the 'Abbasid prince Abū Aḥmad, on return from an expedition, received six robes, a sword, a crown, a cap decorated with precious stones, while other military chiefs were also honored.[9] The following year a Turkish commander, Bughā al-Sharābi, received a robe, crown, and bracelet.[10] In 878/264, the caliph al-Mu'tamid, who had entrusted important powers to his brother (Prince Abū Aḥmad, the future al-Muwaffaq), granted him a robe; then, in 883/270, he similarly honored Ibn Kundāj, the governor of Mosul, who had escorted al-Mu'tamid (in fact, brought him under duress) from Mosul to Samarra.[11] We learn, in this instance, that the "robe" was a brocade (*dibaj*) tunic (*qāb'*), and that the recipient, a military commander, also received two swords.

At the very start of the tenth / end of the third century, several grants of "robes" are noted: the recipients are, in 900/287 Amr al-Sa#ffār, appointed governor of Transoxania, then in 901/288 the Samanid Ismā'īl appointed governor of Sijistan, in 902/289 the vizier al-Qāsim, and in 904/291 the secretary of the army, conqueror of the Tulunids of Egypt, Muḥammad ibn Sulaymān.[12] The practice thus began to spread at this time, directed to a vizier, a new governor of a province, or a victorious military commander. The robe could denote a distinction, but more often it accompanied an investiture, although we do not know if all investitures included this ceremony.

Beginning from the reign of al-Muktadir (that is, from 908/295), the chronicles furnish many accounts of the granting of robes of honor under varied circumstances. We can establish that during this time every vizier at his nomination, which was proclaimed in the course of a public audience given by the caliph, received a robe, not to mention various gifts, sometimes a horse with a golden saddle, and that the vizier so honored was escorted back to his dwelling by the high officers of the state. Military commanders could also be recognized in the same manner but only, it seems, after bringing a victory. They were then additionally granted necklaces and bracelets.[13]

The first chief emir appointed by the caliph in 936/324, Ibn Rā'ik, also received a robe, but the texts specify that this was a double robe to indicate his preeminence over the vizier who, undoubtedly, also received one as before.[14] Subsequently, during the period of the Buyid chief emirs (from 945/334 to 1055/447), political affairs were dominated by the tension between the 'Abbasid caliph, who delegated his powers to the chief emir, and the latter, who governed as he pleased all the while requiring the endorsement of the caliph to maintain his legitimacy. The robes of honor continued to be used in the court of the caliph and in that of the chief emir, who thenceforward instituted the appointment of numerous officials, but the chronicles are sparse in information about these ceremonies. We note nevertheless that the governor of Egypt, al-Ikhshīd, in the course of his nomination in 936/324, received a collar and bracelets, while the Turkish chief emir Badjkam in 938/326 could claim seven robes,[15] and the chief emir Tūzūn (appointed a little later, in 943/331) came into not only a robe but also the jeweled crown and collar usually given to military chiefs.[16] We are told that 'Ali ibn Buwayh, the Buyid emir appointed governor of Fars in 943/331, took care to have witnesses to record that he had received a robe.[17]

A little later, in 945/333, the Buyid emir Aḥmad ibn Buwayh, who was honored with the name "he who makes strong the dynasty" (*Mu'izz al-Dawla*), received when he was appointed chief emir the customary recognition—robes of honor, collar, bracelets, and flag.[18] It seems that by then the established practice was to grant a costume corresponding to "seven" robes, but the sources are not explicit on this subject. These grants of robes and diverse insignia continue during the entire so-called Buyid period.[19]

Little by little, the ceremonies of investiture became more sumptuous, the caliphs seeking to compensate the loss of their powers by a greater magnificence, and the chief emirs piling up honorific distinctions, the better to prove their legitimacy. The investiture of 'Adud al-Dawla, who governed the combined Buyid realm, Iraq and western Iran, from 977/366 to 983/372, was particularly ceremonious. Hilāl al-Ṣābi, a writer of the same century, tells us that when 'Adud al-Dawla, the Buyid emir, came to present himself to the caliph al-Ṭā'i' at Baghdad, once admitted into the audience-hall of the palace, he was invited to kiss the ground before the ruler, which he did, repeating this action several times while drawing near, then kissing one more time the base of the enclosure or *sidilla* where the caliph sat, at which point the ruler declared to him:

> I have decided to grant to you the governance of my subjects, in the east and in the west, which God entrusted to me, likewise the management of all matters, with the exceptions of my private affairs, my means of subsistence, and the internal organization of my residence.

After having repeated this declaration before the qadis of Baghdad and before the distinguished persons who were accompanying the emir, he ordered that the latter be crowned and reclothed in a costume of honor loaded with precious stones. Then the caliph had him presented with two flags, one for the east, the other for the west.

In another passage, the same author adds that 'Adud al-Dawla received also a collar and bracelets, according to the custom for military commanders, as well as a sword decorated in silver, plus the sword that accompanied the robe.[20] Another text notes that one of the successors of 'Adud al-Dawla bore, like his predecessors, a black turban.[21] Turban and crown are presented by certain authors as the "crowns of the Arabs and the Persians," and the granting of the crown, although an ancient practice, seems to correspond to an Iranian tradition.

The same ceremonial was used in Baghdad in 1058/449 at the investiture of the Saldjuk emir Ṭoghrīlbeg, who supplanted the Buyid emirs and received the novel title of sultan, which numerous chiefs of subdominions would bear after him. A chronicler[22] recounts that the sultan entered the audience hall when he was given leave and, as soon as he saw the caliph, kissed the ground and then advanced, repeating this action. When he came to the caliph, who invited him to sit at his side, the caliph declared:

> The prince of believers entrusts to you the countries which God has entrusted to him, and leaves to you to watch over the faithful. . . . Be diligent to promote justice and to repel oppression.

The sultan then went off into a room where he was reclothed in "the seven robes of honor forming a single costume," as well as a crown. He returned to sit close by the caliph, who granted him a sword and gave him the title of "king of the east and the west," then entrusted him with three flags and the document of nomination, declaring:

> Our decree of nomination is read and granted to you in order that you may act in conformity with what we have commanded. May God be favorable to us, as well as to you and to Muslims.

The accounts of the chroniclers, which inform us primarily about the honors granted to great persons, are confirmed by the explanations of an author, Hilāl al-Ṣābi, who wrote a treatise on the ceremonial of the court of Baghdad in the tenth/fourth century and who dedicated a chapter to robes of honor. By his account,[23] it was above all the military commanders who were honored with them, sometimes at their investiture, sometimes after a success. They received what is called in Arabic a *khil'a,* a complete costume comprised of a black robe with an embroidered border and a pocket, a second black robe without pockets, a black turban, a silk tunic, a sword decorated in silver, and two quivers; besides these items, grantees received a horse, a collar, bracelets, and a belt. The emir 'Adud al-Dawla, this author specifies, also received a crown, an honor that military commanders had received in earlier times. The description of *khil'a* is here more precise but uses terms (such as "pocket") that are not precisely defined.

The author continues his account, pointing out that viziers received analogous costumes but without golden borders. In addition, they had a claim to a horse and a saddle. It should be noted that these descriptions apply to the mid-tenth/fourth century and not prior times, when the viziers had precedence over the military commanders. We also remark that the author seems not to know of the "seven robes" noted by the chroniclers for the Buyid period. However, these details excepted, the descriptions agree.

Continuing according to Hilāl al-Ṣābi, there was an additional class of robes, that is the robes granted to the "companions" who were admitted to the intimate company of the sovereign; these costumes included an embroidered turban, two robes of differing types, and a cloak. The robes granted to governors of provinces were different again. The most beautiful cost 300 dinars, the least 30 dinars, without anyone telling us to what this hierarchy corresponded. All that we know is that the caliph often sent out such robes, for example, as favor to 'Ali ibn Buwayh, the governor of Fars. We also have a miniature showing the emir Maḥmūd of Ghazna putting on before courtiers the robe that he has just received.[24]

Of these robes, which were not all "robes of honor" but could be simply court costumes, we have at least one intact example preserved in a museum, and many fragments consisting of the epigraphic strips that were embroidered on the sleeves and, it seems, on the upper part of the garment. These robes of linen with inscriptions embroidered in silk were manufactured in workshops controlled by the caliph. The texts embroidered on them bore the name of *ṭirāz,* which was given by extension to the garments themselves. The fabrication of these *ṭirāz* in the name of the caliph was a caliphal privilege, similar to the minting of coin.[25] It was carried out in workshops that were located primarily in Egypt and in Iran (notably in Bishapur, a town near Shiraz, which was destroyed in the tenth/fourth century), and later at Baghdad.[26] It would seem that the methods of weaving practiced in Egypt and in Iran were introduced into Iraq only in the ninth/third century, which would explain how the use of robes of honor spread only at this time.

We have one example of an intact robe of honor, preserved at The Textile Museum in Washington, D.C.[27] It is a garment bearing the name of the Buyid emir Bāha' al-Dawla, and dating from the year 1000/390. Other surviving fragments with inscriptions are found in several museums. They have been the subject of various publications and the majority of them have been edited in the *Repertoire chronologique d'epigraphie arabe.*[28] A complete edition of these texts, however, does not exist at this time.[29]

The dated inscriptions that figured on these garments bore a prayer for the caliph and usually the name of the vizier who had given the order for their fabrication, as well as the date and the name of the workshop. Here are a few examples belonging to the reigns of the caliphs al-Muqtadir (908/295–932/320) and al-Qādir (991/381–1031/422):

> Blessing and favor of God upon the Caliph Ja'far, the imam al-Muqtadir, commander of the faithful, may God make long his reign! Here is what the vizier 'Ali ibn 'I+sā ordered to be made, by the hands of Shāfi', in the year 303 [being 915 of the Christian era].[30]
>
> Praise to God, master of the worlds, the King, the Truth made known. May God grant his blessing to Muḥammad, the seal of the prophets. Glory from God to the slave of God, Ja'far, the commander al-Muqtadir Billah, commander of the faithful, may God make long his reign. Here is what he ordered made at his own weaving factory, at Bisapur, by the hands of the vizier Ḥamd ibn al'Abbās, the client of the commander of believers, may God glorify him. Which was done in the year 307 [919].[31]
>
> Al-Qādir Billah, commander of the faithful, may God make long his reign and . . . is enemies . . . Bahā 'l-Dawla ordered this made, in his own weaving factory, in the year 390 [1000].[32]

This last inscription shows that even in the period when the caliph delegated the greater part of his powers to the Buyid emirs, he retained the privilege of having woven robes of honor bearing an inscription in his name. We know from another source that the Samanid governor of Transoxiana, Nūḥ ibn Manṣūr, obtained from the Buyid chief emir robes of honor bearing the name of the caliph and himself.[33]

These fragments demonstrate that the practice of granting robes of honor to dignitaries of the Baghdad court continued at least until 1037/428, and the chroniclers affirm that this continued until the arrival of the Saldjuk sultans in 1057/449. From other sources, we learn that in the same period the emir al-Basāsiri, who sided with the Fatimids and had occupied Baghdad for several months, distributed robes of honor in the name of the Fatimid caliph of Cairo.[34] On the other hand, for the period of the Saldjuk sultans the texts and the inscriptions give us little precise information. We know only that in 1086/479, when Malik Shah, the third Saldjuk sultan, went to Baghdad and paid a visit to the caliph, he received "sultan robes" (*al-khila' al-sulṭāniya*) about which the chroniclers give no detail, and that the sovereign declared that he entrusted to him the condition of the lands and of men, ordering him to make justice reign. But when the sultan asked to kiss the hand of the caliph, the latter held out to him only his seal, and the sultan had to content himself with this gesture. Niẓām al-Mulk, the vizier of the Saldjuk sultan, also received a robe of honor.[35]

The granting of robes of honor to delegates of the caliph, whether this was in the capitol or in the provinces, continued until the Mongol invasion of 1258/656, which put an end to the 'Abbasid caliphate of Baghdad. The Turkish emirs of Damascus who succeeded the Saldjuks at the beginning of the twelfth/sixth century received robes of honor the moment the caliph agreed to their investiture, and they in turn distributed robes to the dignitaries around them.[36]

A later author, al-Qalqashandi, summarizes the practice as it was perpetuated over the centuries:

> If the person whom the Caliph appointed was a prince of regions far from the court, the robe of honor [termed *tashrīf*, or "mark of honor"] was carried to him by a messenger of the caliph. It consisted of a robe [*jubba*] of black satin with an embroidered border, a collar, two bracelets of gold . . . , a sword and a horse with a golden saddle, as well as a black flag with the name of the Caliph written in white. It was one of these robes which was sent to the sultan Ṣālaḥ al-Dīn Yūsuf ibn Ayyūb [known in Europe as Saladin, who ruled from 1169/564 to 1193/589] and to his brother al-'Adil. When the robe was granted to the prince of the region, he put on the robe and the turban [*'imāma*], grasped the sword, mounted the horse, and paraded to the palace at the head of his retinue.[37]

We know that Saladin had received in 1180/576 a delegate from the caliph who had come to deliver his diploma of appointment and robes of honor.[38] Al-Qalqashandi states also that the last Ayyubid sultan, al-Nāṣir, received a robe of honor from the 'Abbasid caliph al-Musta'ṣim in the year 1257/655, immediately before the Mongol invasion that ended the 'Abbasid Caliphate of Baghdad. But certainly by this time the granting of robes of honor by the caliph had lost the solemn ceremony that the practice bore in the golden age of the 'Abbasid caliphate.

Notes

1. N. A. Stillman, "Khil'a," in *The Encyclopaedia of Islam.* 2nd ed., ed. H. A. R. Gibb et al. (Leiden: E. J. Brill, 1960). The second edition of *The Encyclopaedia of Islam* is cited hereafter as *EI2,* and the first edition as *EI1.*
2. al-Djahshiyari, *Kitāb al-wuzāra',* ed. M. al-Sakka' et al. (Cairo: 1938), 90.
3. Ibid., 113.
4. A. Northedge, "Samarra," *EI2.*
5. al-Ṭabari, *Kitāb akhb+r al-rusūl wa al-mulūk* (*Annales,* ed. M. J. De Goege et al., 13 vols. (Leiden: E. J. Brill, 1879–1901), 3:1233.
6. Ibid., 3:1302.
7. al-Tanūkhi, *Nishwār al-muḥāḍarah* (Damascus: 1930), 8:13.
8. al-Ṭabari, *Annales,* 3:1647.
9. Ibid., 3:1657.
10. Ibid., 3:1687.
11. Ibid., 3:1127 and 2040.
12. Ibid., 3:2194, 2204, 2244. See also Dominique Sourdel, *Le vizirat 'abbaside* (Damascus: Institut francais de Damas, 1959–60), passim.
13. Sourdel, *Le vizirat,* 676.
14. Ibid., 493.
15. al-Ṣūli, *Akhbār ar-Rādī billah wa'l-Muttaqi billah,* trans. M. Canard, 2 vols. (Algiers: Institut d'etudes orientales, 1946), 1:174. See also H. Busse, *Chalif und Grosskonig* (Beirut: 1969), 216.
16. Miskawayh, *Tadjārib al-umam (The Experiences of Nations),* ed. and trans. H. F. Amedroz and D. S. Margoliouth, *Eclipse of the 'Abbasid Caliphate,* 7 vols. (Oxford: Blackwell, 1920–1921), 2:78.
17. al-Ṣūli, *Akhb+ar ar-Rāḍi,* 2:69.
18. Ibn al-Djawzi, *al-Muntaẓam,* ed. F. Krenkow, 6 vols. (Haydarabad: 1938–1940), 6:340.
19. Busse, *Chalif und Grosskonig,* 216–17. See also Ibn al-Djawzi, *al-Muntaẓam,* 7:267.
20. Hilāl al-Ṣābi, *Rusūm dār al-khilāfa,* ed. M. Awwad, (Baghdad: 1964), 84–85. Also E. A. Salem trans., *The Rules and Regulations of the 'Abbasid Court* (Beirut: 1977), 65–70.
21. Busse, *Chalif und Grosskonig,* 217; and Ibn al-Djawzi, *al-Muntaẓam,* 7:148.
22. Ibn al-Djawzi, *al-Munta#zam,* 7:161–62.
23. Hilāl al-Ṣābi, *Rusūm,* 93–95; Salem translation, 75–77.
24. *EI2,* "Khil'a," plate I.
25. See R. B. Serjeant, "Material for a History of Islamic Textile up to the Mongol Conquest," *Ars Islamica* 9 (1942): 72. The existence of a *Dār al-Ṭirāz* [*Tiraz* office] is already noted during the reign of Harun al-Rashid (786/170–809/193). See also A. Grohmann, "Tiraz," in *The Encyclopaedia of Islam* (including *Supplement*), 1st ed., ed. M. T. Houtsma et al. (Leiden: E. J. Brill, 1913–38).

26. A. Grohmann, "Tiraz," *EI1* and *Supplement.* See also E. Kuhnel and L. Bellinger, *Catalogue of Dated Tiraz Fabrics* (Washington: Textile Museum, 1952).
27. "Harir [Silk]," *EI2,* plate III.
28. E. Combe, J. Sauvaget, and G. Wiet, eds., *Repertoire chronologique d'epigraphie arabe,* 6 vols. (Cairo: Institut francais d'archeologie orientale, 1931–1935). The oldest fragments date from the reigns of the last Umayyad caliph, Marwān II, and the early 'Abbasid caliphs Harūn al-Rashīd, al-Amīn, and al-Ma'mūn (in all, about 744/127 to 831/216). The next dates from the reign of al-Mutawakkil in 855/241.
29. The most important publications are: F. E. Day, "Dated Tiraz in the Collection of the University of Michigan," *Ars Islamica* 4 (1937): 421–46; R. Pfister, "Toiles a inscriptions abbasides et fatimides," *Bulletin d'Etudes Orientales* 11 (1945–1946): 47–90; E. Kuhnel, "Abbasid Silks of the Ninth Century," *Ars Orientalis* 2 (1957): 367–71; M. A. Marzouk, "Five Tiraz Fabrics in the Volkerkunde-Museum of Basel," in *Aus der Welt des islamischen Kunst: Festschrift fur Ernst Kuhnel* (Berlin: Verlag Gebr. Mann, 1957), 283–89. A more comprehensive bibliography undoubtedly will soon be published under the article "Tiraz" in *EI2.*
30. *Repertoire,* 3: number 967. It is not certain that the word *Miṣr,* translated here as "*al-Fusṭāṭ* [the name of the capital]," designates Egypt. See Marzouk, "Five Tiraz Fabrics."
31. *Repertoire,* 3: number 1019.
32. *Repertoire,* 6: number 2079.
33. Serjeant, "Material," 76.
34. See G. Makdisi, *Ibn 'Aqil et la resurgence de l'islam traditionaliste au Xie siecle* (Damascus: Institut francais, 1963), 110.
35. Ibn al-Athīr, *al-Kāmil* (Leiden: E. J. Brill, 1867), 10:156–57.
36. See for example, J. M. Mouton, *La principaute de Damas sous les Seljoukides et les Bourides* (Cairo: Institut francais d'archeologie orientale, 1994), 114 and 150. see also A. M. Edde, La Principanté Ayyoulide d' Alep (Stuttgart: Franz Steiner, 1999), 205
37. al-Qalqashandi, cited in Serjeant, "Material," 77.
38. See A. Hartmann, *an-Nasir li-Din Allah (1180–1225)* (Berlin: Walter de Gruyter, 1975), 86 and n. 123.

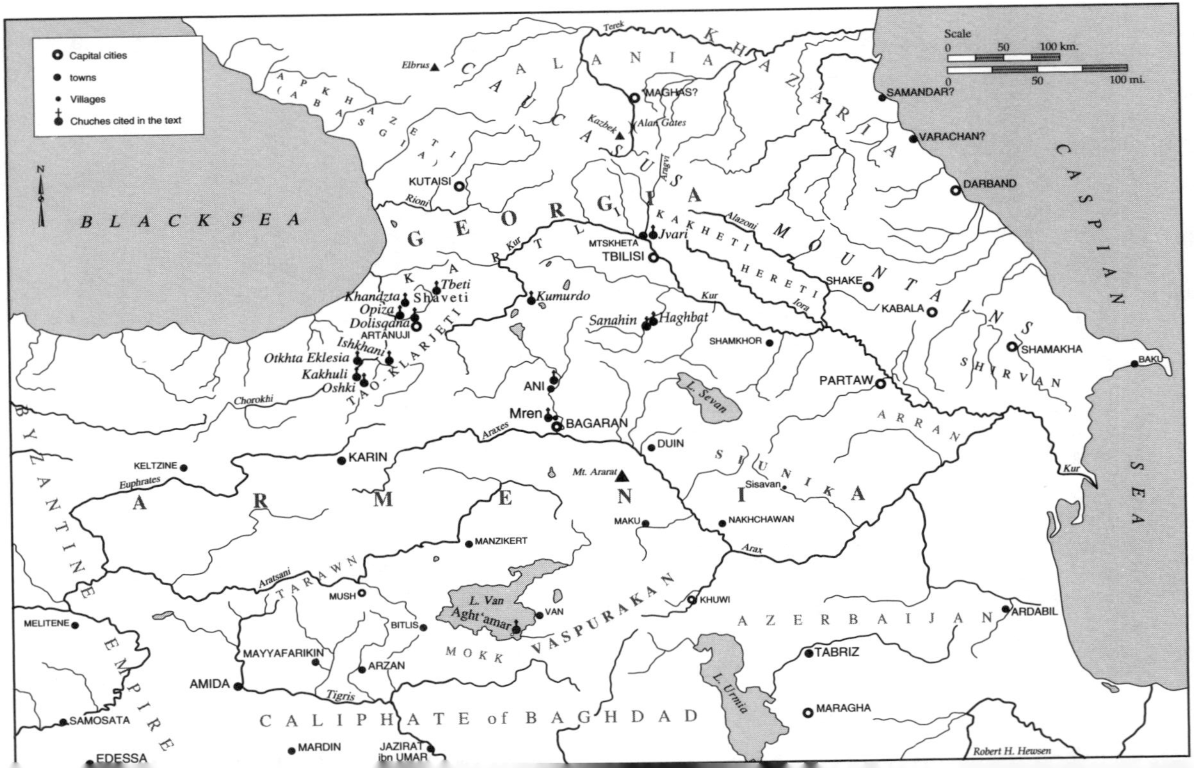
Capital cities
towns
Villages
Chuches cited in the text
Scale
0 50 100 km.
0 50 100 mi.
N
BLACK SEA
CASPIAN SEA
APKHAZETI (ABASGIA)
ALANIA
KHAZARIA
CAUCASUS MOUNTAINS
GEORGIA
KARTLI
KAKHETI
HERETI
TAO-KLARJETI
SHIRVAN
ARRAN
SIUNIKA
ARMENIA
TARAWN
VASPURAKAN
MOKK
AZERBAIJAN
BYZANTINE EMPIRE
CALIPHATE of BAGHDAD
Elbrus
Kazbek
Alan Gates
Terek
Aragvi
Alazoni
Iora
Kur
Rioni
Chorokhi
Araxes
Arax
Euphrates
Aratsani
Tigris
L. Sevan
L. Van
L. Urmia
Mt. Ararat
MAGHAS?
SAMANDAR?
VARACHAN?
DARBAND
KUTAISI
MTSKHETA
Jvari
TBILISI
SHAKE
KABALA
SHAMAKHA
BAKU
Tbeti
Shaveti
Khandzta
Opiza
Dolisqana
ARTANUJI
Ishkhani
Otkhta Eklesia
Kakhuli
Oshki
Kumurdo
Sanahin
Haghbat
SHAMKHOR
PARTAW
ANI
Mren
BAGARAN
DUIN
Sisavan
NAKHCHAWAN
MAKU
KARIN
KELTZINE
MANZIKERT
MUSH
BITLIS
VAN
Aght'amar
KHUWI
ARDABIL
TABRIZ
MARAGHA
MELITENE
MAYYAFARIKIN
ARZAN
AMIDA
SAMOSATA
EDESSA
MARDIN
JAZIRAT ibn UMAR
Robert H. Hewsen

CHAPTER 7

ROBING, POWER, AND LEGITIMACY IN ARMENIA AND GEORGIA

Antony Eastmond and Lynn Jones

Introduction

This chapter addresses the relationship between ceremonial, robes, and the legitimization and display of royal power in Armenia and Georgia. These Christian states of the Caucasus acted as buffers between the Byzantine empire to the west and the Islamic caliphate to the east and southeast, and for much of the Middle Ages they were dominated by one or the other of their more powerful neighbors. This study concentrates on the ninth and tenth centuries, a period when both Armenia and Georgia began to establish their own power and independent position in the region. It examines the different ways in which ceremonial and the gifts of robes and regalia from the emperor in Constantinople or the caliph in Baghdad or Samarra were used to establish or enhance rulership.

As will become clear, Armenia and Georgia were decentralized states, each divided into a number of separate principalities with many opposing family dynasties vying to extend their power over their rivals. Indeed the terms Armenia and Georgia are largely anachronistic: regional loyalties were dominant and ideas of unity were largely conceptual, effected by adherence to a common language or Christian confession rather than to any single political entity.

The principal dynasties in the two countries were closely related, the founder of the Georgian royal Bagrationi family being descended from the Armenian ruling Bagratid family.[1] However, while the Bagratids of Armenia remained heavily influenced by Islam, the Bagrationis of Georgia were increasingly drawn into the sphere of influence of the Christian Byzantine empire. Armenia and Georgia were also separated by doctrinal issues. By the mid-seventh century the Armenian Orthodox Church had broken with the Church of Byzantium and was also separated from the Georgian Church, which had returned to Eastern Orthodoxy.[2] Thus, while Armenia and Georgia were linked by kinship and geographical proximity, they were divided by political influence and theological doctrine. As is demonstrated in the pages that follow, the differences between them determined that robes and ceremonial played very different roles.

Armenia

This chapter seeks to clarify the nature of Armenian kingship in the ninth and tenth centuries by analyzing the textual descriptions of investitures, including the presentation of robes and regalia, and comparing their royal message with that conveyed by royal portraits. The material under examination is limited to that associated with the two most powerful Armenian families of the period, the Bagratids and Artsruni, and for each family a series of questions must be posed. How did a ruler visually characterize his rule? Which cultures were available for appropriation of the iconography or ideology of rulership and which were not? Did royal ceremonial and portraits remain static, or were they altered in response to political upheaval?

In the ninth and tenth centuries Armenia was a vassal state of Islam, administered by an *ostikan* (resident governor) who collected taxes and forwarded them to the caliphal court.[3] In terms of national organization, medieval Armenia was a collection of principalities ruled by the *nakharars* (nobility) and dominated by one presiding prince, traditionally a senior member of the Bagratid family. The presiding prince was recognized as the authority over all other Armenian princes, and was entrusted with the collection and forwarding of taxes to the *ostikan*.[4] In 884–885 the Bagratid presiding prince Ashot I became the first king in four hundred years to rule over a united Armenia.[5] Bagratid rule was undermined by the civil wars constantly raging among the Armenian aristocracy and by challenges from *nakharars* seeking to usurp Bagratid power or to free themselves from Bagratid suzerainty. Chief among the challengers were the Artsruni, rulers of the southern principality of Vaspurakan, who were related by marriage to the Bagratids. In 908 Gagik Artsruni, grandson of the Bagratid king Ashot I, broke the power of Bagratid rule and established an independent kingdom that would briefly eclipse the kingdom of Armenia in regional and international authority.[6]

Two contemporary texts offer a rich and largely untapped source of information on this period. Yovhannes Drasxanakertc'i was the catholicos, or spiritual leader, of the Armenian Church from 897 to 924–925 and wrote

The History of Armenia to illustrate the fatal consequences of civil war to the feuding Armenian princes. Known outside of Armenia as John Catholicos, he began his work under the patronage of the Bagratid kings of Armenia and finished it under the protection of Gagik Artsruni, king of Vaspurakan.[7] The second text, *The History of the House of the Artsruni,* was written by T'ovma [Thomas] Artsruni, a kinsman of Gagik Artsruni and a contemporary of John Catholicos. The work was commissioned by Gagik to glorify the ancestry and accomplishments of his family. Thomas records events through 904, when the narrative is taken up by an anonymous continuator who retells many events previously related by Thomas and who also continues the history of Gagik's reign.[8]

Investiture

The importance of the ceremonial bestowal of rank is evident in the contemporary histories; both texts brim with descriptions of ceremonies in which the caliphate granted honors and titles to members of the Armenian nobility. These ceremonies consistently feature the presentation of lavishly embroidered Islamic robes, jeweled and gilded armaments, and the gift of a horse or mule.[9] The following pages are not concerned with the Islamic presentation of robes as such but rather explore how such ceremonial was appropriated and adapted to characterize Armenian kingship.[10]

Thomas Artsruni describes an Islamic ceremony honoring Armenian princes in his account of the 858 release of Gagik Artsruni's father and grandfather from imprisonment in the caliphal city of Samarra.[11] According to Thomas, the Artsruni princes were promised restoration to their land by the caliph and then were feted in the caliphal dining hall. Thomas stresses the caliph's participation, describing how he personally clothed the princes in rich garments, gave them banners, girt them with swords fastened in jeweled belts, and presented them with a splendidly decorated horse.[12] The Armenian princes then proceeded from the caliphal palace "in glorious splendor and notable honors," to the sound of singing and trumpets, while heralds declared their sovereignty over the land of Vaspurakan.[13] John Catholicos more briefly describes several similar ceremonies, including that in 862 which accorded the status of presiding prince to the Bagratid prince Ashot I. For the occasion the *ostikan* came to Armenia "in accordance with the orders of the caliph," and "invested him with many robes as well as royal insignia."[14] When Ashot's grandson and namesake, Ashot II, was invested as presiding prince in 903/4, the ceremony paralleled that accorded to Ashot I. The *ostikan* presented him with a horse, "ornaments, armor, and multicolored garments," in addition to a "girdle studded with gems."[15] The shared features of these and other ceremonies, as reported by the contemporary historians, indicate that the caliphate employed a standard ceremony to honor Armenian princes and nobility.[16]

Ashot I was elevated to the status of king of Armenia in 884—22 years after his recognition as presiding prince.[17] The decision to grant him royal status was made by the members of the Armenian nobility rather than by the caliph or the *ostikan*. According to John Catholicos: "In view of the nobility of his family, the princes and *nakharars* of Armenia unanimously resolved to raise him up as king over themselves, and informed the caliph through the governor."[18] The caliph demonstrated his agreement by sending the *ostikan* to Armenia with "a royal crown," which was formally presented to Ashot together with royal robes, horses, weapons, and ornaments.[19] A second ceremony of investiture was then performed in a cathedral by the Armenian catholicos, who blessed Ashot and placed a crown upon his head. When Ashot's son, Smbat I, was crowned king of Armenia in 890, the same procedures were followed. First the *ostikan* "came forth to meet him at the place of assembly" and presented Smbat with "a royal diadem," and "robes wrought with gold," as well as horses and armor.[20] The king and his court next "returned to the holy church with the patriarch," who "pronounced the solemn blessings" on Smbat, and "investing him with gold-embroidered robes covered with expressive designs, he placed on his head the royal crown."[21]

In each of these investitures the *ostikan* first ceremonially presented the king of Armenia with a crown, luxurious robes, and other sumptuous gifts in the presence of the assembled Armenian and Islamic armies.[22] Only the gift of a royal crown differentiates this ceremony from those that honored lesser Armenian nobility, confirming that the first recognition of a Bagratid king was effected in an Islamic ceremony. The second recognition of the king was, in contrast, Armenian. The status of the ruler was formally acknowledged in a ceremony performed by the catholicos in the major church of the current Bagratid capital.[23] The catholicos blessed each king, placed a crown on his head, and sometimes also invested him with royal robes.

The textual accounts clearly indicate the separate nature of the Islamic and Armenian ceremonies.[24] The two investitures not only featured different participants, they occurred in different settings and followed different procedures. It may therefore be suggested that the investitures confirmed and displayed different aspects of Armenian kingship. The caliphal gift of Islamic crown and robes, ceremonially presented by the *ostikan*, gave visual expression to the Bagratid king's temporal power.[25] The investment of a crown by the catholicos in a religious ceremony then confirmed the recipient's pious worthiness to rule as a Christian king.[26] The double investiture can be seen as the symbolic unification, in the person of the king of Armenia, of the seemingly disparate aspects of Bagratid rule: Armenian suzerainty to Islam and Armenian Orthodox faith.

A principal emphasis on piety is suggested by the setting of the Armenian investiture and by the prominent role played by the catholicos. The investment of a medieval ruler by the spiritual head of the church was, of course, also known from Byzantium.[27] Certainly the example of the patriarch of Constantinople investing the emperor was a convenient and potent model; initial studies of a text that preserves a later ordination rite of Bagratid kings suggests that much of that rite was derived from the Byzantine model of imperial investiture.[28] It may be suggested, however, that the key to understanding the symbolic importance of the Armenian investiture of a Bagratid king does not lie in the possible emulation of Byzantine ceremonial but is instead found in the catholico's unique role in medieval Armenian society. The successive Sasanid, Byzantine, and Islamic occupations that buffeted Armenia from the fifth through the ninth centuries threatened not only the political integrity of the country but the very existence of Armenian Orthodoxy. During this period the Armenian Church was central to the development of a national cultural identity, and the catholicos was the unifying Armenian figure. Moreover, in the absence of secular unity the catholicos also took on many temporal roles and was, prior to the restoration of a unified Armenia, the most significant Armenian authority.[29]

It is evident from the textual descriptions that the highlight of the Armenian investiture ceremony was the crowning of the new king by the catholicos. Crowns are also invariably listed first by Armenian historians in their descriptions of caliphal gifts. This consistent textual emphasis contrasts with the inconsistent mention of robes for both the Islamic and Armenian ceremonies and indicates that among Armenian regalia the crown was paramount. Its potency as a symbol of the resurrection of a unified nation was explicitly acknowledged by the catholicos: "Also [I shall comment on those] in whose days the glorious crown of the Armenia people was completely destroyed, and [narrate] how once again, through the coronation of the great prince Ashot as our king, we witnessed the renewal of the kingdom which had ceased long ago."[30]

Once a Bagratid king of Armenia had been formally recognized by both the *ostikan* and the patriarch, it was his prerogative to confer honors and titles. Bagratid investment of foreign kings was apparently limited to the elevation of Georgian princes. These investitures took place in Armenia and featured the Bagratid king, who personally invested the Georgian ruler with a crown, royal robes, and a jeweled belt. The ceremonies also included the presentation of gifts, including armor, soldiers, and "other things necessary for travelling."[31] The written accounts of these events suggests that the ceremonies were modeled on the Islamic paradigm.[32]

As the title king of Armenia constituted official recognition by the caliph, it is not surprising that the Byzantine emperor was quick to counter Islamic influence with his own recognition of Bagratid rulers. Basil I (867–886) recognized Ashot I with the title *archōn tōn archōnton* in 884/85, immediately after his investiture by the *ostikan*.[33] *Archōn tōn archōnton* is a literal Greek translation of the Armenian title of presiding prince. It granted the recipient several privileges, chief among them the right to be called the emperor's "beloved son," but did not confer royal status.[34] Because there is no evidence that Ashot traveled to Constantinople, he most likely received his honors from an imperial envoy sent to Armenia. When Ashot's son Smbat I was invested as king in 890, the emperor Leo VI (886–912) was quick to acknowledge him with the same title and also sent him "beautiful weapons, ornaments, robes wrought with gold, goblets, and cups, and girdles of pure gold studded with gems" to confirm his status in the eyes of the Byzantine court.[35] In addition to these distinctions, the Bagratid kings were the yearly recipients of imperial gifts.[36]

Bagratid rule over a unified Armenia was brief. In 908 Gagik Artsruni, prince of Vaspurakan, was elevated to royal status by the *ostikan*. Given the disparate ties of patronage that bound the authors of the contemporary histories, it is not surprising that they provide very different accounts of Gagik's investiture. According to John Catholicos, Gagik went in 907/08 to the *ostikan*'s palace in Partaw. There he was presented with "a royal crown, as well as honors and gifts befitting royalty." The catholicos's low opinion of Gagik's kingship is evident in his remark that when Gagik returned to Vaspurakan he was "bearing something like a crown."[37] While there can be no doubt that this disapproval reflects the catholicos's current allegiance to the Bagratid king and his despair at the fragmentation of Armenia, it also confirms that a second investiture, performed by the catholicos, was indispensable for the declaration of legitimate Armenian kingship. The indelible phrase "something like a crown" in particular suggests that trappings of royal power, such as a crown, imbued the wearer with legitimacy only when bestowed by the proper hands. As we have seen, the proper hands were those of the catholicos.

The anonymous continuator's description of Gagik's elevation is, not surprisingly, much more flattering. According to this account the *ostikan* placed on Gagik's head "a crown of pure gold, artfully made and set with pearls and valuable precious stones, which I am unable to describe. He clothed him in a robe embroidered with gold, a girdle and sword shining with golden ornament."[38] Gagik was then seated upon a splendidly accoutered horse, and soldiers in full armor flanked the newly crowned king while "the sound of drums, trumpets, horns, flutes, lyres and harps shook the camp of the caliphal army."[39]

It is clear from this description that Gagik was invested as king of Vaspurakan in an Islamic ceremony paralleling that accorded to the Bagratid kings of Armenia. Gagik's investiture was, however, set apart from that of the Bagratids by its lack of religious symbolism—an omission that did not escape the notice of the contemporary historians.[40] John Catholicos notes repeatedly that Gagik received his crown *from the hands* of the Islamic governor, effectively contrasting the agent of Gagik's investiture with the participation of the catholicos in the elevation of Bagratid kings.[41] Even the anonymous continuator, the most enthusiastic of Gagik's chroniclers, was unable to conceal the flaw in his patron's investiture and took poetic license to remedy the problem. After describing the ceremony he states, "I do not hesitate to say that his anointing was invisibly performed by the Holy Spirit, according to the apostles' saying: There is no authority save from God; and what is, has been established by God."[42]

Gagik was invested by the *ostikan* on two additional occasions, and in each instance it is clear that the *ostikan* was not representing the caliph but was acting independently.[43] In 919 Gagik received a crown and royal robes from the caliph, and it is clear from the textual account that this recognition accorded Gagik a higher degree of legitimacy than did his earlier investitures at the hands of the *ostikan*. In his account of Gagik's caliphal recognition, the anonymous continuator first extols the great honor accorded to his patron, conveniently bypassing the precedent of the first two Bagratid kings of Armenia, who, as we have seen, were similarly recognized by the caliph. He also refashions Gagik's ancestral heritage into something more royal than the facts admit: "For me this is prodigious to relate, this for me is amazing to hear; it far surpasses my own history and those of others; no one has ever heard tell of it or seen it, to be able to reveal that anyone was honored by the [caliph's] court with the dignity of wearing a crown, especially a Christian and orthodox believer and son of a king, the hereditary and legitimate ruler of Armenia."[44] The anonymous then again resorts to rhetorical embellishment to provide his king with pious validation: "I do not reckon it too audacious to repeat a second time that the tyrant was forced to do this by the will and command of the All-Highest and Lord of all."[45]

This insistent emphasis on Gagik's piety undoubtedly reflects the damage done to his pious persona by his military cooperation with the *ostikan* against his uncle, the Bagratid king Smbat I. In 912/13 Gagik allied his forces with those of the *ostikan* and led the combined armies in a series of campaigns against the Bagratids. These battles resulted in the capture and death of the majority of the Bagratid nobility and brought great destruction to the land. Gagik's military cooperation with the ostikan also resulted in the latter's capture of the Bagratid king. In 914, after being held prisoner for one year, Smbat was tortured and put to death. His body was then crucified and set on display on the walls of Dvin, the former Bagratid capital.[46] While Smbat's death consolidated Gagik Artsruni's temporal power, Gagik's collusion with the *ostikan* severely compromised his pious reputation.

Following Smbat's death, Bagratid rule was fragmented. The *ostikan* refused to recognize the status of Smbat's son and heir, Ashot II, and further undermined his claims to succession by installing his cousin, the *sparapet* (commander-in-chief) Ashot, as anti-king in an Islamic ceremony.[47] Ashot II's subsequent struggle to claim his rightful title demonstrates that the recognition of a Bagratid king of Armenia no longer depended upon ancestral lineage and the support of the *nakharars;* the determining factor was instead the support of the *ostikan*. It is also clear that the catholicos could not independently invest a king without such support.

Unable to secure the royal title from the *ostikan,* Ashot II turned elsewhere for validation of his status. In 914 he was acclaimed king of Armenia by Gurgen, the Georgian duke of Tao in a ceremony that is otherwise not described.[48] This guaranteed Ashot II military assistance in his efforts to defeat the anti-king and provided him with a base in Georgia from which he could conduct his raids into Armenian territory. The Georgian recognition did not, however, advance his claim to kingship within Armenia. Later that same year Ashot II went as an imperial guest to the court at Constantinople.[49] He was granted the title *archōn tōn archōnton,* which as we have seen was also previously accorded to his father and grandfather. The emperor "dressed him [Ashot II] in glorious purple, and gave valuable gold-embroidered robes, byssus with golden borders, and a girdle studded with gems for his waist."[50] He was also given armored horses, "as well as many cups, and utensils, and many gold and silver wares."[51] More importantly, the emperor "put in his command many Roman generals and forces, and sent him back to his land."[52] While the imperial honors accorded to Ashot II were great, he was unable to defeat the anti-king, and his status in Armenia therefore remained unresolved.

Civil war raged between Ashot II and his rival for four years, further devastating the country. In 918 the *ostikan,* needing Ashot II's military support, abruptly recapitulated and agreed to grant him royal status.[53] The ceremony that formally recognized Ashot II as king of Armenia was much altered from the investitures that had recognized his father and grandfather. According to the catholicos, the investiture occurred in conjunction with the previously planned celebration of Ashot II's marriage, undoubtedly because of the suddenness of the *ostikan*'s reversal. The *ostikan* did not come to Armenia, as was usual for the declaration of a Bagratid king, but rather sent "a royal crown and valuable ornaments for robes, both beautiful and becoming," as well as horses, weapons, armor, and a detachment of cavalry. After the marriage ceremony Ashot was invested with "the crown that the *ostikan* had dispatched."[54]

There was, then, no double investiture for the third Bagratid king of Armenia; Ashot II's ceremonial elevation instead combined aspects of the Islamic and Armenian investitures previously accorded to Ashot I and Smbat I. The gift of a crown signaled the support of the *ostikan,* a support more tangibly expressed by the Islamic cavalry. The catholicos then placed the Islamic crown on Ashot's head, a usage that confirms that the symbolic importance of the regalia was secondary to the symbolism embodied by the Armenian ceremonial, in which the catholicos validated the king's pious worthiness.[55] This emphasis on the piety of the king suggests that while the Bagratid ceremonial changed in response to the altered political climate, its symbolic message remained constant. Like the double investiture accorded to the first two Bagratid kings of Armenia, Ashot II's investiture, however hastily arranged, emphasized his pious persona over his temporal power. As we have seen, such pious symbolism was unique to the investiture accorded to a Bagratid king of Armenia.

Royal Portraits

As with royal ceremonial, portraits of medieval rulers could also visually characterize power and piety.[56] Unfortunately, Armenian imagery of any type is poorly documented for the medieval period. The successive foreign invasions of the fifth through ninth centuries have left only a few surviving examples of Armenian portraits; for the tenth and eleventh centuries the preserved works are scarcely more numerous.[57] Because there are no surviving depictions of Bagratid rulers or descriptions of lost portraits from the first half of the tenth century, it at first seems impossible to compare the visual expression of Bagratid kingship with the remarkably clear picture of Bagratid investiture ceremonial provided by textual descriptions. However, Bagratid portraits do survive from the second half of the tenth century. In the following pages it will be demonstrated that these later portraits visually convey the ideology of kingship expressed in the investitures of the first three Bagratid kings of Armenia, and can therefore reasonably serve as iconographical substitutions for the lost images of the earlier Bagratid kings.

Ashot III, the nephew of Ashot II, ruled as Bagratid king of Armenia from 953 to 977.[58] In 966 he and his wife Khosrovanuosh founded a church at Sanahin and placed there portraits of two of their sons, Gurgen and Smbat (figure 7.1). Their sculpted images are high in a niche on the east facade, beneath the gable. The princes are the same height and

Figure 7.1. Sanahin. Gurgen and Smbat Bagratuni, east fascade (966 CE).

wear idntical undecorated tunics carved with deep lines in imitation of flowing drapery. They wear identical peaked headdresses and hold between them a model of the church.[59] Khosrovanuosh also founded a church at Haghbat.[60] Sculptural portraits of Gurgen and Smbat are again placed high on the east facade of the church, and here, as at Sanahin, the two brothers are of equal height and hold between them a model of their church (figure 7.2). However, in this portrait group their relative rank is

Figure 7.2. Haghbat. Gurgen and Bagratuni and Smbat II, east fascade (977 CE).

distinguished by their headdresses.[61] Gurgen, the younger brother, wears a caplike helmet, while Smbat's royal status is indicated by his turban.[62] Both brothers wear undecorated mantles over plain tunics and high riding boots strapped at the ankle. The only ornamental accent is provided by the voluminous cuffs of their tunics, which project beyond the sleeves of their mantles and hang down from their extended arms.

Another royal Bagratid portrait was once part of the church of St. Gregory the Illuminator at Ani. The church was founded in the late tenth century by the Bagratid king Gagik I (989/90–1020), son of Ashot III and brother to Gurgen and Smbat. The church is now in ruins, but in 1906 a life-sized sculpture depicting the king holding a model of his church on his outstretched arms was discovered in the rubble (figure 7.3).[63] The portrait, which was lost during World War I, was the only known example of medieval Armenian figural sculpture in the round. The figure of Gagik I was dressed in a tunic covered by a red mantle, and wore a necklace with a large cross suspended at chest level. The tunic's sleeves terminated with great swags of fabric, exactly like those worn by his brothers in their portraits at Haghbat. The king's royal status was conveyed by an immense white turban.

Figure 7.3. Ani. Church of St. Gregory the Illuminator. Donor relief of King Gagik I (990–1020). (after Thierry).

While the evidence is limited, these portraits suggest a standard representation of Bagratid royal status that features the presentation of a church model, a turban as a sign of royal rank, and robes worn over tunics distinguished by pendant sleeves. Perhaps as important are the elements that are *not* found in the surviving royal images; there are no foreign crowns or robes.[64] The Bagratid portraits of the second half of the tenth century thus visually stress the specifically Armenian nature of their kingship, prominently displaying their piety and eschewing any foreign emblems of power. This interpretation correlates with the ideology of kingship expressed in the investitures of the first three Bagratid kings, in which the recognition of temporal power symbolized in an Islamic ceremony or through the gift of an Islamic crown was secondary to the pious symbolism conveyed through the investiture performed by the catholicos. This shared ideology, as expressed in both ceremonial and portraiture, allows us to view the Bagratid portraits from the end of the tenth century as a continuation of an earlier established tradition of Bagratid royal imagery.

When we turn to examine the visual expression of kingship employed by Gagik Artsruni, we find, in happy contrast to the scarcity of Bagratid portraits, two surviving contemporary images and a textual description of lost portraits. The two extant portraits of Gagik are carved on the exterior of his palace church, constructed on the island of Aght'amar in Lake Van in present-day eastern Turkey. Dedicated to the Holy Cross, the church was built during the years 915 to 921, after Gagik had attained royal status.[65]

The Church of the Holy Cross is best known for its extensive sculptural program—over 200 remarkably well-preserved figures carved in low relief decorate the exterior. The west facade features a depiction of Gagik presenting a model of his church to the figure of Christ (figure 7.4). While this image is on one level a straightforward testimony to Gagik's piety as donor, the king's Islamic regalia forcefully conveys his temporal power. Gagik wears a long-sleeved tunic decorated with concentric circles linked in vertical rows, which is carefully folded back at the lower hem to reveal trousers. A mantle, lavishly decorated with the figures of small birds in medallions, is worn over the tunic and is fastened with a large floral-shaped brooch.[66] The distinctive shape of the mantle, which is shorter in front and trails to mid-calf length behind, emulates those worn by Sasanian kings in surviving portraits.[67]

Gagik's crown has been badly damaged, but photographs taken before the image was vandalized show that it originally featured flaring side wings, emulating the winged form of Sasanian crowns. Further evidence of this emulation is found in the absence of the uppermost section of Gagik's nimbus, indicating that originally the crown also featured a tall,

Figure 7.4. Aght'amar. King Gagik Artsruni, west facade Church of the Holy Cross (915–21 CE).

central projection that extended above the nimbus. Sasanian crowns frequently feature a tall central orb.[68] Abbasid knowledge and emulation of

Sasanian royal iconography is well documented, and the bestowal of Sasanian-influenced crowns by the Abbasid caliphate is known from contemporary portraits of Islamic princes.[69] Gagik's crown certainly bears no resemblance to any type of royal headgear featured in other depictions of Armenian royalty or to any described in textual accounts of lost portraits; like his mantle, Gagik's crown is unique. This apparent uniqueness, combined with the emphasis placed on the caliphal gift of crown and robes in the *History of the House of the Artsruni,* suggests that the sculpture preserves a copy of the robe and crown presented to Gagik by the caliph in 919.[70]

A second, much smaller portrait of Gagik Artsruni is carved in the upper register of the east facade of the Church of the Holy Cross. Here the king is shown sitting cross-legged on a cushion, wearing a loose, undecorated tunic that is cuffed at the sleeves.[71] He reaches with his left hand to pluck from a cluster of grapes dangling above his head and raises a cup of wine to chest-level with his right hand. His image is flanked by two attendants wearing princely costume and by a lion and eagle, animals traditionally associated with royalty. A comparison of Gagik's portrait with a commemorative medallion issued by the reigning caliph al-Moqtadir (912–932) reveals the extent to which Gagik's portrait was modeled after the current symbol of Islamic authority. On the medallion the caliph is shown sitting cross-legged on a low platform throne topped with a cushion, raising a glass to chest-level with his right hand.[72]

The *History of the House of the Artsruni* allows us to reconstruct portraits of Gagik Artsruni that were once displayed in the royal palace of Aght'amar. The palace, which has long since vanished, was originally adjacent to the south facade of the Church of the Holy Cross. According to the anonymous continuator, the palace was lavishly decorated and included depictions of Gagik seated on gilt thrones, surrounded by princely attendants, musicians, dancing women, and men engaged in swordplay and wrestling matches. There were also representations of wild animals, including lions and flocks of birds.[73] This description generally evokes the iconography of Gagik's portrait on the east facade of his palace church, where the king is flanked by princely attendants, a lion, and an eagle. It more specifically evokes the iconography of the Islamic cycle of princely entertainments, which features an enthroned king flanked by noble attendants, musicians, and dancers, and often includes contests of strength, and animals, such as lions, traditionally associated with royalty.[74] Such representations are known from many works surviving from the Umayyad and Abbasid courts, where they were a component of the decorative program of palaces and were also featured on portable luxury goods such as textiles, gold and silver plates, and medallions.[75]

The differences between Gagik's portraits and those depicting Bagratid kings are striking.[76] Gagik chose to stress his power through the appropriation of Islamic courtly iconography and the representation of Islamic regalia. In contrast, Bagratid portraits emphasize piety and do not include foreign regalia. The royal messages conveyed by the Artsruni and Bagratid portraits thus agree with the messages conveyed by their investitures. As has been observed, Gagik's investitures were expressive of his temporal power alone, while the investiture of a Bagratid king of Armenia stressed the piety of the ruler.

Why would Gagik, a Christian king, appropriate Islamic iconography—why did neither he nor the Bagratid kings turn to Byzantium for a visual expression of kingship? The Byzantine empire, the most powerful Christian nation, certainly seems a rich and convenient source for representations of Christian rulership. Yet, because imperial presentations conveyed aspects of Byzantine theological doctrine, Armenian rulers were effectively prevented from any appropriation of imperial iconography.[77] The rupture between Eastern and Armenian Orthodoxy and the resultant continuing disputes posed a real threat to the autonomy of the Armenian Church; these were not merely rarified theological debates. Because the Church was the fount and focal point for Armenian national identity, the possibility of its incorporation by Eastern Orthodoxy was as threatening as Islamic secular domination.[78]

Why then did Gagik not model the visual expression of his kingship on that already established by the Bagratids? It may be suggested that any emulation of the Bagratid model, with its emphasis on the pious worthiness of the ruler, would have shown Gagik's pious persona in an undesirable light. Gagik could not hope to compare his piety favorably with that of the Bagratids; the martyrdom of Smbat I, his subsequent canonization, and the miraculous events associated with the site of his death all boosted the spiritual authority of the Bagratid kings to unparalleled heights.[79] In formulating a visual expression of kingship, Gagik was conceivably faced with limited options. He could emulate the visual expression of rulership associated with Bagratid portraiture, or he could construct a new expression of kingship by drawing from other sources. Gagik's use of the current Islamic iconography of power and his representation of Islamic regalia suggests that he made a conscious effort to distance the visual representation of his kingship from that associated with the Bagratid kings of Armenia. Viewed in this context, his choice of the Islamic paradigm is less surprising. The contemporary histories demonstrate that the Armenian princes and kings had personal knowledge of Islamic palaces and were the frequent recipients of lavish gifts bestowed by the caliph or his representatives. It is clear from this evidence that the Islamic representation of earthly power was familiar to the Armenian upper classes, and that its royal message was understood by its Armenian audience.

It has been suggested above that while the realities of Bagratid rule altered significantly in the early tenth century, the visual characterization of Bagratid kingship through ceremonial and portraiture remained essentially unchanged and continued to emphasize the piety of the kings of Armenia. The most powerful symbol of Bagratid rulership was their investiture by the catholicos. This Armenian ceremonial remained a paradigm that could not be copied and for which there existed no substitute. While Gagik Artsruni's royal portraits and his multiple investitures demonstrated his undeniable temporal power, he could not compete with the pious legitimacy enjoyed by the kings of Armenia, conferred upon them in a uniquely Armenian investiture ceremony.[80]

Georgia

The situation in Georgia in the ninth and tenth centuries has many parallels to that in Armenia in the same period as different families including many branches of the Bagrationi family sought to establish and demonstrate the legitimacy of their power. However, the nature of the surviving material dictates that it be examined in a different manner: the Georgian histories for this period were mostly compiled in the eleventh century and minimize all foreign involvement in Georgian history.[81] As a result they make no mention of the gift of robes to Georgian rulers. The few references to such acts that do exist are very brief and come in non-Georgian sources. Four contemporary Georgian images of rulers survive, and their evidence is consequently more important as a source for Georgian attitudes to the importance of dress in the depiction of power. As will become clear, Georgian and foreign sources differ considerably about the importance of robes in the conferring of legitimacy and the ways in which dress could manifest or construct different aspects of power.

The revival of local power in Georgia began at the turn of the eighth century in the west of the country, those regions furthest from possible Islamic interference. In Apkhazeti (Abasgia in Byzantine sources), members of the Anchabadze family rebelled against the declining Byzantine power in the region and established themselves as kings,[82] and to the south collateral branches of the Bagrationi family established themselves in the regions of Kartli (Iberia in Byzantine sources) and Tao-Klarjeti (which was itself divided among members of the family). This latter region lay on the border of the Byzantine empire, and most Byzantine evidence deals with the interaction between its rulers and the emperor. The eastern province of the country, Kakheti, was cut off from the west by the Arab emirate of Tbilisi and remained more firmly under Islamic influence.

The manner of the establishment of the two most powerful Georgian families is strikingly different: the Anchabadzes seized power for themselves in a vacuum, whereas the Bagrationis were granted lands: the Armenian chronicler Vardan Arewelc'i records that Ashot I Bagrationi (786–826) was given land by the caliph,[83] and was then confirmed in his possessions by the Byzantine emperor Michael I, who granted him the Byzantine court title of *kouropalates.*[84] In 888, the Georgian nobles appointed Ashot's great grandson, Adarnase II (ruled 888–923),[85] as king of Kartli (Iberia), a title that had been suspended since 580; and in 891 he was also granted the title of *kouropalates.*[86] The titles of king of Apkhazeti and king of Kartli seem to have become hereditary, but that of *kouropalates* was not: it, along with the many lesser Byzantine titles, such as *magistros* and *patrikios,* which were also bestowed on Bagrationi rulers, was an honor bestowed from Constantinople.[87] It is with these Byzantine honors and the robes that accompanied them that this part of the paper will mostly be concerned.

According to John Catholicos, Adarnase was crowned as king once more in 897/8 by Smbat I of Armenia: Smbat crowned Adarnase "king with great glory and proper ceremony, outfitting him in armor befitting kings."[88] Later, in 904 Smbat also gave robes and a crown to Adarnase's rival, king Constantine III of Apkhazeti (899–916): "he dressed him in royal robes, placed on his head a golden crown studded with pearls, and girdled his waist with a golden belt set with gems."[89] These ceremonies are similar to the Islamic-style rituals in which the Bagratids honored their nobles. Interestingly, both coronations happened at crucial points in the political and military emergence of Georgia and were largely dictated by Smbat's political needs. Smbat's recognition of Adarnase was bowing to the inevitable after his recognition by the Byzantine emperor and the caliph, and Constantine's was in an effort to gain the allegiance of the Apkhazetian ruler whose power was about to eclipse that of Adarnase as he took control of Kartli.[90] In these cases the gifts of robes and crowns represent the recognition of each ruler's power in Georgia rather than the investiture of their authority. Nevertheless, they both also demonstrate the influence of Armenia over Georgia at the start of the tenth century. The absence of any later such references suggest that this influence was soon to wane.

On Adarnase's death, his lands and titles were divided between his four sons, the eldest, Davit II,[91] becoming king of Kartli and the next Ashot IV,[92] receiving the title of *kouropalates.* The brothers had to defend their position against a number of potential enemies and invaders, including the kings of Armenia and Apkhazeti, the Byzantine emperor, their cousin, Gurgen II of Tao—who was already becoming more influential in Armenian politics,[93] and a third branch of the Bagrationi family based in the strategic and wealthy city of Artanuji, not to mention each other. It is against this complex background that the first mention of robes from a significant power comes: the gift of robes from Byzantium. These formed an increasingly important part of Byzantine diplomacy as the empire became more and more involved in the region.

The first reference comes in the *De administrando imperio,* the diplomatic handbook compiled by Constantine VII Porphyrogennetos in the 950s. This records that the emperor Romanos I Lekapenos (920–944) sent robes of rank to Gurgen II Bagrationi, *eristavi* (governor) of Tao,[94] in order to confer upon him the title of *magistros.*[95] The gift of robes was one part of a diplomatic embassy led by the patrician Constantine, lord admiral, *protospatharios,* and *lictor* in the mid-920s. The honor was to draw Gurgen closer into the Byzantine orbit and thus secure a potentially useful and increasingly powerful ally on the Byzantine eastern frontier. As a by-product, it also served to destabilize Gurgen's relations with his Bagrationi cousins and so keep power in Georgia relatively weak and fragmented. After the death of Adarnase II in 923, the title of *kouropalates* had fallen vacant and Adarnase's four sons were worried that Constantine would offer Gurgen the honor, which they considered should be conferred on one of them. In fact, the final result of Constantine's diplomatic mission was to draw these two rival branches of the family together: Constantine had an extra mission to annex the strategic Georgian city of Artanuji in the Chorokhi valley, and all the Bagrationis united to prevent this as they were determined to preserve the city and its wealth within the family. Romanos had to back down, and in his efforts to pacify the Georgians, he invited Ashot IV to Constantinople to receive the honor of *kouropalates.*[96]

The only other significant reference to the gift of robes also come in histories of Byzantium. They concern Davit II of Tao (961–1000),[97] who was the most important ruler in Georgia in the second half of the tenth century and a formidable builder and patron of the church. Davit was an important ally of Byzantium and seems to have received the rank of *magistros* at the start of his reign. In 979 his aid was vital to the suppression of the revolt of Bardas Skleros against Emperor Basil II (975–1025).[98] Cultural ties with Byzantium also became closer after the foundation of the monastery of Iviron on Mount Athos, which acted as a center for the translation of Greek theological texts into Georgian.[99] However, in 989 Davit joined the revolt of Bardas Phokas against Basil II. The revolt was defeated and, as part of the peace treaty that followed, Davit had to agree to cede his lands to Byzantium on his death. In return, he was confirmed in his position in Georgia and given the higher title of *kouropalates.* The title was accompanied by "sumptuous vestments."[100] Here the title and gifts seem to have been a sop to the Georgian ruler, confirming that normal relations had been restored but at the same time reminding Davit of his position.

Although no other examples of robes being conferred are recorded, it is probable that all such Byzantine promotions were accompanied by the gift of vestments of office. The *Kleterologion* of Philotheos, compiled in 899, emphasizes the importance of robes in the bestowal of these titles: it records that the insignia of the office of *kouropalates* were "a red chiton with gold ornament, a chlamys and a belt, solemnly bestowed by the hand of the emperor in a church of the Lord," and those of *magistros* were "a white chiton with gold epaulettes and a belt of red leather ornamented with precious stones, given by the hand of the emperor."[101] It is clear that in Constantinople vestments were vital to the expression and dignity of office. The sending of robes and different titles to Georgia extended this Byzantine ceremonial abroad, although it is noteworthy that this is not something recorded in the Georgian sources.

The impression given in the texts is that titles and the robes that accompanied them were used to denote power. And from the point of view of Byzantium, they were used to express hierarchical relationships to the imperial throne. By accepting titles from Byzantium and the robes that went with them, the Bagrationis were acknowledging their subordinate position in the Christian world presided over by the Byzantine emperor. In the same way that the Armenian Ashot I accepted robes and a crown from the caliph—and thereby admitted a theoretical (if no longer always actual) position within an Islamic world hierarchy, so too the Bagrationis of Tao-Klarjeti were admitting their junior place in the Byzantine hierarchy. But at the same time they were placing themselves above their family rivals.

Evidence to support this can be found in the Georgian sources, which do record the awarding of titles, if not the robes that accompanied them. Members of the Bagrationi family did not automatically assume the Byzantine titles of *kouropalates* or *magistros* as a hereditary right but instead had to appeal to the emperor for their bestowal.[102] Georgian rulers would even travel to Constantinople to receive the robes from the emperor's hands and thereby guarantee their own legitimacy. As we know from the story of Constantine's botched mission in the 920s, Ashot IV, son of Adarnase II, traveled west to receive the dignity of *kouropalates* from the hands of the emperor himself as part of the attempt to rebuild bridges in Georgio-Byzantine diplomacy.[103] Later in 1030/1, Mariam, the mother of Bagrat IV (1027–1072), traveled to Constantinople to secure the title of *kouropalates* for her son, although by this stage the chronicle claims that the title was "the custom and right of their house."[104]

This desire to accept titles demonstrates the importance and power they held, and there was fierce competition between the various branches of the Bagrationi family to claim them and the prestige that went with them. As such, titles and robes were double-edged swords, and Byzantium was quick to exploit this. The dispute between Gurgen II and Ashot IV for the rank of *kouropalates* shows the potential for open rivalry that the bestowal of titles could provoke. But robes could be manipulated in more insidious ways to provoke civil war and instability among the Bagrationis. One example is recorded in *Kartlis tskhovreba:* "Basil [II] gave them titles: to Gurgen[105] that of *magistros,* and to [his son] Bagrat[106] that of *kouropalates,* so that he might cause mutual enmity between father and son. For by these means he plotted evil. But Gurgen was true and sincere, not at all was his heart perturbed through this ruse, nor through these means was he affected."[107] By promoting the son above the father Basil hoped to ferment a new civil war between Tao-Klarjeti and Kartli, the different regions that the two men then controlled as part of his policy of divide and rule on the frontier.

Titles, then, placed Georgians within a hierarchy of Christian power that could be exploited to enhance, demonstrate, or even diminish authority. Robes were clearly used to signify power, but their transformative power was limited. In Georgian sources, most concern seems to have surrounded the choice of person for any particular title. After that the value of vestments was to provide an outward confirmation of power.

This conclusion finds support in the visual evidence concerning the robes of Georgian rulers in the tenth century, although, as will become clear, this evidence is itself very complex and often at odds with the non-Georgian textual record.

Four images of Bagrationi rulers in Tao-Klarjeti survive from the tenth century. All are donor images associated with the founding or rebuilding of monasteries and churches. As such they are primarily records of piety, but the very fact of their existence demonstrates the donors' concern to commemorate themselves and to display their wealth, position, and devotion to the church. Two images show the sons of Adarnase II, the first king of Kartli (Ashot IV and Davit II at Opiza; Sumbat I at Dolisqana); the third depicts his great-grandsons (Davit III and his brother Bagrat at Oshki). The fourth is of a minor member of another branch of the family, Ashot Kukhi at Tbeti.[108]

The most striking image is that from the monastic church at Opiza in Tao-Klarjeti. In the aftermath of the devastating Arab invasions of the eighth century and under the leadership of the monk St. Gregory of Khandzta, Opiza had played a central role in the revival of the economy and culture of Tao-Klarjeti. Consequently it was much supported by members of the Bagrationi family from the reign of Ashot I onwards.[109] In the

Figure 7.5. Opiza. Donor relief of Ashot IV *kouropalates* and Davit II, king and *magistros,* before Christ (923–937 CE). State Museum of Fine Arts, Tbilisi.

early tenth century, the principal church was substantially remodeled, and a donor panel was set up on the south facade of the church to commemorate this. It is carved on two large blocks of stone (57x64, 58x64cm), and now survives in the State Museum of Fine Arts in Tbilisi (figure 7.5).[110] The left hand panel shows Ashot IV *kouropalates* offering the church to Christ. Christ, seated in majesty, his right hand stretched out to bless the church Ashot offers, dominates the right hand block. Squeezed in at the right-hand edge of this panel is a third figure labeled as Davit, who was Ashot's elder brother, and who held the titles of king of Kartli and *magistros* after the death of his father in 923.

Ashot and Davit wear identical clothes: both have boots with pointed toes, and their robes have stiff triangular collars with buttonlike attachments and a lozenge shaped belt. Other details are lost in the stylistic representation of the robes. These are depicted as a series of gently curving, parallel ridges that produce wonderful abstract patterns and almost totally ignore any attempt to delineate the shape of the cloth or the way it falls over the body. Neither ruler has a crown or halo, and the inscriptions name the three men only as "Ashot," "Jesus Christ," and "Davit." The fourth and most prominent, inscription beneath the building names it as "church."[111]

The figure of Christ is shown essentially in the same way as the two donors, but his clothes are less distinct (there are no identifiable individual features, such as the collar or belt). His authority derives from his halo, his throne, his book, and his gesture of blessing toward the church. All emphasis in the image is on gesture. Hands dominate the panels, while faces and dress are shown with little attempt at differentiation or individualism.

What is immediately apparent from the image is the absence of interest in the depiction of the material trappings of hierarchy and power. This image was, after all, erected by the sons of the first king of Georgia in 300 years, yet there is virtually no indication of the two men's power. Ashot does not name himself as *kouropalates* in this image (although this is probably because of constrictions of space, as he did employ his title in several other inscriptions in the church),[112] and more significantly not only does he not show himself wearing the robes to which he was entitled, but he makes no attempt to distinguish his rank from that of his brother. Given that it was Ashot who traveled to Constantinople in the aftermath of the patrician Constantine's failed mission in order to receive his titles and robes from the emperor, this absence is notable. Ashot needed the emperor's support to demonstrate the source of his authority and, more crucially, to reassert his superiority over his cousin Gurgen II of Tao. Robes acted as the visible manifestation of his right to rule and his superiority over his cousins, yet this sculpture in the most prominent position in one of the most important monasteries in the province makes no reference to it.

It is this panel that also lies behind much of the confusion about the relative seniority of Georgian titles. Davit, the elder brother, had nominally the senior title (*mepe,* or king), yet he is in much the junior position in the image. At the same time he had an inferior Byzantine title (*magistros*), yet no differentiation in rank is apparent. Can Ashot's prominence be solely due to his possibly greater involvement in the rebuilding of the monastery, or was it that his Byzantine title of *kouropalates* carried greater authority?

A similar lack of interest in questions of rank and position can be seen in the image of the youngest of the four sons of Adarnase II, Sumbat I.[113] This image survives *in situ* on the southeast side of the drum of the small church of Dolisqana (figure 7.6). After the deaths of his brothers Davit (d. 937) and then Bagrat (d. 945), Sumbat inherited the title of king of Kartli, after which he built and ornamented the church.[114] Later in 954, when Ashot IV died, Smbat received the title of *kouropalates.*

The image at Dolisqana provides even fewer details about the status of the ruler than that at Opiza. Smbat is shown holding a model of his church, but his figure is depicted in a very crude manner. His robes are merely blocked out in the stone and enlivened only by a series of shallow grooves that are meant to delineate the nature of his dress. Moreover, the image is very small and hard to see clearly in its location high up on the

Figure 7.6. Dolisqana. Donor relief of King Smbat I on southeast side of drum of church (945–954 CE). Photograph by Antony Eastmond.

side of the drum of the church. The only clue to Smbat's actual status comes in the inscription that accompanies the image and is repeated around the window of the south transept of the church. This names Sumbat as king: "Christ exalt our king Sumbat."[115] Once again, any interest in

Figure 7.7. Tbeti. Donor relief of Ashot Kukhi (891–918 CE). State Museum of Fine Arts, Tbilsi.

the appearance of power is denied in the official image of the ruler; the display of piety seems to be the overriding concern.

The extraordinary nature of the images at Opiza and Dolisqana is brought into sharp relief by reference to the one surviving earlier Georgian royal image. This is the donor relief set up by Ashot Kukhi, who held the Georgian title *eristavt-eristavi* (senior provincial governor) and was uncle of Gurgen II.[116] The image comes from the cathedral of Tbeti, which was founded by Ashot Kukhi between 891 and 918, but it is now to be found in the State Museum of Fine Arts in Tbilisi (figure 7.7).[117]

The relief is carved with extraordinary realism and a great concern to depict the details of Ashot's dress. Ashot wears a long-sleeved surcoat embroidered with lions over a chequered tunic. He has heavy boots and wears a turban. Fragments of a halo behind his head demonstrate that he was depicted as possessed of divine as well as earthly authority. Originally, he probably held a model of the cathedral in front of him. The device of a heavily patterned outer garment in imitation of woven silk is similar to that worn by the Armenian Gagik at the contemporary church of Aght'amar (figure 7.4), although its long-sleeved shape is very different: this seems to reflect much older Caucasian traditions, such as the long-sleeved robes worn by donors as seen on seventh-century monuments in the region, such as at Mren in Armenia or Jvari in Mtskheta, the old capital of Georgia.[118] No satisfactory interpretation of Ashot's robes has yet been achieved, largely because almost nothing is known about his history: only two chronicle references mention him, both as founder of Tbeti.[119] Otherwise, he was totally eclipsed by his nephew, Gurgen II. Given that this image was set up during the peak time of Armenian involvement in Georgian affairs—when Sumbat I gave royal regalia to both the kings of Kartli and Apkhazeti—it may reflect Armenian ceremonial, although no record of any such link with Ashot Kukhi survives. Equally, however, these robes may present Ashot's own perception of his power rather than one that derived from the authority invested in robes given by the Byzantine emperor, the caliph, or the Armenian king.

The importance of the image lies in its overall concern for the accurate depiction of robes, all the elements of which seem to be imbued with the symbolism of power. The existence of such an image in an important ecclesiastical center in Tao-Klarjeti in the decade before the creation of the donor panel at Opiza shows that there must have been a radical change in perceptions of art in the intervening years and, more critically, a re-evaluation of the value of displaying ceremonial robes as a sign of status.[120] The precarious position of the Bagrationi family at this time rules out any political reason for such a change, as these rulers were not yet in a position to promote themselves as an independent power, even if only visually. To ascribe the change only to artistic decisions is also an insufficient explanation.

The final images add a further layer of complexity to this picture. They come from the cathedral of Oshki, the largest and architecturally most complex Georgian building of the tenth century. The church was founded in 963—less than a decade after Dolisqana was completed—by Davit III and his brother Bagrat, the grandsons of Bagrat I (the third son of Adarnase II).[121] Oshki was begun very early in the brothers' joint reigns, at a time when Davit held the Byzantine title of *magistros* and his younger brother that of *eristavt-eristavi*.[122] The cathedral was finished after ten years in 973, but in the meantime Bagrat had died in 966. Two images of the brothers survive: one on a large donation panel on the south facade of the church, the other bust portraits on either side of a niche in the southwest pier beneath the dome of the church facing the apse. Both seem to have been erected while both brothers were alive, in the years 963 to 966.[123]

The external image is the most impressive (figure 7.8): it is just under life size (the figures are 1.46m tall) and shows the brothers flanking the Mother of God and St. John the Baptist, who intercede with Christ in the center.[124] Davit's and Bagrat's robes and crowns are depicted with great care, and each holds a model of the cathedral. The contrast with the images of their great uncles at Opiza and Dolisqana is immediate and striking. There has been an absolute return to a concern for realism and detail.

However, unlike the image of Ashot Kukhi from Tbeti, the origins of the dress of Davit and Bagrat can be much more precisely described and analyzed. The brothers wear recognizably Byzantine dress. Davit, who stands on the senior, right-hand side of Christ, wears, clasped over his left shoulder, a chlamys that sits on top of a long-sleeved tunic. The chlamys is decorated with roundels containing birds, and the tunic has palmette roundels. On his head Davit wears a low, flat crown decorated with jewels in a similar pattern to those on the hems of his chlamys and undertunic. Bagrat also wears a chlamys and tunic, both decorated with roundels containing geometric patterns. Bagrat's crown is of the same design as Davit's, but with one important addition: broad, flat pendilia hang down from either side of the crown.[125] The images of Davit and Bagrat inside the church are much smaller than those on the south facade, and consequently contain much less detail (each is 40cm tall), but seem to repeat the tunics and crowns worn on the external images.[126]

Robes here take on a great significance in any attempt to analyze the relationship between the brothers and Byzantium. In 979, Basil II was to turn to Davit as an ally for help in suppressing the revolt of Bardas Skleros, but before that Davit and Bagrat seem to have been regarded in the same way as their Bagrationi predecessors: as merely client rulers whose authority was

Figure 7.8. Oshki. Donor relief of Davit II *magistros* and Bagrat *eristavt-eristavi,* on south facade (963–966 CE). Photograph by Antony Eastmond.

ultimately dependent on Byzantium. But in this image both brothers have chosen to be portrayed in robes of far higher status than their positions in the Byzantine world hierarchy would permit. As was seen from the list in the *Kleterologion,* the robes of *magistros* did not include the chlamys—that was reserved for the ranks of *kouropalates* or above. And more significantly, no one below the person of the emperor was permitted to add pendilia to his crown. Given that we know that Davit received robes of rank when appointed to the rank of *kouropalates* in 989, we may assume that he also received the robes of *magistros* on his accession in 961. But these robes are ignored in the image in favor of far more elevated regalia. So why should the brothers presume so much symbolic power so early in their reigns, and why should they be so interested in displaying it in visual form? Do the images represent a usurpation of imperial authority, as Wachtang Djobadze has concluded?[127]

The little we know of the early years of Davit's and Bagrat's joint reigns gives no hint of any policies as ambitious as the robes they wear might indicate. Only the series of large churches they commissioned, such as Oshki, Khakhuli, or Otkhta Eklesia, and the brothers' closer cultural links with Byzantium give any clues as to the extent of their ambition.[128] Davit alone comes to prominence and only after 979. It is impossible to see these robes in any literal way. Like those of Ashot Kukhi, the brothers' robes seem to be a fiction, although a considerably more realistic one this time. It is possible that the Georgian audience to whom these images were addressed was not well versed in the finer details of Constantinopolitan court protocol, so the brothers could display their potential grandiose political ambitions in their dress. However, the images seem not to have offended Basil II. In the 1020s, Oshki came under Byzantine control, and the emperor twice gave it money for repairs—without ever requiring that such "incorrect" images be altered or removed.[129] It seems that these robes should not be read literally as the usurpation of Byzantine power; rather they were the usurpation of any device to enhance prestige, regardless of any inherent meaning. It is possible that it was the Bagrationis' increasingly close links with the Byzantine world and especially the powerful Phokas family that encouraged this renewed interest in the accurate display of power, but even this cannot explain the radical change from Opiza and Dolisqana to Oshki.[130]

Another intractable problem lies in the relation between the brothers themselves. Davit has gone down in history as the more important figure largely because he survived his brother by thirty-four years and was to play a large role both in Byzantine politics and in the unification of Georgia under Bagrat III. He held the senior title at the outset of their reign—*magistros* as opposed to *eristavt-eristavi*—and in the image is shown in the more prestigious position to the right of Christ. However, details of the image seem also to point to Bagrat as the more important figure, since it is only he who has the pendilia hanging from his crown. This apparent reversal of seniority is comparable to that at Opiza. Further evidence for this can be found in one other—now lost—image from the cathedral of Ishkhani. This was a wall painting seen in 1917 by the Georgian scholar Ekvtime Taqaishvili, who recorded its details.[131] It showed Bagrat *eristavt-eristavi* standing next to his father, Adarnase III *kouropalates,* and his grandfather, Bagrat *magistros* and king of Kartli (the third son of Adarnase II). The image must date from after 958, when Adarnase III received his title of *kouropalates.* Interestingly, it did not include Davit, the elder brother. It suggests that Bagrat was being groomed as successor by his father during his lifetime. In 961 the brothers joined forces to force their father to abdicate and retire to a monastery, where he soon died, and it seems that in the aftermath of this Davit asserted his seniority, although never completely. In the image at Oshki the textual and visual references to rank seem to balance each other out. It suggests that the internal politics and the source of power of Tao-Klarjeti in the 960s were far more complex than now appears from the chronicle records.

The visual evidence of Georgian rulers in the tenth century provides no clear argument about the importance of robes in the display or gaining of power in Georgia. At first sight, this seems to accord with the Georgian sources, which make no reference to robes; but clearly the position is more complex than that. Robes were used by the Bagrationis to display their power to their subjects but never in a literal way. Power relationships were manipulated through the positioning of rulers in the images and through the adoption or creation of robes to convey new messages about the authority of the Bagrationis. Equally, the evidence from non-Georgian sources indicates that the gift of robes to the Bagrationis was important for the maintenance of their position within an international hierarchy of power. These two positions are difficult to reconcile. It would seem that the Bagrationis were very concerned to have their authority recognized by their most powerful neighbors, whether that be Armenia at the start of the tenth century or Byzantium at other times, but that they regarded the title that was awarded as the most significant aspect of that recognition. Robes were an outward sign of power that was open for manipulation. In 904 Constantine III of Apkhazeti took control of Kartli, leaving its king ruler in name only. Despite this and the growing power of the Bagrationis in Tao-Klarjeti, the kings of Kartli retained symbolic, if never actual, authority. And at the end of the century it was on the figure of the king that all machinations for the unification of Georgia centered. Ultimately, power lay with the title and not its appearance. Robes were no more than the outward dressing of that power, and one that could be ignored or manipulated at will.

Notes

Lynn Jones would like to acknowledge the support of a Fellowship for Teachers and Independent Scholars from the National Endowment for the Humanities and to thank the staff of the Byzantine library at Dumbarton Oaks, Washington, D.C. This material comes in part from a forthcoming book examining the visual expression of medieval Armenian kingship.

1. Bagrationi is, in fact, the Georgian equivalent of Bagratid, and will be used in this paper to distinguish the Georgian and the Armenian branches. Some Georgian historians, such as P. Ingoroqva, *Giorgi Merchule* (Tbilisi: Metsniereba, 1954), pp. 76–80, have sought to deny the Armenian descent of the Bagrationis (for a summary see K. Salia, *History of the Georgian Nation* (Paris: Orientaliste, 1980), pp. 127–31), but this has been conclusively demolished by C. Toumanoff, *Studies in Christian Caucasian History* (Georgetown : Georgetown University Press, 1963), 334–36, 407–28.
2. The date of the Armenian-Byzantine break remains the subject of great debate. I follow the chronology proposed by Nina Garsoïan, "Quelques précisions préliminaries sur le schisme entre les Eglises byzantine et armenienne au sujet du Concile de Chalcédoine, III: Les évéchés méridionaux limitrophes de las Mésopotamie," *Revue des Études arméniennes* 23 (1992): 39–80; and "Quelques précisions préliminaires sur le schisme entre les Eglises byzantine et armenienne au sujet du Concile de Chalcédoine, II: La date et les circonstances de las rupture," *L'Arménie et Byzance, Histoire et culture* (Paris, 1996), 99–112.
3. During the reign of Ashot I the *ostikanate* of Armenia was allowed to lapse, and of the former duties expected from Armenian nobility only the collection of taxes remained in place. During the reign of Ashot I's son, Smbat I, the *ostikanates* of Armenia and Azerbaijan were joined, reinstating direct Islamic control over the country. The *ostikan*'s primary residence was in Partaw, in present-day Azerbaijan. The fundamental study of Islamic administration of Armenia, and of Armenian-Islamic interactions, is Aram Ter-Ghewondyan, *The Arab Emirates in Bagratid Armenia,* trans. Nina Garsoïan (Lisbon: Livraria Bertrand, 1976).
4. Yovhannes Drasxanakertc'i, *History of Armenia,* trans. Krikor H. Maksoudian (Atlanta: Scholars Press, 1987), 125. For Bagratid presiding princes in the period preceding the war see Joseph Laurent, *L'Arménie entre Byzance et l'Islam depuis la conquête arabe jusqu'en 886* (Paris: Fontemoing et cie, 1919), rev. Marius Canard (Lisbon: Librarie Bertrand, 1980), 406. All subsequent citations refer to the revised edition.
5. Laurent, *L'Arménie,* 406; Thomas Artsruni, *History of the House of the Artsrunik',* trans. Robert W. Thomson (Detroit: Wayne State University Press, 1985), 270. In 480 CE the Sasanians eradicated the last Arsacid king of

Armenia; in the subsequent four hundred years Armenia was contested by Byzantium, Sasanid Persia, and the Umayyad and Abbasid caliphates.

6. Gagik's mother Sop'i was the daughter of Ashot I. The marriage was intended to conciliate the Artsrunis after they were forced by the caliph to recognize Ashot I as presiding prince. Artsruni, *History,* 270–71; Drasxanakertc'i, *History,* 127.
7. Drasxanakertc'i, *History,* 8, 232. The text reflects his shift in patronage. At first critical of Gagik Artsruni, the catholicos later praises him and notes the deficiencies of Bagratid rule.
8. Two further anonymous continuators take the history beyond the life of Gagik Artsruni; see the comments by R. Thomson in Artsruni, *History,* 16–17.
9. In the descriptions of ceremonies elevating *nakharars* to less than royal status a crown is included only once, in the investiture accorded to Gurgen Artsruni in 852. Gurgen's investiture was a ploy; three days later he was captured and sent to Samarra. The intent to deceive explains the inclusion of a crown, which is properly seen as an enticement meant to lure Gurgen and to insure his capture. Ibid., 216–17.
10. The ceremonial presentation of robes by the Baghdad caliphate is considered in chapter 6 of this volume by Dominique Sourdel.
11. In 852 the caliph al-Mutawakkil (847–861) waged war against the *nakharars* who had united in rebellion against the imposition of new taxes. Those who were not killed in battle were captured and imprisoned in Samarra, then the capital of the Abbasid caliphate. In 858 the caliph, faced with the threat of Byzantine incursions into Armenian territory, released some *nakharars* on the provision that they assist in repelling the perceived aggression. For the Armenian rebellion, captivity in Samarra, and release see ibid., 189–277; Drasxanakertc'i, *History,* 116–26.
12. Artsruni, *History,* 264–66. Only one horse was presented because only the younger prince Derenik, Gagik's father, was actually allowed to return to Armenia after the ceremony; Derenik's father Ashot was released several years later. This small detail inspires confidence in Thomas's account.
13. Ibid., 265–66. Other examples of Artsruni investitures confirm that the ceremony accorded to Ashot and Derenik Artsruni was representative. For the investiture of Gurgen Artsruni, see ibid., 216; for that of Gurgen, son of Apupelch, see ibid., 262.
14. Drasxanakertc'i, *History,* 125. The quasi-royal status granted by this title is documented by the catholicos, who notes that after Ashot's appointment, all *nakharars* aspired to marry into the Bagratid house in order to "be distinguished from the other *nakharar* houses, as members of the royal family." Ibid., 126.
15. Ibid., 157. The catholicos was also honored at the same time by the *ostikan,* who presented him with "robes suitable for a man in my position" and a mule adorned with golden ornaments; evidence that the Islamic ceremony was not only employed to grant an increase in rank, but was also used to

recognize existing status. The temporal powers of the Armenian catholicos are discussed more fully below and in n. 29.

16. For the standardization of ceremonial by the Abbasid caliphate see Aziz Al-Azmeh, *Muslim Kingship: Power and the Sacred in Muslim, Christian, and Pagan Politics* (London: I. B. Taurus, 1997), 134–35.
17. There was no precedent for the internal election or appointment of an Armenian king. In classical Armenia, kingship was designated and supported by the controlling foreign power, and unless removed, succession was hereditary within the designated family. During this period the royal families of Armenia were most often collateral branches of the suzerain dynasty; the Bagratids were, strictly speaking, the first Armenian kings. In the classical period the Bagratids were the equivalent of coronants, and thus in the ninth century could not lay any historical claim to royal status. See [Ps.] P'awstos Buzand, *The Epic Histories Attributed to P'awstos Buzand [Buzandaran Patmut'iwnk'],* trans. and commentary by N. Garsoïan (Cambridge, MA, 1989) 5.44, pp. 228–29; C. Toumanoff, *Christian Caucausian History,* 139; C. Toumanoff, "The Third-Century Armenian Arsacids: A Chronological and Genealogical Commentary," *Revue des Études arméniennes* 6 (1969): 243.
18. Drasxanakertc'i, *History,* 128.
19. Ibid.
20. Ibid., 132.
21. Ibid.
22. Ibid. The "place of assembly" referred to by the catholicos indicates an outdoor setting and has military connotations.
23. The location of Ashot I's Armenian investiture is not specified, but is believed to have been at Bagaran, the current Bagratid capital. Ibid., 274 n. 6; Ter-Ghewondyan, *Arab Emirates,* 59. For Smbat I, the catholicos clearly states that the Armenian investiture took place in a church which he does not identify; the location again is certainly Bagaran. Drasxanakertc'i, *History,* 132. No location is specified for Ashot II's investiture in 918, Drasxanakertc'i, *History,* 205.
24. There is no evidence that the catholicos participated in or was present for the Islamic investiture of robes and crown. Similarly, there is no evidence for the participation or presence of the *ostikan* in the Armenian ceremony.
25. In Abbasid ceremonial the crown was reserved for military recognition of victorious commanders and was not used by the caliph, for whom it was deemed inappropriate; see Al-Azmeh, *Muslim Kingship,* 12. This exclusive use supports the interpretation of its symbolic message, in the Armenian context, as one concerned solely with the temporal power of the king.
26. This is confirmed by the catholicos' characterization of Smbat I's Armenian investiture as "spiritual nuptials." Drasxanakertc'i, *History,* 132.
27. For a discussion of the textual sources and bibliography see Averil Cameron, "The Construction of Court Ritual: The Byzantine Book of

Ceremonies," in *Rituals of Royalty,* ed. David Cannadine and S. Price (Cambridge: Cambridge University Press, 1987), 106–36.

28. S. Peter Cowe, forthcoming, and "New Light on the Evolution of the Byzantine Coronation Liturgy," Abstracts of the Twenty-Second Annual Byzantine Studies Conference, October 24–27, 1996, University of North Carolina at Chapel Hill (Chapel Hill, N.C: University at Chapel Hill, 1997), 11.
29. John Catholicos, for example, represented Bagratid kings in their negotiations with the *ostikan;* see Drasxanakertc'i, History, 163–66. For the catholicos' role in Armenian-Byzantine diplomacy, see ibid., 198. For examples of the catholicos as judge and arbiter of civil disputes, see Artsruni, *History,* 269–70, 284, 286; Drasxanakertc'i, *History,* 154, 202, 204–5.
30. Drasxanakertc'i, *History,* 64. The texts note that many additional crowns and robes were sent to each of the Bagratid kings by the caliph and the *ostikan* during their reigns. As there is no mention of supplementary coronations or investitures associated with these gifts, they are properly seen as honoring the recipients and confirming their temporal status. Ibid., 155, 157. Only Ashot II received additional, formal affirmation of his royal status. After the *ostikan* Yusuf was imprisoned and replaced by Subuk, the latter executed a peace treaty with Ashot in which the king, according to the catholicos, was "granted" the title *shahanshah* (king of kings). The text makes no mention of any coronation or investiture. *Shahanshah* is an Iranian title, and as it was not granted to previous Bagratid kings it seems to have been resurrected specifically to acknowledge Ashot II's preeminence over Gagik Artsruni and the Bagratid anti-king. Ibid., 212, 303 n. 5.
31. Ibid., 151, 159.
32. More frequently, the Bagratid king granted honors and titles to members of the Armenian nobility. The textual descriptions of these ceremonies are brief and neither document nor disprove the emulation of Islamic ceremonial for the bestowal of lesser honors. Artsruni, *History,* 291, 298, 301.
33. Drasxanakertc'i, *History,* 129.
34. Constantine VII Porphyrogenitos, *De ceremoniis aulae byzantinae,* ed. J. J. Reiske (Bonn, 1829–30), II, 48.129. The emperor, considered to be Christ's representative on earth and therefore without equal, did not officially recognize the claim of foreign rulers to the status of king; hence the literal translation of the Armenian title. Because the Armenian rulers were not granted royal status, crowns were not among the imperial gifts. This effectively rules out the possibility that the Armenian investiture of a Bagratid king featured Byzantine crowns.
35. Drasxanakertc'i, *History,* 138. There is no evidence that Smbat visited the Byzantine capital; like his father, he must have received the title from an imperial envoy sent to Armenia. The awarding of the same title to Smbat's son, Ashot II, is discussed below.
36. Ibid., 158.

37. Ibid., 162–63. The catholicos also notes that Yusuf, scheming to dissolve the unanimity between Smbat and Gagik, did not immediately reveal the fact of Gagik's kingship, and that "after a few months," in 908, Gagik returned to Partaw and was "once again crowned by Yusuf." Ibid., 164.
38. Artsruni, *History,* 347–48.
39. Ibid. This version also suggests a different chronology from that presented by the catholicos. According to the anonymous, Gagik was crowned only after the *ostikan* had captured and imprisoned Smbat I in 913. No mention is made of Gagik's role in Smbat's capture. According to the text it was Smbat's imprisonment that left Armenia in need of a king. This chronological manipulation allowed the historian to present Gagik's elevation as necessary for the preservation of the country, and avoided his presentation as a usurper.
40. Although the exact place of Gagik's ceremony is not recorded, as it occurred in Partaw it is unlikely to have taken place in a church.
41. Drasxanakertc'i, *History,* 163, 164, 208.
42. Artsruni, *History,* 348. This also confirms that the importance of the catholicos' role in the investiture of Armenian kings, as conveyed in the *History of Armenia,* does not simply reflect the identity of the author.
43. Ibid., 348–49; Drasxanakertc'i, *History,* 163, 164, 208. The *ostikan,* by fostering enmity between the two most powerful Armenian families, hoped to increase his power and thereby establish his autonomy from the caliph.
44. Artsruni, *History,* 348.
45. Ibid. Gagik's father was a prince, and not a king. His mother was the daughter of Ashot I (see above, n. 6). It is doubtful that the anonymous is referring, however obliquely, to Gagik's maternal grandfather; he is rather inflating Gagik's lineage and therefore his right to royal status.
46. Drasxanakertc'i, *History,* 167–69, 173–77. The anonymous continuator omits any mention of Gagik's alliance with the *ostikan,* and implies that Smbat's capture and murder were achieved by the *ostikan* alone. He also blames Smbat for provoking the *ostikan*'s attack by refusing to negotiate peace treaties or to pay the yearly tax, "as the Lord commanded." Artsruni, *History,* 347.
47. The *ostikan* "crowned the *sparapet* of Armenia as king, and gird up his loins with a sword" in the city of Duin. Drasxanakertc'i, *History,* 202. This is evidently the same Islamic ceremony we have encountered above.
48. Ibid., 179, 294 n. 17. Gurgen is discussed below.
49. The date of Ashot II's imperial visit has been much contested; the arguments are summarized in Steven Runciman, *The Emperor Romanus Lecapenus and His Reign* (Cambridge: Cambridge University Press, 1929), 249–52. I follow the chronology proposed by Adontz, which is now generally accepted by scholars. Nikolai Adontz, *Etudes arméno-byzantines* (Lisbon: Livraria Bertrand, 1965), 265–66.
50. Drasxanakertc'i, *History,* 198. The emperor was Constantine VII Porphyrogenitos, who, as a minor, was undoubtedly represented by his mother the Empress Zoë, who served as her son's regent from 914–919.

51. Ibid.
52. Ibid., 202.
53. For the possible motivations behind the *ostikan*'s abrupt decision to support Ashot II, see Ter-Ghewondyan, *Arab Emirates,* 73–74.
54. Drasxanakertc'i, 205. It is interesting that there was no gift of robes; it is unclear whether this reflects their relative lack of importance, the hasty preparations for the ceremony, or the possibility that the *ostikan*'s presence was required for investiture of robes. It will be remembered from the preceding pages that robes are not mentioned in the description of Ashot I's investiture.
55. For the coronations of Ashot I and Smbat I there is no evidence that Islamic crowns were used in the Armenian investitures; the text is more ambiguous concerning the use of robes. In John Catholicos's description of Smbat I's investiture it is not clear whether the robes "wrought with gold" presented by the *ostikan* were the same as the "gold-embroidered robes covered with expressive designs" with which the catholicos invested Smbat. Ibid., 132.
56. There are, for instance, multiple surviving examples of Byzantine portraits that depict the emperor receiving his crown from the hand of God. For an ivory panel depicting the emperor Constantine VII Porphyrogenitos crowned by Christ, see Adolf Goldschmidt and Kurt Weitzmann,, *Die Byzantinischen Elfenbeinskulpturen des X.-XIII. Jahrhunderts* (Berlin: Deutsche Verlag fur Kunstwissenschaft, 1930), no. 35; 35–36. For a manuscript portrait depicting Constantine IX Monomachos crowned by Christ, see Iohannes Spatharakis, *The Portrait in Byzantine Illuminated Manuscripts* (Leiden: E. J. Brill, 1976), 99–102, fig. 66. For an illumination of Constantine and his empress, Eudokia, crowned by Christ see ibid., 102–106, fig. 68; for an illumination depicting John II Komnenos and his eldest son Alexios being crowned by Christ see ibid., 79–83, fig. 46. A manuscript portrait of an imperial family, including the crowning of the emperor by Christ, is discussed in Jeffrey Anderson, Paul Canart, and Christopher Walter, *The Barberini Psalter. Codex Vaticanus Barberinianus Graecus 372* (Zurich: Belser Verlag, 1989), 15ff., 55–56. An enamel on the Khakhuli Triptych now in the State Museum of Fine Arts in Tbilisi shows Michael VII Doukas and his Georgian empress, Maria, being crowned by Christ; Shalva Amiranashvili, *Medieval Georgian Enamels of Russia,* trans. F. Hirsch and J. Ross, (New York: Abrams, 1964), 93–111.
57. The church of Mren, dating to the second or third decade of the seventh century, retains depictions of the prince Nerseh Kamsarakan and the prince David Saharuni. See Nicole and Michel Thierry, "La Cathédral de Mrèn et sa décoration," *Cahiers Archéologiques* 24 (1975): 73–114. A prince of Siwnik is depicted in the church at Sisavan, dated to 691; see Lucy Der Manuelian, "Armenian Sculptural Images, Fifth to Eighth Centuries," in *Classical Armenian Culture,* University of Pennsylvania Armenian Texts and Studies 4, ed. Thomas J. Samuelian (Chico, CA: Scholars Press, 1984), 185, plate 6. Nothing survives from the eighth and ninth centuries.

58. Ashot II was followed in succession by his brother, Abas, who ruled from 928/29–952.
59. For bibliography see O. Kh. Ghalpaktchian and Adrian Alpago-Novello, *Sanahin,* Documents in Armenian Architecture 3 (Milan: Edizioni Ares, 1980). The portraits have been differently interpreted by Helen Evans, "Kings and Power Bases: Sources for Royal Portraits in Cilician Armenia," in *From Byzantium to Iran: In Honour of Nina Garsoïan,* ed. Jean-Pierre Mahé and Robert W. Thomson (Atlanta: Scholars Press, 1997), 485–507, esp. 488. Evans suggests that the peaked headdresses worn by the princes at Sanahin are meant to imitate Byzantine crowns, and cites as supporting evidence a thirteenth-century Armenian history that records the gift of a crown to Ashot I in 887 by the emperor Basil I. As has been discussed above and in n. 34, no such imperial gifts are recorded in the surviving contemporary Armenian histories.
60. The church was constructed between 976 and 991. The images at Haghbat are carved in much higher relief than their sculptural counterparts at Sanahin. Step'an Mnats'akanian and A. Alpago-Novello, *Haghbat,* Documents in Armenian Architecture 1 (Milan: Edizioni Ares, 1980), 12.
61. Their placement may also reflect their status. The elder brother, Smbat, is to the viewer's right. If a figure of Christ, for example, is imagined accepting the symbolic offer of the church presented by the two princes, Smbat would be on Christ's favored side, at his right hand.
62. The turbans featured here and in the sculpture from Ani, discussed immediately below, reflect the previous assimilation of Islamic modes of dress into the Armenian aristocracy. A turban is also depicted in the portrait of the Georgian Ashot Kuhki, discussed below. This image is dated to 891–918, attesting to the assimilation of turbans in the period contemporary with the first three Bagratid kings of Armenia. It therefore provides supporting evidence that, like their late tenth-century counterparts, the lost portraits of the earliest Bagratid kings of Armenia could also have featured turbans as a sign of royal rank. For a discussion of the contemporary and later use of such "Islamic" dress in Byzantium, see Cyril Mango, "Discontinuity with the Classical Past in Byzantium," in *Byzantium and the Classical Tradition,* ed. Margaret Mullett and Roger Scott (Birmingham: University of Birmingham, 1981) 48–57, esp. 51–52.
63. Nikolai Marr, the supervising archaeologist, suggested that the sculpture was originally located on the north facade of the church. Nikolai Marr, *O rasopkak i rabotax' v' Ani letom 1906 goda,* vol. 10 of *Teksty i razyskaniia po armianogruzinskoi filologii* (St. Petersburg: n.p., 1907), 18–20, figs. 13, 15; Paul Cuneo and A. Alpago-Novello, eds., *Ani,* Documents of Armenian Architecture 12 (Milan, 1984), 92–93.
64. While it is possible that the robes worn by the princes at Sanahin and Haghbat were originally embellished with painted decoration and therefore may have imitated either Islamic or Byzantine embroidered textiles, it should be noted that the dress is not Islamic *in form,* as it is for a portrait

of Gagik Artsruni discussed below. The absence of Byzantine costume is not surprising, as the division between the Byzantine and Armenian Churches rendered it impossible for any Armenian ruler to be depicted on an Armenian Orthodox Church wearing such dress, a difficulty discussed below.

65. The church is all that survives of the tenth-century city of Aght'amar, which originally also featured a royal palace, princely residences, treasuries, gardens, fortified walls, and an enclosed harbor. This is described in Artsruni, *History,* 354–58. Two subsidiary chapels were added to the northeast of the church sometime after the early fourteenth century, and the southern bell tower and the western chapel were added in the eighteenth or early nineteenth centuries. For a discussion of these later constructions see Sirarpie Der Nersessian, *Aght'amar, Church of the Holy Cross* (Cambridge: Cambridge University Press, 1965), 9–10.
66. These birds, with their short beaks and plump bodies, do not appear elsewhere on the Church of the Holy Cross, indicating that they are not a conventional decorative motif. In contrast, the linked concentric circles and the floral brooch that are also part of Gagik's costume can be seen as elements of the sculptor's decorative vocabulary, as they reappear in the dress of other figures carved on the church, for example in the figure of St. Sahak on the south facade. Illustrated in Lynn Jones, "The Church of the Holy Cross and the Iconography of Kingship," *Gesta* 33/2 (1994): 104–117.
67. Gagik's mantle is essentially a cape, shorter in front and trailing to mid-calf length behind. Umayyad portraits are known to have borrowed from the Sasanian tradition of royal representation, and several Umayyad portraits feature such mantles. An example from Qasr al-Hayr West is illustrated in Richard Ettinghausen, *Arab Painting* (Geneva: A. Skira, 1962) fig. 30. For Abbasid emulation see below and n. 69.
68. Der Nersessian, *Aght'amar,* 30–31, was the first to note the similarities between Gagik's crown and Sasanian crowns, although her comparison is restricted to the flaring side wings.
69. For a discussion of Abbasid emulation of Sasanian royal art, see Oleg Grabar, "An introduction to the art of Sasanian Silver," in *Sasanian Silver: Late Antique and Early Medieval Arts of Luxury from Iran. August-September 1967, University of Michigan Museum of Art* (Ann Arbor, MI, University of Michigan Museum of Art, 1967) 20–25. For Abbasid familiarity with, and interest in, Sasanian royal art, see Ar-Rawandi, *Rahat us-Sudur,* ed. Muhammad Igbal (London, 1921), 72; trans. in Thomas W. Arnold and Arnold Grohmann, *The Islamic Book* (Leipzig: Pantheon, 1929), 67; M. J. de Goeje, ed., *Kitab at-Tanbih,* Bilbiotheca Geographorum Arabicorum VIII, 106; trans. Arnold and Grohmann, *Islamic Book,* 1; *Kitab ta'Rikh sinni muluk al-Ard wa-'l Anbiya'* (Berlin: Kaviani-Verlag, 1340 A. H. = 1921/22 A. D.), 34, trans. Arnold and Grohmann, *Islamic Book,* 1–2. As noted above, no examples are from the house of the ruling dynasty, as crowns were generally considered inappropriate for Abbasid caliphs. For examples of caliphal

headdress, see Mehdi Bahrami, "A Gold Medallion the Freer Gallery of Art," in *Archaeologica Orientalia in Memoriam Ernst Herzfeld,* ed. G. C. Miles (New York: J. J. Augustin, 1952) 20, fig. 4a, 17, fig. 2.

70. As discussed above, and in Artsruni, *History,* 348. Der Nersessian, *Aght'amar,* 31, suggests that Gagik's robes and crown represent those he received from the *ostikan* upon his elevation to kingship.

71. This identification of this seated ruler and his princely attendants, human and animal, has generated much scholarly debate. For illustration, discussion and bibliography see Jones, "The Church of the Holy Cross," 108, 116 n. 33, 34, fig. 5. The small size of the crown makes it difficult to read, but it appears to be of a simple, single-tiered construction, without any wings or vertical projections, and thus differs from that worn by Gagik on the west façade.

72. Illustrated in Janine Sourdel-Thomine and Bertold Spuler, eds., *Kunst des Islam,* vol. 4, *Propyläen Kunstgeschichte* (Berlin: Propyläen Verlag, 1973) figs. 155 a, b.

73. Artsruni, *History,* 357–58.

74. There is evidence that the iconography of princely entertainments reflected, to a greater or lesser degree, actual court entertainments; Al-Azmeh, *Muslim Kingship,* 135. Depictions of enthroned rulers accompanied by dancers, musicians, and men engaged in contests of strength have no parallels in contemporary Byzantine art.

75. For palaces see Ernst Herzfeld, *Die Ausgraben von Samarra,* vol. 3 (Berlin: Verlag Reimer, 1927), 38, fig. 23. For textiles, Arnold and Grohmann, *Islamic Book,* 10. For silver, see Arthur U. Pope, ed., *A Survey of Persian Art,* vol. 4, pl. 208 A. For gold medallions, see Sourdel-Thomine and Spuler, *Propyläen Kunstgeschichte,* 267, fig. 204c, fig. 205a. For Fatimid examples, see Edmond Pauty, *Les Bois Sculptés* (Cairo: l'Institut Français d'Archéologie Orientale, 1931), 49–50, pl. XLVII-LVIII; Georges Marçais, "Les figures d'hommes et de bêtes dans les bois sculptés d'époques fâtimite conservés au Musée arabe du Caire," in *Mémoire de l'Institut français, Mélanges Maspero* (Cairo: l'Institut Français d'Archéologie Orientale, 1935), reprinted in Robert Lacoste, ed., *Mélanges d'Histoire et d'Archéologie de l'Occident Musulman,* vol. 1, *Articles et Conférences de Georges Marçais* (Rabat, Algeria: Direction des Beaux-Arts du Gouvernment Général, 1957), 81–92 (pages refer to reprint edition). For multiple Hispano-Umayyad examples and bibliography, see Jerrilynn Dodds, ed., *Al-Andalus: The Art of Islamic Spain* (New York: Abrams, 1992). For use of this iconography in a Christian context, in the extraordinary muqarnas ceiling over the nave of the Capella Palatina in Palermo, see Ugo Monneret de Villard, *Le Pitture Musulmane al Soffitto della Cappella palatina in Palermo* (Rome: State Library, 1950); and William Tronzo, *The Cultures of His Kingdom* (Princeton: Princeton University Press, 1997), 57–62.

76. The locations of the sculptures and their costumes, headdresses, and poses all find different expression in Bagratid and Artsruni portraits. While both

the Artsruni and Bagratid portraits feature the presentation of church models, Gagik alone offers his to the carved figure of Christ. In contrast the Bagratids make symbolic presentations, as there are no sculpted figures to accept them.

77. As we have observed, even the Bagratid kings—the frequent recipients of Byzantine robes—did not include such regalia in their portraits. The seminal work on imperial imagery remains André Grabar, *L'Empereur dans l'art byzantin: Recherches sur l'art officiel de l'empire d'orient* (1936, reprint London: Variorum, 1970).
78. For an example of the harm a visit to the empire could cause to the patriarch's reputation, see Drasxanakertc'i, *History,* 198. The Georgian rulers, who followed Eastern Orthodoxy, did display Byzantine robes in their portraits; see the following discussion.
79. A divine light was seen at the site where Smbat's corpse had been crucified and set on display, and, as attested to by John Catholicos, miraculous cures were effected by the soil which had been saturated with the king's blood. Drasxanakertc'i, *History,* 177. It was not only Gagik's personal piety that compared poorly with that of the Bagratids; his family's pious reputation was compromised by his father and grandfather who, like most *nakharars* imprisoned in Samarra, converted to the Muslim faith and underwent circumcision rather than be put to death. In contrast, the Bagratid presiding prince and later king, Ashot I, was not imprisoned and therefore was not forced to renounce his faith; he remained free through virtue of his cooperation with the occupying Islamic general. This cooperation is presented by both contemporary historians as a noble sacrifice made to preserve Armenia and, consequently, the Armenian church. As a result, Ashot I was not only the most powerful Armenian prince; his piety was uniquely untainted. Ibid., 125–26; Artsruni, *History,* 267. As the majority of the imprisoned Armenians did renounce their faith, it is likely that Gagik could have successfully rehabilitated his family's pious reputation had it not been for the actions of Ashot Artsruni, Gagik's elder brother and prince of Vaspurakan. In 904 Ashot imprisoned his cousin Hasan in a dispute over a fortress. Smbat I dispatched John Catholicos to negotiate a settlement, and Ashot swore an oath in which he agreed to release Hasan unharmed. When Hasan was subsequently blinded by Ashot, the catholicos promptly excommunicated him. Ashot died one year later at the age of twenty-nine. The Artsruni historians concealed the excommunication, noting only that before he died Ashot repented of his sins and undoubtedly received forgiveness. Drasxanakertc'i, *History,* 154–55; Artsruni, *History,* 310–13, 339.
80. If the spiritual prestige of the Bagratid kings was incomparable, their secular powers were secondary to those of Gagik Artsruni. His dominant status was affirmed in 924/25, when the emperor Romanos I Lekapenos (920–944) transferred the title *archōn tōn archōnton* from the Bagratid king and granted it to Gagik. K. H. Maksoudian presents a concise overview of

the controversy surrounding this event, with bibliography, in Drasxanakertc'i, *History,* 22–23. Gagik expended great effort in the subsequent years of his reign to restore his pious reputation. For a consideration of the pious royal message of the sculptures and frescoes of the Church of the Holy Cross at Aght'amar, see Jones, "The Church of the Holy Cross." The emperor Constantine VII Porphyrogenitos (945–959) subsequently recognized both the Artsruni and Bagratid kings as *archōn tōn archōnton,* placing them as equals above all other Armenian rulers. Constantine Porphyrogenitos, *De ceremoniis,* 687, 4–5. A fuller consideration of this topic, and of Gagik's pious deeds and donations, is the subject of a forthcoming book by L. Jones.

81. The relevant chronicles for this period are the anonymous *Matiane kartlisai* (the Book of Kartli), and Sumbat Davitisdze's *Life and History of the Bagrationis,* in S. Q'aukhchishvili ed., *Kartlis tskhovreba* (the Annals of Georgia) (Tbilisi: Sakhelgami, 1955) vol. 1, pp. 249–317, 372–86; *Matiane kartlisai* is translated by Robert W. Thomson, ed., *Rewriting Caucasian History. The Medieval Armenian Adaptation of the Georgian Chronicles. The Original Georgian Texts and the Armenian Adaptation* (Oxford: Oxford University Press, 1996), pp. 255–308; and Sumbat Davitisdze by Gertrud Pätsch, *Das Leben Kartlis. Eine Chronik aus Georgien 300–1200* (Leipzig: Sammlung Dieterich, 1985), pp. 459–81. On the history of the chronicles, see Stephen H. Rapp, *Imagining History at the Crossroads: Persia, Byzantium, and the Architects of the Written Georgian Past* (unpublished Ph.D thesis: University of Michigan, 1997), chap. 6, part 2.
82. *Kartlis tskhovreba* 1 (*Matiane kartlisai*), p. 251, lines 13–15; tr. Thomson, *Rewriting Caucasian History,* p. 258.
83. No Georgian source mentions the caliph in such a capacity.
84. Robert W. Thomson, "The Historical Compilation of Vardan Arewelc'i," *Dumbarton Oaks Papers* 43 (1989): 182.
85. There is no general agreement about the identification and numbering of members of the Bagrationi family. It is very complex as so many collateral branches of the family ruled simultaneously and as certain names recur frequently. In this part of the paper the numbering adopted is that used in Antony Eastmond, *Royal Imagery in Medieval Georgia* (University Park, Pennsylvania: Penn State Press, 1998), p. 261; however, for clarity the identification numbers used in the stemma produced by Cyril Toumanoff, "The Bagratids of Iberia from the Eighth to the Eleventh Century," *Le Muséon* 74 (1961): 5–42, 233–316 will also be cited; in Toumanoff, Adarnase is: No.23, Adarnase IV(II).
86. Cyril Toumanoff, "Armenia and Georgia," in Joan M. Hussey, ed., *The Cambridge Medieval History,* vol. 4, part 1 (Cambridge: Cambridge University Press, 1966), p. 613.
87. The title of *kouropalates* was normally reserved for members of the imperial family. However, it had been used irregularly as an honorific title for rulers in Georgia since the sixth century when the emperor Justin bestowed

it on Tzathe, king of Lazica (Colchis) in 522: Louis Dindorf ed., *Chronicon Paschal* (Bonn: Corpus Scriptorum Historiae Byzantinae, 1832), pp. 163–64; Michael Whitby and Mary Whitby, eds., *Chronicon Paschale 284–628 AD,* Translated Texts for Historians: 7 (Liverpool: Liverpool University Press, 1989), p. 105. The text that describes the ceremony lays great stress on the nature of the robes given to Tzathe. Interestingly, this first example also establishes the importance of these honors as an instrument of international politics: the Persian ruler Koades immediately complained that the bestowal of the honor was a usurpation of his authority. For a general discussion of the title see Rapp, *Imagining History at the Crossroads,* chap. 7, part 1.

88. Drasxanakertc'i, *History,* pp. 150–51.
89. Drasxanakertc'i, *History,* pp. 159. In this text Constantine is called king of Egrisi, an alternative name for Apkhazeti.
90. *Kartlis tskhovreba* 1 (*Matiane kartlisaî*), p. 262, lines 3–7; tr. Thomson, *Rewriting Caucasian History,* pp. 265: "At that time [904] Constantine, king of the Apkhaz, seized Kartli, and became an enemy of the king of Armenia, Sumbat." Nothing else is known about Apkhazetian ritual; and the only known image of a ruler of Apkhazeti is in the church of Kumurdo in Javakheti. On this see Eastmond, *Royal Imagery,* pp. 34–38, 231–32; Valerie Silogava, *Kumurdo tadzris epigrapika* (The Epigraphy of the church of Kumurdo) (Tbilisi: Metsniereba, 1994).
91. = Toumanoff "Bagratids," No. 34, David II.
92. = Toumanoff "Bagratids," No. 35, Ashot II.
93. see above, n. 45. p. 154 and n. 48.
94. = Toumanoff, "Bagratids," No. 25, Gurgen II the Great.
95. Constantine VII Porphyrogennetos, *De administrando imperio,* ed. G. Moravcsik and R. J. H. Jenkins, Dumbarton Oaks Texts: 1 (Washington, D.C.: Dumbarton Oaks, 1967), chap. $46._{49-53}$. Wachtang Djobadze, *Early Medieval Georgian Monasteries in Historic Tao, Klarjeti and Savseti* (Stuttgart: Franz Steiner Verlag, 1992), p. 118, misidentifies this Gurgen as Gurgen I (= Toumanoff, "Bagratids," No. 8, Gurgen I).
96. The full story is related in Constantine VII, *De Administrando Imperio,* chap. 46.49–165.
97. = Toumanoff, "Bagratids," No. 54, Davit II the Great.
98. Z. Avalichvili, "La succession du curopalate David, d'Ibérie, dynaste de Tao," *Byzantion* 8 (1933): 177–202; C. Badridze, "Contribution à l'histoire des relations entre le Tao Géorgie du sud et Byzance. Insurrection de Bardas Skléros," *Bedi Kartlisa* 33 (1975): 162–90.
99. Bernadette Martin-Hisard, "L'Athos, l'Orient et le Caucase au XIe siècle," in Anthony A. M. Bryer and Mary Cunningham, eds., *Mount Athos and Byzantine Monasticism,* Society for the Promotion of Byzantine Studies. Publications: 4 (Aldershot: Variorum, 1996), pp. 239–248.; Hélène Metreveli, "Le rôle de l'Athos dans l'histoire de la culture géorgienne," *Bedi Kartlisa* 40 (1983): 17–26.

100. These robes are mentioned in a number of sources: I. Kratchkovsky and A. A. Vasiliev, ed. & trans., *Histoire de Yahya-Ibn-Sa'id d'Antioche, Continuateur de Sa'id-Ibn-Bitriq,* Patrologia Orientalis: vol. 23 fasc. 3 (Paris: Patrologia Orientalis, 1932), pp. 429–30; John Skylitzes, *Synopsis historiarum,* ed. H. Thurn (Berlin: Walter de Gruyter, 1973), p. $339._{72-79}$. There are some problems with the chronology of Davit's titles as one manuscript, dated earlier by a colophon, names Davit as *kouropalates.* This conflicts with the chronicle accounts. I follow here the chronicle dating since it appears to provide a more compelling explanation of the events of Davit's reign. Djobadze, *Early Medieval Georgian Monasteries,* p. 119 n. 421 claims both these texts refer to the emperor Romanos II and the 979 revolt of Bardas Skleros—a historical impossibility and a misinterpretation.
101. Nicolas Oikonomides, *Les listes de préseance byzantines du IXe et Xe siècle* (Paris: CNRS, 1972), pp. $95._{14-21}$ (*magistros*) and $97._{7-11}$ (*kouropalates*).
102. Constantine VII, *De Administrando Imperio,* chap. $46._{82-91}$.
103. Constantine VII, De Administrando Imperio, chap. $46._{162-5}$.
104. *Kartlis tskhovreba 1 (Matiane kartlisai),* pp. $294._{4}$–$295._{2}$; trans. Thomson, *Rewriting Caucasian History,* pp. 287–88.
105. = Toumanoff, "Bagratids," No. 55, Gurgen I (ruled 975–1008).
106. = Toumanoff, "Bagratids," No. 60, Bagrat III (ruled 1008–1014 as the first king of united Georgia).
107. *Kartlis tskhovreba* 1 (*Matiane kartlisai*), p. $278._{7-10}$; trans. Thomson, *Rewriting Caucasian History,* p. 374.
108. These images are fully described in Eastmond, *Royal Imagery,* pp. 9–34; 221–34.
109. On this site see: V. Beridze, *Architecture de Tao-Klardjétie* (Tbilisi: Khelovneba, 1981), pp. 299–301; Djobadze, *Early Medieval Georgian Monasteries,* pp. 10–13; Eastmond, *Royal Imagery,* pp. 17–19.
110. S. Amiranashvili, *Istoriia gruzinskogo iskusstva* (The History of Georgian Art) (Moscow: Iskusstvo, 1963), pp. 176–77.; N. A. Aladashvili, *Monumental'naia skul'ptura Gruzii* (Monumental Sculpture in Georgia) (Moscow: Iskusstvo, 1977), pp. 68–74.
111. The inscriptions are analyzed by N. Shoshiashvili, *Aghmosavlet da samkhret sakartvelo V-X ss. Kartuli tsartserebis korpusi: Lapidaruli tsartserebi,* vol. 1 (A Corpus of Georgian Inscriptions in East and South Georgia, V-X centuries) (Tbilisi: Metsniereba, 1980), p. 286.
112. These are recorded by Nikolai Marr, *Dnevnik poezdki v Shavshetiiu i Klardzhetiiu* (St. Petersburg: Imperial Press, 1911), pp. 160, 163; Eastmond, *Royal Imagery,* p. 223.
113. = Toumanoff, "Bagratids," No. 37, Sumbat I.
114. Djobadze, *Early Medieval Georgian Monasteries,* pp. 9–15.
115. Marr, *Dnevnik poezdki,* p. 184; Eastmond, *Royal Imagery,* pp. 224–25.
116. In Toumanoff, "Bagratids," Ashot Kukhi = No. 19, Ashot II the Immature.

117. Djobadze, *Early Medieval Georgian Monasteries,* pp. 218–32; Beridze, *Architecture de Tao-Klardjétie,* pp. 309–10. The image was found mounted on the interior north wall of the cathedral by Nikolai Marr in 1911, but he argues that it may well have been moved there from the facade in the course of the rebuilding of the church in the eleventh century: Marr, *Dnevnik poezdki,* pp. 15–16.
118. On these churches and their reliefs, see Thierry, "La cathédrale de Mrèn et sa décoration": 43–77; W. Djobadze, "The Sculptures on the Eastern Façade of the Holy Cross of Mtzkheta," *Oriens Christianus* 44 (1960): 112–35 and 45 (1961): 70–77.
119. *Kartlis tskhovreba* 1 (*Matiane kartlisai*), p. $260._{1-2}$; trans. Thomson, *Rewriting Caucasian History,* p. 372; *Kartlis tskhovreba* 1 (*Sumbat Davitisdze*), p. $380._{9-10}$; tr. Pätsch, *Das Leben Kartlis,* pp. 470–71.
120. The image at Tbeti, and its fascination with dress, also argues against the idea that donor images are not in fact concerned with the presentation of power at all. One possible argument would be to say that Opiza and Dolisqana are concerned only with donations to God and the relation between the earthly donor and God. However, this is to divorce ideas of power and religion in a way that was not conceived in the Byzantine worlds.
121. = Toumanoff, "Bagratids," No. 36, Bagrat.
122. Djobadze, *Early Medieval Georgian Monasteries,* pp. 92–141; Beridze, *Architecture de Tao-Klardjétie,* pp. 297–99. On the reign of Davit III, see Zaza Skhirtladze, "The Mother of All the Churches. Remarks on the Iconographic Programme of the Apse Decoration of Dort Kilise," *Cahiers Archéologiques* 43 (1995): pp.101–116.
123. The evidence for this comes from the inscriptions accompanying the images, which make no distinctions between the brothers, and from the fact that they are depicted with square haloes, normally reserved for living figures.
124. The figure of the Mother of God has now fallen out of place and lies on the ground near the others.
125. Despite the damage that both images have suffered, it is clear that it is only Bagrat's crown that has pendilia, as the surface on either side of Davit's head is quite smooth.
126. The men wear decorated robes with patterns of medallions, and low flat crowns. There is no sign of pendilia on either crown. For an image see Eastmond, *Royal Imagery,* figs. 21 and 22.
127. Wachtang Djobadze, "The Donor Reliefs and the Date of the Church at Oshki," *Byzantinische Zeitschrift* 69 (1976): 50.
128. On these churches see Djobadze, *Early Medieval Georgian Monasteries.*
129. The evidence for this comes in two inscriptions recorded at the church that mention the donations of Basil II and his co-emperor Constantine VIII: Ekvtime Taqaishvili, *Arkheologicheskaia ekspeditsiia 1917-go goda v*

iuzhnye provintsii Gruzii (The archaeological expedition of 1917 to the southern provinces of Georgia) (Tbilisi: Khelovneba, 1952), pp. 63–64.

130. On links with the Phokas family, see Vasiliev Kratchkovsky, *Histoire de Yahya-Ibn-Sa'id,* p. 424.

131. Taqaishvili, *Arkheologicheskaia ekspeditsiia,* pp. 36–37. Unfortunately, even when Taqaishvili saw the wall painting it was too fragmentary to be able to determine any details of the figures or their dress—only the inscriptions survived.

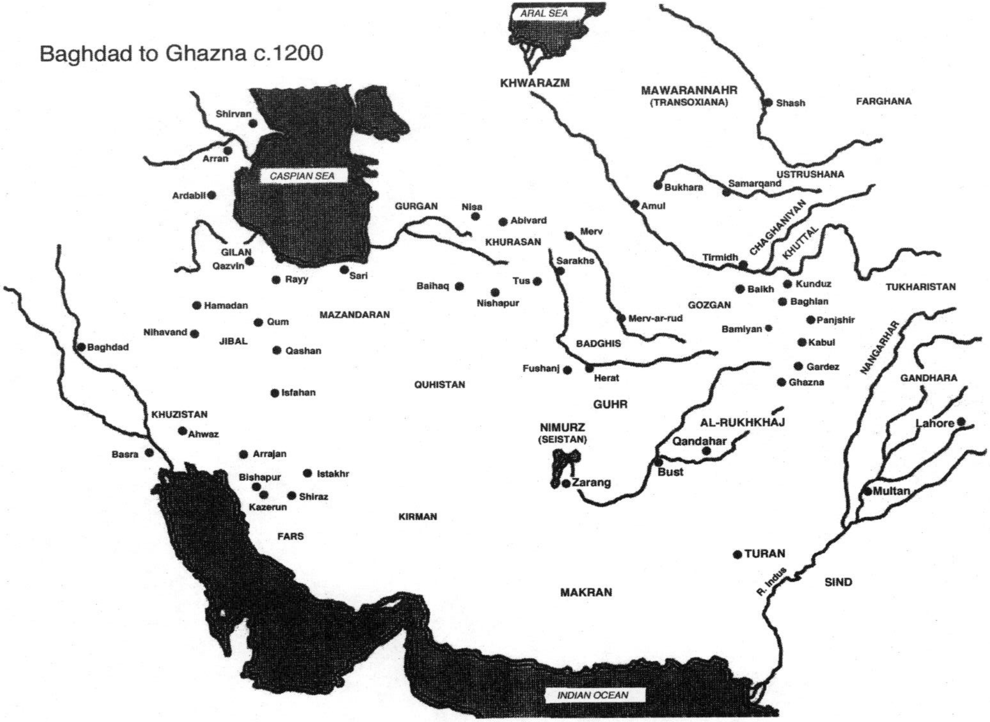

Figure 8.0 Iran, tenth to thirteenth centuries

CHAPTER 8

FROM BAGHDAD TO BUKHARA, FROM GHAZNA TO DELHI: THE *KHIL'A* CEREMONY IN THE TRANSMISSION OF KINGLY POMP AND CIRCUMSTANCE[1]

Gavin R. G. Hambly

Prior to his death in 193/809, the fifth 'Abbāsid caliph, al-Rashīd, made an unusual disposition of the caliphate, bequeathing to his eldest son, al-Amīn, the caliphal office together with the western and central provinces, while endowing his second son, al-Ma'mūn, the offspring of a Persian slave-girl, with the great province of Khurasan north and east of the Iranian Dasht-i Lut and Dasht-i Kavir.[2] This latter charge provided the fiscal and manpower resources for the younger son to challenge the elder, and after a protracted fratricidal struggle, al-Amīn was killed and al-Ma'mūn took his place (198/813). Recognizing the practical problems of administering Khurasan from Baghdad, he appointed his most trusted henchman, Ṭāhir b. al-Ḥusayn, its governor in 205/821.

From this time forward, Khurasan and its adjacent regions—Nimruz,[3] Khwarazm,[4] and Mawarannahr[5]—gradually passed from the direct control of the caliph's government. First, Ṭāhir and his descendants, to 259/873, and then various predominantly Iranian dynasties,[6] established de facto autonomy in the area, to be replaced around 382/992 by Turkish rulers who thereafter adapted themselves in varying degrees to Irano-Islamic norms of kingship and culture.[7] These developments did not, however, fracture the religious unity of the Sunni caliphate. Unlike the Shī'ī Fatimids in North Africa and Egypt (297–567/909–1171) or the Daylamī Būyids in western Iran and Iraq (320–454/932–1062),[8] these Iranian and Turkish dynasts of the eastern provinces of the caliphate were, with few exceptions, ostensibly loyal to Baghdad and inclined to emphasize their formal ties with the caliphal court: in return for ʿAbbāsid approbation, which served a legitimizing function, they were willing to honor the caliph as a distant suzerain, invoke God's blessing upon him in the weekly congregational prayers *(khuṭba),*[9] and imprint his name upon the coinage *(sikka).*[10]

While some of these rulers-to-be were ruffianly adventurers, such as the Ṣaffārid, Yaʿqub b. Layth (d. 265/879), or Mardāwīj b. Ziyār (d. 323/935), most lineages took their responsibilities seriously, maintaining the security of their dominions, enforcing public order, administering justice, and supporting public charities.[11] The ethical premises upon which their rule was based were adumbrated in a justly famous letter that Ṭāhir b. al-Ḥusayn sent to his son and that later generations came to regard as embodying the highest ideals of Islamic rulership.[12]

Rulers, however, need more than admirable ethical precepts to retain their power, and these eastern rulers, in addition to relying upon the loyalty of their military retinues, the competence of traditional bureaucratic elites, and the compliance of their subjects, skillfully employed style and symbol to enhance their prestige. They achieved this not only by emulating the ceremonial splendor of ʿAbbāsid Baghdad but also by drawing upon much older infidel and especially Iranian traditions of kingship.

Long afterward, Ibn Khaldūn (732–808/1332–1406) in his *Muqaddima* (introduction) to his *Kitāb al-ʿIbar,* deplored the way in which the concept of the Islamic ruler, conceived in the first generations of Islam as the leader and guide of the community, had come to approximate to infidel kingship.[13] The outward signs of this inner transformation were the carrying of banners and insignia *(ʿalam),*[14] the blowing of horns and trumpets and the beating of drums, a parasol of state *(čatr)* carried before the ruler,[15] the ruler seated upon a throne, the ruler's name imprinted on the coinage *(sikka),*[16] the use of a seal of state *(muhr),*[17] and the distancing of the ruler from his people by means of tents and tent walls (and, by extension, palaces) to ensure privacy and security, most notably with the adoption of an enclosed space *(maqṣūra)* in which the ruler prayed.[18]

To these attributes of kingship must be added the robe of honor *(khilʿa;* plural, *khilaʿ)*[19] Originally, this was a garment that had been worn by the caliph, in the first Islamic centuries the sole sovereign, who presented it to a deserving subordinate as a mark of honor and appreciation.[20] When, during the ninth and tenth centuries, the eastern dynasts began to acquire a de facto independence of the caliphate, they nevertheless looked to the caliph's government to legitimize and reinforce their authority with diplomas *(ʿahd, manshūr),*[21] accompanied by honorific titles *(laqab)*[22] and robes of honor, and less commonly, banners and parasols.

Such honors usually followed upon acknowledgment of the caliph's authority in public ceremonies involving the oath of allegiance *(bay'a),*[23] binding not only the oath-taker himself but also the entire community. Medieval Islamic society attached profound significance to oaths taken between two persons or to vows made by one man to another. As Roy Mottahedeh has expressed it, "In the Koran, a whole series of covenants between man and his Creator, starting with the primeval covenant of Adam, stand as the archetype and the ultimate guarantee of all solemn and weighty undertakings between one man and another."[24] Thus, at least from early 'Abbāsid times, the *bay'a* had a distinctly religious character; undertakings given to the ruler, initially the caliph, were viewed as undertakings given to Allāh.

Although the relations between the caliphs and the eastern dynasts, which involved the exchange of oaths and honors, were frequently tense or ambiguous, the evidence points to both parties regarding these mutually acknowledged ties as being both meaningful and worth cherishing, and it is surely significant that these ties were replicated at a lower level between the de facto independent dynasts and their own subordinate officials and local vassals, for whom robes of honor in particular became the currency of mutual obligation and loyalty between superior and subaltern.

This spread of the use of insignia and symbols of rulership from the caliphal court to the provincial regimes of Sāmānids, Būyids, and others does not appear to have been due to the mere borrowing or mimicking of caliphal ritual, but was rather the result of a deliberate impetus from the Baghdad court as a means of dealing with the problem of how to maintain some semblance of control over distance provinces.

Although some historical writing has suggested the contrary, it does not appear that it was during periods of weakness but rather during periods of self-confident strength that the 'Abbāsid caliphs vigorously employed insignia and symbols to control remote and potentially dissident subordinates. Thus, the period when ties with the east were strenuously pursued by active and intelligent diplomacy was not the decade following the death of al-Mutawakkil in 247/861 when four fainéant caliphs ruled, but the half-century of revived caliphal power when al-Mu'tamid was caliph (256–279/870–892) and the real ruler was his brother, al-Muwaffaq, and when the latter's son, al-Mu'taḍid (279–289/892–902), and grandson, al-Muktafī (289–295/902–908) reigned. The story is best illustrated by Baghdad's dealings with the first two Ṣaffārid rulers.

From 247/861 until his death in 265/879, Ya'qūb b. Layth aṣ-Ṣaffār was the independent ruler not only of his home region of Sistan but also of Khurasan (which he had seized from the Ṭāhirids), Kabul, Ghazna, Kirman, Fars, and Ahwaz. The 'Abbāsids could do nothing to prevent this accretion of power because they faced even more serious threats elsewhere, especially the revolt of the Zanj in southern Iraq (255–270/869–883).[25] But when Ya'qub died and was succeeded by his brother, 'Amr, the 'Abbāsids set out to bring 'Amr into the framework of the caliphal polity. 'Amr proved compliant and promptly submitted his allegiance to al-Mu'tamid, who formally invested him with the governorships of the provinces of Sistan, Khurasan, Sind, Kirman, and Fars, as well as (in one account) the position of commandant in Baghdad. In 265/879, al-Mu'tamid, according to al-Ṭabarī, sent an envoy to 'Amr "with the document of his investiture, together with a contract and a robe of honor."[26] In the following year, 266/879, when 'Amr appointed as his agent in Baghdad 'Ubayd Allāh b. 'Abd Allā'h b. Ṭāhir, a member of the Ṭāhirid family notoriously hostile to the rest of his kinsfolk, 'Amr personally handed his new deputy a robe of honor and a bar of gold.[27] In 268/881–882, when 'Amr was still in favor at court, al-Ṭabarī records his sending to Baghdad taxes worth five hundred thousand dinars, including "three hundred embroidered and other garments," some no doubt destined to be applied as robes of honor.[28]

It seems that 'Amr temporarily lost favor in the last years of al-Mu'tamid's reign, but with the accession of the active and warlike al-Mu'taḍid in 279/892, 'Amr's reputation was restored.[29] In 284/897, 'Amr put down a rebellion in Rayy, of which al-Mu'taḍid now made him the governor, sending him an envoy to Nishapur with robes of honor, a banner signifying his new gubernatorial appointment, and personal presents from the caliph.[30] Subsequently, al-Mu'taḍid, possibly at the solicitation of 'Amr, appointed the latter governor of Mawarannahr (Transoxiana) in 258/898, and it may have been the price of this appointment that led 'Amr in the following year (286/899) to send to Baghdad a tribute of four million dirhams, "twenty horses with ornamented saddles and bridles inlaid (with silver), one hundred and fifty horses with embroidered saddlecloths, garments, perfume, and falcons," the garments perhaps constituting a complete wardrobe.[31]

Although it has been suggested that in appointing 'Amr governor of Mawarannahr al-Mu'taḍid was deliberately provoking a conflict between him and Ismā'īl b. Aḥmad the Sāmānid, such an assumption may reflect the wisdom of hindsight. 'Amr's legendary defeat at the hands of Ismā'il's forces could hardly have been anticipated by the caliph.[32] The end of the story notwithstanding, 'Amr's relations with al-Mu'tamid and al-Mu'taḍid can be viewed as firmly establishing the "*khil'a* culture," which thereafter prevailed as the basis of relations between Baghdad and the virtually autonomous lands in the east, a policy that came to fruition during the rule of the Sāmānids of Bukhara.

From Baghdad to Bukhara

Previous to the fall of 'Amr in 287/900, when the governors of Khurasan appointed by the 'Abbāsids had experienced increasing difficulty in controlling Mawarannahr, they delegated authority there, with the caliph's approval, to the influential family of Sāmān Khudā of Balkh, reputedly a descendant of Vahrām Čūbīn and the first of his house to adopt Islam. When Ghassan b. 'Abbad became the caliph's governor in Khurasan, he appointed Nūḥ b. Asad b. Sāmān Khudā as ruler of Samarqand, and his brother Aḥmad as ruler of Farghana. This was in 202/817–818. When Ṭāhir b. al-Ḥusayn replaced Ghassān as governor, he not only confirmed Nūḥ's appointment on behalf of the caliph, al-Ma'mūn, but presented him with a robe of honor, further enhancing his stature.[33] When Nūḥ died in 204/819, he had already designated his brother Aḥmad to be his successor, and Aḥmad, in his turn, designated his son, Nasr, who succeeded him in 263/875. Al-Mu'tamid (256–279/870–892) confirmed this appointment.[34] The preceding upheavals in Khurasan, the overthrow of the Ṭāhirids and the rise of Ya'qūb b. Layth, had left the Sāmānids as virtually independent rulers of Mawarannahr; al-Mu'tamid's confirmation of Naṣr's position brought the latter once more within the ring of caliphal authority.

Meanwhile, Nasr had delegated to his brother, Ismā'īl, the government of Bukhara, then in a state of mutiny and insubordination. Arriving in Bukhara with an insufficient force, Ismā'il found the city in the hands of a Khwārazmī adventurer, Ḥusayn b. Muḥammad, whom he was not strong enough to eject. Negotiations ensued, but Ḥusayn b. Muḥammad's troops would transfer their allegiance to Ismā'il only on condition that their leader remained as Ismā'il's deputy. Emulating the pragmatic caliphal approach to such problems, Ismā'il sent Ḥusayn b. Muḥammad a diploma as his deputy, a banner, and a robe of honor, and with these Ḥusayn b. Muḥammad paraded through the city to popular acclamation. The uncertain attitude of the people of Bukhara had obviously prompted Ismā'il to defer to the realities on the ground, but a few days later he made his way into the city and had the *khuṭba* read in the caliph's and his name. However, the situation remained tense in Bukhara until a leading member of the local *'ulamā'* came out on the side of Ismā'il, who shortly afterward felt strong enough to arrest and imprison Ḥusayn b. Muḥammad.[35]

Although Ismā'il had emerged as the most energetic member of the Sāmānid family, Baghdad continued to recognize the seniority of Naṣr until his death in 279/892, when Ismā'il (279–295/892–907) took his place as ruler of Mawarannahr. Meanwhile, the new caliph, al-Mu'taḍid, named 'Amr b. Layth as governor of Mawarannahr. When, however, 'Amr was defeated and captured by Ismā'il and sent to Baghdad, followed shortly afterwards by Ismā'il's repulse of an 'Alīd invasion of Gurgan by Muḥammad b. Zayd, al-Mu'taḍid promptly recognized Ismā'il's de facto rule over not only Mawarannahr but also over Khurasan and Tabaristan, sending him, in 288/901, diplomas confirming his position, together with "a corselet, a crown, and a sword of gold," as well as large sums of money. He also had Ismā'il's dispatch reporting his victory over the 'Alīds read in two of the Friday Mosques of Baghdad, a reminder that these exchanges served a two-way political purpose.[36]

Mīrkhwānd, writing long afterwards but in an informed historiographical tradition, describes how Ismā'il received this caliphal embassy. Al-Mu'taḍid sent Ismā'il robes of honor of great value, rescripts, and diplomas *(aḥkām va manāshīr),* confirming him in the government of Sistan, Khurasan, Mazandaran, Rayy and Isfahan. Ismā'il then put on one by one the robes of honor, and after he had finally selected one to wear, he performed two *rak'at* (an inclination of the head with the palms of the hand coming to rest upon the knees). He then received and kissed the caliph's *manshūr* and rewarded the envoy with one hundred thousand dirhams. Such was the public reverence due to communications from the caliphal throne.[37]

In 289/902, al-Mu'taḍid was succeeded by al-Muktafī, involving the need to reaffirm relations between Baghdad and Bukhara. The new caliph was almost immediately reminded of the valuable services which his Sāmānid warden of the marches provided: following the defeat of the Zaydīs in Tabaristan, one of Ismā'il's army commanders, Muḥammad b. Hārūn, had defected to the 'Alīds and had occupied Rayy. Ismā'il followed him there, defeated his forces and occupied the city. The new caliph responded by sending an embassy to Ismā'il with robes of honor and other gifts, as well as a letter appointing him governor of Rayy in addition to his other charges.[38] The reward for his faith in Ismā'il came with the news of a Sāmānid victory against invading pagan Turks, which was likewise proclaimed from the pulpits of Baghdad.[39] When Ismā'il died in 295/907, al-Muktafī confirmed his son, Aḥmad, as his successor, sending a mission that carried, among many gifts, a banner that the caliph had personally tied.[40]

It perhaps goes without saying that the robe of honor and other forms of regalia would on occasion be employed as instruments of political manipulation. A case in point occurred during the reign of the Sāmānid amīr Nūḥ I (331–343/943–954). Nūḥ's predecessor, Naṣr II, had promoted to be the principal commander of his troops in the west Abū 'Alī Aḥmad b. Muḥtāj, hereditary ruler of the principality of Chaghaniyan north of the Amu-Darya beyond Tirmidh.[41] Nūḥ, rightly, mistrusted Abū 'Alī who, while campaigning in Jibal, decided to rebel against his master. Abū 'Alī recruited for his scheme the brother of the late Naṣr II, Ibrāhīm b. Aḥmad, who was then in the service of the Hamdānid ruler of Mosul, Nāṣir al-Dawla al-Ḥasan (317–358/929–969), intending to put him on the Sāmānid throne in place of Nūḥ. Through the good offices of Nāṣir al-Dawla, Abū 'Alī secured from Baghdad robes of honor and honorific titles for Ibrāhīm b. Aḥmad, which would obviously strengthen the latter's position as a claimant to the throne. There followed a successful march on Bukhara but thereafter the rebellion collapsed, the would-be Sāmānid usurper was captured and blinded by Nūḥ, and Abū 'Alī fled to Chaghaniyan. Why the caliph chose to support this act of rebellion is unclear. He may have been dissatisfied with Nūḥ, but more probably it was a question of expediency: Abū 'Alī with his troops in Hamadan was uncomfortably close to Baghdad, while Nāṣir al-Dawla al-Ḥasan was a formidable northern neighbor in Mosul.[42]

Enough has been said of the relations between Baghdad and Bukhara, which continued until the collapse of Sāmānid rule at the close of the fourth/tenth century. This mutually supportive relationship consisted, on the caliph's part, of impressive ceremonial missions, diplomas of confirmation, robes of honor, and other gifts, in return for which the caliph could rely upon the loyalty of the Sāmānids, and news of their victories, to sustain caliphal prestige. However, there is no evidence that the Sāmānids ever sent tribute or taxes to Baghdad.[43] With other dynasties in the east, the pattern was different, and at its most complex in the case of the Būyids,[44] but it was in the service of the Sāmānids that Alptigin and Sebüktigin, founders of Ghaznavid rule, learnt their statecraft and the tools for binding subordinates with *bay'a, 'ahd,* and the rest. Among these, the *khil'a* came to loom large, as it had among the Sāmānids, raising the question as to whether the Sāmānids and their successors manufactured their own robes of honor. R. B. Sergeant has documented a long history of workshops for *ṭirāz* and a wide variety of textiles in Mawarannahr, including the celebrated *zandanījī* stuff,[45] which Niẓām al-Mulk, writing nearly a century after the demise of the Sāmānids, describes their newly recruited *mamluks* wearing in the form of *zandanījī* garments *(qabā'-ye zandanījī),* perhaps as a kind of livery indicating that they were in the Sāmānid service.[46] It is perhaps significant that when Abu 'Alī b. Muḥtāj, alluded to above, plundered Bukhara in Nūḥ's absence, he carried off the holdings of fine textiles stored in the city.[47]

It should be noted too of the Sāmānids, as of those dynasties that emulated their style and manners, that robes of honor as rewards were never restricted only to military men or bureaucrats but were granted to all whom the ruler wished to honor. The Sāmānid Manṣūr b. Nūḥ b. Naṣr rewarded the celebrated physician Muḥammad b. Zakariyā 'Rāzī (Rhages) for curing his illness with a robe of honor, together with a cloak and turban, a horse, weapons, a male slave, and a concubine.[48] The poet Farrukhī, on presenting the Muḥtājid amīr of Chaghaniyan with a brilliant *qaṣīda,* was even more lavishly rewarded.[49] After Maḥmūd of Ghazna, having quarreled with the polymath scholar al-Bīrūnī over astrological interpretations, sought to reconcile him, he sent him a robe of honor, a richly caparisoned horse, a male slave, a concubine, and a thousand dinars.[50] At the Qarakhanid court at Kashgar, Yūsuf Khāṣṣ Ḥājib was rewarded with a robe of honor by his patron, Tavghach Bughra Khan, for writing the *Qutadghu biliq.*[51] In all these cases, however, there was the same implication as in the political sphere: that the recipient was in some sense bound to the donor.

From Ghazna to Delhi

The Ghaznavids (366–582/977–1186), first as vassals and then as the principal political heirs to the Sāmānids, naturally sought to adopt the political symbolism and style emanating from the Sāmānid court, while at the same time, as *ghāzīs* on the frontiers of the Islamic world, they sought to derive maximum benefit from the good will of the caliphs in acknowledging that particular aspect of their expansionism. The caliphs, for their part, were only too willing to placate successive Ghaznavid rulers, all strict Sunnīs, because during that period, Baghdad and the caliphate were under the hegemony of the Shīʿī Būyids (334/945–447/1055) and threatened by the existence of the Fatimid caliphal regime in Cairo.

Hence, Maḥmūd of Ghazna (388–421/998–1030), while wrapping his sovereignty in all the ceremonial pomp of the Sāmānid court, had little difficulty in extracting from Baghdad the political symbols required to confirm and legitimate his position as a virtually autonomous ruler *de facto* while remaining a loyal servant of the caliph *de jure.* Meanwhile, he developed these symbols as part of the process of confirming the fact of Muslim rule in those lands that he had conquered where hitherto caliphal writ had not run and, in so doing, incorporating them into the *Dār al-Islām.*

As early as 389/999, Maḥmūd sent a *fatḥnāma* (an official announcement of a victory) to the caliph, al-Qādir (381–422/991–1031), announcing that he had restored the caliph's name to the *khuṭba* (the last Sāmānids continued to recognize his deposed predecessor, al-Ṭāʾi [363–381/974–991]). In return, the caliph sent him a *manshūrnāma* appointing him ruler of Khurasan and granting him the titles of *walī amīr al-mu'minīn* and *yamīn al-dawla wa amīn al-milla* ("Helper of the Commander of the Faithful," "Right Hand of the State," and "Trustee for the People"), and a *khilʿa* (see figure 8.1).

In the words of the Ghaznavid historian, Abū Naṣr ʿUtbī, the caliph

> sent a *khil'a,* such as had never before been heard of, for the use of Sultan Saif al-Dawla ["Sword-Bearer of the State," i.e., Maḥmūd]. . . . The sultan sat on his throne and robed himself in his new *khil'a,* professing his allegiance to the successor of the prophet of God. The *amīrs* of Khurasan stood before him in order, with respectful demeanour, and did not take their seats till they were directed. He then bestowed upon the nobles, his slaves, his confidential servants, and his chief friends, valuable robes and choice presents, beyond all calculation . . . and vowed that every year he would undertake a holy war against Hind.[52]

On this great state occasion, which took place in Balkh, can be seen all the later elements of the *khil'a* ceremony as it evolved in the east: the robe of honor accompanying a rescript or diploma granting or confirming office, rank, and titles, proclaiming the recipient's relationship with the caliph in a highly visible setting in which the recipient, in turn, rewarded his own dependents. It would be unwise, however, in contemplating this scene, to assume that Maḥmūd took lightly these important honors from the caliph or that the caliph himself felt merely a titular figure acquiescing in the realities of power-politics. In Maḥmūd's case, it is known that he attached such importance to his status as the agent of caliphal authority that when al-Qādir sent to the Ma'mūnid Khwārazmshāh, Abū'l 'Abbās Ma'mūn b. Ma'mūn (399–407/1009–1017) a *manshūrnāma,* honorifics, a robe of honor, and a banner, the Khwārazmshāh did not dare to receive them publicly in his capital at Gurganj for fear of provoking Maḥmūd.[53] Similarly, al-Qādir, in 414/1023, firmly asserted his right to intervene locally. In that year, Abū 'Alī Ḥasan b. Muḥammad b. 'Abbās, known as Ḥasanak, a long-time servant of Maḥmūd and currently *ra'īs* of Nishapur, performed the hajj, in the course of which he accepted a *khil'a* from the Fatimid caliph, al-Ẓāhir. When the news of this reached Baghdad, al-Qādir wrote to Maḥmūd denouncing Ḥasanak as an Ismā'īlī and calling for his execution. Maḥmūd had no intention of sacrificing his loyal servant whom, two years after, he would appoint his *wazīr,* but the offending garment was sent to Baghdad and publicly burnt.[54]

On another occasion, the Fatimid caliph al-Ḥākim sent a letter to Maḥmūd that he forwarded to Baghdad, where it was also publicly burnt. Later, al-Ḥākim sent to Ghazna an envoy, Tāhartī, whom Maḥmūd arrested, had condemned by the *'ulamā'* and subsequently executed (403/1012–13). For this display of orthodoxy al-Qādir granted him the additional titles of *niẓām al-dīn* ("Regulator of Religion") and *nāṣir al-ḥaqq* ("Defender of Divine Truth").[55] After Maḥmūd's campaign in Kathiawar and his sack of the temple of Somnath in 417/1026, al-Qādir granted him the further title *of kahf al-dawla wa'l-Islām* ("the Refuge of

Figure 8.1 Maḥmūd of Ghazna donning a robe from the Caliph, 389/999 Or.MS.20, fol.121r., Edinburgh University Library. Used by permission.

the State and of Islam").[56] Such public approbation by the caliph, the stately embassies, the gifts of *manshūrnāmas, khila'*, and *laqabs* obviously enhanced and legitimized Maḥmūd's status as the greatest Muslim ruler east of Baghdad.

But Maḥmūd was also himself granting robes of honor to those whose service he wished to reward or whose loyalty he sought to command. In the course of relating the famous anecdote of how Maḥmūd came to feel remorse of his shoddy treatment of the poet Firdawsī, Niẓāmī 'Arūdī describes how Maḥmūd, en route to Ghazna from India, was confronted by a rebellious chieftain in a nearby fortress. Not wishing to be delayed by having to besiege the fort, Maḥmūd sent in an envoy to tell the chieftain that if he would attend the court on the next day and pay homage to Maḥmūd, he would receive a robe of honor and retain his fortress.[57] Here, the receipt of a robe of honor can be seen to be part of a formal process of reconciliation involving the prior receiving of the *bay'a* or oath of allegiance, redolent of the ancient Arab custom of the hand-clasp.[58] Maḥmūd also sent robes of honor to family members on important occasions. In his romance, *Mir'āt-i Mas'ūdi,* 'Abd al-Raḥmān Čishtī attributes to Maḥmūd a nephew, Sālār Mas'ūd Ghāzī, at whose birth, mother and child were sent robes of honor.[59]

Figure 8.2 Portrait of the Būyid ʻAḍud al-Dawla, wearing a robe of honor, on a gold medal minted in Fars, 359/970. After a drawing in Dr. Mehdi Bahrami, *Gurgan Faiences* (Costa Mesa, California: Mazda Publishers, reprinted edition, 1988). Used by permission.

By the time of Maḥmūd's son, Mas'ūd (421–432/1031–1041), it is possible to see how the *khil'a* ceremony had become the common currency of affirmation and reward between superiors and inferiors, made the more popular by the passion for the wearing of luxurious robes and sashes, and other accoutrements, by the ruling elite, a passion reiterated again and again in contemporary chronicles such as those of Bayhaqī. Bayhaqī relates that, at the beginning of the reign, an envoy from the caliph al-Qādir, Bū Muḥammad Hā<u>sh</u>imī, was received by the new sultan in a splendid public ceremony in Nishapur in Sha'bān 421/ August 1030. The envoy brought a *manshūrnāma* investing the new sultan with caliphal authority, together with a string of grandiose *laqabs.* He also brought rich presents including robes of honor, one of which was a black garment, the color of the 'Abbāsids, and presumably once worn by the caliph, as well as pieces of unsewn cloth, and ten richly caparisoned horses, the presentation of which must have made for excellent public theater, which was important for advertising Mas'ūd's claim to the throne of Ghazna, at that time still occupied by his ineffective brother, Muḥammad.[60]

When al-Qādir died a year later, Mas'ūd, who had by now eliminated his older brother, made recognition of the new caliph (al-Qā'im, 422–467/1031–1075) conditional upon Mas'ūd's receipt of a new *manshūrnāma* acknowledging all his present conquests, upon the caliph's prior approval of his anticipated conquests in the west, and upon the caliph's agreeing that he would have no dealings with the Qarakhanids except through Mas'ūd, who would henceforth transmit any robes of honor or honorifics destined for the Qarakhanid court. The last important provision would, in effect, reduce the Qarakhanid dynasty to the status of Ghaznavid dependents.[61] These were harsh demands, considering that Baghdad was still under Būyid control, but Mas'ūd sweetened the pill by a lavish display of Ghaznavid wealth and generosity in the form of gifts to the caliph. When, in 424/1033, al-Qā'im's envoy, al-Sulaymānī, arrived in Nishapur with the desired *manshūrnāma,* the caliph's gifts included robes of honor, horses, a sword, and a turban, the latter presumably the former property of the caliph.

According to Bayhaqī, who was present,

> They brought forward the turban and sword and the Sultan declared, "This turban which I am about to put on with my hand must be wound on by the Supporter of Religion (Nāsir-i Dīn)." He put it on his head after the crown. He drew the sword and said, "The Zanādiqah and Qarāmiṭah must be uprooted, and the *sunnah* of my father Yamīn al-Dawlah wa'l-Dīn thereby observed; moreover, other regions which are in the hands of enemies must be seized by the might of this sword."[62]

Although it is beyond doubt that at the time, the symbolism of the *khil'a* ceremony concerned primarily the caliph and those whom he regarded as his dependents, *khila'* had become normative vehicles for confirming personal and public ties between superiors and subordinates.[63] Bayhaqī relates in detail the circumstances surrounding the elevation to the *wazīrat* of Aḥmad b. Muḥammad b. 'Abd al-Ṣamad, who served thereafter throughout Mas'ūd's reign and into that of Mawdūd. At first, a written agreement *(muwaẓẓaf)* was negotiated between the sultan and his new *wazīr.* The next day, the *wazīr* was publicly acknowledged in full court and the sultan said "you must now put on the robe of office, because we have many important things to attend to." The sultan then signaled to the guard commander, Ḥājib Bilgetigin, to take him to the state wardrobe. The men departed "and remained there till about 12 o'clock, because the astrologer had fixed on that time as auspicious for his putting on the dress."[64] Clearly, Bayhaqī is describing a ceremony of great formality, requiring an assembled court and astrological auspiciousness.

> All the chief men and military officers attended the court, some sitting and others standing. The Khwāja [Aḥmad b. 'Abd al-Ṣamad] then invested himself with his official robes. I stood and saw what passed. What I say is from

> ocular observation, and according to the list I possess, there was a garment of scarlet cloth of Baghdad, embroidered with small flowers; a long turban of the finest muslin, with a delicate lace border; a large chain, and a girdle of one thousand miskals [1 *miskal* = 75 grams], studded with turquoises. Ḥājib Bilgetigin was sitting at the door of the wardrobe, and when the Khwāja came out, he stood up and offered his congratulations, and presented one dinar, one small turban, and two very large turquoises, set in a ring. He wished to walk before him (in procession), but the Khwāja said, upon the life and head of the Sultān, you must walk by my side; tell the other guards to go before. Bilgetigin answered, O great Khwāja, say not so, because you know my friendship, and besides, you are now dressed in the robe of my lord the sultan, to which we, his slaves, must show respect.[65]

He then returned to the sultan's presence, "kissed the ground, approached the throne, and presented a bunch of pearls to the king, which was said to be valued at ten thousand dinars. The Amīr [i.e., Sultan] Mas'ūd gave to the Khwāja a ring set with a turquoise, on which his majesty's name was engraved, and said, this is the seal of state, and I give it to you that the people may know that the Khwāja's authority is next to mine. The Khwāja took the ring, kissed the Amīr's hand and the ground, and returned to his house."[66]

When he returned to court the next day, he left behind the vizieral robe of honor *(khil'a al-wizāra)*.

> He had got a garment made after the old fashion, and a turban of Nishapur or Qa'in, and in these people always saw the great man dressed. May God approve him! I have heard from his companions, such as Abū Ibrāhīm Qa'inī, that he had his reception dress and twenty or thirty other garments all made of the same colour, and these he used to wear for a year, so that people thought he had only one dress, and used to express their surprise that the garment did not wear or fade.[67]

After the Ghaznavid defeat at Dandanqan, there is no record of further Ghaznavid communications with Baghdad. The later Ghaznavids had no Bayhaqī and given the paucity of source material it is largely a matter of assumption, reinforced by numismatic evidence, that presupposes that the formal ties between Ghazna and Baghdad, and the lavish ceremonies that Bayhaqī describes as cementing the two powers in the early history of the dynasty, continued during the long reign of Ibrahim (451–492/1059–1099), a great collector of *laqabs.*[68]

Ibrāhīm's son, Saif al-Dawla Maḥmūd Shāh, who presumably predeceased his father, received a caliphal investiture, perhaps for some notable victory in India from either al-Qā'im or his successor, al-Muqtadī

(467–487/1075–1094), according to the Lahorī poet, Ma'sūd-i Sa'd-i Salmān. The poet also refers to an embassy from al-Mustaẓhir (487–512/1094–1118) to Sultan al-Dawla Arslan Shāh (509–512/1115–1118), which confirmed his position with gifts including a standard and diploma of investiture.[69] Thereafter, and especially following the sack of Ghazna in 545/1150–51 by 'Alā' al-Dīn Ḥusayn Ghūrī, when the last Ghaznavids had withdrawn to Panjab, ties with Baghdad must have become highly tenuous, although probably not forgotten. In any case, the wheel had come full circle. The early Ghaznavids had been dependents upon the Sāmānids, but both Maḥmūd and Mas'ūd I had deliberately assumed a direct relationship with the caliph, but eventually their descendents were compelled to acknowledge first Saljuq and then Ghūrid overlordship.[70]

Between the sack of Ghazna in 545/1150–51 and the establishment of the Delhi sultanate in the first decade of the seventh/thirteenth century, there occurred the intervening period of Ghūrid (or, as contemporaries knew them, Shansabānid) rule,[71] during which this hitherto obscure family was bent, in addition to extending its conquests, upon acquiring the kind of legitimation that the Sāmānids and Ghaznavids had formerly enjoyed by establishing direct ties with Baghdad. It is surely significant of rising Ghūrid pretensions that at his accession in 558/1163, Ghiyāth al-Dīn Muḥammad b. Sām required of his followers an oath of allegiance *(bay'a)* before they formerly raised him to the throne.[72] Later, when he took possession of Ghazna, he elevated his brother, Mu'izz al-Dīn Muḥammad, to a kind of condominium with himself, handing over the former Ghaznavid territories—"the throne of the Maḥmūdīs"—[73] in northwestern India and implicitly the Ghaznavid imperial heritage.

Ghiyāth al-Dīn Muḥammad also undertook to ensure that his status was in no wise inferior to that of the displaced Ghaznavids. He sent two embassies to Baghdad, presumably requesting caliphal confirmation of the Ghūrids' new status and although no record of these survive, mention of two reciprocal missions from Baghdad do. The first came from the caliph al-Mustaḍi' (566–575/1170–1180) and the second from al-Nāṣir (575–622/1180–1225), and they confirmed Ghiyāth al-Dīn Muḥammad in his possessions and included splendid robes of honor. Both caliphs shared a common concern, the enmity of the Khwārazmshāh, 'Alā' al-Dīn Takash (567–596/1172–1200), and sought to use Ghiyāth al-Dīn Muḥammad as a counterweight.[74] On the second occasion, the arrival of the caliph's robe of honor was announced by the beating of drums, which thereafter was performed five times a day, the introduction of the *naubat* being an indication of enhanced status as a ruler.[75]

These caliphal honors implied that Ghiyāth al-Dīn would protect the caliph from the ambitions of the Khwārazmshāhs in the direction of Baghdad. When, however, on the death of Takash, the new Khwārazmshāh, Muḥammad (596–617/1200–1220), sent an embassy to Ghiyāth al-Dīn Muḥammad calling for a renewal of the former friendship between his father and the sultans of Ghur, the Khwārazmshāh declared that he wished to be regarded as Ghiyāth al-Dīn's protegé and, like a son, he urged that the sultan's brother, Mu'izz al-Dīn Muḥammad, marry his (Muḥammad b. Takash's) mother. At the same time, he requested a patent of investiture for Khurasan and Khwarazm, and with it a robe of honor. There could hardly be a better example of the way in which someone who was assuming the role of a subordinate ruler sought in the *manshūrnāma* and *khil'a* confirmation of status from a superior. Ghiyāth al-Dīn firmly rejected the proposal, perhaps mindful of the caliph's displeasure or perhaps the formidable reputation of the Khwārazmshāh's mother, and hostile relations ensued between the two rulers.[76]

In addition to seeking caliphal robes of honor, the Ghūrids followed Ghaznavid precedents by regularly rewarding their followers and servants with what was now becoming the established form of public approbation. To give an example, Ghiyāth al-Dīn Muḥammad rewarded his *wazīr,* Khwāja Saif al-Dīn Maḥmūd, with robes of honor of great value for countering with a polished quatrain an insolent poem by an envoy of the Khwārazmshāh.[77] For another example, Ghiyāth al-Dīn Muḥammad's brother, Mu'izz al-Dīn Muḥammad, involved in an engagement on the banks of the Jhelum, witnessed an outstanding act of courage on the part of a *mamluk* belonging to Quṭb al-Dīn Aybak, and conferred upon him a robe of honor as well as a deed of manumission (the fortunate *mamluk* was the future sultan of Delhi, Shams al-Dīn Iltutmish).[78]

Tāj al-Dīn Yildiz was a favorite *mamluk* of Mu'izz al-Dīn Muḥammad, who had brought him up, trained him, and promoted him until he became *mīrdār*, or head of his master's *mamluk* establishment, around which time, Mu'izz al-Dīn Muḥammad conferred upon him the government of an extensive tract from Gardez eastwards to the Indus and including the Gomul Pass, the southern route from Ghazna to Lahore.[79] Tāj al-Dīn Yildiz presumably held a diploma of investiture from the sultan, and Minhāj-i Sirāj relates how every year, when Mu'izz al-Dīn Muḥammad was en route for India, he would halt in the Karman valley, where Tāj al-Dīn Yildiz maintained his headquarters, and the latter would feast the sultan, his *maliks* and *amīrs,* presenting his guests with a thousand headdresses, quilted tunics, and other lavish gifts.[80] The sultan arranged for the marriage of his protegé's two daughters with Quṭb al-Dīn Aybak and Nāṣir al-Dīn Qabāča. Minhāj-i Sirāj describes how, in the final year of the sultan's life, marching into India for the last time, he halted in the Karman valley, where Tāj al-Dīn Yildiz presented to him, as stipulated, a thousand tunics and headdresses for himself, and then the sultan honored Tāj al-Dīn with his own robe, together with a black banner, his intent being to have Tāj al-Dīn Yildiz succeed him as ruler of Ghazna.[81]

Mu'izz al-Dīn Muḥammad was assassinated in 602/1206, and immediately thereafter Tāj al-Dīn Yildiz encountered opposition to his would-be accession. It is clear that by this time, the late sultan's lieutenants, who were shortly to play a great role in the history of northern India—Quṭb al-Dīn Aybak, Nāṣir al-Dīn Qabāča, Muḥammad *Ba<u>kh</u>tiyar*, and Shams al-Dīn Iltutmish—were already preparing in their respective power-bases to make future bids for de facto independence. In the meanwhile, two Ghūrid contenders emerged to assume Mu'izz al-Dīn Muḥammad's legacy. In the north, around Firuzkuh, the claimant was the late sultan's cousin, Malik al-Hajj 'Alā' al-Dīn Muḥammad. In the south, it was the late sultan's nephew, Ghiyāth al-Dīn Maḥmūd b. Ghiyāth al-Dīn Muḥammad. On being pressed by the Turkish *amīrs* and *maliks* to assume sovereignty, Ghiyāth al-Dīn Maḥmūd indicated that he regarded as his prime objective his father's throne of Firuzkoh and the kingdom of Ghur, and he conferred on Tāj al-Dīn Yildiz the kingdom of Ghazna (the analogy here is with the arrangement in the previous generation between Ghiyāth al-Dīn Muḥammad and Mu'izz al-Dīn Muḥammad). Accordingly, he sent Tāj al-Dīn Yildiz a robe of honor and presumably a *manshūrnāma,* although it is not specifically mentioned in the text, as well as a diploma of manumission.[82] It was now that the great *amīrs* who had formerly been the *mamluks* of Mu'izz al-Dīn Muḥammad (in effect, his *<u>kh</u>u<u>sh</u>dā<u>sh</u>īyya*, although the word is never used)[83] separately sent envoys to Sultān Maḥmūd, perhaps in emulation of Tāj al-Dīn Yildiz, asking for diplomas of manumission and of investiture over the territories which they already ruled *de facto.* While it is perhaps curious that these powerful *amīrs* were sufficiently concerned regarding their status to request formal diplomas of manumission, it is clear that they wanted official confirmation to legitimize their rule in the same way that the Ghaznavids had formerly sought legitimization from Baghdad. Sultān Maḥmūd presumably recognized their concern and acted accordingly. He despatched a *manshūrnāma* and *čatr* (a ceremonial parasol, or canopy of state, which was an ancient symbol of sovereignty)[84] to Tāj al-Dīn Yildiz, and another to Quṭb al-Dīn Aybak in Delhi together with the title of sultan, which in this case signified only a limited gubernatorial rule.[85] It may be assumed that he also sent robes of honor and diplomas to other great *amīrs.*

With Ghiyāth al-Dīn Maḥmūd as nominal suzerain, Tāj al-Dīn Yildiz ruled for some years in Ghazna as his surrogate but, in reality, as a virtually independent ruler.[86] At first, his hold over Ghazna seemed precarious (on one occasion, Quṭb al-Dīn Aybak advanced from Lahore and held the city for forty days), but he gradually reasserted his position so that he was able to send armies into Ghur and Khurasan on behalf of Ghiyāth al-Dīn Maḥmūd, and on another occasion, into Sistan. His relations with his son-in-law, Quṭb al-Dīn Aybak, were presumably cool, but there is perhaps a case for arguing that he claimed a superiority over the *mamluk* commanders holding sway in India on account of his special relationship with the former sultan, Muʿizz al-Dīn Muḥammad. When Quṭb al-Dīn Aybak was killed playing polo in 607/1210, he was briefly succeeded by his son, Ārām Shāh. The latter was overthrown by Aybak's favorite slave, Shams al-Dīn Iltutmish, who had been ruling on Aybak's behalf in Delhi and Bada'un. This bare-faced usurpation, made worse by being directed against the son of his late master,[87] necessitated higher sanction, and Tāj al-Dīn Yildiz obliged by sending Iltutmish a diploma *(ʿahd),* a parasol *(čatr),* and a mace of state *(dūrbāsh).*[88] It may be noted that a somewhat similar example of what may be styled "subinfeudation" had occurred a few years earlier: when Muḥammad *Bakhtiyār* Khaljī returned to Lahore with the spoils of his conquest of Bengal, Quṭb al-Dīn confirmed him as ruler of that newly-conquered region and conferred on him what is described as "a rich robe of honour from his own especial wardrobe," termed *sulṭānī*, presumably meaning that Aybak himself had received it from the hands of Muʿizz al-Dīn Muḥammad.[89]

The fate of Tāj al-Dīn Yildiz, however, illustrates the way in which concern for formal niceties of legitimation easily gave way to raw struggles for power. In 612/1215–16, the Khwārazmshāh ʿAlā' al-Dīn Muḥammad advanced to Ghazna and occupied it. Tāj al-Dīn Yildiz and such forces as he could muster withdrew to beyond the Indus into territory that he had shortly before designated as belonging to Iltutmish. The two warlords met in battle not far from Panipat; Yildiz was defeated, captured, and shortly afterward taken to Bada'un and executed.[90]

With the Khwārazmshāh's capture of Ghazna, ties with the old Ghaznavid-Ghūrid heartland west of the Indus were now severed. Of the great *mamluk* commanders of Sultān Muʿizz al-Dīn Muḥammad b. Sām, Quṭb al-Dīn Aybak was dead; Tāj al-Dīn Yildiz had been eliminated by Iltutmish; and Nāṣir al-Dīn Qabāča, who as ruler of Multan and Sind claimed the right to two canopies of state,[91] would soon be defeated by Iltutmish, supposedly drowning in the Indus near Bhakkar.[92] East of the Indus, Shams al-Dīn Iltutmish alone remained (Muḥammad Bakhtiyār, safely ensconced in Bengal, belonged to the Khalji tribe and had never been a *mamluk*). Such legitimation as all these *de facto* rulers had once enjoyed had flowed from the original caliphal investiture obtained long before by their master Sultān Ghiyāth al-Dīn Muḥammad b. Sām. There was now a vacuum, and it is this that makes significant Iltutmish's determination to open direct communication with Baghdad. The result was an embassy from al-Mustanṣir

(623–640/1226–1242) that reached Delhi in 626/1231 and that provided the occasion for a great display of public theater involving the old sultan, his sons, his *maliks* and *amīrs,* and his entire slave-household. On the day of the envoy's arrival, according to the *Tāj al-Ma'at͟hir* of Sadr al-Dīn Ḥasan Niẓāmī, Iltutmish was presented with a diploma of investiture for the sovereignty of Hindustan, a robe of honor, and the title *sultān mu'aẓẓam* ("Great Sultan"). The next day, the diploma was read publicly in the presence of the sultan and his court, after which he himself gave robes of honor to the caliphal envoys as well as to members of his entourage.[93] This event was to figure predominantly in the minds of later historians. Yaḥyā b. Aḥmad Sirhindī, writing long after, declared:

> The Sultan fulfilled the conditions of reverence and homage, and put on those robes along with his sons, the chiefs, and his old officers. It beggars description how the Sultan felt supreme pleasure and happiness from putting on that robe.[94]

While it is reasonable to suppose that in previous reigns, the caliph's name had continued to be read in the *khuṭba,* Shams al-Dīn Iltutmish renewed the former Ghaznavid and Ghūrid ties with Baghdad, while at the same time using the same forms of ritual allegiance to confirm, reward, and bind subordinates. Thus, on receiving the caliphal robes, he selected one of the finest sets, which he dispatched, together with a red canopy of state, to his son and heir, Nāṣir al-Dīn Maḥmūd, in Bengal.[95] It seems that it is from this time that the caliph's name appeared on the coinage of the Delhi Sultanate. So far as is known, this was the first and only occasion on which an 'Abbāsid caliph sent from Baghdad an *'ahd* for any of the sultans of Delhi. During the twenty-seven years that remained prior to the Mongol sack of Baghdad in 656/1258, five of Iltutmish's descendants reigned in fairly rapid succession and presumably not one had time or occasion to initiate contact with the caliphal court. In 640/1242, al-Musta'sim succeeded al-Mustanṣir and his name appeared on the coins of 'Alā' al-Dīn Mas'ūd Shāh, Nāṣir al-Dīn Maḥmūd Shāh, Ghiyāth al-Dīn Balban, Mu'izz al-Dīn Kayqubād, Jalāl al-Dīn K͟halji, and 'Ala' al-Dīn K͟haljī.[96] Balban, in an inscription on the Jāmi' Masjid at Garhmukteshwar, still described himself in 682/1283 as *nāṣir amīr al-mu'minīn* ("Helper of the Commander of the Faithful") to a nonexistent caliph.[97]

Balban initiated a routine of court ceremonial much more elaborate than had been the case with his predecessors, and in doing so it is assumed that he was harking back to pre-Islamic Sasanid traditions of kingship.[98] But it is conceivable that, aware of the fiction of paying allegiance to a long-dead caliph (al-Musta'sim was murdered in Baghdad in 656/1258, while Balban reigned from 664/1266 to 686/1287), he felt the need further to enhance and legitimate his own authority by even more attention to the externals of kingship, which set a precedent for the more opulent displays of magnificence which characterized the rule of the Khaljīs and Tughluqs.

The Khaljīs retained the fiction of an ongoing caliphate, also styling themselves *nāṣir amīr al-mu'minīn,* but the unstable Quṭb al-Dīn Mubārak Shāh (716–720/1316–1320) dropped the pretence, styling himself caliph and *imām al-a'zam* ("Imam of the Age") and assuming the caliphal regnal name of al-Wāthiq.[99] The first Tughluq sultan, following earlier Khaljī precedent, returned to the role of "helper" of a nonexistent caliph.[100]

It was thus left to Muḥammad b. Tughluq (725–752/1325–1351) to make some sense of this obviously unsatisfactory situation, and he did so by the daring although logical step of recognizing the exiled line of 'Abbāsids living in Cairo under the protection of the Egyptian Mamluk Sultanate. In so doing, he set the seal on his grandiose program of enhancing his power and prestige by territorial expansion, the promotion of far-flung diplomatic contacts, and the adoption of a public ceremonial of unexampled splendor.[101] He may also, in seeking caliphal legitimation, have sought to diminish the prestige of his formidable neighbors, the Il-Khan Abū-Sa'id and the Čaghatayid Khan, Tarmashīrīn.

Muḥammad b. Tughluq must have at some unrecorded point in time dispatched a mission to Cairo to the long-reigning caliph al-Mustakfī I (701–740/1302–1340), seeking caliphal confirmation, and presumably al-Mustakfī's name, and that of his short-reigning successor, al-Wāthiq (740–741/1340–1341), were read in the *khuṭba* in Delhi. However, it was not until after the accession of Ḥākim II (741–753/1341–1352) that, according to Baranī, the caliph's envoy, Hajji Sa'id Sarsarī, arrived in Delhi in 744/1343 with the anticipated robe of honor, a diploma of confirmation, and sonorous titles, causing the sultan and his court to go out of the city on foot to greet the envoy and his gifts.[102] Another mission was then sent to Cairo, returning with a further confirmation of the sultan's status. The Tughluqid court poet, Badr al-Din Čāč, celebrated this latter occasion in a fulsome *qaṣīda:*

> Gabriel, from the firmament of heaven, has proclaimed the glad tidings, that a robe of honor and patent have reached the sultan from the caliph, just as the verses of the Qur'ān honoured Muhammad by their arrival from the court of the immortal God. . . . The imam has give the shah absolute power over all the world, and this intelligence has reached all other shahs throughout the seven climates. The patent of the other sovereigns of the world has been revoked, for an autograph grant has been dispatched from the eternal

> capital. The wells of the envious have become as dry as that of Joseph, now that the Egyptian robe has been received in Hindustan from Canaan. . . . A veritable 'Id has arrived to the faithful, now that twice in one year, a *khil'a* has reached the sultan from the *amir al-mu'minin*. . . .
>
> Yesternight, at the time that the sun, the king with the golden garments, invested itself with a black mantle, and the king of the host of darkness, whose name is the moon, filled the emerald vault with sparks of gold, a robe of honour and a patent of sovereignty arrived, for the king of sea and land, from the lord caliph, the saint of his time, Aḥmad 'Abbās, the imam of God, the heir of the prophet of mankind.[103]

Then, after describing the scene of the reception and grandiloquently paraphrasing the words of the patent, the poet adds,

> The imam has sent a *khil'a,* black as the apple of the eye, calculated to spread the light of the law through the hearts of men. For fear of the justice of thy government, the hart and the lion consort in the forest. May the eyes of thy enemies shed tears of blood. . . . [104]

The splendor of Muḥammad b. Tughluq's court is well attested by contemporary writers.[105] Whether his ostentatious respect for the caliphate was policy or piety, Ibn Baṭṭūṭa, who provides such an intimate vignette of the sultan's court and its ceremonial, relates an interesting story (now impossible to date) regarding the sultan's respect for a member of the 'Abbāsid family, a descendant of the last caliph in Baghdad, al-Musta'sim, who appeared as a refugee at his court. Muḥammad b. Tughluq went out of Delhi to receive him, and when the two met, he dismounted and bowed to the 'Abbāsid prince who did the same. The latter then presented the sultan with robes of honor, one of which Muḥammad b. Tughluq placed over his shoulders and "did homage in the same manner that people do homage to him."[106] A horse was then brought up and the sultan held the stirrup for the 'Abbāsid to mount, after which the two rode together under a single parasol and, what most amazed Ibn Baṭṭūṭa, who had never seen the sultan do such a thing before, Muḥammad b. Tughluq offered him betel nut with his own hand.

Ibn Baṭṭūṭa also describes in some detail the lavish gifts and privileges granted to the caliph's descendant, who proved to be an incorrigible miser, including the assignment of the Delhi suburb of Siri, and recounts how on one occasion he himself accompanied a great *amīr* with three sets of ceremonial robes from the sultan, which had pearl buttons the size of large hazelnuts in place of the usual silk fastenings. The 'Abbāsid prince came out of his house to receive them and the *amīr* helped to robe him.[107] For Ibn Baṭṭūṭa, robing was a normal part of public life. For example, on one occasion, Muḥammad b. Tughluq, returning to his capital, decided to make a number of high appointments. One such appointee, Khudāwandzāda Ḍiyā' al-Dīn, who belonged to a prominent family from Tirmidh, was appointed *amīr dād* (minister of justice) and received in addition to revenue assignments and cash a silk robe of honor with gold embroidery that the sultan himself placed on him. This was called a *ṣūrat al-shīr* ("the face of a lion") because embroidered on the front and back was a figure of a lion (inside was sewn a tag showing the amount of gold thread used for the embroidering).[108] Another recipient of the sultan's generosity was Khudāwandzāda's nephew, Amīr Bakht, who received a similar robe when he was appointed *rasūldār* (chamberlain in charge of missions). Ibn Baṭṭūṭa himself was appointed *qāḍī* of Delhi and was invested with what was called a *miḥrābī* robe of honor, that is to say, one with a representation of a *miḥrāb* embroidered back and front, and a further ten robes were distributed among his companions.[109]

In the *Masālik al-absar,* Shihāb al-Dīn al-'Umarī provides a glittering montage of Muḥammad b. Tughluq on the road or in the hunting field, accompanied by 30,000 horsemen, numerous elephants and a thousand led-horses caparisoned with saddles and bridles studded with diamonds and gems. As he moved from palace to palace in the neighborhood of Delhi, he rode alone, apart from the horsemen carrying his parasol *(čatrbardār),* his mounted bodyguard *(silaḥbardār),* and the chamberlains of the wardrobe *(jāmadār).* Around and behind these walked 12,000 *mamluks* on foot.[110] He stresses the munificence of the sultan and how he rewarded those in his service, whether men of the sword or men of the pen, with gifts of silver and gold, revenue assignments *(iqṭā'),* horses, richly embroidered saddles, jewels, golden girdles, and clothing, but never elephants, which belonged to the sultan alone.[111]

From all this, it is clear that so many sumptuary objects destined for gifts had to be manufactured or at the very least stored within the palace complex, and *al-'Umari* indeed confirms the existence of a large *kārkhāna* (palace workshop). He writes:

> The sultan maintains a *kārkhāna* in Delhi for the embroidery work. There are four-thousand silk-workers who weave and embroider different kinds of cloth for robes of honour and garments. In addition, the cloth imported from China, Iraq and Alexandria is also embroidered here. The sultan distributes every year 200,000 suits of clothes, one lakh (i.e., 100,000 rupees) in the winter and one lakh in the summer. The cloth for the winter garments are imported mostly from Alexandria, while those for the winter are made of cloth woven in the royal *kārkhāna* or around Delhi or imported from China and Iraq. Royal garments are distributed among the residents of *khānqāhs* (Sufi hospices).

> Besides, the sultan has 4,000 embroiderers who make garments for him and his harem. They prepare robes of honour which are granted by the sultan to his officers of state and their ladies.[112]

In a further passage on textiles, he remarks:

> The linen garments which are imported from Alexandria and the land of the Russians are worn only by those whom the sultan honors with them. The others wear tunics and robes of fine cotton. They make garments of this material which resemble the robes (makti') of Baghdad. But these latter, as also those called Nasafi, differ very much from those of India as regards fineness, beauty of color, and delicacy.[113]

Thus, the reign of Muḥammad b. Tughluq saw the fullest elaboration of older traditions of legitimization by means of caliphal recognition (however nominal) and the utilization of ceremonial and gift-giving to reinforce the day-to-day exercise of authority, as it also witnessed the culmination of the Delhi sultanate, while the summation of the process followed during the reign of that most orthodox of the sultans of Delhi, Fīrūẓ Shāh Tughluq (752–790/1351–1388).[114]

Four years after Fīrūẓ Shāh mounted the throne, an embassy arrived in Delhi in 756/1355 from the Cairene caliph, al-Ḥākim II, bringing a diploma confirming the sultan's rule over Hindustan as well as robes of honor.[115] There is no record that his embassy was solicited and therefore perhaps the caliph himself, on learning of the death of Muḥammad b. Tughluq, initiated this contact with his successor. In any case, it must have been very comforting for a sultan facing breakaway movements in Bengal and in the Deccan to have this confirmation of his authority. In the *Fūtūhat-i Fīrūz Shāhī,* the sultan wrote that

> The greatest and best of honours that I obtained through God's mercy was, that by my obedience and piety, and friendliness and submission to the *Khalīfa,* the representative of the Holy Prophet, my authority was confirmed; for it is by his sanction that the power of kings is assured, and no king is secure until he has submitted himself to the *Khalīfa,* and has received a confirmation from the sacred throne. A diploma was sent to me fully confirming my authority as deputy of the *Khilāfat,* and the leader of the faithful was graciously pleased to honour me with the title of "Sa'id al-Salatin." He also bestowed upon me robes, a banner, a sword, a ring and a foot-print as badges of honour and distinction.[116]

The coinage of Fīrūz Shāh bore the name of al-Ḥakīm and, after the latter's death, his two successors, al Mu'taḍid and al-Mutawakkil.[117] His

Tughluqid successors continued the practice, retaining the name of al-Mutawakkil after the latter's demise, presumably because, as Tughluqid rule disintegrated and all contacts with Egypt came to an end, no one in Delhi was informed of the fortunes of the Cairene caliphs.[118] Later sultans of Delhi—Mubārak Shāh II, Muḥammad Shāh IV, 'Ālam Shāh, and Bahlūl Lōdī--used the earlier formula of *nāṣir amīr al-mu'minīn,*[119] but if doing so was little more than reverence for tradition, there can be no doubt that the court ceremonial and the forms and symbols of rulership that had long since traveled from Baghdad via Bukhara and Ghazna to Delhi, and which had seen their zenith under the Tughluqs, survived ubiquitously at most of the later Indo-Islamic courts, and especially at the court of the Mughals.

Conclusions

Throughout most of the Islamic era and in most parts of the Islamic world, the conferring of robes of honor was an ubiquitous symbol of bonding between a superior and an inferior. Whether its origin was sanctified by the Prophet of Islam's own usage or whether its roots lay deep in the traditions of the ancient Near and Middle East, by 'Abbāsid times it had become a normative component of court ceremonial, testified to again and again in the pages of such writers as Ṭabarī, Miskawayh, and Bayhaqī.[120] And yet, interestingly, the practice apparently never became closely associated with the religious institution, although in the appropriate circumstances men of religion *('ulamā', fuqahā'* and Sufi *shaykhs)* could be recipients or donors. The data, in fact, suggests a nondenominational custom of the very widest application in traditional Islamic society, which, if it had ever had any religious significance at one time, had long since lost it, allowing rulers and notables of impeccable religious credentials to use it to honor and reward women and children as well as men, slaves and eunuchs as well as free men, and non-Muslims as well as believers.

Notes

1. Arabic and Persian names and words are transliterated in accordance with the system employed in *The Encyclopaedia of Islam (EI)* with the following two exceptions: the Arabic letter *JIM* is represented by *J* and not *DJ,* and the Arabic letter *QAF* by *Q* and not *Ḳ*. Modern place-names reflect current international usage. Arabic and Persian words for terms are normally given in the singular.
2. Medieval Arab geographers gave the name of Khurasan to the area lying north and east of the central Iranian desert region (Dasht-i Lut and Dasht-i Kavir) as far as the Amu-Darya (Oxus) and upstream as far as the mountains

of Badakhshan. It was divided into four quarters (*rub'*), named after its four principal cities: Nishapur, Marv, Herat, and Balkh. It thus included lands that today are in Iran, Turkmenistan, and Afghanistan. In this chapter, the name Khurasan will be used in the sense indicated above, and not in the restricted present-day usage of the northeasternmost *ustan* of modern Iran, with its capital at Mashhad.

3. Nimruz was the medieval name given to the region lying due south of Khurasan, in what is today Iranian and Afghan Sistan, with its principal urban centers located at Zaranj and Bust.
4. Khwarazm was a fertile region south of the Aral Sea, comprising the lower reaches and delta of the Amu-Darya, with twin capitals at Gurganj and Kath.
5. Mawarannahr (known to the Greeks as Transoxiana and in the nineteenth century as Turkistan) meant "the lands beyond the river," the region between the Amu-Darya and the Syr-Darya (Jaxartes). Its most celebrated cities were Bukhara and Samarand.
6. The most important of these Iranian dynasties were the Ṭāhirids of Nishapur (205–259/821–873), the Ṣaffārids of Nimruz (253-ca. 900/867-ca. 1495), the Sāmānids of Bukhara (204–395/819–1005), and the Ma'munids of Gurganj (385–408/995–1017).
7. These were the Ghaznavids (366–582/977–1186), the Qarakhanids (382–607/992–1211) and the Saljuqs (429–590/1038–1194).
8. The Būyids were Shī'īs from Daylam (now Mazandaran, south of the Caspian Sea), who professed broad Zaydī tendencies at a time when Twelver Shī'īsm had yet to be formulated. Ruling western Iran and much of Iraq, they entered Baghdad as conquerors in 334/945 and thereafter held the 'Abbāsid caliphs in tutelage until they were expelled by the Saljuqs in 447/1055.
9. A. J. Wensinck, "*KHUṬBA,*" *EI* (2), vol. 4, pp. 74–75.
10. J. Allan, "*SIKKA,*" *EI* (1), vol. 7, pp. 423–24.
11. See, for example, Richard N. Frye, *The Golden Age of Persia: The Arabs in the East* (London: Thames and Hudson, 1975), pp. 186–212.
12. This letter was written by Ṭāhir al-Ḥusayn around 205–206/821 to his son 'Abd Allāh b. Ṭāhir on the occasion of al-Ma'mūn appointing the latter as governor of Raqqa and Egypt. See Ibn Khaldūn, *The Muqaddimah,* trans. Franz Rosenthal, 3 vols. (Princeton: Princeton University Press, 1958), vol. 2, pp. 139–56.
13. In this regard, Ibn Khaldūn remarked:

> The Muslims [the generation of the Prophet and the first caliphs] . . . wanted to avoid the coarseness of royal authority and do without royal customs. They also despised pomp, which has nothing whatever to do with the truth. The caliphate then came to be royal authority, and the Muslims learnt to esteem the splendor and luxury of this world. Persian and Byzantine clients, subjects of the preceding (pre-Islamic) dynasties, mixed with them and showed them their ways of ostentation and luxury. (*Ibid.*, vol. 2, p. 50)

14. J. David Weill, "'ALAM," *EI* (2), vol. 1, p. 349; A. Birken, "LIWĀ'," *EI* (2), vol. 4, p. 776.
15. Eleanor Sims, "ČATR," *EI* (2), vol. 2, pp. 77–79.
16. J. Allan, "SIKKA," (1), vol. 7, pp. 423–34.
17. J. Deny, "MUHR," *EI* (1), vol. 6, pp. 701–02.
18. J. Pedersen, "MASDJID," *EI* (2), vol. 6, pp. 660–68 ("the component parts and furnishings of the mosque," pp. 660–668), ("*maqṣūra*," pp. 661–662).
19. N. A. Stillman, "KHIL'A," *EI* (2), vol. 4, pp. 6–7. Closely linked with early Islamic robes of honor was the embroidering in silk or gold thread of the caliph's name upon the borders of garments, and known as *ṭirāz*. See Ibn Khaldūn, *op.cit.*, vol. 2, pp. 65–66, and A. Grohmann, "ṬIRĀZ," *EI* (1), vol. 8, pp. 785–93, and vol. 9, Supplement, pp. 248–50.
20. See the discussion in Paula Sanders, *Ritual, Politics, and the City in Fatimid Egypt* (Albany: State University of New York Press, 1994), pp. 29–30, 78, 128, and 186.
21. J. Schacht, "'AHD," *EI* (2), vol. 1, p. 255; W. Bjorkman, "*MANSHŪR*," *EI* (2), vol. 4, pp. 423–24.
22. C. E. Bosworth, "LAQAB," *EI* (2), vol. 4, pp. 618–31. For an eleventh-century discussion on contemporary honorifics, see Niẓām al-Mulk, *Siyār al-Mulūk,* ed. H. Darke (Tehran: B.T.N.K., A.H. 1345), pp. 189–200. For the English translation see Nizam al-Mulk, *The Book of Government or Rules for Kings,* trans. H. Darke (London: Routledge and Kegan Paul, 1960), pp. 152–63.
23. E. Tynan, "BAY'A," *EI* (2), vol. 1, pp. 1113–14. Its origin lay in the oath of allegiance given to the first caliph, Abū Bakr, in 11/632.
24. Roy P. Mottahedeh, *Loyalty and Leadership in an Early Islamic Society* (Princeton: Princeton University Press, 1980), p. 42. See also pp. 62–66.
25. See Alexandre Popovic, *Révolte des Esclaves en Iraq au IIIe, IXe siècle* (Paris: P. Geunther, 1976).
26. Al-Ṭabarī, *Ta'rīkh al-rusūl wa'l mulūk* (*The History of Prophets and Kings*), vol. 36, *The Revolt of the Zanj,* trans. David Waines (Albany: State University of New York Press, 1992), pp. 203–205. For 'Amr, see W. Barthold, "'AMR B. AL-LAYTH," *EI* (2), vol. 1, pp. 452–53, and C. E. Bosworth, "The Tahirids and Saffarids," in *The Cambridge History of Iran,* vol. 4, ed. R. N. Frye (Cambridge: Cambridge University Press, 1975), pp. 116–210.
27. Al-Ṭabarī, vol. 37, *The 'Abbāsid Recovery,* trans. Philip M. Fields (Albany: State University of New York Press, 1987), p. 1.
28. *Ibid.*, p. 72.
29. *Ibid.*, pp. 160–61, and vol. 38, *The Return of the Caliphate to Baghdad,* trans. Franz Rosenthal (Albany: State University of New York Press, 1985), p. 2.
30. *Ibid.*, p. 64.
31. *Ibid.*, p. 77. According to Rosenthal, the word *kiswa* is often used as a collective with a meaning approximating to a complete wardrobe (p. 77, n. 392). For 'Amr's request for appointment, see *Ibid.*, pp. 70 and 84.
32. *Ibid.*, pp. 84–85.

33. Narshakhī, *Ta'rīkh-i Bukhārā,* trans. R. N. Frye as *The History of Bukhara* (Cambridge, Mass.: Medieval Academy of America, 1954), p. 76.
34. *Ibid.,* 77 and 148, n. 271. Narshakhī, or a copyist, as Frye points out, made a scribal error in attributing this confirmation to al-Wāthiq (227–232/842–847).
35. *Ibid.,* pp. 79–80.
36. Ṭabarī, vol. 38, *The Return of the Caliphate to Baghdad,* pp. 91–92, 95–96, and 112.
37. Charles F. Defremery, ed. and trans., *Histoire des Samanides, A.D. 892–999, par Mirkhond* (Paris, 1845, reprinted Amsterdam: Oriental Press, 1974), Persian text, p. 11; translation, pp. 122–23.
38. Ṭabarī, vol. 38, pp. 117–118.
39. *Ibid.,* pp. 146–147.
40. *Ibid.,* p. 183.
41. B. Spuler, "CHAGHANIYAN," *EI* (2), vol. 2, p.102.
42. C. E. Bosworth, "The Ruler of Chaghaniyan in Early Islamic Times," in *The Arabs, Byzantium and Iran: Studies in Early Islamic History and Culture,* by C E. Bosworth (London:Variorum, 1996), XX: 6.
43. R. N. Frye, "The Samanids," p. 140, in *The Cambridge History of Iran,* vol. 4, pp. 136–61.
44. See especially Roy Mottahedeh, *op. cit.,* pp. 54–57.
45. R. B. Sergeant, *Ars Islamica* 11 (1946), 122–27; Narshakhī, op. cit., pp. 15–16 and 19–20; and D. G. Shepherd and W. B. Henning, "Zandanījī Identified?" *Aus Der Welt Der Islamischen Kunst. Festschrift für Ernst Kuhnel zum 75. Geburstag am 26.10.1957* (Berlin:Verlag Gebr. Mann, 1959), pp. 15–40; and Dorothy G. Shepherd, "Zandanījī Revisited," *Documenta Textilia. Festschrift für Sigrid Muller-Christensen,* ed. M. Flury-Lemberg and K. Stolleis (München: Deutscher Kunstverlag, 1981), pp. 105–122.
46. Niẓām al-Mulk, p. 133; English trans., p. 106. The wearing of liveries or uniforms by *mamluk* units extends back to the time when, according to Mas'ūdī, al-Mu'taṣim (218–227/833–842) dressed his troop of 4,000 Turkish *mamluks* "in brocade with gilded belts and ornaments, distinguishing them by their costume from the rest of the army." Mas'ūdī, *The Meadows of Gold: The 'Abbāsids,* trans. P. Lunde and Caroline Stone (London: Kegan Paul, 1989), p. 228.
47. Bosworth, "Chaghaniyan," *op. cit.,* p. 7.
48. Niẓamī 'Arūḍī Samarqandī, *Chahār Maqāla,* ed. M. Qazvini (London: Luzac & Co., 1927), pp. 82–85: trans. E. G. Browne (London: Luzac & Co., 1921), pp. 115–118.
49. *Ibid.,*Qazvini, pp. 41–46; *Ibid.,* Browne, pp. 58–66.
50. *Ibid.,* Qazvini, pp. 64–65; *Ibid.,* Browne, pp. 92–95.
51. Yūsuf Khāṣṣ Ḥājib, *Kutudgu Bilig,* trans. as *Wisdom of Royal Glory,* trans. R. Dankoff (Chicago: University of Chicago Press, 1983), p. 259. See also W. Barthold, "The Bughra Khan Mentioned in the *Qudatqu Bilik,*" *Bulletin of the School of Oriental Studies* 3 (1923–25): 151–58.

52. H. M. Elliott and J. Dowson, *The History of India as told by its own Historians,* 8 vols. (London: Trubner and Co., 1869), vol. 2, p. 24 (the spelling has been modified in accordance with the transliteration used throughout this essay). See also the version of Ibn Bābā al-Qashānī, quoted in C. E. Bosworth, *The Later Ghaznavids* (New York: Columbia University Press, 1977), p. 136.
53. Abū'l-Faḍl Bayhaqī, *Ta'rīkh-i Ma'sūdī,* ed. Q. Ghani and 'A. A. Fayyad (Teheran, 1324/1945), p. 669.
54. Mahmud's successor, Mas'ūd, who had been treated with arrogance by Ḥasanak, revived at his accession the charges of Ismā'īlī heresy and had him executed in 422/1031. Bayhaqī, pp. 181–83, Elliott and Dowson, vol. 2, pp. 88–100. See M. Nazim, *The Life and Times of Sultān Maḥmud of Ghazna* (Cambridge: Cambridge University Press, 1931) pp. 136–37.
55. Nazim, pp. 164–65.
56. Ibid., p. 165. It is curious that the Niẓām al-Mulk, writing over a century later, stresses in the *Siyāsatnāma* the caliph's reluctance to grant Maḥmūd titles other than the first two he received and relates a prolix tale on that subject., Niẓām al-Mulk, pp. 189–98; English trans. pp. 153–60. See also C. E. Bosworth, "The Titulature of the Early Ghaznavids," *Oriens* 15 (1962): 210–33.
57. Niẓāmī 'Arūḍī Samarqandī, *Chahār Maqāla,* pp. 77–84; English translation, p. 77.
58. E. Tyan, "BAY'A," *EI,* (2), vol. 2, pp. 1113–14.
59. Elliot and Dowson, vol. 2, p. 518.
60. Bayhaqī, pp. 44–49, and Bosworth, "The Imperial Policy of the Early Ghaznawids," *Islamic Studies: Journal of the Central Institute of Islamic Research, Karachi* 1 (1962), p. 64.
61. Bosworth, in fact, is of the opinion that it was apprehension of the Qarakhanids then ruling in Bukhara, Samarkand, and Kashgar that encouraged Mas'ud to boast of being the premier ruler of the Muslim East. Bosworth, "The Imperial Policy of the Early Ghaznavids," p. 65.
62. Bayhaqī, pp. 284–94, quoted in Bosworth, "The Imperial Policy of the Ghaznavids" p. 66.
63. We may discern such garments in the costumes worn by the courtiers painted on the walls of the audience hall of Mas'ūd's palace at Lashkari Bazar. Daniel Schlumberger, "Le Palais Ghaznévide de Lashkari Bazar," *Syria* 29 (1952): 251–70. It is a measure of that common currency that Muḥammad 'Awfi (d. c.630/1232) could eulogize Maḥmūd, using the image of the *khil'a* with *ṭirāz* ornamentation: "the robe of glory and grandeur was richly embroidered by his virtues and triumphs." A. J. Arberry, *Classical Persian Literature* (London: George Allen & Unwin, 1958), p. 53.
64. Elliot and Dowson, vol. 2, p. 68.
65. Elliot and Dowson, vol. 2, pp. 68–69.
66. Elloit and Dawson, vol. 2, p. 69.
67. Elliot and Dawson, vol. 2, p. 70.

68. Bosworth, *Later Ghaznavids,* pp. 78–80.
69. Bosworth, *Later Ghaznavids,* p. 80, and Aziz Ahmad, *Islamic Culture in the Indian Environment* (Oxford: Clarendon Press, 1964), p. 6, quoting Ma'sud b. Sa'd-i b. Salman, *Diwan,* ed. Rashid Yasimi, Tehran, pp. 443, 460 and 113–14. See also Mirza Muhammad Qazwini, "Mas'ud-i-Sa'd-i-Salman," *Journal of the Royal Asiatic Society* (1905): 693–740 and (1906) 11–51; D. C. Ganguly, "The Historical Value of Diwan-i Salman," *Islamic Culture* 16 (1942) 423–28; and E. Thomas, "On the Coins of the Kings of Ghazni," *Journal of the Royal Asiatic Society* 9 (1848) 267–386.
70. Bosworth, *Later Ghaznavids,* pp. 78–79.
71. C. E. Bosworth, "GHŪRIDS," *EI,* (2), vol. 3, pp. 1099–1104.
72. Minhāj-i Sirāj Jūzjānī, *Tabaqāt-i-Nāṣirī,* ed. A. H. Habibi, 2 vols. (Kabul: The Historical Society of Afghanistan, 1963–64); English trans. H. G. Raverty, 2 vols. (Calcutta: The Asiatic Society, 1881). Raverty vol. 1, p. 317.
73. Raverty, vol. 1, p. 377.
74. Habibi, vol. 1, pp. 201–202 and 360–61; Raverty, vol. 1, pp. 242–44 and I:382–83.
75. Habibi, vol. 1, p. 361; Raverty vol. 1, p. 383. Ibn Khaldūn included the beating of drums as part of the *alah,* the display of banners and the playing of music instruments that he regarded as one of the emblems of royal authority. Ibn Khaldūn, 2:38–42. For the practice in Mughal India, see William Irvine, *The Army of the Indian Moghuls* (London, 1903; rpt. New Delhi: Eurasia Pub. House, 1962), pp. 30–31 and 207–209.
76. Habibi, vol. 1, p. 360; Raverty, vol. 1, p. 382.
77. Habibi, vol. 1, p. 366; Raverty, vol. 1, p. 388.
78. Habibi, vol. 1, p. 444; Raverty,vol. 1, p. 605.
79. For Karman, see Raverty, vol. 1, pp. 498–99, n. 7.
80. Habibi, vol. 1, pp. 411–12; Raverty, vol. 1, pp. 498–500.
81. Habibi, vol. 1, pp. 411–12; Raverty, vol. 1, pp. 500–501.
82. Habibi, vol. 1, p. 412; Raverty, vol. 1, pp. 501–502.
83. *K͟hus͟hdās͟hīyya* is a term used for a group of *mamluks* bound by loyalty to a common master and to each other in Mamluk Egypt. See D. Ayalon, *L'Esclavage de Mamlouk* (Jerusalem: The Israel Oriental Society, 1951), pp. 29–31 and 34–37; D. P. Little, *An Introduction to Mamluk Historiography* (Montreal: McGill-Queen's University Press, 1970), pp. 125–26; and R. Irwin, *The Middle East in the Middle Ages: The Early Mamluk Sultanate, 1250–1382* (Carbondale: Southern Illinois University Press, 1986), pp. 65, 88–90 and 154–55. While the term *k͟hus͟hdās͟hīyya* or its Persian equivalent has not been found in the Indian sources (Peter Jackson, "The *Mamluk* Institution in Early Muslim India," *Journal of the Royal Asiatic Society,* 3d ser., 2 [1990]: 351), Minhāj-i Sirāj's practice of referring to the Mu'izzī, Quṭbī and Shamsī *mamluks* surely makes a distinction between members of different slave-households, making it difficult not to assume a bonding comparable to Egyptian *k͟hus͟hdās͟hīyya* practice.
84. See Eleanor Sims, "CATR," *EI,* (2), vol. 2, p. 77–79.

85. Habibi, vol. 1, p.417; Raverty, vol. 1, pp. 524–25.
86. He minted coinage in his own name. See S. Lane-Poole, *The Coins of the Sultans of Dehli in the British Museum* (London: British Museum, 1884), pp. xviii-xix, 10–12, and plate I; Dominique Sourdel, *Inventaire de monnaies musulmanes anciennes du Musée de Caboul* (Damascus: Institut Français de Damas, 1953), pp. 129–32 and plate VI; Edward Thomas, "On the Coins of the Kings of Ghazni," *Journal of the Royal Asiatic Society* 9 (1848):379–80.
87. If the custom of *khushdāshīyya* prevailing in Mamluk Egypt had existed in India, Iltutmish would have been duty-bound to promote the interests of his late master's son.
88. Habibi, vol. 1, p. 444; Raverty, vol. 1, p. 607. For *dūrbāsh*, see J. Burton-Page, "DŪRBASH," *EI* (2) vol. 2, pp. 627–28; see also Raverty, vol. 1, p. 607, n. 5.
89. Habibi, vol. 1, p. 426; Raverty, vol. 1, p. 554.
90. Habibi, vol. 1, pp. 412–13; Raverty, vol. 1, pp. 505–506.
91. Habibi, vol. 1, p. 419; Raverty, vol. 1, p. 532.
92. Habibi, vol. 1, pp. 420–421; Raverty, vol. 1, p. 544.
93. Sadr al-Dīn Ḥasan Niẓāmī, *Tāj al-Ma'athir,* in Elliot and Dowson, vol. 2, p. 243.
94. Yaḥyā b. Aḥmad Sirhindī, *Ta'rīkh-i Mubārak Shāhī,* ed. Hidayat Hosain (Calcutta: Bibliotheca Indica, 1931), p. 19; trans.: *The Ta'rikh-i-Mubarakshāhī,* ed. K. K. Basu (Baroda: Oriental Institute, 1932), p. 19. Khwāja Niẓām al-Dīn Aḥmad echoed the sentiment: "He felt boundless pleasure and happiness, from the putting on of that robe." *Ṭabaqāt-i Akbarī,* trans. B. De, 3 vols. (Calcutta: Bibliotheca Indica, 1911–41), vol. 1, p. 67.
95. Raverty, vol. 1, p. 630. This prince died shortly afterwards, throwing the succession into confusion.
96. Edward Thomas, *Chronicles of the Pathán Kings of Delhi* (London: Trübner & Co., 1871), pp. 122, 127–29, 134, and 141.
97. Ibid., p. 136.
98. K. A. Nizami, *Some Aspects of Religion and Politics in India during the Thirteenth Century* (Aligarh: Aligarh Muslim University, 1961), pp. 92–97.
99. Thomas, *Chronicles of the Pathán Kings,* pp. 179–83.
100. Thomas, *Chronicles of the Pathán Kings,* pp. 186–192.
101. Peter Jackson, "The Mongols and the Delhi Sultanate in the Reign of Muhammad Tughluq (1325–1351), *Central Asiatic Journal* 19 (1975):118–57. Iqtidar Husain Siddiqui, "Sultan Muhammad bin Tughluq's Foreign Policy: A Reappraisal," *Islamic Culture* 62 (1988), 1–22.
102. Elliot and Dowson, vol. 3, pp. 249–50. In his habitual manner of denigrating Muḥammad b. Tughluq, Baranī, in his *Ta'rīkh-i Fīrūz Shāhī,* presents his dealings with the Egyptian 'Abbāsids in a perjorative light.
103. Elliot and Dowson, vol. 3, pp. 567–568. The reference to the receipt of two robes of honor in one year has aroused much controversy; see above, n. 1 on p. 568. I have reduced the use of capital letters in this passage.
104. Elliot and Dowson, vol. 3, p. 569. The mention of the color black refers to traditional 'Abbāsid usage.

105. Ibn Baṭṭūṭa, *Travels,* trans. H. A. R. Gibb and C. F. Beckingham, 4 vols. (Cambridge: Cambridge University Press, 1958–94), vol. 3, pp. 657–70; Shihāb al-Dīn al-'Umarī, *Masālik al Abṣār fi-mamlik al-Amṣār,* trans. I. H. Siddiqi and Q. M. Ahmad, as *A Fourteenth Century Arab Account of India under Sultan Muhammad bin Tughluq* (Aligarh: Siddiqi Publishing House, 1972), pp. 41–46; al-Qalqashandī, *Subh al-A'shā,* trans. Otto Spies, as *An Arab Account of India in the 14th Century* (Stuttgart: Verlag von W. Kohlhammer, 1936), pp. 73–78.
106. Ibn Baṭṭūṭa, vol. 3, p. 680.
107. Ibn Baṭṭūṭa, vol. 3, pp. 679–83.
108. *Ibid.,* vol. 3, pp. 744–746.
109. *Ibid.,* vol. 3, pp. 746–748.
110. Shihāb al-Dīn al-'Umarī, *Masālik al Abṣār, A Fourteenth Century Arab Account of India under Sultan Muhammad bin Tughluq* p. 44. See also M. Zaki, *Arab Accounts of India during the Fourteenth Century* (Delhi: Idarah-i Adabiyat-i Delli, 1981), p. 29.
111. Al-'Umarī, p. 52; Zaki, p. 40.
112. Al-'Umarī, *ibid.,* p. 39; Zaki, *ibid.,* pp. 23–24; Sergeant, *Ars Islamica* 12 (1947): 136–37. Sergeant quotes from al-Qalqashandī, *Subh al-A'shā:* "the Sultan of Delhi has a tiraz factory (dār al-ṭirāz) in which there are four thousand manufacturers of silk (kazzaz), making all kinds of textiles for robes of honor (khil'a), robes (kasawa), and presents (itlakat), besides the cloth of China, Iraq, and Alexandria which is brought there" (p. 136).
113. Sergeant, p. 136.
114. For Muḥammad b. Tughluq's use of the coinage to emphasize his position vis-à-vis the caliphate, see Stanley Lane-Poole, *The Coins of the Sultans of Delhi in the British Museum* (London: British Museum Trustees, 1884), pp. xxv-xxvii.
115. Yaḥyā b. Aḥmad b. Sirhindī, p. 126; trans, p. 131. See also Khwāja Nīẓām al-Dīn Aḥmad, vol. 1, p. 245, where he refers to the sultan's pride and happiness in receiving the mission. Shams-i Sirāj 'Afīf states that robes were also sent to the heir-apparent, Fāth Khan, and to the *wazīr,* Khan-i Jahān. Elliot and Dowson, vol. 3, pp. 342–43.
116. Elliot and Dowson, vol. 3, pp. 342–43. The Prophet's footprint (*qadam*) was placed at the graveside of the sultan's eldest son, Fāth Khan, who predeceased him. The tomb in Delhi, close to Ajmeri Gate, is known as Qadam Sharif.
117. Thomas, pp. 269–99.
118. Thomas, pp. 303–305, 305–310, 311, and 312–17.
119. Thomas, pp. 330–33, 334–37, and 338–40, and 357–64.
120. N. A. Stillman, "*KHIL'A,*" *El* (2), vol. 5, pp. 6–7. See also F. W. Buckler, "Two Instances of Khil'at in the Bible," *Journal of Theological Studies* 23 (1922) 197 ff., and F. W. Buckler, "The Oriental Despot," *Anglican Theological Review* 10 (1927–28) 238–49.

PART THREE

THE LATER MIDDLE AGES:
CA. 1000 CE–CA. 1500 CE

CHAPTER 9

ROBES OF HONOR IN FATIMID EGYPT

Paula Sanders

In memory of Yedida Kalfon Stillman

At its most literal, a *khil'a* (pl. *khila'*) is a garment that has been taken off (*khala'a*) by one person and given to another. The Prophet Muḥammad is said to have given the mantle (*burda*) he was wearing to the poet Ka'b b. Zuhayr. While earlier rulers certainly bestowed such "castoff" garments as honorific robes, the term *khil'a* came into usage only in the Abbasid period (750–1258). In time, it was used to designate any garment bestowed by the ruler upon an official, and court officials were referred to as the "men of robes of honor" (*aṣḥāb al-khil'a*).[1] In a Fatimid account from the North African period, containing rare details about the ritual of bestowal itself, the chamberlain Ja'far tells of an audience with the imam:

> We saw the Mahdi sitting in the middle of the tent on his throne, resplendent like the sun with beauty and gracefulness. Weeping, we threw ourselves down before him, while he laughed and humbly praised God, may his name be blessed, thanked him and exalted him. Then he said to Ṣandal: "Give me the two splendid garments which I have been keeping especially in such-and-such a trunk." He brought them, and the Mahdi donned one of them, and the Qā'im the other. Then he said, "And now the clothing and swords, which I have been keeping for these here!" Then, after he had first clothed Abū 'Abdallāh with his own hand, wound a turban around his head and girded him with a sword, he also clothed me, and that indeed with a garment under which there was yet another, made of Dabīqī linen, and with turban, trousers and slippers, and he girded me with a sword. He clothed and girded Ṭayyib as he had done for me, and then also Muslim, Ṣandal and Abū Ya'qūb.[2]

At a public audience the next morning, these same men whom the imam had clothed and girded with his own hand stood in close proximity to him. The only information about the materials themselves is the detail specifying the base material of Ja'far's costume as Dabīqī linen, a fine textile of Egyptian origins. The Mahdī himself had been wearing a shirt of Dabīqī linen, a wrap from Medina, a turban cloth from Shaṭā wrapped around his head and shoulders, and Arab sandals only days before when he had been rescued from his captivity.[3] Though presumably fine textiles, the emphasis in this early account on the ritual of bestowal itself points to the importance of the imam's hand in bestowal even when the garments themselves were not castoffs.

Later textual sources almost never provide details of the ritual involved in bestowing of robes of honor. We ordinarily do not know in more than a general sense how the garment was conferred: whether it was actually draped upon the recipient, and if so, by whom; whether the recipient removed any outer clothing before donning the garments; whether the recipient, in fact, donned the clothing during the audience or rather took it away with him. Indeed, the texts from which we draw our evidence of later periods employ a shorthand in noting most investments with robes of honor. Most of the time, they describe neither the ceremony nor the garments. By the tenth century, the verb *khala'a 'alayhi* was used only infrequently in its original sense of "casting off" a garment and was scarcely used in the active voice at all. Since robes of honor were often given at the time of an official's appointment, chroniclers adopted the convention of using the passive *khuli'a 'alayhi* ("he was invested with a *khil'a* [robe of honor]") as a shorthand meaning simply that he was appointed to office. In his classic study of Mamluk robes of honor, L. A. Mayer suggests the introduction of the usage *khuli'a 'alayhi* in the Mamluk period (1250–1517): "The essential thing to remember is the official character of the *khil'a*. Any appointment to a higher post implied the offer of a *khil'a*—so much so that not only expressions like *khuli'a 'alaihi bi-niyāba* became common, but that the word *labisa* (*khil'a* or *tashrīf*) became a very common, though sloppy, term for 'being appointed.'"[4] The evidence from Fatimid sources clearly indicates, however, that this usage had been current for at least several centuries in Egypt. The Fatimid court historian al-Musabbiḥī, for example, uses the phrase *khuli'a 'alā* numerous times to denote the appointment of the judge of Tinnīs (an important center for textile production), the head of Ṭālibīs (the descendants of 'Alī b. Abī Ṭālib), the market inspector (*muḥtasib*), various provincial officials, the official charged with announcing the rise of the Nile, the chief of police, the head of the treasury, and other offices in 1024–1025.

Whether castoff or not, these robes bestowed upon officials carried prestige as well as material value. But a true castoff provided something that a mere robe of honor could not, *baraka*. The Fatimid caliphs were Ismā'īlī imams, spiritual guides and authoritative interpreters of religious tradition as well as political leaders. They had *baraka* (literally "blessing"), spiritual charisma, and this *baraka* was transmitted from one imam at the moment of death to his successor. *Baraka* resides only in the imam and radiates from him, much as the divine light emanates from his luminous presence. Believers thus desired proximity to the imam so they might derive the benefits from his *baraka*. The eunuch Jawdhar, who served three Fatimid rulers, wrote to the imam requesting that his homeless mother be permitted to buy a house near the palace because of the *baraka* of the proximity; the imam replied favorably, even sending the woman the purchase price of the property.[5] Objects that the imam had touched could transmit his *baraka*. During the banquet for the New Year, the caliph distributed food with his own hands, the recipient kissed it, and then placed it in his sleeve for the *baraka*.[6] Similarly, the castoff *khil'a* was highly desirable also because of its capacity to transmit the imam's *baraka* to its recipient.

Castoff *khil'as* were especially prized as funeral shrouds, and they might be given in response to a specific request. Shortly before Jawdhar's death, he requested one of the imam's own robes to be used as a shroud upon his death, so that he might thereby receive *baraka*. The imam's response surely exceeded Jawdhar's hopes, for he received "a *khil'a* from our [own] clothing" as well as garments worn by three other Fatimid imams.[7] Archaeological evidence from the Iṣṭabl 'Anṭar excavations in Old Cairo, conducted by Dr. Roland-Pierre Gayraud, confirms the use of caliphal garments as shrouds during the Fatimid era. A number of corpses in this funerary site are shrouded in inscribed textiles, including one wrapped in three different shrouds, two of which contain inscriptions dedicated to different rulers.[8]

Jawdhar's concern about the world to come figures in another telling anecdote, a story told as evidence both of the imam's special quality of *firāsa* (that is, perspicacity or intuition about character) and Jawdhar's special status at court. A few days after Jawdhar entered the service of al-Mahdī, the imam assembled his courtiers and offered them their choice of a large number of robes made of various fabrics. Jawdhar's cohort chose robes of Tustarī, a very fine Iranian brocade; Jawdhar himself chose a robe of 'Attābī (tabby), a striped cotton cloth.[9] But the imam instructed one of his servants to direct Jawdhar to a Tustarī robe. When Jawdhar persevered in his choice of the 'Attābī garment, the imam deduced immediately that he would be a faithful servant, for he had chosen clothing that "resembles shrouds."[10] Taken together, these two stories construct Jawdhar as a paragon of faithful service to the imam, one whose sights are set properly on the world to come (*asbāb al-ākhira*) rather than this world (*asbāb al-dunyā*). But the imam could not allow this man, whose preference for shroudlike 'Attābī over this-worldly Tustarī had revealed him to be a pious servant who would never disappoint the imam's intuition, to quit the audience with only the 'Attābī robe. He ordered that Jawdhar be given both the 'Attābī robe he had chosen and an additional Tustarī robe. This is, in fact, a complicated story that can be properly interpreted only within a universe of discourse in which the commodity, prestige, and efficacy values of robes of honor are recognized as being in a state of constant relation and renegotiation with one another. Even the imam, who recognizes Jawdhar's piety and therefore his suitability for service at his court, feels compelled to reward his servant with the garment carrying the higher prestige value. Whatever state is being marked—whether it is the external sign of Jawdhar's high rank at court or the imam's intuition about his inner character—it is clothing that both reveals and displays it.

Honor and Dishonor: Textiles and Diplomacy

When an ambitious man who was threatening to instigate a rebellion extorted a robe and skullcap from the caliph as his price for backing down, he stipulated that he wanted something that the caliph himself had actually worn (*thiyāb min thiyāb mawlānā . . . allatī yalbis-hā*).[11] Whether castoffs or new garments, textiles were heavily laden with symbolic meaning and played an important role in the political life of the Fatimid court. Garments might be given, as in this case, as an extraordinary measure to quiet a would-be rebel. But they were also a part of the give-and-take of everyday diplomacy. Like other Islamic rulers, the Fatimids honored officials and visitors to their courts with luxury garments, and they often exchanged precious textiles with other rulers in elaborate reciprocal gift-giving.[12] But what was given (and received) as a gift bestowing honor and signaling peaceful relations could easily become a source of disgrace and dishonor.

In the year 414/1024, for example, a caravan of pilgrims from the lands of the Abbasid caliph made their way to Mecca and Madina. Having completed their *ḥajj,* however, they worried that Bedouin pirates would attack their caravan. And so they diverted to Syria, which was then under Fatimid rule. Naturally, their leaders, Ḥasanak and al-Aqsāsī, appointed respectively by the Ghaznavid Sultan Maḥmūd and the Abbasid Caliph al-Qādir (both enemies of the Fatimids), requested the Fatimid caliph's permission to enter his territory. Not only did Fatimid Caliph al-Ẓāhir grant permission, but he also seized the opportunity to secure a diplomatic triumph by showering Ḥasanak and al-Aqsāsī with gifts. Each received a gift including a thousand dinars, numerous garments, and robes of honor (*khila'*), and Ḥasanak also received a horse with a gilded saddle.

But this was no simple act of generosity on the part of the Fatimid caliph: he expected to win the praise of the pilgrims and for his gifts to remind Caliph al-Qādir that the Fatimids, not the Abbasids, controlled access to the sacred cities of Mecca and Madina. As Paul Walker tells us in his analysis of this episode, Caliph al-Ẓāhir's intent was not lost on his Abbasid rival, who not only arrested al-Aqsāsī but also demanded that Sultan Maḥmūd send the horse, garments, and robes of honor that had been given to Ḥasanak. Sultan Maḥmūd complied and the gifts were sent to Baghdad, where the garments were burned publicly, the gold extracted from the textiles, and distributed to the poor.[13]

Some years later, Fatimid Caliph al-Mustanṣir had the opportunity to avenge the Abbasid caliph's insult to his father al-Ẓāhir. In 443/1051, the Abbasids dispatched an ambassador bearing a diploma of investiture, a black banner (black being the Abbasid color), and robes of honor for the Zirid ruler of Tunisia, al-Mu'izz b. Bādīs, who had just renounced the Fatimids and sworn allegiance to the Abbasids. The Abbasid ambassador was captured by the Byzantine emperor, who turned him over to his Fatimid ally, Caliph al-Mustanṣir. The diploma, black banner, and the robes of honor were burned in the parade ground between the two Fatimid palaces (*bayn al-qaṣrayn*). The historian al-Maqrīzī remarks that the Abbasid al-Qādir had done the same thing to the *khil'a* sent by Caliph al-Mustanṣir's father, al-Ẓāhir.[14] But public burning of banners and robes of honor was not the only method of disgracing rival rulers. Both Abbasid and Fatimid caliphs held garments of their rivals hostage in their treasuries. In his biography of Caliph al-Mustanṣir, the historian Ibn Taghrī Birdī reports that at the height of the famines that befell Egypt in the 1050s and 1060s, the caliph had to sell everything in his palace, including the garments belonging to the Abbasids, which they kept out of hatred for them and in order to disgrace them.[15] These garments included robes of the Abbasid caliph al-Ṭā'i' that had been taken when the Abbasid palace in Baghdad was plundered in 381/991, as well as items confiscated during the year when the Turk al-Basāsīrī deposed the Abbasid caliph in favor of the Fatimids in 450/1058.[16]

As these anecdotes show, robes of honor were a site at which economies of prestige value and market value converged. The use of garments to dishonor throws a new symbolic light on the tragic circumstances in which al-Mustanṣir was compelled to sell the contents of his treasuries. This was a calamity not only because of the economic crisis, and not only because of the loss of his legendary treasures, but also because so many of the caliph's treasures were carried to Baghdad, where they could be acquired by members of the Abbasid family or even by ordinary (albeit well-to-do) people, who could in turn put them to almost any use.[17] Indeed, after the public circumstances under which the Costume Treasury (*khizānat al-kisawāt*) had been divested of its contents during the calamitous years of Caliph al-Mustanṣir's reign, the multiplication of robes of honor under Caliph al-Āmir was a highly visible way of communicating several related and equally important things. First, it communicated that the dynasty had recovered its former prosperity. Second, it signaled the recovery of the Egyptian economy, which was based on agriculture and the textile industry.[18] Finally, it announced the restoration of the dynasty's prestige. Some sixty years earlier, the Fatimid caliph had been compelled to sell what portion of his treasuries had not already been taken; his treasuries replenished, garments were now *bestowed* by the caliph, not plundered by his unruly troops.

Gold and Silk: The Commodity Value of Fatimid Court Textiles

Robes of honor were produced in government textile factories, and many had inscribed or ornamental borders.[19] Whether inscribed or not, robes of honor were made of luxury fabrics (primarily fine linens and silks), and they served both as instruments for conveying symbolic power and as economic capital. In fact, the presence of an inscription on a textile may have had less specific charge in the context of the much wider uses of public writing that the Fatimids inaugurated.[20] And the commodity value of the textile must have assumed greater importance than the presence of an inscription, particularly at a time when the production of pseudo and generic inscriptions had become quite common, and when increasingly elaborate ornamentation dominated *ṭirāz* bands.[21] As Irene Bierman has noted, the most frequently recorded detail about costumes is the "commodity value of the textiles as indicated by the presence of gold or gold threads."[22] The bestowing (and receiving) of robes of honor should therefore be understood in the larger context of the economic and social importance of textiles in Fatimid and other medieval Islamic societies, all the more so in view of the fact that textile production was one of the largest industries in the medieval Islamic world.

Indeed, we know remarkably little about robes of honor besides their base materials. There is almost never information about tailoring or color. While the absence of details about tailoring is entirely typical of the period, where many garments were either woven in a single piece or were of a limited number of styles, the absence of color is quite striking, given what S. D. Goitein calls the "color intoxication" of the Fatimid era. We may be justified, then, in concluding that the majority of robes of honor at court were white, the Fatimid color.[23] In the early eleventh century, nearly all of the robes of honor that al-Musabbiḥī mentioned are described as either *muthaqqal* or *mudhahhab,* that is, woven or embroidered with gold.[24] But there is scarcely a mention of silk in al-Musabbiḥī's chronicle. A century later, however, the huge inventory of clothing distributed for the festival in 516/1122 contains numerous garments of both silk and gold, the two materials that most determined the commodity value of a garment. In fact, many garments bestowed during the festival in the later period contained both gold and silk (often woven into or embroidered onto a linen base). For example, all of the eunuchs who served in the caliph's private wardrobe (that is, the chief and his six assistants) received gold outfits, although the outfit intended for the chief was clearly more elaborate. The major domo of the palace (*zimām al-quṣūr*) received a gold outfit while his lieutenants received garments described as "kingly" silk (*ḥarīrī khusrawānī*). The term *khusrawānī* here mostly likely describes silk fabrics embroidered with medallions of crowned heads, the majority of which probably were embroidered in gold.[25] Nonetheless, in the inventory of 516/1122, which is notable for its meticulous attention to the amounts (by weight) of gold in the costumes, the relative amounts of gold and silk in the robes of honor determined their primary descriptor as *mudhahhab* (gold) or *ḥarīrī* (silk).

While the very fact of being one of the *aṣḥāb al-khil'a* (those receiving robes of honor) distinguished elites from commoners, the relative amounts of gold and silk, as well as the number of pieces, in these costumes marked distinctions among the ruling elites. The costumes of the highest ranking, which contained both gold and silk, were designated as *mudhahhab;* those of the lower ranks, containing only silk, were designated as *ḥarīrī*. The gold-silk line might mark distinctions of rank even within the Fatimid family: cousins of the royal family who were courtiers (*al-julasā' min banī al-a'mām*) received a gold outfit (*badla mudhahhaba*), while noncourtier cousins (*ghayr al-julasā'*) received a silk outfit (*badla ḥarīrī*). Similarly, officials performing similar functions at different ranks received gold or silk in accordance with their rank: the chief of the treasury and chief administrator of the diwans received gold outfits while their assistants got silk; the porter of the caliph's parasol got a gold outfit, the five lesser officials charged with the service of the parasol got four articles of clothing, each of a different variety of silk;[26] the head waiter received a gold outfit, and his assistants, silk; the female superintendent of the caliph's private wardrobe (*khizānat al-kiswa al-khāṣṣ*), whose title was Ornament of the Treasurers (*zayn al-khuzzān*), received a gold outfit (*ḥulla*) and her assistants, silk.

The celebration of the festival in 516/1122 was characterized so thoroughly by its extravagant distributions of ceremonial garments that it was designated *'īd al-ḥulal,* the Festival of Gala Costumes, apparently in recognition of the very large number of costumes distributed to women.[27] In fact, this inventory is unique in the amount of information it provides about women of the royal household, who are almost never mentioned by name. There is therefore little comparative material available for a philologically rigorous reconstruction of the precise meaning of the terminology in the text. Most of the women mentioned are called *jiha,* a term that is very well attested in the Mamluk period as a title for notable women.[28] Royal women received outfits with both gold and silk, but the gold clearly was the predominant factor in determining value. The caliph's wife (*al-jiha al-'āliyya*) received a gold outfit (*ḥulla mudhahhaba*) consisting of fifteen pieces. Like the caliph's *badla* (which consisted of eleven items), its most important pieces had ornamental stripes (*muwashshaḥ*), were decorated with goblets (*mujāwam*), and had gold ornamental edges (*muṭraf*) and hems (*mudhāyal*).[29] Princesses of the royal family received gold *ḥullas* consisting of fourteen pieces, while their eunuch guardians received silk *badlas.*[30] A number of garments designated as both gold and silk (*ḥulla mudhahhaba wa-ḥarīrī*) were distributed to the female servants of royal women. On the other hand, the caliph's elite bodyguard of *muḥannak* eunuchs (so-called because of the way they wound the ends of their turbans under their chins) received gold *badlas.* Lower-ranking *muḥannak* eunuchs received a silk outfit (*ḥulla*) consisting of four pieces, plus a wrapper (*lifāfa*) and a *fūṭa* (a long piece of cloth that could serve many different purposes).[31] The most luxurious costumes came in wrappers (*lifāf*) or in chests (*takht*), as in the descriptions of the *kiswa* of 516/1122, a practice known to us from the documents of the Cairo Geniza.[32]

It is clear from this inventory that silk was so readily available that its presence alone was not enough to distinguish a courtier from a non-courtier. By the tenth century, silks of varying quality were readily available at predictable prices in the markets.[33] Although even the finest silks were easily within the reach of the middle and upper classes, gold remained beyond their means. The Fatimid government, ordinarily characterized by a laissez-faire economic policy, kept tight control over the production and distribution of gold in all its forms. As a result, Fatimid coins maintained such a high standard of fineness that they were considered to be an international currency, a fineness that was sustained even during the most serious economic crises of the Fatimid state.[34] The reliability of Fatimid gold coins inspired the production of inferior counterfeit dinars by the Crusaders in the early twelfth century, causing a loss of confidence in Fatimid currency. In response, the Fatimids built a new mint in Cairo in December 1122 and placed it under the strict supervision of the caliph's officials. While in earlier times the Fatimid mint had been supervised by the chief judge, under the reform a new civilian official supervised the mint. The supervisor of the mint also audited the gold thread used in the production of inscribed textiles in the caliph's *ṭirāz* factories.[35]

The relative unavailability of gold, as compared with silk, was also important in helping to distinguish textiles originating from the court.[36] Even the inscribed bands affixed to many court textiles were no guarantee of authenticity; the head of the Jewish community (*nagid*) conferred embroidered silk robes of honor upon scholars.[37] The middle and upper classes also imitated court fashions by giving robes of honor as gifts and wearing made-to-order inscribed borders.[38] Like the *khila'* at court, the robe of honor of the bourgeoisie was ordinarily an ensemble of two to five items. And it was extremely expensive. As Yedida K. Stillman states, "an individual *khil'a* might cost as much as twenty dinars, a sum of money which a lower middle class family could live on for close to a year." The least expensive ensemble recorded in the Cairo Geniza cost fifteen dinars, and one of the most expensive, fifty dinars.[39] The haute bourgeoisie also mirrored the court by placing a high value on castoffs for pious uses. In 1028/9, for example, the merchant prince Joseph Ibn 'Awkal was asked by his factotum in Alexandria to honor him with one of his own cloaks, which he planned to wear on the Day of Atonement.[40]

Robes of Honor and the Culture of Hierarchy

Robes of honor marked relative hierarchies at all levels in Fatimid society, and their meaning was constructed within the framework of hierarchy, however contingent the specific circumstances under which a robe or robes might be conferred. Indeed, conferring robes of honor was not necessarily an expression of power. But it was *always* on some level a recognition and expression of hierarchy. As obvious an observation as this might seem, we should take for granted neither the fact that robes of honor express hierarchy nor that hierarchy was seen as good and even necessary in medieval Islamic societies. The same can be said of the adoption by the bourgeoisie of the practice, which we should not dismiss as mere imitation. It is ideological in the broadest sense, that is, it expresses a cultural and social ideology of hierarchy as opposed to egalitarianism at *all* levels of society. Whether inside or outside the court, conferring robes of honor reflects and magnifies the notion that an orderly society is necessarily a hierarchical society. As Louise Marlow has shown, both Muslim rulers and religious scholars had to come to terms with the constant tension between the realities of highly stratified societies and the pious egalitarianism of the Islamic religious tradition. In the end, the religious tradition, while admitting the realities of social stratification, never fully accepted it.[41] In this area, as in so many others in medieval Islamic societies, court ritual and social practice provided a response to the insistent arguments of religious scholars, coming down firmly on the side of hierarchy.

Notes

1. See *Encyclopaedia of Islam,* New Edition, s.v. *khil'a,* and Yedida Kalfon Stillman, *Female Attire of Medieval Egypt: According to the Trousseau Lists and Cognate Material from the Cairo Geniza* (Ph.D. diss., University of Pennsylvania, 1972), p.17 n.36. The designation was not limited to official works. Jewish courtiers are frequently referred to in this way in the Cairo Geniza, particularly in letters requesting their assistance; see S. D. Goitein, *A Mediterranean Society: The Jewish Communities of the Arab World as Portrayed in the Documents of the Cairo Geniza,* 5 vols. (Berkeley and Los Angeles: University of California Press, 1967–88) 2:351.
2. Muḥammad b. Muḥammad al-Yamanī, *Sīrat al-ḥājib ja'far b. 'alī,* cited in Heinz Halm, *The Empire of the Mahdi: The Rise of the Fatimids,* trans. Michael Bonner (Leiden: E. J. Brill, 1996), p. 138.
3. Halm, p. 134 citing *Sīrat ja'far,* p. 125.
4. L. A. Mayer, *Mamluk Costume* (Geneva: Albert Kundig, 1952), p. 60.
5. Abū 'Alī Manṣūr al-Jūdharī, *Sīrat al-ustādh jūdhar (Jawdhar),* ed. M. Kāmil Ḥusayn and M. 'Abd al-Hādī Sha'īra (Cairo: Dār al-fikr al-'arabī, 1954), pp. 137–38.
6. Paula Sanders, *Ritual, Politics, and the City in Fatimid Cairo* (Albany: State University of New York Press, 1994), p. 28. Taqī al-dīn al-Maqrīzī, *Kitāb al-mawā'iẓ wa'l-i'tibār bi-dhikr al-khiṭaṭ wa'l-āthār,* 2 vols.(Bulaq: Dār al-ṭibā'a al-miṣriyya, 1853; reprint, Beirut: Dār ṣādir, n.d.) 1:453, lines 3–5.
7. *Sīrat al-ustādh jūdhar,* pp. 138–39.
8. Roland-Pierre Gayraud, "Isṭabl 'Antar (Fostat) 1994, Rapport de Fouilles," *Annales Islamologiques* 29 (1995): 1–24; Jochen Sokoly, "Between Life and Death: The Funerary Context of Ṭirāz Textiles," *Islamische Textilkunst des Mittelalters: Aktuelle Probleme* (Riggisberg: Abegg-Stiftung, 1997): 78.
9. Although 'Attābī is most often described as a silk stuff, I follow here Irene Bierman's conclusion that this must refer to a cotton rather than silk cloth; see "Art and Politics: The Impact of Fatimid Uses of *Ṭirāz* Fabrics" (Ph.D. diss., University of Chicago, 1980), p. 78. Carl Johan Lamm, *Cotton in Mediaeval Textiles of the Near East* (Paris: P. Geuthner, 1937), describes it as either cotton or silk, pp. 123, 210, 219. Cf. R. B. Serjeant, *Islamic Textiles: Material for a History up to the Mongol Conquest* (Beirut: Libraire du Liban, 1972), pp. 28–29; Stillman, "Female Attire," p. 21.
10. *Sīrat al-ustādh jawdhar,* pp. 35–36.
11. See Sanders, *Fatimid Cairo,* pp. 29–30, citing *al-Musabbiḥī, Akhbār Miṣr* (Tome Quarantième de la Chronique d'Egypte de Musabbiḥī), ed. Ayman Fu'ād Sayyid and Thierry Bianquis (Cairo: Institut français d'archéologie orientale, 1978), p. 58.

12. See numerous examples in Ibn al-Zubayr, *Kitāb al-dhakhā'ir wa-al-tuḥaf,* ed. M. Hamid Allah (Kuwait: Dā'irat al-maṭbū'āt wa-al-nashr, 1959), recently translated by Ghāda al-Ḥijjāwī al-Qaddūmī under the title *Book of Gifts and Rarities* (Cambridge, Mass.: Harvard Center for Middle Eastern Studies, 1996).
13. For this account, and the analysis of its political implications, I rely heavily on Paul Walker, "Purloined Insignia: Stolen Symbols of legitimacy in the Abbasid-Fatimid Rivalry" (Paper delivered at the Middle East Studies Association, Providence, Rhode Island, November 21–24, 1996), pp. 9–13. I am grateful to Dr. Walker for his permission to cite so extensively from this piece, which is to be incorporated into his forthcoming book on Fatimid religious policy. The Arabic accounts may be found in al-Maqrīzī, *Itti'āẓ al-ḥunafā bi-akhbār al-a'imma al-fāṭimiyyīn al-khulafā,* 3 vols. (Cairo: Al-majlis al-a'lā li'l-shu'ūn al-islāmiyya, 1967–73), 2:138–39 and al-Musabbiḥī, *Akhbār Miṣr,* pp. 22–23 and 28–29. See also Thierry Bianquis, *Damas et la syrie sous la domination fatimide (359–468/969–1076),* 2 vols.(Damascus: Institut Français de Damas, 1989), 2:410–11.
14. See Walker, "Purloined Insignia," pp.12–13; al-Maqrīzī, *Itti'āẓ al-ḥunafā,* 2:214.
15. Abu'l-Maḥāsin Ibn Taghrī Birdī, *Al-Nujūm al-ẓāhira fī mulūk miṣr wa'l-qāhira,* 16 vols. (Cairo: Dār al-kutub, 1929–55; reprint Cairo: Wizārat al-thaqāfa wa-al-irshād al-qawmī, n.d.), 5:16.
16. For the sale of the Abbasid garments in the Fatimid treasuries, see Ibn Taghrī Birdī, *al-Nujūm al-ẓāhira,* 5:16; Serjeant, *Islamic Textiles,* p. 157. The most complete account of the sale (and later looting) of the Fatimid treasuries is in al-Maqrīzī, *Itti'āẓ al-ḥunafā,* 2:279–301. For al-Basāsīrī's looting of the Abbasid palaces, see al-Maqrīzī, *Itti'āẓ al-ḥunafā,* 2:252–53. Al-Maqrīzī says that the Abbasid caliph's turban (*mandīl*), wound with his own hand, and his cloak (*ridā'*) were sent with other objects to Cairo and stored in the Wazir's residence (*dār al-wizāra*). Al-Maqrīzī notes that these (and several other) objects that were the personal property of the Abbasid caliph were returned to the Abbasids by Saladin when he restored Egypt to Abbasid suzerainty after the death of the last Fatimid caliph. This would seem to contradict Ibn Taghrī Birdī's statement that the garments were sold. Other objects sent to Cairo included the Abbasid caliph's mantle (*burda*). Ibn al-Athīr, *Al-Kāmil fī al-tārīkh* (Beirut: Dār ṣādir, 1966), 10:61–62, says that a number of these items turned up in Baghdad with merchants, including items taken when al-Ṭā'i' was deposed and taken by al-Basāsīrī. What is important here is that these items were not merely the property of the Abbasids but were actually worn by the Abbasid caliph. Walker, "Purloined Insignia," pp.14–17, discusses al-Maqrīzī's report at length.
17. See Eliyahu Ashtor, *Histoire des Prix et des Salaries dans l'Orient Médiéval* (Paris: SEVPEN, 1969), p.166, where he notes the appearance of *khila'* in Geniza trousseaux of the 1100s and speculates that the increasing availability of the garments on the open market was a function of the political

turbulence of the twelfth century, when officials and wazirs were often summarily dismissed in rapid succession and, no doubt, sold their robes of honor.

18. See Gladys Frantz-Murphy, *The Agrarian Administration of Egypt from the Arabs to the Ottomans* (Cairo: Institut français d'archéologie orientale, 1986); Goitein, *Mediterranean Society,* 1: 99–108, 222–28.
19. Like other medieval Islamic dynasties, the Fatimids employed a variety of symbols and ceremonial acts to assert and express their legitimacy, authority, and power as rulers. In addition to the formal insignia of sovereignty (*tāj,* scepter, various banners, inkstand, etc.), they closely guarded prerogatives associated with the ruler's name: pronouncing the ruler's name in the sermon at Friday prayer (*khuṭba*), and inscribing his name on coins (*sikka*) and on textiles (*ṭirāz*). The custom of bestowing *khil'as* is clearly related to *ṭirāz*, the prerogative and custom of inscribing the ruler's name on textiles. For a discussion of *ṭirāz*, see Yedida K. Stillman and Paula Sanders in *Encyclopaedia of Islam* (Leiden: E.J. Brill), New Edition, s.v. "ṭirāz."
20. For a complex discussion of the issues involved in interpreting writing on many different media, see Irene Bierman, *Writing Signs: The Fatimid Public Text* (Los Angeles: University of California Press, 1998) and, on writing on textiles in particular, pp. 120–26.
21. On the changes in the character of inscriptions, see Kjeld von Folsach, "Textiles and Society: Some social, political, and religious aspects of Islamic textiles" in Kjeld von Folsach and A.-M. Keblow Bernsted, *Woven Treasures—Textiles from the World of Islam* (Copenhagen: The David Collection, 1993), pp. 14–15. On pseudo and generic inscriptions, see also Veronica Gervers, "Rags to Riches: Medieval Islamic Textiles," *Rotunda* 11 (1978/79): 22–31, and especially p. 28.
22. On the relationship between display value and exchange, see Irene A. Bierman, "Inscribing the City: Fatimid Cairo," in *Islamische Textilkunst des Mittelalters: Aktuelle Probleme,* pp. 105–14.
23. Goitein, *Mediterranean Society,* 4:172–83.
24. Al-Musabbiḥī, *Akhbār Miṣr,* pp. 14, 17, 36, 47, 49, 50, 63. The information provided by al-Musabbiḥī's text is particularly useful because his *Akhbār Miṣr* is one of the very few Fatimid texts that has survived in an original Fatimid-era manuscript. Most Fatimid chronicles survive only as anthologized or cited in Mamluk sources.
25. See Goitein, *Mediterranean Society,* 4:121 n. 93; Ibn al-Zubayr, *Kitāb al-dhakhā'ir wa'l-tuḥaf,* para. 379 and the corresponding translation by al-Qaddūmī *Book of Gifts and Rarities,* p. 233; reported also in al-Maqrīzī, *al-Khiṭaṭ,* 1:413, lines 14–16.
26. The three items with a specified textile are a Sūsa (Tunisia) mantle (*mandīl*), a Damietta *shuqqa* robe, and an Alexandrian *shuqqa* robe. Goitein identifies the *shuqqa* as a type of robe, often referred to also as *maqṭa'*. Though I cannot be certain, my conclusion that these items were silk is based on Goitein's discussion of the varieties of silk that appear in the Ge-

niza, often mentioned by place name without being specifically designated as silk (*ḥarīr*). See *Mediterranean Society,* 4:168–69; Serjeant, *Islamic Textiles,* pp.183–84; Stillman, "Female Attire," s.v. silk. The final item was a *fūṭa,* which was presumably made of silk.

27. Although the terms *badla* and *ḥulla* (pl. *ḥulal*) are attested in the Cairo Geniza for outfits for either men or women (see Stillman, "Female Attire," pp. 73–75), in the inventory, *badla* seems to refer specifically to garments given to men and *ḥulla* to female garments. For the inventory, see al-Maqrīzī, *al-Khiṭaṭ,* 1:410–413; Ayman Fu'ād Sayyid, ed., *Passages de la Chronique d'Égypte d'Ibn al-Ma'mūn* (Cairo: Institut français d'archéologie orientale, 1983), pp. 48–55; Ayman Fu'ād Sayyid, ed., *Le Manuscrit autographe d'al-Mawā'iẓ wa-al-I'tibār fī Dhikr al-Khiṭaṭ wa-al-Āthār de Taqī al-Dīn Aḥmad b. 'Alī b. 'Abd al-Qādir al-Maqrīzī* (London: Al-Furqān Islamic Heritage Foundation, 1995), pp. 219–29.

28. This interpretation is preliminary. With the exception of the two most famous royal women in the Fatimid period, Sitt al-Mulk and the Ṣulayḥid al-Sayyida al-Ḥurra, women are scarcely mentioned in the chronicles. On them, see Yaacov Lev, "The Fāṭimid Princess Sitt al-Mulk," *Journal of Semitic Studies* 32/2 (Autumn 1987): 319–28; H. F. al-Hamdani, "The Life and Times of Queen Saiyida Arwa the Ṣulaiḥid of the Yemen," *J. of the Royal Central Asian Society* 18 (1931): 507–17; Leila al-Imad, "Women and Religion in the Fatimid Caliphate: The Case of al-Sayyidah al-Hurra, Queen of Yemen," *Intellectual Studies on Islam,* ed. Michel M. Mazzaoui and Vera B. Moreen (Salt Lake City: University of Utah Press, 1990), pp.137–44. Epigraphic evidence attests the usage for women of the Fatimid royal family, as well, see Gaston Wiet, *Matériaux pour un corpus inscriptionum arabicarum,* II, Égypte (Cairo: Institut français d'archéologie orientale, 1929) 52/2, no. 591, for an inscription in the name of *al-jiha al-karīma* (dated 533/1139) in the mausoleum of al-Sayyida Ruqayya attributed to the wife of the Caliph al-Āmir; similarly, see Max Van Berchem, *Matériaux pour un corpus inscriptionum arabicarum,* I, Égypte (Cairo: Institut français d'archéologie orientale, 1900), 19, no. 457, for an inscription in the name of *al-jiha al-jalīla* (dated 550/1155).

29. See Goitein, *Mediterranean Society,* 4:378 n.28, citing twelfth-century Geniza documents (*muwashshaḥ*). Goitein, *Mediterranean Society,* 4:331 n. 165 and Maqrīzī, *al-Khiṭaṭ,* 2:129 (*mujāwam*). Goitein, *Mediterranean Society,* 4:323, 462 n. 216 (*muṭraf*). Goitein, *Mediterranean Society,* 4:324 n. 107 (*mudhāyal*).

30. The question of eunuch guardians is a complicated one. Women, especially noble women, are never referred to by name (a protocol that was observed by upper class Christians and Jews as well as Muslims; see Goitein, *Mediterranean Society,* 3:160–62). The inventory lists a number of women with the title *jiha* who, given their placement in the list between "Her Highness" (*al-jiha al-'āliyya*) (who is no doubt to be identified as the caliph's wife), and his brothers, paternal aunts, and courtier cousins, should

almost certainly be understood as royal princesses who are still unmarried. These may well have been the daughters or sisters of al-Āmir. They are designated in the text as: *jihat murshid, jihat 'anbar, al-sayyida jihat ẓill, jihat munjab, jihat maknūn al-qāḍī (sic), and jihat jawhar.* Shaun Marmon, author of *Eunuchs and Sacred Boundaries in Islamic Society* (Oxford and New York: Oxford University Press, 1995), notes that she has seen similar formulations referring to women of the Mamluk households, and suggests a working assumption that the custom of eunuch guardianship for minor women as well as young boys was not unknown among the elites of Fatimid and Mamluk society (personal communication, November 29, 1998). My interpretation must be considered tentative until a systematic study of the subject can be undertaken.

Several of the names in the list (Murshid, 'Anbar, Jawhar) are common eunuch names: see David Ayalon, "The Eunuchs in the Mamluk Sultanate" in *Studies in Memory of Gaston Wiet,* ed. Miriam Rosen-Ayalon (Jerusalem: Institute of Asian and African Studies, Hebrew University of Jerusalem, 1977), pp. 267–95. Jawhar is mentioned twice in connection with the Dār al-Jadīda (New House), an otherwise unidentified location that seems to have housed the royal harem. Murshid is designated as *al-khāṣī* (*sic,* for *al-khaṣī*) (the eunuch). Maknūn ("Hidden") is called *mutawallī khidmat al-jiha al-'āliyya* ("chief in the service of Her Highness"). Such a position could be held only by a eunuch, and this calls into question the designation of Maknūn as *al-qāḍī,* the judge, in three printed editions: the Būlāq edition of Maqrīzī's *al-Khiṭaṭ,* Ayman Fu'ād Sayyid's *Passages de la Chronique d'Egypte d'Ibn al-Ma'mūn,* and Ayman Fu'ād Sayyid's *Manuscrit autograph d'al-Mawā'iẓ wa-al-I'tibār.* I would suggest that Maknūn was in fact a eunuch. I consider it entirely possible that even al-Maqrīzī himself might have misread an earlier manuscript or repeated a copyist's error. Until a critical edition of al-Maqrīzī's *al-Khiṭaṭ* is available (itself a monumental project), the question cannot be resolved.

31. In the Geniza, the *fūṭa* is mostly made of silk, Stillman, "Female Attire," pp. 214–16.
32. See Yedida Kalfon Stillman, "Costume as Cultural Statement: The Esthetics, Economics, and Politics of Islamic Dress," in *The Jews of Medieval Islam: Community, Society, and Identity,* ed. Daniel Frank (Leiden: E. J. Brill, 1995), p. 133; Goitein, *Mediterranean Society,* 1:101–106.
33. Gervers, "Rags to Riches," 26. The standard silk that is mentioned in the Cairo Geniza was converted so easily to cash and at such stable prices that it functioned as a sort of medieval Mediterranean traveler's check. Yedida Kalfon Stillman, "New data on Islamic textiles from the Geniza," *Textile History* 10 (1979): 186; Irene A. Bierman, "Art and Politics," pp. 90–93; Goitein, *Mediterranean Society,* 1:222–24.
34. See Sanders, *Fatimid Cairo,* p. 85 and notes.
35. See Sanders, *Fatimid Cairo,* pp. 85–87 and the sources cited there.

36. In the late twelfth and early thirteenth centuries, the middle classes began to imitate gold thread by using yellow silk (Gervers, "Rags to Riches," 26).
37. Goitein, *Mediterranean Society,* 2:24–25.
38. Stillman, "Female Attire," pp. 16–18; Bierman, "Art and Politics," pp. 92–95; Goitein, *Mediterranean Society,* 4:184.
39. Stillman, "Female Attire," pp. 93–96.
40. Goitein, *Mediterranean Society,* 4:156.
41. For a full discussion of these issues, see Louise Marlow's insightful study, *Hierarchy and egalitarianism in Islamic thought* (Cambridge: Cambridge University Press, 1997).

CHAPTER 10

THE MANTLE OF ROGER II OF SICILY[1]

William Tronzo

The subject of this chapter is one of the most extraordinary examples of the textile art to have come down to us from the entire Middle Ages, the Mantle of Roger II now in the Treasury of the Kunsthistorisches Museum in Vienna (Figure 10.1).[2] The mantle is a half circle of scarlet samite, 345 cm wide and 146 cm long, encrusted with enamels, pearls, and gems, and it displays, in gold and silk embroidery, a figure that is spectacular in its boldness and simplicity: the doubled image of a lion, triumphant over the camel he holds tightly in his grip, to either side of a palm tree that spreads outward from the center. What might have been analogous to the mantle in a certain sense is the contemporary garb of the Byzantine emperor: an anonymous ekphracist of the twelfth century tells us that Manuel I Komnenos wore a robe decorated with addorsed griffins.[3] But nothing quite like it has survived from Byzantium, nor is anything similar attested in the Latin West.[4]

The fact that the mantle has been preserved for us today is due in no small part to its role as the coronation robe of the Holy Roman emperor. The historical circumstances by which it came to play this role are well known. Created in 1133–34 in the tiraz of the palace of Roger II, the first of the Normans to rule Sicily as king, the mantle then passed to the Hohenstaufen through the marriage of Henry VI and Roger's daughter, Constance, and thence, presumably first through their son, Frederick II, and then through his successors to the empire—to the Palatinate, Prague, Karlstein, Nuremburg, and other venues, and finally to Vienna—where it is documented in use from the thirteenth century.[5] At the same time, in hindsight, this usage must seem rather strange, since the Holy Roman emperor was one of the great enemies of the Muslim invaders of Europe in the form of the Turk, and the mantle is decorated, in addition to images,

Figure 10.1. Vienna, Treasury of the Kunsthistorisches Museum, Mantle of Roger II (photo: after Tronzo, *Cultures,* fig. 147).

with a prominent inscription along its curved border in another language of the Muslim nations, Arabic. Presumably this feature was ignored by the later Christian audience, who even went so far as to misunderstand and misrepresent the mantle's history. In the Holy Roman Empire the mantle was believed to have originated with Charlemagne, which is how Dürer represented it in the first image of the object to be disseminated in art.[6]

The later history of the mantle would seem to highlight an interesting phenomenon of selective reading or viewing: what was important about the mantle in the Holy Roman Empire was its presumed pedigree, which the imagery of the piece—the triumphant lions—and the color—imperial red—probably also supported in the view of contemporary users (since these were the conventional signs of rulership in western culture), but not the inscription in Arabic, or, for that matter, the Islamic style of the figures.[7] One might call this reading or viewing disjunctive in the sense that only part of the object is perceived or understood. But has the mantle fared any better in the history of art? It is striking that the rather extensive literature on the mantle, with few exceptions, has focused on the imagery and the inscription separately, with the consequence that little attention has been paid to the relationship between the two.[8] It is entirely possible that there was none, or rather, that nothing beyond the physical proximity of the two was intended to begin with—that the relationship between the words and images on the mantle was casual or circumstantial. But I doubt it, and the point of my paper will be to suggest how our view of the mantle might be enriched by bringing this particular relationship more to the center of our discussion. Within the restricted scope of this essay, however, I shall be able to touch on only the major arguments, and I shall do so quite selectively: style, for one, will not be an issue here.

First the text. My translation is taken from Grabar, based in part on the reading established by Samman: "This is what was made in the royal *khizanah* (treasury or household), full [i.e., the *khizanah*] of (or the royal *khizanah* operating with) happiness, honor, good fortune, perfection, long life, profit, welcome, prosperity, generosity, splendor, glory, perfection, realization of aspirations and hopes, of delights of days and nights, without end or modification, with might, care, sponsorship, protection, happiness, well-being (success), triumph, and sufficiency. In Palermo *(madinah Siquliyah)* in the year 528 [1133–34]."[9] Notwithstanding the difficulties indicated by the alternate readings in parentheses, the text strikes me today as it did when I first studied it several years ago: as a description of the state of life under the rule of King Roger—a perfected earthly existence.[10] I related the text to the words and images on the ceiling of the nave of the Cappella Palatina in Palermo, also created for King Roger—a litany of epithets of the kingdom, visual and verbal, as an emanation of the virtue of the king. I described the ceiling not only as a hymn of praise but also as a call for gratitude on the part of onlookers to be offered to the source of this beneficence, the king.

In his paper Grabar has conveniently summarized the prevailing currents of interpretation of the imagery of the mantle, which are three. The first and perhaps also the most widespread is what might be described as a view of the mantle as a set of conventional royal images, with their roots deep in the visual culture of the Mediterranean and Near Eastern worlds: the palm as the tree of life and the conquering lion as an emblem of the king, with the additional twist here of the camel as an image of the Islamic world (Ifriqiyah?), over which the Normans sought dominion. A second line stresses the presence of the circular motifs on the lion and camel, which are interpreted in the light of medieval (Islamic) images of constellations to yield an image of the heavens (and perhaps even the indication of a date inscribed in the stars relevant to Roger himself). Finally, and following upon this interpretation, there has been an attempt to read the imagery of the front of the mantle in terms of the imagery of the back or lining (which is fragmentary and may or may not be contemporary) as parallel representations of the heavenly and earthly spheres. Since both the strengths and weaknesses of these views have been discussed by Grabar, there is no need to dwell on them now except to say that in each case the deficiencies or difficulties are enough to give one pause. But in the present context one might also adduce the aforementioned inscription, which stands in relationship to these meanings, at best, in a loose or general way.

What I would like to suggest is another reading of the imagery that is more site-specific; it is a reading that I cannot prove, but its validity—to my mind—derives from the degree to which it appears to fit its context. In order to propound it, I shall begin at a different point altogether—with the image of a garden.

In addition to their palace in the city, the Norman kings created a set of residences and pleasure pavilions in the gardens and parks they constructed on the outskirts of Palermo, some of which survive in the form of the edifices of the Favara, the Zisa, and the Cuba, among others.[11] The important role that these places played in the life of the court is indicated in the sources, as well as in the quality of this architecture, in its elaborateness, size, and finish. A case in point is the Zisa, a multistoried structure with grand representational spaces, numerous amenities, and sumptuous decorations.[12] Romuald of Salerno informs us, on the other hand, that King Roger sought to spend much of his time at the Favara, whose present melancholy aspect belies what must have been a very pleasant situation in the twelfth century, in the midst of pools and palm trees.[13] In this context, it is interesting to observe that one of these sub-

Figure 10.2. Bern, Burgerbibliothek, cod. 120 II, fol. 98r, detail, Petrus de Ebulo, "Liber ad honorem augusti sive de rebus Siculis," park of Genoard (photo: Burgerbibliothek Bern)

urban Norman precincts, the park of the Genoard (ǧannat-al-arḍ—paradise on earth), came to be represented in art. In a late-twelfth-century miniature illustrating Petrus de Ebulo's famous poem on Henry VI, "Liber

Figure 10.3. Palermo, Norman Palace, Norman Stanza, detail of mosaic decoration (photo: after Demus, *Norman Mosaics,* fig. 115B)

ad honorem augusti," the park appears, accompanied by its title ("viridarium Genoard"), in the upper left hand corner of the page (beside a representation of the city of Palermo), filled with different kinds of trees, including a palm tree, and birds and a feline (figure 10.2).[14] Giuseppe Bellafiore has claimed that this image is the first representation of an actual garden, as opposed to a fictional or conceptual one such as the Garden of Eden, in the history of European art.[15]

Yet the image is also clearly based on conventions for the representation of garden space in the Middle Ages. The forms of the trees, for instance, mirror those in depictions of landscape settings in the narrative mosaics of the Cappella Palatina and the Cathedral of Monreale.[16] The nature of the image, however, might be brought out more fully by comparing it to another group of images to which it is clearly related. Both the Zisa and the Norman Palace contain rooms decorated with the images of parks or gardens, of which the richest is the palatine chamber known as the Norman Stanza in the Norman Palace.[17] The Stanza decoration is complex but essentially breaks down into units of similar composition of elements symmetrically arranged around a central axis: trees, including the palm with flanking lions (facing the visitor as she or he enters the room), as well as birds and other beasts and mythological creatures (figure 10.3).

The garden depictions thus share a common (although not entirely identical) vocabulary; at the same time, they diverge in the way in which this vocabulary is arranged. Whereas the composition of the Stanza decoration is rigidly symmetrical, in the miniature, it is loose: trees and plants occupy a varying groundline, and the creatures, a feline and birds, are fitted in the interstices. The difference may have been the result of different artists, or media, or dates, or it may reflect a functional differentiation of the two images. A loose or casual arrangement of elements as in the miniature may not have been the ideal backdrop in a chamber of the king destined to play a role in the ceremonial life of the court, but it may have been appropriate as a device to call to mind a place that at least some of those viewing the image might be expected to know.

A third image of the period that makes use of a similar vocabulary is a large follaro *(follis)*, an issue probably of William II (figure 10.4).[18] The obverse and reverse of the coin juxtapose the head of a lion and a palm tree. Philip Grierson once thought that the imagery derived from ancient coins and was symptomatic of an interest in the ancient past of Sicily on the part of Roger II.[19] But this view has recently and convincingly been challenged by Lucia Travaini, who has argued for a later date under William II but without an explanation of the iconography.[20] The palm and the lion, however, are familiar from the contexts that we have explored here, albeit rendered in separate fields and reduced to the quintessential marks of their identification.

The numismatic context may also provide an additional frame of reference for this object. The coinage of Byzantium and other medieval states was conventionally divided between heaven and earth, church and state, on its two sides.[21] Would it not be logical to posit a similar division of realms on the Norman coin, figured here in the favored vocabulary of the Normans? In this case the lion would be understood, as it was commonly understood elsewhere, as an emblem of the king.[22] In another context I suggested that the palm tree on the mantle also carried royal connotations, based on a reading of certain biblical passages, such as Psalm 92.12, "The righteous shall flourish like the palm tree," which appear as citations in a sermon delivered by the court homilist of Roger II, Philagathos of Cerami.[23] But in the twelfth century the motif also carried distinct religious connotations, by which I mean not the palm as an emblem of the martyr's victory over death—an age-old symbol in the Christian church—but the palm as the church, a theme expressed and elaborated by the twelfth-century Augustinian canon, Hugh of Fouilloy, among others.[24] The *arbor palmarum,* a primary symbol of the church in Lambert of St. Omer's *Liber floridus,* completed in 1120, was vividly illustrated in the beautiful manuscript of the text now in the University Library at Ghent, in which the palm was also accompanied by the names of Norman princes.[25]

Even though I have discussed the three Norman images—the manuscript illumination, the mosaic and the coin—sequentially, I do not want to give the impression that they constituted a sequence—chronological or otherwise—or that they were consciously contrived in relationship to one another beyond the fact that they share a visual vocabulary. But this vocabulary is the salient point. In each case, the same or similar elements are employed to very different visual effect and, one might assume, purpose: from the loose and casual concatenation of signs in the miniature that were intended to call to mind an actual place in Palermo, to the highly structured sets of images in the Norman Stanza, set in order according to the principles of art (symmetry, hierarchy), which were meant to serve as the evocation of an ideal place for the presence of the king, to a pair of emblems on the coin of William II that conveyed, on the currency of the state, the mark of the *regnum.* In each case, the individual components of the images were manipulated, by placement above all, to communicate specific messages that seem to have been quite separate one from the other. What links the images, on the other hand, is a common ground in the garden and its inhabitants, and specifically the palm tree and the lion, the world in which royal life was staged and idealized, or, to return to the ceiling in the

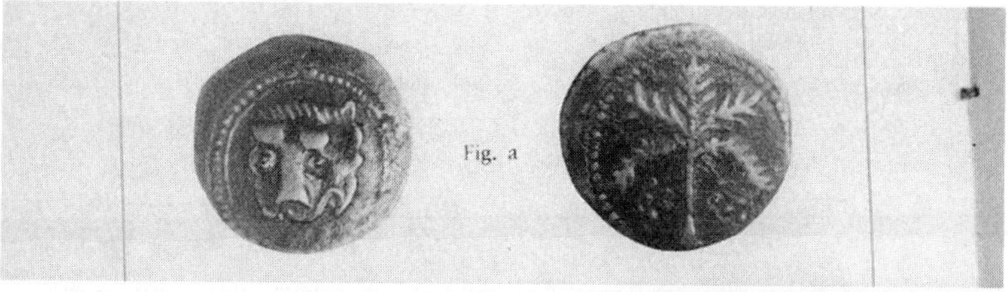

Figure 10.4. Large follaro of William II, obverse and reverse with lion's head and palm tree (photo: after Grierson, "Guglielmo II o Ruggero II?," p. 196, fig. a).

Cappella Palatina and its epithets that were adduced earlier, conceived of as an emanation of the virtue of the king.

Notwithstanding the variety in the previous views of the mantle summarized above, it would not be unfair to say that they all share in essence the conviction that the key to understanding its imagery lies in a diachronic process—some larger tradition—outside Norman Sicily. The fact is, however, that its imagery also had a context within Norman Sicily, into which I would like to insert the mantle.[26] I see the imagery on the mantle as an evocation of a place—the place of the ruler, or perhaps more accurately, of rulership—that belongs to the spectrum of representation embodied in the manuscript and mosaic and on the coin, with of course one additional element in the figure of the camel over which the lion holds sway.

The camel may well have been the image of Africa, or even of the Muslim world, as some have claimed, and thus meant to depict the territorial ambitions of the Norman kings. But the Normans otherwise did not think visually in quite so literal a way, and to equate the camel with such a specific referent misses the larger and overwhelmingly negative frame of reference within which it was often seen. The creature was a pack animal, a beast of burden of the desert; camel drivers in the *De administrando imperio* were persons of the lowest social standing.[27] It was in a ceremony that was a humiliating perversion of the ruler's *adventus* that the true nature of the beast was revealed. It was a "mangy camel" that carried the deposed Byzantine rule, Andronikos I Komnenos, through the streets of Constantinople in the twelfth century, and it was on the back of a camel that the captured anti-pope Gregory VIII was made to enter Rome in 1121.[28] The theme was an ancient one. The hated astrologers of Constantinople were humiliated in this way by the emperor Justinian in the sixth century.[29] The camel, the ignoblest of beasts, was often associated not with the good but with the bad ruler—the usurper, illegitimate, incompetent, and abusive of power.

I shall finish my sketch now with reference to a critical historical issue. The first Norman king, Roger II, did not inherit his office or the right to rule a *regnum;* he was the self-created king of a self-created state, which was heresy in the eyes of many, and hence openly criticized.[30] Roger was called *rex tyrannus,* an illegitimate ruler, and throughout his life he used the varied means he had at his disposal to dispel the specter of doubt his critics had instilled. From the Assizes of Ariano, through his military campaigns in North Africa and Greece, through the building projects in Palermo and elsewhere, the trajectory of his argument can be traced. I would like to suggest that the point was made too in the imagery discussed in this paper, and especially on the mantle, though the latter was not simply about territorial ambitions narrowly framed, as has been claimed. Nor was the mantle some arcane astrological concoction. It spoke to the themes of rulership and may be construed in a number of ways. Here is one: the lion, noble and strong, holds in check the accursed beast—the rightful and powerful ruler prevents the ignoble from rising up, and all under the aegis of the church (and perhaps with the implication that this church is guided and shaped by the king). It is the right and power of the king that guarantees the health of the kingdom, the "happiness, honor, good fortune, perfection . . ." and so on, to return to the inscription on the hem of the mantle, which may now be seen in direct relationship to the mantle's imagery. It may also be seen in relationship to the other images and places (that is, the Genoard) that have been discussed, in which the notion of the kingdom as garden found representation in forms ranging from the three-dimensional to the emblematic.

Notes

1. This paper in an earlier form was presented at the 1998 College Art Association Annual Meeting. I would like to thank Eva Hoffman for the discussion of the mantle that we had both before and after.
2. Erwin Margulies, "Le Manteau impérial du Trésor de Vienne et sa doublure," *Gazette des Beaux Arts* ser. 6, 9 (1933), pp. 360ff.; Ugo Monneret de Villard, "Le tessitura palermitana sotto i normanni e i suoi rapporti con l'arte bizantina," *Miscellanea Giovanni Mercati,* 1 (Vatican City, 1946), pp. 464ff.; Hermann Fillitz, *Die Insignien und Kleinodien des Heiligen Römischen Reiches* (Vienna: A. Scholl, 1954), pp. 23ff, 57f.; Filippo Pottino, "Le vesti regali normanne dette dell'incoronazione," *Atti del convegno internazionale di studi ruggeriani,* 21–25 aprile 1954, 1 (Palermo, 1955), pp. 291ff.; Josef Deér, *The Dynastic Porphyry Tombs of the Norman Period in Sicily* (Cambridge MA: Harvard University Press, 1959), pp. 40ff.; Tarif Al Samman, "Arabische Inschriften auf den Krönungsgewandern des Heiligen Römischen Reiches," *Jahrbuch der kunsthistorischen Sammlungen in Wien* 78

(1982), pp. 7ff.; *Kunsthistorisches Museum Vienna. The Secular and Ecclesiastical Treasuries: Illustrated Guide* (Vienna: Residenz Verlag, 1991), pp. 136ff; David Jacoby, "Silk in Western Byzantium Before the Fourth Crusade," *Byzantinische Zeitschrift* 84/85 (1991/92), pp. 464ff; Rotraud Bauer, "Il manto di Ruggero II," *I normanni, popolo d'Europa 1030–1200* (exhibition catalogue), ed. Mario D'Onofrio (Venice: Marsilio Editori, 1994), pp. 279ff.; William Tronzo, *The Cultures of His Kingdom. Roger II and the Cappella Palatina in Palermo* (Princeton: Princeton University Press, 1997), pp. 142ff; Oleg Grabar, "The So-Called Mantle of Roger II," in "The Experience of Islamic Art," forthcoming. I am grateful to Professor Grabar for allowing me to read his paper before publication.

3. Henry Maguire, "The Heavenly Court," *Byzantine Court Culture from 829 to 1204,* ed. Maguire (Washington, D.C.: Dumbarton Oaks, 1997), pp. 253f.
4. See, for example, Eduard Eichmann, "Von der Kaisergewandung im Mittelalter," *Historisches Jahrbuch* 58 (1938), pp. 273ff.; *Sakrale Gewänder des Mittelalters, Ausstellung im bayerischen Nationalmuseum, München, 8. Juli bis 25 September 1955* (Munich: Hirmer Verlag, 1955); Percy Ernst Schramm and Florentine Mutherich, *Denkmale der deutschen Könige und Kaiser: Ein Beitrag zur Herrschergeschichte von Karl dem Grossen bis Friedrich II. 768–1250* (Munich: Prestel Verlag, 1962), pp. 44ff.; *Die Zeit der Staufer,* 1 (1977), pp. 607ff., 5, pp. 389ff.; Anna Muthesius, *Studies in Byzantine and Islamic Silk Weaving* (London: The Pindar Press, 1995), passim; Guido Fauro, "Le vesti nel 'De ceremoniis aulae byzantinae' di Costantino VII Porfirogenito," in *Arte profana e arte sacra a bisanzio,* ed. Antonio Jacobini and Enrico Zanini (Rome, 1995), pp. 489ff. For a textile attributed to Palermo with the inscription, "operato in regio ergast [erio]," see *Federico e la sicilia: dalla terra alla corona. Arti figurative e arti suntuarie* (exhibition catalogue), ed. Maria Andaloro (Palermo: Ediprint, 1995), p. 99, figs. 13.1–13.2.
5. A convenient summary of this history was made by Rotraud Bauer in *Kunsthistorisches Museum Vienna. The Secular and Ecclesiastical Treasuries* (above, n. 2), pp. 134–36 (with bibliography).
6. Hermann Fillitz, *Die Schatzkammer in Wien. Symbole abendländischen Kaisertums* (Salzburg and Vienna: Residenz Verlag, 1986), fig. 5.
7. The issue of the perception of the mantle is discussed by Grabar in the paper cited above, n. 2.
8. One exception is the paper of Grabar cited above, n. 2, which, however, does not as much seek to view word and image in alignment but as separate phenomena.
9. Ibid.
10. Tronzo, Cultures (as above, n. 2), pp. 60–61.
11. For a recent discussion with bibliography, see Hans Rudolf Meier, *Die normannischen Königspaläste in Palermo. Studien zur hochmittelalterlichen Residenzbaukunst* (Worms: Wernersche Verlagsgesellschaft, 1994). Bauer, above, n. 2, relates these buildings to the mantle but with a different purpose.

12. Ibid., pp. 68ff.
13. Romuald of Salerno, *Chronicon,* in *Rerum Italicarum Scriptores,* ed. Ludovico Antonio Muratori 7 (repr. of 1725 ed., Bologna: Arnaldo Forni Editore, 1977), p. 194. For the poetic description of the Favara by 'Abd ar-Rahman of Trapani, see *Gli arabi in Italia,* ed. Francesco Gabrieli and Umberto Scerrato (Milan: Garzanti, 1993), p. 738 (Italian trans.).
14. *Liber ad honorem augusti sive de rebus Siculis, Codex 120 II der Burgerbibliothek Bern. Eine Bilderchronik der Stauferzeit,* ed. Gereon Becht-Joerdens, Theo Koelzer, and Marilis Staehli (Sigmaringen: Jan Thorbecke Verlag, 1994), fol. 98r, p. 47.
15. Giuseppe Bellafiore, *Giardini e parchi della Palermo normanna* (Palermo: Flaccovio Editore, 1996), p. 27. See also the discussion of Rosario La Duca, *Cartografia generale della città di Palermo e antiche carte della Sicilia* (Naples: Edizioni Scientifiche Italiane, 1975), pp. 15ff.
16. Otto Demus, *The Mosaics of Norman Sicily* (London: Routledge and Kegan Paul Ltd., 1949), Figures 26B-28A, 94A-97B.
17. Ibid., pp. 178ff.
18. Lucia Travaini, "Aspects of the Sicilian Norman Copper Coinage in the Twelfth Century," *Numismatic Chronicle* 151 (1991), pp. 159–74, pl. 26, no. 2.
19. Philip Grierson, "Guglielmo II o Ruggero II? Una attribuzione errata," *Rivista italiana di numismatica e scienze affini* 91 (1989), pp. 195–204.
20. See Travaini above, n. 18.
21. Philip Grierson, *Byzantine Coins* (Berkeley and Los Angeles: University of California Press, 1982), passim.
22. See Deér (above, n. 2), pp. 66ff., and the study of Willy Hartner and Richard Ettinghausen, "The Conquering Lion, The Life Cycle of a Symbol," *Oriens* 17 (1964), pp. 161 ff., esp. pp. 164ff.
23. Tronzo, Cultures (as above, n. 2), 142, n. 31. The Byzantine emperor Manuel I Komnenos was compared to a palm tree; see Henry Maguire, "Images of the Court," in *The Glory of Byzantium: Art and Culture of the Middle Byzantine Era A.D. 843–1261* (exhibition catalogue), ed. Helen C. Evans and William D. Wixom (New York: Metropolitan Museum of Art, 1997), p. 185.
24. Willene B. Clark, "The Illustrated Medieval Aviary and the Lay-Brotherhood," *Gesta* 21 (1982), pp. 63ff.
25. Penelope C. Mayo, "The Crusaders Under the Palm: Allegorical Plants and Cosmic Kingship in the *Liber Floridus," Dumbarton Oaks Papers* 27 (1973), pp. 29ff.
26. The royal garden, of course, had a long history in the Mediterranean world, against the backdrop of which the Norman phenomenon might be viewed with profit; to cite only one of many studies, see, for example, Elizabeth B. Moynihan, *Paradise as a Garden in Persia and Mughal India* (New York: George Braziller, 1979), pp. 5ff.

27. See the entry on "Camels" in the *Oxford Dictionary of Byzantium,* ed. Alexander Kazhdan (New York and Oxford: Oxford University Press, 1991), p. 368. The camel is depicted on the facade of Saint Gilles-du-Gard together with a pair of apes, which were considered wicked creatures in the Middle Ages; see Whitney S. Stoddard, *The Facade of Saint-Gilles-du-Gard. Its Influence on French Sculpture* (Middletown CT: Wesleyan University Press, 1973), p. 59, fig. 71 (I owe this reference to Eva Hoffman). Apart from the context of the biblical narrative, the image of the camel in medieval Sicilian art is rare; see Ugo Monneret de Villard, *Le pitture musulmane al soffitto della Cappella Palatina in Palermo* (Rome: La Libreria dello Stato, 1950), fig. 250 (ceiling of the Cappella Palatina); *Federico II e la Sicilia* (above, n. 4), 1:171 (ivory box in the Cappella Palatina, Palermo). Of course, not all images of the camel carried negative connotations; see Glen Bowersock, *Roman Arabia* (Cambridge, MA: Harvard University Press, 1983), pp. 83f. (use of the image on coins); *The Age of Spirituality: Late Antique and Early Christian Art, Third to Seventh Century,* ed. Kurt Weitzmann (New York, Metropolitan Museum of Art, 1977), p. 578, no. 517 (ivory plaque with St. Menas flanked by camels).
28. Peter Cornelius Claussen, "Renovatio Romae. Erneuerungsphasen römischer Architektur im 11. und 12. Jahrhundert," *Rom im hohen Mittelalter. Studien zu den Romavorstellungen und zur Rompolitik vom 10. bis zum 12. Jahrhundert. Reinhard Elze zur Vollendung seines siebzigsten Lebensjahres gewidmet, ed. Bernhard Schimmelpfennig and Ludwig Schmugge* (Sigmaringen: Jan Thorbecke Verlag, 1992), p. 100.
29. Procopius, *The Secret History,* trans. G. A. Williamson (London: The Folio Society, 1990), p. 55.
30. Helene Wieruzowski, "Roger II of Sicily, *Rex-Tyrannus* in Twelfth-Century Political Thought," *Speculum* 38 (1963), pp. 46–78.

CHAPTER 11

THE ROBE OF SIMPLICITY: INITIATION, ROBING, AND VEILING OF NUNS IN THE MIDDLE AGES

Désirée Koslin

> *". . . he hath couerd my soule inwarde and myn heed with a veyle, that and if I wyll loue ony man better than hym I shall goo to the colour of my veyle and that is euerlastynge deth." In lyke wyse she shewed that her Spouse Cryste Jesu had indued her with a garment all sette with precyous stones, that is to saye with charyte, fayth, hope, humylyte, obedyens, abstynence, and prayer, and inbroudred all thyse fayr vertues in the blake garmente of her body and soule here knytte togyder. . . .*
>
> —John Alcock, Bishop of Ely (1430–1500), ca.1496[1]

Using the humble, black monastic dress[2] as evocative metaphor, Bishop Alcock spoke to the novices and nuns of his diocese in the voice of St. Agnes, an early Christian martyr who was a popular role model and patron saint for many religious women in the Middle Ages. Their clothing and consecration ceremonies were rich in symbolism of ancient standing and are at the core of this essay, which will also discuss the development of the prescribed dress practices of the various religious orders. The medieval nun's "taking of the veil" constituted a voluntary act of submission and an imposition, imparities that resonate in medieval art and literature. This topic deserves attention today, a generation after the decrees of the Second Vatican Council (1962–1965) when distinctive religious dress was all but abolished. The clothing of the religious has not been addressed by the many recent scholars who have focused on medieval religious women. The theme was clearly of great interest, however, to the women themselves, their contemporaries, and to many subsequent generations of proponents as well as detractors of monasticism.[3]

Religious lives were led by many in the Middle Ages, either as individuals or in groups. The former might live in seclusion as anchorites under the guidance of a mentor or reside at home obeying simple vows, especially that of chastity. Institutions for communal living presented a great variety of formal as well as informal organizations, especially toward the end of the medieval period. Best known and documented are the monasteries whose inhabitants, monks or nuns, had taken full vows of chastity, poverty, and obedience. They led cloistered lives under a rule and belonged to an order, such as the Benedictine, Cistercian, or Carthusian, formally accepted and approved by papal authority.

The term *convent* is used here in its medieval sense to designate a foundation whose members had not taken full vows, especially not that of poverty, which allowed them to be active in secular life. Examples of conventual orders are the Mendicant ones, the Augustinian, Carmelite, Dominican, and Franciscan friars and sisters. It is a recurrent pattern in conventual orders that the friars often would have functions in secular life, such as teaching and preaching, whereas the female branches of these orders usually chose or were forced to be enclosed. Therefore the term nun, properly denoting a cloistered or enclosed religious, may also be applied to conventuals such as the Poor Clares who obeyed the Franciscan Rule while living in strictest observance of full vows. Other groups of medieval religious who at first led informal, communal lives were frequently persuaded or forced to adopt the customs of an order while rarely taking full vows.

Somewhat confusingly, the term *order* is also used in a broader, hierarchical sense. Thus the male branches of any given order were designated as First Order, cloistered women constituted the Second Order, and all others, men and women, were identified as Third Order.[4] Such tertiaries would take partial vows only and could remain active in secular society as they also lived chaste, communal lives, much like the Shakers of North America of the recent past.

There were formalities and ceremonies for entry into any of these religious communities, and documents from nonmonastic houses do survive which describe such ceremonies.[5] This essay, however, is primarily concerned with the medieval consecration ceremony of monastic, religious women whose ordination was part of the Rites of the Church. When compared with the other, resplendent robing and investiture rituals for secular persons and high-ranking ecclesiastical clergy, however, the clothing and consecration ceremonies of medieval monastic women in the western

Church present paradoxical, often reductionist features. To begin with, nuns were the only women other than queens and empresses who qualified for an ordination rite performed by a bishop. But the ritual for nuns consisted merely of a Blessing and a Consecration upon taking full vows. This reduced number of rites for the Second Order is in stark contrast to the multiple ones for the male First Order, whose initiation and investiture rituals encompassed several clerical ranks from acolyte and novice to monk, deacon, priest, then perhaps abbot, bishop, or archbishop. The hierarchy of ranks for the Second Order of female religious was short; the office of abbess was the only one sanctified by an episcopal blessing to which women could aspire.[6]

Another distinction is that the magnificent coronation and investiture garments of temporal rulers would be worn just once or only rarely, whereas the insignificant dress of the religious, blessed and imposed at their consecration, would be the permanent, daily and nightly clothing for a lifetime. The splendor of the pattern-woven silks and cloths of gold used for the inauguration of monarchs and high-ranking clergy were similarly in diametrical contrast to the rough, undyed, usually dark wool of the humble dress of both nuns and monks. When thoroughly worn out, these garments would be passed on to the truly poor and replaced by new ones. Only the nun's black veil would be preserved unused for her burial, as it was a memento of her state as a Bride of Christ, *Sponsa Christi,* blessed by the bishop during her veiling ceremony, the *velatio.*

The physical features of the monastic garments, a chafing cincture and rough cloth texture, were designed to remind the wearer at all times of Christ's suffering and apostolic poverty. This visual sartorial message of the dress of the religious was instantly conveyed to any observer, inside or outside the cloister. Monastic attire thus embodied both inner and outer significance of perpetual renunciation and commitment to solemn vows. As *sponsae* or *paranymphae,* bridesmaids, consecrated nuns were joined with Him in Mystical Marriage and committed to a cloistered life after their profession of full vows; from then on they should no longer be seen and were considered dead to the world.

The pronouncedly nuptial aspects of nuns' clothing were also a contradiction to the garments used in the secular, high-status marriage ceremonies of the social milieu from which most nuns were recruited. The expensive and festive attire of worldly weddings was countered by the nun's drab and shapeless woollen garments. The secular bride's primary signifier of beauty was her luxuriant and flowing hair arrangement, which was contrasted by the nun's tonsured hair[7] and black veil. Other traditional nuptial symbols, such as the ring and the crown, were features present both in the ceremony of nuns' consecration and in secular marriages.

The study of the dress of religious women is difficult in many ways. Primary sources contain little written evidence on medieval women generally, a fact often noted in the many recent publications on the topic that have utilized broad interdisciplinary methodologies and interpretive approaches.[8] Information on religious women specifically is of course even more scant, but can be accessed by researching a variety of textual sources, from patristic literature to vernacular satire, and from legal documents to hagiography; these sources have been used here to glean information on the dress of religious women. Such references are usually brief, sometimes perfunctory, and when addressed with emphasis they are usually only negative, describing what clothes not to wear. Conclusions must be reached by a process of elimination. Since clothing and vestimentary signals were of paramount importance in the medieval world, we must however understand that the wearing of appropriate and specific religious clothing was in no way neglected or ignored but rather was part of the common knowledge in the medieval "high context" society, and therefore it was largely unnecessary to record it.[9] Only late in the medieval period do the new or revised orders' customaries become explicit and particular in regard to clothing, a sign of a "low context" society. For example, the "Birgittine" Order of St. Savior, which was approved in 1370, stipulated in great detail the nature of the heavily fulled woollen cloth, its penitential, ash-gray color, the overgarment's sleeve-length, which could extend only to the long finger's tip, the humble buttons of wood for the mantle, and the exact number of pins, four, allowed for securing the headdress.[10]

Visual evidence, primarily in the form of miniatures in manuscripts, also expands our understanding of religious dress in the medieval period. It has provided important material for this essay and has been the basis for a larger study.[11] To take the depictions of dress in this period at face value can, however, be perilous and misleading. Some dress historians have argued that medieval manuscript illustrations of clothing cannot be trusted at all for veracity in either cut, color, or shape due to idealization, artistic license, or ignorance on the part of either patron or artist. It is true that medieval images have frequently been taken out of context and used inappropriately for illustrative purposes by modern authors. It is necessary to pay close attention to issues of patronage, audience, and prevalent conventions, as well as the nature of the text when evaluating medieval illustrations. With such issues accounted for, the immediacy of the visual medium offers new keys to understanding that complement and sometimes transcend the written sources.

Particularly useful are the late medieval miniatures in pontificals, the liturgical texts containing the prayers and ceremonies used by a bishop. The first such compilation appeared in the ninth century, and an expanded version, the *Ordo Romanus,* was introduced in the tenth century. From the thirteenth century these episcopal manuals began to have illustrations punctuating the different sections, usually in the form of historiated initials.[12] It is also at this point that the organization of the pontifical underwent a radical revision undertaken by William Durandus (ca.1230–96);[13] his redaction remained the basis for later editions until revisions were called for at the Second Vatican Council. Durandus was bishop of Mende, France, and his improvements made the pontifical easier to use in its tripartite division of the rites: those relating to persons, to things, and to special functions. The illustrations accompanying the sections usually have a didactic clarity and constitute, for instance, the only medieval depictions we have of monastic consecration rites.[14] Of the extant medieval pontificals, only a small number have illustrations, however, and of these just a few have full cycles depicting the ritual tasks of the bishop. Religious women appear under the five rubrics of the Blessing of the Abbess, the Deaconess, the Widow, and the Blessing and Consecration of Virgins.[15] Even here, however, caveats must be issued since several of these celebrated and luxurious pontificals have been found to contain inaccuracies in the ecclesiastical and ceremonial protocol of their miniatures, which implies ignorance on the artists' part.[16] When seen in their entirety, the many emblematic visuals that accompany the text of the bishop's tasks are nevertheless helpful and instructive because they reflect key points in the ritual frequently combined into one composite image.

These images have not been utilized in the cursory treatment of religious dress in the current literature on dress. If mentioned at all by dress historians, the continuity and ideological antifashion aspect of monastic dress are noted, a proof of this retrograde tendency being the retention of its Latin-based terminology in the various vernaculars.[17] But fashion also informed the dress of the religious, a feature that is manifestly apparent, sometimes even subversively depicted and described in art and literature. The active royal female patronage of various religious orders and monastic foundations was often accompanied by propagandistic art manifestations; therefore, the surviving depictions of the elite women who were religious may also be seen as contributing to secular fashions, adding another layer of meaning and complexity to an investigation of the "humble insignificance" of nuns' clothing.[18]

Dress Practices of the Different Orders

Religious dress in its summarily codified form has held considerable fascination for modern interpreters other than costume historians. On the one hand it is thought possible to describe the monastic imposition of a dress code discipline according to Foucaultian theory in terms of repression and surveillance. That is quite literally the case in the enclosed community.[19] On the other hand, a 'perspectival' approach mediates this partial and very useful truth as frequently banal; late in the Middle Ages we encounter the authentic voices of religious women who described their intimate and meaningful relationship to the apostolic precepts through the actual and metaphorical means of their humble dress.[20]

It is also obvious that this complex sartorial language of visible insignificance was already fully employed in the fourth and fifth centuries when wealthy Roman matrons as new adherents to Christianity spoke their faith through dress (anti)fashions in a society keenly attuned to visual and sensory expressions and perceptions.[21] In so doing, these now spiritually empowered women in fact reverted to the ancient pan-Mediterranean gender divisions of male public and female private presences.[22] The "high context" in which these dress modes functioned without ever being specifically or explicitly described can be seen in a long, slow trajectory toward the "low context" at the end of the period covered here, ca.1500, when signs and emblems, manners of veil-draping, and uniform color-coding of the various orders were necessary for recognition.

The elements of monastic clothing were linked to ancient, apostolic precepts quoted in rules and customaries, the tracts that governed the religious houses. Each order had to obey one of the three Rules approved by papal authority, that of St. Benedict (ca. 480-ca. 550), St. Augustine (354–430), and St. Francis (1181/2–1226).[23] The Benedictines and the reformed Benedictine orders espoused orthodoxy as they observed the contemplative life; this exclusive and increasingly costly existence was made possible by their usually long-established privileges and by significant incomes from dependencies.[24] The orders obeying the Rule of St. Augustine can broadly be said to have chosen this allegiance for one of two distinct economic reasons. The first was by default: while the founder may have preferred his or her new religious foundation to be fully cloistered and contemplative under the Benedictine rule, financial support and therefore ultimately papal approval was lacking, and the more flexible Augustinian Rule therefore provided an acceptable option. The Gilbertines (f.1148), and the Birgittines (f. 1370) are examples of this.[25] The second rationale was a more deliberate choice: the caritative mission of the hospital orders,[26] for instance, was secular service; and the Canonesses'[27] preference was to retain personal property while living enclosed lives, so for these orders the versatile Rule of St. Augustine was adopted since it required no vow of poverty. The orders obeying the Rule of St. Francis (approved 1223), the only autonomous mendicant rule, were by definition not cloistered, although St. Clare (1193/4–1253) insisted on full enclosure for her nuns. Many other female branches of the mendicant orders also chose or were forced to impose full enclosure for all but their tertiary sisters. These were the consequences of constant efforts in Rome, at synods, and at councils to ensure adequate pastoral care, *cura monialium,* of the religious women, a matter largely of financial concern to Rome and to the heads of the First Orders.[28] One of the most powerful decrees enforcing claustration, the bull usually referred to as *Periculoso,* was published in 1298 by Boniface VIII in his *Liber Sextus Decretalium.* Its purpose was to limit and control religious women by imposing strict claustration on all foundations, no matter which Rule they obeyed.[29]

The monastic dress components are few, and will be introduced here to (re)establish a terminology as well as a context for the garments and their variants in the different orders. Their models derived from ancient and classical usage, and to the religious, the simple cuts of the garments and the retention of Latin nomenclature signaled their timeless aspects and origins. The clothes were summarily described in chapter 55 of the Rule of St. Benedict, "Monks must not grumble at the color or coarseness of their clothing, they shall be such as can be procured in the district where they live, or as can be bought at the cheapest price."[30]

The attire consisted of the ankle-length, sleeved tunic, retained in its pervasive, classical form; the cowl, a sometimes hooded, sometimes sleeved overgarment patterned on the foul-weather cloaks of Roman peasants; and the scapular, an apronlike piece of apparel worn during manual labor. It was these three, largely genderless pieces of clothing of apostolic poverty and penitence that all monastics strove to emulate, and the female branches of the orders used equivalents of them. Although these garments underwent changes over the centuries, there was nevertheless a deliberate archaicizing and a conscious adherence to the Benedictine precepts. As these basic dress items developed differently in the various orders, each garment retained aspects of its original significance, and each can be traced to its common origin. We shall see below that all three Rules employed the same terms for the dress of the religious, and the orders that obeyed them shared clothing of the same general appearance. The Rule of St. Augustine, written first for a monastery of virgins in Thagaste, North Africa, was revised when it was reintroduced in the eleventh century for use by Augustinian canons. Apart from the usual instructions against vanity and luxurious dress, few specifics pertaining to clothing are mentioned.[31] The dress prescriptions in the Rule of St. Francis similarly hark back to Benedictine ideals, emphasizing the apostolic poverty of both the cloth quality and the dimensions of the garments.[32]

Thus the simple woollen tunic, with its antique and classical precedents, was worn by all monastics and conventuals. St. Benedict stipulated that it had to be cinched at the waist, night and day, a symbol of chastity and purity derived from biblical instructions. In images of medieval Benedictines, and the orders depending on this rule, the tunic with its cincture is frequently covered by the fully cut *cucullus,* and the tunic is then only glimpsed at sleeves and lower edges. Derived from Benedict's cowl, the *cucullus* with its wide, hanging sleeves denoted the contemplative life—this was not a garment for work. Other, noncloistered orders adopted *cucullae* for those taking part in the divine service.[33] In female dress usage the *cucullus* didn't include a hood, of course, as it was awkward to accommodate it along with a veil. The latter was usually lined with an underveil and complemented with a wimple covering throat and chest.

Many of the reformed orders under the Rule of St. Benedict at first wore only their tunics with the cinched girdle for daily use, in ideological response to the Rule that called for the simplest locally available cloth and a daily practice of manual labor. Later on the well-established orders, such as the Cistercian, become increasingly contemplative since the heavy work was by then assigned to *conversi* brethren or sisters.[34] Late-medieval depictions show Cistercians in *cucullae* over the tunic, although rarely with the voluminous Benedictine sleeves. But St. Bernard, as one of the founders, is usually represented in his cinched tunic, sometimes with a scapular. The scapular was an apronlike garment for work, slipped over the head to protect the tunic. It was usually worn hanging free front and back over the cincture. It is rare to see the monastic, contemplative orders depicted in scapulars, although they presumably did spend part of their day at manual labor. The Augustinian and the mendicant orders, however, had scapulars of various lengths and colors, symbols of their commitment to an active life. The Augustinian Hermit nuns had a particularly voluminous version, whereas the scapulars of the Dominicans and Franciscan were medium-sized, and many hospital orders used small, vestigial scapulars.[35]

The colors of the dress of the religious are described in medieval and later sources as uniform signifiers, but they present many problems in terms of identifications in medieval texts and images. Thus, Black Ladies are considered to be Benedictines, White Ladies are Cistercian, Gray Sisters would be Franciscans, etc.[36] Depictions as well as historical facts belie this simplified scheme, however, and historians have pointed out many inconsistencies: many Augustinian canonesses also wore all black; Gilbertine nuns were at times called White Nuns; the Fontevrault, and Premonstratensian nuns in England used white clothing also. Since neither St. Benedict nor St. Augustine were specific as to dress color, usages developed that sometimes were coordinated into uniform clothing codes through the general chapters of the "federated" orders, such as the Premonstratensian, Cistercian, and the Mendicant ones. These were dictates that limited themselves to the male First Orders, however, to which the female branches stood in precarious and often temporary relationships.[37] This is one reason why there is such diversity of dress color in the images of the religious. Another is the issue of artistic license or ignorance mentioned earlier. Black "Benedictine" clothing had been established by the eighth century but had many variations until it became uniform.[38] Augustinian canonesses and nuns frequently appear in all black in visual representations, but many other colors are also seen. Pierre Hélyot's 1714–19 *Histoire des Ordres Monastiques* offers a helpful hint—the various Augustinian foundations and orders allowed many clothing colors and combinations of colors, but all white was not permitted them as it was clearly reserved for the fully chaste, contemplative nuns.[39] The Humiliati, Fontevrault, Cistercian, Carthusian, Vallombrosan, Olivetan, and Sylvestrine orders considered themselves reformed Benedictines and showed this by using the cheapest, locally produced, and undyed woollens that St. Benedict had suggested—these natural shades range from brown to bleached white in medieval depictions. In representations of Cistercian nuns, a particularly rich extent of such neutral dress colors is seen.[40] For the secular context regarding the use of all white, we may be reminded of Margery Kempe's disconsolate lament at not being allowed to wear white clothing since it was reserved for the fully chaste only; she continued her appeals for dispensation from ecclesiastical authority for this privilege.[41]

The Mendicants dispensed with the *cucullus,* as it was unsuitable to their missionary activities and caritative functions. Instead scapulars served them as humble emblems of their active lives, and in the choir of the conventual church simple mantles would be worn during services. The Dominicans, Augustinians, and Carmelites all adhered to the not-all-white rule, to which the Franciscans added a not-all-black rule, again evoking the ancient Benedictine ideal of undyed, local woollen cloth cinched with a rough, knotted hempen rope. The crisp and uniform dress of the female branch of the Dominican "army of priests" is in stark contrast to the ragged attire of the Franciscans. In her rule, St. Clare urged her sisters to always wear poor clothing, "*vestimentis semper vilibus,*" and made a point of setting an example in penitential garments without fullness or excessive length.[42] Her mantle has survived and is kept in the Convento Santa Chiara in Assisi today. The many lacunae seen in it are the result of pieces having been cut from it, presumably by St. Clare herself, to be used as patches to mend the tunic of St. Francis which is also preserved in Assisi—a very literal deconstruction and moving evidence for the centrality and importance of cloth and clothing in use as relics.[43]

The Consecration of Virgins

So ye must kepe the tresour of your spouse Cryste perteynynge to his faythe and to haue in your remembraunce and wyll to kepe the foure thynges that shall be delyuerd unto you this daye, your veyle and your mantell both beynge of blake and a rynge and a lyght of waxe berynge in your honde, and in kepynge of thyse it shal be shewed as ye loue your husbonde.

—John Alcock, *Exhortacyon*[44]

The central part in the medieval consecration procedure for nuns was the taking of the veil, *velatio,* in mystical union with the Heavenly Bridegroom. Women's veils as signs of matrimony were continuous from pre-Christian times in the Greek and Near Eastern cultural contexts.[45] Current research on religious women in the late Antique and early Christian periods has established that foundations for women's communities existed prior to the period of the desert fathers and early cenobitic, male monasticism.[46] Paul's injunction that women should cover their heads in the church established the transmission of this practice from pagan days,[47] and in the patristic writings the ritual change of clothes, *mutatio vestium,* of a young girl vowed to virginity entailed being dressed in a dark-colored tunic, wrapped in somber cloaks, and having linen garments taken away, as Jerome (ca. 345–420) instructs in his letter to Pacatula, Epistle 128.[48]

That a nun's veil and its dark color were standardized early on in the medieval West and at a considerable distance from Rome is evident in a passage of the prose poem *De Virginitate,* addressed to the nuns at Barking Abbey, England. The author is Aldhelm of Wessex (639–719), bishop of Malmesbury, who rails against the vanity of both genders in a style that we today perceive as misogynist:

> Contrary to the decrees of canon law and the norm of the regular life, vanity and insolence are adopted for one purpose only, that the bodily figure may be adorned with forbidden ornaments and charming decorations, and that the physical appearance may be glamorized in every part and every limb. This consists for either sex in fine linen shirts, in scarlet or blue tunics, in necklines and sleeves embroidered with silk; their shoes trimmed with red-dyed leather; the hair of their forelocks and the curls at their temples are crimped with a curling iron; dark gray veils for the head give way to bright and colored headdresses, which are sewn with interlacings of ribbons and hang down as far as the ankles. Fingernails are sharpened after the manner of falcons or hawks.[49]

By the end of the twelfth century, depictions of nuns point to a modification in the manner of wearing the headveil and its component parts. In earlier images of religious women, a single cloth is seen wrapped around the head, covering the chest, forehead, and shoulders. Later illustrations show the nun's black veil of fine wool or silk placed over an underveil of white linen, which in turn partly covers a wimple. This separate accessory consisted of a cloth that was draped snugly over the chest to cover chin and throat, and it is requisite in depictions of religious women from the thirteenth century onward.[50] It is also shown used by pious upper-class and royal women generally and may well represent a fashion inspired by contacts during the Crusades with the sophisticated cultures to the south and east where women were habitually veiled.

Such elaboration and multiplication of nuns' headdress elements did not escape censure, and the previously quoted Aldhelm is only one in a long series of male ecclesiastic and secular critics who condemn luxurious attire worn by religious women. The 1222 Council of Oxford continued the tradition:

> Since it is necessary that the female sex, so weak against the wiles of the ancient enemy, should be so fortified by many remedies, we decree that nuns and other women dedicated to divine worship shall not wear silken wimple, nor dare to carry silver or golden tiring-pins in their veil. Neither shall they, nor monks nor regular canons, wear belts of silk, or adorned with gold or silver, nor henceforth use burnet or any other unlawful cloth.[51]

Regional variations in the manner of arranging the veil can be seen in medieval representations; a *Legendarium* made for the Dominican Holy Cross convent in Regensburg in 1271, for instance, displays nuns and tertiaries in crisp linen headbands added above the underveil, thereby providing an elevation over which to drape their veils.[52] In other manuscript illustrations the texture of the veil's fabric is frequently rendered in an open cross-hatching indicating a sheer textile, probably the proscribed but apparently ubiquitous silk. Pins as well as embroidered crosses also decorate the black veils of nuns, an emphasis easy to associate with the adherence to prevailing fashions discussed earlier, as well as the nuptial and matrimonial aspects of this garment.

All initiation and ordination rites feature a period of preparation, and for those entering a monastery, this time provided opportunities to test a novice's commitment and suitability for the enclosed life. Training in the daily observances and an ability to read the liturgical books in Latin were also required for those engaged in the divine service. The sources are at some variance on the topic of the suitable age for a young woman's acceptance as a nun and the length of her postulancy, but by the late thirteenth century the age of 25 had been decreed as the minimum age for profession, the taking of full vows, although many exceptions to this seem to have occurred.[53] A novitiate of a year's duration to precede this event is frequently mentioned and seems to have been the norm. The Rule of St. Benedict stipulated that three investigations be held during the novitiate before the postulant could be accepted into the community. In the pontifical, these scrutinies were continued as part of the consecration ceremony.[54]

The pontifical of Durandus has been used here to describe the Consecration of Virgins in detail since it contains greater elaboration, detail, and more pronouncedly nuptial aspects of the ritual when compared to the Roman Ordo, which continued in use during the Middle Ages, even after the introduction of the Durandine model. The nuns-to-be, for instance, are termed *paranymphae* and *sponsae* by Durandus, and they are *ancillae Dei* (God's handmaidens) and *sponsae* in the Ordo Romanus version.[55] There is also a deliberate reiteration in the Durandus version in the multiple benedictions of the discrete articles of clothing and objects that correspond to that of royal coronations and ecclesiastical investitures, a reciprocity and expectation noted by several writers on the topic of Christian rites.[56]

The solemn rites of the Blessing of Virgins and of the Consecration of Virgins took place on designated feast days of the liturgical calendar. Durandus enumerated several options: Epiphany, Birthdays of the Apostles, Easter, Ascension, Pentecost, Assumption of the Virgin, and, "if necessary," on the Sundays surrounding Advent or Lent, leaving out but a very few.[57] On the eve of the chosen feast day, during mass at vespers, the bishop received the virgins and inquired about their age and whether they were chaste and willing to be consecrated. Mass was then celebrated the following day to the end of the Collect, at which point the bishop seated himself, as was stipulated, in a folding chair with armrests in front of the altar. The officiating priest, archdeacon, or other person appointed by the bishop then called forth the novices with *"Prudentes virgines, aptate lampades vestras, ecce sponsus venit, exite obviam ei"* [Wise virgins, prepare you lamps, see the Bridegroom approaching, come greet him].[58] The lighted candles, carried in the right hand, thus symbolized the bridesmaids of the parable in Matthew 25.1–13 of the Wise Virgins, to whom Christ refers as the "light of the World," the candles relating directly to the torches carried in the nuptial processions of antiquity. The young women had been given a tonsure[59] and were dressed in white tunics but without veils, mantles, or *cucullae.* They proceeded to the entrance of the choir where they knelt, holding the lighted candles. The bishop inquired and received affirmative response from the officiating cleric as to whether the virgins were worthy. He then invited them to enter the choir where they again resumed a kneeling position. Antiphonary exchanges followed, the nuns-to-be singing in response to the bishop's incantations. Each novice in turn was asked to approach the bishop; she was interrogated as she again knelt in front of him as to her willingness to live in chastity, to which she would respond affirmatively. He then held her praying hands in his, asking for her vow always to remain chaste, which was then given. He uttered a blessing, and she kissed his hand and returned to the group. When all had confirmed their intentions in this way, the bishop asked the group whether they were willing to be betrothed to Christ, to which they responded as one, "*Volumus*" ("We are willing").[60] The bishop then turned to the altar, kneeling on his folding chair, *super faldistorium*. Behind him and facing the altar were the young women, now prostrate but in an orderly row on the carpet, *super tapeta*. The Litany was begun, whereupon the bishop turned anew to the novices. With his episcopal staff in the left hand, he beseeched Christ to accept the *virgines*. The Litany continued to be sung, with special invocations in the female form, while the novices departed to fetch their tunics and veils, with which they returned to the altar. The bishop blessed the garments one by one, sprinkled holy water on each of them in turn, and repeating his solemn prayers, finally pronounced the clothing consecrated and immaculate.

The nuns' rings were then brought, held in a basin by an assisting clergy. Like the candles, they were ancient tokens of matrimony adopted here as symbols of perpetual chastity of the *Sponsa Christi*. Each was sprinkled with the *aspergillum* and then blessed, and this was followed by a similar procedure for the bridal wreath or crown. The soon-to-be-nuns again left the choir to return dressed in the now sanctified attire of their order, although still carrying the veils in their hands. Singing *Hallelujah* and *Regnum mundi,* they again turned to the altar. Asked a final time by the bishop if they would persist in their virginity, they responded again, "*Volumus,*" whereupon the bishop commenced placing the veil on the head of each nun in turn, covering her shoulders and her chest with it, and letting it fall over the face to the eyebrows, as he intoned for each, "*Accipe, virgo, velamen sacrum, quod perferas sine macula ante tribunal eterni iudicis . . .*" [Virgin, receive the holy veil, which you will bring spotless to the Tribunal of the Last Judgment . . .], to which the nun responded chanting: *"Posuit signum in faciem meam, ut nullum preter eum amatorem admittam"* [He has placed a sign on my face so that none but He can be my Beloved]. A ring was then given to each nun with a further blessing, and the women responded: "*Anulo suo subarravit me dominus meus Iesu Christus et tamquam sponsam decoravit me corona*" [My Lord Jesus Christ has pledged me with his ring and also adorned me as his Spouse with a crown]. As the ceremony approached its completion with the benediction of the crown, the virgins exulted: "*Induit me dominus cyclade auro texta et immensis monilibus suis ornavit me*" [The Lord has endowed me with a gown woven of gold, and has adorned me with his matchless jewels].[61] Returning to their places, the nuns again genuflected. Banns were announced by the bishop against whomever would attempt to molest or pervert the nuns, and blessings were again given for the nun's new life of virginity. In conclusion the bishop read anew from the Gospel of Matthew and gave a final benediction. The consecration ceremony ended with partaking of the Sacrament. During the three days to follow, the newly consecrated nuns remained shrouded with their veils drawn below their chins, covering their faces entirely, while they maintained a strict fast and observed complete silence to mark their departure from the World. On the third day they attended a Mass of the Resurrection, their veils were lifted, and they could again speak. A festive, "nuptial" meal followed their return, or entry as consecrated to the religious community.[62]

The illustrations that are found in the historiated initials of the incipits to the prayers and instructions in the pontificals are of much interest in their sparse detail. There are some standard formats in the representation of novices for the "Ordo ad virginem benedicendam" (Blessing of Virgins), or, in the Durandus version, "De benedictione et consecratione virginum" (Blessing and Consecration of Virgins)[63] that establish two categories of religious women before their Consecration, usually in groups standing or kneeling before the bishop. They are either in secular garments but having had female tonsure *in rotondum,* their hair shorn to the ears. Alternately they are shown in the dress of their order wearing the white veils of the novitiate. The same color of veil was also used to signify widows and tertiary women. To distinguish between these representations, the context is all-important and remarkably consistent. For instance, if other secular persons are present, widows and tertiary women are indicated, and if seen in front of a bishop, a novice is represented. Other illuminations in pontificals display scenes of the bishop and one or more novices during the consecration, for instance at the moment of the imposition of the veil; the nuns-to-be in their black veils carrying tall candles; and receiving the ring from the bishop. An abbess is sometimes present by the bishop's side as the vows are given.

In the consecration rite described above, formulaic and didactic devices were used to impart and emphasize the ordination's symbolic message of a new identity. Unlike temporal ceremonies and rituals in which the sartorial magnificence stood in direct proportion to the status of the office conferred, the new nun's clothing and veil were insignificant and dull, but they marked the transcendent nature of the event. Through the ceremony's many components, a microcosm of ancient initiation rituals had been reenacted, and by taking the veil the nun would transcend, even if temporarily, her bodily needs. Like the coronation ceremonies the consecration ritual of religious women entailed exalted rewards, even if theirs were deferred. In Bishop Alcock's *Exhortacyon* quoted above, marital imagery is most powerfully evoked through the voice of St. Agnes, with her lived experience as *Sponsa Christi*. Under her veil, the nun was encouraged to interiorize her role-model's message and was instructed to see her new, veiled body covered with a fabric "woven of gold," in which her virtues were turned into extraordinary gems for her ultimate, celestial destination as Bride of Christ.

Notes

I am most grateful to Jonathan J. G. Alexander for reading this essay and offering generous and constructive advice; the text has also benefited from discussions with Susan L'Engle.

1. John Alcock (Spousage of a Virgin to Christ) *An Exhortacyon Made to Relygyous Systers,* The English Experience, No. 638 (Amsterdam: Theatrum Orbis Terrarum, 1974).
2. The term *habit* for the clothing of the religious is avoided here as it is imprecise and also designated a specific set of outer garments of medieval Benedictines; see Barbara Harvey, *Monastic Dress in the Middle Ages: Precept and Practice* (Canterbury: The William Memorial Trust, 1988), p. 14.
3. An early compendium is a twelfth-century treatise probably written in Liège, *Libellus de diversibus Ordinibus et Professionibus,* ed. Giles Constable and Bernard Smith (Oxford: Clarendon Press, 1972); from the sixteenth century on, great numbers of illustrated guides to identification of the various orders were published, and an extensive bibliography is included in an important survey, Pierre Hélyot, *Histoire des Orders Religieux et Militaires et des Congregations seculieres de l'un & de l'autre sexe qui ont ésté éstablies jusqu'a present,* 8 vols. (Paris: Nicolas Gosselin, 1714–19). An example of anti-monastic views is Thomas D. Fosbroke, *British Monachism; or Manners and Customs of the Monks and Nuns of England* (London: M. A. Nattali, 1843).
4. These distinctions appear in the twelfth century, when the secular Humiliati brethren and sisters of northern Italy were given this rank; see *The Oxford Dictionary of the Christian Church,* third ed., ed. F. L. Cross and E. A. Livingstone (Oxford: Oxford University Press, 1997), s.v. Henceforth *ODCC.*
5. For instance, a late fifteenth-century manual for a Florentine convent of Franciscan Tertiary women (Oxford, Bodleian Library Canon. Lit.ms 347) contains a series of miniatures depicting the clothing of a sister performed by a priest, not a bishop.
6. Within a monastery or convent for women there were several internal positions, such as chambress, cellaress, and mistress of novices, but these ranks were not included in the episcopal rites. For a description of the administrative system, see the classic by Eileen Power, *Medieval English Nunneries*

c.1275 to 1535 (Cambridge: Cambridge University Press, 1922), esp. chapters 3 and 4.

7. On tonsure as an ancient preparatory element for initiations, see Simone Vierne, *Rite, Roman, Initiation* (Grenoble: Presses Universitaires, 1973), chap. 1. As a rite in Christian context current from eighth century it is believed to have come from the practice of cutting the hair of slaves; see *New Catholic Encyclopedia,* 17 vols. (New York: McGraw-Hill, 1967), s.v., henceforth *NCE.*
8. This brief, chronologically arranged sampling includes scholars from different disciplines who have written recently and specifically on religious women: Elizabeth Makowski, *Canon Law and Cloistered Women: Periculoso and Its Commentators 1298–1545* (Washington, DC: The Catholic University of America Press, 1997); Jeffrey Hamburger, *Nuns As Artists: The Visual Culture of a Medieval Convent* (Berkeley: University of California Press, 1997); Jo Ann K. McNamara, *Sisters in Arms: Catholic Nuns Through Two Millennia* (Cambridge, MA: Harvard University Press, 1996); Gertrude Jaron Lewis, *By women, for women, about women: the Sister-Books of fourteenth-century Germany* (Toronto: Pontifical Institute of Medieval Studies, 1996); Barbara Newman, *From Virile Woman to womanChrist: Studies in Medieval Religion and Literature* (Philadelphia: University of Pennsylvania Press, 1994); Roberta Gilchrist, *Gender and Material Culture: The archaeology of religious women* (London: Routledge, 1994); Penelope D. Johnson, *Equals in Monastic Profession: Religious Women in Medieval France* (Chicago: University of Chicago Press, 1991).
9. These are concepts used by Edward T. Hall in designating societies in which stereotypes play an important role; here a "high context" community, such as the earlier Middle Ages, produces texts that are sketchy because cultural expectations are embedded and shared, whereas a "low context" society, here the later medieval period, requires detailed texts, leaving "little to the imagination." See Edward T. Hall, *Beyond Culture* (Garden City, NY: Doubleday, 1976), esp. pp. 91–101, and his *The Dance of Life: The Other Dimensions of Time* (Garden City, NY: Doubleday, 1983), pp. 59–77. This methodology was introduced to me by reading Jerome H. Neyrey's application of Hall's thought to the early Christian period in his "What's Wrong With This Picture? John 4, Cultural Stereotypes of Women, and Public and Private Space," *Biblical Theology Bulletin* 24/2, 1994, pp. 77–91.
10. *Kulturhistoriskt Lexikon för nordisk medeltid,* 22 vols. (Malmö, Sweden: 1956–78), s.v.
11. See my dissertation, "The Dress of Medieval Religious Women as Seen in the Visual Arts to ca. 1500," Institute of Fine Arts, New York University, 1999.
12. Victor Leroquais, *Les Ponticifaux manuscrits des bibliothèques publiques de France* (Paris: Macon, 1937) remains an important authority on these litur-

gical books; the author has plotted the development based on pontificals in French collections.

13. See expanded treatment in Michel Andrieu, *Le Pontifical Romain au Moyen-Age,* 4 vols. (The Vatican: Biblioteca Apostolica Vaticana, 1938–40), esp. vol. 3, which treats the surviving examples of Durandine pontificals.
14. The Office of Deaconess survived only in the rituals of the pontifical during the later Middle Ages. Once a clerical rank with certain tasks in the Divine Service, deaconesses were abolished already at ecclesiastical council meetings in the sixth century. See *ODCC,* s.v. The Rite for the inauguration of the Abbess is not considered here, as it includes no clothing ceremony; the Widow's blessing is left out for the same reason.
15. That is, in a typical cycle of pontifical illustrations.
16. Leroquais, *Les Pontificaux,* notes "mistakes" on the part of the artists throughout his catalogue, such as depicting the bishop using the wrong hands for rituals and wearing the processional cope instead of the ritual chasuble, etc.
17. See, for instance, Joan Evans, *Dress In Medieval France* (Oxford: Clarendon Press, 1952), p. 67; Françoise Piponnier and Perrine Mane, *Se vêtir au Moyen Âge* (Paris: Adam Biro, 1995), p. 153, and Janet Mayo, *A History of Ecclesiastical Dress* (New York: Holmes & Meier, 1984),p. 33.
18. An example depicts Blanche of Castile, Queen of France, and her daughter, Isabelle of France, in a late fifteenth-century manuscript, *Le livre des faits de Saint Louis, roi de France* (Paris: Bibliothèque nationale de France, ms fr. 2829), available in facsimile.

19 See Michel Foucault, *Discipline and Punish: The Birth of the Prison* (New York: Vintage Books, 1979), esp. Part Three, "Discipline," in which each of his arguments have easy parallels to the cloistered context: its architecture; the training, supervision, and disciplining of its inmates.

20. The term "perspectival" was introduced in an article by Caroline Walker Bynum and Paula Gerson, "Body-Part Reliquaries and Body Parts in the Middle Ages," *Gesta,* Volume 36/1, 1997, pp. 3–7, which addressed the current need for multilayered, "post-modern" responses to topics in medieval studies.

21 Jerome's writings offer many illustrations, for instance his letter to Eustochium, Epistle 22, in *Handmaids of the Lord: Holy Women in Late Antiquity & The Early Middle Ages,* trans. and ed. by Joan M. Petersen (Kalamazoo, MI: Cistercian Publications, 1996), pp. 171–213. See also Elizabeth Schüssler Fiorenza, *In Memory of Her: A Feminist Theological Reconstruction of Christian Origins* (London: SCM, 1983); Ross Shephard Kraemer, *Her Share of the Blessings: Women's Religions Among Pagans, Jews, and Christians in the Greco-Roman World* (New York: Oxford University Press, 1992); and Margaret Y. MacDonald, *Early Christian Women and Pagan Opinion: The Power of Hysterical Women* (Cambridge: Cambridge University Press 1996), which explore similar themes.

22. Jerome Neyrey in "What's Wrong" contrasts traditional gender expectations with the Gospel context, establishing veiling as a literal/metaphorical spatial concept of division between genders.
23 Hélyot, in his *Histoire,* usefully organized his magisterial survey on the various orders under their respective Rules, which first made me aware of the relationships among them in terms of dress as well as other customs.
24. R.W. Southern, *Western Society and the Church in the Middle Ages* (London: Penguin, 1970), for instance pp. 237–40.
25. See Sharon Elkins, *Holy Women of Twelfth-Century England* (Chapel Hill, NC: University of North Carolina Press, 1988) Sally Thompson, *Women Religious: The Founding of English Nunneries after the Norman Conquest* (Oxford: Clarendon Press, 1991), and Bruce Lanier Venarde, "Women, Monasticism, and Social Change: The Foundation of Nunneries in Western Europe, c. 890–c. 1215," Ph.D. diss., Harvard University, 1992, all works that have the founding of medieval women's houses as their focus.
26. See Nicholas Orme and Margaret Webster, *The English Hospital 1070–1570* (New Haven: Yale University Press, 1995), esp. pp. 70–73, and Robert N. Swanson, *Religion and Devotion in Europe, c. 1215-c. 1515* (Cambridge: Cambridge University Press, 1995), for instance pp. 229–31.
27. See Jo Ann McNamara, *Sisters,* who has numerous entries on the long and complicated history of canonesses (index, s.v.) in the Western Church.
28. No recent book on women religious has failed to take up this important delimitation to the aspirations of medieval religious women. The most comprehensive, *longue durée* treatment is found in McNamara, pp. 260–88, a chapter equipped with an exhaustive bibliography.
29. See lucid presentation on *Periculoso* by Elizabeth Makowski, *Canon Law.*
30. Among the many translated editions, see Adalbert de Vogüé, *La règle de Saint Benoît* (Paris: Éditions du Cerf, 1971).
31. For the Latin text, see L. Verheijen, "La règle de saint Augustin," *Études Augustiniennes,* 2 vols. 1967, and in trans. by Agatha Mary Crabb, *The Rule of St. Augustine: An Essay in Understanding* (Villanova, PA: 1992).
32. See Regis J. Armstrong and Ignatius D. Brady, trans. and eds., *Francis and Clare, The Complete Works* (New York: Paulist Press, 1982) pp. 110–11, and pp. 212–13.
33. Leo F. Stelten, *Dictionary of Ecclesiastical Latin* (Peabody, MA: Hendrickson, 1995), takes up 'cucullus-i:m; cowl'; and 'cuculla-ae:f; cowl, choir cloak' The former is used here to designate especially the Benedictine standard monastic garment, and the latter term is used for the other orders' adoption of the wide-sleeved garment for wear during divine service only.
34. On the topic of conversi and lay brothers, see *ODCC,* s.v.; and Swanson *Religion,* 107–108.
35. See *ODCC,* s.v., and discussion in Hélyot on the Poor Clares' use of the scapular, 5:193 and 203.
36. See Thompson, *Women Religious,* pp. 29, 78, 100, and also her earlier "The Problem of the Cistercian Nuns in the Twelfth and Early Thirteenth Cen-

turies" in *Medieval Women,* ed. Derek Baker (Oxford: Blackwell, 1978), pp. 227–52.

37. McNamara returns frequently to this topic and provides especially comprehensive treatment of it in her chapter on "Cura Mulierum," pp. 260–88.
38. Barbara Harvey, *Monastic Dress,* p. 10. This brief case study focused on the monks at Westminster Abbey.
39. Hélyot, *Histoire,* 3:53.
40. One well-known early fourteenth-century manuscript is particularly instructive in this respect, the so-called "La Sainte Abbaye," London: British Library, Yates Thompson 11 (formerly Add. 39843).
41. Margery Kempe, *The Book of Margery of Kempe,* ed. W. Butler-Bowdon (London: Oxford University Press, 1954), for instance p. 135; p. 151; p. 156.
42. Claire D'Assise, *Ecrits: Introduction, Texte Latin, Traduction,* ed. Marie-France Becker et al. (Paris: Éditions du Cerf, 1985), pp. 130–31.
43. Mechtild Flury-Lemberg, *Textile Conservation and Research* (Bern: Abegg-Stiftung, 1988), discusses this garment in detail along with the cowl of St. Francis, pp. 314–17.
44. John Alcock, *Exhortacyon,* unpag. p. 7–8.
45. See Antoinette Clark Wire, *The Corinthian Women Prophets: A Reconstruction through Paul's Rhetoric* (Minneapolis: Fortress Press, 1990).
46. Among the many authors: MacDonald, *Early Christian Women,* p. 125 and Part Two; McNamara, p. 22 and elsewhere; Petersen, *Handmaids,* p .20.
47. Kraemer, *Her Share,* p. 145–48, where she applies Mary Douglas's grid-group theory of cultural patterns in this period.
48. Petersen, pp. 273–78.
49. Aldhelm, *The Prose Works,* ed. and trans. Michael Lapidge and Michael Herren (Ipswich and Cambridge: D. S. Brewer, 1979), pp. 127–28.
50. *Bildwörterbuch der Kleidung und Rüstung,* ed. Harry Kühnel (Stuttgart: Alfred Kröner, 1992), s.v. "Schleier"; "Weihel," "Wimpel." These terms are poorly accounted for in recent English language reference works.
51. Quoted in Eileen Power, *Medieval English Nunneries,* p.585.
52. Today in the Oxford Keble College Library, ms 49, in which these illustrations occur frequently.
53. *ODCC,* s.v. "novice"; "postulant"; "profession"; "vows"; etc.; and under the same terms in Mayke De Jong, *In Samuel's Image: Child Oblation in the Early Medieval West* (Leiden: Brill, 1996), which offers information for the early period. The practice of leaving young children as oblates in monasteries for their education and often for their lifetime was also discouraged and explicitly forbidden in the proceedings of several synods and councils.
54. *NCE,* s.v. "Religious Profession," and E. O. James, *Myth and Ritual: A Historical Study* (Gloucester, MA: Peter Smith, 1973), pp. 95–98.
55. Andrei, Le Pontifical Romain, vol. 2, pp. 414–48; and vol. 3, pp. 411–25.
56. Ibid.; and James, p. 95; *NCE,* p.331.
57. Andrei, vol. 3, p. 411.

58. Ibid., p. 412.
59. *ODCC,* s.v.; *NCE,* s.v.
60. Andrei, vol. 3, p.414.
61. Ibid., p. 420.
62. James, p. 94.
63. Illustrations of women in the pontificals are fewer than those depicting male monastic clergy, reflecting a demographic reality.

CHAPTER 12

THE SUFI ROBE (*KHIRQA*) AS A VEHICLE OF SPIRITUAL AUTHORITY[1]

Jamal J. Elias

The famous and highly influential Andalusian mystic, Ibn 'Arabī (d. 638/1240) provides insight into the nature and significance of the Sufi robe (*khirqa*) in his magisterial work, *al-Futūḥāt al-makkiyya:*

> One of my teachers, 'Alī ibn 'Abd Allāh ibn Jāmi', who was a companion of 'Alī al-Mutawakkil and Qaḍīb al-Bān, had met Khaḍir; he used to live in his garden outside Mosul. Khaḍir had invested him with the *khirqa* in the presence of Qaḍīb al-Bān. He in turn transmitted it to me, on the very same spot in his garden where he had received it from Khaḍir and in the same way that it had been performed in his case. . . . From this time onwards I maintained [the validity and effectiveness of] investiture with the *khirqa* and I invested people with it because I understood that Khaḍir ascribed importance to it. Up until then I was no supporter of investiture with the *khirqa* when understood in this sense: as far as I was concerned it was simply an expression of companionship. . . . So it is that when the masters of spiritual states perceive some imperfection in one of their companions and wish to perfect that person's state, they resort to the custom of meeting with the person alone. The master then takes the piece of clothing he is wearing in the spiritual state he is in at that particular moment, removes it and puts it on the man whom he wishes to guide to perfection. He then holds the man closely to him—and the master's state spreads to his disciple, who thereby attains to the desired perfection. This is the "clothing" as I understand it and as it has been transmitted by our masters.[2]

I have quoted this anecdote of Ibn 'Arabī because it provides several clues about how the concept of the *khirqa* was accepted by him and by medieval Sufis in general. In the first place, there appears to have been a difference between the "western" and "eastern" understandings of the role of the *khirqa,* where by the west one means Spain and North Africa, and by the east Egypt and the Asian Islamic lands. Not only was the *khirqa* much less formal in the west (both in its ritual uses and as a ritual or educational object), but it seems clear that Ibn 'Arabī did not hold in very high regard the many formal uses of the *khirqa* by people in the east.

Furthermore, Ibn 'Arabī recognized Khaḍir (the immortal mystical guide of the unseen realm who is equated in Islamic thought with the Prophet Elijah and the individual who led Alexander on his quest for the fountain of eternal youth) as a legitimate and valued source from which to receive a *khirqa*. Thus not only did Ibn 'Arabī accept the notion of non-physical investiture, that is, investiture by Khaḍir, but it is clear from the above quotation that this kind of investiture was widely accepted as real. Following on this, it was widely understood in the medieval Islamic world that *khirqa*s did not have to be physical objects.

Lastly, the *khirqa* can mean things other than simply being a symbol of the bond between a master and a disciple. It can have a transformative impact on the disciple, in that it carries the master's spiritual state (as if it were carrying perfume), and envelops the disciple in it, thereby helping him to attain the degree of advancement the master wants. In other words, it has tonic powers in addition to its function as a badge of affiliation and spiritual advancement.

In this essay I discuss the various understandings of the *khirqa,* concentrating on the "east" because it is in that region that the role of the *khirqa* seems to become most formalized. Not only did Sufi writers in Iraq, Iran, and Central Asia write about the significance and origin of the Sufi robe, but some, such as Najm al-Dīn Kubrā (d. 618/1221), wrote treatises describing various robes and their significance in meticulous detail.

Imagined Origins of the Sufi Robe

The *khirqa* in the sense of the symbolic bond between an individual and a spiritual master is attested to frequently in Ibn 'Arabī's life. He received his first *khirqa* in 592/1195 in Seville from Khaḍir, to whom he had been introduced by Abū al-'Abbās al-'Uryabī, an illiterate mystical guide whose influence on Ibn 'Arabī's early development seems second only to that of Abū Madyān (d. 594/1197), Ibn 'Arabī's primary mystical guide (although the two of them had never met in this world).[3] He was again invested with the *khirqa* of Khaḍir in Mosul in 601/1204 as outlined in the anecdote from the *Futūḥāt* that I have just quoted.

Ibn 'Arabī's second *khirqa* was received from Taqī al-Dīn 'Abd al-Raḥmān ibn 'Alī al-Tawzarī al-Qasṭallānī. The next was received in 594/1197 in Fez from Muḥammad ibn Qāsim al-Tamīmī al-Fāsī; both of them had received it from Ṣadr al-Dīn ibn Ḥamuwayh. Two other *khirqa*s that he received in the east, one of Khaḍir and one of 'Abd al-Qādir al-Jīlānī, have already been mentioned.

I would like to emphasize the fluidity of movement between investiture at the hands of living, physical human guides and at the hands of Khaḍir.[4] Indeed, the fluidity with which the *khirqa* of Khaḍir is transformed into a "mundane" *khirqa* says much about how similar they were considered to be: both Taqī al-Dīn 'Abd al-Raḥmān ibn 'Alī al-Tawzarī al-Qasṭallānī and Muḥammad ibn Qāsim al-Tamīmī al-Fāsī had received their *khirqa*s from Ṣadr al-Dīn ibn Ḥamuwayh whose grandfather had received it from Khaḍir.[5] This form of investiture is sometimes referred to as an Uwaysi lineage, after the mystical contemporary of Muḥammad named Uways who was believed to receive instruction from the Prophet telepathically. In the sixteenth and seventeenth centuries this form of instruction became prominent and formalized, particularly in Central Asia.[6]

The *khirqa* as a sign of mystico-educational affiliation has a long history and is based to some extent in the Sufi view that the *khirqa* is the most appropriate form of religious dress, derived from the prototypical costume worn by Adam and Eve when they were placed upon the earth. Such a pedigree for the Sufi robe is only fitting, because Sufis view Adam not only as the original human being but also as the first in the chain of prophets culminating in Muḥammad. Muḥammad is viewed by Sufis as the source of authority for Islamic legal and doctrinal prescriptions as well as the first Sufi, all chains of mystical affiliation being traced back to him.[7]

In medieval times, this mystical affiliation was often passed down through symbolic acts, most frequently a ritual grasping of the hand (*'ahd al-yad wa al-iqtidā'*) or the acceptance of the robe (*'ahd al-khirqa*). Al-Qurashī, the earliest known author to discuss Sufi robes of affiliation, mentions five different kinds: (1) that of 'Abd al-Qādir al-Jilānī (d. 561/1166); (2) Aḥmad al-Rifā'ī (d. 570/1175); (3) Shihāb al-Dīn al-Suhrawardī (d. 632/1234); (4) Abū Madyān al-Shu'ayb (d. 594/1197); and (5) Abu Isḥāq al-Kazurūni (d. 426/1034).[8] Al-Wāsiṭī (d. 744/1343) displays a similar understanding of the *khirqa* in using it as the term for Sufi chains of affiliation in his important organizational history of medieval Sufism entitled *Ṭiryāq al-muḥibbīn*.[9]

The importance of the *khirqa* is discussed at some length in several classical Sufi handbooks, most importantly in the *Kashf al-maḥjūb* of 'Alī Hujwīrī (d. 469/1077) and the *'Awārif al-ma'ārif* of Shihāb al-Dīn Abū Ḥafṣ 'Umar al-Suhrawardī (d. 632/1234). According to Hujwīrī, the wearing of a Patched Robe (*muraqqa'a*) is the Sunna (custom) of the Prophet, who is believed to have said: "See that you wear woolen clothing so that you might find the sweetness of faith."[10] Suhrawardī has a longer section on the importance of the *khirqa* that he connects to the custom of the Prophet Muḥammad and earlier prophets even more strongly than does Hujwīrī.[11] He also makes it very clear that the *khirqa* is the symbol of the bond between a master and his disciple and that, as such, it mimics the prophetic, spiritual, and hereditary links between the pre-Islamic prophets. Of particular interest in this connection is the tradition he quotes concerning Abraham who entered into the fire and lost his clothes, whereupon Gabriel gave him a shirt (*qamīṣ*) made from heavenly silk (*ḥarīr al-janna*). On his death, Abraham bequeathed this shirt to Isaac, who left it to Jacob, who made the shirt into a talisman (*ta'wīdh*) that he placed around Joseph's neck. In turn, when Gabriel found Joseph naked in the well where he had been abandoned by his brothers, Gabriel took the shirt out of the talisman and clothed Joseph in it.[12]

The story of the heavenly silken shirt notwithstanding, it is generally agreed in Sufi circles that the most excellent material for making clothing is wool. There are many prophetic traditions (*ḥadīth*) that claim that all the prophets wore wool, and that when Adam and Eve were placed on the earth and made aware of their nakedness, Gabriel brought them a ram that Adam sheared and from which Eve fashioned robes (*khirqa*s) for them both.

In his discussion of the *khirqa,* Suhrawardī makes a distinction between two kinds of investiture, the *khirqat al-tabarruk* (Robe of Blessing) and the *khirqat al-irāda* (Robe of Free Will). The *khirqat al-irāda* is the higher of the two and is given to the true disciple of the master (*al-murīd al-ḥaqīqī*). The *khirqat al-tabarruk* resembles the *khirqat al-irāda,* except that the *khirqat al-tabarruk* represents a much more informal system of affiliation, sometimes little more than a token of encouragement given by a Sufi master to a part-time Sufi.[13] There is no sense that this kind of *khirqa* symbolizes an exclusive bond between an individual and his sole master, for people often received such *khirqa*s from a number of teachers.

> Be assured that there is no stipulation in the obligatory conditions of initiatic investiture and spiritual companionship that this garment [*khirqa*] must be received from one person alone. No one has ever imposed such a condition. . . . Investiture [with the *khirqa*] simply consists of keeping the company of a master and practising his spiritual discipline, and that does not involve any restriction in number. In stating these facts I am referring to certain ignorant people [68] who imagine that one is only entitled to receive the *khirqa* from one person alone.[14]

There can be no doubt, however, that Suhrawardī was drastically simplifying the different varieties of *khirqa*s being given by masters to their disciples in his day. It is conceivable that he was motivated to do so by the important position he held in the court of Baghdad and because of the pivotal role he played in attempts to bring the Sufi orders of Iraq under caliphal authority.[15] By the end of the thirteenth century, documents attest to the existence of a much wider variety of *khirqa*s. The important Iranian Sufi writer 'Ala' al-Dawla Simnānī (d. 736/1336), who is one of the few medieval Sufis to have left substantial autobiographical writings, received a number of different robes from his teacher Nūr al-Dīn Isfarā'inī (d. 717/1317). The first was a *khirqa-yi mulamma'a* (Variegated Robe), brought from Isfarā'inī in 687/1288 by Akhī Sharaf al-Dīn who acted as a go between during the early stages of Simnānī's mystical training. The second was called *al-khirqa al-dhākira* (Robe of Remembrance or Meditation) by Simnānī and was one that Isfarā'inī had worn for ten years while performing the Sufi meditational exercise called *dhikr* before he sent it to Simnānī in 697/1298. Simnānī also mentions a *khirqat al-aṣl* (Robe of Affiliation) connecting Kubrā, to whose school both Simnānī and Isfarā'inī belonged, through a chain of earlier mystics, to the Prophet. He received two *khirqa-yi tabarruks* (Robes of Blessing), which were also traced back to Muḥammad. These were in addition to something called the *khirqa-yi hazār mīkhī* (Tattered or Many-patched robe) which I will discuss later in this essay.[16]

It is not clear if the *khirqat al-aṣl* (Robe of Affiliation) is actually an object or simply a reference to Simnānī's chain of affiliation. It is not inconceivable that he claimed some form of ritual investiture that actually went back to the Prophet, for Simnānī also had a *khirqa* given to him by Isfarā'inī that was supposed to contain a comb belonging to the Prophet. This object had been given by the legendary Indian mystic and contemporary of the Prophet, Abū Riẓā Bābā Ratan, to Kubrā's disciple 'Alī-yi Lālā (d. 642/1244) during the latter's visit to India. From 'Alī-yi Lālā the comb passed to Aḥmad-i Gūrpānī (d. 669/1270) and on to Simnānī's teacher Isfarā'inī. According to the Sufi scholar and poet 'Abd al-Raḥmān Jāmī (d. 898/1492), Simnānī allegedly wrapped the comb in the *khirqa* and the *khirqa* in a piece of paper, although it is equally likely that the comb was itself the *khirqa,* providing further evidence that *khirqa*s can be a variety of symbolic objects and not necessarily robes at all.[17]

It is not clear what the *al-khirqa al-dhākira* (Robe of Remembrance or Meditation) and *khirqat al-aṣl* (Robe of Affiliation) are. Simnānī fails to provide any details concerning the occasion on which he received the latter, and it is quite possible that it was another name for one of the *khirqa*s he had received. It is worth noting that the *al-khirqa al-dhākira* (Robe of Remembrance or Meditation) is mentioned as having been worn by Isfara'ini for ten years while engaging in meditation and was given to Simnānī exactly ten years after he received his first robe (the Variegated Robe or *khirqa-yi mulamma'a*) from Isfarā'inī. One can therefore deduce that in all likelihood, the first robe had also been one worn by Isfarā'inī during his mystical exercises, and that he gave his own robes to his favorite disciple in order to enable Simnānī to benefit from the spiritual power that had been imbued in the robes. The *al-khirqa al-dhākira* (Robe of Remembrance or Meditation) can therefore be understood not as a particular kind of robe but probably a Variegated Robe (*mulamma'a*), which was named according to its function in this context.

The *Khirqa* as a Badge of Progress in Kubrā's *Mukhtaṣar Ādāb al-murīdīn*

One of the most important works discussing the nature and importance of the *khirqa* in Iranian Sufism is known variously as the *Mukhtaṣar fī ādāb al-ṣūfiyya, Ādāb al-ṣūfiyya,* or the *Ādāb al-murīdīn*. There is a unique manuscript by the first title, dated 770/1368, that attributes it to Khwāja 'Abd Allāh Anṣārī (d. 481/1089).[18] Known by its other title, it is ascribed to Najm al-Dīn Kubrā (d. 618/1221). The work has been published in English translation by G. Böwering, and in German (with the Kubrā ascription) by F. Meier.[19] There is also a Persian edition where it is treated as one of Kubrā's works.[20] Böwering maintains that this treatise—call it the *Mukhtaṣar fī ādāb al-ṣūfiyya* or the *Ādāb al-ṣūfiyya*—is almost certainly the work of Khwāja 'Abd Allāh Anṣārī, although he also notes the stylistic and structural difference between the bulk of the treatise and the section on the *khirqa,* which seems to be disproportionately long.[21] In light of the fact that the only manuscripts of the text list it as being one of Kubrā's works, it is conceivable that the part of the treatise that deals with Sufi robing was either revised or entirely reworked by Kubrā, or that a Kubrā treatise somehow got joined to an Anṣārī one shortly after Kubrā's death. This possibility seems more probable when one considers that the section dealing with the *khirqa* is quoted verbatim, almost in its entirety, by Abū al-Mafākhir Yaḥyā Bākharzī (d. 736/1336) in his *Awrād al-aḥbāb,* in which he attributes the writing to Kubrā.[22] Abū al-Mafākhir Yaḥyā Bākharzī's work is very heavily influenced by the teachings of Sayf al-Dīn Bākharzī (d. 659/1261), who was one of Kubrā's closest disciples. It is rather unlikely that either Kubrā deceived his students into believing he had written one of Anṣārī's works, or that Bākharzī attached Kubrā's name to an Anṣārī text and then quoted a section of it in his master's name, or that Kubrā and his students collaborated in the deception.

Kubrā provides a detailed guide to the significance of the fabric color of the Sufi robe as an outward sign of the individual's degree of spiritual advancement. Kubrā's scheme is formal and hierarchical to the point of reminding the reader of Christian ecclesiastical robes. It seems unclear, however that such robes were ever worn by his own students, much less adopted by other Sufis in the greater Iranian world.

According to Kubrā, the basic Sufi robe is either black or dark blue, signifying that the wearer has conquered and slain his carnal soul (*nafs*) and is wearing black so as to mourn it symbolically. If the Sufi has attained the Sufi stage of repentance (*tawba*), he wears a white robe in order to symbolize his cleansed heart and the washing away of worldly concerns. If he has risen above the lower world and is continuing his mystical journey in the supralunar realm, he wears a blue robe representing the color of the sky. If, finally, he has completed all stages of the mystical path and has experienced the lights of all mystical states, he wears a multicolored or variegated robe (*khirqa-yi mulamma'a*).[23] Kubrā's disciple, Bākharzī, reproduces the same hierarchy, except that he attributes the wearing of black wool to Adam, who adopted it on the archangel Gabriel's advice as a symbol of his baseness. Bākharzī also switches the order of the white and blue robes, making the blue robe the symbol of the mystic having turned away from the physical world. In fact, he considers this color to be the most appropriate for Sufis in general.[24] In this prescription, Bākharzī is in agreement with Hujwīrī, who also believes that blue is the most appropriate color for Sufi clothing. This view is partly a matter of practicality, since white or light-colored clothes look dirty sooner than dark ones and are also more coveted by others; but it is also because blue is the color of mourning, symbolizing the physical world's status as a place of bereavement in which the mystic suffers on account of his separation from God.

> A dervish was asked why he wore blue. He replied: "The Apostle [Muḥammad] left three things: poverty, knowledge, and the sword. The sword was taken by potentates, who misused it; knowledge was chosen by savants, who were satisfied with merely teaching it; poverty was chosen by dervishes, who made it a sign of mourning for the calamity of these three classes of men."[25]

There is no indication that any practical considerations play a part in Kubrā's instructions concerning Sufi dress. He continues with prescriptions on how to accessorize the Sufi robe in order to signify higher states of spiritual advancement:

> If he has affixed the seal of security to his exterior and interior, and has made his heart a treasure house of secrets, he shall sew a braid (*farāwīz*) on his robe. If he has sat on the throne of love, has reclined on the couch of knowledge and conformity to God's command, he shall stitch a hem (*kursī*) onto it. If he has put on the armor of opposition to the carnal soul and the devil, and

> has placed on his head the helmet of resistance against temporal power, he shall reinforce the collar (*qabb*).[26]

The material out of which the garment is sewn is similarly a sign of one's location along the hierarchical Sufi path. A roughly sewn coarse garment (*khashin*) signifies that the individual is in a state of combat with his carnal soul. If in the course of this battle he has "wounded himself and bruised himself with a thousand darts of spiritual warfare, has swallowed a thousand cups of poison, and has tortured his nature with the needle of renunciation," he wears a Tattered or Many-Patched Robe (*hazār mīkhī).* If he has successfully rid himself of his worldly existence and has annihilated himself (a Sufi concept commonly called *fanā'*), he should wear a cloak (*labācha*); and lastly, when he has fulfilled all the requirements of both Islamic law and the Sufi path, he wears a mantle (*ridā*) around himself, in imitation of the mantle worn by the Prophet Muḥammad, who is taken by Sufis to be both the exemplar of Islamic ritual behavior and the Sufi path.[27]

Other items of clothing have similar symbolic importance. Wearing a turban (*dastār*) and letting one end of it hang loose, wearing a scarf (*izār*) and folding it a certain way, wearing socks or shoes—all represent a particular level of mystical attainment, as does wearing a face-veil (*rūysutra*).[28] Like them, the other accoutrements of Sufi life mark an individual's mystical status: the prayer rug (*sajjāda*), staff (*'aṣā*), hollowed-out gourd (*rakwa*), ewer (*ibrīq*), satchel (*kinf*), and sandal (*pāyafzār*) all have their own significance, so much so that sandal straps serve as "the guardians of the limbs, the prison of passion, and the purity of body and dress."[29]

The writings of and about Kubrā's many disciples belie the adoption of this extremely formulaic scheme of robing. Their written works and correspondence do not mention them receiving such intricate garments from Kubrā, nor their granting such robes to their own disciples.[30] Licenses and diplomas issued by Kubrā to students such as Sayf al-Dīn Bākharzī, Majd al-Dīn Baghdādī and Sa'd al-Dīn Ḥamuwayī do not mention these robes.[31] The ones that do appear in works relevant to the Kubrāwi school are those that were clearly prevalent in wider Sufi circles: the aforementioned *khirqas* such as that of blessing (*tabarruk*) and of affiliation (*aṣl*) that do not specify a particular color or pattern, the Tattered or Many-Patched Robe (*hazār mīkhī),* and the Patched Robe (*muraqqa'a*). An important but anonymous treatise in a manuscript containing works of Kubrā and his disciples and dated sometime after 722/1322 contains a treatise entitled *Kitāb al-ṭuruq fī ma'rifat al-khirqa,* which mentions the *khirqa-yi tabarruk* (Robe of Blessing) and *khirqa-yi irādat* (Robe of Free-will), as well as a *khirqa-yi taṣawwuf* (Robe of Sufism) and a *khirqa-yi khidmat wa ṣuḥbat* (Robe of Service and

Discipleship).[32] The latter two are not substantially different in signifying the position of the Sufi along the mystical path, nor is any of them mentioned as having a specific color or design. On the other hand, the treatise does talk about five different kinds of garments worn by Sufis as they progress along the mystical path: *dūtā'ī, farjī, ṣadra, mulamma'*, and *dalaq*.[33] All except the *mulamma'* were varieties of robes or cloaks worn in the medieval Iranian world, although their specific patterns are unknown to me. From their names, one can surmise that the *dūtā'ī* was either made from a particular fine cloth or else had two layers or folds in its construction; the *farjī* perhaps was a robe open at the front or else with large sleeve openings; the *ṣadra* prominently featured a belt or vest; and the *dalaq* was a large cloak, perhaps made of fur. The *mulamma'* is the variegated Sufi robe mentioned earlier (*khirqa-yi mulamma'a*), which may, in some contexts, be the same as the Tattered or Many-Patched Robe (*khirqa-yi hazār mīkhī*) and the Patched Robe (*muraqqa'a*).

The Patched Robe

The importance attached by the Sufis to the Patched Robe (*muraqqa'a*) deserves some emphasis. Hujwīrī dwells on this subject in his *Kashf al-maḥjūb*, saying that the origins of the patches lie in the abstemiousness and poverty of the most virtuous religious exemplars: the pre-Islamic prophets, the religious heroes of early Islam, and most importantly, the Prophet. The Prophet is related as having told his wife, 'A'ishā, not to dispose of a worn robe of his but to patch it. The Caliph 'Umar is said to have worn a *muraqqa'a* (Patched Robe) with thirty patches on it. It is clear from Hujwīrī's writing that by his day the patched robe had attained religious significance, for he makes disparaging references to such people as wear patched robes to increase their reputation and status. He advises Sufis to avoid being associated with such individuals in two ways. On the one hand, he deemphasizes the role of symbolic clothing in Sufism: "It is inward glow (*ḥurqat*) that makes the Sufi, not the religious habit (*khirqat*). To the true mystic there is no difference between the mantle (*'abā*) worn by dervishes, and the coat (*qabā*) worn by ordinary people."[34] On the other hand, Hujwīrī advises Sufis on how to patch robes so that they will be distinguishable from the patched robes of people who don such clothing solely for ostentation. He provides exceptional detail on exactly how one should patch a robe, whether the patches should be sewn with random, haphazard stitches, or whether one should taken pains to make straight, even stitches, saying that Sufi masters differ in their opinions on this point. His own judgment is that how the patches are stitched is of less importance than the consideration that they should be stitched on only when needed, not to accessorize the robe.[35] Hujwīrī's emphasis upon avoiding ostentation in dress echoes the opinion of the classical Sufi writer Abū Naṣr al-Sarrāj (d. 378/988), who believed that it did not matter what the mystic wore, any dress that was conveniently available being appropriate as long as it was not something the wearer had longed for or coveted.[36]

An interesting point raised by Hujwīrī is that many masters warn that the patches on the robe should be small, so as to give a clear indication of the painstaking act of devotion it took to sew them on. This emphasis on minute patches might help explain a curious kind of robe that appears in Iranian Sufi circles sometime in the thirteenth/fourteenth century, the *Khirqa-yi hazār mīkhī* (Tattered or Many-Patched Robe). Simnānī received such a robe from his master Isfarā'inī which had belonged to Kubrā and was given by him to Majd al-Dīn Baghdādī who then gave it to 'Alī-yi Lālā. This is perhaps the same as the cap called *kulāh-yi hazār-mīkhī,* allegedly belonging to Kubrā and given to Simnānī by Isfarā'inī sometime in 1305.[37] It is more likely that the Tattered or Many-Patched Robe represents the formalized version of Hujwīrī's *muraqqa'a* (Patched Robe) made with very small patches.

In his *Kitāb al-luma',* Sarrāj discusses the virtues of poor dress, saying that not only is it the example of religious luminaries but that it also prevents the individual from being overly concerned with his appearance and getting caught up in the desire to have more and better clothes. Among the most interesting traditions he quotes to support his opinion is the story of a Sufi mystic who owned only one shirt, which he wore both in winter and in summer. When he was questioned about this, he replied that he used to own many clothes, but that one night he had a dream in which he entered heaven where he found a group of fellow Sufis sitting down to eat. He wanted to join them, but a host of angels came and forced him to stand up, saying that these Sufis were each the possessor of only one shirt, and that he had many and therefore did not belong with them. After that time he made a point of never owning more than one item of clothing.[38]

Conclusion

The above discussion clearly demonstrates the connection between Sufi robes on the one hand and educational and spiritual advancement on the other. Robes are used not just to designate an individual's status along the Sufi path but also to reward and encourage disciples in their progress. However, robes are more than simply representative markers or badges of spiritual status; there was a widespread belief in medieval Sufi circles in an absolute correspondence between the physical and spiritual dimensions of the individual, as a result of which many Sufis believed that the robes themselves could influence an individual's spiritual state in tonic and prophylactic ways. Kubrā's disciple Baghdadi held the opinion that it was acceptable for Sufi masters to give *khirqa*s to their disciples even before they had completed the requisite stages of the Sufi path because the robes would help them progress.[39]

Kubrā maintained that the power of Sufi robes resided in the very letters of the word used to designate them. The word *ṣūf* ("wool," the material from which Sufi robes are made), has an intrinsic value, as do the letters that make up *muraqqa'a* (Patched Robe). Donning these forms of garb help the mystic actualize the qualities inherent in the individual letters of which these words are made up.

> When he puts on wool, he seeks to accomplish what it requires. In fact the word *ṣūf* consists of three letters, *ṣād, waw* and *fā'*. With the *ṣād* he embraces sincerity (*ṣidq*), purity (*ṣafā*), firmness (*ṣalābat*), patience (*ṣabr),* and integrity (*ṣalāḥ*); with the *waw,* loyalty (*wafā*), union (*waṣl*), and ecstasy (*wajd*); and with the *fā'*, freedom from sorrow (*faraj*) and joy of life (*faraḥ*). . . . The word *muraqqa'* also has four letters, *mīm, rā', qāf* and *'ain.* With the *mīm* the novice embraces cognition (*ma'rifat*), love (*maḥabbat*), and humility (*madhallat*); with the *rā'*, compassion (*ra'fat),* mercy (*raḥmat*), ascetic exercise (*riyāḍat*), and tranquility (*rāḥat*); with the *qāf,* contentment (*qanā'at*), nearness to God (*qurbat*) spiritual strength (*quwwat-i ḥāl*), and truthful speech (*qaul-i ṣidq*); with the *'ain,* religious knowledge (*'ilm),* passionate love (*'ishq*), intense zeal (*'uluww-i himmat*), and fidelity to one's vow (*'ahd-i nīkū*).[40]

The treatise entitled *Kitāb al-tūruq fī ma'rifat al-khirqa* complements Kubrā's work by providing the symbolic value of the letters that make up the word *khirqa* (*khā', rā', qāf and hā'*): the *khā'*, stands for acknowledging the destruction of the physical world (*al-iqbāl 'alā kharāb al-dunyā*); the *rā'*, for ascetic exercises of the heart (*riyāḍat al-qalb*) and refusing the pleasures of the lower soul (*rafḍ ḥuẓūẓ al-nafs*); the *qāf* for etiquette of the heart in its closeness to God (*qā'idat al-qalb fī al-qurb ma'a al-rabb*); and the *hā'* for contempt for the physical world (*hawān al-dunā*) and fleeing to God (*harab ilā Allāh ta'ālā*).[41]

There are many examples in the history of Sufism of the use of clothing or other artifacts as talismans. According to one myth, Baghdad was saved from a flood by casting Manṣur al-Ḥallāj's (d. 309/992) *khirqa* into the river.[42] In the Indian context, the garment of the Sufi master Niẓām al-Dīn Abū al-Mu'īd's deceased mother was used to end droughts in Delhi.[43]

The power of clothing to have a transformative or tonic effect on individual Sufis is demonstrated in the conversion experience of Ibn 'Arabī. When he was a young man in Seville, he attended a banquet at which goblets of wine were being passed around. When it was Ibn 'Arabī's turn to drink, he heard a voice say, "Muḥammad, it was not for this that you were created!" Ibn 'Arabī fled the banquet in an agitated state, and on his way home encountered a shepherd. Ibn 'Arabī exchanged his ornate clothing with the coarse cloak of the shepherd, then left the city and spent the next four days meditating in a cemetery. It was during this period of meditation following the exchange of worldly clothing for the cloak of a poor shepherd that Ibn 'Arabī had many mystical experiences that he was to recall in later life.[44]

Abū al-Najīb al-Suhrawardī (d. 563/1168), the uncle of the aforementioned Shihāb al-Dīn al-Suhrawardī, who had much greater influence on Sufi practices in medieval Iran and Iraq than his nephew did, was acutely aware of the spiritual power that was held by Sufi robes. In his *Ādāb al-murīdīn,* he discusses the appropriate manner of treating a *khirqa* thrown off by a mystic in ecstatic throws induced by listening to music (*samā'*). Abū al-Najīb al-Suhrawardī recounts the opinions of a number of different Sufi masters who differ on whether the robe should be given to the musicians and singers or to an individual in the audience. It is clear from his discussion that such a robe was viewed as spiritually charged to the point of being dangerous, and that it was best to consult a Sufi master regarding the disposal of the robe. He also draws a distinction between robes that are discarded in genuine ecstasy and those that are thrown off in order to impress other people with one's propensity for entering trances. The latter robe should not be given to any member of the Sufi group but rather should be donated to a needy person.[45]

One of the opinions regarding the proper disposal of a *khirqa* discarded in ecstasy that Abū al-Najīb al-Suhrawardī attributes to an unnamed Sufi master is that the robe should be cut up and the pieces given to everyone present. This clearly implies a spiritual power inherent within the fabric of the discarded robe, and it is very likely that such sectioned *khirqa*s were the ideal source from which to get patches for one's *muraqqa'* (Patched Robe).

In conclusion, the Sufi *khirqa* represents a variety of forms of spiritual investiture that serve complementary purposes. In the first place, the *khirqa* does not necessarily have to be a robe, since the term *khirqa* is frequently used metaphorically to connote a chain of mystical afilliation connecting the individual Sufi with the Prophet Muḥammad, who is regarded as the model and fountainhead of Islamic spirituality. Even on those occasions when the *khirqa* is actually a Sufi robe, it does not have to be a physical one, since investiture in the spiritual realm is widely regarded as authentic and, indeed, a mark of unusual spiritual distinction. At the same time, the *khirqa* can also serve a transformative or curative function, in that wearing a robe worn by a Sufi master or even patching one's robe with pieces from a *khirqa* imbued with spiritual qualities can help a Sufi advance to a higher mystical level. As such, the physical and spiritual curative and transformative powers of the *khirqa* coexist within the Sufi understanding of the nature and function of the robe, just as there exists a simultaneous understanding of the *khirqa*'s significance as a physical commodity and a nonphysical one.

Notes

1. Earlier versions of this article were presented at the annual meetings of the Muhyiuddin Ibn 'Arabī Society (Berkeley, 1997) and the American Academy of Religion (San Fransisco, 1997).
2. Muḥī al-Dīn Ibn 'Arabī, *Al-futūḥāt al-makkiyya* (Cairo: Maktabat al-thiqāfa al-dīniyya, n.d.), I:187. The significance of the *khirqa* is alluded to again in *Kitāb al-nasab,* MS. Esad Efendi, Süleymaniye Kütüphanesi, Istanbul, folios 90a-b. Translation from Claude Addas, *Quest for the Red Sulphur: The Life of Ibn 'Arabī,* trans. by Peter Kingsley (Cambridge: Islamic Texts Society, 1993), 145–46. This incident occurred in 601/1204 in the Iraqi city of Mosul, two years after Ibn 'arabī received the first "eastern" *khirqa,* that of 'Abd al-Qadir al-Jīlānī (d. 561/1165) which Ibn 'Arabī got at Mecca.
3. Addas, 61–62.
4. For more information on the *khirqa* of Khadir, see Louis Massignon, *Essai sur les origines du lexique technique de la mystique musulmane* (Paris: Paul Geuthner, 1922), 111–12.
5. Shams al-Dīn al-Dhahabī, *Siyar a'lām al-nubalā',* 35 vol. (Beirut: Mu'assasat al-risāla, 1985), vols. 22 and 23. For a discussion of the Ḥamuwayi family, see Jamal J. Elias, "Sufi Lords of Bahrabad" in *Iranian Studies* 27:1–4 (1994), 53–75; Sa'īd Nafīsī, "Khāndān-i Sa'd al-Dīn-i Ḥamawī" in *Kunjkāwīhā-yi 'ilmī wa adabī,* Intishārāt-i dānishgāh-i Tihrān 83 (Tehran: Dānishgāh-i Tihrān, 1950); and Fritz Meier, *Abū Sa'īd-i Abū l-Ḫayr,* Acta Iranica 3rd Series, no. 11 (Leiden: E. J. Brill, 1976), 322–23, note. 22.
6. For information on the Uwaysis, see (among others) J. Baldick, *Imaginary Muslims: The Uwaysi Sufis of Central Asia* (London: I. B. Taurus, 1993); and Ahmet Yašar Ocak, *Veysel Karanî ve Üveysîlik* (Istanbul: Dergah Yayınları, 1982).
7. For information on the early development of the *khirqa,* see Eric Geoffroy, "L'apparition des voies: les *khirqa* primitives (XIIe siècle–début XIIIe siècle)," in *Les voies d'Allah: Les ordres mystiques dans l'islam des origines à aujourd'hui,* edited by Alexandre Popovic and Gilles Veinstein (Paris: Fayard, 1996), 44–54; and J.-L. Michon, "Khirḳa," *Encyclopedia of Islam,* new edition (Leiden: E. J. Brill, 1985), 5:17b–18a.
8. This list appears in an unpublished treatise entitled *Al-Qawā'id al-wafiyya fī aṣl ḥukm al-khirqat al-ṣūfiyya* (Louis Massignon, *The Passion of al-Hallāj,* trans. by Herbert Mason, Bollingen Series, no. 98 (Princeton: Princeton University Press, 1982), 2:107–108.

9. Taqī al-Dīn 'Abd al-Raḥmān al-Wāsiṭī, *Kitāb ṭiryāq al-muḥibīn fī ṭabaqāt khirqat al-mashāyikh al-'ārifīn,* For the publishers, 1887.
10. 'Alī ibn 'Uthmān al-Jullābī al-Hujwīrī, *The Kashf al-maḥjub: The Oldest Treatise on Sufiism,* trans. by R. A. Nicholson, E. J. W. Gibb Memorial, vol. 17 (London: Luzac and Co., 1911; rpt. 1976), 45.
11. Shihāb al-Dīn 'Umar al-Suhrawardī, *Kitāb 'awārif al-ma'ārif,* (Beirut: Dār al-kitāb al-'arabī, 1983), 95–102.
12. Suhrawardī, 100.
13. Suhrawardī, 99.
14. Addas, 67, from *Kitāb nasab al-khirqa,* folios 98a-b.
15. For a detailed study of Suhrawardī and his *'Awārif al-ma'ārif,* see Richard Gramlich, *Die Gaben der Erkenntnisse des 'Umar as-Suhrawardī,* Freiburger Islamstudien, no. 6 (Wiesbaden: Franz Steiner, 1978).
16. Jamal J. Elias, *The Throne Carrier of God: The Life and Thought of 'Alā' ad-dawla as-Simnānī* (Albany: State University of New York Press, 1995), 39–41.
17. Nūr al-Dīn 'Abd al-Raḥmān Jāmī, *Nafaḥāt al 'uns,* edited by Mahdi Tawhidipur (Tehran: Kitābfurūshī-i Sa'dī, 1958), 437.
18. MS 1393, Şehit Ali Paşa, Süleymaniye Kütüphanesi, Istanbul, folios 39a–49a.
19. Fritz Meier, "Ein Knigge für Sufi's," in *Scritti in onore di Giuseppe Furlani, pt. 1, Revista degli studi orientali* 32 (1957), 485–524.
20. Mas'ūd Qasimī, ed., *Ādāb al-ṣūfiyya* (Tehran: Kitābfurūshī-yi Zawwār, 1984).
21. Gerhard Böwering, "The Adab Literature of Classical Sufism: Anṣārī's Code of Conduct," in *Moral Conduct and Authority: The Place of Adab in South Asian Islam,* ed. Barbara D. Metcalf (Berkeley: University of California Press, 1984), 69–70.
22. Abu al-Mafākhir Yaḥyā Bākharzī, *Awrād al-aḥbāb wa fuṣūṣ al-ādāb,* vol. 2, ed. Iraj Afshar (Tehran: Instishārāt-i dānishgāh-i Tihrān, 1966), 23ff. A summary of the contents of this work is available in Muhammad Isa Waley, "A Kubrawi Manual of Sufism: the *Fuṣūṣ al-ādāb* of Yahya Bakharzi," in *The Legacy of Mediaeval Persian Sufism,* ed. Leonard Lewisohn (London: Khaniqahi Nimatullahi Publications, 1992), 289–310.
23. Böwering, 75.
24. Bākharzī, 30–31.
25. Hujwīrī, 53.
26. Böwering, 76.
27. Böwering, 76.
28. Böwering, 76–77.
29. Böwering, 78.
30. An important example of correspondence between masters and their students in the Kubrawi school is that exchanged by Isfarā'inī and Simnānī; see Hermann Landolt, ed., *Correspondence spirituelle échangée entre Nuroddin Esfarayeni et son disciple 'Alaoddawleh Semnani,* Le departement d'iranologie

de l'institut franco-iranien de recherche, no. 21 (Tehran: L'institut franco-iranien de recherche, 1972).

31. Several examples of such licenses are to be found in MS. 2800, Şehit Ali Paşa, Süleymaniye Kütüphanesi, Istanbul.
32. MS. 2800, Şehit Ali Paşa, Süleymaniye Kütüphanesi, Istanbul, folio 64b.
33. *Kitāb al-ṭuruq fī ma'rifat al-khirqa,* MS. 2800, Şehit Ali Paşa, Süleymaniye Kütüphanesi, Istanbul, folios 64a ff.
34. Hujwīrī, 47–48. Kubrā's disciple, Majd al-Dīn al-Baghdādī (d. 616/1219), is one of the few Sufis to make a connection between Sufi robes and the royal practice of giving robes as marks of honor. He claims that this is completely appropriate, since Sufi masters are the kings of the afterlife just as rulers are the kings of this life, hence there should be a correspondence between their practices, although the actions of the kings of the afterlife are more meaningful and better (*Tuḥfat al-barara fī ajwibat al-as'ila al-'ashara,* MS. 1695 Ayasofya, Süleymaniye Kütüphanesi, Istanbul, folios 65b–66a).
35. Hujwīrī, 50.
36. Abū Naṣr al-Sarrāj, *Kitāb al-luma' fī al-taṣawwuf,* ed. 'Abd al-Ḥalīm Maḥmūd (Cairo: Dār al-kutub al-ḥadītha, 1960), 249.
37. Elias, *Throne Carrier,* 41. For the *khirqa-yi hazār mīkhī* see also M. T. Danishpazhuh, "Khirqa-yi hazār mīkhī," *Collected Papers on Islamic Philosophy and Mysticism,* ed. H. Landolt and M. Mohaghegh (Tehran: La branche de Téhéran de l'institut des études islamiques de l'Université McGill, 1971), 147–178.
38. Sarrāj, 248.
39. Baghdādī, folio 66b.
40. Böwering, 74–75. Several of these are the names of stages along the Sufi path as it is described by writers such as Abū Bakr al-Kalābādhī in his *Kitāb al-ta'arruf li madhhab ahl al-taṣawwuf* (Cairo: Maktabat Khānjī, 1933); trans. A.J. Arberry as *The Doctrine of the Ṣūfīs* (Cambridge: Cambridge University Press, 1935; rpt. 1979).
41. *Kitāb al-ṭuruq,* folio 64a.
42. Massignon, *Passion,* 1:628, 2:366.
43. 'Abd al-Ḥaqq Muḥaddith Dihlawī, *Akhār al-akhār,* Urdu trans. Iqbal al-Din Ahmad (Karachi: Dār al-ishā'at, 1963), 487.
44. Addas, 36.
45. Abū al-Najīb al-Suhrawardī, *Ādāb al-murīdīn,* ed. Najīb Māyil-i Hirawī, with Persian trans. by 'Umar ibn Muḥammad ibn Aḥmad Shirkan (Tehran: Intishārāt-i Mawlā, 1984), 281.

CHAPTER 13

THE REGAL SIGNIFICANCE OF THE DALMATIC: THE ROBES OF *LE SACRE*[1] AS REPRESENTED IN SCULPTURE OF NORTHERN MID-TWELFTH-CENTURY FRANCE

Janet Snyder

The act of putting on a mask, a garment, or ornaments to transform appearance and disguise the self implies the choice to modify one's fundamental structure. During the Middle Ages, the prince, abandoning his first identity, took on a divine character through the act of the unction, and became another man: the king.[2] In this reincarnation, he assumed an entirely changed aspect; the new clothes that he put on during the course of the *sacre* expressed the king's experience of a right of passage and revealed his altered state. As part of the rituals associated with his consecration, the king disrobed to wear only a white silk chemise.[3] After the unction at the altar, he was vested in the royal costume: over his chemise he put on a tunic, a dalmatic, and the royal mantle fastened by a fermail on his right shoulder.[4] The man of flesh had transformed himself, becoming the anointed of God and acquiring the superior qualities transferred to him by the cosmos.

During the Middle Ages, the king of the French was in part a lay person and partially religious. Louis VI was interred in his religious vestments; before the battle of Bouvines, Philippe Auguste blessed his soldiers; Louis IX regularly dressed himself in a dalmatic, a vestment that though derived from Roman costume in the thirteenth century was worn by deacons and subdeacons at Mass, and was worn as an ornament by bishops.[5] In the medieval consecration ceremony of the king of the French, the metamorphosis from the quotidian to the sacred occurred with the anointing of the new king with oil. This unction during the *sacre* by holy chrism from the *Sainte Ampoule,* delivered by a dove during the baptism of Clovis, permanently transformed the king's person from an ordinary mortal into a being of higher status, as in an ordination, or as through baptism a Christian might pass into the community of grace.[6] At the *sacre,* the garments of the king articulated the principle that he was simultaneously the anointed of God and a layman, signaling his competence to direct the political affairs of his people.[7]

The *ordo,* the liturgical calendar that specifies the diverse parts of the ceremonial and liturgy associated with the elevation of a the French kings, was revised in the 1130s, during the reign of Louis VII.[8] This *ordo* specifies a ceremonial that broke with the *ordo* prepared by Hincmar for the *sacre* of Charles the Bald in 848 and Louis II in 877.[9] The regal dalmatic, a ceremonial costume worn exclusively by the newly consecrated French king, is not mentioned by name until the *ordos* of the fourteenth century but it is described in the manuscript of the 1250 *ordo.*[10] I have identified the representation of the regal dalmatic among the garments worn by the column-figure sculpture installed between the 1130s and the 1160s along the jambs of churches in northern France. Since few written comments document the hierarchy and value of textiles and clothing in the twelfth century, and the artist-sculptors—the *ymagiers*—clearly illustrate the actual clothing worn by the elite of society, the church portal sculpture programs themselves constitute historical documents for mid-twelfth-century dress.

The dating of the group of church portals believed to have been constructed between the 1130s and the 1160s has been based to a large degree on the style of costume represented in the sculpture installed in the jambs of the doorways. During the twelfth century, high-ranking men and women in northern France dressed themselves in an ensemble comprising chemise, bliaut, and mantle.[11] A new and different period of fashion between the 1130s and the 1160s is illustrated by church portal sculpture at such cathedrals of Chartres and Angers, the royal abbey church of Saint-Denis or the priory church of Saint-Loup de Naud.[12] (Figure 13.1.) The *ymagiers* presented the contemporary clothing in larger-than-life-size statues with an attention to detail normally confined to small-scale sculpture, so that the column-figures of the middle third of the century were carved with such precision that the garment construction can be discerned and the textiles may be identified. Using contemporary vocabulary of the language of dress, the costumes portrayed on the column-figures represent the actual clothing of the elite of northern French society: courtly ladies, knights, powerful spokesmen, bishops, lords, and kings.[13] The costumes of the sculpted figures differ from reliefs made before 1130 at Moissac, and

Figure 13.1. Right jamb column-figure sculpture of the north transept portal, Porte des Valois, of the royal abbey church of Saint-Denis. Photograph by Janet Snyder.

they differ from sculpture representing Old Testament prefigurations of Christ at Senlis, carved after 1165.

Figure 13.2. Detail showing dalmatic heavy appliquéd hem of Porte des Valois R1, north transept portal of Saint-Denis. Photograph by Janet Snyder

The fashion shift observable just after 1130 is most easily recognized in the new version of the woman's bliaut, the *bliaut gironé,*[14] which appeared at court; no examples of this fashion appear after 1170.[15] Extant textiles and fragments of costumes provide compelling evidence showing that the clothing of the column-figures represents actual twelfth-century clothing. The fabric of narrowly pleated *gironées* depicted on column-figures closely resembles the pleated sections of the alb used in the 1160s by Thomas Becket, now preserved in the treasury of the cathedral of Sens.[16]

Though male costume showed the tendency toward slimness in the early twelfth century, men's clothing was much more subtle in its stylistic distinctions than the clothing of women. Cîteaux manuscript illuminations from the 1120s show men in form-fitting bliauts, but elsewhere a man's bliaut appears to have been cut with some fullness through the torso, blousing loosely over a cinch at the natural waistline.[17] Most often, for men as for women, the bliaut neckline was a high, round opening at the base of the throat, closed imperceptibly with an overlap or along the shoulder or with an appliquéed border band of embroidery and jewel forms. The fashions illustrated as being worn by the personages populating the portals would have been constructed of embroidered silks, fine linens, and woollen cloth.

Figure 13.3. Sculpture no. 81 in the destroyed cloister of Notre-Dame-en-Vaux at Chalon-sur-Marne. Photograph by Janet Snyder.

Though among the column-figures many figures wear crowns, few wear the regal dalmatic. In twelfth-century sculpture, this dalmatic was represented as a narrow but not form fitting tunic shorter than the usual man's bliaut. It appears to have been constructed of practically flat, unpleated front and back panels of fine cloth, attached at the shoulders, belted at the natural waistline, open down the sides and finished with a heavy appliquéed border band at the hem (see figure 13.2). In some examples, these tunics have rather short, relatively wide sleeves, much like those of a liturgical dalmatic, while in others dolman sleeves terminate in narrow cuffs.

Among the column-figures, the special status of an anointed king is designated his ensemble, most easily recognized by this knee-length ceremonial dalmatic. When a similar dalmatic was depicted as being worn by prophets, apostles, and angels in manuscript illuminations and painted stained glass, a comparable holy state was signaled. The legibility in portal sculpture programs of the king's sacred status as expressed through his clothing suggests that what appears to be a static arrangement of standing figures may actually function as a large-scale narrative relief. Because the observer might discriminate individual column-figures through sartorial cues, a differentiation would be made clear between the king functioning in his sacerdotal role and, for example, his role as judge or military leader.

The costume of the column-figure king reflects three influences that shaped the French notion of the monarchy. First, his tunic was often the mounted warrior's bliaut, with its center-front and center-back seams open to the hip to ease the straddling of a horse: in Frankish tradition the sovereign was the elected chief of a clan of warriors (see figure 13.3). Second, over this bliaut he donned the dalmatic of the subdeacon: according to Church doctrine the anointed monarch functioned as a member of the clerical hierarchy. Third, the scepter and banderole or codex held by the column-figure represent the impersonal *res* of the state and the written law of the Gallo-Romans. It seems likely that the appearance of this ensemble in a portal program might indicate the patron who commissioned the sculpture was a particular supporter of Louis VII, le Jeune, perhaps condoning the king's efforts to transform the Peace of God into the Peace of the King throughout the region in the 1150s.[18] By including the image of an anointed monarch, the sculpture program's designer acknowledges a divine authorization for the king's acts.

Sixteen of the 136 male column-figures installed between the 1130s and the 1160s for which there is substantial evidence are represented dressed in the dalmatic, as are two smaller figures from cloisters built during the same period. At the basilica church of the Royal Abbey of Saint-Denis, all save one of the column-figures of the north transept portal, the *Porte des Valois,* (L2, L3, R1, R2 and R3) and two of the figures on the west facade (CL1, CR4) wore the regal dalmatic.[19] It is depicted in Paris at Saint-Germain-des-Prés (R2) and on the west facade of Notre-Dame, the cathedral of Paris (RL1, RL3, RR2). Particularly wide and delicately ar-

Figure 13.4. Detail showing dalmitic open side seam and hem border, no. 81 in the destroyed cloister of Notre-Dame-en-Vaux at Chalon-sur-Marne. Photograph by Janet Snyder.

ticulated border patterns decorate the hemlines of the dalmatic at Saint-Maurice at Angers (L2). At Notre-Dame of Vermenton, while the three crowned Magi do not wear the dalmatic, the corners of the open side seam

Figure 13.5. Side view, showing dalmitic open side seam of the figure of King David, found at Saint-Ayoul in Provins, now in the Musée, Maison romane in Provins. Photograph by Janet Snyder.

along the hem of a dalmatic apparently worn without a stole furnish the only identifiable feature of an otherwise destroyed column-figure on the right jamb (R3).

The engraving published in 1739 by Dom Plancher of the portal of Saint-Bénigne in Dijon illustrates significant details of textile pattern and texture for the dalmatics of three column-figures (L1, L4 and R1).[20] Perhaps the clearest illustration of a king wearing the dalmatic over the warrior's bliaut is column 81 from the cloister of Notre-Dame-en-Vaux, Châlons-sur-Marne.[21] (Figures 13.3 and 13.4) The dalmatic affirms the royal-sacerdotal status of the headless figure in a warrior's bliaut identified through the words carved on his banderole as David, found at Saint-Ayoul, now in the Maison Romane in Provins (see figure 13.5). With the curious exception of the column-figure on the right jamb (R2) at Notre-Dame in Paris, these kings also wear their mantles fastened on the right shoulder, as specified in descriptions of the rerobing of the king after consecration.

Comparative sculpted documentation includes the twelfth-century ivory Lewis Chessmen, now in the British Museum. These kings are distinguished because they wear the unpleated, bordered dalmatic-bliaut with their mantles fastened on right shoulders. Further, their hair is dressed in four to six twisted coils lying on their shoulders and back, a "Merovingian" royal hairstyle also seen at Angers (L2), Saint-Bénigne (L1 and L4), Saint-Germain-des-Prés (R2), Notre-Dame of Paris (L3), Porte des Valois (L3 and R3), and the king from the cloister of Notre-Dame-en-Vaux.

Costumes and fabrics carried broad geographical and cultural implications for European audiences. From descriptions in the lais of Marie de France and contemporary romances, it is clear that for the quotidian observer of twelfth-century sculpture not only would the clothing have been recognizable, but a fundamental distinction was drawn between European cloth and goods from east of Venice. Silk, cotton, and cotton-linen blends came from the Middle East and the Orient; gauze originated in Gaza, damask in Damascus; silk and linen, sharb, and *tiraz* came from Egypt, which had the reputation in the Middle Ages as the "land of linen," with the best grades produced along the Lower Nile. Fine extant linens from Islamic *tiraz* correspond in weight and quality to textiles represented in twelfth-century French sculpture.

The fabrics and cut of the costumes of the column-figures identify the personages with the Holy Land in the East. Personages might be Old Testament kings such as David, to whom the king was compared after the unction during the *sacre,*[22] or Solomon, the builder of the Temple of Jerusalem.[23] The symbolism of the royalty of Israel influenced French conceptions of kingship reinforcing the reciprocal inference associating the contemporary French elite with the prestige of the biblical models.

Before 1100 not only price and scarcity but also social rank limited the use of silk and fine cloth to the highest-ranking and most wealthy persons in northern Europe;[24] the Cairo/Fustat Geniza documents indicate that such goods were being shipped from Egypt to Europe since at least the ninth century.[25] Pilgrims' and Crusaders' experiences must have increased the desire of European people for fine Levantine cloth, resulting in an expansion of commercial exchange in the years following the successful First Crusade (1095–1099). In 1106, Louis assisted at the celebration of the marriage of his sister Constance and Robert Guiscard's eldest son Bohémond, the prince of Antioch.[26] Hosted by Countess Adèle of Blois-Champagne, the wedding was celebrated in Chartres with great pomp. Certainly textiles from the East must have figured prominently in this sumptuous celebration of the wedding of a Levantine prince and the daughter of Philippe I, foreshadowing the significance of textiles represented in the sculpture that was installed at Chartres thirty years later.

Twelfth-century costumes combined available goods with exotic imports. Courtly clothing in northern France during the twelfth century was made of linen, wool, and silk, and it was decorated with metallic thread, pearls, and precious jewels. Much of the original polychromy of northern French church portal sculpture has been effaced, though pigments staining the stone indicate the facades were once vibrant with color. Three-dimensional representations of textiles survive in a number of places.[27] Dom Plancher's engravings of Saint-Bénigne in Dijon illustrate pronounced overall textile patterns in addition to the patterned borders.

The adapted clothing of the eleventh and twelfth centuries reflected the impact of the Islamic world on European visitors to the Near East. The broad patterns of embroidery appearing at the hemline of the dalmatic recall the characteristic *tiraz* worn by twelfth-century Muslim princes.[28] The textile-weaving and embroidery workshops, known as *dar al-tiraz* or *dar al-kiswa,* were maintained as a standard part of the Islamic communities from Afghanistan to Spain from the seventh century until about the thirteenth century. The inscribed *tiraz* were destined for the personal usage of the caliph but were also distributed to his familiars, high functionaries, ambassadors, foreign princes, and all those whom he chose to thank or honor. Such textiles had found their way to northern France by the mid-twelfth century.[29]

The language of dress functions as a system of immanent signs, conveying subtle messages between contemporary "authors" and "readers." Although the regal dalmatic is not mentioned by name, the detailed revision of the *ordo* for the consecration of the kings and queens of the French during the reign of Louis VII reveals a strong concern with the propriety of the ritual and its prerogatives, and the church-portal sculpture programs make that concern impressively concrete and present in real time for their community. The precocious representation of the actual clothing of the courts in column-figure sculpture—appearing at northern French churches exclusively during the reign of Louis VII—indicate the representation of the regal dalmatic was intended to articulate the divine authorization of the king. The recognition of its representation in twelfth-century sculpture is the first key to unlocking the code of the meaning embedded in the great sculpture programs of the mid-twelfth century.

Notes

1. *Le sacre* combines the rites of consecration, anointing, and coronation. Its rank as a sacrament and its role in conferring legitimacy on the French king were under debate in the twelfth century. "Le sacre est en quelque sorte la consécration d'un pouvoir par un rite—l'onction—qui confère à celui la reçoit un supplément de légitimité et donc de puissance dont les attributs sont remis ensuite lors du couronnement." Archives nationales, *Le Sacre à propos d'un millénaire 987–1987* (Paris: Archives nationales Musée de l'Histoire de France, 1987), p. 13.
2. J.-P. Bayard and P. de la Perrière, *Les Rites Magiques de la Royaute (*Paris: Friant, 1982), p. 156.
3. Bayard and de la Perrière, *Les Rites Magiques,* p 157
4. See the royal costume descriptions in P. E. Schramm, *Kaiser Könige und Päpste, Gesammelte Aufsätze zur Geschichte des Mittlealters* III (Stuttgart: Anton Hiersemann, 1969), pp. 547–52. See also Archives nationales, *Le Sacre,* p. 54.
5. A. Bonnefin, *Le Sacre royal dans l'histoire de France, permanence d'une valeur fundamentale* (Paris: Bonnefin, 1993), p. 8. Among the Romans, the dalmatic was an outer garment with short sleeves decorated with clavi under which was worn the *tunica romain,* a long gown with narrow sleeves. E. Piltz, *Le costume official des dignitaires byzantins à l'époque paléologue.* Figura Nova Series 26 (Uppsala: Acta Universitatis Upsaliensis, 1994), p. 10. See also Jules Quicherat, *Histoire du Costume en France depuis les Temps les plus reculés jusqu'a la fin du XVIIIe siècle* (Paris: Librairie Hachette et Cie, 1875, 1877), p. 161.
6. A. van Gennep, *Rites of Passage,* trans. M. B. Vizedom and G. L. Caffee (Chicago: University of Chicago Press, 1960), p. 110.
7. Bayard and de la Perrière, *Les Rites Magiques,* p. 162
8. E. A. R. Brown, *"Franks, Burgundians and Aquitanians" and the Royal Coronation Ceremony in France.* Transactions of the American Philosophical Society, fol. 82, part 7(1992), p. 37.
9. Bonnefin, *Le Sacre royal,* pp. 5–6
10. Paris, Bibliothèque national, MS lat. 1246. See Henri Comte de Paris, *Les Rois de France et le Sacr,* with Gaston Ducheta-Suchaux (Paris: Éditions du Rodier, 1996), pp. 150–51.
11. Eugene Viollet-le-Duc, *Dictionaire raisonné du mobilier français,* 3–4 (Paris: V.S. Morel et Cie, 1872), p. 38; Joan Evans, *Dress in Mediaeval France* (Oxford: Clarendon Press, 1952), p. 8; Quicherat, *Histoire du Costume en France,*

p. 147. The *bliaut,* a tunic worn on top of the *chemise,* a linen undergarment, has a closely fitted bodice, an ankle-length wide skirt, and comparatively loose sleeves.

12. Churches with column-figures installed at this time were: Saint-Maurice at Angers, Saint-Lazare at Avalon, Saint-Étienne at Bourges, the west facade of Nortre-Dame of Chartres, Notre-Dame of Corbeil, Saint-Bénigne at Dijon, Notre-Dame du Fort at Étampes, Notre-Dame at Ivry-la-Bataille, Saint-Julien at Le Mans, Saint-Ours, now Notre-Dame du Château, at Loches,the abbey of Notre-Dame of Nesle-la-Reposte, the Saint Anne Portal of Notre-Dame of Paris, Saint-Germain-des-Prés at Paris, the churches of Saint-Ayoul and Saint-Thibaut at Provins, Rochester Cathedral, England, the west facade and the *Porte des Valois* at the royal abbey church of Saint-Denis, Saint-Loup de Naud, Notre-Dame at Vermenton. Most of the sculpture exists in fragments today while some sculpture is known only from engravings published in the eighteenth century.
13. See Janet Snyder, *Clothing as Communication: A Study of Clothing and Textiles in Northern French Early Gothic Sculpture,* Ph.D. dissertation, Columbia University, 1996, and J. Snyder, "Knights and Ladies at the Door: Fictive Clothing in Mid-Twelfth-Century Sculpture," *AVISTA Forum Journal, Association Villard de Honnecourt for the Interdisciplinary Study of Medieval Technology, Science, and Art,* Winter, 1996. pp. 10–14.
14. The term *bliaut gironé* differentiates the two-piece garment with a finely worked waistband from the one-piece bliaut. "The bliaut was cut in two distinct parts, the *cors,* or bodice, and the *gironée,* or skirt." Eunice Goddard, *Women's Costume in French Texts* (Baltimore: The Johns Hopkins University Press, and Paris: Presses universitaires de France, 1929), p. 20
15. In the present discussion, "the court" is construed as the circle of the king and his great vassals, the magnates of the realm, the elite community of these peers who had joined Louis VI when he took up the standard of the Vexin against the threatened invasion of the Holy Roman Emperor in 1124 and called on "all of France to follow." M. Bur, *Suger, abbé de Saint-Denis, régent de France* (Paris: Perrin, 1991), pp. 115–16. See document #348, A. Luchaire, *Louis VI le Gros, Annales de sa vie et de son Règne (1081–1137)* (Paris, 1890; reprint: Brussels: Culture et Civilisation, 1964), p. 160. Du Tillet said the *ordo* prepared for Philippe Auguste in 1179 established the twelve peers of France. See Brown, *"Franks, Burgundians and Aquitanians."*
16. Abbé E. Chartraire, *Inventaire du Trésor de l'église primatiale et métropolitaine de Sens.* Sens, 1897. Ch. de Livas, "Rapport sur les anciens vêtements sacerdotaux et les anciennes étoffes du Trésor de Sens," *La Revue des sociétés savantes,* II. 1897.
17. See the Falconer in the initial Q *Incipit,* Book 35, Gregory the Great, *Moralia in Job,* in Dijon, Bibliothèque municipale, MS. 173, fol. 174, published in C. Oursel, *Miniatures cisterciennes* (Macon: Impr. Protat frères, 1960).

18. By the time Louis VII returned from the Second Crusade in November 1149, temporal and spiritual prerogatives were combined into comprehensive peace so that the peace of the kingdom and of God became one. The rights of the Church were identified as the rights of the king and vice versa. The transition was made from a loose system of government in which an overlord defended quasi-independent lords and enforced the peace of God to the institutional monarchy representing a single body of which the fiefs were integral members who embraced the peace of the king. Eric Bournazel, "Suger and the Capetians" *Abbot Suger and Saint-Denis, A symposium,* ed. Paula Gerson (New York: The Metropolitan Museum of Art, 1981), p. 55. On the Peace of God and the Truce of God, see H. E. J. Cowdrey, "The Peace and Truce of God in the Eleventh Century," *Popes, Monks and Crusaders* 9 (London: The Hambledon Press, 1984), pp. 42–67.
19. The abbreviations L and R refer to the left or right jamb of the portal as the observer faces the door (or the center portal left jamb, etc.), and the column-figures have been numbered on each jamb reading from left to right. As an example, CR4 at Saint-Denis indicates the fourth figure from the door opening on the right jamb of the center portal.
20. Dom Urbain Plancher, *Histoire générale et particulière de Bourgogne* (Dijon, 1739, reprint; Paris: Éditions du Palais Royal, 1974), p. 503.
21. See S. Pressouyre, *Images d'un cloître disparu (Notre-Dame-en-Vaux à Châlons-sur-Marne)* (Bergamo: Joël Cuénot, 1976).
22. " . . . près l'onction des mains, l'archevêque compare le roi et son onction à David oint par Samuel." Comte de Paris, *Les Rois de France et le Sacre,* p. 144.
23. Bayard and de la Perrière, *Les Rites,* p. 162.
24. "Les textes dans lesquels il est question de ces tissus visent exclusivement la noblesse, le haut clergie et les moines; les dons d'ornements liturgiques aux églises émanent de la même classe sociale." E. Sabbe, " L'importation des tissus orientaux en Europe occidentale du haut Moyen Age IX-X siècles," *Revue belge de philologie et d'histoire* (July-December, 1935): 1284.
25. S. D. Goitein, *A Mediterranean Society; the Jewish communities of the Arab world as portrayed in the documents of the Cairo Geniza 2* (Berkeley: University of California, 1967–1993), p. 214.
26. Archives nationales, *Le Sacre,* no. 36, mars 25-mai 26, 1106, Chartres. For a document relating to the marriage, see Luchaire, *Louis VI le Gros, #36: Constance, fille de Philippe I marriage with Bohémond of Antioche.* Also in attendance at the nuptials were Philippe I, the papal legate, and a great many archbishops, bishops, and barons. See Suger, *La Geste de Louis VI.* pp. 66–67.
27. Besides broad carved borders seen at Saint-Denis, Notre-Dame-en-Vaux, Provins, broad bands of fabric were applied to sleeves and thighs at Angers, Bourges, and Chartres, and the hemline of Chartres LL3 appears to have a texture woven into the surface of the cloth. Complex carved

fabric is represented in the vestments of the twelfth-century fragment of an archbishop's *gisànt,* found in the chapel of Saint Joseph in the cathedral of Reims, now in the Palais du Tau and of the late twelfth-century *gisànt* of an abbot now in the Musée de l'Hospice Saint-Roch in Issoudun.

28. See *Figure of a Prince.* Stucco. H. 47 in. Islamic. Sculpture. Persian. c. 1200. Saljuk. The Metropolitan Museum of Art, Cora Timken Burnett collection of Persian miniatures and other Persian art objects, bequest of Cora Timken Burnett, 1956 (57.51.18).
29. Dated examples of silk and linen tapestry textile fragments are, for example, in the collection of the Metropolitan Museum of Art, New York: 11.138.1 (eleventh century); 27.170.1(late eleventh century); 31.106.28ab (1035–1094); 27.170.64 (twelfth century). The ubiquitous *tiraz* workshops produced such uniformly high-quality materials that scholars have difficulty pinpointing the source of particular textile fragments, though the essential fact of their non-European origin was undeniable.

CHAPTER 14

ROBING IN THE MONGOLIAN EMPIRE*

Thomas T. Allsen

In recounting the enthronement of Chinggis Qan (reigned 1206–1227), the historian Hayton (Het'um), a prince of Lesser Armenia long in Mongolian service, says that in those early days they made do with "black felt" because they had no "fairer cloth [*drap*]."[1] Very soon, however, the Mongols enthusiastically embraced a much fairer cloth of state. Indeed, this textile became closely identified with the Mongols and its fame spread across Eurasia from the Far East to the Far West, where it was known as "Tartar cloth" in the languages of Europe.[2] From direct examination of garments designated as *panni tartarici* in early church inventories, we know that this was a drawloom textile mainly made of gold and silk thread.[3] In the Middle East, the same cloth was usually called *nasij,* a shortened form of the Arabic *nasij al-dhahab al-harir,* literally "cloth of gold and silk."[4] In the Chinese sources of this period *nasij* is encountered in the transcription *na-shi-shi,* which on two occasions the *Yuan shi* defines as "gold brocade [*jinjin*]."[5]

Once the Mongols had acquired sufficient supplies through booty, tribute, trade, and court-sponsored production, Chinggis Qan and his successors made lavish use of gold brocade in tents and conveyances and most conspicuously in their official court dress. For formal state occasions the required apparel, according to the chapter on court ceremony in the *Yuan shi,* was a special garment called *zhi-sun* in Chinese; in this same passage this term, derived from the Mongolian *jisün,* "color," is defined as a "robe of one color."[6] The name arises from the fact that the ground threads were of a solid color, while the ornamental weft weaves were of gold thread. In other Chinese texts, interestingly, the same kind of robe is occasionally called *zha-ma,* from the Persian *jamah,* "garment" or "vestment."[7] In any case, these sumptuous robes were given out to courtiers for use at great banquets of state called, appropriately enough, *jisün* feasts (*zhi-sun yan*). Such festivals typically lasted for days and on each the emperor, his court, and guests all donned *jisün* robes of the same color.

Marco Polo describes at length the robing of the imperial guard (*kesig*) in Qubilai's time (reigned 1260–1294). By the Venetian's calculation the guardsmen (*kesigten*) numbered about 12,000, each of whom received robes of one color thirteen times a year for an annual total of 156,000.[8] The scale of these presentations, if not the precise number, is fully sustained by the Chinese sources, which record repeatedly that all guardsmen, as well as imperial relatives, great ministers, personal attendants, and court musicians, had *zhi-sun* robes and that everyone, without exception, was required to wear such garments to imperial feasts.[9] Not unexpectedly, even the considerable resources of the Yuan court were severely strained in consequence of the large amounts of "cash and silk" annually expended on the maintenance of the imperial guard. In the succinct phrase of the *Yuan shi,* "the general budget of the state was regularly exhausted in this fashion."[10]

The massive robing so prevalent in Mongolian political culture of the imperial era served a multitude of purposes. Clear-cut categorization is difficult because its various roles were always intertwined and to a large extent interdependent. In what follows, I try to make some distinctions, however artificial, in an effort to provide a sense of the individual character and overall range of these diverse functions.

Certainly, one of the essential goals of investiture was to demonstrate majesty. A qaghan surrounded by thousands of people bedecked in gold brocade robes communicated to subject and foreigner alike that the Mongolian sovereign possessed vast wealth and great generosity. But this was more than a dazzling display of conspicuous consumption and lavish redistribution of material wealth; it also effectively advertised the ruler's control over the labor of myriad highly skilled artisans collected from every corner of the known world. As Ibn Khaldun long ago argued, powerful courts and dynasties dominate the marketplace for both goods and services.[11] And this kind of domination was yet another proof of majesty, an attribute of kingship that rests upon a ruler's command, real and imagined, of material and spiritual resources as well as organizational skill. Massed servitors swathed in color-coordinated robes of gold brocade constituted an eye-catching and convincing demonstration of such command.

More obviously, of course, investiture ceremonies were a central element in the fashioning of hierarchies. In the Old World at least, the acceptance of vestments was universally understood as the acceptance of subordinate status, social or political. This is clearly evident in the Mongols' conception of interstate relations. The Chinese literatus Yen Fu, writing in the fourteenth century about the achievements of Bayan the Barin, says that the famous general extended the Yuan realm north and south and that in consequence of his military achievements, "all [peoples] accepted our calendar and [all] adopted our mode of dress."[12] The first element, of course, is of Chinese inspiration but the second is particularly Mongolian, and one well understood by their neighbors. Thus, when the ruler of Thailand (Xianguo) wished to reaffirm his allegiance to the Mongols in the 1290s he sent envoys to the Yuan court requesting "clothing of gold thread [*jinlü i*]."[13] Conversely, foreign envoys not wishing to enter the Mongolian "family of nations" tried to avoid the acceptance of clothing or even pieces of cloth from the hands of the Chinggisids. This is particularly true of clerics, who often served as envoys and intercessors to the Mongolian authorities. Understandably, medieval men of the cloth such as the Franciscan Rubruck and the Armenian monk Vartan were very wary of these offers because they already belonged to exclusive corporate entities that used investiture as a major mechanism of defining membership and establishing hierarchy.[14]

For the Mongols, internal politics were similarly ordered. Investiture not only created hierarchy at court, it was also a means of fashioning chains of clientage that was at the very heart of Mongolian princely politics. This is most clearly revealed during succession crises; in such circumstances the consolidation and expansion of a contender's base of support always entailed robing on a large scale. When Baidu (reigned 1295) challenged Ghazan (reigned 1295–1304) for the Il-qan throne in Iran, he first endeavored to win over "men of high position" and he did so, according to contemporary testimony, with extravagant gifts and "royal apparel."[15] Even more telling is the earlier contest between Tegüder/Ahmad (reigned 1281–1284) and Arghun (reigned 1284–1291). In this instance hostilities opened with a lightening strike on textile production centers. In Rashid al-Din's recounting, Tegüder, upon learning of his rival's intentions to challenge him, immediately sent an advanced patrol to Varamin, south of Ray, where

> they seized all three hundred households of artisans who belonged to Arghun, plundered their homes and returned to the [main] army. When Arghun became aware of this situation he sent envoys to the treasury of Gurgan in order to make ready all that was on hand and he sent to the workshops [*kar-khanah-ha*] of Nishapur, Tus and Isfarayin to bring garments [*jamah-ha*]; and in the course of twenty days they conveyed sums of ready money of gold, objects adorned with gold and gems, jewels, and garments to 'Adiliyyah in Gurgan and [Arghun] distributed these things to the military commanders.[16]

A similar tale is told by the Spanish envoy Clavijo, an eyewitness of the behavior of Prince 'Umar, a grandson of Tamerlane who, upon hearing of the latter's demise in 1405 immediately sent to Tabriz and Sultaniyyah for 3,000 gold brocade robes "to bestow on various of his lords" in anticipation of the coming succession struggle.[17]

For these princes, obviously, an ample supply of robes, like weapons, horses, and money, was a strategic commodity necessary for success in political-military competition. In fact, the regular distribution of gold brocade robes was so central to Mongolian court life, politics, and ideology that only under extreme conditions, such as the abortive introduction of Chinese-style paper money (*chao*) into Iran in 1294, were restrictions placed on the production of gilt cloth, and even here an exception was made for gold robes destined for the Il-qan and his senior officials.[18] In other words, what we now think of as "luxuries" were actually necessities in the political economy of traditional states, a reality often ignored in modern scholarship.[19]

The importance attached to luxuries emerges, too, in any examination of imperial courts as "educational" institutions. As Norbert Elias has argued, traditional courts always try to promote new models of conduct designed, quite consciously, to alter and remold the behavior of retainers and clients. Ceremony and etiquette were the principal means by which rough-hewn warriors and provincials were transformed into more presentable and pliable courtiers. The latter were often willing students because the court provided many powerful incentives to change behavior—prestige, rank, quality food, drink, entertainment, and clothing.[20] Thus, in the Mongolian Empire as elsewhere, investiture enhanced the ruler's control over the officers of the realm since robing was part of a larger package of rewards that came to define the good life, a life that could only be had at a price—adherence to court-mandated procedures, ceremonies, and behavioral codes. Naturally, when etiquette was breached, the Yuan court acted swiftly; in response to infractions the imperial guard, Marco Polo tells us, was required to "take away [the offender's] clothes, and to have them again he must redeem them."[21] This confiscation of robes was a most serious business because it meant that the offender had lost his access, his ticket to court banquets with their many attractions and rewards, including, of course, the bestowal of more gold brocade robes.

From the generalized functions of investiture, let us turn to its more specialized applications, two of which reveal the institution's great flexibility and utility. On the one hand, robing was a most effective means of individualizing rewards, of identifying and celebrating admirable deeds judged worthy of emulation. To this end, Chinggisid rulers, following long-established precedents in Iran and the Islamic world, often transferred, on public occasions, clothes they themselves had worn to individuals whose bravery, honesty, or competence pleased them.[22] Chinggis Qan gave a "shred" of his robe to the Uighur king, and later on the Il-qan Abaqa (reigned 1265–1281) granted clothes from his own back to a prince of Lesser Armenia, and Abu Sa'id (reigned 1316–1335) bestowed his own robe on a *qadi* of Shiraz.[23] Individuals so honored were set apart from their fellow courtiers as recipients of their ruler's personal wardrobe and therefore some of his personal aura, his charisma. This in turn conferred a special protection; to strike or insult a man wearing his sovereign's clothes was an act of *lèse majesté*.

At the same time, investiture could also be used to suppress individuality and encourage corporate and collective identity. This is most evident in the Mongols' *jisün* feasts in which the participants, all in robes of one color, were marked off in distinctive fashion from the rest of the qaghan's subjects; this surely created a strong sense of separateness and privilege in relation to all outsiders. But within the elite itself the *jisün* feast can be viewed as an integrative mechanism. Through the massive presentation of robes of one color rank and individuality were masked and social distance reduced during these occasions of celebration and reward. And even though this equality was temporary and contrived, it nonetheless fostered a long-term sense of comradery and a set of shared interests in the continued success of the imperial enterprise. This was a very important matter at a court populated by individuals of the most diverse ethnic, religious, and occupational backgrounds, individuals who had to cooperate and interact with one another if the Mongols' vast imperium was to be administered effectively.

Investiture among the Mongols had, it is apparent, various meanings and functions. Like other successful symbolic systems it, too, was multivalent—that is, open to differing readings, each of which was valid, comprehensible, and relevant to someone.[24] This very malleability and versatility explain why investiture readily crossed so many political and religious boundaries and became, centuries before the Mongols, a pan-Eurasian institution. Its expansive character and transnational appeal is well illustrated in the career of Juansher, a Monophysite prince of Caucasian Albania, who in the middle decades of the seventh century was invested in succession by the Zoroastrian Sasanians, Orthodox Byzantines, and Muslim Ummayads.[25]

This is not to say that the Mongols adopted investiture just because it was a visible part of preceding imperial traditions or because of neighbors' and subject peoples' expectations. The great investment the Chinggisids made in robing and the profound importance they attached to it had in fact very deep roots in steppe society: more specifically, gifts of clothing were integral to the nomads' patrimonial notions of state and society.

Structurally and ideologically the Mongolian government grew out of the personal guard (*kesig*) of Chinggis Qan, an institution that functioned simultaneously as his household establishment.[26] Thus the early qaghans lived in close proximity with their government officials and were expected, as part of their most basic obligations to their retainers, to provide each with food, drink, shelter, and clothing. This responsibility extended as well to foreign visitors who arrived at court, indeed to all guests admitted into the household for any purpose.[27]

Each Chinggisid prince with aspirations fashioned his own personal guard/household establishment that formed the core of his political-military support in any succession struggle and the new government in case of victory. Consequently, politics were highly personalized in the Mongolian empire. There were no neutral, independent civil servants loyal to the dynasty at large, only partisan retainers whose primary loyalty was to the prince who fed and clothed them. Naturally, whenever a prince died all those who made the transition to the new regime had to be invested again to fashion new ties of interdependency. This is why K'urd, an Armenian noble and military commander, was granted robes of honor (Armenian *xilay,* Arabic *khil'a*) by three successive Il-qans in the late thirteenth and early fourteenth centuries.[28]

The precept that rulers feed and clothe followers and in return receive service and unflinching loyalty is the basic formula of nomadic statecraft, one with a long history behind it. The very earliest written materials from the steppe world, the Orkhon inscriptions, include the claim of the Türk ruler Bilge Qaghan (reigned 716–734) that he inherited "people who were foodless on the inside and clotheless on the outside" and that through unstinting efforts he "furnished naked people with clothes."[29] It is interesting to note that the Middle Persian text *Shabuhragan,* written by Mani for the Sasanian ruler Shapur I (reigned 240–272), speaks of the virtue of those who feed the hungry and clothe the naked and the evil of those who refuse to do so.[30] This, of course, parallels closely the message of Matthew 25.35–44, passages Mani knew well. In these particular texts the central concern is with eschatology, not politics, but the phrasing may well have been appropriated by the Türk as a means of giving eloquent voice and wider meaning to indigenous ideas about rulership. But whatever its origin, this same formula reappears in the eleventh century Turkish mirror for princes written by Yusuf Khass Hajib, who reminds his sovereign, the Qarakhanid ruler of Turkestan, that a "prince must give good reward for service, clothing the naked and feeding the hungry."[31]

In the steppe tradition these principles were transmitted orally as well as textually. In the Oghuz epic, "The Story of Bugach Khan," the wife of the legendary Khan Dirse recommends that he "feed the hungry, give clothes to the naked." He follows her advice and achieves success.[32] Most certainly, subjects' expectations and rulers' public deportment were framed by such epic depictions of proper kingly behavior.

That the Mongols firmly and consciously embraced this ancient formula is evident from various contemporary sources. The *Secret History,* the Mongols' own account of the rise of their empire, contains a dramatic episode on this very theme. In 1203, following the defeat of the Kereyid chieftain Ong Qan, his son, Senggüm, fled into the desert to escape capture. Senggüm's equerry, sensing that the political tide had turned toward Chinggis Qan, decided to defect. As he departed, the narrative relates, his wife rebuked him for turning his back on a leader who had provided him with savory meat and gilded clothing. When the equerry reached the Mongolian camp and told his story, Chinggis Qan praised his wife and immediately ordered the defector cut down and abandoned. The message was perfectly clear: the equerry had broken the contract, forsaken "his proper qan," and could now be trusted by no one.[33] Such notions held sway until the end of the Yuan dynasty even though Chinese and Mongolian criteria for loyalty and good service differed markedly. This is brought out in a debate in 1335 between Bayan the Merkid, a Mongolian military officer, and Xu Yufen, a Chinese scholar-official, concerning recruitment to high office. For Xu, not unexpectedly, proper literary education and commitment to honest government were the keys, whereas Bayan openly pushed aspirants of diverse ethnic and occupational backgrounds "who desire beautiful clothing and delicious food."[34] From Bayan's perspective the desire for beautiful robes signaled a candidate's understanding of Mongolian ways and his willingness to play by Mongolian rules. This, clearly, was the kind of man a qaghan could really trust.

Notes

* This essay summarizes arguments in my earlier work, *Commodity and Exchange in the Mongol Empire: A Cultural History of Islamic Textiles* (Cambridge: Cambridge University Press, 1997). I have used this opportunity to add some new material.

1. Hayton, *La flor des estoires de la terre d'Orient,* in *Recueil des historiens des croisades, documents arménien* 2 (Paris: Imprimerie nationale, 1906), pp. 148–49.
2. Paget Toynbee, "Tartar Cloths," *Romania* 24 (1900): 559–64.
3. Anne E. Wardwell, "*Panni Tartarici:* Eastern Islamic Silks Woven with Gold and Silver (Thirteenth and Fourteenth Centuries)," *Islamic Art* 4 (1988–89): 95–133, especially 115–17.
4. R. P. A. Dozy, *Supplément aux dictionnaires arabes* 2 (Leiden: E. J. Brill, 1881), p. 666.
5. *Yuan shi* (Beijing: Zhonghua shuju, 1976), chap. 78, pp. 1931 and 1938.

6. *Yuan shi,* chap. 78, p. 1938.
7. See the discussion of Ye Xinming, "Liang du xunxing zhi yu Shangdu de gongting shenghuo," *Yuan shi luncong* 4 (1992): 154–56.
8. Marco Polo, *The Description of the World* 1, trans. A. C. Moule and Paul Pelliot (London: Routledge, 1938), p. 54.
9. *Yuan shi,* chap. 37, p. 812; chap. 67, p. 1669; and chap. 78, p. 1938.
10. *Yuan shi,* chap. 99, p. 2525. For a full translation, see Hsiao Ch'i-ch'ing, *The Military Establishment of the Yuan Dynasty* (Cambridge: Harvard University Press, 1978), p. 94.
11. Ibn Khaldun, *The Muqaddimah: An Introduction to History,* trans. Franz Rosenthal (New York: Pantheon Books, 1958), 1: 46–47 and 2: 102, 287, and 352.
12. Su Tianjue, *Yuan wenli* (Taibei: Shijie shuju yingxing, 1967), chap. 24, p. 19a.
13. *Yuan shi,* chap. 210, p. 4664. For the historical context, see G. Coedes, *The Indianized States of Southeast Asia* (Honolulu: University of Hawaii Press, 1968), p. 218.
14. Christopher Dawson, ed., *Mongol Mission: Narratives and Letters of the Franciscan Missionaries in Mongolia and China in the Thirteenth and Fourteenth Centuries* (New York: Sheed and Ward, 1955), pp. 196 and 205; Peter Jackson, trans., and David Morgan, ed., *The Mission of Friar William of Rubruck* (London: The Haklyut Society, 1990), pp. 228 and 251; and Robert W. Thomson, "The Historical Compilation of Vardan Arewelc'i," *Dumbarton Oaks Papers* 43 (1989): 221.
15. Bar Hebraeus, *The Chronography of Gregory Abu'l Faraj* 1, trans. Ernest A. Wallis Budge (London: Oxford University Press, 1932), pp. 505–06.
16. Rashid al-Din, *Jami' al-tavarikh* 2, ed. B. Karimi (Tehran: Eqbal, 1959), p. 792.
17. Ruy González de Clavijo, *Embassy to Tamerlane, 1403–1406,* trans. Guy Le Strange (New York and London: Harper Brothers, 1928), p. 327.
18. Karl Jahn, "Paper Currency in Iran: A Contribution to the Cultural and Economic History of Iran in the Mongol Period," *Journal of Asian History* 4 (1970): 121–22.
19. For an insightful discussion of this issue, see Jane Schneider, "Was There a Pre-Capitalist World System?" *Peasant Studies* 6/1 (1977): 20–29.
20. Norbert Elias, *The Civilizing Process,* trans. Edmund Jephcott (Oxford: Blackwell, 1994), pp. 465–75.
21. Marco Polo, *Description of the World,* 1: 219.
22. The precedents are many; see, for example, Juzjani, *Tabaqat-i nasiri* 1, ed. Abd al-Hayy Habibi (Kabul: Anjuman-i tarikh-i Afghanistan, 1963), p. 272, and Juzjani, *Tabaqat-i nasiri* 1, trans. H. G. Raverty (1881; repr. Oriental Books Reprint Corporation: Delhi, 1970), p. 179, who speaks of this practice in Iran on the eve of the Mongolian invasions.
23. Francis W. Cleaves, trans., *The Secret History of the Mongols* (Cambridge: Harvard University Press, 1982), sect. 238, p. 172; Stephannos Orbelian,

Histoire de la Siounie, trans. M. Brosset (St. Petersburg: Academie imperial des sciences, 1864), p. 236; and Ibn Battutah, *The Travels of Ibn Battutah* 2, trans. H. A. R. Gibb (Cambridge: Cambridge University Press for the Hakluyt Society, 1962), p. 304.

24. See the comments of Mircea Eliade, *Images and Symbols: Studies in Religious Symbolism* (Princeton: Princeton University Press, 1991), p. 15, on the "bundle of meanings" contained in every successful religious image.
25. Movses Dasxuranci, *The History of the Caucasian Albanians,* trans. C. J. F. Dowsett (London: Oxford University Press, 1961), pp. 111–12, 116, and 128.
26. For details, see Thomas T. Allsen, "Guard and Government in the Reign of the Grand Qan Möngke, 1251–59," *Harvard Journal of Asiatic Studies* 46 (1986): 495–521.
27. The missionary, Andrew of Perugia, in a letter written in Quanzhou in 1326, refers to an "*alafa* [Arabo-Persian '*alafa,* "stipend"] from the noble Emperor for food and dress of eight persons." See Dawson, *Mongol Mission,* pp. 235 and 236.
28. Avedis K. Sanjian, trans., *Colophons of Armenian Manuscripts: A Source for Middle Eastern History* (Cambridge: Harvard University Press, 1969), p. 74.
29. Talat Tekin, *A Grammar of Orkhon Turkic* (University of Indiana Publications, Uralic and Altaic Series, LXIX; Bloomington, 1968), pp. 267–68.
30. D. N. MacKenzie, "Mani's *Shabuhragan,*" *Bulletin of the School of Oriental and African Studies* 42 (1979): 507 and 509. Hans Joachim Klimkeit, trans., *Gnosis on the Silk Road: Gnostic Parables, Hymns and Prayers from Central Asia* (San Francisco: Harper, 1993), pp. 241, 243, and 249, n. 2, was the first to make these connections.
31. Yusuf Khass Hajib, *Wisdom of Royal Glory (Kutudgu Bilig): A Turko-Islamic Mirror for Princes,* trans. Robert Dankoff (Chicago: University of Chicago Press, 1983), p. 138. The author uses similar phrasing on another occasion, p. 93.
32. Faruk Sümer, Ahmet E. Uysal and Warren S. Walker, trans., *The Book of Dede Korkut* (Austin: University of Texas Press, 1972), pp. 11–12.
33. Cleaves, *Secret History,* sect. 188, pp. 115–16.
34. *Yuan shi,* chap. 142, p. 3405.

CHAPTER 15

FROM PAPAL RED TO CARDINAL PURPLE: EVOLUTION AND CHANGE OF ROBES AT THE PAPAL COURT FROM INNOCENT III TO LEO X, 1216–1521

Bernard Berthod

Introduction

During the three centuries between the deaths of Innocent III and Leo X, the papal court became increasingly important and was also restructured to become distinctively princely. Robes—their form, mode of display, and the configuration of color and materials—positioned each dignitary according to rank: pope, legates, cardinals, and curial officers. During this period, robing prerogatives were successively adopted by legates and cardinals. In the thirteenth century, in contrast to civil society, in which blue was increasingly deployed and ultimately became the royal color, ecclesiastical society preferred red, which soon became the marker of the papal court.[1]

The present work draws upon three types of sources thatcomplement each other: (1) ceremonial books of the papal Curia, (2) iconography from illuminated liturgical manuscripts, and (3) a few significant paintings (which are, however, less reliable than liturgical books). The texts were written by influential members of the papal court—cardinal-deacons, masters of ceremonies, and the like—based upon texts from the period of Innocent III to that of Paris de Grassi. They describe practices of the papal entourage whether in Rome, in Avignon, or on the numerous papal tours. The main texts, recently published and annotated by Marc Dykmans[2] are the *Ordo* of Gregory X (ca. 1273); the *Cérémonial du Cardinal-Evêque* (ca.

1280); the *Cérémonial cardinalice,* a collection of four texts dating from about 1300; *Cardinal Stefaneschi's Ceremonial,* written between 1300 and 1341; the *Cérémonial Long* written at Avignon before 1342; the texts of François de Conzié: the *Cérémonial Complémentaire,* written between 1383 and 1408 and his *Journal* written between 1406 and 1407; the *Ceremonial* of Patriarch Pierre Ameil, written between 1380 and 1400 after the return of the Pope to Rome; and finally the *Ceremonial* of Patrizzi Picolimini, a major (and very precise) work written around 1480 and annotated by John Burckard and Paris de Grassi (who himself also wrote several texts about court practices between 1500 and 1528). Later authors were quite aware of prior texts and noted in minute detail both customs that had fallen into disuse and their replacements. Thus, very few customs could have escaped this close scrutiny, especially since the manuscripts themselves were often annotated by others, thereby adding even more detail.

Using these sources, we shall analyze three aspects of the evolution of ecclesiastical garments: form and manufacture, colors, and quality of the fabric. We shall througout cite the original Latin in order to avoid inaccurate translations.

Papal mantle: *cappa, mantellus,* and *capucius*

One particular garment marked membership in the papal court: the *cappa,* a large outside cloak worn by the pope (*cappa contra aqua).* During the thirteenth century, it signaled one's status as a Roman cardinal, slowly becoming standard ceremonial wear. It is important to note that this cappa was not the red mantle that the pope wore for his investiture and that was a mark of the Roman bishop's authority.

We first find the word *cappa* appearing at the end of the thirteenth century, describing a robe worn by the pope; it is mentioned in Gregory's *Ordo (hoc tamen nota quod papa dedit cum cappa non cum pluviali).*[3] Similary, Stefaneschi's *Cérémonial,* referring to the practices of 1294, mentions a *cappa contra aqua* that the pope wore when he traveled and that was clearly distinguished from the inverstiture mantle.[4] Gregory's *Ordo* does not mention the robe used by cardinals; however, it notes that the first cardinal-deacon removed the *cappa* or the *clamide* in order to put on the dalmatic.[5] The *Cérémonial du cardinal évêque* notes that the cardinal-bishop wore the *cappa comunis* after taking off the liturgical robes. The Stefaneschi *Cérémonial* gives further information: this *cappa* was made of wool, the color not specified, except that members of religious orders had to wear the color of their order. This *cappa* was worn by cardinals after removing liturgical robes, especially for Candlemas, Ash Wednesday, and Palm Sunday. The *cappa* was also worn by the two cardinal-deacons who attended the Pope for Maundy Thursday services. At this period, the cardinal-deacons undertook specific functions but lacked formal titles, so they did not yet employ unique liturgical dress when they participated in the acts of obedience, or celebrated vespers or the papal mass; instead, in those rites, they wore a *cappa de scarlato.*

The *Cérémonial Long* shows how the *cappa* became an outside cloak between 1316 and 1334, worn specifically to assist at vespers during Lent in place of the *pluvial.*[6] The same *Ceremonial* and the *Cérémonial complémentaire* confirm that this *cappa lanea* was put on after removing liturgical garments.[7] These texts, however, give few indications about the form and cut of the garment. About 1340, the papal *cappa* became an enveloping cloak open at the front (*capam . . . a pectore usque ad pedes apertam*)[8] clasped at the throat with a large button, provided with an ample hood (*capucius)* that covered the head; the cardinals' *cappa* had much the same form. We have, for example, an illustration in the fresco painted by Simone Martini in 1320 of the Basilica of Assisi, showing Cardinal Gentile di Montefiore wearing just such a *cappa.* During the first decades of the fifteenth century, however, the open *cappa* was abandoned, superceded by a bell-shaped cloak, typical of the cardinals of Avignon at the beginning of the century, a *clocia* described by François de Conzié that soon became the standard ceremonial garment. From then on it is this bell-shaped cloak that was called a *cappa.*[9] For more elaborate occasions, roman cardinals added a train to it, with a hoop of the hood buttoned at the left shoulder.[10]

Round Cloak and Short Cape as Alternatives to the Cappa

At the end of the fourteenth century, the texts distinguish the *cappa* from a round cloak (*mantellus rotondus).* This *mantellus* was described by Pierre Amiel as a round cloak without a train, open at the front (*in forma circulatari et spherica*) and covering the body entirely; it was fastened under the collar and sleeveless. Lay members wore it in pink while regular clergy wore the color of their orders. Cardinals wore it over the *cotta* (a short surplice) with a simple mitre for the banquet following the ceremonies of Holy Thursday as they had done in the past.[11] Once shortened, the *mantellus rotundus* became the basis for the *mantelletta.* A note, written about 1450 in the margin of Cardinal Pietro Barbo Stefaneschi's copy of *Cérémonial,* confirms the use and form of this pinkish brown cape. This cloak is likewise shown in a portrait of Cardinal Albergati painted by Van Eyk in 1438.[12] Here, the *mantellus* was trimmed with fur and fastened under the collar by two buttons. Patrizi notes that while cardinals were in conclave, they were dressed in rochet and the little mantle (*parvus mantellus).*[13] This round little mantle was more and more frequently worn in place of the *cappa,* especially in less solemn circumstances.

By the end of the fifteenth century, a more convenient garment replaced the *cappa* in less solemn venues, specifically a short cape buttoned at the front and covering the shoulders (*capucius* or *caputius).*[14] Patrizi discriminates between *capucius magnus* worn with the *cappa* and the *capucius parvus* alone. Certainly, Sixtus IV (1471–1784) was the first to wear a *capucius parvus,* replacing the red velvet papal *cappa* with this short cape. His master of ceremonies describes the pope inspecting a church dressed in a long rochet covered by a red short cape (*et supra capucium parvum rubei coloris*)[15]—he is painted as such in 1477 in the fresco of Melozzo da Forli. Patrizi, likewise, shows cardinals wearing a *capucius* on top of the rochet.[16] Cardinal Francesco Gonzaga, painted by Mantegna in the ducal palace of Mantova, wore a similar garment over his rochet, as does Cardinal Lorenzo Pucci kneeling in front of Leo X in Pucci's missal.[17] By the beginning of the sixteenth century, cardinals ordinarly wore a *capucius parvus* (also known as a mozetta), similar in form to the pope's.

The Color Red: Popes, Legates, and Cardinals

The significance of the color red precedes even the Roman civilization and seems rooted deeply in the prehistoric past. This color is, according to Michel Pastoureau, "a historic and fundamental anthropologic fact."[18] Medieval liturgists such as Bruno de Segni wrote that the color red, an imperial privilege, was obtained by the pope during the early Christian period to consolidate the sovereign authority of the roman papacy.[19] Also, red was considered a christic color. Rupert de Deutz, for example, shows Christ "while shining of the stunning white of holyness accented with the red color of the Passion."[20]

At his coronation in 1076, Gregory VII wore a red mantle.[21] The *ordines* of the twelfth century of Albinus (1182) and of Centius (1192) note that the bishop of Rome after election was dressed by the deacon prior with a red liturgical mantle (*pluviale rubeo).*[22] Gregory X's *Ordo* describes in detail various coronations and enumerates, for the first time, different robes, several of which were red. It notes the red mantle, solemnly put on by the leading cardinal-deacon (*postea ponit ei mantum et dicit investio te de papatu romano).*[23] Returning to his his private appartment, the pope replaced the papal red mantle (also called *pluviale)* by a lighter robe, also red (*deponit pluviale et mitram et assumit rubeum mantellum).*[24] Throughout the ceremony, he also wore on red stockings and red shoes (*caligas de panno rubeo).*

In fact, from the fourteenth century onward, papal dress became focused on only two colors, white and red. White was the color for the robe—it was not yet called a cassock—and the linen rochet.[25] Red was the color for the other garments—the mantle of the investiture, the *cappa* that he wore in the chapel when not celebrating Mass, the *mantellus* that he wore inside the papal palace, and shoes. The texts distinguish several hats, for example the two or four hats carried before him in the solemn processions (*capellum pape qui debet esse coopertus de rubeo samito),*[26] the hat he used for travel, and the little cap (biretum) that he wore under the mitre (or thiara). Boniface IX wore just such a cap for matins of Holy Thursday and Good Friday 1391 (*cum capa et sola bireta rubea in capite).*[27] All were of red color.

Easter week was an exception. During this week, papal dress was entirely white, in association with the resurrection of Christ, whose vicar on earth was the pope. This use was described for the first time about 1410 by François de Conzié in a additional note to the *Cérémonial Long:*on Easter day in Cesaraugusta, Benedict XIII came to the chapel in a white wool mantle (*ivit ad capellam cum manto albo de lana).*[28]

Though certainly not the pope, a papal legate had all prerogatives of the Roman pontiff during his mission because he represented the pope himself. As early as the thirteenth century, he wore the papal mantle and other garments characteristic of the pope and had the papal cross carried before him. In the *Chronicles of Constantinople,* George Logothete wrote (1213 CE) that Innocent III's legate, Pelagius, wore red shoes (*calceos rubros induebat).*[29] Innocent IV gave his legate in Poland, a Dominican cardinal, permission to wear a red hat, red shoes, and red gloves (*rubeo galero, rubeis sandalis, ocreis et chirotecis rubeis caput et manus ac pedes tegerent).*[30] The *Hostiensis,* commenting on the decree letter, *Antiqua,* enumerated the papal insignia given to the legate: white horse, red mantle, red shoes, gilded saddle trappings, bridle, spurs, and baldachin.[31] Stefaneschi carefully notes that a legate was not allowed to display these insignia outside his legation territory. Immediately on his return to the Curia, a legate took ordinary cardinal's robes (*demittit cappam rubeam et birretum rubeum et assumit cappam communem et birretum tale sicut alii cardinales portant).*[32]

This usage continued until the end of our period. The form of legate's garments followed the evolution of cardinal's garments, but the red color throughout marked the designation of legate. The legate John Carjaval's *Ceremonia* written by a master of ceremonies between 1446 and 1461 describes both his exterior and interior attire as follows: " . . . outside at all times riding or walking with papal red *cappa*. . . . He gives audience to great princes in the red papal mantle with hood down; to others, with croccia and hood on the head or at least over his shoulders" *[extra domum semper cum cappa proficiscebatur, aliquando pedes aliquando aques. . . . Audienciam magnis principibus dabat cum manto rubeo papali et capucio in capite, reliquis cum croccia et capucio in capite, aut saltem supra spatulas].*[33]

By the middle decades of the fifteenth century, the legate's *cappa* no longer had the papal *cappa* form but instead followed the distinctive cardinal's form. Cardinal Francesco Picolomini for legate Giorgio da Costa (ca. 1476) noted that he was required to go "outside with a large cappa of the cardinal. . . . Inside, when he gives audience, he is to wear a clamys (also called *croccia* and similar to a *mantellus)* open at the front, pleated around shoulders, and extending to the floor. Over his head, he wears a *capucius parvus* like cardinals" *[cum autem exit domo, capam ampiam cardinalarem. . . . In domo, cum dat audienciam, habeat clamidem quam appelant crocciam autem est in forma mantelli ad terram usque, aperti tantum a parte anteriore habens circa humeros crispas circumcirca. In capite autem habebit capucium parvum quo utuntur cardinales].*[34] In addition, Burckard indicates to Cardinal Bernardino de Lunate in 1495 that a legate must wear the "rochet with *capucius (parvus)* and when he goes outside, the *cappa* of cardinals" *[rochetum cum capuccio et cum exit de domo, cappam cardinalarem . . . In domo vero cum dat audientiam habeat clamidem longuam crocciam nuncupatam sutra rochetum et capucium parvum].*[35] Finally, we note that the legate never wore the deep red velvet papal *mozetta* but always a red one similar to the cardinal's *mozetta.*

Although legates ceased wearing red garments when they returned to the Curia, it seems that, as early as the fourteenth century, they perpetuated their embassies and the honors that distinguished them by iconographic representations. Cardinals who were former legates thus had their portraits painted dressed in red garments. For example, Bertrand de Deux, cardinal of Saint-Marc and legate between 1333 and 1345, is portrayed as such in his missal (ca. 1338 / 1348) dressed in a red papal *cappa,* open at the front and lined with ermine (figure 15.1)[36] This dress was far more sumptuous than that of a cardinal's; it is understandable that a former legate preferred portrayal in the legate's red mantle rather than the ordinary garment of a simple curial cardinal.

Robes of Cardinals

In the thirteenth and fourteenth centuries, one cannot distinguish a cardinal's garments from clerical vestments except by the quality of the fabric. The cloak was made of a rather dark cloth, but never red. We have two accurate portraits of Cardinal Stefaneschi, one in his study where he is writing; the other, the altarpiece of Saint-Peter's Basilica in Rome painted by Giotto in 1315, shows the cardinal in more solemn circumstances as a donor kneeling at the feet of Christ.[37] In both portraits, he wears an ample robe tight at the waist and an open cloak. He is depicted by Giotto in a deep-blue V-shaped robe with a purple open cloak over his shoudlers

Figure 15.1. Cardinal Bertrand II in a legate's robe (between 1338 and 1348 CE). Archives of St. Peter, B. 63, f. 188v. Photo by permission of the Vatican Apostolic Library, Vatican City.

Figure 15.2. Cardinal Stefaneschi in his everyday attire, Giotto, from an altar panel at St. Peter's, Pinoteca Vatican, inv. 120.

(*in habitu violaceo quotidiano, tunica silicet et mantello*).[38] The red hat is by his side. He is portrayed in his study by the Master of the Codex of Saint George with the same kind of robe but less open; over the robe he is wearing an orange cloak with a hood (figure 15.2).[39] At the same period, cardinals wore a brownish pink cloak for the banquet of Holy Thursday.[40] During the pontificate of Innoncent VIII (ca.1485), a cardinal's *cappa* was pink or blue. Paris de Grassi (ca.1520) indicates that these colors had been abandonded and that the normal color was violet (*pavonatio*); red was exceptional and reserved for solemnities.[41] This diversity of color is found in numerous frescos of the period, for example, those in the Picolomini Library of Sienna, painted with great attention to detail between 1505 and 1507 by Pintoricchio. All of this evidence suggests that any overall rule about color of cardinal's garments must have been established after the first decades of the sixteenth century.

For mourning, only dark colors were permitted. The *Cérémonial complémentaire* describes a mourning outfit with a dark or black cloak, lined with squirrel fur. This cloak could be of blue cloth for the cardinals created by the late pope and for members of the papal family [*domini cardinales seculares portare capas obscuri, non tamen omnino nigri, folratas de grisiis, vel de sindone blavo obscuro, illi videlicet qui fuerint de genere pape defuncti et etiam alii creati per eum*].[42] Such dress is illustated in a portrait of Saint Jerome in the National Gallery of London painted by Antonello da Messina.[43] Patrizi noted that dark colored *cappa* lined with squirrel fur, which had been worn by cardinals to funeral services and during vacancies in the Holy See, were no longer worn when he wrote in the early sixteenth century.[44]

Regular cardinals, following their respective orders' vows of poverty, the same color as their brothers. An autograph note of Burckard added to Patrizi's manuscript details this practice.[45] Benedictines wore a black *cappa* with black fur; Cistercians and Augustinians wore a black robe with lateral openings for the arms and an ample hood rounded at the front; Dominicans wore a black coat open at the front, with an ample hood ; and Franciscans wore a coat and a *capucius parvus* of dark gray London cloth. Burckard notes the portrait of Franciscan Cardinal Pietro Riario (Sistus IV's nephew) in the vatican fresco of Melozzo da Forli (figure 15.3). Paris de Grassi gives somewhat different norms. In particular, Franciscans wore a black or dark violet cap (*biretum*) and a garment held by a white cord that functions as a belt (*cordula alba pro cinctura*); the other garments (*cappa* and *capucius parvus*) were of dark color, a brown nearly black, the color of leather (*colore taneo*) or like lion skin (*loenato*).[46] We can see just such a coat worn by Saint Bonaventure in the Raphael fresco, the *Dispute of the Holy Sacrament*, painted in 1509 in the apostolic palace apartments.

Acquisition of Red by Cardinals and Prelates: Hats, Caps, and Linings

The primary distinguishing feature of the college of cardinals is the well-known red hat. In the eleventh century, travelers wore such a wide hat covered with wool as a protection from the sun and bad weather. In the following century, this outmoded headgear was worn by clerics in a black color. In the thirteenth century, the form of the hat had changed little; it still shed rain well and was held in position by cords tied under the chin. Those cords were soon ornamented with decorative tassels. The red hat was a privilege granted by Innocent IV at the first Council of Lyon in 1245, "so that Cardinals might be distinguished from Chaplains" as was reported by his biographer Nicolò da Calvi.[47] This headgear was so successful that cardinals wore it even inside the palace or church when they were assisting with council duties. It was then worn with the liturgical *pluvial,* as well as ordinary and traveling outfits. The red hat was placed on the head of new cardinals with a solemnity that only grew in the course of the two following centuries.

The *birettum* (biretta) was a large, round cap covering the head and made from relatively fine wool. The cap was soft, and the cleric fashioned it as he wanted, generally giving it a square form. Tradition holds that it was Paul II who gave cardinals the right to wear a red biretta, though the actual decree has never been located. Its first mention is an addition to the *Cérémonial Long* by Antoine Rébiol, master of ceremonies of Paul II (ca. 1465); this dating of the red biretta for cardinals is, however, questionable because the permit given by Paul II was to wear a *capas de scarlata et birretos de scarlata.*[48] In this usage, the word *scarlatum* designated a fine quality fabric, not the color red. Twenty years later, however, Patrizi mentions this concession in his *Ceremonial* and indicates the red color. Its use began, therefore, about 1480, but was reserved for secular cardinals (*Paulus II instituit quod cardinales bireto rubeo uterentur).*[49]

Red also began to appear in the *cappa* of cardinals, but only at the end of the fifteenth century and then only tentatively. Patrizi indicates that cardinals should wear in the chapel or outside, a large *cappa* of violet, dark blue, bronze, or sometimes red, but rarely.[50] Burckard adds (ca. 1500), *quibus diebus cardinales consueverunt modernis temporis uti cappis de scarlato sive rosacio aut camerlotto rubeo.*[51] Paris de Grassi notes in his *Supplément* that the red *cappa* was to be worn only for great feasts; the usual colors were pink, violet of all shades, and dark colors for mourning and penitence. He outlined the composition of a new cardinal's outfits in his *Instruction to nine new cardinals* (1505); it was to include at least three *cappa* and three mozetta of violet or violet approaching red (*unam de cambelotto cremosino, aliam de*

Figure 15.3. Pope Sixtus IV and his two nephews, the Cardinals della Rovere and Riaro, o.f. m. Mellozo da Forli, Vatican City, Pinoteca, inv. 270.

panno pavonatio, tertiam de cambelotto pavonatio).[52] On the other hand, Patrizi notes that the fur of the hood of the *cappa* was to be replaced by red silk during summer, that is, from Pentecost to All Saints's Day (*utuntur serico rubei coloris loco pellium)*.[53]

Below cardinals in the pontifical hierarchy were other officials, such as curial prelates. What of their access to the color red? At the opening of the fifteenth century, curial prelates normally wore violet-colored dress; for example, master of ceremonies Pietro Burgensis received, on the occasion of the coronation of Nicolas V, eight meters of violet fabric.[54] By the end of our period, however, all curial officers had some access to the color red. Paris de Grassi, in his *Treatise of Ceremonies,* indicates that prelates should wear a robe of violet and, for feasts, a color close to red (*non rubei nec rosini maxime nimium rubentis)*.[55] The chamberlains who oversaw the papal daily service wore a red coat during the service. Outside, they wore a mauve coat with the hood fastened on the left shoulder and lined with red taffeta during summer and with ermine during winter.[56] Thus, even these minor officers and household functionaries came to wear the papal red simply because they were members of the pontifical household.

Fabrics of Curial Dress

In general, the quality of the fabric matched the rank of the official. The papal wardrobe included a large range precious fabrics, rich in silk, velvet, and scarlet. Let us begin with the fabric known as scarlet *(scarlettum);* it was this cloth, tinted red, that gave its name to the color known as scarlet.[57] As early as the end of thirteenth century, the pope's daily dress was in scarlet, put on after removing pluvial and mitre *(infula rubea de scarleto* and *tunicas et vestes de scarleto albo).* In the papal wardrobe, this fabric was either red or white. Cardinal Stefaneschi adds the detail about white color to Gregory X's *Ordo* (1273).[58] Zangger noted in Boniface VIII's inventory "40 shirts in red scarlet and 42 shirts in white scarlet" *[40 brachiatas de scalato rubeo, item 42 brach. de scarlato albo]* (1413), and "4 mantles on red scarlet and some white scarlet for the robes of the Lord" *[4 mantellos de scarlato rubeo; pro robis Domini, de scarlato albo]* (1414).[59] For Good Friday, the pope did not wear a *pluvial* but a *cappa* of red scarlet.[60] Similarly, he wore scarlet when he removed the *pluvial* after the service. This usage survived during Lent until the end of the fifteenth century. For example, for the matins of Holy Wednesday, the pope wore either a mantle with inverted hood over the head or the red scarlet *cappa (manto cum caputio inverso supra caput vel cappa rubea de scarletto).*[61]

A silk fabric often mixed with gold thread known as samit was used for liturgical vestments as early as the twelfth century.[62] Around 1345 and after, it covered the papal hat (*capellum rubeum coopertum de samito rubeo)*[63] and was the fabric of the ermine-lined *biretta (bireta de samito albo foldata de ermenis)* found in the inventories of Innocent VI (1353) and Clement VI's chapel.[64]

During the fourteenth century, except during Lent, the pope wore a *cappa* in satin or in velvet to assiat at liturgical celebrations (*cappa de satanino vel veluto).*[65] From 1430 onwards, the pope asssited at matins on Advent Sundays dressed in a red velvet *cappa (capa de velluto rubeo cum arminiis).*[66] Paris de Grassi confirms, in his *Memory to Leo X,* precisely that during Easter week *capucius* and *biretta* were from white damask (*albo damascenio eisdem bireto et caputio utitur).*[67]

We have noted that cardinals' robes were from scarlet from the early fourteenth century onward; this is the *cappa de scarlato* described by Stefaneschi. Burkhard (ca.1500) who adds that the *cappa* could be made from camelot. Silk appears at the end of the fifteenth century for the red lining of the summer *cappa*. The curial officers kept the use of simple wool, except for the apostolic subdeacon, who wore a lined black silk hat with blue cords and tassels.

Our final discussion is of the mitre, which represents another interesting case of cardinals acquiring certain papal prerogatives and is exactly parallel to the cardinals' acquisition of the color red. The mitre is, of course, a circular hat with two points used by Roman pontiffs as early as the seventh century. After 1150, it became the bishops' liturgical headgear. Roman liturgy provided three mitres according to circumstances—a precious mitre (jeweled), a golden mitre (with embroided banding), and a simple white mitre. Cardinal-bishops and cardinal-priests used all three mitres. Cardinal-deacons used only the white mitre, which they wore with the dalmatic on days when the pope celebrated mass.

The mitre was worn only for liturgy. There are few exceptions until the middle of the fourteenth century. One was during the banquet of Holy Thursday, when the mitre was worn with *mantellus.* At the papal court, the mitre was always white[68] and made of different fabrics, more or less precious according to the class of the prelate or the liturgical context. Only the pope, however, wore a mitre decorated with gold, jewels, or pearls.

Early in the fourteenth century or even before, cardinals wore, during Lent and in particular for the banquet of Holy Thursday, a mitre of modest material called *garnellus*[69] (*cardinales . . . habebunt cottas cum . . . mitris simplicibus de garnello in capite).*[70] Later in the fourteenth century, both the pope and the cardinals wore a similar white mitre for Candlemas, Ash Wednesday, and Palm Sunday[71] (*mitra alba et plana de garnello).*[72] At the end of the fourteenth century, the papal mitre for the first Sunday of Lent was "plain garnellus without pearls" *[albam et planam de garnello sine perlis].*[73] Patriarch Ameil (ca.1400) states precisely that a cardinal-priest who blessed the candles for Candlemas had to wear a "simple mitre of garnellus" *[simplice de garnello]* while the pope wore a golden mitre.[74] In a manuscript written in 1451, in the ritual of *Cérémonial Long, garnello* was replaced by pearl-adorned damask (*damasco imo de perlis).*[75] By the end of the fifteenth century, cardinals are the only prelates who used a damasked silk mitre (*mitre cardinalium sunt ex serico damaschino).*[76] Thus, by the end of our period, we have shown that while staying white, the mitre of cardinals had, in fact, taken over the fabric of the papal mitre. The papal mitre, even during Lent, was required to be distinguished from the college of cardinals by further ornamentation—gold thread, pearls, or jewels.

Conclusion

Beginning in the eleventh century, the power of the cardinals grew; they began to take precedence over other prelates and gain the power exclusively to elect the pontiff (Bulle *in nomine Domini,* by Nicolas II in 1059) and Innocent III ultimately made them his intimate counselors. By the end of the thirteenth and into the fourteenth centuries, they gained more power in direct Church governance. To be a cardinal represented the height of power, each representing a potential pope. The cardinals stood in front of the king at the papal chapel, and papal legates exclusively represented the pope within their domains. The shift toward red (formerly an exclusively papal color) for cardinals' robes symbolized the growing power of the cardinals.

Throughout the long evolution of cural dress, the pope remained master over the form, color, and type of allowed fabrics. He first granted his distinctive mantle to his legates and his red hat to the cardinals; later the popes allowed all cardinals to use the color red in any or all of their vestments. It seems, however, that the cardinals occasionally forced the pope's hand. Cardinals who were papal legates were entitled to dress in red during the terms of their legations and were required to don ordinary cardinal's robes when they returned to the Curia. Nevertheless, several legates, upon their return, sat for portraits in full red vestments, implicitly in violation of canonical law.

These prerogatives, given and taken, did not, however, vitiate the overall shape of papal power as it had been constituted after the Great Schism. This process represented neither a displacement or usurpation of papal power but rather power delegated. The cardinals remained securely subordinate to the pope, with whom they shared Church governance. The *cæremoniale episcoporum,* published in 1600, codified such relationships. During the following centuries, we do not find radical changes but generally stronger aspirations of the clergy to wear red or violet garments.Centuries later, this aspiration reached some kind of apogee during the pontificate of Pius XI (1921–1939), when all ecclesiastical dignitaries, even the lowest, were allowed to dress in some splendor, thus participating in the splendor of the Papal Court and His Holiness's majesty. All of these vanities were withdrawn after the Council ofVatican II; the pope and the cardinals took back the splendor of imperial purple for their exclusive use.

Notes

1. Michel Pastoureau, "Et puis, vint le bleu," *Europe* 654 (983): 43–50.
2. Marc Dykmans, *Le Cérémonial papal de la fin du Moyen-Age à la Renaissance,* 4 volumes, Bibliothèque de l'Institut historique belge, 24–27 (Rome: Institut historique belge, 1975–1984). vol. 1, *Le Cérémonial papal du XIII° siècle* (1975); vol. 2, D*e Rome en Avignon ou le Cérémonial de Jacques Stefaneschi* (Rome, 1981); vol. 3, *Les textes avignonais jusqu'à la fin du grand schisme* (Rome, 1983); vol. 4, *Le retour à Rome ou le Cérémonial du patriarche Pierre Ameil* (Rome, 1984); in abbreviation: text title; ed. Dykmans, vol. 1, 2, 3, or 4; and *L'Oeuvre de Patrizi Piccolomini ou le Cérémonial de la première Renaissance,* 2 volumes (Vatican City: Biblioteca apostolica vaticana, 1980); in

abbreviation: *Patrizi;* ed. Dykmans, vol. 1 or 2.

3. *Ordo de Grégoire X,* ed. Dykmans, 1:194.
4. *Cérémonial de Stefaneschi,* ed. Dykmans, 2: 328.
5. *Ordo de Grégoire X,* ed. Dykmans, 1:159. The dalmatic was a long, loose, wide-sleeved vestment open at the sides, worn by deacons and bishops and by a monarch at his or her coronation.
6. *Cérémonial long,* ed. Dykmans, 3:238.
7. *Cérémonial complémentaire,* ed. Dykmans, 3:315.
8. *Cérémonial long,* ed. Dykmans, 3:161.
9. *Le Diaire de François de Conzié,* of December 11 and 13, 1406; ed. Dykmans, 3:392–93.
10. Correspondence between François de Conzié and Pedro de Luna, nephew of Benedict XIII, January 10, 1409. *Cérémonial complémentaire,* introduction; ed. Dykmans, 3:49.
11. *Cérémonial du patriarche Pierre Ameil,* ed. Dykmans, 4:141, 1.
12. *Kunsthistorisches Museum,* Vienna, inventory number 975.
13. *Patrizi,* ed. Dykmans, 1: 41.
14. Later, this dress will be called mozetta, from the Italian word *mozzo,* which means cut, because it is a reduction *a minima* of the *cappa* with a little hood corresponding to the hood of the *cappa.* Pallavicino in his *Storia del Concilio di Trento* (Montrouge: Migne, 1844), 5; chapter 13 calls the *caputius: cappa breve* or *mozza;* cited by Gaetano Moroni, *Dizionario di erudizione storico-ecclesiastica* (Venezia: Tipografia emiliana, 1847), 47: 31.
15. *Patrizi,* ed. M. Dykmans, 1:184.
16. *Patrizi,* ed. M. Dykmans, 1:41.
17. *Missal of Cardinal Pucci* reproduced in *Biblioteca apostolica vaticana, Liturgie und Andacht im Mittelalter (*Köln: Erzbichöfliches Diözesanmuseum, 1992), 405.
18. Michel Pastoureau, "Vers une histoire de la couleur bleu," *Sublime Indigo* (Fribourg: 1987), p. 21.
19. H.W. Klewitz, "Die Krönung des papstes." *Zeitschrift der Savigny-Stiftung für Rechtsgeschichte* 3 (1941): 120.
20. Cited by Agostino Paravicini Bagliani, *Le corps du pape* (Paris: Seuil, 1997), 106.
21. Cited by Agostino Paravicini Bagliani, *Le corps du pape,* 104.
22. *Le Liber Censuum,* published and annotated by P. Fabre et L. Duchesne (Paris: Fontemoine, 1910), 1:311 and 2:123.
23. *Ordo de Grégoire X,* ed. Dykmans, 1:159
24. *Ordo de Grégoire X,* ed. Dykmans, 1:160
25. The rochet formed part of episcopal church dress since the twelfth century. It is in fact a shortened alb. The Pope wore an alb, the *alba romana,* which was shortened by a sash and produced the same effect.
26. *Cérémonial long,* ed. Dykmans, 3:178.
27. *Cérémonial du patriarche Pierre Ameil,* ed. Dykmans, 4:234.
28. *Cérémonial long,* add ca. 1410; ed. Dykmans, 3:234.

29. Franz Wasner, "Fifteenth-century texts on the ceremonial of the papal Legatus a Latere," *Traditio,* Rome, 14 (1958): 301.
30. Franz Wasner, "Fifteenth-century texts," 301.
31. Franz Wasner, "Fifteenth-century texts," 302.
32. *Cérémonial de Stefaneschi,* ed. Dykmans, 2:500.
33. F. Wasner, "Fifteenth-century texts," p. 326.
34. F. Wasner, "Fifteenth-century texts," p. 329.
35. F. Wasner, "Fifteenth-century texts," p. 343.
36. *Missal of Cardinal Bertrand de Deux,* reproducted in *Biblioteca apostolica vaticana, Liturgie,* 218.
37. Vatican City, *Pinacoteca vaticana,* Inventory number 120.
38. Cited by Dykmans, *Le Cérémonial papal,* 2:118, n.427.
39. *Codex of Saint George,* fol. 17r, reproduced in *Biblioteca apostolica vaticana, Liturgie,* 214; and fol. 41r, reproduced in Gerhart Ladner, *Die päpstbildnisse des Altertums und des Mittelalters* (Rome: Pontificio istituto di archeologia cristiana, 1970), 2:271.
40. *Cérémonial Stefaneschi,* ed. Dykmans, 2:375.
41. Paris de Grassi, *Traité des Cérémonies,* fol. 24v from Mucante edition, cited by Dykmans, "Paris de Grassi," *Ephemerides liturgicae* (1986): 289.
42. *Cérémonial complémentaire,* ed. Dykmans, 3:266.
43. Dated from ca.1475–1476, showing St. Jerome in his study wearing dark red *cappa* of cardinal with a fur-lined hood. London, National Gallery, inventory number 1418.
44. *Patrizi,* ed. Dykmans, 2:503.
45. Marc Dykmans, "L'habit de chapelle des prélats des ordres religieux," *Patrizi,* 2:541. Burckard does not distinguish between the dress of cardinals and of the other prelates.
46. Cited by M. Dykmans, "Paris de Grassi," *Ephemerides liturgicae* (1985): 415.
47. F. Pagnotti, "Niccolò da Calvi e la sua vita d'Innocento IV con una breve intraduzione sulla istoriografia pontificia dei secoli XIII e XIV," *Archivio della reale Società di storia patria* 21 (1898): 97.
48. Vatican City, Biblioteca Apostolica vaticana, MS Vat. Borgia lat. 409. Text for Candlemas in *Cérémonial long, l'Année liturgique,* chapter 78. Manuscript annotated by Antoine Rébiol, papal master of ceremonies from Nicolas V (1447) to Sixtus IV (1484); ed. Dykmans, 3:182–83.
49. *Patrizi,* ed. Dykmans, 2:503.
50. *Patrizi,* ed. Dykmans, 2:503.
51. *Patrizi,* ed. Dykmans, 2:531.
52. Paris de Grassi, *Instruction aux neuf nouveaux cardinaux, le 12 décembre 1505,* Vatican City, Biblioteca Apostolica vaticana, MS Vat. lat. 4739, fol. 148; cited by M. Dykmans, "Paris de Grassi," 412.
53. *Patrizi,* ed. Dykmans, 2:503.
54. *Registres aux Mandats,* Rome, Archivio di Stato, MS Cam, I, reg. 831, fol.19v; cited by Dykmans, "Le cérémonial de Nicolas V," *Revue d'histoire ecclésiastique* 63 (1968): 375, n. 2.

55. Paris de Grassi, *Traité des Cérémonies,* fol. 24v from Mucante edition; cited by M. Dykmans, "Paris de Grassi," 289.
56. Paris de Grassi, *Traité des Cérémonies,* fol. 279 from Mucante edition; cited by Dykmans, "Paris de Grassi," 314.
57. See, on fabrics, Bernard Berthod, "Etoffes à la Cour papale du XIII° au XV° siècle," *Bulletin du CIETA* 74 (1998): 53–61.
58. *Cérémonial Stefaneschi,* ed. Dykmans, 2:268.
59. Kurt Zangger, *Contribution à la terminologie des tissus en ancien français attestés dans les textes français, provençaux, italiens, espagnols, allemands et latins* (Bienne: Shüller, 1945), 54. The author thanks Dr. Peter Honneger and Mrs. Elisabeth Scheidegger, curators at *Abegg-Stiftung* who have permitted him to consult the work of Zangger. See also E. Molinier, "Inventaire du Trésor du Saint-Siège sous Boniface VIII (1295)," *Bibliothèque de l'Ecole des Chartes* 43 (1882): 19–310 and 626–46.
60. *Cérémonial long, la messe papale,* ed. Dykmans, 3:161.
61. *Patrizi,* ed. Dykmans, 2:365. The papal *cappa* differed from that of cardinals by the position of hood, which was *inverso,* that is, inside out; around 1480, this configuration was dropped in favor of that of the cardinals.
62. Elisabeth Hardouin-Fugier, Bernard Berthod, and Martine Chavent-Fusaro, *Dictionnaire historique des Etoffes* (Paris: L'Amateur, 1994), 339.
63. *Cérémonial long,* ed. Dykmans, 3:180.
64. Hermann Hoberg, *Die Inventare des päpstlichen Schatzes in Avignon 1314–1376,* (Vatican City: Bibiloteca apostolica vaticana, 1944), 196–284.
65. *Cérémonial complémentaire,* ed. Dykmans, 3:314.
66. *Cérémonial long, l'année liturgique* the copy of cardinal Prospero Colonna, ca. 1430; ed. Dykmans, 3:242.
67. Vatican City, Biblioteca Apostolica vaticana, MS Borghese I 568 fols. 262v–265. Cited by Dykmans, *Paris de Grassi,* op. cit. (1986): 329–31.
68. The only exception is when a cardinal or a hight prelate celebrates pontifically in front of the pope. He can wear a precious mitre if litugical time permits. See *Cérémonial du Patriarche Pierre Ameil,* 10; ed. Dykmans, t. 4, p. 70.
69. This fabric is cited in price lists of salt tax of Sienna from 1388 to 1452, defined by Maria Assunta Ceppari as a fabric of cotton and wool or short or piled cotton and very simple dress that takes the name of this fabric. M. A. Ceppari, *Drappi, velluti, taffettà e altre cose, antichi tessuti a Sienna e nel suo territorio* (Sienna: Nuova Immagine, 1994), p. 249 and 75n.
70. *Cérémonial Stefaneschi,* ch. 87 § 7; ed. Dykmans, t. 2, p. 375.
71. *Cérémonial Stefaneschi,* chap. 78, §15–16; ed. Dykmans, t. 2, p. 356.
72. *Cérémonial long, l'année liturgique,* § 2; ed. Dykmans, t. 3, p. 183.
73. *Cerémonial du Patriarche Pierre Ameil,* § 253; ed. Dykmans, t. 4, p. 105.
74. *Cérémonial du Patriarche Pierre Ameil,* § 112–13; ed. Dykmans, t. 4, p. 85.
75. *Cérémonial long, l'année liturgique,* § 2, apparat.; ed. Dykmans, t. 3, p. 183.
76. Patrizi, § 1576; ed. Dykmans, t. 2, p. 499.

CHAPTER 16

ROBING AND ITS SIGNIFICANCE IN ENGLISH MYSTERY PLAYS

Martial Rose

Introduction

English medieval mystery plays flourished during the fifteenth and the first half of the sixteenth centuries. They were performed in cities and country towns as out-of-door productions, at first at the time of the feast of Corpus Christi (first Thursday after Trinity Sunday), but later over the Whitsun holiday. An early characteristic of the Corpus Christi celebration was an elaborate procession in which the Host was carried aloft in the company of the district's chief ecclesiastical and lay representatives clad in their ceremonial robes.

The plays told stories of selected parts of the Old and New Testaments. The selection was largely based on the readings of the church year that illustrated how events in the Old Testament were fulfilled in the New. Apocryphal elements abounded, and some of the action, such as the death of Cain, bore little in common with the biblical version. The plays were in the vernacular, in contrast to Latin of the liturgy, and in contrast to the Latin or Anglo-French of contemporary liturgical drama. The mystery plays asserted an aggressive championing of the vernacular at the expense of Latin and French, which were frequently held up to ridicule. Such a class attitude also informed the political and social stance within the text of the plays. These plays, from the end of the fourteenth century to well into the sixteenth century, were often amended if not wholly rewritten. New versions would reflect changing contemporary religious, political, and social pressures, among which was the oppression exerted by the ruling class and their "maintenance men," the hired, liveried henchmen who acted as their masters' "heavies" and feathered their own nest at the same time. Current fashions of dress were often the butt of the authors' humor.

The few extant manuscripts of the mystery plays are compilations by anonymous authors, most probably minor clergy or friars whose preaching medium was the vernacular. A central civic authority, a religious guild, or a trade guild most likely commissioned the writing or rewriting of these extant texts. At York and Chester, the trade guilds under the supervision of the appropriate civic control presented the plays. At Wakefield, the role of the earlier religious guilds gave way in the sixteenth century to trade guilds. In Lincoln, however, a religious guild, St. Anne's, remained most influential in mounting the plays.

In each case presentation was in contemporary costume, and the guild accounts furnish fascinating details of properties and costumes used. The plays at York, for instance, were sectioned out among a great number of competing guilds, forty-eight in the extant manuscript. On the whole no play would last longer than thirty minutes. There was keen rivalry between guilds to mount a production of the highest standards, for example, in the management of properties and costuming, and efforts were made to secure the best actors within the guild, or even to poach talent from elsewhere. Medieval guild records cast light on such practices.

The mystery plays were finally suppressed in the reign of Queen Elizabeth, as much for political as for religious reasons. The plays had originated as part of a religious festival, celebrated throughout Europe. But in England their popular appeal, bringing large groups of people together in a legitimate activity through which was frequently expressed political and social unease, was considered a threat to the peace of the realm. The suppression of the plays was easily accomplished in the south of England near the seat of government. In the north, where the old faith lingered more tenaciously, suppression was not effective until about 1576, the year that the very first professional theater opened in London. (It would be of some interest to know to what extent the great wardrobes of the mystery plays were absorbed into those of the burgeoning professional theater.)

Fortunately, the story of the mystery plays does not end with their Elizabethan suppression. Largely forgotten and certainly unperformed for centuries, the plays were rediscovered by researchers in the twentieth century. Today, mystery plays have been revived in all their medieval glory both in their original cities and in many additional sites worldwide.

The Paradox

The monarchs of medieval England followed a well-established tradition of wearing their crowns on certain festival occasions, prominent among which were Christmas, the New Year, and Easter. Winchester and Westminster were the centers at which coronations took place for the late Anglo-Saxon and Norman kings. The royal mint was also located in these two centers, which became especially identified with the monarch, crowned and in his full regalia, showing largesse to his subjects. During the reigns of the Angevin and Plantagent monarchs, however, Winchester diminished in importance. These monarchs, together with the Lancastrian and York kings of the fifteenth century, found it essential to move about the country—establishing their authority, sitting in judgment on wrong-doers, hearing the pleas of the plaintiffs, and above all, showing themselves in their majestic splendor and dispensing their royal gifts where their favor fell.

The magnificence of their robes and the richness of the gifts that they were able to bestow helped to distance the monarchs from their subjects. Generally, it was a distinction that the subjects expected and revered. When kingly magnificence, however, spilt over into wanton extravagance enriching a handful of favorites to the economic detriment of the country, as in the last decade of Richard II's reign, public reaction was to smooth the path for his usurping successor, Henry Bolingbroke. On the other hand, when the king's subjects perceived that their monarch lacked all sense of kingly magnificence and seemed content to leave the management of his state to incompetent counselors or even to his wife (as was the case with Henry VI), the usurper's path to power was again eased.

It was during the fifteenth century under the Lancastrian and Yorkist monarchs that the mystery plays were at their peak. The supreme figure of authority was God, who appeared in most of the Old Testament plays: creating the universe; instructing Noah about building the ark; directing Abraham to sacrifice his only son, Isaac; speaking to Moses out of the burning bush. In the New Testament plays, God's intervention was less direct and took place more through the agency of angels to Mary and Joseph; to the shepherds and the Magi; to John before the baptism of Christ; and to the three Marys at the Resurrection.

Various extant texts and guild accounts make clear the grandeur of the figures of God and his angels. The plays prescribe comparable magnificence for the appearances of those who set themselves up against God's will: Lucifer, Pharaoh, Caesar Augustus, King Herod, and the high priests, Annas and Caiaphas.

In radical contrast to these magnificently robed figures is the character of Jesus, who was humbly dressed in the plays and who, on his way to becoming the savior of the world, was divested of what few garments he had and crucified nearly naked on the cross. This King of kings offered his largesse to men in a way far removed from that shown by those medieval monarchs or by those masterful tyrants in the mystery plays.

Heaven

The overarching presence of God was felt throughout the mystery plays (figure 16.1). In most of the extant cycles he had a substantial speaking part in the first section of the Old Testament plays, and even when he was not speaking references were made to his overlooking presence. The Son of God and the Holy Ghost were at times also depicted with God in heaven. In *The Parliament of Heaven* of the *N-Town Play,* both had speaking roles, and they took part with God in an impressive stage action to mark the Immaculate Conception. The stage direction in *The Salutation and Conception* reads as follows:

> Here the Holy Ghost descends with three beams to our Lady, the Son of the Godhead next with three beams to the Holy Ghost, the Father godly with three beams to the Son. And so enter all three into her bosom.

The material contact through the three sets of three beams, from God the Father, God the Son, and God the Holy Ghost, to the bosom of Mary exemplifies the concreteness of medieval imagery. In these plays, the costuming of the Trinity before the incarnation might not distinguish among the three crowned and robed figures sitting on thrones, apart from the positioning. The Son would be on God's right and the Holy Ghost on his left. The costuming of the Trinity at the last judgment would show Christ wearing his crown of thorns and displaying the stigmata.

In the *N-Town Play* Anima Christi, the Spirit of Christ, appeared once Christ has died on the cross. Anima Christi's function was to go down to the gates of hell to challenge, overcome, and bind Satan and his fellow demons, and then to break down the gates of hell and lead to paradise those souls awaiting redemption, Adam and Eve and the prophets. Anima Christi carried a cross staff from the top of which flew a red cross pennant. Such confrontations at the gates of hell between Anima Christi or, in the other cycles, Christ with Satan and his fallen angels, were presented in the plays as the action of a castle siege or as knights errant about to engage in combat.

In Norwich the Grocers were responsible for the play *Paradise,* which tells the story of Adam and Eve's fall and their expulsion from paradise. The Grocers' accounts for 1534 list the players with various payments for expenses—in pence (contracted to "d") and shillings (contracted to "s"). Twelve pence made a shilling. For example, "a new wig and a crown for the Serpent" cost 6d. God the Father was played by Jeffrey Tybnam, who was paid 16d—not necessarily a professional fee but rather out-of-pocket expenses. Tybnam was paid considerably more than twice as much as any

Figure 16.1. God blesses his Creation. Norwich Cathedral ceiling boss, ca.1470. Photo copyright Julia Hedgecoe. Used by permission.

of the other players: Adam, 6d; Eve, Angel, and Serpent, 4d each. It was perhaps the importance of the role, a senior rank Tybnam held within the Grocers' Guild, or even the cost of the maintenance of God's costume from year to year that was responsible for his high fee. The props and costumes were a steady expense. In 1565, for example, a mask and a wig were made for God the Father, and a coat and ape's skin for an angel. And in that year provision was made for a painted coat, hose, and tail for the Serpent and also a white wig.

No women would have acted any of the parts in the plays at Norwich, but the upper part of the Serpent was often shown as feminine. To Eve the serpent is an attractive figure. When Adam returns from his walk in the garden Eve tells him:

> An angel came from God's grace
> And gave me an apple from this tree[1]

It was not until after the Serpent has received God's curse that he is condemned to wriggle on his belly:

> On thy womb then shalt thou glide,
> And be ay ful of enmity.[2]

Angels appeared in feathered costumes or ape's skins. They were invariably winged. The Mercers of York were responsible for the presentation of *The Judgement Day.* In their pageant documents of 1433, reference is made to six great angels holding the signs of Christ's passion. One of them carried a latten (an alloy of copper and zinc) banner and wore on his head a gilded iron cross. Such a cross probably indicated archangelic status. The same account then refers to four smaller gilded angels holding other signs of the passion, and nine yet smaller angels, painted red, to run about in heaven. Mention in this document is also made of a requirement for two pairs of angels' wings tipped with iron.[3] The actors playing the parts of angels did so mostly in bare feet. This was so that they could not be mistaken for cloven-hoofed devils pretending to be angels.[4] Contemporary iconography shows the archangel Michael expelling Adam and Eve from paradise with a flaming sword, and the archangel Gabriel, as the ambassador from God to the Virgin Mary, carrying in his hand a scepter, the symbol of his office. The two angels appearing in the Chester *Resurrection* were played by boys in white garments. Mary Salome approaching the tomb said:

> Two children I see there sitting
> all of white is their clothing.[5]

The angel in the York *Resurrection* was also apparently played by a boy. The first Mary said:

> Sisters! a young child as we go
> Making mourning,
> I see it sit where we went to
> In white clothing.[6]

The accounts of the Coventry Cappers, the guild that had the responsibility for the *Resurrection,* itemized payments for the cast in the 1530–1550 period. Two angels received 4d each whereas other payments were as follows:

> Pilate . . . 4s; God . . . 16d; Spirit of God . . . 16d; Mary . . . 12d;
> 2 bishops . . . 2s

This Coventry "God" was paid the same as the Norwich "God," which was, as we have seen, far in excess of the receipts of all the other players. In Coventry, however, it was the actor playing Pilate who received the most money. The role of Pilate was given to an actor virtually of professional status; his costume and his properties, as we shall see later, also accord with that status. In contrast, the boys playing the angels in their simple white garments were paid the minimum rate.

Pilate, Pharaoh, Herod, and Satan were among the parts most highly rewarded. To their costume and properties most attention was paid. The clothing of Jesus is given scant reference in the guild records, and indeed the actor playing Jesus was only moderately remunerated. But the actor playing God was well rewarded. For instance, in the Coventry Drapers' play of the *Last Judgement* Robert Croo (the actor in 1562) received 3s 4d. The Drapers' accounts in 1565 record "a pair of gloves for God . . . 2d, 3 yards of red sendall (a rich silken material) . . . 20d."

The majesty of God was also conveyed by a special mask and wig. "A face and hair of the Father" is an entry in the Norwich Grocers' accounts for 1563. The York Mercers' accounts provided for a gilded visor for God. And in the Chester mystery plays in 1567–1568, God had his face gilded for 12d. The actor playing the part of the twelve-year old Jesus in *The Doctors* is named in the Smiths' accounts "the little god." In 1563–1564, he had his face gilded for 12d and a horse provided for him for 3d.

The magnificence of God is shown in the first group of plays that deals with the creation, and in the last play the *Last Judgement.* In York the first group consisted of *The Creation and the Fall of Lucifer, The Creation to the Fifth Day, God Creates Adam and Eve, Adam and Eve in the Garden of Eden,*

Man's Disobedience and Fall, and *Adam and Eve Driven from Eden.* God and his angels are dominant; the Son and the Holy Ghost do not appear. The Son, however takes a prominent part in *The Judgement Day* of York as he does in all the plays about Doomsday. In the Chester version God appears surrounded by his angels, whom he instructs to show the instruments of Christ's passion: the cross, the crown of thorns, the sponge, the spear, and the nails. Both good and evil souls await their doom. Jesus descends in a cloud that stays suspended above the earth, from where he passes judgment on all, as the angels showing the instruments of his passion stand by.

The first and the last plays with scenes of creation and judgment required large casts. The guilds that produced these plays were usually appropriately chosen for their wealth, organizational skills, and for their ready access to the materials specially required in the plays. The Chester Tanners were responsible for *The Fall of Lucifer,* and the Drapers for *Adam and Eve.* The Towneley play of the *Creation and the Fall of Adam and Eve* was also, in the sixteenth century, the responsibility of the Tanners. It was the York Tanners who staged the *Creation.* In the Coventry plays there is reference to God's coat of white leather comprising six skins.[7] White leather was also a stage convention for conveying nudity. The York Drapers were standing by to clothe Adam and Eve after the Fall. The Chester Weavers, were, however, even more purposefully employed as the guild responsible for Chester's *Judgement.* They were not only able to emphasize the grandeur of God and his angels but could provide the rich materials in which so many of the damned souls were dressed, and for which those souls in their vanity and pride were condemned to "the everlasting bonfire."

Middle-Earth and Hell

The hierarchical structure of the Middle Ages was mirrored in the staging of the mystery plays in which all the action is played out in heaven, middle-earth, or hell. But hell was provided for Lucifer and the fallen angles before middle-earth became available for man. In the Towneley cycle, after the fifth day's work of creation, God retired. The Cherubim praised God and singled out Lucifer whom God had made brighter than all other angels:

> We love thee, Lord, bright are we,
> But none of us so bright as he.[8]

God in introducing himself as all powerful, alpha and omega, never refers to his personal appearance. In contrast, Lucifer's first speech is wholly concerned with his physical comeliness:

I am so fair and bright,
From me comes all this light
This glamour and this glee.[9]

He presumes to sit in God's throne, which precipitates the fall to hell of Lucifer and his attendant angels. As they fall they turn from angels to devils. Both their garments and their faces change in their descent; they shed their angelic outer costume and wings to reveal demons underneath. In the Chester play of *Lucifer,* it is clear that masks too have been changed. The Second Demon turning on Satan says, "the devil may speed thy stinking face." The extraordinarily high expense in the Coventry Drapers' accounts for 1568 underlines the dramatic importance and the popular appeal of the devils': "paid to the two devils . . . 3s. 4d, paid for making the two devils' masks . . . 10s."[10]

While the part of God in the Old Testament plays was substantial, his speeches, apart from his presence in the Garden of Eden, were usually made from God's throne on high. When he needed to communicate at middle-earth level, he sent his angels: for instance, in the Chester play of *Balaack and Balaam* or in the Nativity sequences in each of the cycles. Satan's intervention, on the other hand, was treated very differently. Satan brought about the fall of Adam and Eve in Paradise. Within touching distance of them he offered Eve the apple. Their nakedness at their creation was one of their glories. Following their fall they became ashamed of their nakedness, and God, in the Chester play of *Adam* presented by the Drapers, put "garments of skin upon them."

Satan's temptation of Christ in the plays followed in broad outline the biblical version, a dialogue between two superhuman beings. But there are a number of examples when Satan rubbed shoulders with the men and women of middle-earth, with grim humor reminding them of their sins, prominent among which is their penchant for extravagant and even absurd styles of dress.

Passion Play 1 of the *N-Town Play* followed two plays of Christ's ministry, *The Woman Taken in Adultery* and *The Raising of Lazarus.* A prologue was written to lead the audience towards *The Conspiracy* and *The Betrayal.* Satan spoke the first 124 lines of the prologue and John the Baptist the last 41 lines. John's speech urged repentance, but Satan as he walked among the audience noted their peculiar sins and gleefully promised them damnation. As he approached different members of the audience, he remarked both on his own dress and on the fashions of the age to which he drew the attention of his listeners: long pointed shoes of fine cordovan leather; costly crimson hose; fine silver points; the best Holland cloth—as yet not paid for; a French waistcoat of the finest material; a doublet stuffed with cotton wool that made the wearer look quite out of proportion with two small legs and a great body; and long hair overlapping the collar, with sidelocks infested with lice.

Satan's account, written in the middle of the fifteenth century against the dress fashions of the time, accorded with the sumptuary laws of the period, which were aimed at restricting such sartorial excesses in the vain hope that through proclamation and prescription each member of society would dress according to his degree and be so recognized. A range of colors, fabrics, furs, and styles of dress and headdress were set aside for exclusive use of the nobility. The gentry were prescribed their clothing according to their income. Laws placed special limits upon commoners wearing furs or fabrics purchased from abroad. It would seem, however, that from the introduction of sumptuary laws in the fourteenth century until the end of the sixteenth century no strict enforcement took place; the result was a blurring in rank and worth as the lower orders aped the styles of the higher. In a world that was held together by a close observation of rank and order, such a blurring was a recipe for chaos. The church repeatedly deplored such a situation, although many a churchman, such as Chaucer's Monk, was in the front rank of the offenders. The churchmen in the fifteenth century who wrote and rewrote the mystery plays exposed not just the extravagance and absurdity of fashionable dress but often identified the wearers, especially those who overreached their class and pocket, as sinners beyond redemption.

The N-Town Play is noted for its extended stage directions, which give details of the clothing of many of the characters. The plays of Christ's passion that follow Satan's and John the Baptist's *Prologue* are rich in references. The forces of evil conspire against Jesus through guile, false witness, corrupt trials, and violence to bring about his death. The chief actors in the earlier part of this sequence are Annas and Caiaphas and four doctors of law. The stage direction that begins the *Conspiracy* is as follows:

> Here shall Annas show himself on his stage arrayed as a bishop of the old law in a scarlet gown, and over that a blue tabard furred with white, and a mitre on his head after the old law. Two doctors stand by him in furred hoods, and one stands before them with his staff of office. And each of them on their heads wears a furred cap with a great tassel in the crown. And one stands before them as a Saracen who will act as messenger.[11]

When Caiaphas appeared he was dressed similarly to Annas except that his tabard was red, furred with white.[12] And when the next two doctors of law, Rewfyn and Leyon, entered they were dressed in furred tabards with furred hoods about their necks.[13] The impression given was one of color, class, and authority. The bishops and lawyers were wrapped in furs and flaunted their power, even to the extent of having a Saracen serving as their messenger. Annas and Caiaphas were seen as bishops rather than high priests of the Jewish faith. They were not, however, parodied as corrupt bishops of the English church. Such treatment would have been alien to medieval literary practice. They were treated as the enemies of Christ. The presence of the Saracen emphasized this. The audience neither demanded nor expected an accurate historical setting. The Saracen, like the oaths sworn to Mohammed by Pharaoh, Caesar Augustus, Pilate, or Herod, was a sign of the enmity shown to Christ especially by "foreigners," epitomizing the crusading struggle between good and evil.

Plays about Doomsday often contained reference to the sinful indulgence of overdressing. In the Chester Weavers *Judgement* the Saved Queen repented her earthly yearning to be dressed in rich, soft silks and velvets. In the Towneley *Judgement,* the demons carried scrolls in which the sins of the Evil Souls were listed, including the common addiction to the latest fashions. Tutivillus, the arch devil, enjoyed tormenting his victims, one of whom was a woman with a horned headdress, a sign of the devil himself:[14]

> If she be never so foul a dowd, with her nets and her pins,
> The shrew can her shroud, both her cheeks and her chins;
> She can caper full proud with japes and with gins,
> Her head high in a cloud, but not shamed by her sins
>   Or evil;
> With this powder and paint,
> She plans to look quaint,
> She may smile like a saint,
> But at heart is a devil.
> She is horned like a cow, and full secret her sin;
> Her side gaiter hangs down, furred with a cat's skin . . . [15]

Tutivillus declared that such fashions "bring wedlock to break." And he criticized such excesses as pranked up gowns with shoulders set ridiculously high, stuffed with flock, and the practice of men being scantily clad below the waist:

> Yet of the sins seven something special
> Now quickly to reckon that runs over all;
> These lads that strut even as lords most royal,
> To be pictured even in royal robes withal,
> As kings:
> His tail may none dock it,
> A codpiece like a pocket,

He scorns not to cock it
When he his tail wrings.
His buttocks they bulge like a fulling mill clog,
His head like a stook bristles like a hog,
His blown up belly filled full like a frog,
This Jelian Juke drives he no dog
To shelter.
But with your yellow locks
For all your many mocks,
Ye shall climb on hell's cross
With a halfpenny halter.[16]

The 1463 sumptuary statute attempted to restrict such masculine exposure as Tutivillus comments on to the upper classes. Only the nobility were allowed any item of clothing "unless it be of such a length that the same, he being upright, may cover his members and buttocks."[17]

Within the Old and New Testament plays, Pharaoh, Caesar August, Pilate, Herod, and the high priests Annas and Caiaphas were archetypal "overdressed" sinful tyrants (figure 16.2). Their rich costumes and accessories, such as crowns, mitres, and scepters, frequently appear in guilds' accounts. In 1571, for example, the Chester Coopers recorded a payment of 6d for the carrying of Pilate's clothes.[18] Like other heavily costumed actors, such as Satan, those playing tyrants received high payments. We might speculate that the success of the play depended on their elaborate dress and bombastic behavior more than on the restrained action and costumes of Jesus, the Virgin Mary, or the angels. An example from the Coventry Smiths' accounts of 1477 underlines the disparity between payments to the actor playing Jesus and other characters in a play in the Passion sequence:

To Jesus for gloves and all	22d
To Herod	3s. 8d
To Pilate	3s. 4d
To Pilate's wife	2s. 0d
To Caiaphas	2s. 6d
To Annas	2s. 2d
To the beadle	3s. 0d

A tyrant's entry was often preceded by retainers warning the audience of their lord's approach; he then appeared, often flailing about with his scepter, a bludgeon stuffed with straw, or in the case of the Coventry Pilate with a pole-axe. In the Coventry *Pageant of the Shearmen and Tailors,* Herod made his appearance brandishing a falchion, a short curved sword:

Figure 16.2. Pharaoh drowning in the Red Sea. Norwich Cathedral ceiling boss, ca. 1470. Photo copyright Julia Hedgecoe. Used by permission.

Behold my countenance and my colour,
Brighter than the sun in the middle of the day.
From where can you find more powerful succour,
Than to behold my person that is so gay?
My falchion and my fashion, with my gorgeous array . . .[19]

Crowds eagerly awaited the spectacular costumes and banter of the overlords and the tormenting devils. The chief agent of devilry in the mid-fifteenth-century morality play *Mankind,* for example, had his approach announced by the rest of the cast but would not make his appearance until a collection was taken.[20] Given the popularity of the "overdressed" sinful characters, what would keep the audience focused on Christ, poorly arrayed and, in the sections with Annas and Caiaphas, Pilate and Herod, almost silent?

The Robing of Christ

In stark contrast to the gay silks, velvets, and furs associated with the "tyrants," Christ's own garments were utterly unremarkable. In the N-Town *Conspiracy with Judas,* Leyon, for example, one of the doctors of law, while plotting with Judas the arrest of Christ admits that as each of the disciples is dressed in exactly the same way as their master they might well arrest the wrong man. And it is for that reason that Judas says, "Take the man that I shall kiss."[21]

In the mystery plays, the birth of Jesus Christ was heralded through prophecy, through the journey of the Magi, through the warnings given to Caesar Augustus and King Herod. Christ's Nativity scene, in all of the extant plays, emphasizes his nakedness, vulnerability, and cold.

In the Towneley *Second Shepherds' Play,* for example, the shepherds arrived at the manger immediately after Mak the sheepstealer and his wife Gill conspired to put a stolen sheep in their cot and pretend it was their newborn child. The shepherds eventually recovered their sheep, identifying it in the cradle as the Devil himself:

Will you see how they swaddle
His four feet in the middle.
Saw I never in a cradle
A horned lad ere now.[22]

The Devil in the cradle was well wrapped up. When the shepherds turned to the manger of the true Christ-child, the third shepherd recalled the words of the angel:

In a crib was he laid;
He was poorly arrayed,
Both meek and mild.[23]

They worshiped the babe with gifts: a bob of cherries, a bird, and a tennis ball—humble gifts but in their symbolism matching those to be given by the three Kings. The midwinter gift of a bob of cherries symbolized the blood of Christ, which promised regeneration; the bird represented the Holy Spirit; the tennis ball stood for Christ's kingship. As they leave the infant Christ, the second shepherd remarks, "But he lies full cold." The shepherds of the Coventry *Pageant of the Shearmen and Taylors* searched about their persons for gifts for the child and offered a pipe, a hat, and a pair of mittens.

The vulnerability of Christ's nakedness reappeared in crucial moments in the plays of his adulthood, portending both vulnerability and power—at baptism in the river Jordan and disrobing to wash his disciples' feet, but especially when he was stripped, mocked, and tortured prior to Crucifixion (figure 16.3). The plays of Christ's passion are among the very finest in the cycles. Their intensity, cruelty, and outright violence were moderated by moments of plaintive lyricism from Christ or the Virgin Mary. In the Towneley *Buffeting,* for example, the action was tempestuous with Christ both verbally and physically assaulted by the four Torturers. Caiaphas, whom Annas was quite unable to calm, screamed abuse but provoked barely a single word from Christ. True power was vested in silence and nakedness. In the York play of the *Second Trial Before Pilate,* the soldiers stripped Christ of his garments on Pilate's command: "Unclothe him, cuff him, and clout him about."[24] The soldiers then described the part of the body of Christ they intended to scourge: "I shall heartily hit on his hips and haunch."[25] Although Christ was naked they referred to their blows as though they were falling on a fur coat or a cloak.[26] Christ's flesh and blood were his clothes—the best clothes that he had, however bruised and bloodied. Following the scourging the soldiers mockingly called him their king, thrust onto his head a crown of thorns, put on him a purple gown, pushed him down upon a stool, placed a round reed into his hand as a scepter and hailed him as king, duke, and mighty lord.[27] (Pilate has already in this play referred to himself as "duke.")[28]

Christ's seamless robe and other garments were of considerable interest in the mystery plays. Let us focus on the Chester play in which soldiers diced for Christ's garments before the crucifixion and on the Towneley version entitled *The Talents,* which was set after the crucifixion and wholly devoted to quarreling and dicing for the robe. In the Chester play, the Four Jews distributed among them the rest of Christ's clothes without argument

Figure 16.3. Cruxifiction. Norwich cathedral ceiling boss, ca.1470. Photo copyright Julia Hedgecoe. Used by permission.

(kirtle, cloak, doublet), but they diced for the seamless coat, believing that "in all Jerusalem is none such a garment."[29] The Fourth Jew had the winning throw and claimed the garment. At that moment Caiaphas appeared and berated the Jews for dallying so long before nailing Christ to the cross.

> Men, for cock's face,
> how long shall pewee—arse
> stand naked in that place?
> Go nail him on the tree![30]

George Herbert's line from "The Sacrifice" catches the irony of Christ's vulnerability: "Man stole the fruit, but I must climb the tree."[31] In climbing the tree to redeem mankind, Christ shed all his clothes.

In the gospel of St. Luke, a press of people eagerly crowded about Christ and a woman with an issue of blood twelve years touched the hem of his garment and was immediately healed.[32] Christ's seamless coat, with its magical potency, became a greatly desired relic in the Middle Ages. It is interesting that in neither the Chester nor the Towneley account of the coat is reference made to its healing properties. The Soldiers or Torturers who mocked Christ as their king with purple gown, crown of thorns, and scepter of reed were as unaware of Christ's true kingship as they were of the sublime healing potential of the seamless robe.

Just as in the medieval original, modern revivals of the Towneley play of *The Talents* begin with a long speech from Pilate, the first stanza of which is in Latin: the following stanzas are partly in Latin, partly in the vernacular. Like other mystery play tyrants, he calls for silence, threatens the audience and demands that they kneel to him. He proclaims his lineage, his authority, his power, swearing by Mohammed. The use of French or Latin, the waving of falchions, and the strutting and storming are part of the entertainment, as much as the elaborate costumes worn by such characters as Pilate or Herod. Like its medieval predecessor, today's audience is, of course, not quelled but taunts Pilate. *The Talents* follows the extremely moving *Crucifixion,* and both audiences need the release of emotions through the comedic and the burlesque.

After Pilate delivered his tirade he felt in need of a rest and asked his servant to tuck him into bed: "Boy, lay me down softly and wrap me well from cold."[33] The three Torturers entered, also swearing by Mohammed. Their purpose was to divide Christ's garments among them. They believed that whoever won the seamless coat would enjoy good fortune. They diced for the garment, quarreled among themselves, and decided to put the matter to Pilate, who immediately claimed the coat as his, brushing aside suggestions that it should be cut by a falchion into four equal parts.[34] The play ended with the disgruntled Torturers each inveighing against the vice of dicing, while Pilate, in possession of the coat, bid farewell to the audience in French and for good measure commended them to Mohammed.

Conclusion: The Power of Christ's Nakedness

The revival of the Christian church in the thirteenth and fourteenth centuries owed more perhaps to the life and work of St. Francis of Assisi than to anyone else. His rejection of the luxurious life associated with his youth is epitomized in his removing his clothes in the presence of his father and leaving his home and family. The tenor of the mystery plays reinforces this rejection of worldly possessions and temporal power. In contrast to King Herod's cruelty even the ass and the ox in the stable draw near to comfort the infant child:

> Mary. Ah! Joseph, husband, my child grows cold,
> And we have no fire to warm him with.
> Joseph. Now in my arms I shall him fold,
> King of kings by field and frith;
> He might have had better if truth were told,
> Than the breathing of beasts to warm him with.[35]

The coming of the three kings on their caparisoned horses, with their retinue and rich gifts, could not present a greater contrast to the naked and vulnerable Jesus.[36]

Christ entered Jerusalem on Palm Sunday, garlanded with flowers and with cloaks spread in his path; yet within a week he would be stripped of his own garments. Virtually naked, he would be crucified and entombed and rise to heaven. In the final scene of the mystery plays such as the Chester *Judgement,* God appears in heaven in the plentitude of his power, an awe- inspiring figure of majesty. He ordered his angels to blow their trumpets and summon every man, dead and alive, to a general reckoning. When all were assembled Jesus descended from heaven in a cloud to pass judgment. He wore his crown of thorns and showed to all the stigmata. He drew attention to his blood that was shed for man, and at this stage the wound in his side began to bleed afresh.[37] The Towneley *Judgement* also has Christ showing his wounds to those gathered waiting for their doom:

> Here may ye see my wounds so wide,
> That I suffered for your misdeed.
> Through heart, head, foot, hand and side,
> Nor for my guilt, but for your misdeed.[38]

Christ in judgment did not appear in the panoply of his power but as the suffering servant of mankind, almost naked. George Herbert, who had so deep an understanding of medieval thought, in his poem "The Bag," reflects the measure of Christ's love for man in his descent from his throne on high.[39] The second and third verses are as follows:

> Hast thou not heard, that my Lord Jesus died?
> Then let me tell thee a strange story.
> The God of power, as he did ride
> In his majestic robes of glory,
> Resolved to light; and so one day
> He did descend, undressing all the way."
> When he was come, as travelers are wont,
> He did repair unto an inn.
> Both then, and after, many a brunt
> He did endure to cancel sin:
> And having given the rest before,
> Here he gave up his life to pay our score.[40]

The poem concludes with Christ showing his wounded side to mankind and inviting all to be saved by his blood. Herbert's poem captures the pattern of the mystery plays in which Christ left his glorious vestments in heaven, and while on earth was steadily divested of what little remained. Of infinitely more value for the salvation of mankind was not his clothing but his body and his blood: "Hoc est corpus meum. . . . This is my body which is given for you. . . . This is my blood which is shed for you."

Notes

All quotations from medieval texts have been adapted to make them more intelligible to the reader.

1. *Norwich Grocers' Play,* version A, in Norman Davies, ed., *Non-Cycle Plays and Fragments* (London: Oxford University Press, 1970), p. 10.
2. *York Mystery* Plays, ed. Lucy T. Smith (New York: Russell and Russell, repr. ed., 1963), p. 27.
3. Alexandra F. Johnston and Margaret Rogerson, *Records of Early English Drama: York* (Toronto: University of Toronto Press,1979), pp. 55–56.
4. William Shakespeare, *Othello* V.:ii.26. Othello, snared by the devilish machinations of Iago, says, "I look down towards his feet; but that's a fable."
5. *The Chester Mystery Plays* 1, ed. R. M. Lumiansky and David Mills (Oxford: Oxford University Press, 1974), p. 362.
6. *York Mystery,* Smith, p. 408.
7. Hardin Craig, *English Religious Drama* (London: Oxford University Press,1955), p. 296.

8. *The Towneley Plays,* ed. George England (London, Oxford University Press, 1897), p. 3.
9. Ibid.
10. R.W. Ingram, *Records of Early English Drama: Coventry (*Toronto: Manchester University Press), p. 247.
11. *The N-Town Play* 1, ed. Stephen Spector 1 (London: Oxford University Press, 1991), p. 252.
12. *N-Town, p. 253.*
13. *N-Town, p. 255.*
14. Frances Baldwin, *Sumptuary Legislation and Personal Regulation in England* (Baltimore: Johns Hopkins University Press, 1926), p. 91.
15. Martial Rose, *The Wakefield Mystery Plays* (New York: W.W. Norton, 1961), p. 530.
16. Rose, *Wakefield,* p. 532.
17. Alan Hunt, *Governance of the Consuming Passions* (New York: St. Martin's Press, 1996), p. 307.
18. Lawrence M. Clopper, *Records of Early English Drama: Chester* (Toronto: Manchester University Press, 1979), p. 95.
19. Hardin Craig, *Two Coventry Corpus Christi Plays* (London: EETS, 1957, repr. 1967), pp. 507–11.
20. *The Macro Plays,* ed. Mark Eccles (Oxford: Oxford University Press, 1969), pp. 168–69.
21. *N-Town Plays,* p. 275.
22. Rose, *Wakefield,* p. 229
23. Rose, *Wakefield,* p. 232
24. Smith, *York Mystery,* p. 324
25. Smith, *York Mystery,* p. 332
26. Ibid.
27. Smith, *York Mystery,* p. 333
28. Smith, *York Mystery,* p. 320
29. Lumiansky and Mills, *Chester Mystery,* p. 308
30. Lumiansky and Mills, *Chester Mystery,* p. 310
31. James Tobin, *George Herbert* (St. Ives: Penguin Books, 1997), p. 29.
32. Luke 8.44.
33. Rose, *Wakefield,* p. 433.
34. Rose, *Wakefield,* p. 440.
35. Craig, *Corpus Christi,* lines 287–92.
36. Ingram, *Records of Early English,* p. 58." . . . for horse hire to Herod . . . 3d." Rose, *Wakefield,* pp. 237–39: the three kings enter on horseback.
37. Lumiansky, *Chester Mystery,* p. 453
38. Rose, *Wakefield,* p. 535
39. Rosamund Tuve, *A Reading of George Herbert* (Chicago: University of Chicago Press, 1952)
40. Tobin, *Herbert,* p. 142.

CHAPTER 17

ROBING CEREMONIALS IN LATE MAMLUK EGYPT: HALLOWED TRADITIONS, SHIFTING PROTOCOLS

Carl F. Petry

The final decades of the Mamluk Sultanate based in Cairo witnessed the assiduous maintenance of court-sponsored ceremonials in which robing figured ubiquitously. The impression of imperial continuity these ceremonials aimed to project was in fact something of a facade masking shifts in concepts of prestige on the part of the Mamluk ruling oligarchy. The following essay seeks to indicate the circumstances of robe granting while discerning such shifts as revealed by alterations in its rituals. The study is derived from hundreds of references to robing ceremonials by four prominent chronicles of the late Mamluk period.[1] These references often provided detailed descriptions of robe granting that disclosed protocols of bestowal, gradations of fineness, types of fabric or fur, ranges of colors, and styles of weaves evolving from centuries of precedent. Since the Mamluk Sultanate drew its ceremonial traditions from cultures in northwestern Africa, southwest Asia, and the Mediterranean, the precedents inspiring the multiplicity of robes were profuse.

While my study acknowledges the significance of these precedents, it does not attempt to trace either the evolution of robe-granting in Egypt or the diversity of its origins. Both objectives exceed the scope of an essay. This chapter rather focuses on the institution of robing as practiced in the Mamluk Sultanate during the reigns of its last prominent rulers: Sultans al-Ashraf Qāytbāy (872–901 H. / 1468–1496 CE) and Qānṣūh Al-Ghawrī (906–922/1501–1516). The regime over which they presided was at once conservative and keenly aware of its custodianship of a venerable ceremonial heritage, yet simultaneously prepared to denigrate or even abandon certain aspects of this heritage as it experimented with a variety of innovations. The analysis addresses the changing protocol of robing in the context of its functions: (1) investiture of military or civilian officials, (2) their subsequent promotion to higher ranks, (3) commemoration of sovereignty in ceremonials augmenting the monarch's stature, (4) confirmation of elite status on the part of militarists and civilians, (5) rewarding services rendered by military and civilian personnel, and (6) reconciliation following their dismissal or punishment. A glossary of technical terms is appended.

Investiture

Investiture in office was statistically the most frequent occasion for robing. So closely were robes tied to appointment that the tri-consonant root for this garment in Arabic (khā-lām-'ayin) became synonymous with the verb for investiture, in its fourth form: akhla'a 'alā—to confer upon.[2] The standard robe of investiture was a *khil'a,* a sleeveless mantle draped over the shoulders and extending below the waist. While woven of fine wool and richly colored in crimson, blue or white, the *khil'a* lacked either fur lining or trim, or elaborate embroidery of gold and silver thread. Bestowal of a *khil'a* marked a military man's entry into the lower and medial ranks of the ruling oligarchy. The chroniclers mentioned granting of the khil'a in the context of appointment to such offices as chief guard *(ra's nawba),*[3] second executive adjutant *(dawādār thānī),*[4] second chamberlain *(ḥājib thānī),*[5] chief of police *(wālī al-shurṭa),*[6] intendant of provision stores *(shādd al-sharabkhānāh),*[7] officer of the horse *(amīr akhūr),*[8] officer of council *(amīr majlis),*[9] intendant of granaries *(shādd al-shuwan),*[10]chief steward *(ustādār al-ṣuḥba),*[11] chief chamberlain *(ḥājib al-ḥujjāb),*[12] and provincial governors *(nuwwāb)* in Syria.[13]

Investiture in more senior military offices warranted bestowal of a *kāmiliyya.* This was an elaborate garment with broad sleeves. While woven of wool, sections of the *kāmiliyya* were covered with velvet *(mukhmal),* its hue often subtly contrasting with that of the underlying fabric. Its lapels and interior *(maqlab)* were lined with fur, typically sable *(sammūr)* imported from territories north of the Black Sea. The *kāmiliyya's* wool or velvet surfaces were decorated with embroidered brocades *(zarkash),* their gold and silver threads intertwining to create intricate patterns depicting blazons of prominent Mamluk cohorts.

The chronicler al-Ṣayrafī described an investiture ceremony involving presentation of a *kāmiliyya* when he discussed the appointment of the amir Barqūq al-Nāṣirī as viceroy of Damascus province *(niyābat al-Shām)* in Rabī' II 875 / September 1470.[14] His comments emphasized both the elevation of an officer to a rank just below the sultan's and the nuanced complexities of his installation. Al-Ṣayrafī observed that the sultan, Qāytbāy, honored him in the central courtyard of the citadel, but presented only a horse with golden saddle *(sarj dhahab)* and brocaded mantle *(kānbūsh bi-zarkash)*. The Amir Barqūq then descended down the citadel ramp accompanied by his peers, the senior commanders *(muqaddamūn)*. These officers each gave the new viceroy a mount with gold saddle and embroidered mantle, eighteen all told. He received these in stages as his progressed from the citadel heights and crossed the Rumayla Square.

The robing ceremony took place later at al-Raydāniyya, a parade ground north of Cairo where Egyptian army units frequently convened before proceeding toward Ghazza and the Palestinian corridor. The sultan's chief minister or confidential secretary *(kātib al-sirr)*, Zayn al-Dīn ibn Muzhir, reminded Barqūq "that he had not departed from obedience to his great imām," the sultan, and draped him with a splendid *kāmiliyya* fashioned of velvet with sable lining. Receipt of this garment confirmed Barqūq as viceroy of Syria, and this robe was conferred in exchange for his oath of loyalty. That the sultan's first minister gave the *kāmiliyya* and extracted the loyalty pledge was unusual since the monarch himself ordinarily presided over this rite. By granting a peer's gifts of horse, saddle and mantle, Sultan Qāytbāy chose to emphasize the tie of camaraderie *(khushdāshiyya)* that bound these two men of near-equal status in bonds of mutual respect. Barqūq's formal installation occurred at the hands of Qāytbāy's confidential secretary who represented the regime itself as an institution that confirmed the viceroy in his new office.

By contrast with appointees to high-ranking military offices, individuals installed in senior civilian posts rarely received the *kāmiliyya*. The majority were granted woollen *khil'as*. Even Mamluk amirs invested in lucrative bureaucratic sinecures made do with them. Of thirty-one references to bureaucratic appointments (not including the judiciary), only two mentioned a different garment. Those receiving *khil'as* were designated finance minister *(wazīr)*,[15] secretary of the department dispensing stipends to the monarch's purchased troops *(kātib al-mamālīk al-sulṭāniyya)*,[16] supervisor of a mystic hospice *(nāẓir al-khānqāh)*,[17] superintendent of the royal harem *(zimām)* and chief treasurer *(khāzindār)*,[18] senior eunuch intendant in Medina *(shaykh al-khuddām)*,[19] collector of minority taxes *(nāẓir al-jawālī)*,[20] accountant of deeds *(mustawfī al-ṣuḥba)*,[21] accountant in the privy fund *(mustawfī al-khāṣṣ)*,[22] supervisor of the royal hospital (*nāẓir al-bīmāristān al-manṣūrī)*,[23] supervisor of the privy fund *(nāẓir al-khāṣṣ)*,[24] senior merchant of mamluks *(mu'allim al-mu'allimīn)*,[25] intendant of the army bureau *(mutawallī dīwān al-jaysh)*,[26] chief physician *(ra' īs al-ṭibb)*,[27] deputy confidential secretary *(nā'ib kātib al-sirr)*,[28] supervisor of charitable trusts *(nāẓir al-awqāf)*,[29] confidential secretary in Damascus,[30] supervisor of the army bureau *(nāẓir al-jaysh)*,[31] market inspector *(muḥtasib)*,[32] and supervisor of fiscal bureaus *(nāẓir al-dawla)*.[33]

One individual chosen for the vizierate vehemently refused his designation. Ibn Iyās stated that a eunuch amir, Khushqadam al-Aḥmadī, rejected his *khil'a* of investiture sent by Sultan Qāytbāy in Jumādā I 879 / September-October 1474.[34] Striking his cheeks and weeping, Khushqadam claimed that he could not accept the post due to his poverty. "But the sultan paid no heed to his words and Khushqadam was forced to don the *khil'a* and return with it to his house." The vizierate in the late Mamluk period imposed a severe financial burden on its incumbent, who was expected to turn over substantial sums to his sovereign on a rigorously monitored schedule. In this instance, the profferment of a robe seems to have been a pyrrhic honor.

Other garments of civilian investiture appeared, although much less frequently. When the grand amir Yashbak min Mahdī was installed in the vizierate by Qāytbāy in Rabī' II 873 / November 1468, he received two satin capes *(aṭlasayn)* embroidered with patterns of date clusters *(mutamarran)* and two sleeveless woollen mantles *(fawqānī)* brocaded with gold and silver thread. These were to be draped over his marshal's *(atābak)* uniform.[35] In Ṣafar 875 / August 1470, Qāytbāy designated a senior judge *(qāḍī)*, Tāj al-Dīn ibn al-Maqsī, supervisor of the privy fund *(nāẓir al-khāṣṣ)*. He was granted an embroidered headcloth *(ṭarḥa)* with no mention of a robe.[36] Unlike the unfortunate Khushqadam who bewailed his appointment, the installation of Ibn al-Maqsī was a festive event. He was permitted to ride a horse with a gold saddle and brocaded mantle, an unusual privilege for a civilian. As he proceeded through the streets of Cairo, tapers illuminated his route, which was decorated with banners. Heralds announced his arrival at several stations. Throughout Qāytbāy's reign, individuals appointed to senior judicial posts also received *khil'as*.[37] No distinctions according to legal affiliation *(madhhab)* or court location (in the capital or provinces) were mentioned. But Ibn Iyās used the term *tashrīf* in three of four references to judicial designations during Al-Ghawrī's reign that merited a robe.[38] The root of *tashrīf* connoted honor as in a diploma of appointment, but the context of these incidents indicated a garment. Ibn Iyās provided no details about its appearance.

Civilians who enjoyed exceptional status and had penetrated the monarch's coterie of advisors did receive the lustrous *kāmiliyya* upon their installation. When Qāytbāy appointed the qāḍī Badr al-Dīn ibn Muzhir supervisor of the privy fund in Rajab 876 / January 1472, he was draped with a sable-trimmed *kāmiliyya*.[39] Al-Ṣayrafī also mentioned the headcloth *(ṭarḥa)* "as per tradition." The chronicler went on to discuss the circumstances of this appointment at length since it had sparked some controversy. Badr al-Dīn had risen to prominence in the shadow of his eminent father, Zayn al-Dīn, one of Qāytbāy's most esteemed counselors. Allegations of corrupt fiscal dealings in the junior muzhir's judicial career had surfaced, and al-Ṣayrafī questioned the wisdom of his placement in one of the regime's most important financial posts.

Chroniclers noted the *kāmiliyya* on the occasion of three other appointees: a supervisor of the sultan's special bureau *(nāẓir al-mufrad),*[40] market inspector (also granted to the aforementioned Badr ibn Muzhir a year later),[41] and *wazīr* under Al-Ghawrī[42] Al-Ṣayrafī reiterated his ambivalence over Ibn Muzhir's propriety, claiming that Qāytbāy had heard complaints raised over the rectitude of his judgments in court. But after discussing these with Ibn Muzhir's father, the sultan gave Badr a *kāmiliyya* of red velvet with sable trim. This award seems to have been reserved for civil officials who were uniquely privileged within the sovereign's intimate circle. None of these designations indicated distinction in previous offices. They all implied special conditions for preferment that were either unknown to the chroniclers or too delicate to elaborate on openly.

Promotion to Higher Rank

Ceremonials commemorating promotion of individuals to more advanced offices did not differ significantly from their initial investitures. The majority of references to promotions of Mamluk amirs mentioned the *khil'a* as their robe of confirmation.[43] In fact, the chroniclers devoted fewer words to description of garments than to financial benefits resulting from the enhanced rank. They emphasized the robe as distinct from the verb of appointment, *akhla'a,* when a political issue complicated the ceremony. Ibn Taghrī-Birdī and al-Ṣayrafī both mentioned the *khil'a* conferred upon the viceroy of Syria, Azbak min Ṭuṭukh, upon his designation as marshal *(atābak)* only because he declined it.[44] Azbak's predecessor, Jānibak al-Īnālī, still occupied the marshalship, having been captured by the Dhū'l-Qadrid rebel Sūwār in southeastern Anatolia. Both authors noted that Qāytbāy and Azbak secretly rejoiced in Jānibak's misfortune, since they were close comrades whose mutual trust was unshakable. Azbak felt compelled to make a show of propriety out of deference to his rival who had, after all, been captured in the line of duty. Jānibak belonged to the powerful faction of officers advanced by Sultan Īnāl (857–865/1453–1461). Qāytbāy had been obligated to grant Jānibak the marshalship to secure his own ascension, but he seized upon this opportunity to replace him with a loyal confidant. Azbak had turned down his *khil'a* of promotion the first time but subsequently allowed Qāytbāy to drape it over his shoulders. Acceptance of the robe itself thus would seem to have marked formal acceptance of succession to higher office.

Promotion of amirs to governorships in the Syrian provinces did not routinely occasion bestowal of a robe more elaborate than the *khil'a*.[45] For advancement in Cairo or the Syrian capitals, the incidence of other garments signaled shifts in protocol marking the change in rank. When al-Malaṭī observed that Yashbak min Mahdī was granted the vizierate in Rabī' II 873 / November 1468, along with his other executive offices (an unprecedented event), he claimed that Yashbak received a *kāmiliyya,* "rather than the traditional *khil'a* reserved for amirs."[46] In Dhū'l-Ḥijja 885 / February 1481, Qāytbāy summoned Almās, intendant of provisions *(shādd al-sharabkhānāh),* to the citadel. Almās had been slated for the viceroyship of Damascus, but when he ascended to the sultan's presence, no *khil'a* was presented to him.[47] Al-Ṣayrafī stated that the supervisor of the privy bureau *(nāẓir al-khāṣṣ),* who traditionally prepared the robes of installation, had arrived with two satin capes *(aṭlasayn)* embroidered with the date pattern *(mutamarran),* and a sleeveless mantle (fawqānī) with brocaded lapels *(ṭirāz)*. But Qāytbāy withheld them, apparently due to a dispute between him and Almās over the latter's wish to retain the lucrative intendantship. Ultimately, the two settled on a delayed combination of the offices. Almās would keep the proceeds from the bureau of provisions in Cairo even while being stationed in Damascus, although not immediately. Al-Ṣayrafī may have been hinting at a covert arrangement whereby Almā temporarily turned over receipts from the *sharabkhānāh* to his sovereign in return for the prestigious viceroyship in Damascus. Whatever the details, which remain speculative, Almās never donned either a *khil'a* or *kāmiliyya*. The satin capes and fur-trimmed *fawqānī* were bestowed only upon resolution of the two men's differences. By implication, the financial arrangements of this settlement counted for more than ceremonial tradition.

The splendid *kāmiliyya,* strangely enough, figured minimally in military promotions. One of the few occasions for its appearance occurred when Qānṣūh Al-Ghawrī designated his nephew, Ṭūmānbāy, as his regent when he departed al-Raydāniyya for Syria in Rabī' II 922 / May 1516 to confront the Ottoman sultan Selim I.[48] Ṭūmānbāy had accompanied his uncle to the bivouac, where he bade him good fortune on his ominous venture. Al-Ghawrī draped him with a *kāmiliyya* and proclaimed him "viceroy of the absence" *(nā'ib al-ghayba)* until he returned. The most unusual reference to a garment of military promotion occurred in Muḥarram 886 / March 1481, when Ibn Iyās described Qāytbāy's advancement of the precocious young officer, Qānṣūh min Ṭarābāy, later known as "Five Hundred" *(Khamsmi'a),* to master of the horse *(amīr akhūr).*[49] Ibn Iyās stated that this Qānṣūh (not to be confused with al-Ghawrī) was currently serving as deputy adjutant *(nā'ib al-dawādār)* and wore a modest headpiece *(kāfiyya)* trimmed with beaver fur *(qundus)*. When he became amīr akhūr, the sultan sent him fabric suitable for a turban *(takhfīfa)* more appropriate to his heightened station.

Civilians promoted to higher offices also received the *khil'a*. Both *dīwānī* bureaucrats and Sharī'a judges donned the unlined wool cape as confirmation of their appointment. Of twelve references to civil promotions, only one mentioned a *kāmiliyya:* to a prominent Jew named Ya'qūb whom Ibn Iyās titled a *mu'allim* (senior merchant).[50] Sultan al-Ghawrī made him director *(mutaḥaddith)* of the mint (Dār al-Ḍarb) after his predecessor had fled to escape embezzlement charges. Al-Ghawrī draped him with a kāmiliyya of blue wool with sable trim, "and he descended from the Citadel with high honors." Award of the more elaborate robe seems to have been reserved for an experienced financier who took over one of the most important fiscal agencies in Cairo. The *kāmiliyya* acknowledged the significance associated with the appointment in the monarch's eyes. That its recipient was not a Muslim evoked no comment from Ibn Iyās.

Both references to promotions of qāḍīs noted the khil'a, although in one instance, the nominee's receipt of his robe was delayed until a dispute over a rival's candidacy was resolved.[51] The individual involved was Sarī al-Dīn ibn al-Shiḥna who, in Jumādā II 876 / November 1471, was only a youthful deputy *(nā'ib)* in the Ḥanafī court. Sultan Qāytbāy had dismissed an individual named al-Sharīf al-Wafā'ī from the senior Ḥanafī judgeship over rumors of sexual impropriety among his staff. Another *nā'ib,* Shams al-Dīn al-Amshāṭī, also coveted the post, and Al-Ṣayrafī mentioned the withholding of Ibn al-Shiḥna's *khil'a* until questions over the validity of charges against al-Wafā'ī had been resolved. Al-Ṣayrafī did not report who ultimately succeeded al-Wafā'ī in this episode but noted that Ibn al-Shiḥna's installation was kept in abeyance since his robe was not presented.

An intriguing incident depicting the meteoric rise of a humble orphan boy to Sultan al-Ghawrī's intimate circle occurred in Ṣafar 922 / March-April 1516.[52] Al-Ghawrī had fired his barber, 'Alam al-Dīn, over the latter's careless gossip about his patron's travails with a boil. The sultan forbade his return to the citadel and ordered his steward *(muhtār)* to "search for a (new) barber to shave my head." The steward presented several possible candidates, none of whom appealed to al-Ghawrī Then the steward informed him about one 'Abd al-Razzāq, a beardless youth who lived nearby in the Vizier Gate district. While only an orphan and thus of low status, he was known to be adept at shaving. Al-Ghawrī summoned him, found his skills pleasing and appointed him royal barber on the spot. He commemorated 'Abd al-Razzāq's new job with a festive mantle *(kiswa ḥāfila),* a draft horse *(kadīsh)* and a mule *(bughl)*. "Thus in one instant, this youth became the sultan's barber. What is ordained shall not be prevented since God heals broken hearts. The slave [rises] by good fortune rather than by his father's or grandfather's [legacy]. As the saying goes: 'Fate favors some among the masses and all they do turns out well.'"

Commemoration of Sovereignty

The Mamluk sultanate was ruled by an absolute monarch who, however, belonged to no royal family. With the exception of several princes descended from al-Manṣūr Qalāwūn (678–689/1279–1290) through his son al-Nāṣir Muḥammad (709–741/1310–1341), all prominent sultans initiated their careers as slaves imported from either the Kipjak regions of Central Asia or Circassian districts of the Caucasus.[53] As peers of their senior officers, these individuals enjoyed no augmented stature above them. Having emerged from an oligarchy composed of amirs who were all potential contestants for the supreme office, Mamluk sultans were keenly aware of their regime's lack of dynastic legitimacy.

The sultanate's architect, al-Ẓāhir Baybars (658–676/1260–1277), had reestablished the 'Abbasid Caliphate in Cairo after its ignominious demise in Baghdad by the Mongols in 656/1258 to lend its venerable aura to his regime, which had its origins in murder and usurpation.[54] The caliphs still enjoyed their formal prerogative of primacy in the Mamluk court during Qāytbāy's and Al-Ghawrī's reigns, although they remained figureheads with no genuine authority. It is interesting that the chroniclers of the late period did not dwell on robing rituals with regard to either the caliphs' installation or their ceremonial duties. Nor was robing central to the sultan's own enthronement, which underscored the derivation of his legitimacy from the caliph's administration of an oath to rule justly and pledges of obedience *(bay'a)* to him from the four *qāḍis* and senior amirs. The sultan swore his oath on a Koran held out to him by the caliph while the former was seated under the Abbasids' black banner. He wore a black *jubba* or sleeved tunic of cotton and/or silk rather than wool. His close adjutants girded him with a sword symbolizing his supreme military authority. After his enthronement, the new sultan descended from the citadel in formal procession, his newly appointed marshal *(atābak)* holding a bird *(ṭayr)* and parasol *(qubba)* over his head.[55] Since the conferral of robes remained the sultan's exclusive privilege, no one was entitled to place them on him.

Several sultans were acutely sensitive to their origin as slaves, and none sought to compensate for it more generously than al-Ashraf Qāytbāy. The chroniclers described his magnanimous treatment of three sons of former rulers: al-Manṣūr 'Uthmān ibn Jaqmaq (857/1453), al-Manṣūr ibn Khushqadam and al-Mu'ayyad Aḥmad ibn Īnāl (865/1461). While the sincerity of Qāytbāy's empathy with the insecurity of these individuals cannot be denied, his extension of royal status to them clearly aimed at edifying the regime's prestige after a tumultuous period of in-fighting. Ibn Taghrī-Birdī, Al-Ṣayrafī, and al-Malaṭī provided minute details on the reception granted al-Manṣūr 'Uthmān after Qāytbāy summoned him from prison in Alexandria.

This prince arrived at the citadel on the third of Shawwāl 873 / 16 April 1469.[56] He had officially come to request the sultan's permission for his departure on the annual pilgrimage (Ḥajj). After entering the reception hall *(Duhaysha),* he approached Qāytbāy, who was seated on his round throne *(al-mudawara).* Before the young man could prostrate himself, Qāytbāy stood up to embrace him as an equal. The sultan conducted 'Uthmān to a window that looked out over the courtyard and the city below, where they sat together talking for an hour. Then, to conclude the audience, Qāytbāy presented 'Uthmān with a *kāmiliyya* of red velvet with sable trim. Over this was draped a brocaded *fawqānī.* He then conducted the prince to the courtyard, where a horse with gold saddle and brocaded mantle was waiting. Before 'Uthmān departed, he stopped by the harem entrance to convey his greetings to Qāytbāy's wife and her staff. Both Ibn Taghrī-Birdī and Al-Ṣayrafī praised Qāytbāy's magnaminity, which restored a tradition of respect and continuity to the ruling establishment. 'Uthmān in practice remained a glorified prisoner upon his return to Alexandria. But Qāytbāy's decency honored not only his stature but that of his father. His reception reaffirmed the dignity of the sultanic institution after it had been discredited during the interregnum that preceded Qāytbāy's enthronement.

Qāytbāy received 'Uthmān again a week later. After granting him a second *kāmiliyya,* he offered the prince a choice between permanent residence in Mecca, an effective exile, or a return to guarded seclusion in Alexandria. 'Uthmān opted for Alexandria, stating that the jurist Abū Ḥanīfa had found Mecca distasteful and that he concurred with his opinion.[57] 'Uthmān then departed on the Ḥajj, returning to Cairo in Muḥarram 874 / July-August 1469.[58] His sister, who had married the marshal *(atābak)* Azbak min Ṭuṭukh, had requested news about her brother's future. Qāytbāy sent a special envoy to her who also wore a *kāmiliyya.* The sultan hosted 'Uthmān in Cairo for more than a month as his guest, playing polo with him as a comrade.[59] 'Uthmān visited Qāytbāy five years later in Dhū'l-Ḥijja 878 / April-May 1474.[60] On this occasion, he received only a *khil'a* but was permitted to wear a sultan's uniform with gold blazons during the polo matches. 'Uthmān remained in Cairo two months, dividing his time between the Citadel and his sister's residence. Ibn Iyās noted that the purpose of this visit was personal. The prince wanted to spend time with the sultan, who graciously indulged his wish.

Qāytbāy also received Sultan Khushqadam's son, a child of five, in Shawwāl 876 / March-April 1472.[61] The details of his audience were touching. The prince ascended to the Duhaysha wearing an amir's uniform, presumably tailored to his diminutive size. When he entered the hall, Qāytbāy ordered him seated at his side as a peer. After the four *qāḍīs* entered, both Qāytbāy and the little boy stood to greet them. The sultan then bestowed a silk *khil'a* on the prince before he descended. Seven years later, in Rabī' II 884 / May-June 1479, Qāytbāy allowed the former sultan al-Mu'ayyad Aḥmad ibn Īnāl to return to Cairo from Alexandria.[62] Aḥmad's mother, the Princess (Khawand) Zaynab, a widow who enjoyed enormous prestige in the capital, was ill and verging on death. Zaynab had requested Qāytbāy's permission to allow the former sultan's return so that she could bid him farewell before she expired. Qāytbāy honored her plea and extended Aḥmad a co-ruler's welcome when he presented himself at the Citadel with his own son, 'Alī. Both received *khil'as.* After the Khawand Zaynab had died and the two prepared to depart for Alexandria, Qāytbāy received them again and draped them with khil'as. Ibn Iyās noted that Aḥmad presented the sultan with a large gift of money, a portion of the inheritance he had from his mother's estate. This ceremony may have represented a face-saving means of restoring the patrimony of Zaynab's husband, Īnāl, to the royal coffers. Many sultans simply confiscated their predecessors' assets outright upon their deaths. But Qāytbāy wished to preserve the facade of integrity for the sultanic institution and had left Zaynab in charge of her husband's wealth until her own death.

Qāytbāy's eventual successor, Qānṣūh Al-Ghawrī, did not share his predecessor's sensitivity over the status of former sultans' progeny. Having come to the throne under trying circumstances as a convenience candidate, he was understandably paranoid over his colleagues' support and incessantly extracted loyalty oaths from them. On one of these occasions, in Ramaḍān 912 / January 1507, Ibn Iyās mentioned the distribution of woolen tunics *(silārīs)* trimmed with sable to the assembled amirs.[63] This garment, which came into fashion during the reign of al-Nāṣir Muḥammad when his Amīr Silār wore it, seems to have been closely—although not exclusively—associated with officers. It was not awarded to commemorate investiture or promotion but did remain the sultan's prerogative to grant. The *silārī's* precise function is not discernible from its discussion in the sources, but its dispensation during rituals intended to reaffirm ties of mutual dependence between the sultan and his subordinates implies its role in the augmentation of the sovereign's primacy.

The distinction of royal status was manifested in the outfits sultans wore during formal progressions. These were more varied than the *khil'as* and *kāmiliyyas* they gave out to their military and civilian staffs. Qāytbāy and Al-

Ghawrī seem to have contrasted in the importance they placed on their appearance. Qāytbāy did not depart from traditional styles, while Al-Ghawrī sported a wider range of garments and colors. This difference may in part reflect idiosyncracies in narrative emphasis, although Qāytbāy's reign overall was described by more narrative authors than Al-Ghawrī's. In any case, Qāytbāy's processional regalia were described in detail only once. Al-Ṣayrafī discussed his progression through the streets of Cairo in Dhū'l-Ḥijja 873 / June-July 1469 during the visit of an ambassador from Ḥasan ibn Qarāyuluk, the ruler of Iran.[64] Qāytbāy wore a white *fawqānī* woven of Ba'labakkī cotton cloth, with black brocade. His golden sword and horse bearing an embroidered mantle and gold saddle conformed with precedents set by his forebears. But Al-Ṣayrafī also noted a symbolic saddle *(ghāshiyya)* that the sultan carried in his hands while riding in the progression. Al-Ṣayrafī did not elaborate on the *ghāshiyya's* purpose but al-Qalqashandī, author of the vast manual of Diplomatic, *Ṣubḥ al-A'shā,* stated that it was made of leather stitched or pierced with gold insignia *(adīm makhrūza).*[65] Unique to royal processionals in Egypt, it enhanced the monarch's stature and was saluted by his retainers as he rode by. Al-Ṣayrafī may have mentioned its appearance in this instance because Qāytbāy wished to impress upon the ambassador the special aura surrounding his office.

The historian Ibn Iyās personally witnessed Qānṣūh Al-Ghawrī's progressions and dwelled on variations in his regalia. During Al-Ghawrī's return to Cairo from the Fayyūm in Dhū'l-Qa'da 918 / January-February 1513, he met the Caliph al-Mutawakkil at the latter's estate in Dahshūr.[66] Al-Ghawrī presented the caliph with an extraordinary *silārī* tunic from his own wardrobe. "It was said that the sable lining alone cost three hundred dinars (gold coins)." Upon his arrival in Cairo, Al-Ghawrī distributed *kāmiliyyas* from his collection to senior officers and the Ḥanafī *qāḍī* (the previously mentioned Ibn al-Shiḥna who was now the sultan's senior legal counselor).[67] Ibn Iyās noted these gifts in the context of his distaste over Al-Ghawrī's penchant for extravagance. But his remarks were in keeping with his description of the sultan's outfits in subsequent progressions. Ibn Iyās mentioned the small turban *(takhfīfa)* and a *silārī* tunic white outside and green within,[68] a *silārī* violet in color *(banfasjī)* lined with lynx *(washaq),*[69] and a red velvet *kāmiliyya* with sable trim.[70] Ibn Iyās did not approve of Al-Ghawrī's departure from traditional riding outfits worn by previous rulers. His detailed descriptions aimed at criticism of hollow display rather than praise for mastery of showmanship. Nonetheless, the diversity of Al-Ghawrī's ceremonial apparel connoted deliberate choices by an individual with a keen eye for a vivid impression during processions that were truly spectacular.[71] Whatever Al-Ghawrī's personal inclinations toward luxury, he was alert to the symbolic value of royal pomp. The incidence of the *silārī* in varying hues suggests its versatility, in contrast with the *kāmiliyya* that was more restricted in both design and purpose.

Confirmation of Elite Status

Members of the civil and military elites received robes in recognition of their positions at consistories *(mawākib)* scheduled throughout the year. These reviews determined the formal agenda of the sultanic court. Garments conferred at these ceremonies of confirmation *(inẓār)* varied, but rarely included the costly *kāmiliyyas* reserved for investitures or promotions. The *khil'a* and *fawqānī* were typical for these occasions. Al-Ṣayrafī described such a confirmation review for amirs early in Qāytbāy's reign.[72] "The month (of Jumādā I 873 / December 17, 1468) began on the twenty-second of Hatūr (the solar Coptic month). The sultan wore the wool uniform *(qumāsh)* customary for the winter season. He conferred *fawqāniyāt* on the amirs of 1000 at the Harem Gate as per tradition every year. The sultan gave a *fawqānī* he was wearing himself to his guard captain *(ra's nawba)*. He did the same every Friday for (an officer) without one, continuing in this fashion until winter's end."

Some 12 years after this consistory, on the Festival of Sacrifice ('Īd al-Naḥr)—10 Dhū'l-Ḥijja 885 / February 10, 1481, Al-Ṣayrafī noted Qāytbāy's break with custom in deference to the death of his closest comrade, the *dawādār* (adjutant) Yashbak min Mahdī.[73] The monarch usually bestowed a robe on his marshal *(atābak)* on this occasion. But since Yashbak had perished during his abortive attempt to conquer a principality for himself on the Iranian frontier, Qāytbāy refrained from doing so.

Qānṣūh Al-Ghawrī was less inclined than Qāytbāy toward upholding continuity in tradition. He introduced innovations during reviews consistent with his flair for display. Ibn Iyās's depiction of a confirmation ceremony presided over by Al-Ghawrī late in his reign contrasts with Al-Ṣayrafī's remarks for 873.[74] The sultan "proceeded to the Nilometer *(miqyās)* to which he had invited all the senior amirs *(muqaddamīn)*. They sat together in the pavilion *(qaṣr)* he had built adjacent to the *miqyās*. He hosted them to a sumptuous banquet and lodged them in tents on the Nile shore across from al-Jīza (Giza). They were served various kinds of sweets and fruits. The sultan remained there to mid-afternoon and then boarded the royal barge *(ḥarāqa)* and proceeded (downstream) to Būlāq. An awning of yellow satin had been installed on the barge. It was said that he draped the officers that day with *silārī* tunics lined with lynx *(washaq)* or sable *(sammūr)*. Truly, a royal excursion." We shall see that Al-Ghawrī was stingier when he recognized notables whose status was rooted in the past.

Civilians who merited robes included the senior judges *(qāḍīs)* of the four schools *(madhhabs)* of law, other eminent jurists *(fuqahā')*, scholastics *('ulamā')*, preachers *(khaṭībs)* and prayer leaders *(imāms)* in the capital's prominent mosques. *Khil'as* were distributed to them during major festivals of the Muslim calendar, in particular the feast of fast-breaking *('Īd al-Fiṭr)* held in Shawwāl,[75] and the Prophet's birthday *('Īd al-Mawlid al-Nabawī)* in Rabī' I.[76] The holy month of Ramaḍān occasioned many formal observances of piety in the court. Most noteworthy of these was the recitation of the entire *Ṣaḥīḥ* or collection of Prophetic Traditions *(ḥadīth)* by al-Bukhārī in the citadel courtyard. All the notable *'ulamā'* attending received robes acknowledging them as legal arbiters and interpreters of the learned sciences. The narrative sources mentioned robing of civilians at these recitations more frequently than any other ritual observance: fourteen references.

Al-Ṣayrafī described one session during Qāytbāy's reign in detail.[77]

> On Wednesday the twenty-eighth [of Ramaḍān 875 / March 20, 1471] al-Bukhārī was recited in the Citadel before the sultan. It was a festive occasion attended by the four qāḍīs, except for the Ḥanbalī judge who was indisposed. . . . Also, the scholastics *('ulamā')*, learned *(fuḍalā')*, students *(ṭalaba)*, officers *(umarā')*, guard captains *(ru'ūs al-nawb)*, elite troops *(khāṣṣakiyya)* and members of professions *(aṣḥāb al-waẓa'if)*. The reciter *(qāri')* was the Shaykh and Imām Burhān al-Dīn al-Karakī, prayer leader to His Majesty. Headcloths *(ṭaraḥāt)* were bestowed on *(khala'a 'alā)* the judges and reciter. Pelts of sable *(sammūr)* were conferred upon the most senior shaykhs . . . while the remainder received squirrel *(sinjāb)* skins. Purses *(ṣurar)* were distributed: those with the most containing 3000 dinars, those with the least 1000.

The official responsible for preparation of these robes supervised the privy fund *(nāẓir al-khāṣṣ)*. During the Circassian Mamluk period, his office had supplanted fiscal duties formerly administered by the prime minister *(wazīr)*.[78] Once again, Al-Ṣayrafī provided a detailed statement about his formal presentation of the robes.[79]

> On the twenty-seventh [of Ramaḍān 876 / March 8, 1472] the Qāḍī Badr al-Dīn ibn Muzhir, confidential secretary, ascended to bring the robes *(khila')* which were customarily provided by the *nāẓir al-khāṣṣ* [C.P.: he held both posts simultaneously]. He brought approximately 1000. The sultan bestowed a *kāmiliyya* with sable lining and granted him a horse with a gold saddle and brocaded mantle. His procession of departure was splendid, since officials, notables and luminaries rode with him. I learned that two days earlier, the Qāḍī Nāẓir al-Khāṣṣ had presented himself for an audience. Since some of his clasps and tassles were unfastened, the sultan beckoned him so

> that he could fasten his collar (ṭawq) with his own hands in the soldiers' presence. This was an example of his [Qāytbāy's] respect that he showed him [Ibn Muzhir].

Al-Ṣayrafī's comments were motivated by more than his penchant for recounting minutiae. He served as a deputy judge *(nā'ib qāḍī)* through much of Qāytbāy's reign and witnessed royal consistories first-hand. This sultan regarded the upholding of ceremonial tradition as a major duty, and showered honors on the civil elite. His eventual successor Al-Ghawrī was less inclined to bestow largesse upon notables solely to reaffirm their venerable stature. He was readier to reward tangible services they provided him, services that often deviated from hallowed traditions.

Rewards for Service

Robing figured prominently in acknowledgment of services rendered to the regime. These typically involved the restoration of order after unrest in Cairo, or the provision of revenue collected by overt or covert means. The ceremonials were extraordinary events if the individual being recognized had assisted the sultan in exceptional ways, and the robe he received was appropriate for the occasion. An example of individuals copiously rewarded for bolstering their sovereign at a tense moment occurred early in Qāytbāy's tenure when two loyal officers apprehended the former sultan Timurbughā in Dhū'l-Ḥijja 872 / July 1468.[80] This man had been Qāytbāy's comrade and when he failed to consolidate a viable regime, he went into honorable exile in Alexandria. Under the influence of several amirs in Syria chafing at the prospect of Qāytbāy's long-term rule, Timurbughā took flight for the Palestine frontier where his supporters would proclaim him sultan. He was captured in Ghazza by one Arghūn Shāh al-Ashrafī and sent back to Cairo in custody of Qāytbāy's right-hand man, Yashbak min Mahdī. The details of a lengthy confession that Timurbughā wrote personally to his former *khushdāsh* explaining his action shed light on the Mamluk concept of political morality, but they are not germane to the ceremonial in which Qāytbāy expressed his gratitude.

Al-Malaṭī and Ibn Iyās differed in their report about who received robes. Al- Malaṭi stated that Arghūn Shāh returned to Cairo himself for an audience with Qāytbāy after he had turned Timurbughā over to Yashbak. Qāytbāy thanked him and granted a splendid *khil'a.* Ibn Iyās claimed that Yashbak took charge of the prisoner in Bilbays and conducted him back to Cairo. It was he who received the *khil'a* along with a horse bearing a gold saddle and brocaded mantle. The veracity of these contrasting versions cannot be ascertained. While Ibn Iyās was not an eyewitness, he mentioned resentment among Timurbughā's supporters. Yashbak's stance was already so formidable that Qāytbāy could rely on him to stave off a revolt by them when Timurbughā arrived at the citadel.

The provision of revenue ranked very high in the hierarchy of services provided to the sultan, since his appetite for cash remained insatiable. It was therefore predictable that those who yielded copious sums were munificently honored. When the amir Yashbak received the vizierate from Qāytbāy in Rabī' I 873 / October 1469, he immediately reaffirmed his own deputy, Qāsim Shughayta, who actually administered the office—backed by his patron's clout.[81] Yashbak readily turned over the *wazīr's* robes of installation—the satin aṭlas with date pattern stitching and the *fawqānīs* with embroidered brocade—to Qāsim. Ibn Taghrī-Birdī remarked: "Scarcely had Yashbak placed the robe on his back then he (Qāsim) addressed himself to cutting the rations of soldiers who took more than their rank warranted. As for the turbaned *(muta'ammamīn*—the *'ulamā'),* he reduced the receipts from their posts. They remained secure [in them], but he [Qāsim] demanded that they return what had formerly been granted them [in excess]." Ibn Taghrī-Birdī observed wryly that only those in the military and civil establishments of Qāytbāy's predecessors who had profited corruptly from the instability of the interregnum had any reason to fear Yashbak's and Qāsim's inquisition. A year later, in Sha'bān 874 / February 1470, Yashbak returned from a crop and livestock inventory of Upper Egypt. He presented Qāytbāy with cash and grain worth 200,000 dinars, "an unprecedented sum."[82] Once again, Qāytbāy draped his adjutant with a splendid robe befitting the scale of his donation.

The sale of offices and acceptance of bribes had become routine procedures in the late sultanate. The fineness of robes granted to the aspirants was determined by the amounts they offered. Al-Ṣayrafī stated that Qāytbāy draped one Shams al-Dīn Muḥammad ibn 'Abd al-Raḥmān with a sable-lined *kāmiliyya* when he paid 10,000 dinars for the lucrative post of moneychanger *(ṣayrafī)* in the Red Sea port of Jidda.[83] When an individual named Quṭb al-Dīn al-Khayḍarī turned over 30,000 dinars for the Shāfi'ī judgeship of Damascus, Qāytbāy conferred two *kāmiliyyas* of white wool lined with sable.[84]

Procurement of revenue by illegal ploys, including extortion, merited a robe of honor even from Qāytbāy, whose biographers described as the paragon of rectitude in government. Ibn Iyās decried his appointment of a furrier *(farrā')* as supervisor of charitable trusts *(awqāf)* in Ṣafar 887 / March-April 1482.[85] His entry is worth quoting:

> The sultan robed a commoner from the dregs of society called Muḥammad ibn al-'Aẓama. He had gained an untoward influence over the sultan, who

> ultimately made him nāẓir al-awqāf. A severe public outcry followed his installation. He had connived to supply the sultan with a monthly sum [derived] from *waqf* proceeds. He contrived suits against property of notables, men and women, and slanted litigation against them on behalf of their trusts. He placed them in debt for both past and future. He extorted vast sums from them and his gate became more sinister than that of the prefect of police *(wālī)*. He surrounded himself with a gang of hooligans who alerted him to a diverse array of schemes. The appointment of this vile creature was one of al-Ashraf Qāytbāy's worst acts. The sultan accepted the sums handed over to him without questioning their sources.

Qānṣūh Al-Ghawrī was more forthright and less burdened with a show of scruples in his quest for revenue. His reign was famous in the annals of historians generations after his death for his draconian yet effective techniques of amassing funds. He also appointed an adept procurer, one 'Alī ibn Abī'l-Jūd, as supervisor of charitable trusts in Jumādā I 908 / November 1502.[86] Ibn Iyās waxed fulsomely on the ploys of this master "of wickedness and corruption." Ibn Abī'l-Jūd donned a tunic *(ṭawq)* of office and wore yellow riding boots with spurs, usually a privilege of officers, when he rode his horse. He combined the posts of supervisor of charitable trusts, royal bailiff *(bardadār), wazīr* and supervisor of the privy fund simultaneously. Ibn Iyās's litany of his extortion is too lengthy to repeat. But he made clear the connection between the importance of his service to Al-Ghawrī and the status the sultan allowed him to assume. Al-Ghawrī reserved his big rewards for persons who were uniquely valuable to him. These individuals had earned their eminence by deeds, however unsavory, rather than from ascribed rank.

Al-Ghawrī surrounded himself with intimates, few of whom belonged to traditional elites of Cairene society. Ibn Iyās mentioned one individual permitted to wear a *silārī* tunic whose eminence was unusual even within this group of parvenus. He was 'Ajam al-Dīn al-Shinqājī, Al-Ghawrī's familiar *(nadīm)* and comic *(mudḥiq)*.[87] He had become known as a performer of sleight-of-hand tricks and juggling. When he made Al-Ghawrī's acquaintance, the latter drew him into his circle and elevated him to notable rank. Al-Ghawrī sent him as an emissary to Damascus in Shawwāl 921 / November-December 1515 with gifts that included two elephants for the provincial governors. Ibn Iyās derided his stature, which he claimed "exceeded that of any previous associate of Egypt's rulers." The *silārīs* consigned to him for bestowal on the governors were lined with sable and lynx. Ibn Iyās ridiculed al- Shinqājī's influence as "one of the errors of our age," since he was only a magician and buffoon. But his prominence in Al-Ghawrī's entourage suggests the sultan's studied goal of demeaning the status of traditional elites while raising men of no formal standing to favor—and dependence on him for their fortunes. Their receipt of robes symbolized the transformation in rank that was the sultan's prerogative to impose.

The esteem attached to the robe itself began to wane in the context of the regime's shifting priorities. As the sultanate downplayed its reaffirmation of traditional status groups while placating individuals who furthered its interests in creative ways, the quality of garments conferred to commemorate status began to decline. Ibn Iyās first noted a reduction in the number of *khil'as* granted to legal scholars *(fuqahā')* in Ramaḍān 872 / August-September 1487 during the recitation of Bukhārī's Ṣaḥīḥ a.[88] He reported a reduction by half, with many persons who expected a robe denied outright. Sultan Qāytbāy faced serious cash shortfalls because of expenses imposed by the Ottoman wars. "In those days, the sultan had become very miserly." Two decades later, Qānṣūh Al-Ghawrī was allowing the Bukhārī recitation observance to lapse. He ceased to use the vast embroidered tent that Qāytbāy had commissioned for the event, and was cutting back on both the number and quality of robes granted.[89]

During the Festival of Fastbreaking ('Īd al-Fiṭr) in Shawwāl 912 / February-March 1507, Ibn Iyās discerned the tie between devaluing traditional status and deterioration of robes. "On the day of 'Īd al-Fiṭr, the sultan distributed khil'as *to those entitled to them* [emphasis mine]. The robes were exceedingly crude *(ghāya waḥāsha),* made of dyed cotton cloth and worth no more than three dinars each. Previously, these robes had been woven of colored silk and trimmed with squirrel fur *(sinjāb)."*[90] Throughout the remainder of Al-Ghawrī's reign, the quality of robes distributed to established notables was mediocre.[91] Yet to persons designated for an innovative duty, the sultan conferred distinctive garments. When Al-Ghawrī placed a former governor of Aleppo in charge of his new corps of musketeers in Jumādā II 912 / October-November 1506, he allowed him to wear a royal turban *(takhfīfa)* with two projecting horns, chosen from his own collection.[92] No cheap cotton wrap awaited him but a *silārī* trimmed with lynx. Ibn Iyās was less amazed by Al-Ghawrī's willingness to share an emblem of sovereignty by granting a royal headdress than he was over this officer's compensation. The new corps commander received no rent from a land allotment *(iqṭā'),* the normative means of paying senior officers with many retainers. He was stipended directly—and handsomely—from a reserve fund *(dhakhīra)* that drew its revenues on estates reverting to crown authority. Qānṣūh Al-Ghawrī was progressively whittling away the percentage of income his senior amirs—all potential rivals—received from allotments they controlled and might alienate. This last noteworthy ruler of Egypt before the Ottoman invasion thus kept his store of sumptuous ceremonial garments for rewarding appointees tangibly useful to his designs. He signaled his contempt for traditional elites who often obstructed his plans by dispensing robes that proclaimed their insignificance.

Reconciliation and Restoration

Conferral of robes was so closely associated with reconciliation that its occurrence was virtually ubiquitous in these rituals. A recently enthroned sultan customarily recalled officers whom his predecessor had exiled from Cairo to ensure their loyalty to him. Qāytbāy began summoning amirs banished by Khushqadam in Jumādā II 872 / January 1468, many of whom had been close comrades. Each received a *kāmiliyya* with sable trim during his audience with Qāytbāy at the Citadel. Al-Ṣayrafī described the poignant example of Iyās al-Ṭawīl (the Tall) who had served as governor of Tripoli (Ṭarābulus) in Syria during Khushqadam's reign.[93] Having returned directly to Egypt from an expedition against the Franks in Cyprus without permission, Iyās had incurred Khushqadam's wrath. It was Qāytbāy, then an officer himself, who had been ordered to arrest Iyās and send him to prison in Alexandria. When Iyās ascended to the reception hall, he kissed his old comrade's hand. Qāytbāy draped him with a *kāmiliyya* of red velvet with a sable cape. His processional horse predictably bore a gold saddle and brocaded mantle. But Al-Ṣayrafī noted that Iyās rode (or mounted) the horse on a wooden chair, apparently to compensate for infirmities he incurred while languishing in a dungeon.

Late in his reign, Qānṣūh Al-Ghawrī released two old rivals from confinement in Alexandria, his former atābak, Qāyt al-Rajabī, and the previous sultan, al-Ẓāhir Qānṣūh, who had conspired against him.[94] Al-Ghawrī sent his steward *(muhtār)* with two vests *(badanas)* of sable and squirrel, and two robes *(thawb)* of Ba'labakkī cotton cloth for each, along with 1,000 dinars. Qānṣūh and Qāyt were to remain in their jail cells but free of chains.

Officers who had aroused their sovereigns' ire often strove to restore themselves to favor. Ibn Iyās commented on an incident between Qāytbāy and the amir Khayrbak min Ḥadīd. Following a heated exchange, Khayrbak recused himself for several days.[95] Qāytbāy then invited him to participate in a polo match at the citadel. During the game, Qāytbāy dropped his mallet, which Khayrbak immediately retrieved. Qāytbāy granted him a *khil'a* and a horse from his own stock. Mamluk sultans rarely allowed a personal quarrel to smolder into an irreconcilable feud, unless an attempt at deposition or assassination was suspected. Sultans regarded themselves as social peers of their powerful subordinates whose loyalty they required to govern effectively. Temper flares or verbal insults were the inevitable consequence of close interaction. The conferral of robes, so symbolic of investiture or promotion, served as visible manifestations of the sultan's readiness to forgive a slight for the sake of harmony in the ruling oligarchy. And some reconciliations could be humorous. Ibn Iyās described a prank Qāytbāy played on the amir Azbak al-Yūsufī. He sent him a robe of investiture along with an appointment to the governorship of 'Ayntāb far away in the Anatolian march.[96] Azbak was alarmed over the prospect of assignment to such a remote outback. Qāytbāy let him fret several days before he sent his marshal to release him from the charge.

Civilian officials rarely enjoyed the banter of peers. The threat of intimidation by their patrons lurked behind all appointments. Al-Ṣayrafī commented on the case of one Ibn Zawīn, whom Qāytbāy had designated as inspector of agrarian land *(kāshif al-turāb)* in the Delta province of Gharbiyya.[97] During the ceremony, two amirs rebuked Ibn Zawīn before the sultan for his wickedness and depravity. Qāytbāy then reviled Ibn Zawīn himself but compelled him to swear an oath of probity rather than withdrawing his appointment. A third officer stood up to defame the hapless Ibn Zawīn to his face: "Who has nominated this Jew, this dog upon the Muslims?" In a fit of temper, Qāytbāy then stripped Ibn Zawīn of his robe and cast it over the accusing amir—thereby saddling him with the post. He refused to heed the amir's protestations until several of his aides interceded. They removed the robe from the officer and gave it back to Ibn Zawīn who was finally confirmed "after 1,000 efforts." The political nuances of this enigmatic incident can only be surmised, but Qāytbāy obviously became angry over conflicting assertions about Ibn Zawīn's fitness for the position. Ibn Zawīn's installation may have been a foregone conclusion despite a show of indignation over his alleged corruption. The sultan may indeed have valued his nefarious talents and targeted him for this post, whatever his past record. If so, the amirs' denunciations against Ibn Zawīn and their rebuttals could have been staged to neutralize more widespread opposition to his installation.

Some of the most noteworthy cases of reconciliation occurred when wealthy civilians suffered confiscation of their assets. After the sultan was satisfied that they had in fact turned over what he suspected they held, these individuals were restored to favor. Qāytbāy arrested Shihāb al-Dīn al-'Aynī, the chief minister of his predecessor, Khushqadam, immediately after his enthronement. He demanded all assets al-'Aynī had acquired during his tenure in Khushqadam's cabinet, claiming that these exceeded 300,000 dinars.[98] Qāytbāy harassed al-'Aynī relentlessly, eventually seizing cash, provisions and real estate worth the extraordinary figure of a million dinars—far beyond initial expectations. But once he had reclaimed al-'Aynī's gains, Qāytbāy released him to retire with a sable-lined *kāmiliyya*. Very few individuals who had amassed great wealth under a rival's patronage were subjected to physical torture. Once they acknowledged the sultan's claim to their assets, they were set free with full honors and often resumed their financial activities to rebuild their fortunes.

Ibn Taghrī-Birdī and al-Malaṭī linked the term *riḍā'* (conciliation) to the robe al-'Aynī received. Its prominence in a ritual of closure and restoration quite likely stemmed from its antiquity as an instrument that formalized a sovereign's act, whether of investiture, promotion, augmentation of royal stature, reward, or reconciliation and restitution. This essay has traced shifts in emphasis and function during robing ceremonials of the Mamluk sultanate in its final decades. Traditional elites were pointedly reminded of their diminished prestige by the crude garments they received, while new players in the game of patronage and power proclaimed their significance in robes designated for the influential. The institution of robing was modified to suit the changing circumstances of sovereign protocol in this medieval Egyptian regime. But its centrality to such protocol continued undiminished into the Ottoman era that followed.

Glossary

Sources: R. Dozy, *Supplément aux dictionnaires arabes,* 2 vols. (Leiden: E. J. Brill, 1881); J. G. Hava, *Al-Faraid Arabic-English Dictionary* (Beirut: Catholic Press, 1964); Leo A. Mayer, *Mamluk Costume: A Survey* (Geneva: A. Kundig, 1952); Hans Wehr, *A Dictionary of Modern Written Arabic,* ed, J. Milton Cowan (London: George Allen and Unwin, 1966).

AṬLAS:	satin robe (Dozy 2: 53; Hava 435; Wehr 20).
BADANA:	sleeveless tunic, woven of silk, frequently worn by Jews (Dozy 1: 58).
BA'LABAKKĪ:	cloth named after Lebanese town of Baalbak, white cotton or silk (Dozy 1: 100).
BAND:	standard; bannād: standard bearer (Dozy 1: 117; Hava 47).
BANFASJĪ:	violet colored (Hava 47)
BARKUSTŪNĀT:	trappings worn by horse during processions (Dozy 1: 77).
FAWQĀNĪ:	robe or mantle worn over the jubba (Dozy 2: 298; Mayer 58–60).
GHĀSHIYYA:	saddle made of leather, embroidered with gold, carried by sultan during processions (Dozy 2: 214 claims that it was carried by bearer in front of sultan).
JUBBA:	long outer garment, open in front with wide sleeves, woven of cotton or linen (Wehr 110).
JŪKHA:	cloth gown with full sleeves (Dozy 1: 230, Hava 103).
KĀMILIYYA:	fur-lined robe with sleeves, woven of wool or velvet (Dozy 2: 497; Mayer 62–63).
KĀNBŪSH:	mantle for horse, chabraque (Dozy 2: 499; Hava 669; Mayer 58).
KHAFF:	boot made of yellow leather (Hava 176).

KHIL'A: robe of honor woven of wool, without sleeves or fur lining (Hava 181; Mayer 56–62; Wehr 256).

KISWA: clothing, uniform (Hava 655).

KŪFIYYA: square headcloth, diagonally folded (Dozy 2: 508; Hava 670; Wehr 846).

MAQLAB: inverse, interior (Dozy 2: 399; Wehr 785).

MIHMAZ: spur (Dozy 2: 772; Hava 836).

MUFARRIYYA: fur-lined gown (Hava 560).

MUKHMAL: velvet, velours, nappy silk (Dozy 1: 406; Hava 186; Wehr 262).

MUTAMMAR: cloth of cotton or satin embroidered with date pattern (Dozy 1: 152; Mayer 58, 63).

QUNDUS(z): beaver (Dozy 2: 418; Hava 629; Wehr 792).

SAMMŪR: sable, sometimes confused with beaver by Arabic authors (Dozy 2: 683; Hava 335; Wehr 432).

ṢANJAQ: banner, standard (Dozy 1: 846).

SARJ: saddle (Wehr 406).

SHAṬFA: fabric forming essential part of flag held over sultan's head during processions (Dozy 1: 759).

SHIQQA: woollen or linen cloth, frequently used for tents (Dozy 1: 775).

SILĀRĪ: sleeveless tunic, in vogue during reign of Sultan al-Nāṣir Muḥammad (709–741/1310–1341) when worn by his amīr silār (herald) (Dozy 1: 673; Mayer 57 [rendered sallārī]).

SINJĀB: gray squirrel, miniver (Dozy 1: 691; Hava 339).

TAKHFĪFA: small turban, when worn by royalty woven of silk or satin and folded around special ornaments such as horns (Dozy 1: 386; Hava 176).

ṬARḤA: head cloth (Dozy 2: 31; Mayer 60).

ṬARṬŪR: headpiece worn by Egyptian bedouin, placed on head of criminal or vanquished enemy (Dozy 2: 36).

TASHRĪF: a robe also called a falbala, worn over uniform (Dozy 1: 750); honor, regard shown (Hava 361; Mayer 56, 60, 62).

ṬAWQ: collar of gown, often embroidered (Hava 442).

THAWB: ample flowing robe woven of silk, sleeves equal length of garment, often rose or violet in color (Dozy 1: 166; Hava 74; Mayer 63).

ṬIRĀZ: embroidered trim or lapels of a garment (Dozy 2: 35; Hava 430; Mayer 59, 64; Wehr 557).

WASHAQ: lynx (Dozy 2: 816; Wehr 1071).

ZARKASH: brocade, gold and silver embroidery (Dozy 1: 589; Hava 288; Mayer 62; Wehr 376).

Notes

1. Jamāl al-Dīn Yūsuf ibn Taghrī-Birdī (813–874 H. / 1411–1469 CE), *Ḥawādith al-Duhūr f Madā al-Ayyām wa'l-Shuhūr* (Episodes of the Epochs

which pass in Weeks and Months), ed. William Popper, vol. 7, nos. 1–4 of *University of California Publications in Semitic Philology* (Berkeley: University of California Press, 1930–42); Nūr al-Dīn 'Alī ibn Dā'ūd al-Jawharī al-Ṣayrafī (819-ca. 900 / 1416–1495), *Inbā' al-Haṣr bi-Abnā' al-'Aṣr* (Informing the Lion [Sultan Qāytbāy] about Scions of the Age), ed. Ḥasan Ḥabashī (Cairo: Dār al-Fikrī al-'Arabī, 1970); Zayn al-Dīn 'Abd al-Bāsiṭ ibn Khalīl al-Malaṭī (844–920 / 1440–1514), *Al-Rawḍ al-Bāsim fī Ḥawādith al-'Umr wa'l-Tarājim* (Gardens Smiling upon Events of Lifetimes and Lifestories), ms. (Rome: Vatican Library, Arabo 729); Abū' l-Barakāt Muḥammad ibn Iyās (852–930 / 1448–1524), *Badā'ī' al-Zuhūr fī Waqā'ī' al-Duhūr* (Marvels Blossoming among Incidents of the Epochs), ed. M. Mustafa, H. Roemer, and H. Ritter, vols. 3–5 (Cairo and Wiesbaden: Bibliotheca Islamica, 1960–63).

2. On use of the verb akhla'a 'alā: *Badā'i'* 3: 5 (atābak appointed at outset of Qāytbāy's reign); 3: 6 (Qāytbāy enrobes several new executive officers); *Rawḍ* f. 175-b (Qāytbāy enrobes Yashbak min Mahdī as new dawādār); *Badā'i'* 3: 7 (Qāytbāy holds review to enrobe several more executive officers); *Rawḍ* f. 176-b (Qāytbāy enrobes new amīr akhūr); *Ḥawādith* 7–4: 619–20 (Qāytbāy grants robes of investiture to several executive officers).
3. *Inbā'* 27, 159; *Badā'i'* 3: 90.
4. *Ḥawādith* 7–4: 684.
5. *Inbā'* 61; *Badā'i'* 3: 31, 114.
6. *Badā'i'* 3: 32.
7. *Inbā'* 139.
8. *Badā'i'* 3: 39, 109.
9. *Inbā'* 159.
10. *Badā'i'* 3: 114.
11. *Badā'i'* 3: 155.
12. *Badā'i'* 3: 108, 158.
13. *Badā'i'* 3: 54 (governor of Ḥamāh); *Inbā'* 511 (governor of Damascus); *Badā'i'* 3: 306 (governor of Ṣafad), 4: 82 (governor of al-Karak), 207 (governor of 'Ayntāb), 295 (governor of Kakhtā).
14. *Inbā'* 218.
15. *Ḥawādith* 7–4: 626; *Rawḍ* f. 179; *Badā'i'* 3: 207, 234; 4: 47.
16. *Inbā'* 8; *Badā'i'* 3: 18, 147.
17. *Rawḍ* f. 206-b.
18. *Badā'i'* 3: 25.
19. *Badā'i'* 3: 31.
20. *Inbā'* 120; *Badā'i'* 3: 37, 107.
21. *Inbā'* 135.
22. *Inbā'* 152.
23. *Inbā'* 157.
24. *Inbā'* 164; *Badā'i'* 3: 148, 181.
25. *Badā'i'* 3: 44; *Inbā'* 489.
26. *Badā'i'* 3: 133.
27. *Badā'i'* 3: 134.

28. *Badā'i'* 3: 143.
29. *Badā'i'* 3: 209, 317.
30. *Badā'i'* 3: 218.
31. *Badā'i'* 3: 221.
32. *Badā'i'* 3: 239.
33. *Badā'i'* 4: 60.
34. *Badā'i'* 3: 99.
35. *Ḥawādith* 7–4: 682; *Inbā'* 23.
36. *Inbā'* 208.
37. Twelve references during his reign.
38. *Badā'i'* 4: 13, 350, 477; for the khil'a, 4: 22.
39. *Inbā'* 392.
40. *Inbā'* 481.
41. *Inbā'* 489.
42. *Badā'i'* 4: 390.
43. For promotions to military offices in Cairo, thirty-one references mention khil'as, while eight mention other garments.
44. *Ḥawādith* 7–4: 676; *Inbā'* 14.
45. For Syria, twenty-five references to the khil'a, four to other garments.
46. *Rawḍ* f. 205-b. Al-Malaṭī did not mention either the satin aṭlas or sleeveless fawqānī. See note 35.
47. *Inbā'* 497.
48. *Badā'i'* 5: 46.
49. *Badā'i'* 3: 179.
50. *Badā'i'* 4: 283.
51. *Inbā'* 360.
52. *Badā'i'* 5: 20.
53. On the tradition of slave succession in the Mamluk sultanate, see David Ayalon, "Aspects of the Mamlūk Phenomenon: A. The Importance of the Mamlūk Institution; B. Ayyūbids, Kurds and Turks," *Der Islam* 53 (1976): 196–225; 55 (1977): 1–32; Ulrich Haarmann, "Miṣr, 5: The Mamlūk Period," *Enclyclopaedia of Islam,* 2nd ed. (Leiden, E. J. Brill, ongoing) 8: 165–67; R. Stephen Humphreys, "The Emergence of the Mamlūk Army," *Studia Islamica* 45 (1977): 67–100; 46 (1977): 147–82; idem., "Mamlūk Dynasty," *Dictionary of the Middle Ages,* ed. Joseph R. Strayer (New York: Scribners, 1987) 8: 73–74; Robert Irwin, *The Middle East in the Middle Ages: The Early Mamlūk Sultanate, 1250–1382* (London: Croom Helm, 1986).
54. On the establishment of the 'Abbāsid Caliph in Cairo, see P. M. Holt, "Some Observations on the 'Abbāsid Caliphate in Cairo," *Bulletin of the School of Oriental and African Studies* 47 (1984): 501–507; Peter Thorau, *The Lion of Egypt: Sultan Baybars I and the Near East in the Thirteenth Century* (London: Longman, 1987): 110–19.
55. These details taken from descriptions of Qāytbāy's enthronement: *Rawḍ* f. 170; *Badā'i'* 4: 3.
56. *Ḥawādith* 7–4: 706; *Inbā'* 61; *Raw* f. 219.

57. *Ḥawādith* 7–4: 707; *Inbā'* 64.
58. *Inbā'* 125, 126, 127; *Badā'i'* 3: 37.
59. *Badā'i'* 3: 38.
60. *Badā'i'* 3: 95.
61. *Inbā'* 416; *Badā'i'* 3: 69.
62. *Badā'i'* 3: 154, 157.
63. *Badā'i'* 4: 103.
64. *Inbā'* 75.
65. al-Qalqashandī, *Ṣubḥ al-A'shā fī Ṣinā'at al-Inshā'* (Dawn for the Benighted Regarding the Craft of Diplomatic) ed. Muḥammad 'Abd al-Rasūl Ibrāhīm (Cairo: Dār al-Kutub al-Khidiwiyya, 1913–20) 4: 7.
66. *Badā'i'* 4: 291.
67. *Badā'i'* 4: 292.
68. *Badā'i'* 4: 367.
69. *Badā'i'* 4: 413.
70. *Badā'i'* 4: 418.
71. The procession in which al-Ghawrī wore the violet silārī tunic marked his departure for an inspection trip to the port of Alexandria on 1 Dhū'l-Qa'da 920 / December 18, 1514 (see n. 69). After he descended from the citadel to the Hippodrome (Maydān al-Rumayla), forty-five horses laden with hair-woven pack saddles (ajlāl sha'r) and halters (maqāwid) set out, followed by thirteen lines of dromedaries bearing saddles (akwār) embroidered with gold thread and velvet. Fifty more horses departed after them, each with a gold saddle and mantle of yellow silk. The sultan's elite corps of troops (khāṣṣakiyya) marched behind these horses. Al-Ghawrī's entourage of staff officials (mubāshirūn) and senior officers (muqaddamūn) then preceded him, his own position at the very end staged to impress the throng after such a lavish display.
72. *Inbā'* 43.
73. *Inbā'* 495.
74. *Badā'i'* 4: 250 (14 Dhū'l-Qa'da 917 / February 2, 1512).
75. On civil robe distribution during the 'Īd al-Fiṭr: *Badā'i'* 3: 274; 4: 88, 104, 127, 145.
76. On civil robes for the 'Īd al-Mawlid: *Inbā'* 140.
77. Inbā' 263.
78. For the office of the supervisor of the sultan's privy bureau (nāẓir al-khāṣṣ), see William Popper, *Egypt and Syria under the Circassian Sultans, 1382–1468 A.D.: Systematic Notes to Ibn Taghri Birdi's Chronicles of Egypt; University of California Publications in Semitic Philology* (Berkeley: University of California Press, 1955) 15: 97.
79. Inbā' 413.
80. *Rawḍ* f. 186; *Badā'i'* 3: 16.
81. *Ḥawādith* 7–4: 682.
82. *Inbā'* 161.
83. *Inbā'* 406.

84. *Badā'i'* 3: 192.
85. *Badā'i'* 4: 44.
86. *Badā'i'* 4: 481.
87. *Badā'i'* 3: 243.
88. *Badā'i'* 4: 88.
89. *Badā'i'* 4: 104.
90. *Badā'i'* 4: 247 (khil'as of cheap cotton with dyed spider motif, no brocade); 4: 248 (khil'as a disgrace [subba]); 4: 286 (less than half the traditional number available); 4: 340 (poor quality); 4: 478 (poor quality due to avarice of nāẓir al-khāṣṣ).
91. *Badā'i'* 4: 100.
92. *Inbā'* 437.
93. *Badā'i'* 4: 425.
94. *Badā'i'* 3: 87.
95. *Badā'i'* 3: 64.
96. *Inbā'* 398.
97. *Ḥawādith* 7–4: 626; *Rawḍ* f. 180; *Badā'i'* 3: 10.

CHAPTER 18

ROBES, KINGS, AND SEMIOTIC AMBIGUITY

Stewart Gordon

Rather than broad theory that seeks to explains all investiture in all settings, I propose a "middle range" hypothesis specific to the investiture tradition that began in Central Asia; it seeks to explain some of the major questions that arise from our essays: Why did this tradition survive in a recognizable form for almost two thousand years in spite of vast changes in governmental structure? Why did it spread across much of Asia, some of Europe, and parts of Africa? How did it find usage in Christianity, Islam, Buddhism, Judaism, Confucianism, Hinduism, and various "barbarian" settings from Russia to sub-Saharan Africa? How is it that a tremendous variety of people received robes, such as particularly adept court dancers, sons of kings, diplomatic envoys, military commanders, nuns, and Sufi holy men? How is it that robing sometimes meant promotion and sometimes signaled defeat? How is it that robes sometimes honored single individuals and other times whole groups, such as all of the leaders going on a campaign? How is it that kings were sometimes robed by a high clergyman and other times they robed themselves? Why was the robing ceremony sometimes so simple as to be nonverbal, and other times included oaths and even written contracts? Why was the robe in some settings accompanied by items of real wealth—gold, silver, jewels—and other times not?

The ability of the ceremony to survive for centuries, adapt to a great number of local settings, and be used for seemingly contradictory purposes suggests that the robe in this tradition was, in semiotic terms, a complex sign with a high degree of ambiguity, a sign that meant little and much simultaneously. The sign could be "uncoupled" so that it meant different things to the giver than to the receiver. Nevertheless, robing became neither so empty of meaning nor so rigidly defined that its use became inappropriate and was dropped.

We might usefully contrast the Central Asian tradition containing great semiotic ambiguity with the even older robing tradition of the Old Testament that contained virtually no semiotic ambiguity. Recall Leviticus, in which God (speaking through the priests) declared that only the house of Aaron and the family of Levi were eligible to be priests. The word of God unambiguously and semiotically defined the practice and meaning of priestly investiture and, further, precisely defined priestly rules that separated them spatially and ritually from followers and unbelievers. God threatened the ultimate sanction for deviation, death to the whole Jewish community.

The rich semiotic ambiguity of Central Asian investiture comes, I believe, from two separate usages. First, the robe and its presentation had a diplomatic use. It was about boundaries and making someone beyond one's boundaries "acceptable," part of a "metropolitan" system. (We find this explicit in early relations between China and the nomads, as well as between China and Tibet.) Robes were given to a single person, a leader, and did not involve any written treaty or specific obligations. Thus it was likely that the giver put quite different meanings on the bestowal than the receiver, and the whole interchange was infused with the fluid politics of the moment. Each side could come away satisfied with only a minimal acceptance of what the other side meant. Semiotic ambiguity was particularly rich when the receiver sought the robes, as was often the case.

Perhaps one way to approach this diplomatic use of robing is comparatively to explore the notion of the "barbarian." We find many using the term and many referents in our long historical period—China and the steppe nomads, Rome and the tribes to the north, Constantinople and the steppe dwellers, Alexander and the groups he encountered in the Caucasus, Islam and the Hindu kings of southern India. In the case of Constantinople, for example, for a group to move from "barbarian" status to acceptability within the empire meant conversion to Christianity, the king taking a Christian wife, and his accepting luxurious robes and gold. While the metropolitan power might send the "barbarian" literacy, priests, and notions of courtly luxury, we should not think of this as a one-way movement. The metropolitan power always received a variety of rewards from the relationship, such as art motifs, new military skills, border security, shifts in possible political alliances, tribute, and recognition of their religion. Robes were a small portable piece of the empire that the "barbarian" leader could carry back to his followers without any particular obligations.

Second, in a quite separate usage, robes became central to a system of fealty. Here let us focus again on the original use of the luxury robes within the Central Asian nomadic war band. Note that I explicitly do not use the word *exchange* in this context. A warrior did not negotiate to bring a certain quality of horse or armor, or negotiate payment of a certain number of ounces of silver or bushels of grain. Fealty was something quite different. A warrior offered to serve; the leader agreed to be his leader. In Central Asian practice, this interaction was virtually nonverbal. The warrior merely stood in his armor before the king and slightly bowed his head; the leader nodded agreement. Certainly, there were implicit expectations on both sides. The follower would fight and die for his leader. The leader would fight by his side, eat and drink with him, and share whatever fortune might bring. The leader remained first among equals as long as the band was relatively successful. Everyone in the system recognized that if a leader could no longer maintain his followers, they had the choice to stay and suffer or without shame seek service with another leader.

It is perhaps worth reminding the reader that these were not exclusively war bands. They were first and foremost nomadic bands based on herds of cattle, sheep, goats, and horses. Their economics included trading the animals and wool to towns and sedentary agriculturalists for grain, iron, and other necessities. The nomads also turned the wool into carpets and other woven items for use and trade. Their ecology and spatial rhythm followed the yearly cycle of the grasses of the steppe. The band included women and children, who were left behind during raids.[1]

In this system of fealty, the robe was not generally given upon entrance to service (though in the Mongol empire it was). In early use, the robe was a personal recognition by the leader of the follower's successful and loyal service, recognition of special status before the full band. It fell almost within the realm of booty, real wealth in luxury fabric that the leader shared with his followers. Thus it does not seem surprising that luxury robes became associated with other objects of war booty—gold, silver, jewels, decorated weapons, and slaves.[2]

Over the ensuing centuries, monarchies based on a war-band tradition in various regions—China, Persia, Byzantium, the Muslim kingdoms in India, and France—experimented with administrative structures that gave the king more stability, power, and income. Note that I am explicitly not accepting any teleology of "state formation" or even the idea that there might be common "stages." In many of these experiments, the king attempted to impose regular taxes collected by salaried officials who had written job descriptions.

What is fascinating is that over the course of a thousand years these geographically dispersed experiments at bureaucracy and hierarchy did not displace fealty and its ceremonies, like robing. Rather, bureaucracy often ended up underneath fealty in an uneasy relationship. Perhaps one example will illustrate what I mean. In the sixteenth century (and after three hundred years of Muslim rule), the Mughal empire in India indeed had written tax contracts, tax collectors, carefully structured assessment guidelines, and officials who dealt with everything from the royal workshops to the branding of horses among low-level soldiers. Nevertheless, an elite above this bureaucracy was structured by fealty—a war band writ large. Known as the *mansabdars* (that is, men holding a grant for the maintenance of troops), this elite consisted of only a few thousand men, each—father and son—known to the emperor and raised to this rank in a simple ceremony of fealty before him. No specific duties were attached to being a mansabdar. It was assumed and expected that any member of this elite would lead troops, even if his family had been administrators for generations. Likewise, it was expected that this elite would share in the king's prosperity either from peaceful development or expansion by war.[3]

In the Mughal empire, ties of fealty were renewed regularly in face-to-face encounters between the mansabdars and the emperor at court, in conference, and on the hunt. Robing was the ceremony that recognized successful service, whether in war or peace, and was especially used to maintain these ties when distance precluded face-to-face contact. Robes arrived in far- flung provinces by special emissary. The recipient faced the capital, bowed deeply and prostrated, put on the robe before his troops and subordinates, placed the warrant on his forehead, and bowed deeply again.[4] Such a system also had its problems. Since all mansabdars in a province or on a campaign received robes regularly and all treasured their direct relation to the emperor, there was no pretense of a unified command structure. In spite of a nominal commander, each mansabdar was leader of "his" men. At best, there were discussions about what strategy to follow; those who disagreed often sent their views directly to the emperor.[5] Readers more familiar with Europe will surely recognize both the structure of fealty and similar problems of divided command throughout the Middle Ages.

Whenever a king tried to adapt robing away from first-among-equals fealty toward bureaucracy or hierarchy, the process was surprisingly similar. The king used his power to simplify the meaning of the robe semiotically, to wring ambiguity out of its presentation, control its exact meaning, and formalize the personal ceremony. This process is particularly clear in the assertion of papal authority over clerics throughout Western Europe by the addition to investiture of written ceremony, sworn oaths, and written warrants of duties. It is perhaps worth suggesting a few more examples of this process. As early as the eleventh century in Iran, certain robes of honor had become robes of office, the very name of the office stitched into the robe.[6] As early as the tenth century, the Byzantine emperor before a campaign bestowed to the army robes whose worth was carefully "ranked" to match the rank of the soldiers. The exact monetary value was stitched into robes bestowed in Ottoman Turkey. In France, at the time of Louis XIV, a bureaucratic "nobility of the robe" was created in contrast to the "nobility of the sword" based on fealty.

Nevertheless, the fealty aspects and semiotic ambiguity never completely disappeared from investiture. In spite of developing bureaucracy at the end of the Middle Ages, it was enormously useful that personal bestowal of the robe meant that the "hand of the king" was in direct relationship to the receiver. Even in the normal run of things, any king, whether strong or weak, needed a way to keep a relationship with officeholders, especially when offices were heritable. A king could demand of "his" man (as marked with the robe) actions and loyalty that he could not ask of a mere salaried employee.[7] Kingship in its many forms was also characterized by periodic crises in which just this sort of loyalty might make the difference, such as succession, or the frequent plots against him by his own nobility, or a failure in war, or an unpopular marriage, or a serious rebellion. For many in service, this personal aspect, characterized by robing, kept the king—if only in imagination—as a companion and accessible. As we have emphasized, the receiver could show the robe to his followers or clients with a rather different meaning than the one in which it was bestowed.

There are, perhaps, some broader conclusions and questions that emerge from our study.

First, I now regard it as extremely likely that a unified robing tradition was the basis of investiture in Central Asia, China, Tibet, Persia, Byzantium, Eastern Europe, the Islamic world including North and sub-Saharan Africa, and by extension Korea, India, Japan, and Islamicized Southeast Asia. As a corollary, in these regions if we find an investiture ceremony with telltale signs of horses and robing, or robing combined with jeweled weapons, daggers, and swords, or luxurious robes from the hand of the king donned in court, we cannot treat the phenomenon as a simply "local" culture. It may well be part of a larger semiotic and ceremonial metalanguage, and therefore we should look for connections to larger political structures or possibly only to distantly remembered larger traditions. In no case can we discount any of this as mere "spectacle," no matter how distant in the past or how removed the court from our own experience.

Second, robing among kings in Western Europe in the Middle Ages remains problematic. We find investiture regularly as a feature of coronation. Nevertheless, while European kingship was certainly influenced by the Central Asian tradition, robing never became so central to fealty or diplomacy in Europe as it did in the broad regions just mentioned. Perhaps there was too strong an indigenous tradition of fealty, or a lack of influence of Constantinople when traditions of kingship were emerging from the warrior band, or some other reason.

Third, the place in Western Europe that investiture flourished was in the Church. Virtually every feature we find in statecraft in the Middle East appeared in the developing ecclesiastical hierarchy. Throughout the Middle Ages, the ceremony seems to have retained aspects of fealty and personal loyalty in spite of steady movement to specify and "normalize" offices through oaths and warrants. There were all too real politics of the meaning of robes and who had the right to wear certain colors and fabrics. Perhaps the reason why robing flourished in the Church and not in secular states has to do with the very complex, shifting relationships between the two realms.

Fourth, as researchers, we must be open to the possibility that common people outside the court understood the meaning of robing ceremonies. I suggest only one example. At the death of a Mughal emperor, his immediate male relatives generally fought it out for the throne. Losers were sometimes paraded though the capital in a "disinvestiture" ceremony. Rather than on a fine horse with golden trappings, the loser rode backwards on a mangy donkey. Rather than luxurious robes, the loser worn cheap, torn, and filthy garments. The populace knew precisely what this meant and mocked him in every street. (It's possible that the populace of the Book of Esther—a millennium and a half earlier—would have equally understood this "disinvestiture.")

Finally, I believe that this study validates cross-disciplinary, transcultural attempts to trace the rise and spread of important symbolic meanings across broad geographic areas and long historical periods. We could not know what we now know about robing from only isolated local studies. Research that crosses disciplines and regional boundaries is worth the difficulties of unfamiliar vocabularies and place names. We have found the process exciting and fruitful and recommend it to others.

Notes

1. Unlike Europe, in this nomadic setting fealty did not include the grant of land on which the family settled. Wealth was calculated in animals, and the only way to keep and develop herds was to be able to range over large areas of the steppe.
2. Some fabulous robes became part of a circulation of "wonderful objects" in a broad region that stretched at least from the Middle East to India and onward to China as early as the eleventh century. Great kings sent presents to each other (as marks of the greatness of the giver and the receiver) that included objects made in their workshops, war booty, items received as gift or tribute, purchased curiosities, and items of alleged antiquity. We have

glimpses of this circulation in various courtly accounts, but the overall pattern has yet to be worked out. See Oleg Grabar, "The Shared Culture of Objects," in Henry Maguire, ed., *Byzantine Court Culture from 829 to 1204* (Washington, DC: Dumbarton Oaks, 1997), pp. 115 –30.

3. As we might expect, codified law accreted to the transactions of trade and many of the relations between the empire and those who paid taxes. Nevertheless, mansabdars remained largely above this system. Commoners could hardly haul them into court. It was only by written appeal to the emperor that redress against mansabdars by commoners was possible.
4. Warrants were usually general, confirming or enlarging the number of troops in a man's grant rather than highly specific lists of duties or responsibilities of office.
5. See the autobiography of a low-level mansabdar who served in Bengal in the early decades of the seventeenth century, *Baharistan-I-Ghaybi,* trans. M. I. Borah (Gauhati, Assam: Government of Assam, 1936), pp. 75–113. Mughal rulers for more than one hundred years resisted the elite becoming "landed": Two methods were to separate mansabdars from their estates by requiring that they serve in some distant area and nominally sequestering estates at death. Placing mansabdars far away and jeopardizing heritability made fealty ceremonies and practices particularly critical.
6. A famous example of this type of robe is found in the collection of The Textile Museum, Washington, DC.
7 A wonderful example of this mixing of "office" with the robe retaining the personal "hand of the king" was the annual ceremony at which the Byzantine Emperor paid heads of departments, witnessed by Liutprand, Bishop of Cremona, in 950 CE. One interesting detail is that robes substituted for money, when money was in short supply. The ceremony is discussed in Nicolas Oikonomides, "Title and Income at the Byzantine Court" in Henry Maguire, ed., *Byzantine Court Culture from 829 to 1204,* pp. 199–201.

CONTRIBUTORS

THOMAS T. ALLSEN'S books include *Mongol Imperialism: The Policies of the Grand Qan Mönke in China, Russia and the Islamic Lands, 1251–1259* and *Commodity and Exchange in the Mongol Empire: A Cultural History of Islamic Textiles.* He teaches at Trenton State College

BERNARD BERTHOD is a historian, doctor ès-Lettres, curator of Museum of Fourvière, Lyon, and a specialist in the history of ecclesiastical garments. He has curated many exhibitions about liturgical art and is the author of several books in this field, including *Paramentica: tissues lyonnais et Arts Sacrè, Dictionanaire historiques des Etoffes,* and *Dictionairre des Arts liturgiques.*

ANNEMARIE WEYL CARR is Professor of Art History at Southern Methodist University. Her books include *Byzantine Illumination, 1150–1250: The Study of a Provincial Tradition* and *A Byzantine Masterpiece Recovered: The Thirteenth-Century Murals of Lysi, Cyprus.* She wrote her chapter for this volume during a year as Lilly Endowment Fellow in Religion and Humanities at the National Humanities Center, North Carolina.

ANTONY EASTMOND is a Research Fellow in the History of Art, University of Warwick. He is the author of *Royal Imagery in Medieval Georgia* and a number of articles on art and culture in Byzantium and the Caucasus. He is currently working on the role of art in the construction of identity in the Eastern Christian world.

JAMAL J. ELIAS is Associate Professor of Religion at Amherst College. His publications include *The Throne Carrier of God: The Life and Thought of 'Ala' ad-dawla as-Simanī, Death Before Dying: Mystical Poems of Sultan Bahū,* and *Islam* in the Prentice Hall/Routledge *Religions of the World* series.

STEWART GORDON is a Research Fellow at the Center for South Asian Studies at the University of Michigan. His books include *The Marathas: 1600–1818* and *Marathas, Marauders, and State Formation in Eighteenth Century India.* His articles have explored kingly legitimacy, processes of conquest, and development of trade and credit networks.

GAVIN R. G. HAMBLY's books include *Cities of Mughal India: Delhi, Agra, and Fatehpur Sikri* and *Women in the Medieval Islamic World: Power, Patronage, and Piety.* He served as an editor and contributor to vol. 7 of *The Cambridge History of Iran.* He is a Professor of History at the University of Texas at Dallas.

LYNN JONES is a specialist in the art and architecture of Byzantium and the Caucasus and is completing an examination of the visual expression of medieval Armenian kingship.

DÉSIRÉE KOSLIN is Adjunct Assistant Professor at the Fashion Institute of Technology. Her recent thesis is entitled "The Dress of Religious Women as seen in the Visual arts from the Early Middle Ages to c. 1500." Her research interests include textiles and dress of the medieval period.

XINRU LIU is Director, Department of Ancient and Medieval History, Chinese Academy of Social Sciences, Beijing. Her books include *Silk and Religion: An Exploration of Material Life and the Thought of People, Ad 600 –1200* and *Ancient India and Ancient China: Trade and Religious Exchanges, AD 1–600.*

MICHAEL MOORE has taught medieval history at Wellesley College, and was Mellon Foreign Area Fellow at the Library of Congress. He is currently the Carolyn Grant Fay Postdoctoral Teaching Fellow with the Honors College of the University of Houston, Texas.

CARL F. PETRY is Professor of History at Northwestern University. His books include *The Civilian Elite of Cairo in the Later Middle Ages,* and *Protectors of Praetorians? The Last Mamluk Sultans and Egypt's Waning as a Great Power.* He also served as editor and contributor to vol.1 of the *Cambridge History of Egypt.*

JENNY ROSE received her PhD in Iranian Studies from Columbia University. Her recent publications include articles on childbirth and divorce in the Zoroastrian religion in the *Encyclopaedia Iranica*, and a series of textbooks on story and symbol in the world's religions.

MARTIAL ROSE was an Open Exhibitioner in English at King's College, Cambridge and, until his recent retirement, Principal of King Alfred's College, Winchester. His many books include *The Wakefield Mystery Plays* and *Stories in Stone: The Medieval Roof Carvings of Norwich Cathedral.*

PAULA SANDERS is Associate Professor of History and Director of the Program for the Study of Women and Gender at Rice University. Her published research has focused on the history and culture of the Fatimid dynasty, gender in medieval Islamic thought, and the history of Cairo.

JANET SNYDER is Assistant Professor of Art History at West Virginia University. Her published research centers on women in the arts of medieval Europe, fictive and actual medieval costume, and the use of masks.

DOMINIQUE SOURDEL is a member of the French Institute for the Study of Arabic at Damascus and chief of the Conference of Muslim Civilization at the University of Algiers. He was Professor at the University of Bordeaux and until his recent retirement Professor at the University of Paris–Sorbonne. He is the author of numerous books and articles on Muslim history, especially in the early period.

WILLIAM TRONZO has published widely on Medieval and Renaissance art and architecture. In addition to numerous fellowships, he has held research appointments at the Dumbarton Oaks Center for Byzantine Studies and the Bibliotheca Hertziana (Rome). He currently teaches in the Newcomb Department of Art, Tulane University.

INDEX

Southern Methodist Univ.
3 2177 01659 9704